To Jim —
Best of luck!
Bill Martin

Jim, I hope you
enjoy all I
have to offer
from front to
back! This
is a marvelous
read!
XOXOXO
♡ Kyra

Data Driven Investing

PROFESSIONAL EDITION

Data Driven Investing

PROFESSIONAL EDITION

Bill Matson, MBA, CPA, CFA, FLMI

and Mitchell R. Hardy

With assistance from

Denis R. Desharnais
and Susan W. Bailey, MBA

Illustrated by Stephen J. Kurth
Special Foreword by R. Foster Winans

DATA DRIVEN PUBLISHING, LLC

Published By:

Data Driven Publishing, LLC
P.O. Box 340
Newburyport, MA 01950
www.datadrivenpublishing.com

Hardy, Mitch.
    Data driven investing / Mitch Hardy, Bill Matson. -- Professional ed.
    p. cm.
    Includes bibliographical references and index.
    ISBN 0-9755842-0-0
    1. Stocks--United States. 2. Investments--United States   I. Matson, Bill.   II. Title
HG4661.H29 2004   332.63'22
                                QB104-200247

To our parents
and to our children.

Executive Table of Contents

Front Matter

Special Foreword by R. Foster Winans.. xx
Authors' Foreword xxv
Introduction xxix

Part One   Our Data Driven Approach To Investing 1

Chapter 1   The Stock Market In The Information Age...................................3
Chapter 2   Data Driven Investing..7

Part Two   Our Data Driven Approach to Stock Selection 13

Chapter 3   The Fed Effect...15
Chapter 4   Value Stocks..21
Chapter 5   Growth Stocks 35
Chapter 6   Value Versus Growth 47
Chapter 7   Buying High Relative Strength Stocks...57
Chapter 8   Buying Nanocap Stocks 65
Chapter 9   The Presidential Election Cycle 77
Chapter 10   The Combined Fed-Election Cycle...93
Chapter 11   The Fed-Election Cycle & Stock Selection Strategy 117
Chapter 12   Sell-Side Analysts' Research 229
Chapter 13   Profiting From Deficiencies In GAAP 247
Chapter 14   Fundamental Analysis 263
Chapter 15   Final Thoughts On Stock Selection Strategies...........................289

Part Three   Our Data Driven Trading Tactics....................................... 293

Chapter 16   Understanding The Psychology Of Investing 295
Chapter 17   Trading To Win 327

After Matter

Afterword   VideoFinancials & The Future Of Wall Street 375
Appendix A   What Do Performance Figures Really Mean?.............................379
Appendix B   Our Backtesting Methodology 389
Appendix C   Brokerage Statements 393
Appendix D   Glossary 464
Index 493
About the Authors..502

Table of Contents

Front Matter

List of Exhibits.. xiv

Acknowledgements xix

Special Foreword... xx

Authors' Foreword xxv

Introduction xxix

Part One Our Data Driven Approach To Investing.......................... 1

Chapter 1 The Stock Market In The Information Age 3

Chapter 2 Data Driven Investing 7
   Key Elements of Our Approach to Investing..........................8
   Strategies for Selecting Stocks 9
   Trading Tactics 10
   Integrating Stock Selection Strategy and Trading Tactics...................11

Part Two Our Data Driven Approach to Stock Selection 13

Chapter 3 The Fed Effect 15
   The Power Of The Fed Effect..19

Chapter 4 Value Stocks 21
   What Is A Value Stock?...21
   Selecting Value Stocks...22
   Notes On Methodology..22
   Performance Of Value Strategies 23
   Low Price To Earnings (P/E) 23
   Low Price To Sales (P/S) 24
   Low Price To Book Value (P/BV) 27
   Low Price To Cash Flow (P/CF).....................................29
   Comparison Of Value Strategies 31
   Value Investing Is A Winner! 34

Chapter 5 Growth Stocks..35
   What is a Growth Stock? 35
   Selecting Growth Stocks 36
   Performance of Growth Strategies...................................36
   High Price to Earnings (P/E) 37
   High Price to Sales (P/S) 40
   High Price to Book Value (P/BV)....................................40
   High Price to Cash Flow (P/CF).....................................43
   Comparison of Growth Strategies....................................43
   None of the Growth Strategies Beat the Market......................46

Chapter 6 Value Versus Growth 47

Chapter 7 Buying High Relative Strength Stocks 57
    Relative Strength Versus Momentum...57
    Returns For Relative Strength Strategies 59
    Relative Strength And Year-End Trading Patterns 61
    Shifts In The Balance From High Relative Strength To Low Relative Strength 61
    The Importance Of Relative Strength Varies 62
    Market Capitalization 65

Chapter 8 Buying Nanocap Stocks 65
    Notes On Methodology...66
    Returns By Market Capitalization 69
    The Nanocap Advantage...69
    The Financial Services Industry Has Little Use For Nanocaps 69
    Nanocaps Are Perfect For Individual Investors..70
    Are Nanocaps Too Risky For Most Investors? 70
    Nanocaps Can Be Challenging To Trade...73
    Technology Makes It Possible 74
    Are There Ever Good Times To Own Large Caps? 76
    Nanocaps Are Key To Our Success 76

Chapter 9 The Presidential Election Cycle 77
    The Election Cycle Effect..77
    The President's Role in Formulating Economic Policy 80
    Are Presidents Motivated by Party Ideology?...81
    Or Are Presidents Motivated by Their Desire to Retain Power?.............83
    Politics and the Election Cycle...85
    Monetary Policy and the Election Cycle 87
    Big Rocks and Small Rocks...89

Chapter 10 The Combined Fed-Election Cycle 93
    The Fed Cycle...95
    The Fed's Independence from Political Control 95
    Fed Policy and Interest Rates 96
    Interest Rates and Stock Prices...98
    The Cycle of Fed Policy Changes 99
    The Fed Effect 101
    The Combined Fed-Election Cycle 102
    Returns for the S&P 500...102
    Returns for Individual Groups 107
    Market Capitalization and the Combined Fed-Election Cycle 110
    Value Versus Growth and the Combined Fed-Election Cycle...............111
    Relative Strength and the Combined Fed-Election Cycle.....................112
    Returns for Individual Groups When Fed Policy is Aggressive 112
    Market Capitalization in Aggressive Years 113
    Value Versus Growth in Aggressive Years..115
    Relative Strength in Aggressive Years..115
    The Combined Fed-Election Cycle and Stock Selection 116

Chapter 11 The Fed-Election Cycle & Stock Selection Strategy......................117
    Analysis of Historical Data 118
    Methodology..118
    Presentation of Historical Data...119
    The Fed-Election Cycle and Market Cap-Based Strategies 120

The Fed-Election Cycle and Nanocaps..120
The 15 Best Years for Large Caps..122
The 15 Best Years for Nanocaps..123
The Fed-Election Cycle and Small Caps..123
The Best Years for Large Caps...127
The 15 Best Years for $100 Million Companies 128
Other Small Market Cap Strategies...128
The Fed-Election Cycle and the S&P 500..129
The Fed-Election Cycle and Value Versus Growth Strategies 162
The Fed-Election Cycle and Price/Earnings 162
The 15 Best Years for High P/E Stocks..163
The 15 Best Years for Low P/E Stocks 164
The Fed-Election Cycle and Price/Sales..165
The 15 Best Years for High P/S Stocks 166
The 15 Best Years for Low P/S Stocks 167
The Fed-Election Cycle and Price/Book Value 168
The 15 Best Years for High P/BV Stocks..169
The 15 Best Years for Low P/BV Stocks 170
The Fed-Election Cycle and Price/Cash Flow..171
The 15 Best Years for High P/CF Stocks 172
The 15 Best Years for Low P/CF Stocks 173
The Fed-Election Cycle and Value Versus Growth.....................................173
The 15 Best Years for Growth 175
The 15 Best Years for Value..175
The Fed-Election Cycle and Relative Strength 201
The 15 Best Years for Low Relative Strength 202
The 15 Best Years for High Relative Strength...203
The Fed-Election Cycle and Stock Selection Strategy................................209
The Best Performing Styles for Each Phase of the Fed-Election Cycle 209
Early Election Cycle, Expansive Fed Policy 210
Late Election Cycle, Expansive Fed Policy 212
Early Election Cycle, Restrictive Fed Policy 213
Late Election Cycle, Restrictive Fed Policy...213
Strategy for Shifting Styles According to the Fed-Election Cycle.......................215
Predicting Style Shifts..216
Earnings Expectations 216
The Yield Curve of Interest Rates..218
Inflation 219
Heteroskedasticity 221
Large Caps Versus Small Company Stocks..224
Implementing the Fed-Election Cycle Strategy: Practical Considerations..........227

Chapter 12 Sell-Side Analysts' Research 229
The Role of the Analyst in a Large Brokerage Firm 230
Supporting Brokerage Operations..230
Supporting Investment Banking Operations..231
External Influences on Analysts' Opinions..232
Analysts' Bias Toward Optimism 234
Analysts' Slow Reaction to New Information...235
Decision Rules for Analyst Recommendations...236
Earnings Forecasts 237
Earnings Surprises and the "Sergei Bubka Gambit" 238
Positive Earnings Surprises...238
The Brokerage Analyst's Future: Reform or Extinction? 241

Chapter 13 Profiting From Deficiencies In GAAP 247
    The Information "GAAP" 248
    GAAP: Generally Accepted Accounting Principles 248
    Historical Cost Basis Accounting 249
    Other Distortions Caused by GAAP 251
    Hi-Q versus Lo-Q 252
    The Information GAAP – Conclusions: 257
    Earnings Manipulation and Financial Reporting Fraud 258
    How to Identify Questionable Financial Reports 259

Chapter 14 Fundamental Analysis 263
    The Role of Fundamental Analysis in Our Stock Selection Strategy 264
    The Importance of a Systematic Approach 265
    Industry Attractiveness 266
    Definition of an Industry 268
    Division of Profits Across Industries 269
    The Company's Competitive Position 270
    Strategy and Execution 270
    The Company's Competitors 273
    The Company's Competitive Position—Additional Considerations 274
    Customers 274
    Products (or Services) 275
    Distribution Channels 275
    Tangible Assets 276
    Intangible Assets 276
    Suppliers and Sub-Contractors 277
    Labor 278
    Legal and Regulatory Issues 279
    The Company's Financial Strength 281
    Recent Cash Flow Trends 281
    Evaluation of Financial Resources 282
    Adequacy of Future Cash Flows 285
    The Quality of the Management Team 286

Chapter 15 Final Thoughts On Stock Selection Strategies 289

Part Three Our Data Driven Trading Tactics 293

Chapter 16 Understanding The Psychology Of Investing 295
    Four Major Psychological Biases 297
    Trend Biases 297
    Loss Aversion Biases 298
    Conservatism Biases 298
    Cognitive Biases 298
    Five Classes of Psychological Factors 299
    Narrow-Minded Stubbornness 299
    The Halo Effect (a Cognitive Bias) 300
    Devotion to Status Quo 304
    Conservatism (a Conservatism Bias) 306
    Anchoring (a Conservatism/Cognitive Bias) 307
    Loss Aversion 308
    The Endowment Effect (a Loss Aversion/Cognitive Bias) 311
    Inattentiveness 312
    Availability and Vividness (Cognitive Biases) 314
    Inaccurate Evaluation of Disjunctive vs. Conjunctive Events (a Cognitive Bias) 316

Illusory and Invisible Correlations (Trend/Conservatism/Cognitive Biases) 318
Overconfidence and Calibration (Cognitive Biases) 321
Unsupported Optimism 323
Investment Trap (a Loss Aversion/Cognitive Bias) 323

Chapter 17 Trading To Win 327
Reacting to News Stories 327
Monitoring News and Price Movements...................................329
Decision Points 329
Evaluating News...................................331
Good News Stories 332
Examples of Bad News 332
How to Place Orders 333
Mechanics of Placing Orders 333
Pricing Orders Appropriately...................................339
Seven Simple Rules...................................345
Shopkeeper Trades 346
A Visit to the Trading Room...................................348
Big Picture Issues...................................363
Exploiting Calendar-Related Trading Patterns 363
Buy Losers in Late December 364
Aggressively Buying Small Companies in December...................................366
Being More Bearish Between June and September 366
Selling Friday Afternoon and Buying Monday Morning...................................367
Buying Spinoffs About One Month After They Begin Trading...................................368
Buying Power Management...................................370
Tax Minimization...................................370
Risk Management...................................371

Afterword VideoFinancials & The Future Of Wall Street...................................375

Appendix A What Do Performance Figures Really Mean? 379

Appendix B Our Backtesting Methodology 389

Appendix C Brokerage Statements 393

Appendix D Glossary...................................464

Index 493

About the Authors...................................502

List of Exhibits

Part 1

Exhibit Name	Page Number
1 Data Driven Test Portfolio vs. S&P 500 - Growth	xxx
2 Data Driven Test Portfolio vs. S&P 500 - Returns	xxxi

Part 2

3	Fed Funds Rate Changes vs. S&P 500 Total Returns	16
4	The Fed Effect	18
5	Value Strategy - Low Price to Earnings (P/E)	25
6	Value Strategy - Low Price to Sales (P/S)	26
7	Value Strategy - Low Price to Book Value (P/BV)	28
8	Value Strategy - Low Price to Cash Flow (P/CF)	30
9	Comparison of Value Strategies– Graphs	32
10	Comparison of Value Strategies– Table	33
11	Growth Strategy - High Price to Earnings (P/E)	38
12	Growth Strategy - High Price to Sales (P/S)	39
13	Growth Strategy - High Price to Book Value (P/BV)	41
14	Growth Strategy - High Price to Cash Flow (P/CF)	42
15	Comparison of Growth Strategies– Graphs	44
16	Comparison of Growth Strategies– Table	45
17	Growth and Value Strategies vs. S&P 500– Graphs	50
18	Growth and Value Strategies vs. S&P 500– Table	51
19	Comparison of Growth vs. Value Strategies' Returns– Graphs	52
20	Comparison of Growth vs. Value Strategies' Returns– Table	53
21	Comparison of Growth vs. Value Strategies vs. Growth Less Value Index Returns	55
22	High Relative Strength vs. Low Relative Strength	60
23	Returns by Market Capitalization– Graphs	67
24	Returns by Market Capitalization– Table	68
25	Nanocap Risk	72
26	The Presidential Election Cycle - Returns	78
27	Monetary Policy and the Election Cycle	91
28	Market Cap and the Election Cycle– Returns	92
29	S&P 500 Returns by Fed-Election Cycle Phase - Current Years' Rates	104
30	S&P 500 Returns by Fed-Election Cycle Phase - Prior Years' Rates	106
	S&P 500 Returns/Number of Years in Each Phase	107
31	Fed-Election Cycle Summary of Returns - All Years	109
32	Fed-Election Cycle Summary of Returns - Aggressive Years	114
33A	Returns by Market Cap by Fed-Election Cycle - Current Years' Rates 100 Smallest Market Caps Over $10 Million vs. 100 Largest	132
33B	Returns by Market Cap by Fed-Election Cycle - Current Years' Rates	

     100 Smallest Market Caps Over $10 Million vs. 100 Largest vs. S&P 500 133

33C   Returns by Market Cap by Fed-Election Cycle - Prior Years' Rates
     100 Smallest Market Caps Over $10 Million vs. 100 Largest 134

33D   Returns by Market Cap by Fed-Election Cycle - Prior Years' Rates
     100 Smallest Market Caps Over $10 Million vs. 100 Largest vs. S&P 500 135

33E   Small Cap vs. Large Cap and the Fed-Election Cycle
     100 Smallest Market Caps Over $10 Million– Best & Worst Years vs. S&P 500 136

34A   Returns by Market Cap by Fed-Election Cycle - Current Years' Rates
     100 Smallest Market Caps Over $100 Million vs. 100 Largest 137

34B   Returns by Market Cap by Fed-Election Cycle - Current Years' Rates
     100 Smallest Market Caps Over $100 Million vs. 100 Largest vs. S&P 500 138

34C   Returns by Market Cap by Fed-Election Cycle - Prior Years' Rates
     100 Smallest Market Caps Over $100 Million vs. 100 Largest 139

34D   Returns by Market Cap by Fed-Election Cycle - Prior Years' Rates
     100 Smallest Market Caps Over $100 Million vs. 100 Largest vs. S&P 500 140

34E   Small Cap vs. Large Cap and the Fed-Election Cycle
     100 Smallest Market Caps Over $100 Million– Best & Worst Years vs. S&P 500 ..141

35A   Returns by Market Cap by Fed-Election Cycle - Current Years' Rates
     100 Smallest Market Caps Over $250 Million vs. 100 Largest 142

35B   Returns by Market Cap by Fed-Election Cycle - Current Years' Rates
     100 Smallest Market Caps Over $250 Million vs. 100 Largest vs. S&P 500 143

35C   Returns by Market Cap by Fed-Election Cycle - Prior Years' Rates
     100 Smallest Market Caps Over $250 Million vs. 100 Largest 144

35D   Returns by Market Cap by Fed-Election Cycle - Prior Years' Rates
     100 Smallest Market Caps Over $250 Million vs. 100 Largest vs. S&P 500 145

35E   Small Cap vs. Large Cap and the Fed-Election Cycle
     100 Smallest Market Caps Over $250 Million– Best & Worst Years vs. S&P 500 ..146

36A   Returns by Market Cap by Fed-Election Cycle - Current Years' Rates
     100 Smallest Market Caps Over $500 Million vs. 100 Largest 147

36B   Returns by Market Cap by Fed-Election Cycle - Current Years' Rates
     100 Smallest Market Caps Over $500 Million vs. 100 Largest vs. S&P 500 148

36C   Returns by Market Cap by Fed-Election Cycle - Prior Years' Rates
     100 Smallest Market Caps Over $500 Million vs. 100 Largest 149

36D   Returns by Market Cap by Fed-Election Cycle - Prior Years' Rates
     100 Smallest Market Caps Over $500 Million vs. 100 Largest vs. S&P 500 150

36E   Small Cap vs. Large Cap and the Fed-Election Cycle
     100 Smallest Market Caps Over $500 Million– Best & Worst Years vs. S&P 500 ..151

37A   Returns by Market Cap by Fed-Election Cycle - Current Years' Rates
     100 Smallest Market Caps Over $1 Billion vs. 100 Largest....................................152

37B   Returns by Market Cap by Fed-Election Cycle - Current Years' Rates
     100 Smallest Market Caps Over $1 Billion vs. 100 Largest vs. S&P 500 153

37C   Returns by Market Cap by Fed-Election Cycle - Prior Years' Rates
     100 Smallest Market Caps Over $1 Billion vs. 100 Largest....................................154

37D   Returns by Market Cap by Fed-Election Cycle - Prior Years' Rates
     100 Smallest Market Caps Over $1 Billion vs. 100 Largest vs. S&P 500 155

37E   Small Cap vs. Large Cap and the Fed-Election Cycle

100 Smallest Market Caps Over $1 Billion– Best & Worst Years vs. S&P 500 156

38A   Returns by Market Cap by Fed-Election Cycle - Current Years' Rates
        S&P 500– Graph & Table...157

38B   Returns by Market Cap by Fed-Election Cycle - Current Years' Rates
        S&P 500– Graphs..158

38C   Returns by Market Cap by Fed-Election Cycle - Prior Years' Rates
        S&P 500– Graph & Table...159

38D   Returns by Market Cap by Fed-Election Cycle - Prior Years' Rates
        S&P 500– Graphs..160

38E   Small Cap vs. Large Cap and the Fed-Election Cycle
        S&P 500– Best & Worst Years vs. 100 Largest 161

39A   Returns by Value & Growth by Fed Election Cycle - Current Years' Rates
        Price to Earnings 176

39B   Returns by Value & Growth by Fed Election Cycle - Current Years' Rates
        Price to Earnings vs. S&P 500..177

39C   Returns by Value & Growth by Fed Election Cycle - Prior Years' Rates
        Price to Earnings 178

39D   Returns by Value & Growth by Fed Election Cycle - Prior Years' Rates
        Price to Earnings vs. S&P 500..179

39E   Value vs. Growth and the Fed-Election Cycle
        Price to Earnings– Best & Worst Years 180

40A   Returns by Value & Growth by Fed Election Cycle - Current Years' Rates
        Price to Sales 181

40B   Returns by Value & Growth by Fed Election Cycle - Current Years' Rates
        Price to Sales vs. S&P 500..182

40C   Returns by Value & Growth by Fed-Election Cycle - Prior Years' Rates
        Price to Sales 183

40D   Returns by Value & Growth by Fed Election Cycle - Prior Years' Rates
        Price to Sales vs. S&P 500..184

40E   Value vs. Growth and the Fed-Election Cycle
        Price to Sales– Best & Worst Years..185

41A   Returns by Value & Growth by Fed Election Cycle - Current Years' Rates
        Price to Book Value..186

41B   Returns by Value & Growth by Fed Election Cycle - Current Years' Rates
        Price to Book Value vs. S&P 500..187

41C   Returns by Value & Growth by Fed Election Cycle - Prior Years' Rates
        Price to Book Value..188

41D   Returns by Value & Growth by Fed Election Cycle - Prior Years' Rates
        Price to Book Value vs. S&P 500..189

41E   Value vs. Growth and the Fed-Election Cycle
        Price to Book Value– Best & Worst Years 190

42A   Returns by Value & Growth by Fed Election Cycle - Current Years' Rates
        Price to Cash Flow 191

42B   Returns by Value & Growth by Fed Election Cycle - Current Years' Rates
        Price to Cash Flow vs. S&P 500..192

42C   Returns by Value & Growth by Fed-Election Cycle - Prior Years' Rates

	Price to Cash Flow	193
42D	Returns by Value & Growth by Fed Election Cycle - Prior Years' Rates Price to Cash Flow vs. S&P 500	194
42E	Value vs. Growth and the Fed-Election Cycle Price to Cash Flow– Best & Worst Years	195
43A	Returns by Value & Growth by Fed-Election Cycle - Current Years' Rates Value Index Minus Growth Index	196
43B	Returns by Value & Growth by Fed Election Cycle - Current Years' Rates Value Index Minus Growth Index vs. S&P 500	197
43C	Returns by Value & Growth by Fed-Election Cycle - Prior Years' Rates Value Index Minus Growth Index	198
43D	Returns by Value & Growth by Fed Election Cycle - Prior Years' Rates Value Index Minus Growth Index vs. S&P 500	199
43E	Value vs. Growth and the Fed-Election Cycle Value Index Minus Growth Index– Best & Worst Years	200
44A	Returns by Relative Strength by Fed Election Cycle– Current Years' Rates	204
44B	Returns by Relative Strength by Fed-Election Cycle vs. S&P 500– Current Years' Rates	205
44C	Returns by Relative Strength by Fed-Election Cycle– Prior Years' Rates	206
44D	Returns by Relative Strength by Fed-Election Cycle vs. S&P 500– Prior Years' Rates	207
44E	High Relative Strength vs. Low Relative Strength and the Fed-Election Cycle Best & Worst Years	208
45	The Fed-Election Cycle and Stock Selection Strategy	211
	The Yield Curve	218
46	Growth vs. Value and Inflation	223
47	How Mutual Funds and Brokerages Keep the Market "Efficient"	245

Part 3

48	How Psychological Factors Cause Market Inefficiencies	325
49	The VideoFinancials Paradigm	378
50A	Test Portfolio Performance Summary	394
50B	Test Portfolio Monthly Returns vs. S&P 500	395

Acknowledgements

Many people contributed to the creation of this book, and many others contributed to the ideas, methods, and mindset from which it arose. The authors would like to acknowledge each and every one of them by name, but that would be impossible, for several reasons.

Some of the individuals who inspired us hold high positions in the financial services industry, and their careers might suffer were they to become publicly associated with the more controversial aspects of our message. Other names have been left off the list due to the polite convention which requires us to obtain the consent of each individual so listed. This latter group includes many well-known public figures whose example inspired and educated us, but from whom it would have been difficult (if not impossible) to obtain consent. In any event, our best efforts to list each and every person who influenced, inspired, and supported our work would necessarily fail; we would be bound to miss an important name or two and so run the risk of offending those we seek to honor.

Recognizing our limitations, we nevertheless want to acknowledge by name certain individuals whose contributions to our book and to our lives have been especially meaningful. These include: Stephanie Barnes, Stan Harrison, Paige Stover Haugue and her associates at The Ictus Initiative, Dr. Edward Michna, M.D., Amanda Percival, Jim Percival, Herve Tessier, Stephen Tessier, and Alan Zucchino.

We also wish to express our gratitude to Standard and Poor's, a division of The McGraw-Hill Companies, Inc. for use of Compustat® and Index Services data, and to Fidelity Investments for permission to reproduce Mr. Matson's brokerage statements.

Finally, among those whose contributions influenced our work, three individuals deserve special recognition: Susan W. Bailey, who supported and influenced the writing of this book at every stage of its four-year course of development; Denis R. Desharnais, whose work with the S&P Compustat® database made our quantitative analysis possible; and Stephen J. Kurth, whose contributions in the development of the exhibits and the design and layout of the text made this book the esthetically pleasing product that it has become.

To all those who inspired and assisted us, whether named and unnamed, we wish to express our profound gratitude.

Special Foreword

When you've interviewed as many analysts, portfolio managers, and economists as I did at *The Wall Street Journal*, you discover a depressing truth: most of these richly-rewarded people are wrong most of the time. For each of my "Heard on the Street" columns, I had to interview a half-dozen or more of the best and brightest of Wall Street. Out of the 1500 or so people I encountered, perhaps five truly impressed me with their wisdom and vision.

The best of the best was Hamilton S. Gregg II, a silver-haired, impeccably-dressed gentleman who sat in my shabby newsroom office one afternoon while I chain-smoked and scribbled. He explained how he invested his clients' money giving extra weight to demographics. His thesis was simple: Gregg was forecasting a "Golden Age" in the U.S. economy based on Census Bureau birth and population data. The numbers told him that in the years to follow there would be a tightening of the available labor pool which would raise incomes, unleash a spending binge, and drive the Dow Jones Industrial Average to unthinkable heights.

That was in 1983. My alternating co-author on the column guffawed when he read the column the next day. "A 'Golden Age'!" he snorted from the other side of the cubicle wall. "Give me a break. You oughta be ashamed of yourself writing something as ridiculous as that."

I admit I was worried. Maybe my colleague was right. Maybe the guy was a flake, and I'd end up the blushing fool. But 21 years later, we can look back on the Golden Age he forecast, and forgive him for his lowball target; when the Dow was trading at an all-time high of 1200, he predicted Dow 5000. His forecast was considered so outrageous, my editors refused to print it.

Data drove Gregg's investment decisions: not analysts' recommendations; not stockbrokers flogging the latest dog on the firm's list; and certainly not talking heads on television. Data - the DNA of science and business - is the basis of intelligent investing.

If you had followed some of Mr. Gregg's advice (baby boomers are going to start having lots of kids), you would have bought Toys"R"Us for about $7.50 a share and ten years later been able to sell at $40, a 433% gain versus 150% for the Dow.

Other memorable investors I met included a guy who'd made a fortune in coin-operated video games because he was curious why every Saturday morning his kids begged him for rolls of quarters. He followed them and found a store full of boys pumping money into boxes. That was data.

Another person - Robert Prechter, the legendary technical market analyst named "Guru of the 1980's" and still a force to be reckoned with - told me how he mined mountains of data on past market activity to predict (accurately, it turned out) both the Great Bull Market and the Crash of October, 1987.

What happened to our stock markets during the 1990's was not data driven, and the result was chaos and disaster. Like past financial crazes - Tulipmania in 17th century Holland or the South Seas Bubble in 18th century England - the New Economy of the 1990's was driven by hype, greed, and old-fashioned corruption.

Like the inflated prices of tulip bulbs and the overblown expectations of Britain's trade with Asia, grandiose predictions about the Internet encouraged otherwise bright people to abandon their senses and, more importantly, ignore the hard facts – the data – that betrayed the hype. Companies with modest sales and no profits became, for a time, more valuable than long-established brand names heavy with tangible assets and cash.

The Internet was a revolution, alright. But like most revolutions, a lot of blood was spilled along the way.

The only reason people invest in the stock market is because they think they know something others don't. The only way to invest intelligently in the stock market is by *knowing* that you know something others don't. That knowledge comes from data, not some breathless story about a hot stock that's "gonna go to a hundred," or a new invention that "everyone in America will want to buy."

Data takes many forms, as you will learn in the pages of this important and ground-breaking book. Data is charts, historical trends and patterns, performance of large versus small company stocks, performance of the stock market relative to interest rates and Federal Reserve policy, how stocks anticipate and react to news, company fundamentals, demographics, and so on.

There are several common misconceptions or assumed rules that the authors of this book debunk, and rightly so. Principal among them is that the stock market is an efficient pricing mechanism. Very smart people have earned millions studying and trying to prove this theory, even winning Nobel Prizes for their research.

Efficient Market Theory says that stock prices reflect all information and expectations and that securities can't be overpriced or underpriced long enough to profit from them. Under Efficient Market Theory, Warren Buffett could not possibly become the richest man, and the most successful investor, in the world. We know from that bit of data how inefficient is Efficient Market Theory.

John Kay, a *Financial Times* columnist, put it best when he described the basic problem with Efficient Market Theory. It's like saying, "There is no point bending down to pick up a $10 bill because someone will have done it already. But if there is no point in bending down to pick it up, it will still be there."

Yet Wall Street, and many investors, are embracing Efficient Market Theory more than ever, sparking a surge in the amount of money being parked in index mutual funds. According to the Investment Company Institute, the fund industry's trade association, the number of exchange-traded domestic stock index funds jumped in the year ended March 2004 by 32%, to 87. As of March 2004, the gross issuance of shares in these funds for the year-to-date was more than twice what it had been a year earlier.

Wall Street continues to sell, and investors continue to buy into, the flawed argument that you can't beat the market. It's a message many people are receptive to after the slaughter of the post-bubble boom. Investors fed up with the bad behavior of analysts, brokers, mutual fund managers, and corporate leadership are turning index funds into the mattresses of the new millennium.

What is even more astonishing is that, because of fees that are sometimes very steep, index funds virtually guarantee their long-term investors that they will do worse than the market! You will never equal the market's return if you have to pay to do it. It's simple math.

The authors of this book know something that most people don't, and you should. Markets are notoriously inefficient, and opportunities for superior returns are always present. The data prove it, and there are many common sense reasons why: insider trading, corruption, bad or unethical analysis, brokerage houses hawking stocks for the wrong reasons, trading desks that continue to find ways to fleece their customers, mob psychology, and the best reason of all - the unexpected.

Terrorism, war, scandals, election results, mad cow disease, SARS - any number of unexpected events create volatility which makes markets inefficient. Inefficiency is the engine of opportunity.

Of all the factors, the one I believe has the most impact on inefficiency is insider trading in all its forms, both legal and illegal – sometimes it's hard to know the difference. Insider trading is common. It happens all day, every day, and anyone who doubts this need only look at a few statistics:

During the boom years of 1993-1998, members of the United States Senate who traded in stocks beat the market by 12 percentage points, according to a study by the Center for Responsive Politics in Washington. By comparison, corporate insiders beat the market by 5%, while the typical household underperformed by 1.4%.

Are senators and corporate insiders smarter than the rest of us? Don't bet on it. What seems more likely is that government officials run across all kinds of market-moving information because government regulation always affects stock prices. If you sit on the banking committee, everything that committee does is important news to Wall Street, and has the power to move prices. These senators also probably have juicy tips whispered into their ears by friends and lobbyists eager to trade for a favor.

Logic also tells you that corporate insiders are not waiting for you to figure out that business is booming, or the company's principal product is so flawed they're going to have to issue a massive recall. They may not trade themselves, but you can bet plenty of relatives, friends, and others are getting a piece of the action. And all of this takes place below the radar, so subtly that the SEC and Justice Department never catch on, can't make a case, or don't have the manpower to prosecute. Everyone may be speeding, but only a few get caught.

The brokerage industry and all of Wall Street thrives on one form of inside information or another. We now know about many of the abuses on the floor of the New York Stock Exchange, cheating on prices of mutual fund shares, and bogus research analysis. Now that those golden geese have been butchered, the brokerage industry is cooking up new ways to cheat customers, especially the big institutions.

In a refreshingly candid report released in September 2003, Bernstein Research described in detail how the big brokerage houses are becoming "counterparties" to their customers. In practice, that sometimes means brokers, in addition to earning a commission, are trading against their own customers, anticipating their orders, going into the market ahead of them, and scalping an extra buck.

They do it all with sophisticated computer programs that can guess ahead of time the big program trades of their customers - a battle of the bytes.

The Bernstein Report, in a tiny footnote buried in the middle of a dense, 32-page document, assures us that, with respect to certain uses of client demand data, "This is not 'front-running.' Trading in front of client orders is not acceptable behavior in the equity market, but using aggregate demand data captured from execution activity to trade in other securities is acceptable."

According to industry insiders I've spoken with, this is the moral equivalent of automated insider trading, and the practice is spreading within the industry, even though it's not in customers' best interests.

Regulators in other parts of the world have begun drawing lines in the sand. In early 2004, a major brokerage house - Deutsche Morgan Grenfell – was caught in the act of trading in anticipation of a program order by one of its customers, and fined over $300,000 by the Financial Services Authority, a British quasi-governmental regulatory agency, for "failing to... manage its conflicts of interests."

Insider trading occurs at all levels.

When I wrote the "Heard on the Street" column, it was a common occurrence that a stock I was researching for the next day's paper would light up or sag based on my reporting. The analysts and traders I interviewed could easily divine what I was writing about and whether it was positive or negative. They violated no law by jumping into the market for those stocks ahead of the *Wall Street Journal* hitting the newsstands the next morning.

So what's an individual investor or an ethical financial advisor to do in an inefficient market? Forget about inside information, for starters. Forget about fads, tips, and gut instinct.

The answer is to let data drive your investment choices. In the following pages you will learn about basic, common sense, easy-to-understand data; sources for data; and an overall strategy that begins with facts and ends with opportunities to exploit all these market inefficiencies.

The game on Wall Street is changing forever. Make sure you change with it.

— R. Foster Winans

Authors' Foreword

Wall Street will be a very different place in 2014.

Our capital markets will no longer be built on a foundation of self-serving securities salespeople who don't understand the products they sell, brokerage analysts who don't believe their own recommendations, and investment bankers free to corrupt the work of those analysts.

Vast numbers of ordinary, hard-working people will no longer entrust their retirement accounts to mutual funds that are simply too big to get out of their own way.

And the traditional brokerage and investment management industries will have shrunk considerably, unless they can evolve into creatures more in tune with investors' growing insistence on getting their investment advice from competent, ethical professionals, supported by research with integrity.

A generation ago, investors began to realize that whole life insurance policies paying 3% interest were a bad deal, and the life insurance business hasn't been the same since. Today, investors are becoming aware of the performance disadvantages of mutual funds and the scandalous practices of Wall Street's biggest names, and the financial services industry is on the verge of a more far-reaching restructuring.

Despite recent gains, the 2000-2002 market declines have led increasing numbers of investors to reassess the wisdom of putting money into actively managed equity mutual funds. The underperformance of these funds relative to major indices could be overlooked during the great bull market of the 1980's and 1990's. But investors whose portfolios are losing value month after month might well begin to question why they would pay sales charges of 6% or 7% and annual expenses of 1%, 2%, or more, to be in funds that consistently underperform the S&P 500.

The problems with mutual funds go beyond a few headline-grabbing practices – like late trading and market timing – that cheat small investors. Indeed, most mutual fund portfolio managers are honest and competent. For the most part, their performance shortcomings result from having impossibly large sums to manage. Even Peter Lynch's legendary performance at Fidelity Magellan suffered late in his career as mountains of cash were thrust upon his fund, though in his case this meant beating the S&P 500 by 2% a year rather than his usual 30%.

The big Wall Street firms used to benefit from name recognition, but now it is their curse. They used to steamroll small competitors with their armies of salespeople and slick brochures, but those advantages are becoming irrelevant overhead. Meanwhile, an SEC regulation known as "Reg FD" has sharply curtailed the privileged access to stock price-moving information that many brokerage analysts and mutual funds enjoyed in the past, and "Do Not Call" legislation has restricted use of the stockbrokers' primary sales technique: the cold call.

The old model of big brokerages selling the products of big mutual funds was built to work in a pre-Internet world. Back then, marketing campaigns involving TV ads, millions of phone calls, and expensive marketing brochures enjoyed advantages arising from huge economies of scale. But today, anyone with a few thousand dollars and an investment story to tell can build a website with the potential to reach millions of viewers 24 hours a day.

Who, then, will manage our trillions of dollars in equity investments, if not large, full-service brokerage firms or mutual funds doomed, as a group, to underperform the market?

Advances in information technology, combined with the advent of online discount brokerage firms, make it easier for individual investors to trade stocks, but probably only a minority will ever possess the skills or have the time required to effectively manage their own money.

A growing number of investors will have their investments managed by highly qualified, independent investment advisors.

Independent investment advisors have been around for a long time, mostly serving the needs of the very well-to-do, but less affluent investors have not entrusted their portfolios to independent money managers to the same extent.

Reg FD

"Reg FD" is an SEC regulation that restricts the "selective disclosure" of non-public information by an issuer of a publicly traded security. Under Reg FD, anyone acting on behalf of a publicly traded company who discloses material, non-public information to a securities market professional or holder of the company's securities must also disclose the information to the public – simultaneously, if the disclosure is intentional, or "promptly," if the disclosure is unintentional.

In formulating Reg FD, the SEC noted that selective disclosure of information (such as advance warnings of earnings results) provides unfair advantages to a privileged few, leading to a loss of investor confidence in the integrity of our capital markets.

The SEC also cited the potential for corporate executives to use their power to selectively disclose or withhold information as a way of gaining favor with analysts and pressuring them to report favorably on their companies. The SEC expressed its concern that analysts who publish negative views of a company are sometimes excluded from subsequent meetings with management. (cont'd.)

It's not difficult to speculate on the factors that might have led some of these investors to hesitate before retaining the services of an independent investment advisor. No doubt, many found reassurance in the thought of turning their money over to a big company rather than some "fly by night" outfit. Some might have had a bad experience with an unscrupulous or unqualified advisor, or heard horror stories from a friend who had had a bad experience.

Perhaps they felt safer dealing with Merrill Lynch, Janus, or Putnam, rather than the fellow down on Main Street.

Investors who may have considered leaving one of the big, scandal-plagued companies might have been unsure of how to go about picking an advisor. Or they might have thought that advisors only dealt with the very wealthy. Maybe they were put off by the 1-2% fees that the typical independent advisor charges (although they didn't hesitate to pay 5% to stockbrokers to get into mutual funds with even higher, albeit hidden, ongoing charges).

But as investors learn more about assessing an investment advisor's professional qualifications (and become more aware of the significance of professional qualifications like the Chartered Financial Analyst® designation), and as they learn to better evaluate advisors' performance figures, they will gain confidence in their ability to select an advisor (or advisors) who will meet their needs.

Furthermore, as they become better informed (due to new disclosure mandates) of the high costs and poor performance associated with most actively managed equity mutual funds, more investors will come to view the fees charged by independent advisors as a very good bargain. Meanwhile, expanded use of information technology will make it more feasible for independent advisors to accept smaller accounts.

With more and more investors leaving big brokerage and mutual funds, the need for independent investment advisors will increase. Many of the most highly qualified of these will be drawn from the roughly 50,000 holders of CFA® charters.

In the coming years, we expect that many more CFA charterholders will set up independent money management practices that:

1. Handle manageable amounts of money (rather than billions of dollars, or even tens of billions, as some mutual funds do today);

2. Manage funds with sensitivity to the tax situation of each individual client (unlike the mutual funds who, in 2000, managed to create huge amounts

---

The SEC also observed that, whereas issuers once had to rely on analysts to serve as information intermediaries, advances in information technology now provide a variety of methods for them to communicate directly with the market. Analysts might still provide value to investors by using their education, judgment, and expertise to analyze information, but they should not continue in the role of information gatekeepers.

The CFA Edge

The Chartered Financial Analyst® designation is earned, in part, by passing three annually administered, six hour written exams that thoroughly test candidates' knowledge in such areas as ethics, equity valuation, economics, accounting, and portfolio management (among others).

While a CFA charter does not guarantee an ability to consistently beat the market (nothing does), it's hard to imagine that anyone could earn a CFA charter without being motivated by a passion for the investment world.

We certainly wouldn't entrust a significant portion of our wealth to anyone who wasn't similarly motivated and competent, because, in addition to the extensive expertise required, the holder of a CFA charter is held accountable to the high standards of the AIMR® Code of Ethics.

of taxable income for many investors who had actually suffered enormous losses); and,

3. Use technology to improve performance and manage client accounts.

For now, even as the news media devote more and more air time to the failings of the conventional financial services industry, the "experts" go on appearing on television and radio programs to tell investors that they have no choice but to continue investing through traditional brokerage houses and mutual fund companies.

Nothing could be further from the truth!

Whether you are an investor who wants to take responsibility for managing your own portfolio of stocks or one who would prefer to work with an independent investment advisor, **Data Driven Investing**™ was researched, developed, and tested to prove that it is possible for you to outperform the big guys and beat the market over the long haul.

Although past performance is never a guarantee of future results, the 788% earned on the personal assets in our test portfolio over the past 45 months is an indication of what can happen when a reasonably competent portfolio manager puts a manageable amount of money to work in the stock market.

— Bill Matson and Mitch Hardy

April, 2004

Introduction

Over a recent 45 month period, during what eventually came to be considered the worst bear market since the Great Depression, we achieved compound annual growth rates of 79.0% in a highly diversified portfolio of mostly U.S. equities. During a period in which the S&P 500 index lost about 18% of its value, our portfolio gained 788%. One dollar invested on July 1, 2000 grew to $8.88 by March 31, 2004.

Exhibits 1 and 2 show our monthly and cumulative returns versus the S&P 500.

We ran this test portfolio with our own personal funds in order to test and refine the investing methodology that is explained in this book. Our methodology is derived from an analysis of strategies that would have achieved superior returns over a 52-year period, as demonstrated by extensive backtesting of historical data, and it employs trading tactics which take full advantage of the new Internet technologies and low commissions available to online traders.

Several factors led us to conclude that investors need a book like *Data Driven Investing— Professional Edition*.

While we were developing and testing our methods, the American public and its leadership were struggling through a stock market meltdown of horrific proportions.

During this deep bear market, which destroyed trillions of dollars in wealth, stock market losses were sustained by a much wider cross section of the population than ever before – including millions of investors who are in the market through 401k plans, IRA's, and mutual funds.

After the deflation of the high tech, dot.com investment bubble, the market was hammered down by one corporate accounting scandal after another. The market values of multi-billion dollar companies, like Enron, World-Com, Global Crossing, Tyco, Adelphia, and Xerox were compromised, if

The Nature of Superior Performance

We would be the first to admit that "past performance is no guarantee of future returns." In fact, we have written an entire appendix (see **Appendix A**) to explain why our test portfolio's advantage over the S&P 500 would be very difficult to maintain. It is essential reading for anyone who truly wants to understand how advantage in the investment world can be gained and lost, and how investors can be misled by performance claims.

Our test portfolio performance figures, if quoted in the absence of their context, are a perfect case in point. Although the figures do have meaning, careful scrutiny is required to deduce the nature and significance of this meaning.

A recurring theme of this book is that the market can be beaten by those who are willing to work at it. Your advantage over the S&P 500 should be a function of the volume of data you process and the wisdom with which you process it. It's rather like counting cards at a blackjack table – dull, mechanical work – but over time the payoff usually makes it all worthwhile.

Exhibit 1: Data Driven Test Portfolio vs. S&P 500 - Growth

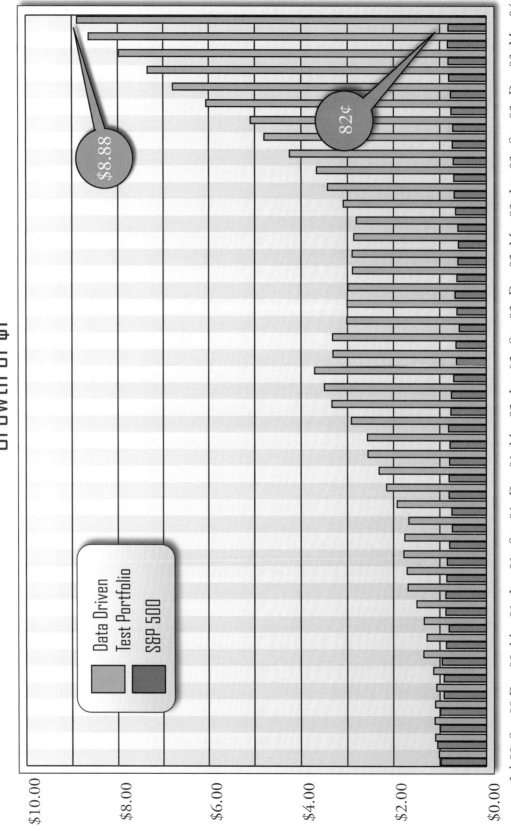

Data Driven Test Portfolio vs. S&P 500
Growth of $1

Exhibit 2: Data Driven Test Portfolio vs. S&P 500 - Returns

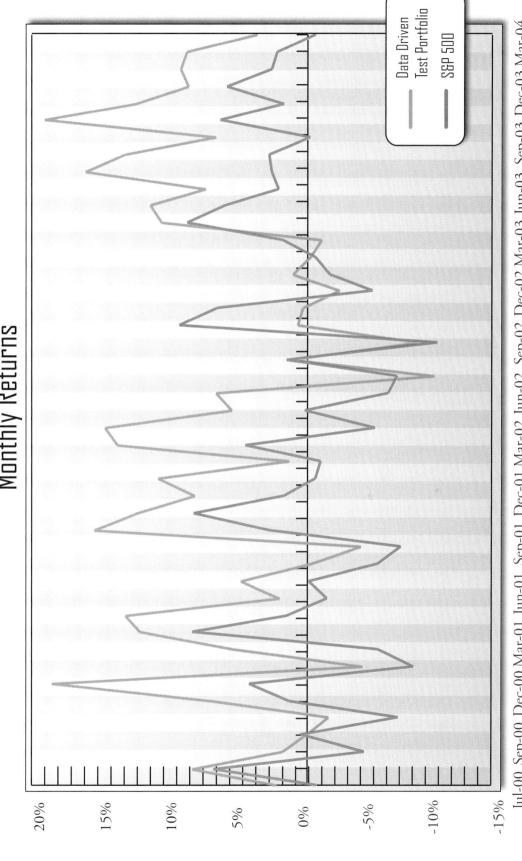

Data Driven Test Portfolio vs. S&P 500
Monthly Returns

not destroyed. Along the way, Arthur Andersen, an accounting firm formerly known for rock solid integrity, came to symbolize all that is wrong with the accounting profession.

Hard on the heels of the accounting scandals, more of Wall Street's dirty linen came to light with revelations that brokerage analysts were touting stocks that they privately considered losers, in return for investment banking deals involving millions of dollars in fees. And recently, longstanding problems in the mutual fund industry have surfaced as additional evidence that the game is rigged in favor of insiders.

None of the problems that have rocked Wall Street are new. The stock market has always been challenging for individual investors. What has changed, however, is that the investing public has become more and more aware of its vulnerability to a flawed system and unscrupulous investment professionals.

In response to this growing awareness, our leaders and the news media have been calling for reforms. President Bush has given major speeches on corporate accountability in an effort to boost markets. Congress has passed new laws and conducted hearing after hearing to determine what went wrong and how to fix it. Major structural changes have been proposed regarding oversight of the accounting profession and regulation of corporate behavior.

If fully implemented, some of these reforms might ameliorate the most flagrant abuses – which may eventually make investors feel better about the stock market – but we are skeptical that fundamental, structural problems will be fixed by legislation and regulation.

In a rapidly rising, "irrationally exuberant" market, many investors can make money, as many did during the dot.com era. In more normal market conditions, only those with some kind of edge can earn solid returns.

So, where is the individual investor to turn?

Interest rates on bank and money market accounts are usually too low to be helpful in funding a child's education or a comfortable retirement.

Mutual funds are not a good answer for most investors. The majority of mutual funds return less than market averages. Moreover, many – including some index funds* – carry high sales charges that further reduce returns. And, as we are learning, many have permitted practices that benefit insiders at the expense of ordinary fund investors. According to an analysis recently quoted by New York Attorney General Eliot Spitzer, practices such as market timing

---

* Even index funds underperform the market after sales commissions and fund expenses are deducted.

and late trading allowed a favored few to siphon as much as 2 percentage points off the already sub-par returns available to average investors.

Investing in stocks through a full service broker definitely isn't the answer. Full service brokers charge high commissions and push stocks recommended by their in-house analysts, who are, for a variety of reasons, rarely devoted to serving the interests of retail clients.

The answer to the investing needs of individuals will not be found in any of the traditional approaches. No conceivable amount of reform legislation or regulation can fix a system that is so fundamentally skewed toward the interests of professionals and insiders.

Fortunately, advances in information technology have created new alternatives that can level the playing field for the individual investor.

Access to timely information through the Internet, combined with low cost trading through online brokerage firms, provides individuals with opportunities that were previously only available to professionals. Real-time information necessary to trade intelligently can be obtained directly, bypassing the traditional broker. Many formerly uneconomical trading maneuvers have been made potentially profitable by low commissions.

In particular, web-based trading greatly facilitates the trading of stocks in very small companies. The superior returns from nanocaps (defined as companies with market caps of between $10 million and $100 million) are well documented, and, now, the enhanced flow of information, easy access to real-time bid and ask quotations, and low commission rates make nanocap investing much more attractive to individuals and small fund managers. Managers of multi-billion dollar portfolios, however, continue to be excluded from this opportunity by the sheer size of their funds under management. They move money in amounts that are simply too large to be profitably invested in nanocaps.

Granted, do-it-yourself online investing requires significant expertise and a commitment of time and effort that few of us are willing or able to make. A good alternative is provided by qualified, independent investment advisors who use the new tools and refrain from taking on more assets than they can properly handle.

Our test portfolio showed what can be achieved through such an approach. Using personal funds (but adjusting for a hypothetical 1.5% annual management fee), we earned 788% over 45 months, a compound annual return of over 79% in a down market. This was achieved mostly through long positions

Open-End Mutual Funds

When you buy an open-end mutual fund share, you are buying a share in the ownership of an investment pool. Unlike a typical corporation, which issues (i.e., sells) shares that are then traded in the secondary market (e.g., on stock exchanges), there is no secondary market for open-end mutual fund shares. The fund (i.e., the pool) is always the buyer or seller of the shares.

By law, the mutual fund must buy and sell its shares at "net asset value (NAV)," which is the per share amount of the fund's assets minus its liabilities. However, the fund can add on a sales charge (commission) when you buy shares, and it can subtract a redemption charge when you sell the shares back to the fund.

It also can charge you for some of its ongoing marketing and operating expenses. Unless you look very carefully, you don't see these operating expenses coming out. You only see a reduction in the NAV.

Never buy a mutual fund share without knowing exactly what sales and redemption charges will be assessed, and what the fund's "expense ratio" is. Then compare.

Profiting From Predictable Behaviors

Virtually every investment move we make is based in some way upon decision rules informed by over 50 years of historical data. The strategies we find to be most successful owe their effectiveness to either quirks in the psychology of investors or perverse incentives acting upon the analysts and accountants who influence investor behavior. Strategies rooted in well-established, predictable patterns of human behavior are, in our opinion, the ones most likely to enjoy continuing success.

Causality or Coincidence?

Our stock selection criteria are not based on chance relationships. There are very good real world causes underlying the past successes of strategies based upon these criteria. Fed policy changes, for instance, affect the spread between long-term and short-term interest rates, which affects the relative desirability of value stocks and growth stocks. When short-term rates fall significantly faster than long-term rates, the cash flows that growth companies project for the distant future become less desirable relative to the here-and-now cash flows of value companies. Would it surprise anyone to learn that presidential administrations change their behaviors in predictable ways as elections approach? Stocks have done particularly well at these times.

in the stocks of small companies, not through some exotic trading scheme that happened to benefit from a run of luck.

And this was no mere theoretical exercise. We invested real money through an online broker, in an amount sufficient to achieve extensive diversification with dozens of stocks. Our gains were not the result of winning one or two big gambles, but instead were earned through disciplined trading, with moderate risk. We hedged by purchasing put options and generally avoided naked short selling.

For readers who would like to see how we did it, we have taken the unprecedented step of publishing our brokerage statements in **Appendix C.**

We call our approach **Data Driven Investing**™ because our trading is driven by the interaction of new data with decision rules rooted in decades of historical data. We don't trade on emotion, interesting stories, or any desire to buy what is fashionable. Instead, we apply research into the psychology of decision making to better understand and predict the actions of our fellow traders.

The ongoing development of our strategy for stock selection relies heavily on analysis of historical data. We use the best and most comprehensive source of stock market data available, Standard and Poor's Compustat database. Using the Compustat database, we backtested numerous investment strategies over the 52-year period from 1951 through 2002.

With additional data on interest rates, we then tested those strategies against the backdrop of Federal Reserve monetary policy and Election Cycles. This led to our discovery that the best choice of investment style has been determined, with remarkable consistency, by the Fed's interest rate policy and the Presidential Election Cycle. From this knowledge, we fashioned a dynamic strategy for selecting stocks in coordination with the two cycles that are among the most powerful determinants of stock market returns.

You probably already know that Fed policy profoundly affects stock prices. But do you know the best kinds of stocks to buy when Fed policy changes direction? And do you know when it's best to avoid major commitments in the stock market? Do you know when the market is most likely to reward risk-takers, and when risk-takers tend to get crushed?

You will find answers to such questions in **Part Two** of *Data Driven Investing— Professional Edition.*

Data Driven Investing– Professional Edition is the first book to present and explain detailed analyses of over five decades of Compustat data, and (so far as we know) the only one ever to correlate returns for different investment styles with the monetary and political cycles. To our knowledge, only one other book (*What Works on Wall Street* by James O'Shaughnessy) has ever attempted to present an extensive analysis of the Compustat database, but that book was substantially narrower in scope.

Quantitative analysis of large databases like Compustat is one of the best ways we know of to gain insight into investment strategies that are likely to succeed. Large institutional investors use quantitative research extensively to improve their returns (although much of the work performed by Wall Street's math wizards involves financial engineering of exotic derivative securities).

Unfortunately, quantitative work with large databases is difficult and expensive, and hardly any of it becomes publicly available, except for highly technical, narrowly focused academic research papers. Very little has been published for a wider audience. As a result, individual investors rarely have access to the knowledge that is gained.

We wrote *Data Driven Investing– Professional Edition* to make our research available to all investors and to provide a comprehensive review of the ideas and methods we consider most important to long-term success in the stock market.

In Part One of this book, we trace recent developments leading up to the Information Age stock market and provide an overview of our data driven approach to investing.

In Part Two, we explain how we developed the quantitative screens we use to select stocks for our "watch list."

Part Three is devoted to the tactics we employ to initiate trades in conjunction with news stories and significant price changes.

A significant portion of *Data Driven Investing– Professional Edition* is devoted to an explanation of the day-by-day, hour-by-hour trading tactics we use to improve our returns, because successful investing goes far beyond stock picking.

Despite the revolutionary changes brought about by web-based trading, very little useful information has been published to show do-it-yourself investors how and when to place orders, or how to price them. Many traders miss out on opportunities by entering buy and sell orders in the same old, traditional ways.

Fed Policy & Investment Style

Not long ago, we created an unpublished survey of the most significant publications available on the topic of equity investing.

In our search for the best literature and techniques available, we examined many such works, but found nothing that dealt with the relationships between Federal Reserve interest rate policy and returns from various investment styles.

Data Driven Investing— Professional Edition is the first book to show how different investment styles have performed through five decades of interest rate and Presidential Election Cycles.

The Nuances of Order Entry

Until the early 1990's, most small investors gave their orders to salespeople who manually recorded the orders on paper tickets. In large, state-of-the-art brokerage offices, these tickets would then be placed in plastic cylinders that were dropped into order chutes and transported to the offices' wire rooms through intricate systems of chutes powered by a vacuum. When they got around to it, the wire room personnel would enter the orders via teletype. As orders were filled, New York would send back teletype confirmations. Eventually, these confirmations would get routed back to the salespeople, who would relay the information to the client when, and if, he or she called to ask.
(cont'd.)

If you wanted to buy a stock, you entered an order to "buy at the market." If you wanted to sell, you sold "at the market." That is, you were blindly accepting whatever the market prices happened to be.

Brokers actively discouraged limit orders, which only execute at a specified price (or better). A favorite saying of sales managers was "limit orders limit production" (i.e., commissions), meaning that salespeople placing limit orders would inevitably earn less money for themselves and the firm. (Unfilled limit orders don't generate commissions, whereas market orders are almost always filled.)

Investors used to be more justified in entering market orders, due to the logistical difficulties associated with adjusting limit orders. But now market orders typically make sense only when the trading spread is very small (i.e., when the difference between the bid and asked prices is 1% or less). It only takes a few seconds to adjust an online order. Nevertheless, investors are still encouraged to enter market orders by their brokers, even their online brokers.

Though order entry technology has leaped ahead, the old economics still apply to the brokers. Limit orders still limit their production. Commissions are lost when limit orders go unfilled. And brokerage firms' traders make less money when they can't buy stock at low-ball bid prices and sell at inflated asked prices.

Online investors have been empowered to start taking money back from these traders, but few of them know how to do it. A major objective of this book is to show them how.

We provide explanations and examples to help individual investors learn to trade like professionals (and professional traders learn to trade nanocaps). In particular, we emphasize the critical importance of reacting quickly and confidently to news stories, based on an understanding of the psychological factors that influence investor decision-making.

We also explain how and why we invest aggressively in nanocaps, and show how a nanocap fund that is kept to a reasonably limited size can be successfully traded through the aid of technology. And, we present data showing that the level of risk associated with a properly diversified portfolio of nanocaps is much lower than commonly perceived.

Most of the methods we discuss in *Data Driven Investing– Professional Edition* are techniques we use regularly. Others are included because they are important to understand, if only because other investors use them. We put a great deal of emphasis on understanding, and exploiting, our fellow traders' reactions.

We have included chapters on financial statement and fundamental analysis, not because we use them as primary stock selection methods, but because they help us interpret news stories. Chapter 13 covers the market inefficiencies (read: investment opportunities) created by misleading or fraudulent accounting and financial reporting, and discusses techniques for discovering when someone is "cooking the books." Chapter 14 outlines an approach to fundamental analysis based on competitive analysis, industry attractiveness, financial strength, and management quality.

While *Data Driven Investing– Professional Edition* provides a comprehensive approach to investing, readers should be cautioned that a significant amount of professional expertise and judgment is often required in the application of our ideas.

In most situations, it would be neither possible nor desirable to apply all of the techniques we describe in this book, because investment opportunities usually demand quick decisions based on imperfect information.

In this regard, our methods are like golf clubs. We carry a full bag of clubs around the course, but we don't use all 14 of them on every hole!

Also, it helps to bear in mind that learning to invest successfully is like learning to play scratch golf. It can't be done by simply reading a book. It takes good equipment, good instruction, and lots of practice.

Part One

OUR DATA DRIVEN
APPROACH TO INVESTING

In Part One, we trace recent developments leading up to the Information Age stock market and provide a general overview of our data driven approach to investing. In addition, we outline the key elements of our stock selection strategy and trading tactics.

Chapter 1

THE STOCK MARKET IN THE INFORMATION AGE

Widely held beliefs concerning the underlying mechanisms thought to govern stock price movements have undergone considerable change in recent years.

For almost a half century, the view of the market taught at business schools and held by a large percentage of investment professionals has been that the stock market is "efficient," i.e., that no one can consistently outperform the risk-adjusted market return.

Efficient Market Theory is multi-faceted, controversial and, in our view, patently absurd.

Efficient Market Theory forms the basis for an analytical construct known as portfolio optimization, which assumes that no stock is inherently a better investment than any other stock. Though it is acknowledged that some stocks are riskier bets than others, it is also assumed that the potential for reward is always exactly commensurate with risk. According to this line of thought, the only way to maximize a portfolio's risk-adjusted return is by maximizing its diversification.

The practical application of this theory entails buying stocks in all sectors, however overvalued they might appear to be, in order to maximize diversification. The wisdom of this approach went effectively unchallenged for decades.

Then, in the 1990's, along came the dot.com craze, when the market ascribed astronomical valuations to companies that, in many cases, had never produced a product or a dollar of earnings. We were told that mankind had entered a new era driven by technological innovations that would change every aspect of life as we know it, including the behavior of stock markets.

It Pays To Be Skillful

According to the conventional wisdom, one's expected return from stocks is purely a function of the risk one is willing to assume. One's prowess in selecting or trading stocks should make no difference in one's returns.

But through sheer idiocy or self-destructive intent, one could choose strategies that are guaranteed to lose money (by regularly placing market orders to buy and sell thinly-traded stocks, for example). And it's safe to say that, at any given time, there are plenty of misguided, if not self-destructive, participants in the stock market. So, if some of their strategies are doomed, isn't it reasonable to expect that other, more sensible, strategies are likely to do better than an average that includes the results of the financially suicidal?

Shouldn't an investor who makes fewer mistakes than the average investor be likely to beat market averages?

(cont'd)

Some games are so rigged (e.g., roulette or slots) as to have a negative expected value for all who play (except the house). The stock market does not fit this description since, over the long-term, gains for the average stock have been excellent. It is an "inherently profitable game," in that the expected value for a typical passive participant (such as an owner of an S&P 500 index fund) is greater than zero - in the long-term, anyway.

Any inherently profitable game that can be consistently lost by the actively incompetent should afford advantages to the actively skillful which are not available to the passive. In a 35-number roulette game with a 36:1 payoff (an inherently profitable game), over the long run all players are likely to win about as often as the player who always bets on the same number (i.e., the passive player), however whimsical their strategies for selecting numbers to bet upon might be.

Long-term stock market returns for any given investor, on the other hand, are likely to approximate:

a) the average market return
   PLUS or MINUS
b) a return component attributable to skill (or its lack)
   MINUS
c) market impact costs (driven by amount of assets managed)
   MINUS
d) brokerage commissions.

This reality is clearly at odds with the notion of an efficient stock market.

Revenue figures, hard assets, earnings, and cash flow became less relevant to valuation than the creativity of a hot young company's business model or the iconoclasm inherent in its paradigm.

Many industry veterans saw this for the speculative bubble that it was, but as the market reached new high after new high, more and more of these older, wiser professionals succumbed to the sirens of the brave new information era. Unfortunately for many, this period happened to coincide with the entrance into the market by vast numbers of new investors, individuals investing through their 401k accounts who wanted a piece of the action. No one wanted to be left behind in one of the biggest run-ups in market history.

True believers in Efficient Market Theory were compelled to mindlessly buy into the speculative frenzy by the dictates of their imperative to diversify as broadly as possible. Indeed, any portfolio not sporting a healthy slug of richly-priced tech stocks was, according to the prevailing wisdom, poorly diversified.

Upon the collapse of the dot.com market, investors began to return to traditional notions of valuation, only to be assaulted by a barrage of financial reporting frauds and revelations of dishonest brokerage analyst recommendations. These scandals profoundly affected investors' ability to evaluate stocks. Unable to believe the reported earnings for prior periods, and facing the prospect that analysts (or management) might be lying about prospects for future earnings, investors feel hard-pressed to make informed judgments concerning which stocks to own.

Thus, we have seen perceptions shift from faith in an "efficient market" to belief in the "new era of mankind" market and then, sadly, to the current widely held view that the market is rigged in favor of insiders.

No doubt conventional thinking about the equity markets will continue to evolve. Whatever the prevailing wisdom turns out to be in the next phase, we continue to believe that investors can prosper in the stock market by aligning their strategies with the market's predictable response to certain key factors.

We mentioned two such factors in the introduction to this book: Federal Reserve policy and the Presidential Election Cycle. These two factors have influenced stock prices in highly predictable ways over many years, through times of chaos, crisis, and uncertainty, as well as during periods of order and prosperity.

We identified these key factors – and measured their effects on different investment styles – by analyzing more than five decades of historical market data, and we tested their practical worth in over three years of real world application.

Until recently, it would not have been possible for an individual or small firm to engage in this kind of analysis. Nor would it have been possible for us to develop *Data Driven Investing– Professional Edition*, with its emphasis on quantitative stock selection strategies, quick reaction to breaking news, and fast, cheap on-line trading.

Information Age technologies are facilitating a fundamental realignment of opportunity away from big institutions and in favor of individuals and independent investment advisors. The Internet provides a convenient way to gather information on stocks and monitor news sources. Computing technology enables individuals to perform the kinds of analysis that formerly took teams of research assistants. And on-line, discount brokerage firms enable anyone with Internet access to enter trades for as little as $7.

Of course, the advantages provided by the Information Age stock market mean little to those who lack the expertise to exploit them.

Data Driven Investing– Professional Edition is dedicated to the proposition that individual investors and small firms can beat the market by learning and applying strategies that have worked consistently over long periods in the past, and by utilizing information technologies to stay informed and achieve better control over their trading.

Chapter 2

DATA DRIVEN INVESTING

We believe that, in any field of endeavor, success is a function of the wisdom of one's decision rules and the discipline with which those rules are applied. Nowhere is this more true than in the field of investing.

Very broadly speaking, our rules for investing are:

Rule #1: Select stocks to own (and to avoid) based ONLY upon strategies that have worked consistently over long periods in the past.

Rule #2: Employ trading tactics based on well-established patterns of investor behavior.

Rule #3: Develop pre-determined action plans so that the response to new data is swift, automatic, and appropriate. Closely monitor news sources for stories and react as quickly as possible to news of material events.

Rule #4: Stay with the program. Don't deviate from rules 1-3, no matter how tempting the opportunity seems at the time.

We call our approach **Data Driven Investing**™ because the strategies we derive from our analysis of historical data interact continuously with real-time data to drive our investment process.

The Data Driven Philosophy

The data driven approach is a pretty good approach to life in general. If you study what has worked well in the past and consistently apply this knowledge to whatever you are doing, your chances of success will probably be better than they otherwise would have been – especially if you are prepared to use this knowledge on a moment's notice when an opportunity arises.

Good luck, it is said, occurs when preparation meets opportunity. Preparation is all about the analysis of past data and the development of contingency plans. Exploitation of an opportunity requires the recognition of similarities between the opportunity and the contingency for which a plan has been devised, in addition to the ability to react swiftly and decisively.

You can't expect to exploit opportunities if you don't have plans for finding and reacting to them.

Key Elements of Our Approach to Investing

Data Driven Investing– Professional Edition consists of a number of elements which, in organizing this book, have been grouped into:

- Strategies for selecting stocks; and,

- Trading tactics

We will cover strategies for selecting stocks in Part Two. Trading tactics will be presented in Part Three.

Our strategies and tactics combine to form a three step process.

The first step is to identify the types of stocks that are likely to achieve superior returns. We accomplish this by analyzing decades of historical market data to determine the quantitative characteristics of stocks that have consistently performed well in each of the various monetary and political climates.

The next step is to run quantitative screens to identify stocks possessing these characteristics. There are thousands of publicly traded companies from which to choose. Running screens allows us to better focus our attention on a "watch list" of suitable candidates.

The third step is to employ time-tested tactics to trade stocks in response to breaking news. The trading tactics that determine how and when we place our orders are derived both from analysis of historical data and experience gained while risking real money.

Success in the market requires more than just picking the right stocks. The timing, pricing, and type of orders we enter can significantly affect performance. Successful trading also depends on the discipline and consistency with which we apply our tactics.

While we speak of this as a three step, sequential process, in practice all three tasks may be performed more or less continuously. We constantly seek to develop and maintain a watch list of the most desirable stocks to own, and we apply our tactics to enter trades whenever breaking news creates an opportunity to buy or sell a watch list stock.

How We Develop Screening Criteria

Data driven investing should not be confused with what is commonly referred to as "technical analysis." We do not study short-term patterns in stock charts to predict the movements of individual stocks or the market as a whole. Instead, we examine how fundamental forces that move equity markets – such as Federal Reserve monetary policy – affect traditional methods of picking stocks (e.g., ratios of price to earnings, price to book value, etc.), in order to develop the quantitative stock screening criteria that serve as the first level of our selection process.

Strategies for Selecting Stocks

Our approach to selecting stocks involves:

- **Reacting to Federal Reserve Policy:** Federal Reserve Bank monetary policy exerts a profound and predictable influence on the behavior of stock and commodity prices. The Fed Policy Cycle, alternating between expansive and restrictive phases, determines the kinds of stocks we buy and sell.

- **Buying High Relative Strength Stocks:** The relative strength measure compares a given stock's return over a defined period of time to the returns of all other stocks in a given group. For example, a stock with a 12-month relative strength of 90 has outperformed 90% of the stocks in its group during the past 12 months. Stocks with high relative strength tend to outperform market indices most of the time. One notable exception is "tax season" (late December through early February), when low relative strength stocks are usually the best choice.*

- **Buying Nanocap Stocks:** Other things being equal, we focus on stocks whose market capitalization is under $100 million, thereby profiting from the well-established pattern – supported by decades of market data – that the smaller the market value of a company, the better its stock price performance is likely to be.

- **Reacting to the Election Cycle:** The four-year Presidential Election Cycle exerts a strong, predictable influence on stock market behavior. Our data clearly indicate that overall market performance improves in the years leading up to an election. Furthermore, the Election Cycle Effect, interacting with the Fed Effect, affects the performance of different investment styles in different ways.

- **Buying Stocks with Minimal Analyst Coverage:** In general, companies that receive little or no coverage by brokerage analysts present better opportunities, because analyst coverage tends to drive stock prices higher than they would otherwise be. Wall Street coverage reduces the potential for profiting from market inefficiencies and increases the likelihood of trading losses. (The absence of analyst coverage contributes to the superior performance of nanocaps. Few stocks with market caps under $100 million are well covered by analysts.) However, we nearly always avoid very large companies with minimal analyst coverage. Brokerage analysts tend to avoid covering large cap companies with problems, rather than issue neutral or negative reports on them.

It Pays To Be In Style

The Fed Effect on stock prices affects different classes of stocks in different ways. While the Fed was lowering rates in 2001-2002, the overall market fell, contrary to conventional expectations, but carefully selected value stocks still did quite well.

The Politics Behind The Election Cycle Effect

One theory attempting to explain the Election Cycle Effect suggests that presidential administrations tend to save initiatives favorable for stocks until later in their terms, in an effort to concentrate the market's gains during re-election campaigns. The Bush administration's activities immediately following the 2002 mid-term elections suggest this possibility.

Harvey Pitt, the colossally unpopular SEC Chairman, and Paul O'Neill, considered by many a failed Secretary of the Treasury, resigned shortly after the mid-term elections. About the same time, the administration's proposal to eliminate the double-taxation of dividends and capital gains was floated. The market responded with big gains in 2003, despite temporary setbacks caused by the Iraq war.

* Source: Stock Traders Almanac 2002, page 112.

- **Profiting From Deficiencies in GAAP Accounting Rules:** We take advantage of differences between a company's true economic condition and performance, and its condition and performance as reported according to GAAP accounting principles.

- **Profiting from Fundamental Analysis:** We employ fundamental analysis to evaluate news stories within the context of the subject firms' industry attractiveness, competitive position, financial resources, and management quality. This helps us assess the impact of new developments on critical earnings and cash flow trends.

Trading Tactics

The key elements of the tactics with which we trade stocks can be summarized as:

- **Understanding and Applying the Psychology of Investing:** When buying or selling shares, we remain acutely aware that we are interacting with real people, who are motivated by the same psychological underpinnings that drive us all. Prejudices, preferences, fears, and illusions impair investors' ability to make rational decisions and delay their reactions to new information, leading to predictable patterns of behavior which can be exploited to our profit.

- **Reacting to News Stories and Significant Price Changes:** We react swiftly and surely to news stories and significant price changes affecting the companies on our watch list. Usually, when a company meeting our selection criteria is the subject of a "good news" story, we try to be first in line to buy. When a company we own is the subject of a "bad news" story, we sell immediately in most cases.

- **Responding to Volume:** Our trading decisions are informed by volume, meaning that our evaluation of events (such as price movements and news stories) is partly based on the volume of other investors' trades entered in response. Market reactions confirmed by high volume are more credible and likely to be sustained than reactions accompanied by low volume.

- **Profiting from the Impatience of Others:** On thinly-traded stocks with wide bid-ask spreads, we enter standing orders to buy and sell shares at the edges of the spread. We call this tactic *shopkeeper trading*, because by maintaining an "inventory" of open orders, we supply convenience (i.e., liquidity) similar to the way the owner of a retail store provides a quick, convenient way to make purchases. We earn the spread whenever impatient traders enter market orders to buy or sell (except in the rare instances when these traders have correctly anticipated a significant price trend – then we lose).

- **Profiting from Established Trading Patterns:** We trade on the basis of short-term patterns established over many years. Examples include tax-motivated year-end trading patterns (e.g., the "January Effect"), weekly patterns that often lead to temporarily depressed Monday morning prices, and patterns in the trading of spinoff stocks.*

- **Making Money from Losers:** We buy put options or short sell in situations where a falling stock price is highly predictable, such as when an overpriced stock is the subject of a very bad news story. When a company reports its first quarterly profit following an extended period of losses, we often buy the stock before the market can fully respond to the turnaround.

- **Staying Fully Invested:** Except during conditions we call "Panic Years" (see Chapter 11), we typically remain fully invested in equities, augmenting our exposure with margin borrowing. Whenever our portfolio runs out of buying power, we sell the worst performers and reinvest the proceeds in stocks associated with good news stories.

- **Hedging Against Catastrophe:** We cross-hedge a portion of our holdings in order to reduce our overall risk. We typically buy put options on the NASDAQ 100 index (i.e., QQQ's) or richly-priced growth stocks during Fed-Election Cycle phases that favor value stocks, switching to puts on the Dow Jones Industrial Average (DIA's) during phases that favor growth stocks.

Integrating Stock Selection Strategy and Trading Tactics

To summarize our data driven approach to investing, we continuously refine our stock selection criteria by backtesting investment strategies against the backdrop of critical cycles, such as the Federal Reserve monetary and Presidential Election Cycles. We periodically run quantitative screens to update a watch list of stocks possessing the appropriate criteria, focusing primarily on nanocap stocks (defined as companies with market caps of between $10 million and $100 million).

We carefully monitor news sources, especially the Internet, for news stories affecting the companies on our watch list. We also watch for significant price changes on these stocks (because significant price movements often presage news events). When a news story breaks or a significant price change occurs, we swiftly implement predetermined actions in response.

A Really Stupid Thing To Do

Placing a market order to buy or sell a thinly-traded stock is usually a really stupid thing to do – but lots of people do it anyway.

Shopkeeper trades provide a way to profit from such stupidity.

Why Spinoffs Bounce Back

When a company spins off a business unit, it issues shares in the newly formed corporation to its existing shareholders.

The recipients of these shares often sell them shortly thereafter, prompted by brokers who earn easy money by telling clients to unload the stock and buy something "more in line with their financial plans." Also, many institutional investors are forced to sell spinoff shares due to prohibitions against their investing in small cap stocks.

In general, share prices of spinoff companies bounce back after this initial sell-off.

---

* "Institutional Demand and Security Price Pressure: The Case of Corporate Spinoffs," *Financial Analysts Journal*, Sept./Oct. 1993 by Brown and Brooke, and "Restructuring Through Spinoffs" *Journal of Financial Economics*, 1993, by Cusatis, Miles, and Woolridge.

We buy stocks on the watch list when good news stories break. When there is bad news or a significant price decline on heavy volume, we usually sell the affected stock immediately.

We try to stay fully invested, including buying on margin, and cull our losing positions whenever we run out of purchasing power in order to free up funds for new purchases. We hedge against catastrophe with put options on major market indices.

Part Two

OUR DATA DRIVEN
STOCK SELECTION STRATEGY

In Part Two, we explain how we developed the quantitative screens used to select stocks for our "watch list." We review the analyses of long-term historical data that lead us to a better understanding of the effects of Federal Reserve monetary policy, the Presidential Election Cycle, the nanocap advantage, and relative strength on the performance of value versus growth strategies, and we state our theories regarding the underlying reasons for their effectiveness.

Chapter 3

THE FED EFFECT

Federal Reserve Bank monetary policy exerts a profound and predictable influence on the behavior of stock and commodity prices. The Fed Policy Cycle, alternating between expansive and restrictive phases, determines the kinds of stocks we buy and sell.

Even a casual observer of the stock market knows that when the Federal Reserve Bank lowers interest rates, investors usually bid stock prices higher – and when the Fed raises rates, the market usually reacts negatively.

When the Fed lowers rates, it is said to be pursuing an expansive policy, because lower rates encourage economic growth. Economic growth leads to higher corporate earnings, and lower interest rates increase the current value of future dividends and capital gains – all of which is positive for stock prices.

When the Fed raises rates, it is said to be pursuing a restrictive policy, because higher rates restrict the rate of economic growth. Slower economic growth puts pressure on corporate earnings, and higher interest rates reduce the current value of dividends and capital gains – all of which is negative for stock prices.

The relationship between interest rates and stock prices can be seen in **Exhibit 3**, which plots changes in the Fed Funds rate against the S&P 500 total return. With few exceptions over the past five decades, lower rates were associated with higher returns, and vice versa.

Obviously the market likes lower interest rates, but how much does it like them? How much of an effect does Federal Reserve policy have on equity market returns?

Interpreting Fed Policy

Throughout most of its 90 year history, the Fed has managed the nation's money supply – and economy – primarily by setting short-term interest rates.

Originally, the discount rate (the rate charged by the Fed for loans to member banks) was considered the most important gauge of Fed policy. For most of the past 3-4 decades, Fed policy has been inferred from changes in the Fed Funds rate (the rate charged for overnight loans between member banks). However, during a four year period beginning in October 1979, the Fed gave up setting interest rates altogether and switched to managing the quantity of unborrowed reserves directly. (This allowed the Fed Funds rate to fluctuate rather dramatically, as can be seen in **Exhibit 3**.)

These changes in the Fed's approach to managing the money supply complicate somewhat the task of measuring the impact of Fed policy on stock market returns.
(cont'd.)

Exhibit 3: Fed Funds Rate Changes vs. S&P 500 Total Returns

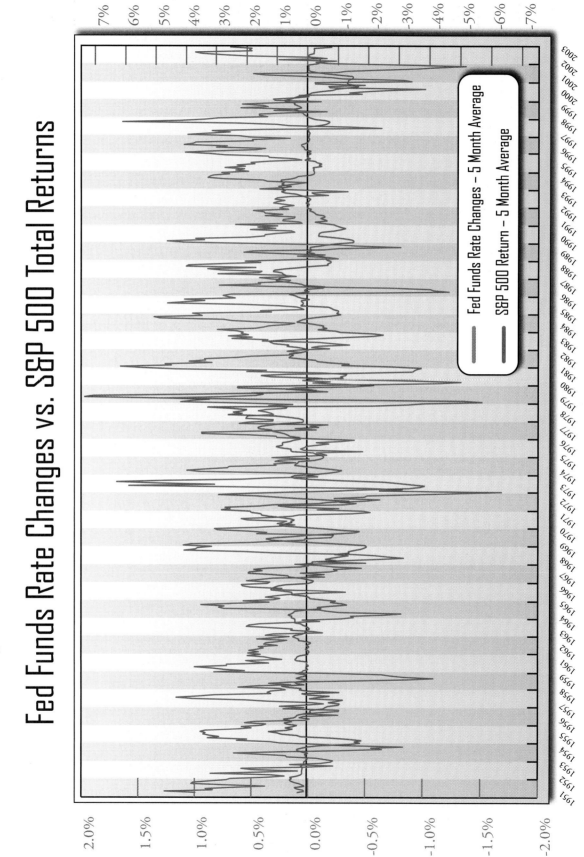

Fed Funds Rate Changes vs. S&P 500 Total Returns

Fed Funds Rate Changes – 5 Month Average

S&P 500 Return – 5 Month Average

The answer, as will be seen, is that Federal Reserve interest rate policy has a substantial effect on the market's performance.

Monthly averages of the daily closing Fed Funds rate are available from the Fed's historical database going back to July 1954. **Exhibit 4** shows the average monthly performance of the S&P 500 for this period, comparing the index's performance during months in which the Fed Funds rate rose to its performance during months in which the rate declined.

During months in which the Fed Funds rate fell, the S&P 500 gained an average of 1.48% per month. During months in which the Fed Funds rate rose, the S&P 500 returned just 0.57%. The S&P 500 had a positive total return in 65% of the months during expansive periods, compared to 59% for restrictive phases.

A difference in performance of 0.91% per month may not sound huge, at first reading, but it amounts to an annual performance advantage of 11.5%. By any measure, this is a significant difference in returns.

It has been said that the job of the Federal Reserve Bank is to take away the punch bowl just when the party is getting good. While that punch bowl is on the table, though, investors have every reason to celebrate.

Furthermore, as **Exhibit 4** shows, there were notable differences in seasonal patterns during months when the Fed Funds rate was falling, compared to months in which it rose.

When rates were falling, the average S&P 500 total return was greater than 1% in nine months of the year. Only one month (September) had a negative return (-0.73%). Two months had positive returns of less than 1%.

January was the best month in which to own the S&P 500 when the Fed Funds rate was falling, returning an average of 2.5%. Average returns were strong through the remainder of the winter and spring months, as was the percentage of profitable months.

There was an obvious slump in returns during the summer months (except for July), which persisted through September. September was easily the worst month for the S&P 500 when the Fed Funds rate was falling. Besides having a negative average return, it was the only month with less than a 50% probability of earning a profit. The typical year ended with good returns in October, November, and December.

Fed policy may be inferred from changes in the discount rate, changes in the actual Fed Funds rate (which fluctuates daily), or from changes in the Fed's *target* for the Fed Funds rate (which wasn't even publicly announced until recently).

For our purposes, we are interested only in directional changes in the Fed's interest rate policy. If the most recent directional change was an increase in rates, we consider the Fed to be pursuing a restrictive policy. If the most recent directional change was a decrease, we consider the Fed to be pursuing an expansive policy.

In determining directional changes in Fed policy, it makes little difference whether we base our characterization of Fed policy on changes in the discount rate, Fed Funds actual rate, the Fed Funds target rate, or some combination of these rates.

All of the Fed Policy Cycle analysis presented in *Data Driven Investing– Professional Edition* is based on changes in the Fed Funds actual rate because, of the options available, it is the rate for which the best historical data is available.

Exhibit 4: The Fed Effect

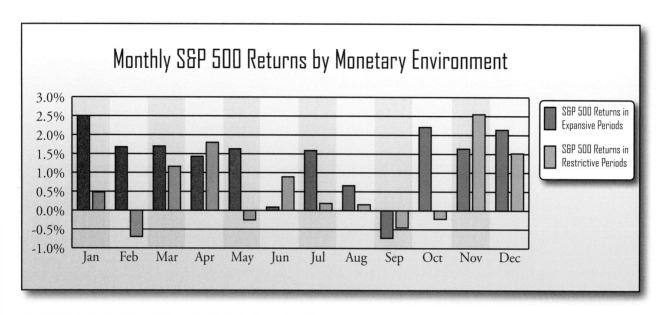

S&P 500 Returns by Monetary Environment, 1954-2003

		Expansive Periods					Restrictive Periods					
	Rank	S&P 500 Average Return	Total Number of Months	# of Months Positive	% of Months Positive	Rank	S&P 500 Average Return	Total Number of Months	# of Months Positive	% of Months Positive	Rank	Advantage When Fed is Expansive
January	1	2.50%	27	17	63%	6	0.48%	22	13	59%	3	2.02%
February	5	1.68%	20	15	75%	12	-0.70%	29	12	41%	2	2.38%
March	4	1.70%	20	15	75%	4	1.16%	29	20	69%	7	0.54%
April	9	1.43%	18	12	67%	2	1.80%	31	23	74%	10	-0.37%
May	7	1.63%	19	13	68%	10	-0.25%	30	17	57%	4	1.88%
June	11	0.09%	16	8	50%	5	0.89%	33	20	61%	11	-0.80%
July	8	1.59%	25	15	60%	7	0.19%	24	10	42%	5	1.40%
August	10	0.66%	16	10	63%	8	0.16%	34	18	53%	8	0.50%
September	12	-0.73%	23	10	43%	11	-0.45%	27	12	44%	9	-0.28%
October	2	2.21%	29	19	66%	9	-0.22%	21	14	67%	1	2.43%
November	6	1.64%	27	18	67%	1	2.55%	23	17	74%	12	-0.91%
December	3	2.14%	30	24	80%	3	1.52%	20	15	75%	6	0.62%
All Months		1.48%	270	176	65%		0.57%	323	191	59%		0.91%

Returns during the months in which rates rose followed an entirely different pattern.

Four of the months had negative average returns, while another four had returns of less than 1%. Only four months had positive average returns of greater than 1%: March, April, November, and December.

Average returns in the month of January were marginal. February was the worst month of the year to hold the S&P 500 when rates were rising, with an average return of -0.70% and the lowest probability of achieving a positive return (41%). Returns were better in the early spring, but then were marginal, at best, until November, which had the best average returns (2.55%) when rates were rising. December was the third best month, with an average return of 1.52%.

The Power of the Fed Effect

Clearly, Federal Reserve interest rate policy has a powerful effect on stock performance.

The best opportunities for gains occur during periods of expansive monetary policy, particularly during the non-summer months. During expansive phases, the prices of many stocks increase, and the challenge for investors is to find bargain stocks.

Restrictive periods pose a different problem. Fewer stocks do well, and the challenge is to find investments that can prosper in a more difficult environment.

Furthermore, the different seasonal patterns of trading we observed in expansive versus restrictive months suggest that other factors may be interacting with the Fed Effect to affect market performance.

This knowledge might not be especially useful but for one other important fact: Federal Reserve monetary policy affects different classes of stocks in different ways. This creates the opportunity to craft strategies based on these differences. Other factors interacting with the Fed Effect – things like tax law, investor psychology, and the Presidential Election Cycle – add to the opportunity.

Strategies built around an understanding of the Fed Effect have a high probability of achieving outstanding performance during expansive periods and respectable performance during restrictive periods. Our test portfolio results demonstrate what can be achieved with such strategies.

A substantial part of *Data Driven Investing– Professional Edition* will be devoted to the development of stock selection strategies for each phase of the key cycles that drive the market, chief among them the Fed Cycle. Investors need not accept low returns during restrictive phases. Winning strategies exist for such difficult periods, strategies that are different from those which have performed well during expansive phases.

However, this chapter's brief discussion of the Fed Effect is just a starting point. Additional background is required to fully understand the Fed Effect and investment strategies based on it.

Before we can complete our explanation of the Fed Effect, we need to lay some groundwork by discussing value and growth stocks, relative strength, market capitalization, and the Presidential Election Cycle.

We'll begin with an explanation of what we mean by value stocks and growth stocks.

Chapter 4

VALUE STOCKS

Value investing is a style that has many adherents, among them some of the most successful investors of all time. Many books – and a great deal of media commentary – have been devoted to value investing. Scan the lists of mutual funds and you can find scores of "value funds."

Value strategies have something of an image problem in certain quarters. They are seen by some as humdrum, boring, and perhaps not suitable for highly intelligent, highly charged young individuals who are willing to take more risks because they want their money to grow fast.

Value strategies will never have the allure of growth strategies. They might be suitable for old folks who can't afford to take any chances, but they will never be seen as exciting, or fun.

But do they make money?

What is a Value Stock?

Let's start by defining what we mean by a "value stock."

A value stock is one whose price is low in comparison to certain figures derived from the company's financial statements, such as earnings, sales, book value, or cash flow.

Practically speaking, the relationship between a stock's price in the open market and the company's financial results is expressed as a ratio between the price per share and per share amounts for earnings, sales, book value, or cash flow. For convenience sake, we'll refer to these as price ratios.

For our purposes, a value stock is one with price ratios that are among the lowest of all public companies.

Selecting Value Stocks

Some of the traditional ways to measure the relationship of a stock's market price to its value include:

- **Low Price to Earnings (P/E):** stock price divided by earnings per share

- **Low Price to Sales (P/S):** stock price divided by sales per share

- **Low Price to Cash Flow (P/CF):** stock price divided by cash flow per share

- **Low Price to Book Value (P/BV):** stock price divided by book value per share

In this chapter, we will compare the returns that would have been earned by stock selection strategies based on these four commonly-used measures of value.

Before we launch into this comparison, however, we need to briefly explain our analytical methodology.

Notes on Methodology

Following Rule #1 of **Data Driven Investing**™, we are looking for strategies that have worked consistently over long periods in the past.

We began, therefore, by calculating the returns that would hypothetically have been earned over a 52 year period (1951-2002) by portfolios consisting of the 100 stocks with the lowest positive P/E, P/S, P/CF, or P/BV ratios.

At the beginning of each year, the portfolios were reconstructed to include only the 100 "cheapest" stocks, as measured by the prior year's earnings, sales, cash flow, or book value and the stocks' year-end price. The average and compound returns earned by each of these four value stock selection strategies over the entire 52 year period were then compared to those of the other strategies as well as to the returns earned by the S&P 500.

Backtesting

The returns which are calculated for each value strategy are "hypothetical" in the sense that we don't actually know that anyone has followed such a strategy for 52 years.

However, by using historical stock price data and real financial statement data from real companies, it is possible to simulate the performance of a strategy. This technique is known as *backtesting*.

There are several ways to calculate ratios derived from income statement figures, such as P/E, P/S, and P/CF. For example, to calculate P/E, one could use the previous fiscal year's reported earnings, the last four quarters' reported earnings, last quarter's earnings multiplied by four, or forecasted earnings for some future period. The best choice depends on circumstances.

When calculating ratios derived from balance sheet figures, such as P/BV, book value per share is usually obtained using the most recent financial statements available.

Our calculations were derived from data on companies with market values in excess of an inflation-adjusted $10 million (in 2002 dollars) included in the Standard and Poor's Compustat Active and Research Database for the period from 1950 through 2002. Transaction costs were ignored. Dividends were added in calculating the total return for each year.

Interested readers can find a more detailed discussion of our methodology in Appendix B.

Performance of Value Strategies

Exhibits 5-8 show the results for each value strategy. In addition to return figures, the tables show the strategies' performance advantage over the "market" (i.e., the amount by which the strategies' returns exceed the S&P 500 returns). Bear in mind that the "advantage" can sometimes be negative, meaning the strategy underperformed the S&P 500. The exhibits also show:

- The growth of $1 invested in the portfolio at the beginning of the study period,

- The number of years out of 52 that the strategy beat the S&P 500,

- The arithmetic average of the return calculations, and

- The compound rates of return for the entire 52 year period.

Low Price to Earnings (P/E)

We'll start with one of the most commonly used measures of value, the price to earnings ratio (P/E). (**Exhibit 5**)

Many investors focus on earnings as the primary determinant of a company's worth. Proponents of the low P/E strategy advise investors to beware of paying too much for earnings. According to this point of view, a dollar of earn-

---

Look-Ahead Bias

"Look-ahead" bias is a potential weakness in backtesting.

It results when the study relies on information that would not have been available to an investor at the time the investment decisions were assumed to have been made. An example would be a study of returns for stocks purchased on the basis of earnings data that was not actually available at the time the stock was bought.

To address concerns regarding both look-ahead bias and stale data, we performed our backtests with both lagged and unlagged data.

Lagging the data by one year (e.g. constructing portfolios in 1952 on the basis of 1950 financial statement data) led to significant differences in portfolio returns. However, the return patterns we derived from lagged data were remarkably consistent in supporting the conclusions we reached with unlagged data.

Skeptical readers may confirm our most significant conclusions through side-by-side comparisons of our backtest results with those presented by James O'Shaughnessy in *What Works on Wall Street*.

O'Shaughnessy used lagged data to construct his portfolios, and his methodology differed from ours in several important respects. Consequently, his portfolios' return figures significantly differ from ours.

Nevertheless, the return *patterns* that emerge from his figures serve to confirm our most significant conclusions regarding the effects of Fed policy and the Election Cycle on returns to differing investment styles.

ings from sales of chewing gum is identical to a dollar of earnings from sales of banking services.

It follows that the P/E ratio would be the single most reliable measure of whether a stock is fairly valued. Our analysis is consistent with this view.

Exhibit 5 shows that buying the 100 stocks with the lowest positive P/E ratios each year would have earned a compounded annual return of 30.7%, versus 11.2% for the S&P 500. The low P/E strategy beat the S&P 500 in 43 years out of 52.

Over the entire 52 year period, the low P/E portfolio would have beaten the S&P 500 by an average of 21.2% per year. $1 invested in the low P/E port-folio would have grown to a total of $1,130,230(!) over 52 years, versus $254 for the S&P 500. The low P/E strategy would have lost money in eight years out of 52.

Exhibit 5 includes two graphs, one showing the growth in value of a $1 in-vestment invested in the low P/E strategy versus the same amount invested in the S&P 500 index, and the other displaying the performance advantage of the strategy over the S&P 500.

As noted above, the performance advantage is equal to the strategy's returns minus the S&P 500 index returns. Therefore, on the graph, the zero line represents the index's returns relative to the strategy's returns. Bars displayed above the zero line indicate years in which the strategy outperformed the S&P 500. Bars falling into negative territory indicate years in which the strat-egy underperformed the S&P 500.

As the chart shows graphically, the low P/E strategy beat the S&P 500 regu-larly and, more often than not, by a substantial amount.

This suggests that a simple-minded strategy of buying the 100 companies with the lowest positive P/E ratios at each year end would have paid off hand-somely over time.

Low Price to Sales (P/S)

Price to sales (P/S) is another widely-used measure of value.

As **Exhibit 6** shows, a strategy based on buying the 100 stocks with the lowest P/S ratios each year would have produced a compound annual rate of return of 21.1%, not as much as the low P/E strategy, but significantly more than the 11.2% compound return produced by the S&P 500. The low P/S strategy

Exhibit 5: Value Strategy - Low Price to Earnings (P/E)

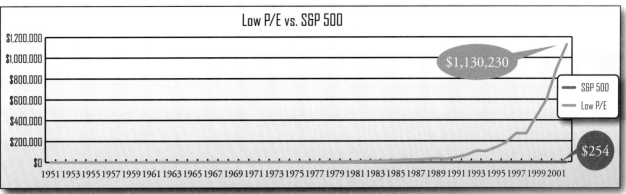

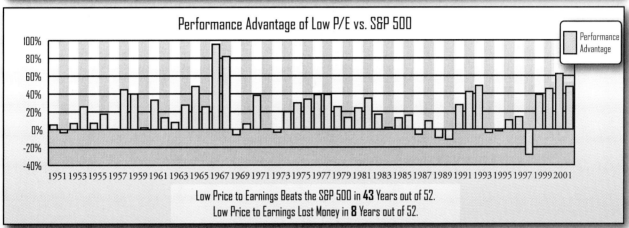

Low Price to Earnings Beats the S&P 500 in **43** Years out of 52.
Low Price to Earnings Lost Money in **8** Years out of 52.

Year	Portfolio Returns	S&P 500 Returns	Performance Advantage	Portfolio Value	S&P 500 Value	Value Differential	Year	Portfolio Returns	S&P 500 Returns	Performance Advantage	Portfolio Value	S&P 500 Value	Value Differential
1951	28.84%	23.37%	5.47%	$1	$1	$0	1977	31.73%	-7.16%	38.88%	$1,364	$13	$1,352
1952	14.29%	17.71%	-3.43%	$1	$1	$0	1978	45.34%	6.39%	38.94%	$1,983	$13	$1,970
1953	5.86%	-1.17%	7.02%	$2	$1	$0	1979	43.61%	18.19%	25.42%	$2,848	$16	$2,832
1954	76.93%	51.23%	25.70%	$3	$2	$1	1980	44.81%	31.52%	13.29%	$4,124	$21	$4,103
1955	38.24%	30.96%	7.27%	$4	$3	$1	1981	19.03%	-4.85%	23.88%	$4,909	$20	$4,889
1956	23.88%	6.44%	17.44%	$5	$3	$2	1982	55.15%	20.37%	34.79%	$7,616	$24	$7,592
1957	-10.20%	-10.48%	0.28%	$4	$3	$2	1983	39.11%	22.31%	16.80%	$10,594	$29	$10,565
1958	87.15%	42.44%	44.72%	$8	$4	$4	1984	7.93%	5.97%	1.96%	$11,434	$31	$11,404
1959	51.65%	11.79%	39.86%	$12	$4	$8	1985	43.77%	31.06%	12.71%	$16,439	$41	$16,399
1960	2.26%	0.28%	1.98%	$12	$4	$8	1986	34.05%	18.54%	15.51%	$22,037	$48	$21,989
1961	59.62%	26.60%	33.02%	$20	$5	$14	1987	-0.26%	5.67%	-5.93%	$21,980	$51	$21,929
1962	4.37%	-8.83%	13.21%	$21	$5	$16	1988	25.67%	16.35%	9.33%	$27,623	$59	$27,564
1963	30.51%	22.50%	8.00%	$27	$6	$21	1989	21.53%	31.23%	-9.70%	$33,569	$78	$33,491
1964	43.73%	16.30%	27.42%	$38	$7	$31	1990	-14.63%	-3.14%	-11.49%	$28,658	$75	$28,583
1965	60.52%	12.27%	48.24%	$62	$8	$54	1991	57.43%	30.00%	27.43%	$45,116	$98	$45,019
1966	15.45%	-9.99%	25.44%	$71	$7	$64	1992	49.49%	7.43%	42.05%	$67,442	$105	$67,338
1967	119.22%	23.73%	95.50%	$156	$9	$147	1993	58.80%	9.94%	48.86%	$107,099	$115	$106,983
1968	92.62%	10.84%	81.78%	$301	$10	$291	1994	-2.75%	1.28%	-4.03%	$104,155	$117	$104,039
1969	-14.43%	-8.32%	-6.11%	$258	$9	$249	1995	35.21%	37.11%	-1.90%	$140,832	$160	$140,672
1970	9.57%	3.33%	6.24%	$282	$9	$273	1996	33.05%	22.68%	10.37%	$187,380	$196	$187,184
1971	52.32%	14.15%	38.17%	$430	$11	$419	1997	46.91%	33.10%	13.81%	$275,278	$261	$275,016
1972	19.35%	18.88%	0.47%	$513	$13	$500	1998	-0.19%	28.34%	-28.53%	$274,753	$336	$274,417
1973	-17.86%	-14.50%	-3.35%	$421	$11	$411	1999	59.76%	20.88%	38.88%	$438,947	$406	$438,541
1974	-6.27%	-26.03%	19.75%	$395	$8	$387	2000	36.35%	-9.03%	45.38%	$598,501	$369	$598,132
1975	66.58%	36.92%	29.67%	$658	$11	$647	2001	50.19%	-11.85%	62.04%	$898,865	$325	$898,540
1976	57.42%	23.64%	33.78%	$1,036	$14	$1,022	2002	25.74%	-21.97%	47.71%	$1,130,230	$254	$1,129,976

Average Return	33.82%	12.59%	21.23%	
Compound Return	30.74%	11.23%	19.50%	

Exhibit 6: Value Strategy - Low Price to Sales (P/S)

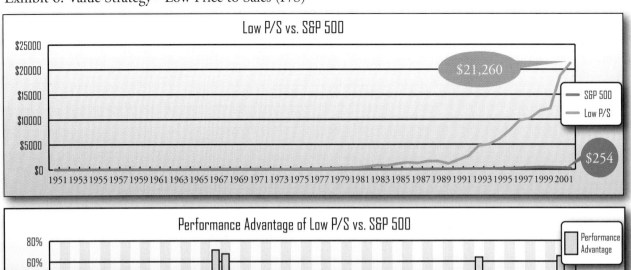

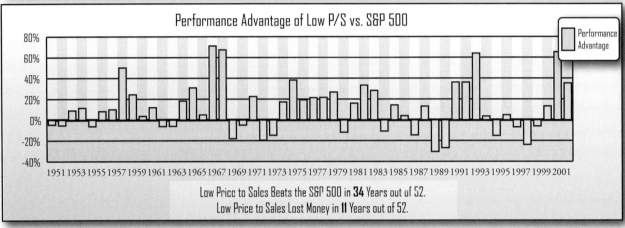

Low Price to Sales Beats the S&P 500 in **34** Years out of 52.
Low Price to Sales Lost Money in **11** Years out of 52.

Year	Portfolio Returns	S&P 500 Returns	Performance Advantage	Portfolio Value	S&P 500 Value	Value Differential	Year	Portfolio Returns	S&P 500 Returns	Performance Advantage	Portfolio Value	S&P 500 Value	Value Differential
1951	18.79%	23.37%	-4.58%	$1	$1	$(0)	1977	14.17%	-7.16%	21.33%	$143	$13	$130
1952	12.38%	17.71%	-5.33%	$1	$1	$(0)	1978	27.98%	6.39%	21.59%	$183	$13	$169
1953	7.81%	-1.17%	8.98%	$1	$1	$0	1979	44.92%	18.19%	26.73%	$265	$16	$249
1954	62.65%	51.23%	11.42%	$2	$2	$0	1980	19.54%	31.52%	-11.97%	$317	$21	$296
1955	24.76%	30.96%	-6.20%	$3	$3	$0	1981	11.22%	-4.85%	16.07%	$352	$20	$333
1956	14.67%	6.44%	8.23%	$3	$3	$0	1982	53.64%	20.37%	33.27%	$541	$24	$517
1957	-0.50%	-10.48%	9.97%	$3	$3	$1	1983	50.57%	22.31%	28.26%	$815	$29	$786
1958	92.43%	42.44%	50.00%	$6	$4	$3	1984	-4.91%	5.97%	-10.88%	$775	$31	$744
1959	36.12%	11.79%	24.33%	$9	$4	$4	1985	45.36%	31.06%	14.30%	$1,127	$41	$1,086
1960	3.85%	0.28%	3.57%	$9	$4	$5	1986	22.56%	18.54%	4.02%	$1,381	$48	$1,333
1961	38.50%	26.60%	11.89%	$13	$5	$7	1987	-8.95%	5.67%	-14.62%	$1,257	$51	$1,206
1962	-14.99%	-8.83%	-6.15%	$11	$5	$6	1988	29.48%	16.35%	13.13%	$1,628	$59	$1,569
1963	16.51%	22.50%	-6.00%	$12	$6	$6	1989	0.70%	31.23%	-30.53%	$1,639	$78	$1,562
1964	34.56%	16.30%	18.26%	$17	$7	$10	1990	-30.06%	-3.14%	-26.92%	$1,146	$75	$1,071
1965	43.08%	12.27%	30.81%	$24	$8	$16	1991	66.19%	30.00%	36.19%	$1,905	$98	$1,808
1966	-5.07%	-9.99%	4.91%	$23	$7	$16	1992	43.54%	7.43%	36.10%	$2,735	$105	$2,630
1967	94.84%	23.73%	71.11%	$44	$9	$35	1993	74.00%	9.94%	64.06%	$4,758	$115	$4,643
1968	78.23%	10.84%	67.38%	$79	$10	$69	1994	4.85%	1.28%	3.57%	$4,989	$117	$4,872
1969	-26.40%	-8.32%	-18.08%	$58	$9	$49	1995	21.89%	37.11%	-15.22%	$6,081	$160	$5,921
1970	-1.55%	3.33%	-4.88%	$57	$9	$48	1996	27.50%	22.68%	4.82%	$7,754	$196	$7,557
1971	36.61%	14.15%	22.46%	$78	$11	$67	1997	26.13%	33.10%	-6.97%	$9,780	$261	$9,518
1972	-0.68%	18.88%	-19.57%	$78	$13	$65	1998	4.50%	28.34%	-23.84%	$10,220	$336	$9,884
1973	-29.33%	-14.50%	-14.83%	$55	$11	$44	1999	14.79%	20.88%	-6.10%	$11,731	$406	$11,325
1974	-8.82%	-26.03%	17.21%	$50	$8	$42	2000	4.18%	-9.03%	13.21%	$12,221	$369	$11,852
1975	75.14%	36.92%	38.22%	$88	$11	$77	2001	53.50%	-11.85%	65.35%	$18,759	$325	$18,434
1976	42.91%	23.64%	19.27%	$125	$14	$112	2002	13.33%	-21.97%	35.30%	$21,260	$254	$21,006
							Average Return	24.56%	12.59%	11.97%			
							Compound Return	21.12%	11.23%	9.89%			

would have performed somewhat less reliably than the P/E strategy, beating the S&P 500 in 34 out of 52 years.

The average annual return would have been 12.0% better than the S&P 500, and a $1 investment would have grown to $21,260 in 52 years, significantly better than the $254 produced by the S&P 500, but nothing like the growth that would have been achieved by the low P/E strategy. The low P/S strategy would have lost money in 11 years out of 52.

Clearly, a strategy of buying stocks with low P/S ratios would have performed well, but not as well as stocks with low P/E ratios.

Low Price to Book Value (P/BV)

A strategy based on low price to book value (P/BV) can entail a variety of difficulties.

Book value is the net worth of a company as shown on its balance sheet and defined under generally accepted accounting principles (GAAP) as the arithmetic result of subtracting liabilities from assets.

But book value quality can vary from firm to firm. Problems can arise in comparing the book value of companies in different industries or those with products in differing stages of their life cycles. A new company with a patent to turn sea water into gasoline might have a book value substantially less than an older industrial firm operating in a dying market. Except in extreme cases involving assets that have become obsolete or unmarketable, GAAP makes no distinction between book values associated with promising new product lines and those associated with marginal operations.

During the period starting in the late 1960's, when inflation was a major economic problem, GAAP-compliant financial statements prepared on the basis of historical costs that were substantially out of date made the concept of book value progressively less meaningful.

Nevertheless, despite these concerns, a stock selection strategy based on low P/BV has proven profitable over the long-term.

As shown in **Exhibit 7**, a strategy of buying the 100 stocks with the lowest P/BV ratios each year would have earned a compound annual rate of return of 23.1% versus 11.2% for the S&P 500.

The low P/BV strategy would have beaten the S&P 500 in 37 years out of 52 and by an average of 13.8% per year over the period. $1 invested in a low

Exhibit 7: Value Strategy - Low Price to Book Value (P/BV)

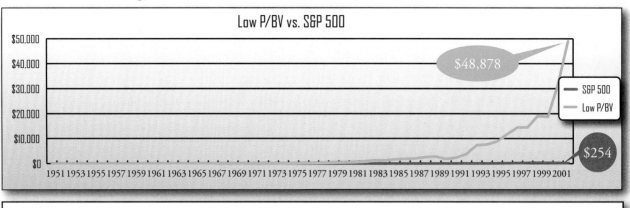

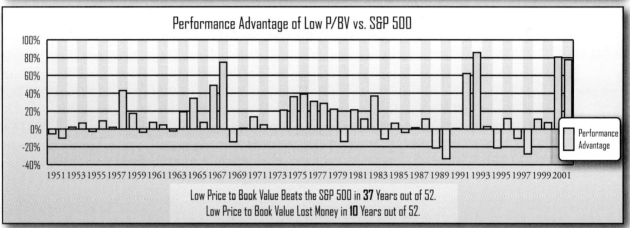

Low Price to Book Value Beats the S&P 500 in **37** Years out of 52.
Low Price to Book Value Lost Money in **10** Years out of 52.

Year	Portfolio Returns	S&P 500 Returns	Return Advantage	Portfolio Value	S&P 500 Value	Value Differential	Year	Portfolio Returns	S&P 500 Returns	Return Advantage	Portfolio Value	S&P 500 Value	Value Differential
1951	18.00%	23.37%	-5.37%	$1	$1	$0	1977	23.70%	-7.16%	30.86%	$216	$13	$204
1952	7.40%	17.71%	-10.31%	$1	$1	$0	1978	35.00%	6.39%	28.61%	$292	$13	$279
1953	1.00%	-1.17%	2.17%	$1	$1	$0	1979	40.30%	18.19%	22.11%	$410	$16	$394
1954	57.90%	51.23%	6.67%	$2	$2	$0	1980	17.30%	31.52%	-14.22%	$481	$21	$460
1955	28.20%	30.96%	-2.76%	$3	$3	$0	1981	16.50%	-4.85%	21.35%	$560	$20	$540
1956	15.60%	6.44%	9.16%	$3	$3	$0	1982	31.50%	20.37%	11.13%	$736	$24	$713
1957	-8.50%	-10.48%	1.98%	$3	$3	$0	1983	59.20%	22.31%	36.89%	$1,172	$29	$1,143
1958	85.40%	42.44%	42.96%	$5	$4	$1	1984	-5.30%	5.97%	-11.27%	$1,110	$31	$1,079
1959	29.20%	11.79%	17.41%	$7	$4	$2	1985	37.50%	31.06%	6.44%	$1,527	$41	$1,486
1960	-3.40%	0.28%	-3.68%	$6	$4	$2	1986	14.50%	18.54%	-4.04%	$1,748	$48	$1,700
1961	34.00%	26.60%	7.40%	$8	$5	$3	1987	7.10%	5.67%	1.43%	$1,872	$51	$1,821
1962	-4.30%	-8.83%	4.53%	$8	$5	$3	1988	27.50%	16.35%	11.15%	$2,387	$59	$2,328
1963	20.20%	22.50%	-2.30%	$10	$6	$4	1989	9.80%	31.23%	-21.43%	$2,621	$78	$2,543
1964	35.50%	16.30%	19.20%	$13	$7	$6	1990	-36.60%	-3.14%	-33.46%	$1,662	$75	$1,586
1965	46.60%	12.27%	34.33%	$19	$8	$11	1991	30.60%	30.00%	0.60%	$2,170	$98	$2,072
1966	-2.70%	-9.99%	7.29%	$19	$7	$12	1992	69.50%	7.43%	62.07%	$3,678	$105	$3,573
1967	72.50%	23.73%	48.77%	$33	$9	$24	1993	95.70%	9.94%	85.76%	$7,198	$115	$7,083
1968	85.60%	10.84%	74.76%	$60	$10	$51	1994	4.00%	1.28%	2.72%	$7,486	$117	$7,369
1969	-22.90%	-8.32%	-14.58%	$47	$9	$38	1995	15.80%	37.11%	-21.31%	$8,669	$160	$8,509
1970	4.20%	3.33%	0.87%	$49	$9	$39	1996	34.40%	22.68%	11.72%	$11,651	$196	$11,454
1971	27.70%	14.15%	13.55%	$62	$11	$51	1997	22.50%	33.10%	-10.60%	$14,272	$261	$14,011
1972	23.50%	18.88%	4.62%	$77	$13	$64	1998	0.40%	28.34%	-27.94%	$14,329	$336	$13,994
1973	-14.60%	-14.50%	-0.10%	$65	$11	$55	1999	32.00%	20.88%	11.12%	$18,915	$406	$18,509
1974	-5.00%	-26.03%	21.03%	$62	$8	$54	2000	-1.80%	-9.03%	7.23%	$18,574	$369	$18,205
1975	73.00%	36.92%	36.08%	$108	$11	$97	2001	68.90%	-11.85%	80.75%	$31,372	$325	$31,047
1976	62.60%	23.64%	38.96%	$175	$14	$161	2002	55.80%	-21.97%	77.77%	$48,878	$254	$48,624
							Average Return	26.39%	12.59%	13.81%			
							Compound Return	23.08%	11.23%	11.84%			

P/BV strategy would have grown to $48,878 over 52 years, versus $254 for the S&P 500.

The low P/BV strategy would have lost money in 10 out of 52 years. So, not as good as low P/E, but significantly better than low P/S.

Low Price to Cash Flow (P/CF)

When business valuation experts are called upon to estimate the value of a company, one of the analytical methods they typically employ is the discounting of future cash flows arising from the business. These professionals tend to be more concerned with cash flow than earnings, sales, or book value. In such circumstances, the present value of future cash flows is often accepted as the soundest estimate of a company's worth.

Sophisticated institutional investors with large research staffs and computerized stock valuation models tend to look at public companies in much the same way. This is one of the reasons a change in interest rates (or changes in anything that would affect cash flow, such as a change in earnings assumptions) has an immediate effect on the presumed valuation (and stock prices) of large public companies.

Individual investors are less likely to use cash flow as a measure of value. It takes fairly sophisticated analysis and a lot of data to use discounted cash flow as a method of gauging stock prices.

Discounted cash flow analysis is rarely applied to smaller companies. The cost of the analysis may be difficult to justify when only a few thousand dollars worth of a company's stock is likely to be available at reasonable prices. An accurate analysis may be impossible due to a lack of readily available information, since less information tends to be available on small companies than on large ones. Moreover, cash flow is susceptible to manipulation through the timing of payments to vendors and the intensity of receivables collection efforts.

The price to cash flow (P/CF) ratio is sometimes used as a shorthand replacement for discounted cash flow analysis. How useful a measure of value is it? **Exhibit 8** shows the results of a stock selection strategy based on a low ratio of price to cash flow (P/CF).

A strategy of buying the 100 stocks with the lowest P/CF ratios each year would have earned a compound annual return of 29.6% versus 11.2% for the S&P 500. Low P/CF strategy would have beaten the S&P 500 in 39 years out of 52 and by an average of 20.7% per year over the period studied.

Exhibit 8: Value Strategy - Low Price to Cash Flow (P/CF)

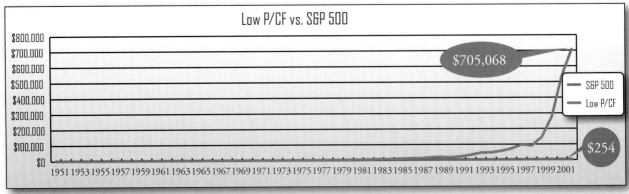

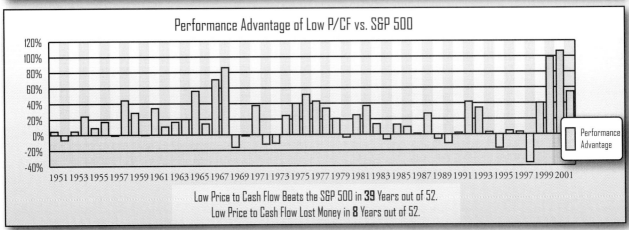

Low Price to Cash Flow Beats the S&P 500 in **39** Years out of 52.
Low Price to Cash Flow Lost Money in **8** Years out of 52.

Year	Portfolio Returns	S&P 500 Returns	Performance Advantage	Portfolio Value	S&P 500 Value	Value Differential	Year	Portfolio Returns	S&P 500 Returns	Performance Advantage	Portfolio Value	S&P 500 Value	Value Differential
1951	28.10%	23.37%	4.73%	$1	$1	$0	1977	35.60%	-7.16%	42.76%	$820	$13	$807
1952	11.20%	17.71%	-6.51%	$1	$1	$0	1978	40.10%	6.39%	33.71%	$1,148	$13	$1,135
1953	3.60%	-1.17%	4.77%	$1	$1	$0	1979	38.60%	18.19%	20.41%	$1,591	$16	$1,575
1954	75.20%	51.23%	23.97%	$3	$2	$0	1980	27.80%	31.52%	-3.72%	$2,034	$21	$2,013
1955	40.00%	30.96%	9.04%	$4	$3	$1	1981	20.20%	-4.85%	25.05%	$2,444	$20	$2,425
1956	23.30%	6.44%	16.86%	$4	$3	$1	1982	57.10%	20.37%	36.73%	$3,840	$24	$3,816
1957	-11.50%	-10.48%	-1.02%	$4	$3	$1	1983	35.80%	22.31%	13.49%	$5,215	$29	$5,186
1958	86.70%	42.44%	44.26%	$7	$4	$4	1984	-0.20%	5.97%	-6.17%	$5,205	$31	$5,174
1959	40.10%	11.79%	28.31%	$10	$4	$6	1985	43.90%	31.06%	12.84%	$7,490	$41	$7,449
1960	-0.20%	0.28%	-0.48%	$10	$4	$6	1986	28.40%	18.54%	9.86%	$9,617	$48	$9,568
1961	60.70%	26.60%	34.10%	$17	$5	$11	1987	6.70%	5.67%	1.03%	$10,261	$51	$10,210
1962	1.70%	-8.83%	10.53%	$17	$5	$12	1988	43.20%	16.35%	26.85%	$14,694	$59	$14,634
1963	39.00%	22.50%	16.50%	$23	$6	$17	1989	25.50%	31.23%	-5.73%	$18,440	$78	$18,363
1964	36.20%	16.30%	19.90%	$32	$7	$25	1990	-14.60%	-3.14%	-11.46%	$15,748	$75	$15,673
1965	68.30%	12.27%	56.03%	$54	$8	$46	1991	32.10%	30.00%	2.10%	$20,803	$98	$20,706
1966	4.20%	-9.99%	14.19%	$56	$7	$49	1992	49.20%	7.43%	41.77%	$31,038	$105	$30,934
1967	94.40%	23.73%	70.67%	$109	$9	$100	1993	44.10%	9.94%	34.16%	$44,726	$115	$44,611
1968	96.90%	10.84%	86.06%	$214	$10	$204	1994	4.20%	1.28%	2.92%	$46,605	$117	$46,488
1969	-24.40%	-8.32%	-16.08%	$162	$9	$153	1995	19.60%	37.11%	-17.51%	$55,739	$160	$55,579
1970	1.80%	3.33%	-1.53%	$165	$9	$155	1996	27.50%	22.68%	4.82%	$71,068	$196	$70,871
1971	51.60%	14.15%	37.45%	$250	$11	$239	1997	36.30%	33.10%	3.20%	$96,865	$261	$96,604
1972	6.70%	18.88%	-12.18%	$267	$13	$254	1998	-7.80%	28.34%	-36.14%	$89,310	$336	$88,974
1973	-25.70%	-14.50%	-11.20%	$198	$11	$187	1999	61.10%	20.88%	40.22%	$143,878	$406	$143,472
1974	-1.50%	-26.03%	24.53%	$195	$8	$187	2000	90.10%	-9.03%	99.13%	$273,512	$369	$273,143
1975	76.90%	36.92%	39.98%	$345	$11	$334	2001	94.70%	-11.85%	106.55%	$532,528	$325	$532,203
1976	75.10%	23.64%	51.46%	$604	$14	$591	2002	32.40%	-21.97%	54.37%	$705,068	$254	$704,814

Average Return	33.27%	12.59%	20.68%
Compound Return	29.56%	11.23%	18.32%

$1 invested in a low P/CF strategy would have grown to $705,068 over the 52 year period, versus $254 for the S&P 500. The low P/CF strategy would have lost money in 8 out of 52 years.

It would appear that low P/CF is an excellent indicator of value.

Comparison of Value Strategies

Now let's compare these four value strategies. (**Exhibits 9 and 10.**)

The usefulness of any stock selection strategy lies in its ability to consistently outperform the market, represented here as the S&P 500. All of the four value strategies we have considered meet this standard.

Low P/E clearly was the best of the four strategies, with a compound return of a very impressive 30.7%. Moreover, low P/E would have performed consistently better than the S&P 500 and consistently better than the other value strategies. It would have beaten the S&P 500 in 43 out of 52 years (i.e., 83% of the years), and it would have outperformed low P/S, low P/BV, and low P/CF in 73%, 69%, and 60%, respectively, of the years. It would have lost money in just eight out of 52 years (15%) of the years studied.

Low P/CF had the next best results, returning a compounded 29.6%, also very impressive. The performance of low P/CF would have been only slightly less consistent than low P/E, beating the S&P 500 in 39 of 52 years (75% of the time), and outperforming low P/E, low P/S, and low P/BV in 40%, 71%, 75%, respectively, of the years. Only low P/E would have consistently outperformed it. Low P/CF would have lost money in just eight out of 52 years (15%), the same as low P/E.

Low P/BV had the third best results, returning a compounded 23.1%, but it was a slightly less consistent performer than either P/E or P/CF. The low P/BV strategy would have beaten the S&P 500 in 37 out of 52 years, and it would have outperformed low P/E, low P/S, and low P/CF in 31%, 50%, and 25%, respectively, of the years. Put another way, it would have consistently beaten the S&P 500 but consistently underperformed the two best value measures. Low P/BV would have lost money in 10 out of 52 years (19%).

The low P/S stocks underperformed the other three value-oriented portfolios. Nevertheless, low P/S would have outperformed the S&P 500 fairly consistently, earning a compound rate of return of 21.1% while beating the S&P 500 in 34 of 52 years (65%) and losing money in 11 out of 52 years (21%).

Exhibit 9: Comparison of Value Strategies– Graphs

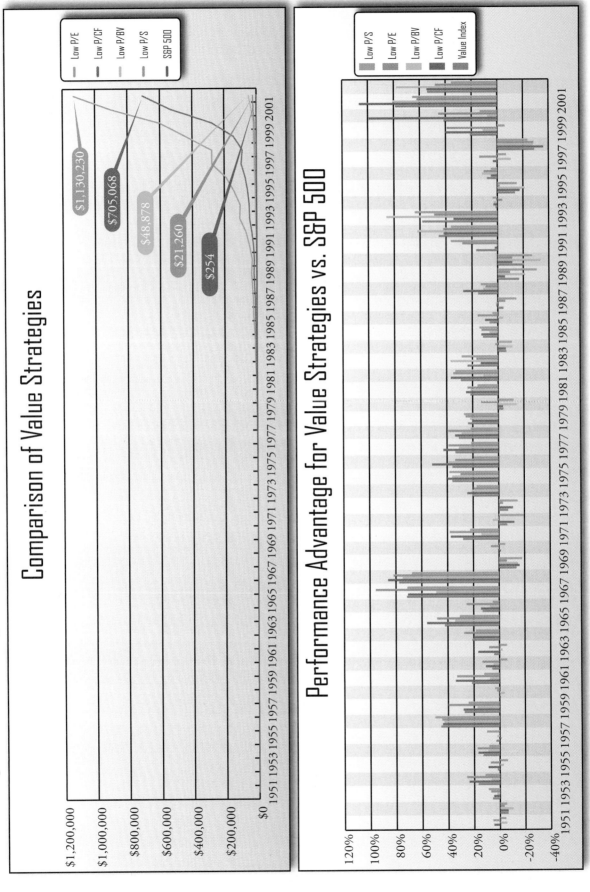

Comparison of Value Strategies

Low P/E
Low P/CF
Low P/BV
Low P/S
S&P 500

$1,130,230
$705,068
$48,878
$21,260
$254

$1,200,000
$1,000,000
$800,000
$600,000
$400,000
$200,000
$0

1951 1953 1955 1957 1959 1961 1963 1965 1967 1969 1971 1973 1975 1977 1979 1981 1983 1985 1987 1989 1991 1993 1995 1997 1999 2001

Performance Advantage for Value Strategies vs. S&P 500

Low P/S
Low P/E
Low P/BV
Low P/CF
Value Index

120%
100%
80%
60%
40%
20%
0%
-20%
-40%

1951 1953 1955 1957 1959 1961 1963 1965 1967 1969 1971 1973 1975 1977 1979 1981 1983 1985 1987 1989 1991 1993 1995 1997 1999 2001

Exhibit 10: Comparison of Value Strategies– Table

							Comparison to S&P 500				
Year	S&P 500 Returns	Low P/E Strategy	Low P/S Strategy	Low P/BV Strategy	Low P/CF Strategy	Value Index	Low P/E Strategy	Low P/S Strategy	Low P/BV Strategy	Low P/CF Strategy	Value Index
1951	23.37%	28.84%	18.79%	18.00%	28.10%	23.43%	5.47%	-4.58%	-5.37%	4.73%	0.06%
1952	17.71%	14.29%	12.38%	7.40%	11.20%	11.32%	-3.43%	-5.33%	-10.31%	-6.51%	-6.39%
1953	-1.17%	5.86%	7.81%	1.00%	3.60%	4.57%	7.02%	8.98%	2.17%	4.77%	5.73%
1954	51.23%	76.93%	62.65%	57.90%	75.20%	68.17%	25.70%	11.42%	6.67%	23.97%	16.94%
1955	30.96%	38.24%	24.76%	28.20%	40.00%	32.80%	7.27%	-6.20%	-2.76%	9.04%	1.84%
1956	6.44%	23.88%	14.67%	15.60%	23.30%	19.36%	17.44%	8.23%	9.16%	16.86%	12.92%
1957	-10.48%	-10.20%	-0.50%	-8.50%	-11.50%	-7.68%	0.28%	9.97%	1.98%	-1.02%	2.80%
1958	42.44%	87.15%	92.43%	85.40%	86.70%	87.92%	44.72%	50.00%	42.96%	44.26%	45.49%
1959	11.79%	51.65%	36.12%	29.20%	40.10%	39.27%	39.86%	24.33%	17.41%	28.31%	27.48%
1960	0.28%	2.26%	3.85%	-3.40%	-0.20%	0.63%	1.98%	3.57%	-3.68%	-0.48%	0.34%
1961	26.60%	59.62%	38.50%	34.00%	60.70%	48.20%	33.02%	11.89%	7.40%	34.10%	21.60%
1962	-8.83%	4.37%	-14.99%	-4.30%	1.70%	-3.30%	13.21%	-6.15%	4.53%	10.53%	5.53%
1963	22.50%	30.51%	16.51%	20.20%	39.00%	26.55%	8.00%	-6.00%	-2.30%	16.50%	4.05%
1964	16.30%	43.73%	34.56%	35.50%	36.20%	37.50%	27.42%	18.26%	19.20%	19.90%	21.19%
1965	12.27%	60.52%	43.08%	46.60%	68.30%	54.62%	48.24%	30.81%	34.33%	56.03%	42.35%
1966	-9.99%	15.45%	-5.07%	-2.70%	4.20%	2.97%	25.44%	4.91%	7.29%	14.19%	12.96%
1967	23.73%	119.22%	94.84%	72.50%	94.40%	95.24%	95.50%	71.11%	48.77%	70.67%	71.51%
1968	10.84%	92.62%	78.23%	85.60%	96.90%	88.34%	81.78%	67.38%	74.76%	86.06%	77.50%
1969	-8.32%	-14.43%	-26.40%	-22.90%	-24.40%	-22.03%	-6.11%	-18.08%	-14.58%	-16.08%	-13.71%
1970	3.33%	9.57%	-1.55%	4.20%	1.80%	3.51%	6.24%	-4.88%	0.87%	-1.53%	0.17%
1971	14.15%	52.32%	36.61%	27.70%	51.60%	42.06%	38.17%	22.46%	13.55%	37.45%	27.91%
1972	18.88%	19.35%	-0.68%	23.50%	6.70%	12.22%	0.47%	-19.57%	4.62%	-12.18%	-6.67%
1973	-14.50%	-17.86%	-29.33%	-14.60%	-25.70%	-21.87%	-3.35%	-14.83%	-0.10%	-11.20%	-7.37%
1974	-26.03%	-6.27%	-8.82%	-5.00%	-1.50%	-5.40%	19.75%	17.21%	21.03%	24.53%	20.63%
1975	36.92%	66.58%	75.14%	73.00%	76.90%	72.91%	29.67%	38.22%	36.08%	39.98%	35.99%
1976	23.64%	57.42%	42.91%	62.60%	75.10%	59.51%	33.78%	19.27%	38.96%	51.46%	35.87%
1977	-7.16%	31.73%	14.17%	23.70%	35.60%	26.30%	38.88%	21.33%	30.86%	42.76%	33.46%
1978	6.39%	45.34%	27.98%	35.00%	40.10%	37.10%	38.94%	21.59%	28.61%	33.71%	30.71%
1979	18.19%	43.61%	44.92%	40.30%	38.60%	41.86%	25.42%	26.73%	22.11%	20.41%	23.67%
1980	31.52%	44.81%	19.54%	17.30%	27.80%	27.36%	13.29%	-11.97%	-14.22%	-3.72%	-4.15%
1981	-4.85%	19.03%	11.22%	16.50%	20.20%	16.74%	23.88%	16.07%	21.35%	25.05%	21.58%
1982	20.37%	55.15%	53.64%	31.50%	57.10%	49.35%	34.79%	33.27%	11.13%	36.73%	28.98%
1983	22.31%	39.11%	50.57%	59.20%	35.80%	46.17%	16.80%	28.26%	36.89%	13.49%	23.86%
1984	5.97%	7.93%	-4.91%	-5.30%	-0.20%	-0.62%	1.96%	-10.88%	-11.27%	-6.17%	-6.59%
1985	31.06%	43.77%	45.36%	37.50%	43.90%	42.63%	12.71%	14.30%	6.44%	12.84%	11.57%
1986	18.54%	34.05%	22.56%	14.50%	28.40%	24.88%	15.51%	4.02%	-4.04%	9.86%	6.34%
1987	5.67%	-0.26%	-8.95%	7.10%	6.70%	1.15%	-5.93%	-14.62%	1.43%	1.03%	-4.52%
1988	16.35%	25.67%	29.48%	27.50%	43.20%	31.46%	9.33%	13.13%	11.15%	26.85%	15.12%
1989	31.23%	21.53%	0.70%	9.80%	25.50%	14.38%	-9.70%	-30.53%	-21.43%	-5.73%	-16.85%
1990	-3.14%	-14.63%	-30.06%	-36.60%	-14.60%	-23.97%	-11.49%	-26.92%	-33.46%	-11.46%	-20.83%
1991	30.00%	57.43%	66.19%	30.60%	32.10%	46.58%	27.43%	36.19%	0.60%	2.10%	16.58%
1992	7.43%	49.49%	43.54%	69.50%	49.20%	52.93%	42.05%	36.10%	62.07%	41.77%	45.50%
1993	9.94%	58.80%	74.00%	95.70%	44.10%	68.15%	48.86%	64.06%	85.76%	34.16%	58.21%
1994	1.28%	-2.75%	4.85%	4.00%	4.20%	2.58%	-4.03%	3.57%	2.72%	2.92%	1.29%
1995	37.11%	35.21%	21.89%	15.80%	19.60%	23.13%	-1.90%	-15.22%	-21.31%	-17.51%	-13.99%
1996	22.68%	33.05%	27.50%	34.40%	27.50%	30.61%	10.37%	4.82%	11.72%	4.82%	7.93%
1997	33.10%	46.91%	26.13%	22.50%	36.30%	32.96%	13.81%	-6.97%	-10.60%	3.20%	-0.14%
1998	28.34%	-0.19%	4.50%	0.40%	-7.80%	-0.77%	-28.53%	-23.84%	-27.94%	-36.14%	-29.11%
1999	20.88%	59.76%	14.79%	32.00%	61.10%	41.91%	38.88%	-6.10%	11.12%	40.22%	21.03%
2000	-9.03%	36.35%	4.18%	-1.80%	90.10%	32.21%	45.38%	13.21%	7.23%	99.13%	41.24%
2001	-11.85%	50.19%	53.50%	68.90%	94.70%	66.82%	62.04%	65.35%	80.75%	106.55%	78.67%
2002	-21.97%	25.74%	13.33%	55.80%	32.40%	31.82%	47.71%	35.30%	77.77%	54.37%	53.78%

	S&P 500 Returns	Low P/E Strategy	Low P/S Strategy	Low P/BV Strategy	Low P/CF Strategy	Value Index
Average Return	12.59%	33.82%	24.56%	26.39%	33.27%	29.51%
Compound Return	11.23%	30.74%	21.12%	23.08%	29.56%	26.42%
Years Beating S&P 500	N/A	43	34	37	39	40
Years Losing Money	13	8	11	10	8	8

% of Years Strategy on Left Beats Other Value Strategies

	P/E	P/S	P/BV	P/CF
P/E	N/A	73%	69%	60%
P/S	27%	N/A	50%	27%
P/BV	31%	50%	N/A	25%
P/CF	40%	71%	75%	N/A

Thus, low P/E and low P/CF were the best of the four value strategies over the 52 year study period.

Low P/E is the selection criterion we rely on most heavily when we are looking to buy value stocks. Low P/CF is problematic due to the potential for short-term manipulation of the reported figures, but it can be very useful in some circumstances: for example, in assessing a potential turn-around situation.

Value Investing is a Winner!

Exhibit 9 provides two charts, one showing the superior growth in the low P/E and low P/CF portfolios, and another one showing the performance advantage of each value measure relative to the S&P 500 return.

The second chart shows how the four value strategies perform relative to the S&P 500, beating it in most years.

Exhibit 9 also includes a "Value Index" which is nothing more than a simple arithmetic average of the annual returns for the four value strategies. The index provides a clearer picture of the behavior of value stocks relative to the market. We will refer to it later in Part Two.

The Value Index's average returns would have beaten the S&P 500 in 40 years out of 52, with only eight money losing years, demonstrating conclusively that value investing has been an excellent, time-tested strategy for beating the market consistently.

Still, there were those 12 years when value stocks underperformed the market. Even though value investing beats the market in most years, there are apparently some conditions under which value doesn't do as well.

What are the conditions that lead to value stocks' underperformance?

As we will show in Chapter 11, the conditions that lead to the underperformance of value stocks can be traced to the effects of Federal Reserve Bank policy changes.

Chapter 5

GROWTH STOCKS

A lot of investors seem to gravitate toward growth stock strategies. Maybe it's something about the term "growth." What investor wouldn't prefer to own stock in a "growing" company? What investor wouldn't prefer to watch his investment "grow?"

The growth style is treated with a great deal of respect by the financial services industry.

There are many growth mutual funds.

And every business day, stockbrokers, mutual fund salespeople, and investment advisors pitch these funds to investors, counseling them to include some "growth" stocks or "growth mutual funds" in their portfolios, "for diversification."

Is this a wise thing to do?

What is a Growth Stock?

Let's start by defining what we mean by a growth stock.

Many growth stocks are well-known, exciting, "story" stocks. A "growth company" tends to be one that achieves sustained earnings and sales growth or unusually high profit margins through significant competitive advantages, such as proprietary technologies, innovative distribution methods, and exceptional marketing or branding capabilities. Often, a growth company is one whose competitive advantages enable it to dominate (or at least share dominion) in its markets.

The stock market tends to reward this kind of superior operating performance with higher stock prices. Prices rise, not only to acknowledge the company's current level of success, but also to reflect the expectation that the company will be ever more successful in the future.

As a result, the price ratios for growth stocks will generally be higher than for value stocks.

Therefore, for our purposes, we'll define a growth stock as one with price ratios that are among the highest of all public companies.

Selecting Growth Stocks

Let's look at the returns that would have been earned by selecting growth stocks on the basis of these ratios, i.e.:

- **High Price to Earnings (P/E):** stock price divided by earnings per share

- **High Price to Sales (P/S):** stock price divided by sales per share

- **High Price to Book Value (P/BV):** stock price divided by the last reported book value per share

- **High Price to Cash Flow (P/CF):** stock price divided by cash flow per share

Once again we will compare the returns that would have been earned during 1951-2002 by stock selection strategies based on these four price ratios.

The methodology used for this analysis is identical to that used to backtest the value strategies (see Chapter 4), except that, in this case, we calculated the returns that would have been earned through a strategy of owning the 100 stocks with the highest P/E, P/S, P/CF, or P/BV ratios.

As before, we'll compare the average and compound returns earned by each strategy over the 52 year study period (1951-2002) to those of the other growth strategies, as well as to those earned by the S&P 500.

Performance of Growth Strategies

Exhibits 10-14 show the results for each growth strategy. In addition to return figures, the tables show the strategies' performance advantage over the "market" (i.e., the amount by which the strategies' returns exceed the S&P

500 returns). Remember, the "advantage" can be negative, meaning that the strategy underperformed the S&P 500.

The exhibits also show:

- The growth of $1 invested in the portfolio at the beginning of the study period,

- The number of years out of 52 that the strategy beat the S&P 500,

- The arithmetic average of the return calculations, and

- The compound rates of return for the entire 52 year period.

High Price to Earnings (P/E)

As **Exhibit 11** shows, a strategy of buying the 100 stocks with the highest P/E ratios each year would have earned a compound annual rate of return of 7.2%, a full 4 percentage points less than the 11.2% earned by the S&P 500.

The high P/E strategy would have beaten the S&P 500 in 23 years out of 52, but, over the entire period, the S&P 500 would have beaten the high P/E portfolio by an average of 1.3% per year. In any case, the high P/E strategy hasn't beaten the S&P 500 very often or by very much over the last 20 years.

$1 invested in the high P/E portfolio in 1951 would have grown to $38 after 52 years, versus $254 for the S&P 500. The high P/E strategy would have lost money in 17 years out of 52.

An investor might have done better with an S&P 500 index fund, depending, of course, on the amount of sales charges and expenses charged.

As usual, **Exhibit 11** includes two charts. The top chart shows the growth in the value of $1 invested in the high P/E strategy versus the same amount invested in the S&P 500. This shows how badly the high P/E strategy has performed over time compared to the S&P 500.

The second chart shows the performance advantage of the high P/E strategy over the S&P 500. This shows graphically how infrequently the high P/E strategy outperforms the index.

Exhibit 11: Growth Strategy - High Price to Earnings (P/E)

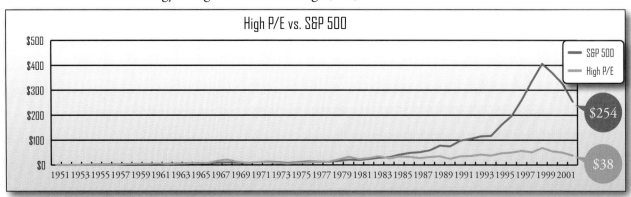

High P/E vs. S&P 500

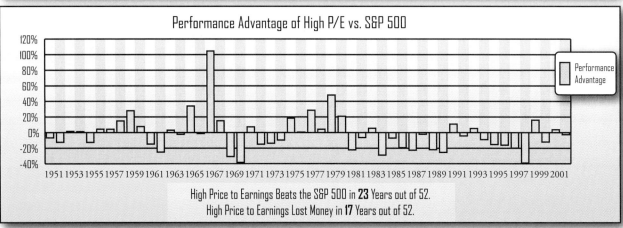

Performance Advantage of High P/E vs. S&P 500

High Price to Earnings Beats the S&P 500 in **23** Years out of 52.
High Price to Earnings Lost Money in **17** Years out of 52.

Year	Portfolio Returns	S&P 500 Returns	Performance Advantage	Portfolio Value	S&P 500 Value	Value Differential	Year	Portfolio Returns	S&P 500 Returns	Performance Advantage	Portfolio Value	S&P 500 Value	Value Differential
1951	16.67%	23.37%	-6.70%	$1	$1	$0	1977	21.39%	-7.16%	28.54%	$12	$13	$(1)
1952	5.31%	17.71%	-12.40%	$1	$1	$0	1978	10.67%	6.39%	4.28%	$13	$13	$0
1953	0.41%	-1.17%	1.58%	$1	$1	$0	1979	66.21%	18.19%	48.03%	$22	$16	$6
1954	52.40%	51.23%	1.17%	$2	$2	$0	1980	52.32%	31.52%	20.80%	$33	$21	$12
1955	18.41%	30.96%	-12.56%	$2	$3	$(1)	1981	-26.95%	-4.85%	-22.10%	$24	$20	$4
1956	10.79%	6.44%	4.34%	$2	$3	$(1)	1982	14.00%	20.37%	-6.37%	$28	$24	$4
1957	-6.15%	-10.48%	4.33%	$2	$3	$0	1983	27.84%	22.31%	5.53%	$35	$29	$6
1958	57.33%	42.44%	14.89%	$4	$4	$0	1984	-22.85%	5.97%	-28.81%	$27	$31	$(4)
1959	39.73%	11.79%	27.94%	$5	$4	$1	1985	24.03%	31.06%	-7.02%	$34	$41	$(7)
1960	7.99%	0.28%	7.71%	$5	$4	$1	1986	-0.79%	18.54%	-19.33%	$33	$48	$(15)
1961	11.92%	26.60%	-14.69%	$6	$5	$1	1987	-16.87%	5.67%	-22.53%	$28	$51	$(23)
1962	-33.80%	-8.83%	-24.97%	$4	$5	$(1)	1988	14.23%	16.35%	-2.11%	$32	$59	$(27)
1963	25.51%	22.50%	3.00%	$5	$6	$(1)	1989	9.39%	31.23%	-21.84%	$35	$78	$(43)
1964	14.11%	16.30%	-2.19%	$6	$7	$(1)	1990	-28.44%	-3.14%	-25.30%	$25	$75	$(50)
1965	46.27%	12.27%	34.00%	$9	$8	$1	1991	40.87%	30.00%	10.87%	$35	$98	$(63)
1966	-11.24%	-9.99%	-1.25%	$8	$7	$0	1992	3.20%	7.43%	-4.23%	$36	$105	$(69)
1967	128.33%	23.73%	104.60%	$17	$9	$8	1993	15.20%	9.94%	5.26%	$42	$115	$(74)
1968	25.93%	10.84%	15.09%	$22	$10	$12	1994	-7.66%	1.28%	-8.95%	$38	$117	$(78)
1969	-38.96%	-8.32%	-30.64%	$13	$9	$4	1995	21.88%	37.11%	-15.23%	$47	$160	$(113)
1970	-34.86%	3.33%	-38.20%	$9	$9	$(1)	1996	6.70%	22.68%	-15.98%	$50	$196	$(146)
1971	21.42%	14.15%	7.27%	$11	$11	$0	1997	13.30%	33.10%	-19.80%	$57	$261	$(205)
1972	3.96%	18.88%	-14.92%	$11	$13	$(2)	1998	-10.77%	28.34%	-39.11%	$51	$336	$(285)
1973	-28.17%	-14.50%	-13.67%	$8	$11	$(3)	1999	36.85%	20.88%	15.97%	$69	$406	$(336)
1974	-35.60%	-26.03%	-9.58%	$5	$8	$(3)	2000	-21.04%	-9.03%	-12.01%	$55	$369	$(314)
1975	55.21%	36.92%	18.29%	$8	$11	$(3)	2001	-8.04%	-11.85%	3.81%	$50	$325	$(275)
1976	24.18%	23.64%	0.54%	$10	$14	$(4)	2002	-24.51%	-21.97%	-2.54%	$38	$254	$(216)

| | | | | | | | Average Returns | 11.29% | 12.59% | -1.29% | | | |
| | | | | | | | Compound Returns | 7.24% | 11.23% | -3.99% | | | |

Exhibit 12: Growth Strategy - High Price to Sales (P/S)

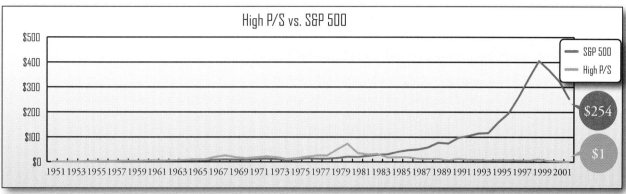

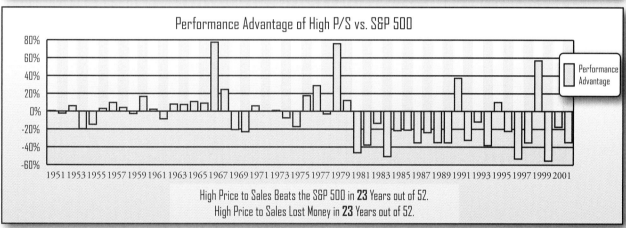

High Price to Sales Beats the S&P 500 in **23** Years out of 52.
High Price to Sales Lost Money in **23** Years out of 52.

Year	Portfolio Returns	S&P 500 Returns	Performance Advantage	Portfolio Value	S&P 500 Value	Value Differential	Year	Portfolio Returns	S&P 500 Returns	Performance Advantage	Portfolio Value	S&P 500 Value	Value Differential
1951	23.87%	23.37%	0.50%	$1	$1	$0	1977	21.66%	-7.16%	28.82%	$26	$13	$13
1952	15.40%	17.71%	-2.31%	$1	$1	$0	1978	3.38%	6.39%	-3.01%	$26	$13	$13
1953	4.81%	-1.17%	5.98%	$1	$1	$0	1979	93.99%	18.19%	75.80%	$51	$16	$35
1954	31.52%	51.23%	-19.71%	$2	$2	$0	1980	43.53%	31.52%	12.01%	$74	$21	$53
1955	16.20%	30.96%	-14.76%	$2	$3	$(1)	1981	-51.23%	-4.85%	-46.38%	$36	$20	$16
1956	9.39%	6.44%	2.95%	$3	$3	$(1)	1982	-17.43%	20.37%	-37.79%	$30	$24	$6
1957	-0.82%	-10.48%	9.66%	$2	$3	$0	1983	8.80%	22.31%	-13.51%	$32	$29	$3
1958	46.51%	42.44%	4.07%	$4	$4	$0	1984	-44.74%	5.97%	-50.71%	$18	$31	$(13)
1959	9.13%	11.79%	-2.66%	$4	$4	$0	1985	9.38%	31.06%	-21.68%	$19	$41	$(21)
1960	16.95%	0.28%	16.67%	$5	$4	$0	1986	-2.55%	18.54%	-21.09%	$19	$48	$(29)
1961	28.72%	26.60%	2.12%	$6	$5	$1	1987	-29.57%	5.67%	-35.24%	$13	$51	$(37)
1962	-17.41%	-8.83%	-8.58%	$5	$5	$0	1988	-7.51%	16.35%	-23.86%	$12	$59	$(47)
1963	30.46%	22.50%	7.95%	$6	$6	$0	1989	-3.83%	31.23%	-35.06%	$12	$78	$(66)
1964	23.80%	16.30%	7.49%	$8	$7	$1	1990	-38.37%	-3.14%	-35.23%	$7	$75	$(68)
1965	23.09%	12.27%	10.82%	$10	$8	$2	1991	67.22%	30.00%	37.22%	$12	$98	$(85)
1966	-1.01%	-9.99%	8.98%	$10	$7	$3	1992	-24.98%	7.43%	-32.42%	$9	$105	$(96)
1967	101.16%	23.73%	77.43%	$20	$9	$11	1993	-1.92%	9.94%	-11.86%	$9	$115	$(106)
1968	35.33%	10.84%	24.49%	$26	$10	$17	1994	-36.99%	1.28%	-38.27%	$6	$117	$(111)
1969	-28.89%	-8.32%	-20.57%	$19	$9	$10	1995	47.10%	37.11%	9.99%	$8	$160	$(152)
1970	-19.70%	3.33%	-23.04%	$15	$9	$6	1996	0.34%	22.68%	-22.35%	$8	$196	$(188)
1971	20.15%	14.15%	6.00%	$18	$11	$7	1997	-20.05%	33.10%	-53.15%	$7	$261	$(255)
1972	19.05%	18.88%	0.17%	$22	$13	$9	1998	-6.75%	28.34%	-35.09%	$6	$336	$(329)
1973	-13.60%	-14.50%	0.90%	$19	$11	$8	1999	77.85%	20.88%	56.96%	$11	$406	$(394)
1974	-33.49%	-26.03%	-7.47%	$12	$8	$4	2000	-64.49%	-9.03%	-55.45%	$4	$369	$(365)
1975	19.67%	36.92%	-17.24%	$15	$11	$4	2001	-29.44%	-11.85%	-17.59%	$3	$325	$(322)
1976	41.24%	23.64%	17.60%	$21	$14	$7	2002	-56.73%	-21.97%	-34.77%	$1	$254	$(253)

	Average Returns	6.50%	12.59%	-6.08%
	Compound Returns	0.36%	11.23%	-10.88%

High Price to Sales (P/S)

Exhibit 12 shows that a strategy based on buying the 100 stocks with the highest P/S ratios each year would have produced a compound annual rate of return of just 0.4%! Over the same period, an index fund mirroring the S&P 500 would have earned a compounded 11.2% return, minus sales charges and expenses. In this case, an investor would almost certainly have been better off with the index fund, even if he had paid the highest sales charges and expenses in the industry!

It's true that the high P/S strategy would have managed to beat the S&P 500 in 23 out of 52 years, but it also would have lost money in 23 of the years. During the most recent two decades, the high P/S strategy has performed abysmally relative to the S&P 500, except for three years when it beat the index by substantial amounts.

The annual return for this strategy would have been an average of 6.1% lower than the S&P 500, and a $1 investment would have been worth just $1 after 52 years!

This looks like one stock selection strategy we would want to avoid, doesn't it?

Well, most of the time, yes. But, as badly as this strategy would have performed over the entire 52-year period, there were certain years when it would have been one of the best, returning handsome profits.

High Price to Book Value (P/BV)

Exhibit 13 shows the results of a strategy of selecting the 100 stocks with the highest P/BV ratio each year. The high P/BV strategy would have earned a compound return of 2.5%, significantly less than what the S&P 500 returned (11.2%).

The high P/BV strategy would have beaten the S&P 500 in 23 years, but it would have underperformed the index by an average of 4.5% per year, and it would have lost money in 21 years. Similar to the pattern observed with high P/E and high P/S, high P/BV performed very poorly relative to the S&P 500 during most of the past two decades – except for a few years, when high P/BV would have beaten the index by as much as 63.3%.

$1 invested in this strategy in 1951 would have only grown to $4 after 52 years, well short of an investment in the S&P 500.

Exhibit 13: Growth Strategy - High Price to Book Value (P/BV)

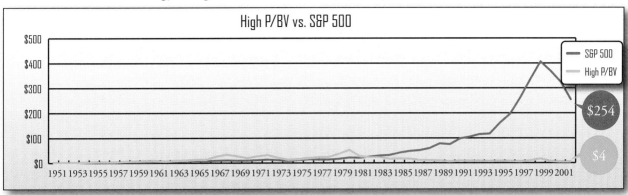

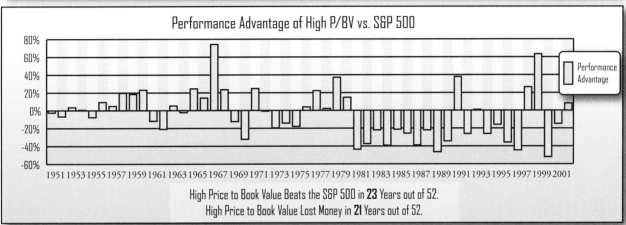

High Price to Book Value Beats the S&P 500 in **23** Years out of 52.
High Price to Book Value Lost Money in **21** Years out of 52.

Year	Portfolio Returns	S&P 500 Returns	Performance Advantage	Portfolio Value	S&P 500 Value	Value Differential	Year	Portfolio Returns	S&P 500 Returns	Performance Advantage	Portfolio Value	S&P 500 Value	Value Differential
1951	20.90%	23.37%	-2.47%	$1	$1	$0	1977	15.10%	-7.16%	22.26%	$21	$13	$8
1952	10.90%	17.71%	-6.81%	$1	$1	$0	1978	8.50%	6.39%	2.11%	$22	$13	$9
1953	2.30%	-1.17%	3.47%	$1	$1	$0	1979	55.40%	18.19%	37.21%	$35	$16	$19
1954	51.80%	51.23%	0.57%	$2	$2	$0	1980	46.10%	31.52%	14.58%	$51	$21	$30
1955	23.30%	30.96%	-7.66%	$3	$3	$0	1981	-48.40%	-4.85%	-43.55%	$26	$20	$6
1956	15.70%	6.44%	9.26%	$3	$3	$0	1982	-17.00%	20.37%	-37.37%	$22	$24	$(2)
1957	-5.60%	-10.48%	4.88%	$3	$3	$0	1983	0.30%	22.31%	-22.01%	$22	$29	$(7)
1958	62.10%	42.44%	19.66%	$5	$4	$1	1984	-33.20%	5.97%	-39.17%	$15	$31	$(16)
1959	30.20%	11.79%	18.41%	$6	$4	$2	1985	9.80%	31.06%	-21.26%	$16	$41	$(25)
1960	23.40%	0.28%	23.12%	$7	$4	$3	1986	-7.10%	18.54%	-25.64%	$15	$48	$(33)
1961	14.70%	26.60%	-11.90%	$8	$5	$3	1987	-33.20%	5.67%	-38.87%	$10	$51	$(41)
1962	-29.80%	-8.83%	-20.97%	$6	$5	$1	1988	-5.70%	16.35%	-22.05%	$9	$59	$(50)
1963	27.80%	22.50%	5.30%	$8	$6	$1	1989	-15.30%	31.23%	-46.53%	$8	$78	$(70)
1964	14.00%	16.30%	-2.30%	$9	$7	$1	1990	-37.60%	-3.14%	-34.46%	$5	$75	$(70)
1965	36.80%	12.27%	24.53%	$12	$8	$4	1991	67.90%	30.00%	37.90%	$8	$98	$(89)
1966	4.00%	-9.99%	13.99%	$12	$7	$5	1992	-18.70%	7.43%	-26.13%	$7	$105	$(98)
1967	98.00%	23.73%	74.27%	$24	$9	$15	1993	10.90%	9.94%	0.96%	$7	$115	$(108)
1968	34.30%	10.84%	23.46%	$32	$10	$23	1994	-24.90%	1.28%	-26.18%	$6	$117	$(111)
1969	-20.80%	-8.32%	-12.48%	$26	$9	$17	1995	21.20%	37.11%	-15.91%	$7	$160	$(153)
1970	-28.90%	3.33%	-32.23%	$18	$9	$9	1996	-13.10%	22.68%	-35.78%	$6	$196	$(191)
1971	38.90%	14.15%	24.75%	$25	$11	$15	1997	-11.50%	33.10%	-44.60%	$5	$261	$(256)
1972	18.10%	18.88%	-0.78%	$30	$13	$17	1998	54.70%	28.34%	26.36%	$8	$336	$(327)
1973	-34.10%	-14.50%	-19.60%	$20	$11	$9	1999	84.20%	20.88%	63.32%	$15	$406	$(391)
1974	-40.30%	-26.03%	-14.27%	$12	$8	$4	2000	-61.10%	-9.03%	-52.07%	$6	$369	$(363)
1975	19.00%	36.92%	-17.92%	$14	$11	$3	2001	-26.80%	-11.85%	-14.95%	$4	$325	$(321)
1976	27.50%	23.64%	3.86%	$18	$14	$4	2002	-14.00%	-21.97%	7.97%	$4	$254	$(250)

Average Returns	8.09%	12.59%	-4.50%
Compound Returns	2.52%	11.23%	-8.71%

Exhibit 14: Growth Strategy - High Price to Cash Flow (P/CF)

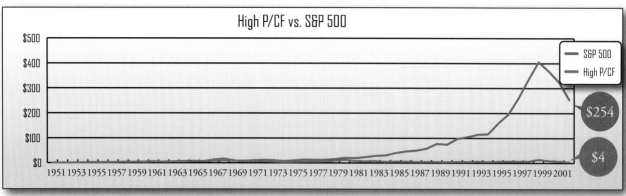

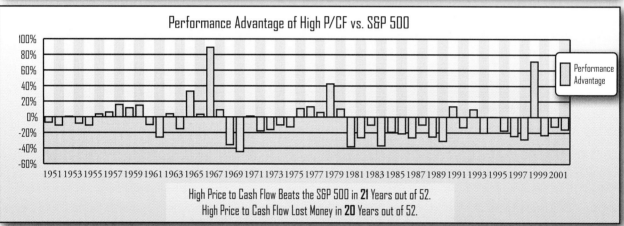

High Price to Cash Flow Beats the S&P 500 in **21** Years out of 52.
High Price to Cash Flow Lost Money in **20** Years out of 52.

Year	Portfolio Returns	S&P 500 Returns	Performance Advantage	Portfolio Value	S&P 500 Value	Value Differential	Year	Portfolio Returns	S&P 500 Returns	Performance Advantage	Portfolio Value	S&P 500 Value	Value Differential
1951	16.40%	23.37%	-6.97%	$1	$1	$(0)	1977	5.90%	-7.16%	13.06%	$5	$13	$(7)
1952	7.00%	17.71%	-10.71%	$1	$1	$(0)	1978	12.20%	6.39%	5.81%	$6	$13	$(8)
1953	-0.60%	-1.17%	0.57%	$1	$1	$(0)	1979	60.80%	18.19%	42.61%	$9	$16	$(7)
1954	43.00%	51.23%	-8.23%	$2	$2	$(0)	1980	41.70%	31.52%	10.18%	$13	$21	$(8)
1955	20.30%	30.96%	-10.66%	$2	$3	$(1)	1981	-42.70%	-4.85%	-37.85%	$8	$20	$(12)
1956	10.00%	6.44%	3.56%	$2	$3	$(1)	1982	-6.00%	20.37%	-26.37%	$7	$24	$(17)
1957	-4.40%	-10.48%	6.08%	$2	$3	$(0)	1983	12.10%	22.31%	-10.21%	$8	$29	$(21)
1958	58.10%	42.44%	15.66%	$4	$4	$(0)	1984	-30.70%	5.97%	-36.67%	$5	$31	$(25)
1959	23.30%	11.79%	11.51%	$4	$4	$0	1985	11.80%	31.06%	-19.26%	$6	$41	$(34)
1960	15.10%	0.28%	14.82%	$5	$4	$1	1986	-2.70%	18.54%	-21.24%	$6	$48	$(42)
1961	16.70%	26.60%	-9.90%	$6	$5	$0	1987	-20.70%	5.67%	-26.37%	$5	$51	$(46)
1962	-34.80%	-8.83%	-25.97%	$4	$5	$(1)	1988	6.40%	16.35%	-9.95%	$5	$59	$(54)
1963	26.40%	22.50%	3.90%	$5	$6	$(1)	1989	6.00%	31.23%	-25.23%	$5	$78	$(72)
1964	1.10%	16.30%	-15.20%	$5	$7	$(2)	1990	-33.90%	-3.14%	-30.76%	$4	$75	$(72)
1965	45.30%	12.27%	33.03%	$7	$8	$(1)	1991	43.40%	30.00%	13.40%	$5	$98	$(93)
1966	-6.70%	-9.99%	3.29%	$7	$7	$(1)	1992	-5.80%	7.43%	-13.23%	$5	$105	$(100)
1967	112.90%	23.73%	89.17%	$14	$9	$5	1993	19.60%	9.94%	9.66%	$6	$115	$(110)
1968	19.90%	10.84%	9.06%	$17	$10	$7	1994	-18.90%	1.28%	-20.18%	$5	$117	$(112)
1969	-43.80%	-8.32%	-35.48%	$10	$9	$0	1995	37.20%	37.11%	0.09%	$6	$160	$(154)
1970	-41.00%	3.33%	-44.33%	$6	$9	$(4)	1996	5.30%	22.68%	-17.38%	$7	$196	$(190)
1971	15.20%	14.15%	1.05%	$6	$11	$(4)	1997	8.80%	33.10%	-24.30%	$7	$261	$(254)
1972	1.10%	18.88%	-17.78%	$7	$13	$(6)	1998	-0.20%	28.34%	-28.54%	$7	$336	$(328)
1973	-30.50%	-14.50%	-16.00%	$5	$11	$(6)	1999	92.20%	20.88%	71.32%	$14	$406	$(392)
1974	-36.20%	-26.03%	-10.17%	$3	$8	$(5)	2000	-32.10%	-9.03%	-23.07%	$9	$369	$(360)
1975	24.30%	36.92%	-12.62%	$4	$11	$(7)	2001	-24.00%	-11.85%	-12.15%	$7	$325	$(318)
1976	34.40%	23.64%	10.76%	$5	$14	$(9)	2002	-37.70%	-21.97%	-15.73%	$4	$254	$(249)

	Average Return	7.70%	12.59%	-4.88%
	Compound Return	2.92%	11.23%	-8.31%

High Price to Cash Flow (P/CF)

The performance of the high P/CF strategy, shown in **Exhibit 14**, was similar to that of the other growth strategies. This strategy would have produced a compound return of 2.9%, beating the S&P 500 in 21 years while earning an average of 4.9% less than the index and losing money in 20 out of 52 years. A $1 investment would have grown to just $4 after 52 years.

Comparison of Growth Strategies

Now let's compare the four growth strategies. (**Exhibits 15** and **16.**)

If, as we said in reference to value strategies, the usefulness of a stock selection strategy lies in its ability to consistently outperform the market, then none of the four growth strategies we have considered pass that test.

High P/E clearly would have been the best of the four growth strategies, earning a compound return of 7.2%.

In beating the S&P 500 23 out of 52 years (i.e., 44% of the time), high P/E's track record vis-à-vis the S&P 500 would have been similar to that of high P/S and high P/BV, and slightly better than that of high P/CF. High P/E would have outperformed high P/S, high P/BV, and high P/CF 56%, 58%, and 71%, respectively, of the time. It would have lost money in 17 out of 52 years (33%) of the years studied.

The relative performance of the other growth strategies was mixed.

High P/CF would have had the second best returns (2.9% compounded), but its consistency vis-a-vis the S&P 500 would have been the worst of the four growth strategies. It would only have beaten the S&P 500 in 21 out of 52 years (40% of the time).

On the other hand, high P/CF would have lost money less often (38% of the time) than high P/S or high P/BV. It would have beaten high P/S and high P/BV, respectively, 54% and 56% of the time.

High P/BV would have had the third best results, with a compound return of 2.5%, and average consistency (for a growth strategy) relative to the S&P 500 and the other growth strategies.

High P/S was the worst performing growth strategy, barely breaking even after 52 years, and losing money in almost one year out of two.

Exhibit 15: Comparison of Growth Strategies– Graphs

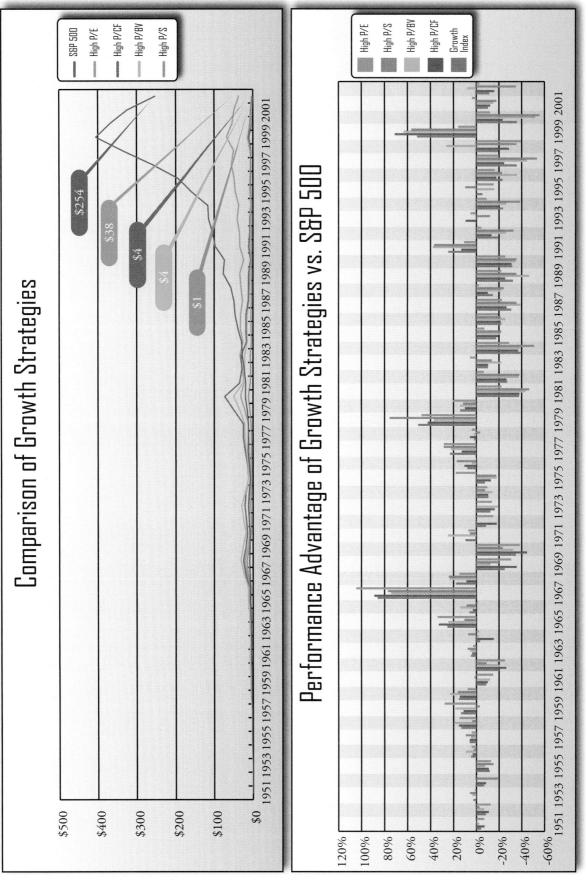

Comparison of Growth Strategies

Performance Advantage of Growth Strategies vs. S&P 500

Exhibit 16: Comparison of Growth Strategies– Table

	Returns for Growth Strategies						Comparison to S&P 500				
Year	S&P500 Returns	High P/E Strategy	High P/S Strategy	High P/BV Strategy	High P/CF Strategy	Growth Index	High P/E Strategy	High P/S Strategy	High P/BV Strategy	High P/CF Strategy	Growth Index
1951	23.37%	16.67%	23.87%	20.90%	16.40%	19.46%	-6.70%	0.50%	-2.47%	-6.97%	-3.91%
1952	17.71%	5.31%	15.40%	10.90%	7.00%	9.65%	-12.40%	-2.31%	-6.81%	-10.71%	-8.06%
1953	-1.17%	0.41%	4.81%	2.30%	-0.60%	1.73%	1.58%	5.98%	3.47%	0.57%	2.90%
1954	51.23%	52.40%	31.52%	51.80%	43.00%	44.68%	1.17%	-19.71%	0.57%	-8.23%	-6.55%
1955	30.96%	18.41%	16.20%	23.30%	20.30%	19.55%	-12.56%	-14.76%	-7.66%	-10.66%	-11.41%
1956	6.44%	10.79%	9.39%	15.70%	10.00%	11.47%	4.34%	2.95%	9.26%	3.56%	5.03%
1957	-10.48%	-6.15%	-0.82%	-5.60%	-4.40%	-4.24%	4.33%	9.66%	4.88%	6.08%	6.24%
1958	42.44%	57.33%	46.51%	62.10%	58.10%	56.01%	14.89%	4.07%	19.66%	15.66%	13.57%
1959	11.79%	39.73%	9.13%	30.20%	23.30%	25.59%	27.94%	-2.66%	18.41%	11.51%	13.80%
1960	0.28%	7.99%	16.95%	23.40%	15.10%	15.86%	7.71%	16.67%	23.12%	14.82%	15.58%
1961	26.60%	11.92%	28.72%	14.70%	16.70%	18.01%	-14.69%	2.12%	-11.90%	-9.90%	-8.59%
1962	-8.83%	-33.80%	-17.41%	-29.80%	-34.80%	-28.95%	-24.97%	-8.58%	-20.97%	-25.97%	-20.12%
1963	22.50%	25.51%	30.46%	27.80%	26.40%	27.54%	3.00%	7.95%	5.30%	3.90%	5.04%
1964	16.30%	14.11%	23.80%	14.00%	1.10%	13.25%	-2.19%	7.49%	-2.30%	-15.20%	-3.05%
1965	12.27%	46.27%	23.09%	36.80%	45.30%	37.87%	34.00%	10.82%	24.53%	33.03%	25.60%
1966	-9.99%	-11.24%	-1.01%	4.00%	-6.70%	-3.74%	-1.25%	8.98%	13.99%	3.29%	6.25%
1967	23.73%	128.33%	101.16%	98.00%	112.90%	110.10%	104.60%	77.43%	74.27%	89.17%	86.37%
1968	10.84%	25.93%	35.33%	34.30%	19.90%	28.87%	15.09%	24.49%	23.46%	9.06%	18.02%
1969	-8.32%	-38.96%	-28.89%	-20.80%	-43.80%	-33.11%	-30.64%	-20.57%	-12.48%	-35.48%	-24.79%
1970	3.33%	-34.86%	-19.70%	-28.90%	-41.00%	-31.12%	-38.20%	-23.04%	-32.23%	-44.33%	-34.45%
1971	14.15%	21.42%	20.15%	38.90%	15.20%	23.92%	7.27%	6.00%	24.75%	1.05%	9.77%
1972	18.88%	3.96%	19.05%	18.10%	1.10%	10.55%	-14.92%	0.17%	-0.78%	-17.78%	-8.33%
1973	-14.50%	-28.17%	-13.60%	-34.10%	-30.50%	-26.59%	-13.67%	0.90%	-19.60%	-16.00%	-12.09%
1974	-26.03%	-35.60%	-33.49%	-40.30%	-36.20%	-36.40%	-9.58%	-7.47%	-14.27%	-10.17%	-10.37%
1975	36.92%	55.21%	19.67%	19.00%	24.30%	29.54%	18.29%	-17.24%	-17.92%	-12.62%	-7.37%
1976	23.64%	24.18%	41.24%	27.50%	34.40%	31.83%	0.54%	17.60%	3.86%	10.76%	8.19%
1977	-7.16%	21.39%	21.66%	15.10%	5.90%	16.01%	28.54%	28.82%	22.26%	13.06%	23.17%
1978	6.39%	10.67%	3.38%	8.50%	12.20%	8.69%	4.28%	-3.01%	2.11%	5.81%	2.30%
1979	18.19%	66.21%	93.99%	55.40%	60.80%	69.10%	48.03%	75.80%	37.21%	42.61%	50.91%
1980	31.52%	52.32%	43.53%	46.10%	41.70%	45.91%	20.80%	12.01%	14.58%	10.18%	14.39%
1981	-4.85%	-26.95%	-51.23%	-48.40%	-42.70%	-42.32%	-22.10%	-46.38%	-43.55%	-37.85%	-37.47%
1982	20.37%	14.00%	-17.43%	-17.00%	-6.00%	-6.61%	-6.37%	-37.79%	-37.37%	-26.37%	-26.97%
1983	22.31%	27.84%	8.80%	0.30%	12.10%	12.26%	5.53%	-13.51%	-22.01%	-10.21%	-10.05%
1984	5.97%	-22.85%	-44.74%	-33.20%	-30.70%	-32.87%	-28.81%	-50.71%	-39.17%	-36.67%	-38.84%
1985	31.06%	24.03%	9.38%	9.80%	11.80%	13.75%	-7.02%	-21.68%	-21.26%	-19.26%	-17.30%
1986	18.54%	-0.79%	-2.55%	-7.10%	-2.70%	-3.29%	-19.33%	-21.09%	-25.64%	-21.24%	-21.82%
1987	5.67%	-16.87%	-29.57%	-33.20%	-20.70%	-25.09%	-22.53%	-35.24%	-38.87%	-26.37%	-30.75%
1988	16.35%	14.23%	-7.51%	-5.70%	6.40%	1.86%	-2.11%	-23.86%	-22.05%	-9.95%	-14.49%
1989	31.23%	9.39%	-3.83%	-15.30%	6.00%	-0.93%	-21.84%	-35.06%	-46.53%	-25.23%	-32.17%
1990	-3.14%	-28.44%	-38.37%	-37.60%	-33.90%	-34.58%	-25.30%	-35.23%	-34.46%	-30.76%	-31.44%
1991	30.00%	40.87%	67.22%	67.90%	43.40%	54.85%	10.87%	37.22%	37.90%	13.40%	24.85%
1992	7.43%	3.20%	-24.98%	-18.70%	-5.80%	-11.57%	-4.23%	-32.42%	-26.13%	-13.23%	-19.00%
1993	9.94%	15.20%	-1.92%	10.90%	19.60%	10.95%	5.26%	-11.86%	0.96%	9.66%	1.00%
1994	1.28%	-7.66%	-36.99%	-24.90%	-18.90%	-22.11%	-8.95%	-38.27%	-26.18%	-20.18%	-23.40%
1995	37.11%	21.88%	47.10%	21.20%	37.20%	31.85%	-15.23%	9.99%	-15.91%	0.09%	-5.27%
1996	22.68%	6.70%	0.34%	-13.10%	5.30%	-0.19%	-15.98%	-22.35%	-35.78%	-17.38%	-22.87%
1997	33.10%	13.30%	-20.05%	-11.50%	8.80%	-2.36%	-19.80%	-53.15%	-44.60%	-24.30%	-35.46%
1998	28.34%	-10.77%	-6.75%	54.70%	-0.20%	9.24%	-39.11%	-35.09%	26.36%	-28.54%	-19.09%
1999	20.88%	36.85%	77.85%	84.20%	92.20%	72.77%	15.97%	56.96%	63.32%	71.32%	51.89%
2000	-9.03%	-21.04%	-64.49%	-61.10%	-32.10%	-44.68%	-12.01%	-55.45%	-52.07%	-23.07%	-35.65%
2001	-11.85%	-8.04%	-29.44%	-26.80%	-24.00%	-22.07%	3.81%	-17.59%	-14.95%	-12.15%	-10.22%
2002	-21.97%	-24.51%	-56.73%	-14.00%	-37.70%	-33.24%	-2.54%	-34.77%	7.97%	-15.73%	-11.27%

	S&P 500 Returns	High P/E Strategy	High P/S Strategy	High P/BV Strategy	High P/CF Strategy	Growth Index
Average Returns	12.59%	11.29%	6.50%	8.09%	7.70%	8.40%
Compound Returns	11.23%	7.24%	0.36%	2.52%	2.92%	3.80%
Years Beating S&P 500	N/A	23	23	23	21	20
Years Losing Money	13	17	23	21	20	21

% of Years Strategy on Left Beats Other Growth Strategies

	P/E	P/S	P/BV	P/CF
P/E	N/A	56%	58%	71%
P/S	44%	N/A	46%	46%
P/BV	42%	54%	N/A	44%
P/CF	29%	54%	56%	N/A

When we are looking to buy growth stocks, high P/E is the selection criterion we rely on most often. High P/BV is useful for finding young growth companies, as is high P/CF. High P/CF can also indicate a company that is growing so rapidly that it is barely able to finance its growth. High P/S can be dangerous; we generally avoid stocks with high P/S ratios.

None of the Growth Strategies Beat the Market

Clearly, none of the growth stock selection strategies we have discussed thus far even came close to beating the market over our 52 year study period.

Exhibit 15 provides two charts, one showing how the growth strategies' portfolios all fall well short of the S&P 500 portfolio's growth in value, and another one showing how the annual returns for each growth strategy stack up against the annual performance of the S&P 500.

The second chart shows how rarely the growth strategies outperform the S&P 500. It also shows that, compared to the value strategies, there is less uniformity among the growth strategies in their performance vis-à-vis the S&P 500. This indicates the possibility that different types of growth stocks might sometimes have different reactions to circumstances. We'll come back to this point later, when we examine whether there are any patterns to such differences.

Exhibit 16 includes a "Growth Index," similar to the Value Index, which, again, is simply an arithmetic average of the annual returns for the four growth strategies. The index provides a clearer picture of the behavior of growth stocks relative to the market, and, along with the Growth Index, it will receive additional attention later in Part Two.

The Growth Index's average returns would have beaten the S&P 500 in 20 years out of 52, with 21 money losing years, demonstrating conclusively that the growth style is not one that can be relied upon to consistently beat the market.

But what about all of those years when growth stocks do outperform the S&P 500? Even though growth stocks underperform on average, there are some situations in which growth stocks outperform the market by a wide margin.

So, what are the conditions that lead growth stocks to outperform the market? We will arrive at the answer to this question in Chapter 11, when we will show how the conditions that lead growth stocks to have good years can be traced to the effects of Federal Reserve Bank policy changes.

Meanwhile, we will continue laying the groundwork for that discussion by proceeding to a more in-depth comparison of the value and growth styles of investing in Chapter 6.

Chapter 6

VALUE VERSUS GROWTH

Considering their dismal performance, it is not unreasonable to question the wisdom of buying and holding growth stocks – or growth mutual funds.

All of the brokers, mutual fund sales reps, and advisors who tell investors that they should always keep some growth stocks – or growth funds – in their portfolios for the sake of diversification are passing along some singularly bad advice.

We have yet to find a growth strategy that will perform well year in and year out, over a long period. More often than not, over the last five decades, growth strategies underperformed the market. Indeed, they lost money 40% of the time.

The performance data exhibited in Chapter 5 should make it clear that buying and holding growth stocks for the sake of diversification is a losing proposition.

Are growth stocks ever a good investment?

Perhaps. The data presented thus far suggests that there might be good times to own growth stocks. However, we repeat: owning them "all of the time," using a buy and hold approach, is a really bad idea.

Value investing is different. It is a viable strategy to employ using a buy and hold approach. This stodgy, boring method of stock selection beats the market over the long term by a comfortable margin. An investor whose sole stock selection strategy was to always hold the 100 lowest P/E stocks would have outperformed the market in 40 of the past 52 years. He would have earned very good returns, and he would rarely have lost money.

Yet, there have been years in which the value strategies underperformed the market, and there were times when growth strategies beat the market.

This raises an important question: Are the conditions which are good for growth stocks the same conditions that cause value stocks to underperform? In other words, do value stocks do poorly when growth stocks do well?

If this were true, then an investor could significantly improve his returns by shifting assets between value and growth at the right times. If not, then the investor would probably be better off staying with value stocks all of the time.

In either case, the concept involved is completely different from the conventional advice to maintain a balance between value and growth stocks in order to be diversified. In the absence of other considerations (such as a desire to exploit tax loss selling), we never want to be buying value and growth at the same time. We might want to buy growth instead of value at certain times, but only if we can identify conditions under which the returns from growth would be predictably higher than those from value.

To get at this question, we compared the performance of each of the growth strategies and value strategies. First, we compared them to the S&P 500. Then, we compared each growth strategy to its corresponding value strategy.

Exhibit 17 shows the performance advantage of each growth and value strategy over the S&P 500.

As previously explained, performance advantage refers to the difference in returns, calculated as the strategies' returns minus the S&P 500 returns. Thus, when the performance advantage is positive, the strategy outperformed the S&P 500. When it is negative, the strategy underperformed the S&P 500.

Exhibits 18 and **19** represent these calculations graphically, as well as in table form. The two charts included in **Exhibit 17** are identical to the charts we presented in **Exhibit 9** (Comparison of Value Strategies– Graphs) and **Exhibit 15** (Comparison of Growth Strategies– Graphs). They are reproduced here for ease of comparison.

Comparing these two charts, and focusing on the periods in which the growth strategies beat the S&P 500 (these are the years for which the columns appear above the "zero" line in the first graph), we can see that there have indeed been a number of occasions when the performance advantage for growth stocks moves in the opposite direction from that for value stocks.

Growth Versus Value In Recent Years

Comparing the two charts shown on **Exhibit 17** yields some fascinating insights into some recent market history.

Notice how, in the years leading up to the dot.com bull market, the balance between growth and value steadily shifted in favor of growth, until the height of the bubble.

Then, when the bubble burst, the balance shifted dramatically back in favor of value stocks, as investors rediscovered traditional methods of valuing stocks.

In other words, there have been a significant number of occasions when growth stocks have beaten the market, while, at the same time, value stocks were underperforming the market. Of course, most of the time, the opposite was true.

We then compared the growth strategies directly to the value strategies in an attempt to bring the shifting balance between growth stock returns and value stock returns into clearer focus. **Exhibits 19** and **20** present this comparison.

The first chart appearing in **Exhibit 19** shows the returns for the Value and Growth Indices, along with returns for the S&P 500. Three conclusions can be drawn from this chart.

First, in general, returns for both the Growth and the Value Indices tend to fluctuate more or less in the same pattern as returns for the S&P 500. Most of the time, the returns for both growth and value stocks improve in a rising market, but by significantly different amounts. Most of the time, the returns for both growth and value stocks decline in a falling market, but again, by quite different amounts.

Second, returns for the Value Index tend to be higher than returns for the S&P 500, and returns for the Growth Index tend to be lower. This is just a restatement of our observation that value usually outperforms the market, while growth tends to underperform the market.

Third, and most importantly, the relative positions of value and growth change from time to time. In other words, there are indeed times when the growth outperforms the value.

The chart in **Exhibit 21** compares each growth strategy to its corresponding value strategy, i.e., the Growth Index minus the Value Index, high P/E minus low P/E, high P/S minus low P/S, and so on.

Every instance where the columns in this chart appear above the "zero" line represents a year when the growth strategy outperformed the value strategy.

A couple of conclusions can be drawn from this exhibit.

First, the growth strategy beat the value strategy in years that growth did exceptionally well compared to the market. We can see this by comparing this chart to **Exhibit 17**. Eight of the ten years in which growth beat value were also years in which growth beat the S&P 500. Value didn't perform poorly during these years; in seven of the 10 years in which growth beat value, both growth and value beat the market.

Exhibit 17: Growth and Value Strategies vs. S&P 500– Graphs

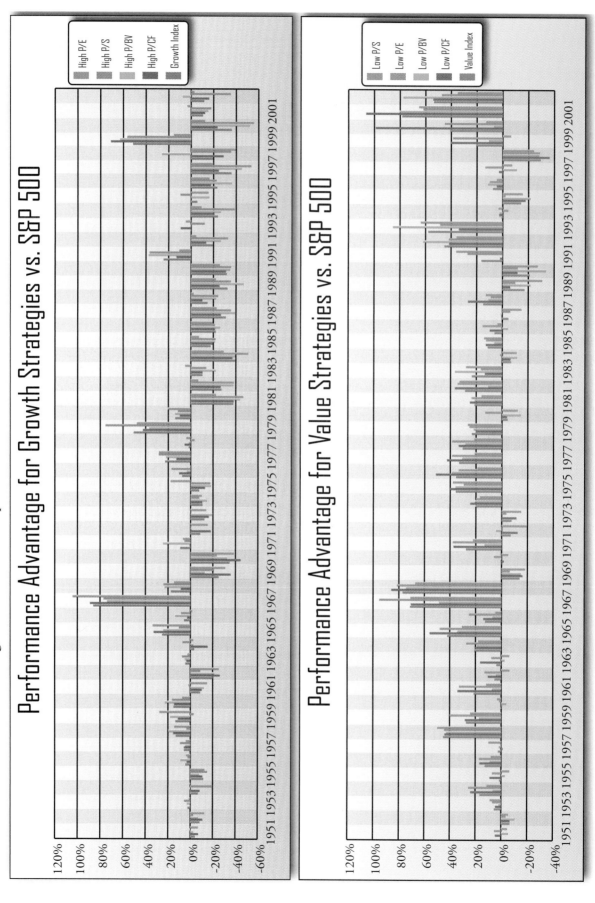

Performance Advantage for Growth Strategies vs. S&P 500

Legend: High P/E, High P/S, High P/BV, High P/CF, Growth Index

Performance Advantage for Value Strategies vs. S&P 500

Legend: Low P/S, Low P/E, Low P/BV, Low P/CF, Value Index

Exhibit 18: Growth and Value Strategies vs. S&P 500– Table

Year	S&P500 Returns	Growth Index	Comparison to S&P 500					Value Index	Comparison to S&P 500				Value Index
			High P/E Strategy	High P/S Strategy	High P/BV Strategy	High P/CF Strategy	Growth Index		Low P/E Strategy	Low P/S Strategy	Low P/BV Strategy	Low P/CF Strategy	
1951	23.37%	19.46%	-6.70%	0.50%	-2.47%	-6.97%	-3.91%	23.43%	5.47%	-4.58%	-5.37%	4.73%	0.06%
1952	17.71%	9.65%	-12.40%	-2.31%	-6.81%	-10.71%	-8.06%	11.32%	-3.43%	-5.33%	-10.31%	-6.51%	-6.39%
1953	-1.17%	1.73%	1.58%	5.98%	3.47%	0.57%	2.90%	4.57%	7.02%	8.98%	2.17%	4.77%	5.73%
1954	51.23%	44.68%	1.17%	-19.71%	0.57%	-8.23%	-6.55%	68.17%	25.70%	11.42%	6.67%	23.97%	16.94%
1955	30.96%	19.55%	-12.56%	-14.76%	-7.66%	-10.66%	-11.41%	32.80%	7.27%	-6.20%	-2.76%	9.04%	1.84%
1956	6.44%	11.47%	4.34%	2.95%	9.26%	3.56%	5.03%	19.36%	17.44%	8.23%	9.16%	16.86%	12.92%
1957	-10.48%	-4.24%	4.33%	9.66%	4.88%	6.08%	6.24%	-7.68%	0.28%	9.97%	1.98%	-1.02%	2.80%
1958	42.44%	56.01%	14.89%	4.07%	19.66%	15.66%	13.57%	87.92%	44.72%	50.00%	42.96%	44.26%	45.49%
1959	11.79%	25.59%	27.94%	-2.66%	18.41%	11.51%	13.80%	39.27%	39.86%	24.33%	17.41%	28.31%	27.48%
1960	0.28%	15.86%	7.71%	16.67%	23.12%	14.82%	15.58%	0.63%	1.98%	3.57%	-3.68%	-0.48%	0.34%
1961	26.60%	18.01%	-14.69%	2.12%	-11.90%	-9.90%	-8.59%	48.20%	33.02%	11.89%	7.40%	34.10%	21.60%
1962	-8.83%	-28.95%	-24.97%	-8.58%	-20.97%	-25.97%	-20.12%	-3.30%	13.21%	-6.15%	4.53%	10.53%	5.53%
1963	22.50%	27.54%	3.00%	7.95%	5.30%	3.90%	5.04%	26.55%	8.00%	-6.00%	-2.30%	16.50%	4.05%
1964	16.30%	13.25%	-2.19%	7.49%	-2.30%	-15.20%	-3.05%	37.50%	27.42%	18.26%	19.20%	19.90%	21.19%
1965	12.27%	37.87%	34.00%	10.82%	24.53%	33.03%	25.60%	54.62%	48.24%	30.81%	34.33%	56.03%	42.35%
1966	-9.99%	-3.74%	-1.25%	8.98%	13.99%	3.29%	6.25%	2.97%	25.44%	4.91%	7.29%	14.19%	12.96%
1967	23.73%	110.10%	104.60%	77.43%	74.27%	89.17%	86.37%	95.24%	95.50%	71.11%	48.77%	70.67%	71.51%
1968	10.84%	28.87%	15.09%	24.49%	23.46%	9.06%	18.02%	88.34%	81.78%	67.38%	74.76%	86.06%	77.50%
1969	-8.32%	-33.11%	-30.64%	-20.57%	-12.48%	-35.48%	-24.79%	-22.03%	-6.11%	-18.08%	-14.58%	-16.08%	-13.71%
1970	3.33%	-31.12%	-38.20%	-23.04%	-32.23%	-44.33%	-34.45%	3.51%	6.24%	-4.88%	0.87%	-1.53%	0.17%
1971	14.15%	23.92%	7.27%	6.00%	24.75%	1.05%	9.77%	42.06%	38.17%	22.46%	13.55%	37.45%	27.91%
1972	18.88%	10.55%	-14.92%	0.17%	-0.78%	-17.78%	-8.33%	12.22%	0.47%	-19.57%	4.62%	-12.18%	-6.67%
1973	-14.50%	-26.59%	-13.67%	0.90%	-19.60%	-16.00%	-12.09%	-21.87%	-3.35%	-14.83%	-0.10%	-11.20%	-7.37%
1974	-26.03%	-36.40%	-9.58%	-7.47%	-14.27%	-10.17%	-10.37%	-5.40%	19.75%	17.21%	21.03%	24.53%	20.63%
1975	36.92%	29.54%	18.29%	-17.24%	-17.92%	-12.62%	-7.37%	72.91%	29.67%	38.22%	36.08%	39.98%	35.99%
1976	23.64%	31.83%	0.54%	17.60%	3.86%	10.76%	8.19%	59.51%	33.78%	19.27%	38.96%	51.46%	35.87%
1977	-7.16%	16.01%	28.54%	28.82%	22.26%	13.06%	23.17%	26.30%	38.88%	21.33%	30.86%	42.76%	33.46%
1978	6.39%	8.69%	4.28%	-3.01%	2.11%	5.81%	2.30%	37.10%	38.94%	21.59%	28.61%	33.71%	30.71%
1979	18.19%	69.10%	48.03%	75.80%	37.21%	42.61%	50.91%	41.86%	25.42%	26.73%	22.11%	20.41%	23.67%
1980	31.52%	45.91%	20.80%	12.01%	14.58%	10.18%	14.39%	27.36%	13.29%	-11.97%	-14.22%	-3.72%	-4.15%
1981	-4.85%	-42.32%	-22.10%	-46.38%	-43.55%	-37.85%	-37.47%	16.74%	23.88%	16.07%	21.35%	25.05%	21.58%
1982	20.37%	-6.61%	-6.37%	-37.79%	-37.37%	-26.37%	-26.97%	49.35%	34.79%	33.27%	11.13%	36.73%	28.98%
1983	22.31%	12.26%	5.53%	-13.51%	-22.01%	-10.21%	-10.05%	46.17%	16.80%	28.26%	36.89%	13.49%	23.86%
1984	5.97%	-32.87%	-28.81%	-50.71%	-39.17%	-36.67%	-38.84%	-0.62%	1.96%	-10.88%	-11.27%	-6.17%	-6.59%
1985	31.06%	13.75%	-7.02%	-21.68%	-21.26%	-19.26%	-17.30%	42.63%	12.71%	14.30%	6.44%	12.84%	11.57%
1986	18.54%	-3.29%	-19.33%	-21.09%	-25.64%	-21.24%	-21.82%	24.88%	15.51%	4.02%	-4.04%	9.86%	6.34%
1987	5.67%	-25.09%	-22.53%	-35.24%	-38.87%	-26.37%	-30.75%	1.15%	-5.93%	-14.62%	1.43%	1.03%	-4.52%
1988	16.35%	1.86%	-2.11%	-23.86%	-22.05%	-9.95%	-14.49%	31.46%	9.33%	13.13%	11.15%	26.85%	15.12%
1989	31.23%	-0.93%	-21.84%	-35.06%	-46.53%	-25.23%	-32.17%	14.38%	-9.70%	-30.53%	-21.43%	-5.73%	-16.85%
1990	-3.14%	-34.58%	-25.30%	-35.23%	-34.46%	-30.76%	-31.44%	-23.97%	-11.49%	-26.92%	-33.46%	-11.46%	-20.83%
1991	30.00%	54.85%	10.87%	37.22%	37.90%	13.40%	24.85%	46.58%	27.43%	36.19%	0.60%	2.10%	16.58%
1992	7.43%	-11.57%	-4.23%	-32.42%	-26.13%	-13.23%	-19.00%	52.93%	42.05%	36.10%	62.07%	41.77%	45.50%
1993	9.94%	10.95%	5.26%	-11.86%	0.96%	9.66%	1.00%	68.15%	48.86%	64.06%	85.76%	34.16%	58.21%
1994	1.28%	-22.11%	-8.95%	-38.27%	-26.18%	-20.18%	-23.40%	2.58%	-4.03%	3.57%	2.72%	2.92%	1.29%
1995	37.11%	31.85%	-15.23%	9.99%	-15.91%	0.09%	-5.27%	23.13%	-1.90%	-15.22%	-21.31%	-17.51%	-13.99%
1996	22.68%	-0.19%	-15.98%	-22.35%	-35.78%	-17.38%	-22.87%	30.61%	10.37%	4.82%	11.72%	4.82%	7.93%
1997	33.10%	-2.36%	-19.80%	-53.15%	-44.60%	-24.30%	-35.46%	32.96%	13.81%	-6.97%	-10.60%	3.20%	-0.14%
1998	28.34%	9.24%	-39.11%	-35.09%	26.36%	-28.54%	-19.09%	-0.77%	-28.53%	-23.84%	-27.94%	-36.14%	-29.11%
1999	20.88%	72.77%	15.97%	56.96%	63.32%	71.32%	51.89%	41.91%	38.88%	-6.10%	11.12%	40.22%	21.03%
2000	-9.03%	-44.68%	-12.01%	-55.45%	-52.07%	-23.07%	-35.65%	32.21%	45.38%	13.21%	7.23%	99.13%	41.24%
2001	-11.85%	-22.07%	3.81%	-17.59%	-14.95%	-12.15%	-10.22%	66.82%	62.04%	65.35%	80.75%	106.55%	78.67%
2002	-21.97%	-33.24%	-2.54%	-34.77%	7.97%	-15.73%	-11.27%	31.82%	47.71%	35.30%	77.77%	54.37%	53.78%
Average Returns	12.59%	8.40%	-1.29%	-6.08%	-4.50%	-4.88%	-4.19%	29.51%	21.23%	11.97%	13.81%	20.68%	16.92%
Compound Returns	11.23%	3.80%						26.42%					
Years Strategy Beats S&P 500		20	23	23	23	21	20	40	43	34	37	39	40

Exhibit 19: Comparison of Growth vs. Value Strategies' Returns– Graphs

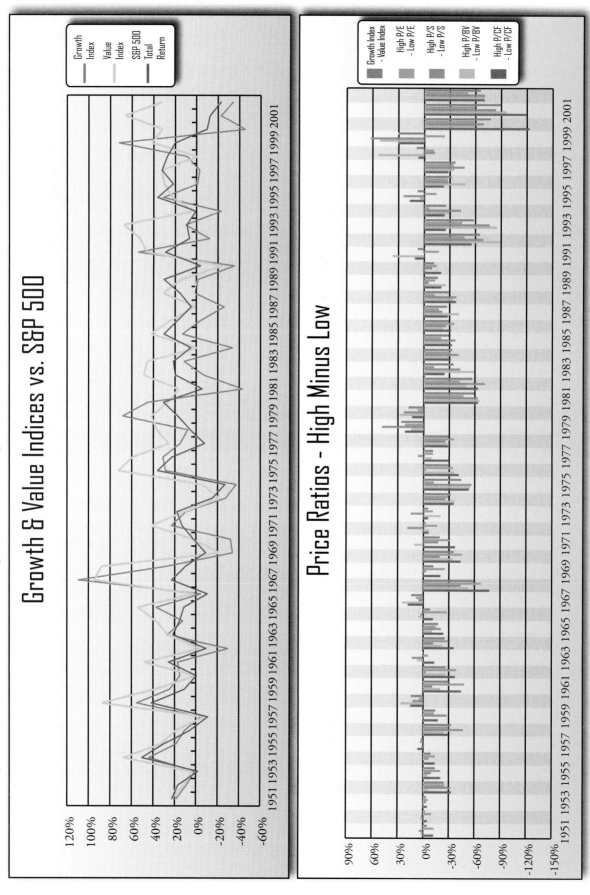

Exhibit 20: Comparison of Growth vs. Value Strategies– Table

	Growth Strategies						Value Strategies									
Year	S&P500 Returns	Growth Index	High P/E Strategy	High P/S Strategy	High P/BV Strategy	High P/CF Strategy	Value Index	Low P/E Strategy	Low P/S Strategy	Low P/BV Strategy	Low P/CF Strategy	Growth Index - Value Index	High P/E - Low P/E	High P/S - Low P/S	High P/BV - Low P/BV	High P/CF - Low P/CF
1951	23.37%	19.46%	16.67%	23.87%	20.90%	16.40%	23.43%	28.84%	18.79%	18.00%	28.10%	-3.97%	-12.17%	5.08%	2.90%	-11.70%
1952	17.71%	9.65%	5.31%	15.40%	10.90%	7.00%	11.32%	14.29%	12.38%	7.40%	11.20%	-1.66%	-8.98%	3.02%	3.50%	-4.20%
1953	-1.17%	1.73%	0.41%	4.81%	2.30%	-0.60%	4.57%	5.86%	7.81%	1.00%	3.60%	-2.83%	-5.44%	-3.00%	1.30%	-4.20%
1954	51.23%	44.68%	52.40%	31.52%	51.80%	43.00%	68.17%	76.93%	62.65%	57.90%	75.20%	-23.49%	-24.52%	-31.13%	-6.10%	-32.20%
1955	30.96%	19.55%	18.41%	16.20%	23.30%	20.30%	32.80%	38.24%	24.76%	28.20%	40.00%	-13.25%	-19.83%	-8.57%	-4.90%	-19.70%
1956	6.44%	11.47%	10.79%	9.39%	15.70%	10.00%	19.36%	23.88%	14.67%	15.60%	23.30%	-7.89%	-13.09%	-5.28%	0.10%	-13.30%
1957	-10.48%	-4.24%	-6.15%	-0.82%	-5.60%	-4.40%	-7.68%	-10.20%	-0.50%	-8.50%	-11.50%	3.43%	4.05%	-0.32%	2.90%	7.10%
1958	42.44%	56.01%	57.33%	46.51%	62.10%	58.10%	87.92%	87.15%	92.43%	85.40%	86.70%	-31.91%	-29.82%	-45.92%	-23.30%	-28.60%
1959	11.79%	25.59%	39.73%	9.13%	30.20%	23.30%	39.27%	51.65%	36.12%	29.20%	40.10%	-13.68%	-11.92%	-26.99%	1.00%	-16.80%
1960	0.28%	15.86%	7.99%	16.95%	23.40%	15.10%	0.63%	2.26%	3.85%	-3.40%	-0.20%	15.23%	5.73%	13.10%	26.80%	15.30%
1961	26.60%	18.01%	11.92%	28.72%	14.70%	16.70%	48.20%	59.62%	38.50%	34.00%	60.70%	-30.19%	-47.70%	-9.77%	-19.30%	-44.00%
1962	-8.83%	-28.95%	-33.80%	-17.41%	-29.80%	-34.80%	-3.30%	4.37%	-14.99%	-4.30%	1.70%	-25.65%	-38.17%	-2.42%	-25.50%	-36.50%
1963	22.50%	27.54%	25.51%	30.46%	27.80%	26.40%	26.55%	30.51%	16.51%	20.20%	39.00%	0.99%	-5.00%	13.95%	7.60%	-12.60%
1964	16.30%	13.25%	14.11%	23.80%	14.00%	1.10%	37.50%	43.73%	34.56%	35.50%	36.20%	-24.24%	-29.61%	-10.76%	-21.50%	-35.10%
1965	12.27%	37.87%	46.27%	23.09%	36.80%	45.30%	54.62%	60.52%	43.08%	46.60%	68.30%	-16.76%	-14.24%	-19.99%	-9.80%	-23.00%
1966	-9.99%	-3.74%	-11.24%	-1.01%	4.00%	-6.70%	2.97%	15.45%	-5.07%	-2.70%	4.20%	-6.71%	-26.69%	4.07%	6.70%	-10.90%
1967	23.73%	110.10%	128.33%	101.16%	98.00%	112.90%	95.24%	119.22%	94.84%	72.50%	94.40%	14.86%	9.10%	6.32%	25.50%	18.50%
1968	10.84%	28.87%	25.93%	35.33%	34.30%	19.90%	88.34%	92.62%	78.23%	85.60%	96.90%	-59.47%	-66.69%	-42.90%	-51.30%	-77.00%
1969	-8.32%	-33.11%	-38.96%	-28.89%	-20.80%	-43.80%	-22.03%	-14.43%	-26.40%	-22.90%	-24.40%	-11.08%	-24.53%	-2.49%	2.10%	-19.40%
1970	3.33%	-31.12%	-34.86%	-19.70%	-28.90%	-41.00%	3.51%	9.57%	-1.55%	4.20%	1.80%	-34.62%	-44.43%	-18.16%	-33.10%	-42.80%
1971	14.15%	23.92%	21.42%	20.15%	38.90%	15.20%	42.06%	52.32%	36.61%	27.70%	51.60%	-18.14%	-30.90%	-16.46%	11.20%	-36.40%
1972	18.88%	10.55%	3.96%	19.05%	18.10%	1.10%	12.22%	19.35%	-0.68%	23.50%	6.70%	-1.66%	-15.39%	19.73%	-5.40%	-5.60%
1973	-14.50%	-26.59%	-28.17%	-13.60%	-34.10%	-30.50%	-21.87%	-17.86%	-29.33%	-14.60%	-25.70%	-4.72%	-10.32%	15.73%	-19.50%	-4.80%
1974	-26.03%	-36.40%	-35.60%	-33.49%	-40.30%	-36.20%	-5.40%	-6.27%	-8.82%	-5.00%	-1.50%	-31.00%	-29.33%	-24.68%	-35.30%	-34.70%
1975	36.92%	29.54%	55.21%	19.67%	19.00%	24.30%	72.91%	66.58%	75.14%	73.00%	76.90%	-43.36%	-11.38%	-55.46%	-54.00%	-52.60%
1976	23.64%	31.83%	24.18%	41.24%	27.50%	34.40%	59.51%	57.42%	42.91%	62.60%	75.10%	-27.68%	-33.24%	-1.67%	-35.10%	-40.70%
1977	-7.16%	16.01%	21.39%	21.66%	15.10%	5.90%	26.30%	31.73%	14.17%	23.70%	35.60%	-10.29%	-10.34%	7.49%	-8.60%	-29.70%
1978	6.39%	8.69%	10.67%	3.38%	8.50%	12.20%	37.10%	45.34%	27.98%	35.00%	40.10%	-28.42%	-34.66%	-24.60%	-26.50%	-27.90%
1979	18.19%	69.10%	66.21%	93.99%	55.40%	60.80%	41.86%	43.61%	44.92%	40.30%	38.60%	27.24%	22.60%	49.07%	15.10%	22.20%
1980	31.52%	45.91%	52.32%	43.53%	46.10%	41.70%	27.36%	44.81%	19.54%	17.30%	27.80%	18.55%	7.50%	23.99%	28.80%	13.90%
1981	-4.85%	-42.32%	-26.95%	-51.23%	-48.40%	-42.70%	16.74%	19.03%	11.22%	16.50%	20.20%	-59.06%	-45.98%	-62.45%	-64.90%	-62.90%
1982	20.37%	-6.61%	14.00%	-17.43%	-17.00%	-6.00%	49.35%	55.15%	53.64%	31.50%	57.10%	-55.95%	-41.15%	-71.06%	-48.50%	-63.10%
1983	22.31%	12.26%	27.84%	8.80%	0.30%	12.10%	46.17%	39.11%	50.57%	59.20%	35.80%	-33.91%	-11.27%	-41.78%	-58.90%	-23.70%
1984	5.97%	-32.87%	-22.85%	-44.74%	-33.20%	-30.70%	-0.62%	7.93%	-4.91%	-5.30%	-0.20%	-32.25%	-30.78%	-39.83%	-27.90%	-30.50%
1985	31.06%	13.75%	24.03%	9.38%	9.80%	11.80%	42.63%	43.77%	45.36%	37.50%	43.90%	-28.88%	-19.74%	-35.98%	-27.70%	-32.10%
1986	18.54%	-3.29%	-0.79%	-2.55%	-7.10%	-2.70%	24.88%	34.05%	22.56%	14.50%	28.40%	-28.16%	-34.85%	-25.11%	-21.60%	-31.10%
1987	5.67%	-25.09%	-16.87%	-29.57%	-33.20%	-20.70%	1.15%	-0.26%	-8.95%	7.10%	6.70%	-26.23%	-16.60%	-20.62%	-40.30%	-27.40%
1988	16.35%	1.86%	14.23%	-7.51%	-5.70%	6.40%	31.46%	25.67%	29.48%	27.50%	43.20%	-29.61%	-11.44%	-36.99%	-33.20%	-36.80%
1989	31.23%	-0.93%	9.39%	-3.83%	-15.30%	6.00%	14.38%	21.53%	0.70%	9.80%	25.50%	-15.32%	-12.13%	-4.53%	-25.10%	-19.50%
1990	-3.14%	-34.58%	-28.44%	-38.37%	-37.60%	-33.90%	-23.97%	-14.63%	-30.06%	-36.60%	-14.60%	-10.60%	-13.81%	-8.30%	-1.00%	-19.30%
1991	30.00%	54.85%	40.87%	67.22%	67.90%	43.40%	46.58%	57.43%	66.19%	30.60%	32.10%	8.27%	-16.56%	1.03%	37.30%	11.30%
1992	7.43%	-11.57%	3.20%	-24.98%	-18.70%	-5.80%	52.93%	49.49%	43.54%	69.50%	49.20%	-64.50%	-46.28%	-68.52%	-88.20%	-55.00%
1993	9.94%	10.95%	15.20%	-1.92%	10.90%	19.60%	68.15%	58.80%	74.00%	95.70%	44.10%	-57.20%	-43.60%	-75.92%	-84.80%	-24.50%
1994	1.28%	-22.11%	-7.66%	-36.99%	-24.90%	-18.90%	2.58%	-2.75%	4.85%	4.00%	4.20%	-24.69%	-4.91%	-41.84%	-28.90%	-23.10%
1995	37.11%	31.85%	21.88%	47.10%	21.20%	37.20%	23.13%	35.21%	21.89%	15.80%	19.60%	8.72%	-13.33%	25.21%	5.40%	17.60%
1996	22.68%	-0.19%	6.70%	0.34%	-13.10%	5.30%	30.61%	33.05%	27.50%	34.40%	27.50%	-30.80%	-26.35%	-27.16%	-47.50%	-22.20%
1997	33.10%	-2.36%	13.30%	-20.05%	-11.50%	8.80%	32.96%	46.91%	26.13%	22.50%	36.30%	-35.32%	-33.61%	-46.18%	-34.00%	-27.50%
1998	28.34%	9.24%	-10.77%	-6.75%	54.70%	-0.20%	-0.77%	-0.19%	4.50%	0.40%	-7.80%	10.02%	-10.58%	-11.25%	54.30%	7.60%
1999	20.88%	72.77%	36.85%	77.85%	84.20%	92.20%	41.91%	59.76%	14.79%	32.00%	61.10%	30.86%	-22.91%	63.06%	52.20%	31.10%
2000	-9.03%	-44.68%	-21.04%	-64.49%	-61.10%	-32.10%	32.21%	36.35%	4.18%	-1.80%	90.10%	-76.89%	-57.39%	-68.66%	-59.30%	-122.20%
2001	-11.85%	-22.07%	-8.04%	-29.44%	-26.80%	-24.00%	66.82%	50.19%	53.50%	68.90%	94.70%	-88.89%	-58.23%	-82.94%	-95.70%	-118.70%
2002	-21.97%	-33.24%	-24.51%	-56.73%	-14.00%	-37.70%	31.82%	25.74%	13.33%	55.80%	32.40%	-65.05%	-50.25%	-70.07%	-69.80%	-70.10%

Average Returns:

| 12.59% | 8.40% | 11.29% | 6.50% | 8.09% | 7.70% | 29.51% | 33.82% | 24.56% | 26.39% | 33.27% | -21.11% | -22.52% | -18.06% | -18.30% | -25.57% |

Compound Returns:

| 11.23% | 3.80% | 7.24% | 0.36% | 2.52% | 2.92% | 26.42% | 30.74% | 21.12% | 23.08% | 29.56% | | | | | |

Yrs Strategy Beats S&P 500:

| | 20 | 23 | 23 | 23 | 21 | 40 | 43 | 34 | 37 | 39 | | | | | |

Second, there are significant differences among the four price ratios in this comparison. As the table shows, high P/E beat low P/E only five times, but high P/BV beat low P/BV 18 times. This reminds us that there are different kinds of growth stocks and different kinds of value stocks. Differences in the behavior of the four price ratios can be seen in **Exhibit 21**.

We will return to these points in Chapter 11 in our detailed discussion of the Fed-Election Cycle and stock selection strategies.

For now, the important points to remember are:

- There have been plenty of times when growth beat the market (i.e., the S&P 500), and

- There have also been a number of times when growth beat value.

This answers part of the question we posed earlier in this chapter.

Since growth sometimes outperforms value, then, at least in theory, we should be able to improve our returns by shifting assets from value stocks to growth stocks at the appropriate times.

Of course, we can't do this without knowing more about the conditions that favor growth over value. We need to know how to spot these conditions as they begin to arise, before they are fully developed, so we can buy growth stocks before their prices start climbing. Just as importantly, we need to be able to identify the point at which the pendulum starts swinging back in favor of value stocks, so we can shift back into value stocks at the appropriate time.

The conditions favoring growth stocks over value stocks are largely a function of Federal Reserve monetary policy, as we have previously noted. Moreover, the practical knowledge of when to shift into – and out of – growth stocks is just one of the principal benefits of understanding the Combined Fed-Election Cycle.

All of this will be thoroughly explained in Chapter 11 as part of our broader discussion of the best stock selection criteria to employ during each phase of the monetary and Election Cycles.

But first, we need to review the effects of relative strength, market capitalization, and the Election Cycle to complete the foundation for understanding and implementing our stock selection strategy.

Exhibit 21: Comparison of Growth vs. Value Strategies vs. Growth Less Value Index Returns

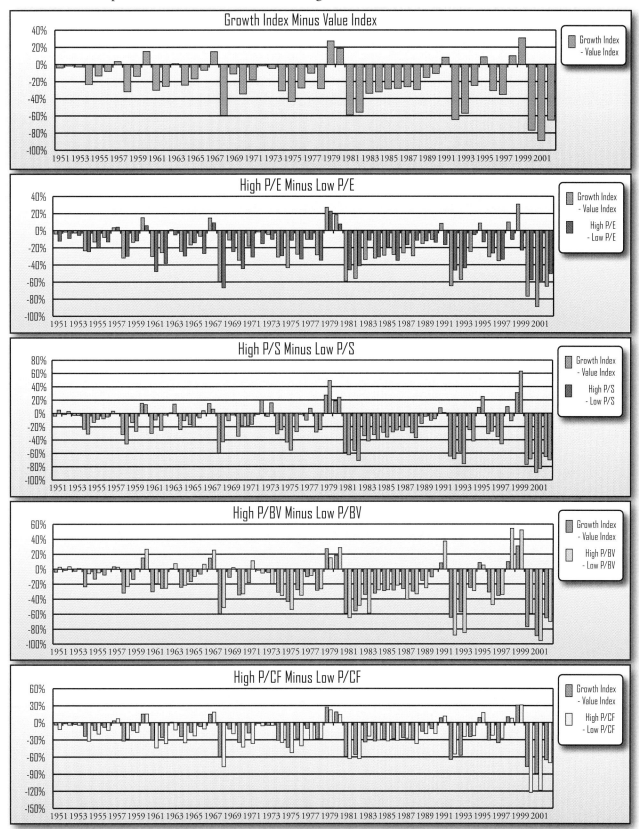

Chapter 7

BUYING HIGH RELATIVE STRENGTH STOCKS

The relative strength measure compares a given stock's return over a defined period of time to the returns of all other stocks in a given group. For example, a stock with a 12-month relative strength of 90 has outperformed 90% of the stocks in its group during the past 12 months. Stocks with high relative strength tend to outperform market indices most of the time. One notable exception is "tax season" (late December through early February), when low relative strength stocks are usually the best choice.

Relative Strength Versus Momentum

The concept of buying relative strength must be distinguished from momentum investing, with which it is sometimes confused. Actually, these are two very different approaches to investing.

There is an old saying on Wall Street that the market is perfectly rational in the long run, but perfectly irrational in the short run. Rational investors bet on relative strength, while irrational investors put their money on momentum.

Relative strength, as we define and employ it, is sustained price appreciation occurring over an extended period of time – at least several quarters if not several years. This kind of sustained appreciation is typically supported by a foundation of earnings growth that consistently exceeds expectations.

Momentum investing, on the other hand, focuses on rapid, short-term price appreciation that takes place over a period of days, or even hours. Momentum investing is driven by hopes, dreams, and visions rather than by solid operating performance. Momentum investors often buy stocks simply because they are going up, without ever attempting to determine if the price gains are propelled by real growth in sales, earnings, and cash flow.

A company whose stock price steadily increases over a period of a year or more is likely to be achieving substantial improvement in operating results. A stock that started going up just a few days ago might well be driven by Internet message board postings that sound thoroughly compelling but are utterly bogus. The day-trading momentum investor buys stocks that are going up in the hope of selling them to a greater fool a few hours later.

It's easy to understand why many investors (excepting contrarians) are attracted to stocks that have posted price gains. There is a feeling that the market has validated the premise that these are good stocks to own. Such feelings are deeply rooted in human behavioral patterns that cause individuals to follow the herd. It somehow feels right to many of us to buy stocks that lots of other investors have been buying, similar to the way people often feel compelled to adopt the beliefs of those around them because it feels better to conform, to fit in, rather than to be left out.

In addition, most of us are susceptible to a cognitive failure known as "trend bias." Trend bias, as the term suggests, is the notion that observed patterns of change will extend indefinitely into the future. Thus, investors who have seen a stock price that has been steadily rising are prone to believe that it will continue to rise indefinitely.

In any event, high relative strength is often a good predictor of future price gains, and therefore it has become an important element in our stock selection strategy.

Nevertheless, the need to distinguish between trends with solid foundations and temporary phenomena is a practical difficulty in screening for relative strength. We need to separate the strong companies whose price gains reflect excellent fundamentals from the stocks whose momentum is ephemeral or based on smoke and mirrors.

We accomplish this in several ways.

First, we rely only on relative strength observed over sufficiently long periods of time, never less than least three months, usually longer. This eliminates many, but not all, of the stocks whose gains represent unsupported momentum.

Second, we rarely buy any stock solely on the basis of relative strength (except during year-end tax season). We combine a screen for high relative strength with screens pertaining to criteria such as market capitalization and value/growth.

Finally, we make an effort to determine whether investors have been buying the stock for good, solid reasons. If a stock has good fundamentals, high relative strength makes it even more likely to be a winner.

"The trend is your friend" only if the trend is established over a significant period of time and is supported by strong fundamentals.

Returns for Relative Strength Strategies

How important is relative strength to a stock's future performance? The returns for strategies based on relative strength are presented in **Exhibit 22**.

This table compares a strategy of buying stocks with the highest relative strength to the strategy of buying stocks with the lowest relative strength. Each year, portfolios were reconstructed from relative strength rankings based on the prior 52-week period using an approach similar to that used for backtesting returns for value and growth strategies.

A number of popular theories have been advanced suggesting that it's better to buy stocks with the worst recent performance. The rationale is that the winners have already had their run and have topped out, but losers can only go up.

The data presented in **Exhibit 22** ought to lay to rest any question of whether a strategy of buying proven winners is better than buying underperforming laggards.

The strategy of buying the 100 stocks with the highest prior-year returns would have earned an average return of 20.0% (13.8% compounded). The strategy of buying last year's losers, i.e., the 100 stocks with the lowest prior-year returns, would have earned an average of 8.3% (2.7% compounded).

The high relative strength strategy would have beaten the S&P 500 in 31 out of 51 years (61% of the time), while it would have lost money in 17 years.

The low relative strength strategy would have beaten the S&P 500 in just 21 of 51 years (41% of the time), while it would have lost money in 21 of the years.

Exhibit 22: High Relative Strength vs. Low Relative Strength

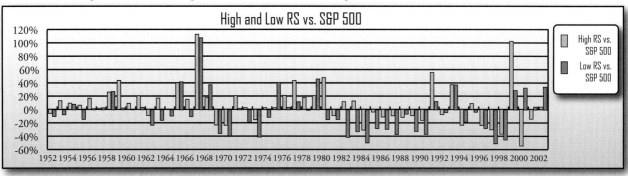

Year	S&P 500 Returns	High Relative Strength	Low Relative Strength	High RS vs. Low RS	High RS vs. S&P 500	Low RS vs. S&P 500	Year	S&P 500 Returns	High Relative Strength	Low Relative Strength	High RS vs. Low RS	High RS vs. S&P 500	Low RS vs. S&P 500
1952	17.71%	11.82%	8.01%	3.80%	-5.89%	-9.70%	1977	-7.16%	36.34%	5.01%	31.33%	43.50%	12.16%
1953	-1.17%	11.90%	-8.32%	20.22%	13.07%	-7.15%	1978	6.39%	24.30%	5.81%	18.48%	17.90%	-0.58%
1954	51.23%	60.62%	59.74%	0.88%	9.40%	8.51%	1979	18.19%	38.75%	64.73%	-25.98%	20.56%	46.54%
1955	30.96%	37.28%	16.82%	20.46%	6.32%	-14.14%	1980	31.52%	79.45%	17.03%	62.42%	47.93%	-14.49%
1956	6.44%	23.23%	8.26%	14.96%	16.79%	1.82%	1981	-4.85%	-14.14%	-19.09%	4.95%	-9.29%	-14.24%
1957	-10.48%	-8.71%	-7.44%	-1.28%	1.76%	3.04%	1982	20.37%	31.98%	-20.65%	52.63%	11.61%	-41.02%
1958	42.44%	68.36%	69.91%	-1.55%	25.93%	27.48%	1983	22.31%	34.96%	-10.12%	45.08%	12.65%	-32.43%
1959	11.79%	55.53%	14.56%	40.97%	43.74%	2.77%	1984	5.97%	-24.91%	-43.36%	18.45%	-30.87%	-49.32%
1960	0.28%	9.35%	1.07%	8.28%	9.07%	0.79%	1985	31.06%	27.17%	3.29%	23.88%	-3.88%	-27.77%
1961	26.60%	46.88%	30.34%	16.54%	20.28%	3.74%	1986	18.54%	7.22%	-10.45%	17.67%	-11.32%	-28.99%
1962	-8.83%	-18.03%	-31.81%	13.79%	-9.20%	-22.98%	1987	5.67%	-3.86%	-31.18%	27.33%	-9.52%	-36.85%
1963	22.50%	39.43%	6.98%	32.45%	16.93%	-15.52%	1988	16.35%	4.57%	10.15%	-5.58%	-11.78%	-6.20%
1964	16.30%	16.79%	7.16%	9.63%	0.49%	-9.14%	1989	31.23%	21.95%	-1.00%	22.95%	-9.28%	-32.23%
1965	12.27%	52.32%	54.51%	-2.19%	40.05%	42.24%	1990	-3.14%	-19.41%	-39.59%	20.18%	-16.27%	-36.45%
1966	-9.99%	4.94%	-20.10%	25.05%	14.93%	-10.12%	1991	30.00%	85.61%	42.69%	42.93%	55.61%	12.68%
1967	23.73%	136.47%	131.90%	4.57%	112.75%	108.17%	1992	7.43%	-0.21%	3.54%	-3.75%	-7.64%	-3.89%
1968	10.84%	28.40%	48.74%	-20.34%	17.56%	37.89%	1993	9.94%	47.27%	47.70%	-0.43%	37.33%	37.76%
1969	-8.32%	-31.71%	-43.63%	11.92%	-23.39%	-35.31%	1994	1.28%	-22.36%	-17.00%	-5.36%	-23.65%	-18.28%
1970	3.33%	-20.47%	-35.59%	15.12%	-23.81%	-38.92%	1995	37.11%	46.10%	33.83%	12.27%	8.99%	-3.28%
1971	14.15%	34.57%	16.36%	18.21%	20.42%	2.21%	1996	22.68%	-1.14%	-4.89%	3.75%	-23.82%	-27.57%
1972	18.88%	21.34%	0.44%	20.90%	2.46%	-18.44%	1997	33.10%	2.79%	-17.40%	20.19%	-30.31%	-50.50%
1973	-14.50%	-29.95%	-55.13%	25.18%	-15.45%	-40.63%	1998	28.34%	-8.49%	-16.44%	7.94%	-36.83%	-44.78%
1974	-26.03%	-23.53%	-37.20%	13.67%	2.50%	-11.17%	1999	20.88%	123.22%	50.00%	73.22%	102.34%	29.12%
1975	36.92%	39.33%	78.29%	-38.96%	2.41%	41.37%	2000	-9.03%	-63.58%	24.13%	-87.71%	-54.54%	33.17%
1976	23.64%	44.61%	27.30%	17.31%	20.97%	3.66%	2001	-11.85%	-26.31%	-7.44%	-18.87%	-14.46%	4.41%
							2002	-21.97%	-18.30%	12.67%	-30.98%	3.66%	34.64%
Average Returns	12.37%	20.00%	8.30%		11.70%	7.62%	-4.08%						
Compound Returns	11.01%	13.84%	2.70%										
Years Beating S&P 500	N/A	31	21										
Years Losing Money	13	17	21										

By comparison, the S&P 500 lost money in 13 of the 51 years.

Exhibit 22, in the first graph, shows the performance advantage of high and low relative strength versus the S&P 500.

This makes it fairly clear that buying last year's winners was usually better than buying last year's losers.

That having been said, however, there is nothing particularly noteworthy about either the compound returns of the high relative strength strategy or its consistency in beating the market. As we mentioned earlier, screening for high relative strength is most useful when done in conjunction with other criteria, except during year-end tax season.

Relative Strength and Year-End Trading Patterns

At year-end, relative strength data helps us in understanding (and profiting from) tax-related trading patterns.

For example, a screen for stocks with high relative strength (based on current year's price increases) in December produces a list of stocks that many investors are unlikely to sell until January of the following year, due to their desire to defer taxes on their profits. A similar screen performed for low relative strength produces a list of stocks that are good candidates for tax loss-related selling late in the current year.

Screening for both high and low relative strength at year-end can provide lots of opportunities to buy and sell stocks based on such trading patterns. We'll discuss this in more detail in Part Three.

Shifts in the Balance from High Relative Strength to Low Relative Strength

A little earlier, we noted that buying last year's winners is usually a better strategy than buying last year's losers. An exception to this general rule applies to occasions when the previous year's returns for high relative strength were unusually large.

The second of the two graphs in **Exhibit 22** shows graphically that the advantage has usually shifted to low relative strength when the prior year's returns for high relative strength were significantly above average.

This appears to indicate that, when the previous year's winners rise so fast that they become overvalued, buyers shift their attention away from these stocks.

Any substantial decline in the performance of high relative strength stocks combined with a substantial improvement in the performance of low relative strength stocks indicates that investors are cycling out of one class of stocks into another.

The shift could be from value to growth (or vice versa), from small cap to large cap (or vice versa), or between other classes of stocks we haven't identified.

In Chapter 11, we will show how the Combined Fed-Election Cycle can be used to predict when growth stocks are likely to outperform value stocks, and when large caps are likely to outperform small caps. We'll also show how a drop in the performance of high relative strength stocks combined with an increase in the returns from low relative strength stocks can be used to confirm that one of these predictable shifts is underway.

The Importance of Relative Strength Varies

The importance of relative strength as a stock selection criterion can vary among types of stocks and between phases of the Fed-Election Cycle.

For example, our experience suggests that relative strength may be a more important consideration with small cap stocks than with large caps.

A small cap stock with low relative strength might have suffered neglect merely by being overlooked by investors, but, more often than not, there are good reasons why it hasn't attracted more buyers. And while a small company's problems are likely to remain unreported longer than a big company's, every small company with problems seems to have some shareholders who know what's going on and are selling on the information.

Problems that would cause a large cap stock to have low relative strength tend to be widely reported. A small cap's low relative strength may be the only indication we have that something is wrong.

Consequently, except for year-end gambits and turnaround situations (explained in Part Three), we generally avoid buying small caps with low relative strength.

A small cap company with very high relative strength, on the other hand, may be overvalued. Here too, the concerns are different with small caps.

Large caps are somewhat less likely to become grossly overvalued under the scrutiny of securities analysts, institutional investors, and media (except for the highest of the high-flyers). All of that attention can serve as a kind of governor to help prevent these stocks from going too far too fast.

Small cap, thinly-traded stocks do not get very much attention from institutional analysts or the media, so they lack this restraint on their stock price.

We usually avoid the possibility of letting an overvalued small cap slip through our screen by combining a value criterion, such as low P/E, with the screen for high relative strength.

Chapter 8

BUYING NANOCAP STOCKS

Other things being equal, we focus on stocks whose market capitalization is under $100 million, thereby profiting from the well-established pattern – supported by decades of market data – that the smaller the market value of a company, the better its stock price performance is likely to be.

Market Capitalization

A company's size (i.e., market capitalization) is one of the most powerful determinants of its stock's performance.

One would think that this fact would be more widely acknowledged by the financial services industry – and more widely reported by financial journalists.

It has long been common practice in the industry to rank publicly traded companies into groups based on their size in order to compare one group's performance against another's.

Plenty of indices have been created to track the performance of different sized companies: the Standard and Poor's 100, 500, 400 MidCap, and 600 Small-Caps, for example, or the Russell 1000, 2000, and 3000 Indices.

Mutual fund companies have created arrays of large cap, mid cap, small cap, and microcap funds, and the financial media regularly reports on the performance of these funds.

The significant performance advantage that very small companies maintain over big companies should be apparent to all.

Market Cap Defined
Market capitalization means the total market value of a company, defined as its stock's price multiplied by the number of its shares outstanding.

Do Lots of Bad Ideas Equal One Good Idea?

Investment advisors who recommend diversification by market cap may not always realize it, but they are perpetuating the myth of an "efficient" stock market.

As the foundation of modern financial theory, Efficient Market Theory is taught in all of the top graduate business schools. According to its proponents, any diversification is good because it pushes your return closer to the market average, and, if the myth is to be believed, average performance is the best an investor can hope for in the long run.

(Proponents of the Efficient Market Theory tend to have trouble accepting that anyone could ever earn the kind of returns achieved in the **Data Driven Investing**™ test portfolio.)

The Efficient Market Hypothesis is more than just an analytical construct confined to the ivory towers of academia, however.

It is also the foundation of the modern financial services industry.

It is the "big idea" that enables stockbrokers and mutual fund sales reps to convince otherwise sensible people to make ill-advised investments in the belief that a large enough collection of bad ideas will somehow add up to one good idea.

Yet, somehow, despite all of the readily available evidence, a majority of investors persist in believing that big companies are better investments than small companies.

Maybe it's a matter of perspective – five decades worth of performance data certainly can bring perspective. Or maybe it's just that the market cap indices don't reach all the way down to $10 million dollar companies.

In any event, people who sell mutual funds and investment advisors of all stripes usually advise investors to own small cap funds in addition to large cap funds, in order to be diversified by market cap.

But performance patterns established over decades prove that it rarely makes sense to hold both at the same time.

The general rule is that small is beautiful, and tiny is even better.

Exhibits 23 and **24** provide a summary of the performance history (1951-2002) of seven different market cap groupings.

Notes on Methodology

For each of the 52 years from 1951 to 2002, all of the companies included in the Compustat database were ranked according to their market capitalization at the end of the previous year.

Then, six groups of companies were selected for each year. One group included the 100 largest companies in the database for that year. The next five groups included the 100 smallest companies at each level of inflation-adjusted market cap. For example, the $10 million group included the 100 smallest companies with market caps of at least $10 million. The $100 million group included the 100 smallest companies with market caps of at least $100 million, and so on. The S&P 500 was included for comparison, providing the seventh group.

Finally, the current year's returns for the 100 companies included in each group were averaged.

The approach used was similar to that used in backtesting returns for the price ratios discussed in Chapters 4-6.

Exhibit 23: Returns by Market Capitalization– Graphs

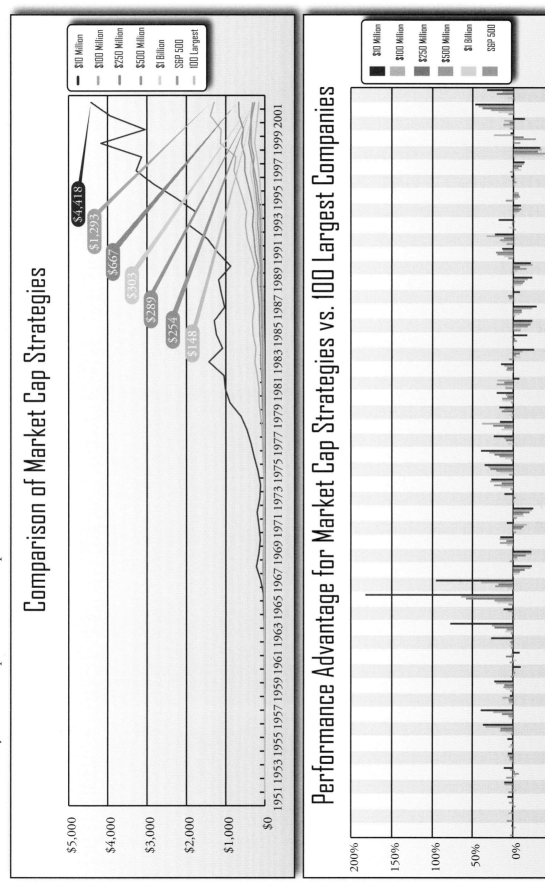

Comparison of Market Cap Strategies

$4,418
$1,293
$667
$303
$289
$254
$148

Legend: $10 Million, $100 Million, $250 Million, $500 Million, $1 Billion, S&P 500, 100 Largest

1951 1953 1955 1957 1959 1961 1963 1965 1967 1969 1971 1973 1975 1977 1979 1981 1983 1985 1987 1989 1991 1993 1995 1997 1999 2001

$5,000
$4,000
$3,000
$2,000
$1,000
$0

Performance Advantage for Market Cap Strategies vs. 100 Largest Companies

Legend: $10 Million, $100 Million, $250 Million, $500 Million, $1 Billion, S&P 500

1951 1953 1955 1957 1959 1961 1963 1965 1967 1969 1971 1973 1975 1977 1979 1981 1983 1985 1987 1989 1991 1993 1995 1997 1999 2001

200%
150%
100%
50%
0%
-50%

Exhibit 24: Returns by Market Capitalization– Table

			Returns by Market Cap					Comparison to 100 Largest Companies					
Year	100 Largest Companies	S&P 500 Returns	$1 Billion	$500 Million	$250 Million	$100 Million	$10 Million	S&P500 Returns	$1 Billion	$500 Million	$250 Million	$100 Million	$10 Million
1951	20.74%	23.37%	20.92%	21.18%	21.47%	17.08%	22.13%	2.63%	0.18%	0.44%	0.73%	-3.65%	1.39%
1952	10.78%	17.71%	10.66%	10.68%	10.80%	15.75%	12.16%	6.93%	-0.12%	-0.10%	0.02%	4.97%	1.38%
1953	2.38%	-1.17%	3.38%	6.71%	1.83%	3.64%	8.61%	-3.55%	1.00%	4.33%	-0.55%	1.26%	6.23%
1954	46.32%	51.23%	41.07%	47.40%	47.51%	56.32%	56.60%	4.91%	-5.24%	1.08%	1.19%	10.00%	10.28%
1955	23.37%	30.96%	18.98%	15.58%	20.64%	26.47%	34.26%	7.59%	-4.39%	-7.79%	-2.73%	3.09%	10.89%
1956	8.72%	6.44%	12.32%	12.24%	12.80%	14.78%	14.62%	-2.28%	3.60%	3.51%	4.08%	6.06%	5.89%
1957	-8.43%	-10.48%	-3.57%	-5.71%	-8.22%	-7.73%	-2.00%	-2.04%	4.86%	2.72%	0.22%	0.70%	6.44%
1958	40.66%	42.44%	48.79%	56.02%	55.85%	74.19%	77.47%	1.77%	8.13%	15.36%	15.19%	33.53%	36.81%
1959	11.89%	11.79%	15.78%	17.10%	25.19%	35.90%	51.38%	-0.10%	3.89%	5.20%	13.30%	24.01%	39.48%
1960	0.53%	0.28%	5.69%	5.06%	5.84%	13.25%	4.15%	-0.25%	5.15%	4.53%	5.31%	12.72%	3.62%
1961	23.50%	26.60%	32.03%	34.98%	33.96%	44.45%	46.34%	3.11%	8.53%	11.49%	10.46%	20.95%	22.85%
1962	-11.40%	-8.83%	-14.34%	-14.64%	-12.75%	-11.27%	-21.13%	2.56%	-2.95%	-3.24%	-1.36%	0.13%	-9.73%
1963	18.86%	22.50%	14.25%	18.11%	27.57%	21.08%	10.48%	3.64%	-4.61%	-0.75%	8.71%	2.22%	-8.38%
1964	14.16%	16.30%	18.53%	16.06%	17.52%	15.44%	40.91%	2.15%	4.37%	1.91%	3.36%	1.28%	26.76%
1965	10.00%	12.27%	19.28%	17.49%	32.89%	35.90%	87.69%	2.27%	9.27%	7.49%	22.89%	25.90%	77.69%
1966	-7.59%	-9.99%	-7.47%	-6.68%	-6.54%	-1.80%	3.84%	-2.40%	0.12%	0.91%	1.05%	5.78%	11.43%
1967	18.53%	23.73%	38.29%	41.13%	76.28%	82.23%	200.57%	5.20%	19.76%	22.60%	57.75%	63.71%	182.04%
1968	12.69%	10.84%	20.00%	34.54%	30.59%	51.64%	108.23%	-1.85%	7.31%	21.85%	17.90%	38.95%	95.54%
1969	-7.28%	-8.32%	-15.00%	-16.05%	-21.77%	-28.96%	-30.45%	-1.03%	-7.72%	-8.77%	-14.48%	-21.68%	-23.16%
1970	-0.53%	3.33%	-6.42%	-6.02%	-16.15%	-23.36%	-23.22%	3.87%	-5.89%	-5.49%	-15.61%	-22.83%	-22.69%
1971	15.87%	14.15%	23.42%	31.91%	24.27%	32.14%	31.56%	-1.72%	7.55%	16.04%	8.40%	16.27%	15.69%
1972	22.78%	18.88%	22.04%	11.83%	9.76%	5.11%	30.42%	-3.90%	-0.74%	-10.94%	-13.02%	-17.67%	7.64%
1973	-9.58%	-14.50%	-23.14%	-22.11%	-29.69%	-32.92%	-34.45%	-4.92%	-13.56%	-12.53%	-20.11%	-23.34%	-24.87%
1974	-26.39%	-26.03%	-28.99%	-27.30%	-29.15%	-28.34%	-15.87%	0.36%	-2.60%	-0.91%	-2.76%	-1.95%	10.52%
1975	33.98%	36.92%	48.74%	57.41%	48.21%	62.51%	60.78%	2.94%	14.76%	23.43%	14.23%	28.53%	26.80%
1976	18.91%	23.64%	34.14%	39.43%	47.12%	49.40%	53.84%	4.73%	15.23%	20.52%	28.22%	30.50%	34.94%
1977	-9.25%	-7.16%	0.40%	7.33%	13.87%	19.96%	30.12%	2.09%	9.65%	16.58%	23.12%	29.21%	39.37%
1978	5.90%	6.39%	11.82%	6.90%	14.77%	17.16%	29.55%	0.49%	5.92%	1.00%	8.87%	11.26%	23.65%
1979	17.67%	18.19%	31.71%	28.41%	42.35%	56.04%	33.92%	0.52%	14.05%	10.74%	24.68%	38.38%	16.25%
1980	29.86%	31.52%	34.79%	29.16%	44.01%	40.37%	46.78%	1.65%	4.93%	-0.71%	14.15%	10.51%	16.91%
1981	-7.26%	-4.85%	5.80%	6.13%	0.18%	1.57%	12.98%	2.41%	13.06%	13.39%	7.44%	8.83%	20.24%
1982	11.03%	20.37%	20.89%	31.06%	22.15%	30.03%	3.40%	9.34%	9.86%	20.04%	11.13%	19.00%	-7.63%
1983	22.30%	22.31%	23.10%	30.57%	29.93%	33.17%	37.23%	0.01%	0.81%	8.27%	7.63%	10.87%	14.93%
1984	1.28%	5.97%	-8.40%	-2.28%	-6.70%	-10.54%	-24.36%	4.69%	-9.68%	-3.55%	-7.97%	-11.82%	-25.64%
1985	31.75%	31.06%	30.35%	26.98%	29.51%	33.50%	14.45%	-0.69%	-1.40%	-4.76%	-2.24%	1.75%	-17.29%
1986	27.77%	18.54%	17.98%	9.61%	6.62%	5.37%	4.42%	-9.23%	-9.79%	-18.15%	-21.15%	-22.40%	-23.35%
1987	8.20%	5.67%	0.04%	-2.58%	-2.29%	-15.28%	-20.52%	-2.53%	-8.16%	-10.78%	-10.49%	-23.48%	-28.72%
1988	16.01%	16.35%	21.10%	20.90%	22.50%	15.75%	7.85%	0.34%	5.09%	4.89%	6.49%	-0.26%	-8.15%
1989	29.96%	31.23%	20.12%	17.85%	16.16%	11.88%	6.61%	1.28%	-9.83%	-12.10%	-13.80%	-18.07%	-23.35%
1990	-4.64%	-3.14%	-10.71%	-21.28%	-12.71%	-28.74%	-26.23%	1.50%	-6.07%	-16.63%	-8.07%	-24.10%	-21.58%
1991	24.21%	30.00%	35.36%	43.69%	45.69%	36.78%	37.90%	5.80%	11.16%	19.49%	21.48%	12.58%	13.69%
1992	-0.69%	7.43%	13.17%	15.41%	10.90%	32.14%	21.86%	8.12%	13.86%	16.09%	11.59%	32.83%	22.55%
1993	13.39%	9.94%	18.60%	13.14%	15.24%	10.99%	31.39%	-3.45%	5.21%	-0.25%	1.85%	-2.40%	18.00%
1994	1.49%	1.28%	-3.27%	-6.15%	-8.10%	-5.44%	-7.97%	-0.21%	-4.77%	-7.64%	-9.59%	-6.93%	-9.46%
1995	27.97%	37.11%	22.33%	19.48%	21.06%	21.29%	27.94%	9.14%	-5.64%	-8.48%	-6.90%	-6.68%	-0.03%
1996	22.07%	22.68%	19.56%	18.10%	23.50%	19.73%	24.67%	0.61%	-2.50%	-3.96%	1.43%	-2.34%	2.60%
1997	29.44%	33.10%	19.66%	22.98%	19.10%	16.31%	15.71%	3.66%	-9.78%	-6.47%	-10.35%	-13.13%	-13.73%
1998	28.67%	28.34%	-8.96%	-12.80%	-1.16%	-6.03%	-4.16%	-0.33%	-37.63%	-41.47%	-29.83%	-34.70%	-32.83%
1999	29.67%	20.88%	30.33%	2.00%	17.07%	53.30%	33.00%	-8.78%	0.67%	-27.67%	-12.60%	23.64%	3.33%
2000	-12.75%	-9.03%	-1.30%	-0.64%	-8.01%	-1.62%	-26.94%	3.72%	11.45%	12.11%	4.74%	11.13%	-14.19%
2001	-17.83%	-11.85%	0.54%	9.55%	20.28%	24.68%	28.96%	5.97%	18.36%	27.37%	38.10%	42.51%	46.79%
2002	-19.65%	-21.97%	-12.97%	-19.32%	1.11%	-6.77%	12.48%	-2.31%	6.69%	0.33%	20.77%	12.88%	32.14%

	100 Largest Companies	S&P 500 Return	$1 Billion	$500 Million	$250 Million	$100 Million	$10 Million
Average Returns	11.35%	12.59%	13.10%	13.28%	15.44%	17.86%	22.69%
Compound Returns	10.08%	11.23%	11.62%	11.51%	13.32%	14.77%	17.52%
Years Losing Money	14	13	13	14	13	14	12
Years Beating 100 Largest Companies	N/A	33	31	29	33	34	34

% of Years Strategy on Left Beat Other Market Cap Strategies

	100 Largest	S&P	$1B	$500 M	$250 M	$100 M	$10 M
100 Largest	N/A	37%	40%	44%	37%	35%	35%
S&P 500	63%	N/A	40%	48%	40%	42%	38%
$1 Billion	60%	60%	N/A	48%	42%	37%	33%
$500 Million	56%	52%	52%	N/A	42%	40%	37%
$250 Million	63%	60%	58%	58%	N/A	38%	37%
$100 Million	65%	58%	63%	60%	62%	N/A	42%
$10 Million	65%	62%	67%	63%	63%	58%	N/A

Returns by Market Capitalization

As **Exhibit 24** clearly shows, investment returns were inversely proportionate to size; that is, on average, the smaller the company, the greater the return. The smallest companies had the best returns over the 52 year study period, gaining an average of 22.7% per year (17.5% compounded).

These tiny, $10 million companies beat the returns produced by the 100 biggest companies in America in 34 years out of 52 (i.e., 65% of the time). They lost money less often than any of the larger market cap groupings by posting negative returns in just 12 years out of 52 (23% of the time)

There was a fairly substantial step down in the performance of the next market cap grouping. The $100 million companies earned an average of 17.9% (14.8% compounded), almost five percentage points less than companies one tenth their size.

The returns got smaller and smaller as the companies got bigger and bigger. The 100 largest companies earned just 11.4% (10.1% compounded), and thus underperformed the S&P 500.

The Nanocap Advantage

Even though the $10 million companies (referred to hereinafter as *nanocaps*) had by far the best returns, beat the market consistently over the past five decades, and rarely lost money, they would not be recommended by most stockbrokers, mutual fund salespeople, or investment advisors.

Why not?

The Financial Services Industry has Little Use for Nanocaps

Stockbrokers don't generally recommend nanocaps because $10 million companies are too small to warrant analyst coverage, and brokers rarely recommend anything that isn't touted by their firms' analysts. In fact, most big brokerage firms have policies prohibiting, or at least strongly discouraging, brokers from recommending any stock that is not covered by their in-house analysts.

Mutual fund sales people don't recommend nanocaps because mutual fund companies typically don't have any nanocap funds to sell. They might have funds that are described as "small cap," or even "microcap," but, in the world of big mutual funds, a "microcap" stock can be a fairly substantial enterprise. The average mutual fund is simply too big to successfully trade the stocks of $10 million companies.

Investment advisors typically do not recommend nanocaps either, due to the widespread misperception (held by the advisors as well as their clients) that small companies, as a group, are substantially riskier than big companies.

Nanocaps are Perfect for Individual Investors

Do these objections to nanocaps have any basis in fact? Or, for that matter, do they have any relevance to an investor intrigued by the superior performance of nanocaps?

The fact that nanocaps are not covered by brokerage analysts enhances, rather than detracts from, their desirability. The lack of analyst coverage creates innumerable opportunities for profiting from information-related market inefficiencies. This point will be dealt with in greater depth in Chapter 12, but, for now, suffice it to say it is much easier to discover hidden value in an obscure nanocap company than it is in a multibillion dollar company followed by a dozen brokerage analysts.

Mutual funds managing more than a few hundred million dollars will probably never be able to profitably trade nanocaps, but this too is an advantage for individual investors and their independent investment advisors. How? An individual who trades General Electric stock is competing against thousands of the best minds on Wall Street to buy and sell at the best price. When he trades a nanocap, he is often competing against a mere handful of others like himself. And it would be a mistake to imagine that trading stocks isn't intensely competitive just because you cannot see the competition.

Are Nanocaps Too Risky for Most Investors?

One charge that gets leveled at nanocaps more than any other is that very small companies are just too risky for most investors.

Are they?

There are several ways of looking at this question.

One way to look at the risk of nanocaps is to ask whether an investor would be more likely to lose money with a portfolio of nanocaps than he would with a portfolio of larger companies. The answer to this question is "no, a nanocap portfolio is not more likely to lose money than a portfolio consisting of large caps." As we noted above, nanocaps actually had fewer losing years during the past 52 than any other market cap grouping.

Financial theorists measure a stock's risk in terms of its "beta," which is business school jargon for saying that a stock whose price fluctuates more widely than the market fluctuates is defined as being more risky.

Nanocaps certainly fit this description. When both the S&P 500 and our nanocap portfolio lost money – which happened seven times between 1951 and 2002 – the average loss for the nanocap portfolio was nearly twice that of the S&P 500. On the other hand, when nanocaps and the S&P 500 both made money, which happened 34 times in 52 years, the nanocaps' average returns were 77% higher than the S&P 500 index's return.

The theoretical concept of risk is not quite the same as the everyday concept of risk. Knowing the facts, an investor might well consider nanocaps' volatility more of an attraction than a defect. He might be very happy to accept a 13% chance of losing 96% more than the market in return for a 65% chance of achieving returns 77% higher than the market.

Remember, though, that the concept of beta came from people whose holy grail is to match the market, not beat it.

Ultimately, when investors think of the risk involved in nanocap stocks, they tend to focus on the risk associated with individual companies. They avoid nanocaps because they assume that failure is far more likely for a very small business than for a larger, more established firm.

Actually, the failure rate for nanocap companies is astonishingly small.

Exhibit 25 shows the percentage of nanocap companies that failed within five years after being selected as one of the companies to be included in the portfolios constructed for our nanocap backtest. **25A** includes only known bankruptcies or liquidations, while **25B** adds in cases where there might have been a bankruptcy or liquidation, but where the data is ambiguous.

Data for liquidations was available from 1970-2002. Because we wanted to look at each nanocap portfolio's failure rate over a five year period, we were left with 28 portfolios to consider, i.e., those constructed between 1970 and 1997.

Exhibit 25 A & B: Nanocap Risk

Risk of Bankruptcy/Liquidation, 100 Smallest Market Cap Companies with Inflation-Adjusted Market Caps > $10 Million

	Exhibit 25A		Exhibit 25B	
	Number of Known Bankruptcies and Liquidations within 5 Years	% of Known Bankruptcies and Liquidations - Annual Average	Number of Known & Possible Bankruptcies and Liquidations within 5 Years	% of Known & Possible Bankruptcies and Liquidations - Annual Average
1970	7	1.4%	14	2.8%
1971	2	0.4%	7	1.4%
1972	7	1.4%	12	2.4%
1973	7	1.4%	7	1.4%
1974	3	0.6%	3	0.6%
1975	2	0.4%	2	0.4%
1976	5	1.0%	5	1.0%
1977	3	0.6%	3	0.6%
1978	2	0.4%	6	1.2%
1979	1	0.2%	4	0.8%
1980	4	0.8%	8	1.6%
1981	0	0.0%	11	2.2%
1982	5	1.0%	15	3.0%
1983	4	0.8%	10	2.0%
1984	3	0.6%	5	1.0%
1985	3	0.6%	8	1.6%
1986	2	0.4%	15	3.0%
1987	6	1.2%	12	2.4%
1988	1	0.2%	7	1.4%
1989	0	0.0%	3	0.6%
1990	2	0.4%	4	0.8%
1991	3	0.6%	11	2.2%
1992	3	0.6%	7	1.4%
1993	0	0.0%	9	1.8%
1994	4	0.8%	9	1.8%
1995	3	0.6%	10	2.0%
1996	6	1.2%	16	3.2%
1997	1	0.2%	8	1.6%
28 Year Average		0.6%		1.7%

The average annual failure rate for these 28 portfolios, using the most pessimistic assumptions (as presented in **Exhibit 25B**), is 1.7%. No portfolio had an average annual rate of known bankruptcies and liquidations greater than 1.4%

Bear in mind, however, that liquidation does not necessarily equal catastrophe. Our test portfolio, for example, actually made money on its holdings of Storage Networks, which we bought a few months prior to its liquidation.

Thus, nanocaps had a surprisingly low failure rate to go along with superior returns. Apparently, once a company has passed the test of a public offering, it is extremely unlikely to fail.

Diversification is a good way to deal with risk, but instead of holding both large caps and small caps, a portfolio should be diversified into a collection of nanocaps that is large enough to spread the risk of any particular company failing.

Then, to the extent that nanocaps' downside risk is still considered a problem, risk could be further reduced by allocating assets to cash or fixed income investments.

In practice, it is easier to attain a sufficient level of diversification in a portfolio of nanocaps than it is in a portfolio of large companies. There are thousands of good opportunities among nanocap companies at any point in time, and even a small portfolio can include enough companies to effectively diversify.

Thus, the risks of failure associated with nanocaps can be easily managed.

Nevertheless, for deep-seated psychological reasons (which we will get into in Part Three), investors with million-dollar portfolios tend to feel worse about losing 100% of a $5,000 nanocap investment than about losing 10% of a $100,000 investment in GE. Irrational as this may sound, such an attitude toward risk is the rule rather than the exception among investors.

Hopefully, the data presented in **Exhibit 25** will lay to rest the doubts of anyone who is attracted to nanocaps' superior returns but worried about their risk.

Nanocaps Can be Challenging to Trade

Lest we present too one-sided of a view of nanocaps, we should point out that there are some very real difficulties involved in trading them.

Investing in nanocaps is very different from investing in large cap stocks.

For one thing, it can be hard to get good information on such small companies. Next to nothing is available in the way of professionally produced analysis. There are rarely analysts' research reports or earnings forecasts on which to base investment decisions.

Investors are mostly on their own when it comes to figuring out what a nano-cap company does or where it is headed. Nevertheless, as we noted earlier, this creates more opportunities than problems for investors who are willing to do a little digging.

Nanocaps are almost always thinly-traded. Attempts to buy or sell often drive their prices up or down dramatically. As a result, it is difficult to acquire large positions in these companies without incurring unacceptably large trading costs, and it can also be very difficult to unload a large position quickly – for a decent price, anyway.

Here again, difficulties can become opportunities in the hands of investors who learn to trade intelligently. Part Three of *Data Driven Investing– Professional Edition* was written to show our readers how to do just that.

Nevertheless, trading nanocaps requires more effort than trading large caps.

After all of the information needed to make an informed decision has been gathered and analyzed, it very well might require multiple orders entered over the course of several days to establish a desired position. And all of this effort will be for naught if the investor does not succeed in the competitive aspect of trading – pricing his orders correctly, holding back when appropriate, or forging ahead at the right times.

Technology Makes it Possible

Fortunately for individual traders and independent investment advisors, Internet and computing technologies are causing a revolution in investing just at the time when they are most needed.

Frankly, many of our most profitable trading techniques – especially our focus on nanocaps – would have been impossible in the pre-Internet world.

Without the ability to search web-based news sources to get information on the companies we trade, without the availability of online discount brokerage firms charging less than $10 per trade, and without the improvements in computer and database technologies that facilitate our analysis of historical data, automate our stock screening task, and make it possible to keep track of hundreds of positions and thousands of trades, **Data Driven Investing**™ would be impossible.

Technology has made it easier to invest substantial and increasing amounts of capital in diversified portfolios of nanocap stocks. As a result, it is now feasible for an independent advisor to efficiently manage a nanocap fund which is large enough to be viable.

Consequently, for the first time in history, nanocaps can be made available to all individual investors: those who manage their own portfolios, as well as those who prefer to employ experts to do this for them.

At the beginning of this book, we expressed our conviction that a fundamental realignment of financial services away from huge institutions and in the direction of independent investment advisors is underway.

Technology made this realignment possible, and technology, combined with the industry's own arrogance and greed, is accelerating the trend.

On-line trading has become easy, effective, fast, and cheap. In fact, it has become significantly easier, more effective, faster, and cheaper than the traditional approach.

The old-fashioned stockbroker, who tried for years to pass himself off as a trusted financial advisor – often successfully, and even while functioning as a hawker of products he often didn't understand and didn't believe in – is headed toward extinction. Recent "Do Not Call" legislation was the final nail in the coffin.

The next major advance will involve improvements in the flow of information and analysis to individual investors.

Currently, investors must choose between an unrestricted flood of raw information available through the Internet, on one side, and the unsatisfactory, often biased and corrupt analysis available from brokerage firm analysts on the other.

In the very near future, high quality research prepared by independent analysts will become available over the web at low cost. Instead of funding research through a corrupt system of investment banking fees and brokerage sales commissions, research will be funded directly by its users.

The cost of this research will be low enough to place it in the hands of every trader who wants it, because its production costs will be spread over many users and because technology will lower the cost of its distribution.

Nanocap stocks will benefit from a democratic, web-based system of research more than any other group of companies. Small public companies will have new opportunities to work with independent research firms and get the word out to investors on their plans and operating performance. Investors will be encouraged to buy these stocks when reliable information becomes more available.

Are There Ever Good Times to Own Large Caps?

After all of the praise we have heaped on nanocaps, readers might wonder whether we are ignoring the evidence presented in Exhibit 19, which shows clearly that there were plenty of times when large caps beat the smaller companies.

There are indeed conditions which favor large caps over small caps. Most often, these are times which are unfavorable for stocks in general.

Large caps appear to do best in poor market conditions. Perhaps this is because investors consider them to be a safer refuge in difficult times.

Nanocaps are Key to Our Success

A substantial portion of the success we have had with our test portfolio is attributable to our heavy nanocap commitment. We are convinced that investing in the stocks of very small companies is an important element in any strategy for beating the market consistently over time.

At the same time, we can state unequivocally that trading nanocap stocks requires more effort and expertise than trading large cap stocks. This fact should be carefully weighed by investors who are considering whether or not to trade nanocaps.

Chapter 9

THE PRESIDENTIAL ELECTION CYCLE

The four-year Presidential Election Cycle exerts a strong, predictable influence on stock market behavior. Our data clearly indicate that overall market performance improves in the years leading up to an election. Furthermore, the Election Cycle Effect, interacting with the Fed Effect, affects the performance of different investment styles in different ways.

The Election Cycle Effect

The Election Cycle Effect is a well-known – by people who ponder such things – pattern of stock market behavior, one whose existence has been confirmed by numerous studies.

The pattern is very simple to describe: returns in the second half of a presidential term tend to be significantly better than returns in the first half.

Exhibit 26 shows the Election Cycle Effect on returns for the S&P 500. (The four year Presidential Election Cycle is defined as beginning on January 1st of the first year of a president's term.)

Over a recent 52 year period (1951-2002), the S&P 500 gained an average of 7.2% per year in the first two years of the cycle, versus an average of 18.0% in years three and four.

The persistence of the Election Cycle Effect can be seen in the second chart shown in **Exhibit 26** and is reflected in the following statistics.

Exhibit 26: The Presidential Election Cycle– Returns

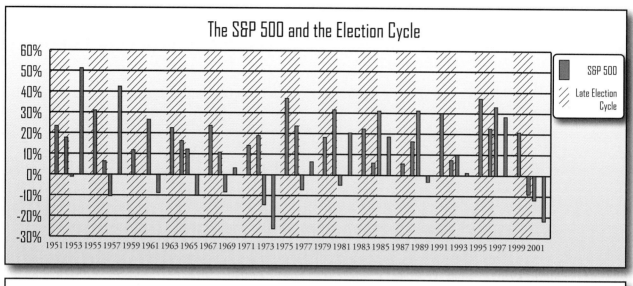

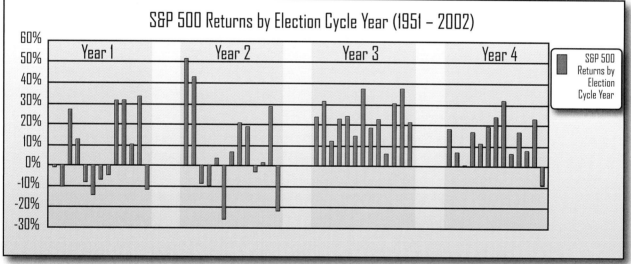

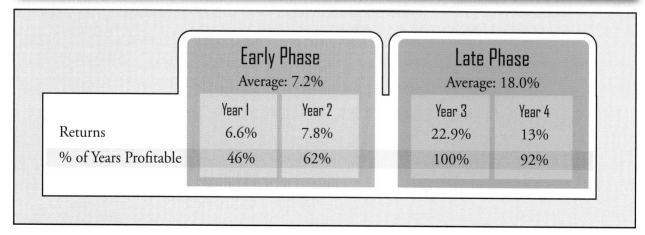

	Early Phase Average: 7.2%		Late Phase Average: 18.0%	
	Year 1	Year 2	Year 3	Year 4
Returns	6.6%	7.8%	22.9%	13%
% of Years Profitable	46%	62%	100%	92%

Returns in the second half of the cycle exceeded those in the first half in eight of the last 12 presidential terms.

In the first years of presidential terms, from Eisenhower's first to George W. Bush's first, the S&P 500 index lost money 54% of the time. In the second years, it did better, losing money 38% of the time.

Thus, the S&P 500 lost money in 46% of the first-half years. By contrast, it made money in 96% of the second-half years.

In fact, the S&P 500 returned a profit in the third year of every presidential term included in our study period (i.e., since 1951). We have to go all the way back to 1939 to find a year when the index lost money (a mere 0.76%) in the third year of an Election Cycle.

The market has done very well in election years, too. The S&P 500 made money in every presidential election year since the first time Eisenhower defeated Stevenson save one – the infamous Y2K.

The first year of the new millennium was an oddity in several respects. For one thing, it brought us the first presidential election ever settled by the Supreme Court. In addition, the market suffered from turmoil in the technology sector caused by a dramatic decline in orders related to the Y2K computer bug.

As a result, the S&P 500 experienced its first election year loss since 1940, an election year marked by fears of economic depression and world war.

Over the 50 years since Eisenhower's first inauguration, the S&P 500 made money 37 times (i.e., 74% of the time). Of the 13 years in which the S&P 500 lost money, 12 occurred early in the Election Cycle (7 in Year 1 and 5 in year 2), but only one occurred late in the Election Cycle (in 2000).

Clearly, the U.S. Presidential Election Cycle exerts a powerful influence on stock market performance.

But what causes the Election Cycle Effect?

And, perhaps more to the point: how can an understanding of the Election Cycle Effect lead to a workable investment strategy?

It wouldn't be practical simply to avoid stocks during the early half of the Election Cycle. Where would we find alternative investments that consistently provide better returns than the 7.2% average earned by the S&P 500 during early cycle years (with similar risk and liquidity)?

Instead, we need to identify groups of stocks that have consistently achieved above average performance early in the cycle.

And we need to consider the Fed Effect.

We have already seen, in Chapter 3, what a powerful influence monetary policy has on performance. It doesn't require a great leap of imagination to suppose that there might be connections between these two powerful drivers of stock prices, or that the best strategy for reacting to the Election Cycle would also take the monetary cycle into account.

In the next two chapters, we will lay out just such a strategy – one that reflects both the Election Cycle and Fed policy. We'll present data drawn from over five decades of stock market history to demonstrate, for arguably the first time ever, how the interaction of Fed policy with the Presidential Election Cycle drives overall market performance, and, more importantly, how it drives the relative performance of specific groups of stocks.

Before we begin our discussion of investment strategies, we need to briefly review the likely causes of the Election Cycle Effect. This will shed useful light on the material which follows.

The President's Role in Formulating Economic Policy

Attempts to explain the Election Cycle Effect on stock market returns naturally focus on the president's role in formulating economic policy, and, more specifically, on the factors that influence presidential economic policy decisions.

We Americans tend to give our presidents 100% of the credit for practically everything good that happens in the country, and 100% of the blame for practically everything bad that happens. This is especially true in the realm of economic affairs.

Whether credit or blame is deserved—or not—the president, as our highest nationally elected leader, is held accountable for the nation's economic performance and, it would seem, for the personal well-being of each and every individual citizen.

> ### Our Exclusive
>
> We don't claim to be the first to observe the interrelationships among Fed policy, the Election Cycle, and the performance of various equity investment styles.
>
> We do believe, however, that we are the first to publish our findings.

Actually, there is a legal, as well as a political, basis for holding presidents responsible for the economy.

During the early half of the 20th century, a series of laws were passed that, collectively, define the president's preeminent role and principal responsibilities in the formation of economic policies. These include, among others, the Budget and Accounting Act of 1921, the Reorganization Act of 1939, and the Employment Act of 1946.

These laws codify the political reality: i.e., that the president's role in formulating economic policy is paramount.

How do presidents exercise this power? What factors influence a president's economic policy choices, and how are a president's economic policies implemented?

Are Presidents Motivated by Party Ideology?

For much of our history, the conventional wisdom held that a president's economic policy objectives were shaped by his party's ideology. According to this line of thought, each party has its own "brand" of economics.

The Democratic brand of economics is perceived as favoring workers over business owners. Its primary objectives include low unemployment, workplace regulation, and social insurance for workers.

The Republican brand is thought to favor business owners over workers. Its primary objectives are low inflation, unregulated markets, and limited taxation.

Presidential economic policy decisions are seen as being directed toward the fulfillment of these partisan objectives. Democratic presidents are supposed to push for liberal causes like the expansion of social welfare programs, trade legislation that protects workers, and low interest rates. Republican presidents are expected to be in favor of free trade, fiscal restraint, and a Fed that is ever vigilant against the wealth-destroying scourge of inflation.

There are several problems with the ideological/partisan model of presidential economic policy-making.

For one thing, as Ralph Nader pointed out in his 2000 campaign, it is becoming increasingly difficult to discern any real differences between the economic policies of Democrats and Republicans. The ideological/partisan model would not have predicted that Ronald Reagan would run huge budget deficits, or that Bill Clinton would be in favor of NAFTA, nor would it have predicted George Bush's expansion of Medicare drug benefits.

For another thing, Federal Reserve policy has historically run counter to the notion of Democrats as anti-unemployment and Republicans as anti-inflation. Although the White House does not directly control Fed policy, everyone on the Fed's Board of Governors, including the chairman, is a presidential appointee. Alan Greenspan has been reappointed four times since 1987, by presidents of both parties. Presumably, he would not have been reappointed if his policies had been seriously misaligned with any of these presidents' objectives.

The Fed pursued an expansive monetary policy in just 25% of the years (1951-2002) in which Democrats held the White House. Under Republican presidents, Fed policy was expansive 50% of the time. (Over the entire period from 1951 to 2002, Fed policy was expansive 40% of the time.)

Could this be a sign of the Fed's political leaning? Or does it suggest that the Fed strives for a balance between fiscal and monetary policy, tightening to offset the perceived profligacy of Democrats and easing to accompany the fiscal restraint of Republicans?

The difference in Federal Reserve monetary policy under Democrat presidents compared to Republican presidents was even more pronounced during the crucial second year of the Election Cycle.

The second year of the Election Cycle is important because it is when a president's new initiatives (enacted in the first year of his term) really begin to take hold. It is, arguably, the year in which the president's policies are likely to achieve their greatest impact.

During the second years of Democratic presidents' terms, the Fed has been much more likely (80% to 20%) to have pursued a restrictive monetary policy. During the second year of Republican presidents' terms, the Fed was much more likely (75% to 25%) to have pursued an expansive monetary policy.

If presidents are motivated primarily by partisan ideology in their choice of economic policy objectives, then presidents of both parties have been largely ineffective in getting the Fed on board with their parties' agendas.

Moreover, if the ideological/partisan model explained how presidents made economic policy choices, then—to the extent that the Election Cycle Effect is produced by real economic factors—the effect would differ according to which party held power. There would be a "Democratic Election Cycle Effect" and a "Republican Election Cycle Effect."

In fact, however, no significant difference in the pattern exists. Returns for the S&P 500 averaged 9.2% in the first two years of Democratic presidents' terms, versus 19.5% in the last two years. Under Republican presidents, returns averaged 6.0% in the first two years versus 17.0% in the last two years.

In other words, knowing which party holds the presidency doesn't tell us anything that could form the basis of a strategy for reacting to the Election Cycle Effect.

Thus, the ideological/partisan model of presidential economic decision making provides no insight into the Election Cycle Effect and no basis for a profitable investment strategy.

Or Are Presidents Motivated by Their Desire to Retain Power?

A very different view of how presidents make economic policy decisions, one that views them as being primarily motivated by their desire to be re-elected, has largely displaced the ideological/partisan model.

According to proponents of this view, which emerged in the mid-1970's as a result of work done by Professors William Nordhaus[1] and Edward Tufte[2], a president's economic policy choices are driven primarily by his desire to retain power, for himself (in the case of a first term president) or for his party. Rather than pursuing ideological objectives—or even pursuing economic prosperity as a generalized goal—presidents instead are seen as adopting policies that stimulate short-term economic activity in ways that improve their chances of re-election by targeting economic benefits to key blocs of voters in the months leading up to the election.

For a president facing an upcoming election, the quickest fixes would usually involve increasing or accelerating:

- Transfer payments,

- Tax cuts,

- Public spending, and

- Public employment.

[1] "The Political Business Cycle," *Review of Economic Studies*, 1975

[2] *Political Control of the Economy*, 1978

Playing Politics with the Fiscal Calendar

One of the more interesting bits of evidence supporting the "re-election model" of presidential economic decision making is the change in the government's fiscal year, which occurred in 1977.

Public spending tends to cluster around the government's fiscal year-end. As the year draws to a close, spending increases as agencies try to use up (to avoid losing) their budget authority. Spending continues at a high level when the new year begins and new funds become available.

By moving the fiscal year-end to September 30, the year-end spending increase was shifted from June/July to September/October– i.e., closer to the election.

In addition, presidents might curry favor with voters by delaying implementation of economically unfavorable measures (e.g., tax increases and military base closings) until after the election.

Besides putting more cash in the pockets of key constituencies through measures such as these, presidents could also employ psychological means ("talking up" the economy) to improve voters' perceptions of their economic performance, which would tend to enhance the economic and political effectiveness of their pre-election stimulus packages.

Measures such as these would be useful to a president seeking re-election, because they would tend to have a more or less immediate impact on the economy, and because they could be directed at key voting blocs. Furthermore, in many cases, they could be implemented through bureaucratic procedures without passing any new laws.

The "re-election model" of presidential economic decision making does not preclude presidential attempts to influence the broader fiscal and monetary policies of the government and Federal Reserve. It simply views these attempts as being motivated by electoral concerns, and it emphasizes the president's need for short-term results.

An impressive array of economic statistics has been cited to support this view of presidential policy making. The statistics generally show that economically favorable items, such as increases in Social Security and veteran's benefits, tend to go into effect two to three months prior to elections, while economically unfavorable items, such as payroll tax increases, tend to become effective after the election.

Nevertheless, there are limits to a president's ability to manipulate economic policy for the purpose of improving his prospects of re-election.

For one thing, the Fed has proven remarkably resistant to presidential arm-twisting.

Presumably, a president facing an election would prefer that the Fed adopt an expansive monetary policy, but, in fact, the Fed has maintained a restrictive policy in eight of the last 13 election years. The Fed has been even-handed in its treatment of administrations facing an election. The Fed maintained a restrictive policy in three of the five election years (60%) in which the sitting president was a Democrat and five of the eight of the election years (63%) in which the sitting president was a Republican.

Another problem with the "re-election model" is that there are significant disincentives for a president to be seen as manipulating the economy for his own re-election. Presidents prefer to be seen as "presidential," and, then too, there is the reality that economic stimuli do not always produce the intended effects. A president who gets it wrong will be criticized both for his ineffectiveness and for abusing the power of his office to further his own personal ambitions.

And then there is the problem of the opposition party. If economic gains are seen as accruing to the benefit of the party in power, the opposition party may refuse to cooperate. This further limits a president's ability to implement economic policies for purely political purposes.

Presidential control of the economy is simply not as great as it is commonly perceived to be. Notwithstanding a president's statutory and political authority, control over economic policy is still divided among the White House, Congress, and the Fed. Moreover, the nature of our free enterprise system serves to render our economy inherently unmanageable. A president's power to unilaterally mandate economic change is, thus, quite limited.

This is not to say that a president's policies do not affect the economy in meaningful ways, but it might suggest that a president's economic power depends more upon the force of his personality than upon his actual spending authority. Whatever else one might say about our presidents, they are invariably masters of persuasion.

We cannot overlook two key facts:

- Economic data clearly follows a market-friendly pattern during presidential election campaigns.

- Electoral success is strongly associated with a rising stock market. Since 1835, only one president (Franklin Delano Roosevelt in 1940) has won re-election as the stock market was falling in the last two years of his term.

The circumstantial evidence leads us to believe that presidents employ a variety of means late in their terms to temporarily improve economic performance and investor sentiment. These politically motivated policies contribute to the Election Cycle Effect.

Politics and the Election Cycle

A president starts a new term with fresh political capital and an agenda of controversial new initiatives. Congress, even if not of the same party as the president, is at least mindful of the recently elected (or re-elected) president's mandate from the people. This creates conditions favoring the passage of new legislation, but it also creates uncertainty. (It's not always easy to predict the economic effects of a new law as it winds its way through the legislative process.) Disliking uncertainty, the market performs poorly as new presidential terms begin.

Later in a president's term, the bloom is off the rose. Problems have arisen, political capital has been spent, and the opposition party in Congress has become bolder, more willing to challenge the president. This forces the president to espouse more conventional policies. The parties compete with each other to bestow federal largesse on key constituencies. Increases in fiscal stimulus and soft-pedaling of radical, new initiatives lead to a growing sense of confidence, creating conditions which favor a market advance.

As election time draws near, political competition intensifies. Politicians of both parties avoid the political risks associated with new initiatives, and they actively block any initiatives their opponents might advance. Gridlock sets in. Legislation with no chance of passing gets introduced solely for the sake of winning political points with voters. The only bills likely to make it through Congress are voter-friendly giveaways for which both parties try to take credit, and which neither party wants to be seen as blocking.

It's been said many times that the stock market hates uncertainty. The period with the greatest uncertainty, from the market's point of view, is the first two years of a president's term. There's no telling what will come out of Washington when a newly inaugurated president starts pushing his legislative program through a cooperative Congress.

On the other hand, the market loves legislative gridlock. The old chestnut, "That government governs best which governs least" describes the market's attitude perfectly. When the only legislation coming out of Washington is a series of short-term economic stimulus packages, the market feels safe from the politicians.

But what about the election itself? Doesn't that create uncertainty?

Actually, the market's reaction to election outcomes is mixed. Although the market tends to celebrate a Republican victory with a run-up in prices, the effect is very short-lived. On average, the market appears to marginally prefer having a Democrat in the White House.

In any case, the outcome of the election tends to have very little lasting impact on returns. From this we can reasonably infer that uncertainty over the outcome is also of little consequence.

Earlier, we saw how presidential efforts to win re-election contribute to the Election Cycle Effect. Political tension between the White House and Congress also contributes to this phenomenon. Together, they create a "political cycle" which gives rise to the Election Cycle Effect on stocks.

Thus, we can summarize our explanation for the Election Cycle Effect as follows.

Presidents and members of the House and Senate, acting primarily in pursuit of their political self-interest, follow predictable patterns of behavior which have consequences for the economy and the stock market. The patterns revolve around presidential elections, in that distance to the next election is the principal determinant of an office holder's actions. The greater the distance to the next election, the more likely an office holder will be to act in ways which are detrimental to the economy and stock market. The closer it gets to election time, the more likely an office holder will be to adopt courses of action which are favorable for the economy and stock market.

Monetary Policy and the Election Cycle

If politicians' jockeying for political advantage causes the Election Cycle Effect, then how does the Fed's monetary cycle interact with this process?

Let's begin by looking at Fed policy changes as the Election Cycle progresses. **Exhibit 27** plots the average S&P 500 return versus the probability that the Fed will pursue a restrictive policy (i.e., raise interest rates) for each year of the Election Cycle.

During the 1951-2002 period, the Fed was more likely to pursue a restrictive policy than an expansive policy in every year of the Election Cycle except Year 2. As **Exhibit 27** also shows, Year 3 of the cycle was by far the best year to own the S&P 500.

If we consider **Exhibit 27** in the context of the political cycle we described earlier, a picture begins to emerge of a "typical Election Cycle," which might look something like this:

Year 1: The Election Cycle begins as a new president is inaugurated. The economy is beginning to weaken, due to a combination of restrictive monetary policy and reductions (from pre-election levels) in fiscal and psychological stimulus. (Nine of the 20 recessions which have occurred during the 20th century started in the first year of the Election Cycle.) Meanwhile, there is uncertainty surrounding the passage of the president's legislative agenda, which contains a number of controversial items. The stock market looks at this picture and gets defensive. Overall returns are weak.

Year 2: In the second year of the president's term, economic weakness causes the Fed to adopt an expansive monetary policy. Disappointing earnings reports and uncertainty over the long-term effects of the new legislation coming out of Washington continue to weigh the stock market down. Government officials, looking for ways to get the economy growing again, start pushing in earnest for a fiscal stimulus package immediately after the mid-term elections. Controversial presidential appointees often resign shortly after these elections and are replaced by mainstreamers who are less likely to rock the boat.

Year 3: In the term's third year, the pump priming begins to pay off. The economic party is in full swing, due to implementation of a fiscal stimulus package and the lagging benefits of the prior year's expansive monetary policy. Growth is strong, and corporate profits are up sharply. Meanwhile, although the Fed has begun to tighten up, interest rates are still low enough not to bother anyone much. The stock market has its best year of the cycle.

Year 4: The fourth year of the term – an election year - sees government fiscal and psychological stimulus peaking. However, some investors are starting to focus on the rising short-term interest rates brought about by the Fed's continued restrictive policy. Bond yields have become high enough to entice some investors' money away from the stock market. The stock market continues to do well, though not quite so well as in Year 3.

Does this sound familiar?

Of course, there is no such thing as a "typical" Election Cycle. We developed this construct to illustrate some of the interrelationships between Fed policy and the political and economic cycles. Fed policy directly affects, and is affected by, the economic policies adopted by office holders.

These interrelationships– among Fed policy, the political cycle, fiscal policy, the economy, and the stock market – help to explain why the relative performance of certain groups of stocks varies according to the Combined Fed-Election Cycle. They help to explain, for example, why growth stocks tend to outperform value stocks under certain conditions, or why, under other circumstances, large cap stocks provide one of the few safe havens available.

Starting in Chapter 10, we'll show how these different investment styles perform in each phase of the Combined Fed-Election Cycle. In our discussion of the patterns which emerge, we will draw on our example of the "typical" Election Cycle.

But before we proceed to Chapter 10, there is one more important matter to deal with in regard to the Election Cycle Effect.

Big Rocks and Small Rocks

The Election Cycle Effect has more impact on small cap stocks than on large cap stocks.

Exhibit 28 shows how companies of various sizes performed (1951-2002) in each half of the Election Cycle.

Returns for the 100 largest companies averaged 6.6% early in the Election Cycle, versus 16.1% late in the Election Cycle. In other words, their late cycle returns were 142% higher than their early cycle returns.

For smaller sized companies, the difference between early cycle returns and late cycle returns – i.e., the Election Cycle Effect - was significantly greater than 142%. For companies with market caps between $100 million and $1 billion, the late cycle return was 234-254% higher than the early cycle return. The nanocap group ($10 million market cap) had a somewhat smaller spread (187%) between early cycle returns and late cycle returns.

Why would the Election Cycle affect smaller companies more than larger companies?

From the market's perspective, the Election Cycle Effect could be likened to a force of nature, like a wind blowing across an open field. Early in the Election Cycle, the wind blows hardly at all. Later in the cycle, it blows hard.

To the extent that Washington has any impact on the stock market early in a presidential term, the impact is mostly negative. Stocks move sluggishly early in the Election Cycle.

Later in a presidential term, the fiscal and psychological stimulus coming out of Washington becomes like a tailwind for the market, and stocks advance rapidly.

A strong wind blowing across an open field moves small particles of dirt and stone easily but has little impact on larger rocks.

Big companies are, well, big. Big objects are hard to move. No matter how hard the wind blows, it will not move them as far or as fast as smaller objects. The prices of large cap stocks simply aren't as volatile as those of small caps.

Volatility & Risk

Volatility in a stock price is considered risky by conventional financial theorists. Therefore, large cap stocks, whose prices are less volatile than small cap stocks, are considered safer.

There is a practical problem with this theory, however. The mean returns of very small cap stocks are much higher than those of large caps. The fluctuations around this mean are greater for nanocaps than large caps; however, as a group, the 100 largest companies' stocks have had, historically, more losing years than nanocaps (14 versus 12 during 1951-2002). The higher mean returns of nanocap stocks have, in effect, cushioned investors against this volatility.

Although individual nanocap stocks have a greater potential for large losses than large caps, these risks can be neutralized through diversification. By owning a wide variety of nanocaps and increasing the allocation of assets to cash, rather than owning large caps, it is possible to both increase potential returns and lower overall portfolio risk.

Investors who want to derive the greatest possible benefit from the Election Cycle Effect would want to own small cap companies late in the Election Cycle. The average late Election Cycle return for $100 million companies is 27.8%. For $10 million companies, it's 33.7%.

After the election, when the wind stops blowing—i.e., when governmental stimulus is withdrawn—large cap companies' inertia keeps them rolling along even as small caps settle to the ground. The average returns for very large companies actually exceed those of some small cap groups early in the Election Cycle.

This advantage of large caps over some small caps early in the cycle may be small, but it is significant, because it is an exception to the general rule: that returns are inversely proportionate to company size.

Later on, we'll see that large caps have an even greater advantage over small caps when Fed policy is restrictive early in the Election Cycle, but that the advantage disappears entirely when Fed policy is expansive. In other words, large caps outperform small caps when the Fed-Election Cycle is least favorable for stocks. This is a manifestation of investors' "flight to quality."

Large caps may outperform some small caps under certain conditions, but they rarely outperform nanocaps. As will soon become apparent, nanocaps achieve superior returns at almost every point in the Fed-Election Cycle. The only exception occurs when the Fed is aggressively restrictive early in the Election Cycle.

Although nanocaps benefit greatly from governmental stimulus late in the Election Cycle, they do not seem to be affected by the withdrawal of that stimulus to the same extent as larger companies. Very small companies are often capable of thriving in spite of unfavorable macroeconomic conditions.

Exhibit 27: Monetary Policy and the Election Cycle

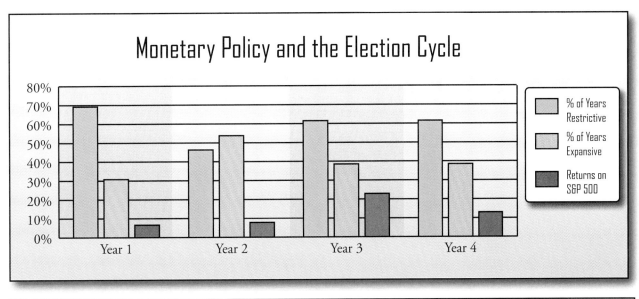

	Year 1	Year 2	Year 3	Year 4	All Years
S&P 500 Returns	6.6%	7.8%	22.9%	13.0%	
% Restrictive	69.2%	46.2%	61.5%	61.5%	59.6%
% Expansive	30.8%	53.8%	38.5%	38.5%	40.4%

Exhibit 28: Market Cap and the Election Cycle– Returns

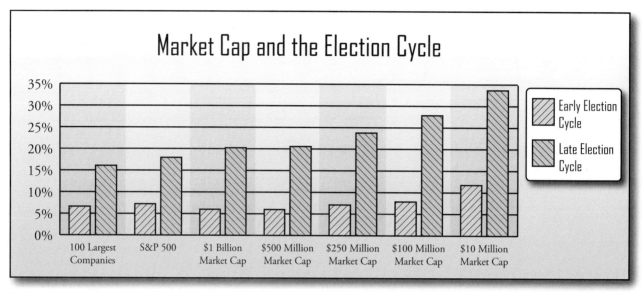

	Early Election Cycle		Late Election Cycle	
	Average Returns	% Years Profitable	Average Returns	% Years Profitable
100 Largest Companies	6.63%	54%	16.06%	92%
S&P 500	7.23%	54%	17.95%	96%
$1 Billion Market Cap	6.00%	58%	20.21%	92%
$500 Million Market Cap	6.00%	58%	20.56%	88%
$250 Million Market Cap	7.11%	62%	23.77%	88%
$100 Million Market Cap	7.87%	58%	27.84%	88%
$10 Million Market Cap	11.74%	65%	33.65%	88%

Chapter 10

THE COMBINED FED-ELECTION CYCLE

In our discussion up to this point, we've compared the historical performance of various investment styles based on value, growth, market capitalization, and relative strength, and we've analyzed the impact of Fed policy and election-oriented economic stimulus on equity returns.

Our analysis of over five decades of stock market data has yielded a number of useful insights.

We've learned that value stocks usually outperform growth stocks, and that small caps tend to outperform large caps.

We've learned that nanocaps, as a group, consistently produce returns superior to those of larger companies—and that nanocaps are significantly less risky than commonly thought.

In addition, we've established that high relative strength stocks tend to outperform the market's laggards.

Furthermore, we have demonstrated the strong influence that Fed policy exerts on overall market performance, and we've shown that an expansive monetary policy generally leads to significantly higher returns.

And, finally, we have seen how political forces in Washington conspire to create a powerful Election Cycle Effect that causes stocks, especially small caps, to perform significantly better in the second half of presidential terms.

Merely knowing that value usually beats growth, that nanocaps usually beat larger companies, and that high relative strength usually beats low relative strength would be enough to fashion a solid stock selection strategy. Based on historical experience, the chances are good that such a strategy would outperform the market over the long term. An investor who never owned anything except high relative strength nanocap value stocks would probably do very well most of the time.

Occasionally, however, growth stocks will outperform value stocks, or large caps will beat nanocaps. Every now and then, low relative strength stocks—last year's losers—will outperform high relative strength stocks. And when they do, the high relative strength nanocap value strategy will not be the best approach.

But what if we had a way of knowing when growth would be likely to outperform value, or when large caps would be likely to outperform small caps?

We became interested in this question as we were investigating the impact of Fed policy and the Presidential Election Cycle on stock market performance. Considering how powerfully these two cycles affect the overall market, it seemed reasonable to suppose that they might also underlie shifts in the relative performance of different investing styles.

Our results are presented in this chapter and the next. They will show how the Combined Fed-Election Cycle affects the relative performance of:

- Value versus growth;

- Small caps (or nanocaps) versus large caps; and

- High relative strength versus low relative strength.

Our analysis will reveal that, in most cases, small cap value stocks with high relative strength have provided the best returns - as we would expect - but it will also show that certain phases of the Fed-Election Cycle have consistently coincided with superior performance by growth, large cap, or low relative strength stocks.

There are good reasons to believe that these patterns are caused by factors associated with the Fed-Election Cycle. However, whether the Fed-Election Cycle causes the patterns we have observed or merely coincides with them for reasons unknown, the correlations are significant enough to indicate the utility of aligning stock selection criteria with the monetary and electoral environment.

In Chapter 10, we'll provide a summary-level overview of the Combined Fed-Election Cycle and its effects.

We'll begin by briefly reviewing the Fed's role in the management of our economy. As we examine the impact of Fed policy on stock prices, we'll emphasize the interrelationships between Fed policy and the Election Cycle.

Then, we'll show how different equity styles have performed in each phase of the Fed-Election Cycle and suggest ways in which the cycle might affect our stock selection criteria.

In Chapter 11, we'll present theories to explain how factors associated with the Fed-Election Cycle might lead to shifts in the relative performance of different investing styles. And, focusing on the practical application of our findings, we'll examine the historical performance data in greater detail in order to determine more precisely when changes in stock selection criteria are likely to be profitable.

The Fed Cycle

The Fed's Independence from Political Control

The Federal Reserve System is the central bank of the United States. It consists of 12 regional Federal Reserve banks overseen by a seven-member Board of Governors.

The Fed is responsible for overseeing the nation's banking system, providing banking services to the national government, and fostering the nation's economic health through judicious exercise of monetary policy. The Fed's principal policy aim is to maintain conditions necessary for sustainable (i.e., non-inflationary) economic growth.

What sets the Fed apart from the central banks of many other countries is its independence from political control.

The seven members of the Board of Governors are appointed by the president and confirmed by the Senate to serve 14-year terms. The Chairman of the Fed's Board of Governors is appointed to a four-year term. Once appointed and confirmed, the members of the Board and its Chairman are - officially at least - free to carry out their responsibilities without further interference from elected officials.

The Fed's Job

The Fed controls the cost and availability of money and credit by setting the discount rate, the Fed Funds rate, and reserve requirements, as well as by conducting open market operations.

Commercial banks operate by taking in deposits and lending them to creditworthy customers. They are not permitted to lend 100% of their depositors' money, however, but must keep a certain portion in reserve to cover withdrawals. The Fed's authority to set reserve requirements gives it control over the amount of money banks can lend.

Banks have the option of borrowing to increase their reserves.

They can borrow from the Fed in order to meet the Fed's reserve requirements or increase the amount they can lend to their customers. The rate banks pay for loans from the Fed is known as the discount rate.
(cont'd.)

In practice, however, the Fed's discount window is rarely used. Instead, commercial banks generally borrow from each other in order to meet reserve requirements. At the end of each business day, after totaling up all of the balances in deposit and loan accounts, some banks have more funds on hand than they need to meet the Fed's reserve requirements, while other banks fall short. Banks with reserve shortfalls borrow from those with excess reserves. The rate charged for these overnight loans between banks is known as the Fed Funds rate.

The Fed's control of short-term interest rates is augmented by its conduct of open market operations. Open market operations provide the Fed the ability to fine-tune short-term rates on a day-to-day basis.

For example, the Fed purchases U.S. government obligations in order to increase the money supply and lower interest rates. When it sells government bonds, it reduces the money supply and raises rates.

Nevertheless, it would be naïve to think that the Fed operates entirely free from political concerns. The Fed has come to be regarded as an independent voice in the formulation of economic policy, and rightly so, but it does not operate in a political vacuum.

The political factors that lead to the Election Cycle Effect indirectly influence Fed policy *because fiscal policies advanced by the president and Congress influence the Fed's formulation of monetary policy.* This would explain why Fed policy is more likely to be restrictive in election years than in any other year of the Election Cycle. Election years mark the point in the cycle when fiscal policy is most likely to be *expansive.*

Thus, the Fed operates independently of the rest of the government, but its policy decisions are, to a large extent, reactions to the economic policies of government officials.

Fed Policy and Interest Rates

The Fed's ability to affect the economy and securities markets derives primarily from its authority to determine the cost and availability of money and credit. Except for a brief period in the late 1970's and early 1980's, when the Fed experimented with managing money supply targets directly, Fed policy has been effected principally through its control of interest rates.

The Fed's power to determine interest rates extends only to short-term rates. Long-term rates are determined by supply and demand forces exerted by lenders and borrowers through the credit markets. Nevertheless, Fed policies have an indirect influence on long-term rates. Lenders and sophisticated borrowers pay careful attention to the Fed's stance on inflation, and thus, when rates change, short-term and long-term rates usually (but not always) move in the same direction.

Interest rate changes affect economic output in a number of ways.

Rate reductions encourage consumers and businesses to spend more (by financing purchases with lower-cost borrowed funds), which tends to increase aggregate demand for goods and services. Rising demand provides an incentive for producers to increase supply, while lower rates make it more economical for them to finance the expansion of production capacity.

Lower interest rates lead to economic growth, but only to the extent consumers and businesses are willing to take on more debt. Prudent borrowers take on additional debt only when they are confident their income will grow fast enough to repay the debt.

Rate increases have opposite effects. Increased borrowing costs reduce demand by making purchases financed with credit more expensive. Falling demand reduces producers' willingness to expand production at the same time as higher rates increase the cost of expansion.

The Fed uses its power over short-term interest rates to control the rate of economic growth, lowering rates when the economy is growing too slowly (or shrinking, as in a recession) and raising rates when economic growth creates inflationary pressures on prices. Fed policy is considered expansive when the Fed lowers rates because rate reductions generally lead to economic expansion. Rate increases are considered restrictive because higher rates tend to restrict economic growth.

Although the Fed plays a central role in the management of our nation's economy, Fed policy has not always been easy to divine.

Fed watchers have traditionally focused on two key short-term interest rates as being the best indicators of Fed policy. These are the discount rate and the Fed Funds rate.

The discount rate is the rate at which the Fed makes loans to member banks, and for many years it was considered the most reliable indicator of Fed policy. It has been largely supplanted in this regard by the Fed Funds rate, the rate charged for overnight loans between member banks.

Back when occasional changes in the discount rate were considered the best indicator of Fed policy, some discount rate changes indicated policy decisions, while others were mere technical adjustments required to bring the rate in line with market rates. In other words, sometimes the Fed took the leading role in setting rates, and other times the Fed followed the market.

The Fed Funds rate was even more problematic as an indicator of Fed policy than the discount rate. The actual Fed Funds rate fluctuates daily due to market forces. Until 1994, when the Fed began to announce its target for the Fed Funds rate at the conclusion of each Federal Open Market Committee meeting, investors were stuck reading Fed policy in the tea leaves of semi-random, day-to-day fluctuations in the actual rate.

Nowadays, the Fed announces its targets for the discount rate[1] as well as the Fed Funds rate, and even Alan Greenspan, who became famous for his ability to wax eloquent while saying nothing at all, occasionally makes an unambig-

Margin Requirements
In addition to setting short-term interest rates, the Fed also has the authority to set margin requirements for stock purchases.

---

[1] On 31 October 2002, the Fed approved the establishment of primary and secondary credit programs, each with its own discount rate.

uous statement about the direction of Fed policy. As a result, investors now have a clearer sense of the Fed's intentions than they had in the past.

If it was often difficult for investors to discern Fed policy at the time it was implemented, it's somewhat less difficult to determine Fed policy changes retroactively.

In order to study the effects of Fed policy changes over the 52 years from 1951 to 2002, it was necessary for us to characterize each year as either expansive or restrictive on the basis of historical interest rate data.

Our options were to use the discount rate, the actual Fed Funds rate, the Fed Funds target rate, or various combinations of these rates. In the end, we settled on a formula based on changes in the actual Fed Funds rate (measured as the current year's average rate less the prior year's year-end rate) as the most reliable method of characterizing each year's Fed policy.

Readers who wish to learn more about the methodology used in our analysis of the Fed-Election Cycle are invited to examine Appendix B.

Interest Rates and Stock Prices

Domestic investors feel the Fed's impact on the stock market in two fundamental ways. (For foreign investors, the Fed's ability to affect exchange rates is an additional consideration.)

When interest rates change, the change affects the rate at which future cash flows are discounted, which has an immediate impact on the market's appraisal of a company's value. (Estimating the net present value of a company's future cash flows is one method for judging its value.) Other things being equal, lowering the interest rate used to discount a company's future cash flows will increase their net present value (assuming the company's future cash flows are positive). This is one reason why stock prices typically rise when an unexpected rate cut is announced.

In addition to this immediate, direct impact on stock prices, interest rate changes also have delayed effects through their impact on future earnings. Rate changes affect profitability in two ways: by affecting the overall level of economic growth (which affects individual companies' sales) and by affecting borrowing costs.

The Cycle of Fed Policy Changes

The Fed Policy Cycle moves through expansive and restrictive phases.

As noted earlier, an expansive Fed policy creates a favorable climate for economic growth by lowering interest rates. Lower interest rates stimulate demand and lower the cost of expanding production capacity.

In the initial stages of an economic recovery, demand tends to rise faster than supply because, generally speaking, business leaders prefer to see evidence of a sustained increase in demand before investing in new production capacity. When aggregate demand goes up faster than supply, prices of goods and services tend to rise.

In the later stages of a recovery, businesses respond to rising demand– and rising goods prices– by expanding production capacity. Expanding production creates more demand for raw materials and labor, causing upward pressure on commodity prices and wages.

When labor costs rise, workers have more money to spend, which creates more demand for goods. The result is known as an "inflation spiral" because rising labor costs lead to rising prices for goods and services, which leads to rising production, which leads to increased demand for workers, which leads to rising labor costs, and so on.

Once an inflation spiral has started, it can be very difficult to stop without severe economic dislocation. Traditionally, an inflation spiral continued until the economy was thrown into recession by rising interest rates. Rate increases dampen consumers' willingness to finance purchases with credit, which reduces demand. Falling demand reduces businesses' incentive to increase production capacity at the same time that rate increases raise the cost of financing new investments in plant and equipment.

The problem with this approach, of course, is that the "cure" (a recession) was often worse than the disease (inflation). Consequently, the Fed tries to nip inflation in the bud by raising short-term rates *before* the economy becomes overheated. The Fed's responsibility, as the saying goes, is to take away the punch bowl just as the party is really starting to get good.

Thus, Fed Policy cycles from expansive—when the economy is growing slowly and inflation is low—to restrictive, when the economy is growing briskly and inflationary pressures are starting to appear.

Over the 52-year period from 1951 to 2002, Fed policy went through 10½ cycles by our count—that is, the Fed changed the direction of monetary policy 21 times.

During this period, the Fed was far more likely to maintain a restrictive policy than an expansive policy. Fed policy was restrictive in 31 of the 52 years and expansive in 21.

The average annual return for the S&P 500 in restrictive phases was 10.6%, versus 15.5% for expansive years—more proof that the stock market much prefers rate cuts to rate increases.

The average length of a cycle was 4.8 years. Restrictive phases lasted 2.9 years, on average, versus 1.9 years for expansive phases.

Earlier, we suggested that the Fed Policy Cycle is linked to the Election Cycle. The principal connection between the two is the fiscal pump-priming that occurs late in the Presidential Election Cycle. The economic policy choices of elected officials affect the Fed's ability to achieve its primary objective—healthy economic growth—and therefore the Fed must include them in its calculations.

Other things being equal, when government spending rises faster than government income, aggregate demand increases. Expansive fiscal policy tends to create inflationary pressures, which the Fed must offset with restrictive monetary policy. As previously noted, Fed policy is more likely to be restrictive in election years than in any other year of the Presidential Election Cycle.

During our 52-year study period, there were two restrictive phases that lasted for exceptionally long periods. During the Eisenhower administration, Fed policy remained restrictive for seven consecutive years. Then, during the "guns and butter" years of the 1960's, when the combination of a "War on Poverty" and the war in Vietnam led to severe inflation, the Fed maintained a restrictive phase that lasted five years.

If we leave these two unusually long restrictive phases out of our analysis, a slightly different picture of the "typical" Fed Policy Cycle emerges. During the 36 years from 1967 to 2002, the average length of a Fed Policy Cycle was 4.25 years—pretty close to the length of the Election Cycle. During this period, restrictive phases lasted an average of 2.25 years, and expansive phases lasted an average of two years. No phase lasted longer than three years.

The similarity between the length of the Fed Cycle over the past 36 years and the length of the Election Cycle could be merely coincidental, but it may also be seen as further circumstantial evidence that the Election Cycle influences the Fed Cycle in predictable ways.

The length of a Fed Cycle is significant for another reason. The longer the Fed sustains a policy, the more impact it tends to have on the stock market. Recall that interest rate changes have both immediate and delayed effects on stock prices. When the Fed sustains a policy direction for two or more years, the delayed effects of early rate changes tend to exaggerate the immediate impact of subsequent changes.

Suppose that, in Year One, the Fed adopts an expansive policy. The Fed's rate cuts have an immediate, positive impact on stock prices because they increase the net present value of companies' future cash flows.

In Year Two, the delayed effects of the Year One rate cuts (economic growth and lower borrowing costs) cause corporate earnings to increase. Stock prices rise in response to these earning improvements. If the Fed makes additional rate cuts in Year Two, the combination of earnings growth and lower interest rates can be extremely bullish.

The Fed Effect

In general, the Fed Effect has been strongest when Fed policy has been sustained and aggressive. The longer the Fed maintains a policy, and the larger the rate changes it makes during that phase, the greater will be its impact on stock prices.

When the Fed adopts an expansive policy, the "liquidity"—that is, the increase in money supply—which the Fed provides to the economy is like water on a garden. Businesses are the plants in the garden. As long as the garden gets plenty of water (but not too much), almost everything grows well.

When the Fed attempts to restrict economic growth by raising interest rates, it is restricting the water supply to our "garden." The greater the severity and duration of the "dry spell," the more effect it will have on the plants' growth.

When a Fed-imposed "drought" begins, investors' first reaction often reflects a presumption that all of the businesses will be equally devastated. The initiation of a restrictive phase is frequently marked by a general decline in prices as the market absorbs the news. As time goes by and the monetary drought persists, however, investors begin to notice that some drought-resistant companies have outgrown the others, which are unable to thrive without a copious supply of liquidity.

Some companies, like some plants, are vigorous and adaptable. They are capable of thriving in an environment that is harsh and unforgiving. Other companies wither away if they're not provided with the economic equivalent of warm sunshine and gentle rains.

It should come as no surprise that differences exist in the way different kinds of companies react to the Fed-Election Cycle. The different phases of the cycle represent different economic, political, and monetary environments, and they're not all equally favorable for stock prices. As we will soon see, companies that thrive in one phase do not necessarily thrive in all phases.

The Combined Fed-Election Cycle

Returns for the S&P 500

In Chapter 9, we presented our conception of a "typical Election Cycle" in which government leaders implement fiscal and "psychological" stimulus programs during the second half of presidential terms. As we've seen, these stimuli create an Election Cycle Effect on stock prices that significantly enhances returns.

Similarly, we've seen how Fed Policy Cycles lead to a Fed Effect on stock prices that causes returns to be significantly higher in expansive phases than in restrictive phases.

We've compared each of these key cycles to forces of nature. From the perspective of investors, they may as well be natural forces, inasmuch as they exert tremendous influence on investment performance and are beyond the control of those affected.

When both cycles are in their "good" phases, the effect on the stock market is unambiguous. The combined forces of political/fiscal stimulus and expansive monetary policy are to the stock market like a fair breeze and a following sea are to a sailing ship. Everything moves in the right direction, and it's easy to make headway.

When both are in their "bad" phases, the combined effects are equally unambiguous. In such times, it may be all an investor can do to avoid being blown off course. Smart investors look for ways to safely weather these "storms."

When the forces push in opposite directions, they tend to create aberrant "weather."

When Fed policy is expansive early in the Election Cycle, or when the Fed is restrictive late in the Election Cycle, strange things happen. The market moves in unusual (but predictable) directions. High relative strength stocks hold less of an advantage over low relative strength stocks, indicating that investors are giving up on yesterday's winners and looking for opportunities among yesterday's overlooked companies. The normal primacy of value over growth becomes extreme in expansive, early Election Cycle years, and practically disappears in restrictive, late Election Cycle years.

The four phases of the Combined Fed-Election Cycle are:

- Expansive Fed policy Early in the Election Cycle

- Expansive Fed policy Late in the Election Cycle

- Restrictive Fed policy Early in the Election Cycle

- Restrictive Fed policy Late in the Election Cycle

Exhibit 29 shows how the S&P 500 performed in each of these phases during the period 1951-2002. As the graph shows, the best years for the market tend to coincide with years in which Fed policy and the Election Cycle were both favorable.

When the Fed was expansive late in the Election Cycle, annual S&P 500 returns averaged a solid 19.6%, compared to 16.9% when the Fed was restrictive late in the Election Cycle.

When the Fed was expansive early in the Election Cycle, returns averaged 11.7%, but when the Fed was restrictive early in the Election Cycle, they averaged just 3.9%.

Overall, the pattern of returns for the S&P 500 conforms to our expectations. Annual returns for the S&P 500 averaged 17.9% late in the Election Cycle versus 7.2% in the early half. When Fed policy was expansive, returns averaged 15.5%, but when Fed policy was restrictive, returns averaged 10.6%.

As we would also expect, the pattern is even more pronounced if we only look at years in which the Fed was aggressively expansive or aggressively restrictive. (We'll define Fed policy as "aggressive" if the change in the Fed Funds rate– measured as the current year's average rate less the prior year's year-end rate– is more than one percentage point.)

Exhibit 29: S&P 500 Returns by Fed-Election Cycle Phase – Current Years' Rates

S&P 500 and the Fed-Election Cycle

Legend:
- S&P 500
- Late Election Cycle
- Expansive Fed Cycle

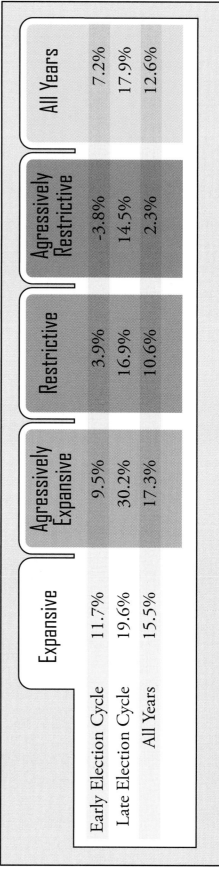

	Expansive	Agressively Expansive	Restrictive	Agressively Restrictive	All Years
Early Election Cycle	11.7%	9.5%	3.9%	-3.8%	7.2%
Late Election Cycle	19.6%	30.2%	16.9%	14.5%	17.9%
All Years	15.5%	17.3%	10.6%	2.3%	12.6%

When the Fed was aggressively expansive late in the Election Cycle, annual S&P 500 returns averaged an outstanding 30.2%, compared to 14.5% when the Fed was aggressively restrictive late in the Election Cycle.

When the Fed was aggressively expansive early in the Election Cycle, the annual S&P 500 return averaged 9.5%. But when the Fed was aggressively restrictive early in the Election Cycle, the S&P 500 lost an average of 3.8% per year.

Exhibit 30 shows the average annual returns for the S&P 500 by Fed-Election Cycle phase, except that in this case the years are categorized using the prior year's Fed Cycle phase. The objective here is to reveal any delayed effects of the Fed policy (as well as to preempt any criticism that our analyses lack practical value due to look-ahead bias).

The patterns revealed in **Exhibit 30** are similar to those shown in the previous exhibit, with one exception. The average returns for late Election Cycle years following restrictive years were actually higher than those following expansive years.

Late in the Election Cycle, the average return in years that followed an aggressively restrictive year was 28.9%. Many of the years included in this average followed multi-year restrictive phases in which the Fed raised rates aggressively. The exceptionally strong returns for the S&P 500 under these circumstances often reflected the market's celebration of the initiation of an expansive policy after a protracted period of restrictive monetary policy.

Ten of the S&P 500's best 15 years occurred when Fed policy was expansive (the average return for these ten years being 29.7%). Of these 10 good years, seven occurred when Fed policy was expansive in a year following one in which Fed policy was restrictive (average return: 31.0%). This suggests that the salutary market effects of an expansive policy are particularly strong when the policy is first initiated.

On the other hand, 10 of the S&P 500's 15 worst years occurred when Fed policy was restrictive (average return for these 10 years was -9.4%). Of these 10 bad years, eight occurred when Fed policy had been restrictive for at least two years (the average return for these years was -9.8%). Thirteen of the 15 worst years occurred early in the Election Cycle. Obviously, prolonged restrictive periods, especially when they occur early in the Election Cycle, are bad times to be invested in the S&P 500.

More Look-Ahead Bias?

The issue of look-ahead bias arises because we cannot know until the end of the current year what the final average Fed Funds rate will be for the current year. Using prior year figures allows us to backtest strategies that would have been possible to implement.

Using current year figures, on the other hand, helps us determine the best response to interest rate changes as they occur. Also, one might argue that it is possible to estimate a year's average Fed Funds rate with reasonable precision long before December 31st.

Exhibit 30: S&P 500 Returns by Fed-Election Cycle Phase – Prior Years' Rates

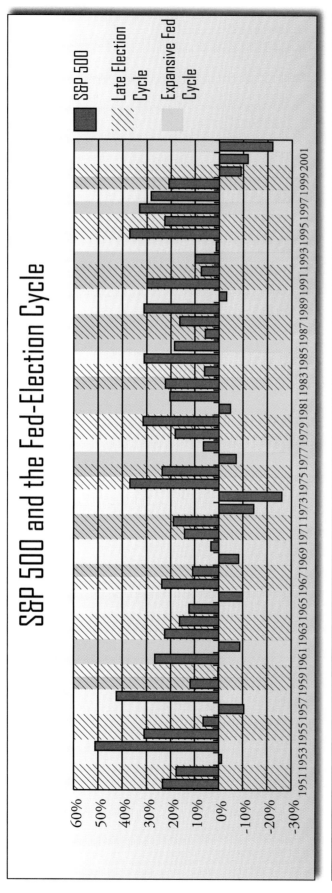

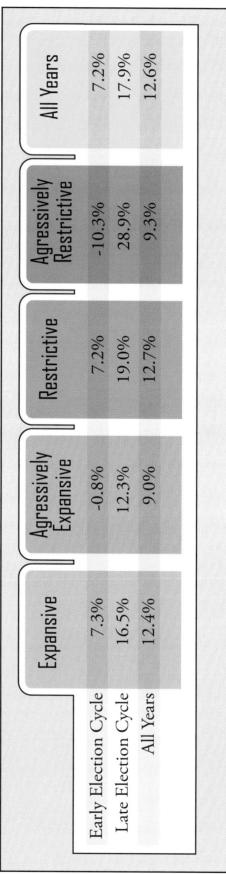

	Expansive	Agressively Expansive	Restrictive	Agressively Restrictive	All Years
Early Election Cycle	7.3%	-0.8%	7.2%	-10.3%	7.2%
Late Election Cycle	16.5%	12.3%	19.0%	28.9%	17.9%
All Years	12.4%	9.0%	12.7%	9.3%	12.6%

The tables which follow show how the market is affected by both the current year's Fed-Election Cycle phase and the prior year's phase.

S&P 500 Returns

This Year	Prior Year Expansive		Prior Year Restrictive	
	Early Cycle	Late Cycle	Early Cycle	Late Cycle
E+EC	5.6%	10.9%	17.7%	9.6%
E+LC	16.6%	15.5%	30.3%	18.2%
R+EC	-8.8%	12.0%	4.6%	1.5%
R+LC	18.3%	15.4%	27.2%	7.5%

Number of Years in Each Phase

This Year	Prior Year Expansive		Prior Year Restrictive	
	Early Cycle	Late Cycle	Early Cycle	Late Cycle
E+EC	3	2	4	2
E+LC	3	2	2	3
R+EC	1	3	5	6
R+LC	3	3	4	5

Clearly, the worst years to be invested in the S&P 500 were the second years of the Election Cycle when the Fed had just commenced a restrictive policy (-8.8%) or early in the cycle when the Fed was maintaining a restrictive policy from the prior year (1.5% to 4.6%).

The best years to be invested in the S&P 500 were the third years of an Election Cycle, either when the Fed had just switched to an expansive policy (30.3%) or when the Fed had maintained a restrictive policy from the prior year (27.2%). Although restrictive monetary policy is, in general, bad for stock prices, it's important to remember that the Fed maintains a restrictive policy to rein in economic growth. With the economy already doing well as the third year of a presidential term commences, the combination of a strong economy and the added push of the Election Cycle Effect appears to outweigh the bearish impact of restrictive monetary policy.

Returns for Individual Groups

Now that we've seen the effects of the Combined Fed-Election Cycle on a broad market index, we're ready to examine how this combined cycle affects returns to different equity styles. We will start at a summary level in this chapter, and then drill down into the details in Chapter 11.

Exhibit 31 summarizes performance data for the following groups:

- Value stocks versus growth stocks;

- Small caps (or nanocaps) versus large caps; and

- High relative strength versus low relative strength

Most of the groups shown on **Exhibit 31** should be self-explanatory.

Under market cap, the 100 largest companies are just that, i.e., the largest 100 companies (by market cap) in the Compustat database. The exhibit also displays performance data for five groups of "small" companies, ranging in size from nanocaps ($10 million market cap) up to $1 billion companies (based on constant 2002 dollars). Note that the performance data for each of these groups represents an average derived from an annual selection of the 100 smallest companies with market caps in excess of the indicated size. For example, the performance of the $250 million group is an average of an annual selection of the 100 smallest companies with a market cap greater than $250 million (on an inflation-adjusted basis).

For value stocks, the performance data was derived from an annual selection of 100 stocks with the *lowest* positive P/E, P/S, P/BV, and P/CF ratios. For growth stocks, the performance data was derived from an annual selection of 100 stocks with the *highest* P/E, P/S, P/BV, and P/CF ratios. The Value and Growth Indices represent averages of these four price ratios.

Similarly, the performance data for high and low relative strength was derived from an annual selection of the 100 stocks with the highest and lowest relative strength values.

In all cases except relative strength, the figures are derived from 52 years of performance data (1951-2002). In the case of relative strength, the figures are derived from 51 years of performance data (because the calculation of relative strength requires stock prices from two years).

Exhibit 31 is organized to compare returns for value stocks, small caps, and high relative strength stocks—i.e., the groups that usually achieve the best performance—to growth stocks, large caps, and low relative strength stocks (i.e., the groups that usually underperform).

To avoid confusion, it's important to understand the organization of this exhibit.

Exhibit 31: Fed-Election Cycle Summary of Returns– All Years

Market Capitalization

Small Companies by Market Cap:	Small Companies				100 Largest Companies				Difference Between Small Companies & 100 Largest Companies			
	Expansive Early	Expansive Late	Restrictive Early	Restrictive Late	Expansive Early	Expansive Late	Restrictive Early	Restrictive Late	Expansive Early	Expansive Late	Restrictive Early	Restrictive Late
Smallest 100 > $10 Million	13.4%	46.2%	10.6%	25.8%					3.0%	29.0%	6.6%	10.4%
Smallest 100 > $100 Million	13.5%	35.3%	3.7%	23.2%					3.2%	18.2%	-0.2%	7.8%
Smallest 100 > $250 Million	12.7%	32.4%	3.0%	18.4%					2.4%	15.2%	-0.9%	3.0%
Smallest 100 > $500 Million	10.4%	27.9%	2.7%	16.0%					0.1%	10.7%	-1.2%	0.6%
Smallest 100 > $1 Billion	10.7%	25.3%	2.6%	17.0%					0.4%	8.2%	-1.4%	1.6%
S&P 500	11.7%	19.6%	3.9%	16.9%								
100 Largest Companies					10.3%	17.1%	3.9%	15.4%				

Relative Strength

	Highest Relative Strength				Lowest Relative Strength				Difference Between Highest & Lowest RS			
	Expansive Early	Expansive Late	Restrictive Early	Restrictive Late	Expansive Early	Expansive Late	Restrictive Early	Restrictive Late	Expansive Early	Expansive Late	Restrictive Early	Restrictive Late
High RS vs. Low RS	6.8%	42.4%	8.5%	26.2%	-3.0%	28.2%	-4.4%	16.0%	9.8%	14.2%	13.0%	10.2%

Value vs. Growth

Positive Price Ratios	Lowest (Value Stocks)				Highest (Growth Stocks)				Difference Between Value & Growth			
	Expansive Early	Expansive Late	Restrictive Early	Restrictive Late	Expansive Early	Expansive Late	Restrictive Early	Restrictive Late	Expansive Early	Expansive Late	Restrictive Early	Restrictive Late
P/S	27.6%	40.1%	11.8%	24.8%	-12.5%	25.6%	-4.9%	18.4%	40.1%	14.5%	16.7%	6.4%
P/BV	28.4%	39.1%	15.9%	26.9%	-3.5%	25.6%	-3.5%	16.0%	31.9%	13.6%	19.4%	10.9%
P/CF	36.7%	44.1%	18.4%	38.1%	-9.2%	26.6%	-2.3%	17.0%	45.9%	17.5%	20.7%	21.1%
P/E	33.6%	48.2%	21.1%	36.9%	-2.5%	32.3%	0.5%	17.7%	36.1%	15.9%	20.6%	19.2%
Index	31.6%	42.9%	16.8%	31.7%	-6.9%	27.5%	-2.6%	17.3%	38.5%	15.4%	19.3%	14.4%

Returns by Fed-Election Cycle phase for value stocks, small caps (of various sizes), and high relative strength stocks are shown on the *left* of **Exhibit 31.**

Returns for growth stocks, large caps, and low relative strength stocks are shown in the *middle* of the exhibit.

The columns on the *right* show the differences in performance, i.e., value minus growth, small caps minus large caps (using returns for the 100 largest companies), and high relative strength minus low relative strength.

Focusing on the differences between stock groups, as shown on the right hand side of **Exhibit 31,** provides a good way to compare the performance of these groups in each phase of the Fed-Election Cycle.

Thus, positive numbers indicate the normal superiority of value over growth, or small size over large size. The higher the number, the greater the superiority of value stocks or small caps over growth stocks or large caps.

Negative numbers indicate phases of the Fed-Election Cycle in which the "normal" relationships are inverted, i.e., where growth outperforms value, or large caps outperform small caps. In some cases, the numbers get fairly small without actually becoming negative. This indicates that value outperformed growth, or small caps outperformed large caps, on average, but it also suggests that there were plenty of years in that phase in which growth outperformed value or large caps outperformed small caps.

Market Capitalization and the Combined Fed-Election Cycle

Our comparison of small caps to large caps **(Exhibit 31)** shows that *nanocaps outperformed all larger-company groupings in every phase of the Combined Fed-Election Cycle.*

In general, small caps (excluding nanocaps) outperformed the largest companies in all phases of the Combined Fed-Election Cycle, with one exception.

The exception—the only phase in which the 100 largest companies outperformed small caps (excluding nanocaps)—was the Restrictive/Early Election Cycle phase. It's no coincidence that this phase was also the worst of the four phases for the market as a whole.

We call these Restrictive/Early Election Cycle years "Panic Years" because both cycles (the Fed Cycle and the Election Cycle) are in their "bad" phases, and because overall market performance in these years has been so bad. The superiority of large caps over small caps in this phase is the result of investors' defensiveness in the face of poor market conditions. This is an example of what is often called "flight to quality." Note that, while large caps outperformed small caps by margins ranging from 0.2% to 1.4%, the average performance of large caps in this phase was nothing special: 3.9%.

If the Restrictive/Early Election Cycle phase was the worst one to be invested in small caps, its opposite, the Expansive/Late Election Cycle phase, was the best. In this phase, nanocaps really shined, returning 46.2% on average. Other small cap groupings had average returns ranging from 25.3% for $1 billion market cap companies up to 35.3% for $100 million market cap companies. Small caps also had their biggest advantage over large caps in this phase, with a return advantage ranging from 8.2% for $1 billion companies to 29.0% for nanocaps.

In the two "mixed phases," i.e., Expansive/Early Election Cycle and Restrictive/Late Election Cycle, small caps outperformed large caps by modest margins.

Value Versus Growth and the Combined Fed-Election Cycle

Value beat growth by the widest margin when the Fed was expansive early in the Election Cycle. Our Value Index outperformed the Growth Index by 38.5%. The Expansive/Early Election Cycle phase was good for value stocks (the Value Index returned 31.6%), but it was the worst time to be invested in growth stocks. The Growth Index actually showed a loss of 6.9% in this phase.

Growth stocks had their best performance late in the Election Cycle when the Fed was expansive (the Growth Index earned 27.5% on average in this phase). Of course, as we would expect, this phase was also the best of the four for the broader market (the S&P 500 returned 19.6%). However, because the Expansive/Late Election Cycle phase was also the best for value stocks (the Value Index earned 42.9%), value stocks maintained a substantial performance advantage over growth stocks in the phase.

When the Fed was restrictive early in the Election Cycle, returns for value stocks were considerably lower (this was the worst phase for the Value Index, with an average return of 16.8%) than they were in either of the expansive phases, but returns for growth stocks were non-existent. In fact, the Growth Index *lost* 2.6%.

The Restrictive/Late Election Cycle phase yielded the most interesting results. Returns for both value and growth stocks were solid, if unspectacular, but the difference between value and growth was the least of any phase. This suggests that the Restrictive/Late Election Cycle phase may provide the best opportunities for an investor to profitably switch into growth stocks. We'll look at this phase more closely in Chapter 11.

Relative Strength and the Combined Fed-Election Cycle

In Chapter 7, we observed that, over the course of the entire 52-year study period, high relative strength outperformed low relative strength. **Exhibit 31** confirms that high relative strength outperforms low relative strength in all phases of the Fed-Election Cycle. And, since high relative strength normally outperforms low relative strength, we tend to avoid low relative strength stocks under most circumstances.

However, we also noted that a reduction in this normal return advantage of high relative strength over low relative strength indicates a shift in the market between two (or more) major groups. We can apply this knowledge to confirm that shifts in the relative performance of value versus growth or small cap versus large cap truly indicate major shifts that represent trading opportunities.

Exhibit 31 shows that the two phases with the smallest average difference between high and low relative strength are the Expansive/Early phase and the Restrictive/Late phase.

The Expansive/Early phase is when value has its greatest performance advantage over growth. The Restrictive/Late phase is when value has its smallest performance advantage over growth.

Thus, it appears that the significant shifts in the relative attractiveness of value versus growth stocks occurring during these phases represent trading opportunities. Under these circumstances, low relative strength should not be considered a reason to exclude a stock from consideration.

Returns for Individual Groups When Fed Policy is Aggressive

Earlier, we noted how relatively large changes in interest rates (i.e., when Fed policy was "aggressive") tend to exaggerate the Fed Effect. Let's look at the returns for each of our stock groupings, but this time we'll only include the years in which Fed policy was aggressive.

Exhibit 32 shows these returns, and, for the most part, yields conclusions similar to those we derived from **Exhibit 31**.

Market Capitalization in Aggressive Years

Nanocaps outperformed larger companies in most phases when Fed policy was "aggressive," except during "Panic Years" (Early Election Cycle/Restrictive phase). Nanocaps returned an average of 99.7% (!) when the Fed was aggressively expansive late in the Election Cycle, and 71.1% when the Fed was aggressively restrictive late in the Election Cycle.

Small caps had their best performance both in absolute terms and relative to large caps late in the Election Cycle. They had returns ranging from 40.8% to 60.5% when the Fed was expansive late in the Election Cycle, and returns ranging from 25.9% to 53.8% when the Fed was restrictive late in the Election Cycle.

As before, large caps outperformed small caps in "Panic Years," this time by 5.0% to 10.2 %. In addition, as we noted, large caps achieved the highly unusual feat of outperforming nanocaps, by 8.5%.

One difference that can be seen in the "aggressive" years compared to "all" years is the margin by which small caps outperform large caps in the Restrictive/Late Election Cycle phase. Using figures from all years (as shown in **Exhibit 31**), the difference between small caps and large caps was modest. In aggressively restrictive years (**Exhibit 32**), small caps did significantly better, while the average returns for large caps were about the same. As a result, small caps outperformed large caps by amounts ranging from 10.7% to 38.7%.

A similar thing happened with nanocaps. They outperformed large caps by 55.9% when the Fed was aggressively restrictive late in the Election Cycle, compared to 10.4% when we consider all Restrictive/Late Election Cycle years.

A little earlier, we suggested that the Restrictive/Late Election Cycle phase might offer the best conditions for growth stocks to outperform value stocks. Now we see that when Fed policy is aggressively restrictive in this phase, the performance of small caps soars.

Bearing in mind that an aggressively restrictive Fed policy implies the likelihood of a booming economy, a picture begins to take shape. Good economic

Exhibit 32: Fed-Election Cycle Summary of Returns – Aggressive Years

Market Capitalization

Fed-Election Cycle Phases — Small Companies

Small Companies by Market Cap:	Aggressively Expansive Early	Aggressively Expansive Late	Aggressively Restrictive Early	Aggressively Restrictive Late
Smallest 100 > $10 million	20.1%	99.7%	-10.8%	71.1%
Smallest 100 > $100 million	16.5%	60.5%	-12.5%	53.8%
Smallest 100 > $250 million	13.4%	56.7%	-11.2%	36.5%
Smallest 100 > $500 million	15.1%	47.4%	-9.4%	31.5%
Smallest 100 > $1 billion	13.3%	40.8%	-7.4%	25.9%
S&P 500	9.5%	30.2%	-3.8%	14.5%

Fed-Election Cycle Phases — Large Companies

	Aggressively Expansive Early	Aggressively Expansive Late	Aggressively Restrictive Early	Aggressively Restrictive Late
100 Largest Companies	8.6%	25.6%	-2.4%	15.2%

Fed-Election Cycle Phases — Difference Between Small Companies & 100 Largest Companies

	Aggressively Expansive Early	Aggressively Expansive Late	Aggressively Restrictive Early	Aggressively Restrictive Late
Smallest 100 > $10 million	11.6%	74.2%	-8.5%	55.9%
Smallest 100 > $100 million	7.9%	34.9%	-10.2%	38.7%
Smallest 100 > $250 million	4.8%	31.2%	-8.8%	21.3%
Smallest 100 > $500 million	6.5%	21.8%	-7.0%	16.3%
Smallest 100 > $1 billion	4.8%	15.2%	-5.0%	10.7%

Relative Strength

Fed-Election Cycle Phases

	Aggressively Expansive Early	Aggressively Expansive Late	Aggressively Restrictive Early	Aggressively Restrictive Late
Highest Relative Strength — High RS vs. Low RS	2.9%	87.1%	-14.9%	33.6%
Lowest Relative Strength — High RS vs. Low RS	-0.5%	84.3%	-27.5%	56.7%
Difference Between Highest & Lowest RS — High RS vs. Low RS	3.5%	2.8%	12.6%	-23.2%

Value vs. Growth

Fed-Election Cycle Phases — Lowest (Value Stocks)

Positive Price Ratios	Aggressively Expansive Early	Aggressively Expansive Late	Aggressively Restrictive Early	Aggressively Restrictive Late
P/S	35.6%	78.7%	-5.7%	61.6%
P/BV	37.9%	58.7%	0.4%	63.0%
P/CF	46.4%	67.8%	-1.5%	67.8%
P/E	40.0%	81.1%	2.6%	68.1%
Index	40.0%	71.6%	-1.1%	65.1%

Fed-Election Cycle Phases — Highest (Growth Stocks)

	Aggressively Expansive Early	Aggressively Expansive Late	Aggressively Restrictive Early	Aggressively Restrictive Late
P/S	-11.3%	62.7%	-19.0%	64.7%
P/BV	-9.8%	61.6%	-17.8%	44.9%
P/CF	-10.5%	60.2%	-20.3%	40.4%
P/E	-2.7%	74.8%	-16.0%	46.1%
Index	-8.6%	64.8%	-18.3%	49.0%

Fed-Election Cycle Phases — Difference Between Value & Growth

	Aggressively Expansive Early	Aggressively Expansive Late	Aggressively Restrictive Early	Aggressively Restrictive Late
P/S	46.9%	16.0%	13.3%	-3.1%
P/BV	47.7%	-2.9%	18.2%	18.1%
P/CF	56.8%	7.6%	18.8%	27.4%
P/E	42.7%	6.3%	18.6%	22.0%
Index	48.5%	6.7%	17.2%	16.1%

times, plus governmental stimulus (real and psychological) apparently lead to a stock market that rewards risk-takers. We'll call these "Euphoric Years." In Chapter 11, we'll bring this picture into sharper focus.

Value Versus Growth in Aggressive Years

Similar to what we saw in **Exhibit 31**, value stocks had their best returns when the Fed was aggressively expansive late in the Election Cycle (the Value Index returned 71.6%). Value also outperformed growth by the widest margin (48.5%) when the Fed was aggressively expansive early in the Election Cycle.

The average return for value stocks was significantly higher in Aggressively Restrictive/Late Election Cycle years compared to all Restrictive/Late Election Cycle years—65.1% versus 31.7%.

Even more interesting, the difference in the average performance of growth stocks in Aggressively Restrictive/Late Election Cycle years over all Restrictive/Late Election Cycle years was even more pronounced—49.0% versus 17.3%. *As a result, high P/E (growth) stocks actually outperformed low P/E (value) stocks, 64.7% to 61.6%.* This is more evidence that Euphoric Years tend to be good for growth stocks.

However, there were some anomalous results in the comparison of value to growth. While high P/E beat low P/E when the Fed was aggressively restrictive late in the Election Cycle (by 3.1%), the differences in the other price ratios actually widened in favor of value. In addition, the difference between value and growth *narrowed* considerably in the Expansive/Late Election Cycle phase, mostly due to the better performance of growth stocks.

Relative Strength in Aggressive Years

The return advantage of high relative strength over low relative strength narrowed considerably in aggressive years, except during the Aggressively Restrictive/Early Election Cycle phase—i.e., Panic Years—suggesting that aggressive Fed policy exaggerated the shifts between value and growth occurring in the market.

In fact, in the Aggressively Restrictive/Late Election Cycle phase, low relative strength actually outperformed high relative strength, by 23.2%. Combined with the figures we saw for value and growth, this is more evidence that investors should adjust their strategies in the Restrictive/Late Election Cycle phase.

The Combined Fed-Election Cycle and Stock Selection

In Chapter 10, we've shown how the combined forces of Fed policy and the Election Cycle Effect influence the performance of different equity styles.

We've shown how the relative performance of large caps versus small caps, value versus growth, and high versus low relative strength has correlated with the four phases of the Combined Fed-Election Cycle. In addition, we've provided further evidence of the consistency with which nanocaps outperform the stocks of larger companies.

Based on these findings, we can begin to outline a stock selection strategy aligned with the Fed-Election Cycle.

Our strategy would have us purchase nanocaps at all times except when the Fed is being restrictive (especially aggressively restrictive) early in the Election Cycle. During these Panic Years, we would switch to buying large caps as a defensive move.

If we weren't able to find enough opportunities among nanocaps, we would seek candidates for purchase among the next smallest groups, especially late in the Election Cycle.

Our strategy would have us buy value stocks most of the time, especially when Fed policy was expansive. It would also lead us to buy value stocks early in the Election Cycle when Fed policy was restrictive, but we would strongly consider buying growth stocks late in the Election Cycle when the Fed was restrictive (particularly when the Fed was aggressively restrictive).

This is a good start, but more remains to be accomplished in Chapter 11.

In the next chapter, we'll complete our analysis of the Combined Fed-Election Cycle and flesh out our strategy for buying stocks in accordance with the two most powerful determinants of stock market performance.

We'll present our theories for why stocks react as they do to the Fed-Election Cycle, and we'll go over some of the practical issues involved with implementing our strategy. In particular, we'll define more precisely when growth would be likely to outperform value, and when large caps would be likely to outperform small caps.

Chapter 11

THE FED-ELECTION CYCLE & STOCK
SELECTION STRATEGY

In Chapter 10, we showed how the two most powerful determinants of stock market performance combine to affect returns from equity investments.

We showed that the market's best years occurred *late* in the Election Cycle when Fed policy was *expansive* and, conversely, that its worst years occurred *early* in the Election Cycle when Fed policy was *restrictive.*

More significantly, we correlated shifts in the relative performance of different equity styles with phase changes in the Fed-Election Cycle. And, based on this analysis, we outlined a strategy for rotating styles through the cycle's four primary phases.

In Chapter 11, we will refine our strategy for reacting to the Fed-Election Cycle.

We'll begin with a detailed examination of the historical performance of 19 stock selection strategies in various monetary/electoral environments and show how the duration and aggressiveness of Fed policy affects returns.

Each strategy will be compared to its antithesis. We'll start with strategies based on market cap. Five small cap strategies will be compared to the 100 largest companies in the Compustat database. We'll also compare the S&P 500 to the 100 largest companies. Then, for each price ratio (P/E, P/S, P/BV, P/CF), we'll compare the value strategy to the growth strategy (e.g., high P/E versus low P/E). We'll do the same for the Value and Growth Indices. Finally, we'll compare high relative strength to low relative strength.

As we review the performance figures, we'll focus on identifying the particular monetary, politico-economic, and market conditions associated with each shift in the relative performance of opposing styles.

But then, venturing beyond merely identifying the market conditions that correlate with each performance shift, we'll explore the likely causes of these shifts. Our explanation will focus on certain economic and psychological factors associated with the Fed-Election Cycle which affect the relative performance of alternative equity styles. These factors include: earnings expectations, inflation, the yield curve of interest rates, and market psychology.

Finally, we will conclude our analysis of the Fed-Election Cycle with some suggestions regarding the practical application of our findings.

Analysis of Historical Data

Methodology

We undertook the analysis presented in this chapter in order to compare the historical performance of various stock selection strategies in different monetary and electoral environments.

In simplest terms, our methodology is comprised of two basic steps.

We began by developing hypothetical annual return figures for each strategy through a technique known as backtesting. This involved the selection of a 100-stock portfolio at the beginning of each year based on the criteria defined by the strategy. The portfolio would be held for one year and the return calculated, and then a new portfolio would be selected for the following year.

Using the low P/E strategy as an example, a portfolio consisting of the 100 stocks with the lowest P/E ratios would be selected at the beginning of each year. At the end of that year, the returns for those 100 stocks would be calculated and averaged, and then a new 100-stock portfolio would be selected for the following year.

After calculating the hypothetical annual returns for each strategy, our next step was to characterize Fed policy for each year based on changes in the Fed Funds rate. This enabled us to classify each year in our study period into one of the four phases of the Fed-Election Cycle and then average the returns for each phase.

Profitable Strategies

Identifying strategies that would have made money in the past is relatively easy to accomplish. The challenge in analyzing historical market data is to determine which of these strategies are likely to be profitable in the future.

Our odds of success are improved when we focus on strategies that:

a.) Have been profitable in the past, and
b.) Exploit predictable patterns

Given the predictability of the Fed's reaction to economic cycles, the economy's reaction to Fed policy, and the behavior of politicians, it's no surprise that the Fed-Election Cycle gives rise to tradable strategies.

We classified each of the 52 years in our study period as either expansive or restrictive, based on the direction of the change in the Fed Funds rate. The change is defined as the difference between the average Fed Funds rate for the year in question minus the year-end rate for the previous year.

(cont'd.)

Our analysis compares the backtested performance of 19 alternative stock selection strategies using hypothetical return figures for the 52-year period from 1951-2002. Annual return figures were derived from financial statements and stock price data drawn from the Standard and Poor's Compustat database. Our Fed Cycle analysis is based on interest rate data provided by the Fed.

This summary vastly simplified our analytical methodology. A more complete explanation is provided in Appendix B.

Presentation of Historical Data

Our backtest analysis of the hypothetical performance of 19 alternative stock selection strategies over the 52-year period from 1951-2002 is presented in 60 exhibits– Exhibits 33A–44E.

Deviating somewhat from our practice in earlier chapters, the exhibits included in Chapter 11 will be presented in groups based on style, rather than being interspersed throughout the text as before.

Exhibits 33A - 38E pertain to market cap-based selection criteria and are reproduced on pages 132 through 161.

Exhibits 39A - 43E pertain to value- and growth-based selection criteria and are reproduced on pages 176 through 200.

Exhibits 44A - 44E provide performance data for relative strength and are reproduced on pages 204 through 208.

When we use the "prior years" interest rates, the 1952 rate change is used to characterize 1953 Fed policy, the 1953 rate change is used to characterize 1954 Fed policy, and so on. This avoids something called "look-ahead bias."

Look-ahead bias occurs whenever you backtest an investment strategy using information that would not have been available to an investor at the time investment decisions were presumed to have been made.

When we use the current years' interest rates, the 1952 rate change is used to characterize 1952 Fed policy, the 1953 rate change is used to characterize 1953 Fed policy, and so on. This shows the link between "current" interest rates and stock market returns more clearly, but it does involve some look-ahead bias. In most cases, though, the Fed policy for any given year is knowable long before year-end, so the look-ahead bias involved would be minimal.

Note:

Large caps and *100 largest companies* are synonymous in this chapter.

The Fed-Election Cycle and Market Cap-Based Strategies

The Fed-Election Cycle and Nanocaps

Exhibit 33A compares the performance of nanocaps (the 100 smallest companies with inflation-adjusted market caps over $10 million) to that of the 100 largest companies in each phase of the Fed-Election Cycle.

The bar chart at the top of the exhibit illustrates the performance advantage of nanocaps. Bars appearing above the zero line indicate years in which nanocaps outperformed large caps.

Nanocaps outperformed the 100 largest companies in 34 (65%) of the 52 years between 1951 and 2002, by an average of 26.6% in those 34 years. Large caps outperformed the nanocaps 18 times during this period (34.6%), by an average of 17.5%.

Nanocaps did not do well vis-à-vis large caps in the great bull markets of the 1980's and 1990's. They underperformed the 100 largest companies in 12 of the 17 years between 1984 and 2000. But the large caps' run of dominance came to an end when the dot.com bubble burst. In 2001-2002, they underperformed nanocaps by an average of 39.5%.

The nanocap group's performance was apparently driven more by the Election Cycle Effect than the Fed Effect. Nanocaps averaged annual returns of 33.6% late in the Election Cycle, versus an average of 11.7% during the early years of the cycle. They responded to an expansive Fed policy with average annual returns of 29.0%, versus the 18.4% they returned when Fed policy was restrictive.

Nanocaps made money, on average, in every phase of the Fed-Election Cycle, except when the Fed was aggressively restrictive early in the Election Cycle. The superior performance of nanocaps was most evident late in the Election Cycle.

The 100 largest companies averaged returns of 16.1% late in the Election Cycle, versus 6.6% during the early years of the cycle. They responded to an expansive Fed policy with average annual returns of 13.6%, versus the 9.8% they returned when Fed policy was restrictive.

Large caps made money, on average, in every phase of the Fed-Election Cycle, except when the Fed was *aggressively restrictive* early in the Election Cycle.

Nanocaps' best performance vis-à-vis large caps occurred late in the Election Cycle when Fed policy was expansive. Nanocaps' performance advantage during this phase was 29.0%. During the late Election Cycle years when Fed policy was *aggressively expansive,* nanocaps' performance advantage was 74.2%.

Nanocaps' second best performance occurred late in the Election Cycle when Fed policy was *aggressively restrictive.* During those years, nanocaps' performance advantage averaged 55.9% per year.

Large caps' best performance vis-à-vis nanocaps occurred early in the Election Cycle.

Large caps actually outperformed nanocaps when Fed policy was *aggressively restrictive* early in the Election Cycle. The 100 largest companies lost an average of 2.4% during these years, but nanocaps' losses averaged 10.8%. This was the only phase in which nanocaps lost money, and the only one in which large caps outperformed nanocaps.

Large caps' performance advantage over nanocaps in Aggressively Restrictive/ Early Election Cycle years resulted from a fairly typical investor reaction to unfavorable market conditions. Times of market turmoil often result in a "flight to quality," as investors shift money into asset classes with lower perceived risk.

Exhibit 33B compares nanocaps' performance to that of large caps (and compares them both to returns for the S&P 500) for each phase of the Fed-Election Cycle.

Exhibit 33B illustrates what we saw in **Exhibit 33A,** i.e., that nanocaps' performance is strongest during Expansive/Late Election Cycle years and worst during early Election Cycle years.

Exhibits 33C–33D are similar to **Exhibits 33A–33B,** except that the years are categorized according to Fed policy in the prior year.

The overall results presented in **Exhibits 33C–33D** are nearly identical to those we saw using the current years' rates to characterize Fed policy, except that the differences in performance between expansive years and restrictive years were smaller. This shows that the delayed effects of Fed policy were less pronounced than the immediate effects, as we might expect. It also indicates that our conclusions are not significantly affected by look-ahead bias.

The 100 largest companies had their best years vis-à-vis nanocaps early in the Election Cycle when Fed policy had been restrictive in the prior year. During Prior Year Restrictive/Early Election Cycle years, nanocaps outperformed the large caps by a small margin. However, during the years when Fed policy was *aggressively* restrictive in the prior year, large caps outperformed the nanocaps by an average of 11.8%.

Exhibit 33E presents a different approach to the performance comparison between nanocaps and large caps. In this case, we rank the years in our study according to the differences between the annual returns for nanocaps and those of the 100 largest companies. Then, we compare the 15 best years for nanocaps to the 15 best years for large caps.

The 15 Best Years for Large Caps

During the 15 best years for large caps, the 100 largest companies gained an average of 8.8%, while nanocaps lost an average of 11.2%. During these years, the average return for the S&P 500 was 9.2%, well below its 52-year average of 12.6%.

The S&P 500 had below-average returns in nine out of the 15 best years for large caps. Five of the six years in which the S&P had above-average returns were early in the Election Cycle.

Eleven of the 15 best years for large caps occurred early in the Election Cycle. In three of the four years occurring late in the Election Cycle, the S&P had below-average returns. Three of the four late Election Cycle years were restrictive years preceded by restrictive years.

Fed policy was restrictive in nine of the 15 best years for large caps, and seven of the nine years were preceded by another restrictive year. 11 of the 15 best years for large caps were preceded by restrictive years.

In 13 of the 15 best years for large caps, Fed policy was restrictive in the current year, the prior year, or both (eight years being the corresponding figure for expansive policy).

Thus, large caps are mostly likely to outperform nanocaps in early Election Cycle bear markets when monetary policy is aggressively restrictive.

The 15 Best Years for Nanocaps

During the 15 years in which nanocaps' performance advantage over large caps was greatest, nanocaps averaged returns of 57.5% per year, versus 9.0% for large caps. The S&P 500 averaged 11.5% during these years, close to its 52-year average.

Fed policy was expansive in nine of the 15 best years. In five of these nine years, Fed policy was expansive in the prior year as well.

Nanocaps' 15 best years were about evenly split between the two halves of the Election Cycle.

Almost all of the difference between nanocaps' best and worst years vis-à-vis large caps resulted from a difference in the performance of nanocaps. There was very little difference in the performance of large caps during these years.

Nanocaps outperform large caps by the widest margin late in the Election Cycle. As we noted in Chapter 9, the Election Cycle Effect apparently has more impact on small caps than on large caps.

Nanocaps tend to outperform large caps in almost all monetary/electoral environments, the only exception being Aggressively Restrictive/Early Election Cycle years.

The term we use to describe Restrictive/Early Election Cycle years is "Panic Years." The Aggressively Restrictive/Early Election Cycle years, in which nanocaps tend to underperform large caps, could be thought of as "Extreme Panic Years."

The Fed-Election Cycle and Small Caps

Having dealt with nanocaps as a special case, we'll turn our attention to the performance of small cap stocks ranging in size from a market cap of $100 million up to $1 billion.

As we saw in Chapter 8, an inverse relationship exists between a company's size (as measured by market cap) and its performance. The larger the company, the smaller its returns are likely to be.

On the other hand, companies with market caps of $100 million or more tend to be significantly easier to trade than nanocaps. Information tends to be

Note:

In the rest of this chapter, the term *small caps* refers to the 100 smallest companies with market caps greater than an inflation-adjusted $100 million.

more widely available on these larger companies, and funds can be invested in them more quickly. Consequently, small caps tend to be a more practical investment than nanocaps for institutions (mutual funds, for example) and the super-wealthy.

Exhibits 34A - 37E present performance data for the 100 smallest companies with inflation-adjusted market caps exceeding $100 million, $250 million, $500 million, and $1 billion.

We will examine the returns for $100 million companies in detail, but then skip over the details for the other small company market groupings. Returns for these companies follow the patterns set by $100 million companies, albeit with progressively smaller returns as company size increases, so it would be repetitious to examine each of these market cap groupings in detail.

Exhibit 34A compares the performance of $100 million companies to that of the 100 largest companies in each phase of the Fed-Election Cycle.

The bar chart at the top of the exhibit illustrates the performance advantage of $100 million companies over the 100 largest companies. Bars appearing above the zero line indicate years in which $100 million companies outperformed the large caps.

$100 million companies outperformed the 100 largest companies in 34 (65%) of the 52 years between 1951 and 2002, by an average of 17.5% per year. Large caps outperformed the $100 million companies 18 times during 1951-2002, by an average of 14.3%.

$100 million companies averaged annual returns of 27.8% late in the Election Cycle, versus an average of 7.9% during the early years of the cycle. They responded to an expansive Fed policy with average annual returns of 23.9%, versus the 13.8% they returned when Fed policy was restrictive.

$100 million companies made money, on average, in every phase of the Fed-Election Cycle, except when the Fed was aggressively restrictive early in the Election Cycle. The superior performance of these small cap companies was most evident late in the Election Cycle.

The performance pattern of $100 million companies was very similar to that of nanocaps, except that the performance advantage of $100 million companies over large caps was smaller than that of nanocaps.

Over the 52-year period from 1951-2002, the $100 million companies' best performance vis-à-vis large caps occurred late in the Election Cycle when Fed policy was expansive or aggressively restrictive. The small caps' performance advantage during the Expansive/Late Election Cycle phase was 18.2%. During late Election Cycle years when Fed policy was *aggressively expansive,* this advantage rose to 34.9%.

$100 million companies outperformed large caps by their widest margin (39.7%) late in the Election Cycle when Fed policy was aggressively restrictive. The $100 million strategy did extremely well in Aggressively Restrictive/Late Election Cycle years, earning a 53.8% average annual return, *almost as much as the strategy did in Aggressively Expansive/Late Election Cycle years (60.5%).*

This is very similar to the pattern we observed in the nanocap returns. Does it imply that Fed policy has little effect on the performance of very small companies?

Not exactly.

It is apparent from **Exhibit 33A** that the Election Cycle Effect is a stronger driver of small caps' performance than the Fed Effect, as it is with nanocaps. The Fed Effect is, nonetheless, a significant factor, especially when Fed policy is expansive. It may be less of a factor when the Fed is restrictive.

The term we use to characterize Restrictive/Late Election Cycle years is "Euphoric." Aggressively Restrictive/Late Election Cycle years are, therefore, "Extreme Euphoric Years."

When the Fed pursues an aggressively restrictive policy late in the Election Cycle, it is typically doing so to rein in an economy that is responding to fiscal stimulus by growing too fast. Quite often, in these circumstances, a kind of "euphoria" overtakes the market. Stock prices rise rapidly in response to rosy earnings reports and vigorous encouragement by the incumbent administration. Investors tend to become more interested in "high-flyers" – risky, but fast-growing companies - and less interested in large, mature companies that turn in solid, though less exciting, results.

Among the companies that attract more than their usual share of buying interest in Euphoric Years are small caps and nanocaps.

In general, large caps' best performance vis-à-vis $100 million companies occurred early in the Election Cycle.

> ### Supplemental Reading
>
> For an in-depth look at how fiscal stimulus has been used to influence voters, we heartily recommend Edward Tufte's *Political Control of the Economy.*

Large caps outperformed $100 million companies by a slight margin (0.2%) in Panic Years (i.e., when Fed policy was restrictive early in the Election Cycle).

When Fed policy was *aggressively restrictive* early in the Election Cycle—Extreme Panic Years—the 100 largest companies outperformed the $100 million group by 10.2% (mostly due to small caps' average annual loss of 12.5%).

As was the case with nanocaps, returns for large caps exceeded those of small caps in Extreme Panic Years. Moreover, large caps outperformed the $100 million companies in Panic Years as well. (Nanocaps lost to large caps—by 8.5%—in Extreme Panic Years, but overall in Panic Years, they beat large caps by 6.6%.)

A quick review of **Exhibits 33A–37A** will show that companies with market caps ranging from $100 million to $1 billion underperformed the 100 largest companies in Panic Years. Moreover, the performance disadvantage of these smaller companies was larger for $250 million companies than it was for $100 million companies, larger still for $500 million companies, and yet larger for $1 billion companies. In fact, every market cap group between $100 million and $1 billion performed worse in Panic Years than groups of its smaller peers.

The opposite is true in Extreme Panic Years. During these years, average returns generally fell as company size decreased (though nanocaps did manage to outperform the $100 million and $250 million groups.) A flight to quality occurred in these years, as investors favored stocks with large market caps—and, thus, lower perceived risk. Companies perceived as risky were very much out of favor in Extreme Panic Years.

Of all the small market cap strategies we backtested, nanocaps was the only one that beat the 100 largest companies in Panic Years. Nanocaps' consistency in the face of inhospitable market conditions is yet one more reason to consider owning them.

Recall that, in Chapter 9, we likened the Election Cycle to a strong wind that blows small bits of gravel further than larger rocks. We explained that when the wind stops blowing (early in the Election Cycle), the larger rocks' inertia keeps them rolling along, but smaller particles settle to earth.

Nanocaps, as a group, usually don't settle to earth when the wind stops blowing. Unless market conditions are truly terrible, they soar high above, in the jet stream.

Exhibit 34B compares $100 million companies' performance to that of large caps (and compares them both to returns for the S&P 500) for each phase of the Fed-Election Cycle. This exhibit illustrates what we learned from **Exhibit 34A**, i.e., that $100 million companies' performance is strongest late in the Election Cycle and weakest during Panic Years (Restrictive/Early Election Cycle).

Exhibits 34C–34D are similar to **Exhibits 34A–34B,** except that the years are categorized according to Fed policy in the prior year.

The overall results presented in **Exhibits 34C–34D** are nearly identical to those we saw using the current years' interest rate changes to characterize Fed policy.

The 100 largest companies had their best years vis-à-vis $100 million companies early in the Election Cycle when Fed policy had been restrictive in the prior year.

Exhibit 34E compares the 15 best years for $100 million companies to the 15 best years for the 100 largest companies, ranking the years according to the differences between the annual returns for $100 million companies and those of the 100 largest companies.

The Best Years for Large Caps

During the 15 best years for large caps, the 100 largest companies gained an average of 12.7%, while the $100 million strategy lost an average of 4.0%. During these years, the S&P 500 gained 12.7%, almost exactly equal to its 52-year average.

The S&P 500 had below-average returns in eight of the 15 best years for large caps. Four of the seven years in which the S&P 500 had above-average returns were early in the Election Cycle.

Ten of the 15 best years for large caps occurred early in the Election Cycle.

Fed policy was restrictive in nine of the 15 best years for large caps, and six of the nine years were preceded by another restrictive year. Ten of the 15 best years for large caps were preceded by restrictive years.

In 13 of the 15 best years for large caps, Fed policy was restrictive in the current year, the prior year, or both (nine years being the corresponding figure for expansive policy).

Thus, large caps are most likely to outperform $100 million companies in early Election Cycle bear markets during periods of restrictive monetary policy.

The 15 Best Years for $100 Million Companies

During the 15 years in which $100 million companies' performance advantage over large caps was greatest, they averaged returns of 45.6% per year, versus 14.4% for large caps. The S&P 500 averaged 16.7% during these years, significantly higher than its 52-year average of 12.6%.

The S&P 500 had above average returns in nine of the 15 best years for $100 million companies. In four of the six below-average years, Fed policy was restrictive.

Nine of the $100 million companies' 15 best years vis-à-vis large caps occurred late in the Election Cycle. In four of the six early Election Cycle years, Fed policy was expansive.

Nine of the $100 million companies' 15 best years versus large caps occurred when Fed policy was expansive. In five of these nine years, Fed policy was expansive in the prior year as well.

Our conclusions regarding $100 million companies are similar to those for nanocaps.

$100 million companies tend to outperform large caps in almost all monetary/electoral environments, the only exception being Panic Years. However, the performance advantage for $100 million companies over large caps during the Expansive/Early Election Cycle tends to be small.

$100 million companies tend to do best relative to large caps when Fed policy is expansive.

Thus, $100 million companies are most likely to outperform large caps in late Election Cycle bull markets during periods of expansive monetary policy.

Other Small Market Cap Strategies

As we noted earlier, the performance patterns for small companies ranging up to $1 billion in market cap are virtually identical to those of $100 million companies, except that the returns in each phase become progressively smaller as company size increases. Naturally, the performance advantage of small companies vis-à-vis large caps also gets progressively smaller as we compare progressively larger companies to the 100 largest companies.

Since any conclusions we reach concerning small companies and the Fed-Election Cycle would apply to all of the small market cap strategies, it would be repetitious to review the performance data for each one of these strategies.

The performance figures for the other small company strategies we backtested ($250 million, $500 million, and $1 billion market caps) are provided as **Exhibits 35A–37E.**

The Fed-Election Cycle and the S&P 500

Exhibits 38A–38E present the performance of the S&P 500 in the same format we used for nanocaps and small caps.

Since the S&P 500 index is comprised of large company stocks, its performance figures tend to be very similar to those for the 100 largest companies. Consequently, a comparison between the two groups will not reveal any significant trading opportunities.

However, since the S&P 500 can be considered a proxy for "the market," reviewing its performance in different phases of the Fed-Election Cycle helps to confirm the validity of our Fed-Election Cycle analysis.

Exhibit 38A compares the performance of the S&P 500 Index to that of the 100 largest companies in each phase of the Fed-Election Cycle. This shows that, as a broad market average, the S&P 500 conforms to our expectations concerning the effects of monetary policy and the Election Cycle.

The S&P 500 performed better late in the Election Cycle, averaging annual returns of 17.9%, than it did early in the cycle, when it averaged 7.2%.

The index's returns were better when Fed policy was expansive (15.5% per year) than when Fed policy was restrictive (10.6%). As we would expect, an aggressively expansive Fed policy yields returns that are significantly higher (17.3%), and an aggressively restrictive Fed policy results in returns that are significantly lower (2.3%).

The best years for the S&P 500 occurred when Fed policy was expansive late in the Election Cycle. Its average annual return was 19.6% when both cycles were working in the market's favor. When the Fed was aggressively expansive late in the Election Cycle, the average annual return for the S&P 500 jumped to 30.2%.

The S&P 500 achieved its second best performance during Euphoric Years (Restrictive/Late Election Cycle years), with returns averaging 16.9%. Note, however, that the index's performance got worse when the Fed was aggressively restrictive late in the Election Cycle. Although this result is not surprising, it is the opposite of the pattern we observed with nanocaps and small caps. Apparently, there is a flight from quality during Extreme Euphoric Years that favors the performance of nanocaps and small caps.

The worst years for the S&P 500 occurred when the Fed was restrictive early in the Election Cycle, i.e., Panic Years. It returned an average of 3.9% during these years. And when the Fed was aggressively restrictive early in the Election Cycle (Extreme Panic Years), the S&P 500 actually lost an average of 3.8%. This was the only phase in which the S&P 500 lost money.

Exhibit 38B illustrates these patterns in the performance of the S&P 500.

Exhibits 38C–38D summarize the performance data for the S&P 500 by Fed-Election Cycle phase, except that, here, the years are categorized according Fed policy in the prior year.

These exhibits show that when Fed policy was expansive in the prior year, the current year's returns tended to be about the same as returns in years following restrictive years.

However, an aggressive Fed policy in the prior year had a powerful effect on returns. Returns tended to be lower in years following an aggressively expansive policy. Following a year of aggressively restrictive policy, they were significantly lower early in the Election Cycle, but much higher late in the cycle.

The Fed rarely maintains an aggressive monetary policy for more than one year. This happened just twice in our 52-year study period, in 1968-1969 and 1978-1979. On each of these occasions, the Fed was aggressively restrictive for two consecutive years. Most of the time, an aggressive Fed policy is followed either by a directional change or, at a minimum, a less aggressive policy.

Smaller rate cuts, or even rate increases, usually occur in the year following an aggressively expansive policy. This would account for the low returns in years following aggressively expansive policy years. Even if Fed policy does not actually change direction, the market tends to perceive the Fed's less aggressive stance as a policy change and reacts accordingly.

Things get more complicated when the Fed has been aggressively restrictive. If the Fed has been aggressively raising interest rates, chances are good that the sub-par fiscal stimulus associated with the early portion of the Election Cycle will result in a weak economy, anemic corporate profits, and poor equity returns. Even if the Fed abruptly changes course and turns expansive, things often get worse before they get better.

If, on the other hand, the economy has been strong enough to warrant an aggressively restrictive Fed policy, odds are that the late Election Cycle's strong fiscal stimulus will act like gasoline on a fire, affording a favorable environment for stocks.

Exhibit 38E shows the 15 best and 15 worst years for the S&P 500.

In its 15 best years, the S&P 500 averaged a return of 19.1%. Ten of its best years occurred late in the Election Cycle, confirming the influence of the Election Cycle Effect.

However, seven of the S&P 500's best years occurred in restrictive years that followed a prior restrictive year, apparently contradicting the evidence we have seen for the Fed Effect. Wouldn't a restrictive policy lasting two years lead to lower returns?

Not necessarily, or at least not right away.

The Fed adopts a restrictive policy when the economy is growing briskly and inflationary pressures are building, but the Fed's rate increases take time to achieve their purpose. In the meantime, the bearish effects of Fed policy can be overwhelmed by the bullish effects of a strong economy, growing profits, and market momentum. Thus, it should come as no surprise that the market would often advance in restrictive years.

Fed policy was restrictive in 31 (60%) of the 52 years included in our study period, while the total return for the S&P 500 was positive in 39 (75%) of the 52 years. Obviously, there have been many years which the market rose while Fed policy was restrictive—22 to be exact. In 14 of these years, the S&P 500 gained well in excess of its 12.6% average.

When stock prices advance rapidly in the face of restrictive Fed policy, a kind of euphoria overtakes the market. These are times when sober, value-oriented investing is punished, and risk-taking is rewarded. Prices advance rapidly, especially for nanocaps, small caps, and, as we will see, growth stocks. Since these circumstances arise most often late in the Election Cycle, we refer to Restrictive/Late Election Cycle years as Euphoric Years.

We will revisit this topic in the discussion of value versus growth which follows.

Exhibit 33A: Returns by Market Cap by Fed-Election Cycle – Current Years' Rates
100 Smallest Market Caps Over $10 Million vs. 100 Largest

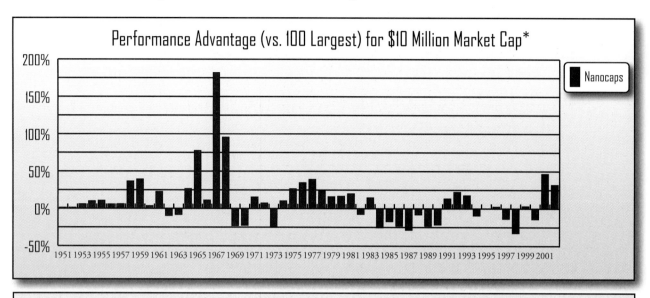

	Expansive	Aggressively Expansive	Restrictive	Aggressively Restrictive	All Years
$10 Million Market Cap*					
Early Election Cycle	13.4%	20.1%	10.6%	-10.8%	11.7%
Late Election Cycle	46.2%	99.7%	25.8%	71.1%	33.6%
All Years	29.0%	50.0%	18.4%	16.5%	22.7%
100 Largest Companies					
Early Election Cycle	10.3%	8.6%	3.9%	-2.4%	6.6%
Late Election Cycle	17.1%	25.6%	15.4%	15.2%	16.1%
All Years	13.6%	14.9%	9.8%	3.5%	11.3%
Difference in Returns (Small Cap Minus Large Cap)					
Early Election Cycle	3.0%	11.6%	6.6%	-8.5%	5.1%
Late Election Cycle	29.0%	74.2%	10.4%	55.9%	17.6%
All Years	15.4%	35.0%	8.6%	13.0%	11.3%

* 100 smallest companies with inflation-adjusted market cap > $10 Million

Exhibit 33B: Returns by Market Cap by Fed-Election Cycle– Current Years' Rates
100 Smallest Market Caps Over $10 Million vs. 100 Largest vs. S&P 500

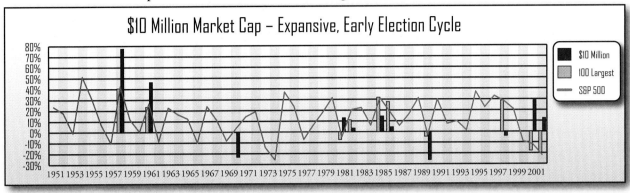

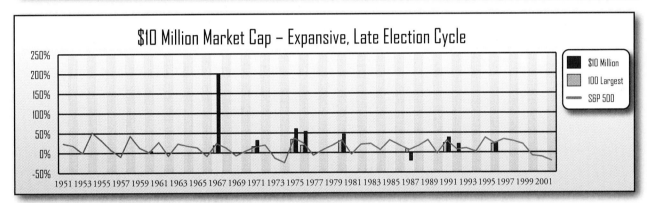

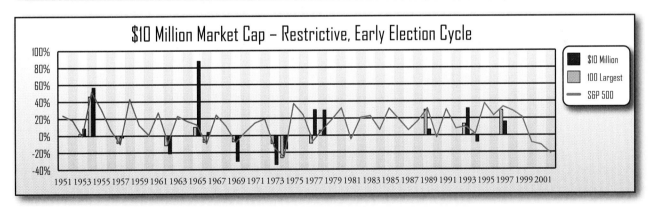

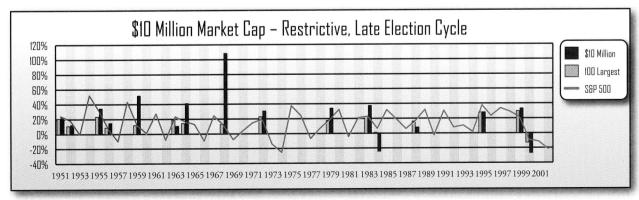

Exhibit 33C: Returns by Market Cap by Fed-Election Cycle – Prior Years' Rates
100 Smallest Market Caps Over $10 Million vs. 100 Largest

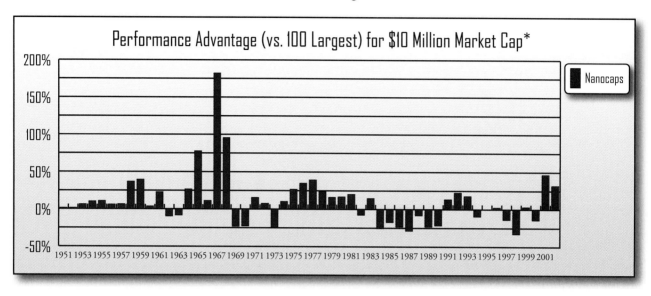

	Expansive	Aggressively Expansive	Restrictive	Aggressively Restrictive	All Years
$10 Million Market Cap*					
Early Election Cycle	15.1%	7.9%	10.0%	-23.2%	11.7%
Late Election Cycle	35.7%	41.1%	32.1%	36.2%	33.6%
All Years	26.4%	32.8%	20.4%	6.5%	22.7%
100 Largest Companies					
Early Election Cycle	6.4%	-4.3%	6.8%	-11.4%	6.6%
Late Election Cycle	16.5%	11.1%	15.7%	25.2%	16.1%
All Years	12.0%	7.3%	11.0%	6.9%	11.3%
Difference in Returns (Small Cap Minus Large Cap)					
Early Election Cycle	8.7%	12.3%	3.2%	-11.8%	5.1%
Late Election Cycle	19.2%	29.9%	16.4%	11.0%	17.6%
All Years	14.5%	25.5%	9.4%	-0.4%	11.3%

* 100 smallest companies with inflation-adjusted market cap > $10 Million

Exhibit 33D: Returns by Market Cap by Fed-Election Cycle– Prior Years' Rates
100 Smallest Market Caps Over $10 Million vs. 100 Largest vs. S&P 500

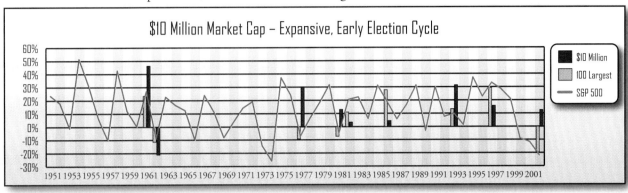

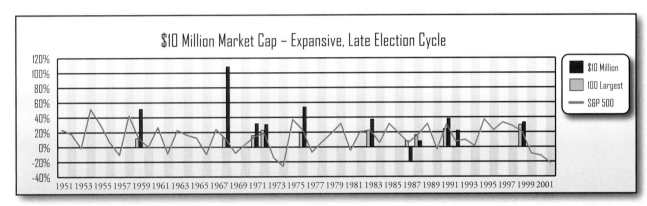

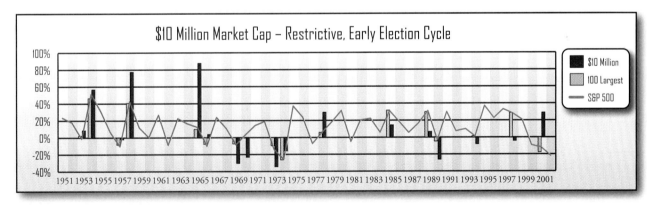

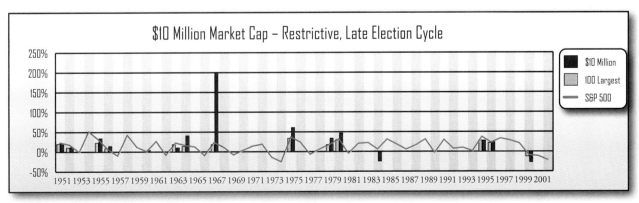

Exhibit 33E: Small Cap vs. Large Cap and the Fed-Election Cycle
100 Smallest Market Caps Over $10 Million– Best & Worst Years vs. 100 Largest

	Fed Policy Analysis			Election Cycle	
	Current Year	Prior Year			
		Expansive	Restrictive	Early	Late
The Best 15 Years for Small Cap:					
Expansive	9	5	4	5	4
Restrictive	6	3	3	3	3
Totals:				8	7
The Best 15 Years for Large Cap:					
Expansive	6	2	4	5	1
Restrictive	9	2	7	6	3
Totals:				11	4
Small Cap Minus Large Cap					
Expansive	3	3	0	0	3
Restrictive	-3	1	-4	-3	0
Totals:				-3	3

The Best 15 Years for Large Cap vs. Small Cap

The Best 15 Years for Large Cap Stocks:

Year	S&P500 Returns	100 Largest Companies	Market Cap > $10 Million	Small Cap - Large Cap
1963	22.50%	18.86%	10.48%	-8.38%
1994	1.28%	1.49%	-7.97%	-9.46%
1962	-8.83%	-11.40%	-21.13%	-9.73%
1997	33.10%	29.44%	15.71%	-13.73%
2000	-9.03%	-12.75%	-26.94%	-14.19%
1985	31.06%	31.75%	14.45%	-17.29%
1990	-3.14%	-4.64%	-26.23%	-21.58%
1970	3.33%	-0.53%	-23.22%	-22.69%
1969	-8.32%	-7.28%	-30.45%	-23.16%
1986	18.54%	27.77%	4.42%	-23.35%
1989	31.23%	29.96%	6.61%	-23.35%
1973	-14.50%	-9.58%	-34.45%	-24.87%
1984	5.97%	1.28%	-24.36%	-25.64%
1987	5.67%	8.20%	-20.52%	-28.72%
1998	28.34%	28.67%	-4.16%	-32.83%
Average Returns	9.15%	8.75%	-11.18%	-19.93%

The Best 15 Years for Small Cap Stocks:

Year	S&P500 Returns	100 Largest Companies	Market Cap > $10 Million	Small Cap - Large Cap
1967	23.73%	18.53%	200.57%	182.04%
1968	10.84%	12.69%	108.23%	95.54%
1965	12.27%	10.00%	87.69%	77.69%
2001	-11.85%	-17.83%	28.96%	46.79%
1959	11.79%	11.89%	51.38%	39.48%
1977	-7.16%	-9.25%	30.12%	39.37%
1958	42.44%	40.66%	77.47%	36.81%
1976	23.64%	18.91%	53.84%	34.94%
2002	-21.97%	-19.65%	12.48%	32.14%
1975	36.92%	33.98%	60.78%	26.80%
1964	16.30%	14.16%	40.91%	26.76%
1978	6.39%	5.90%	29.55%	23.65%
1961	26.60%	23.50%	46.34%	22.85%
1992	7.43%	-0.69%	21.86%	22.55%
1981	-4.85%	-7.26%	12.98%	20.24%
Average Returns	11.50%	9.04%	57.54%	48.51%

Exhibit 34A: Returns by Market Cap by Fed-Election Cycle– Current Years' Rates
100 Smallest Market Caps Over $100 Million vs. 100 Largest

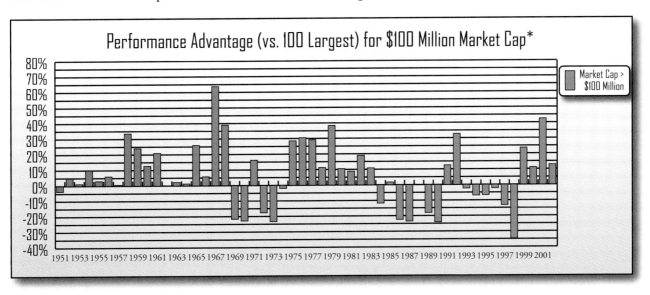

	Expansive	Aggressively Expansive	Restrictive	Aggressively Restrictive	All Years
$100 Million Market Cap*					
Early Election Cycle	13.5%	16.5%	3.7%	-12.5%	7.9%
Late Election Cycle	35.3%	60.5%	23.2%	53.8%	27.8%
All Years	23.9%	33.0%	13.8%	9.6%	17.9%
100 Largest Companies					
Early Election Cycle	10.3%	8.6%	3.9%	-2.4%	6.6%
Late Election Cycle	17.1%	25.6%	15.4%	15.2%	16.1%
All Years	13.6%	14.9%	9.8%	3.5%	11.3%
Difference in Returns (Small Cap Minus Large Cap)					
Early Election Cycle	3.2%	7.9%	-0.2%	-10.2%	1.2%
Late Election Cycle	18.2%	34.9%	7.8%	38.7%	11.8%
All Years	10.3%	18.1%	3.9%	6.1%	6.5%

100 smallest companies with inflation-adjusted market cap > $100 Million

Exhibit 34B: Returns by Market Cap by Fed-Election Cycle– Current Years' Rates
100 Smallest Market Caps Over $100 Million vs. 100 Largest vs. S&P 500

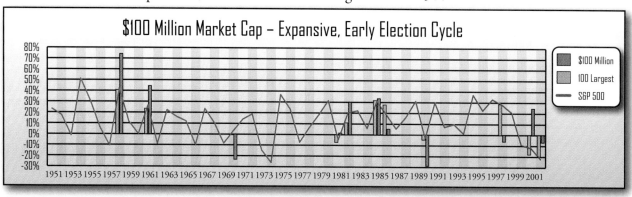

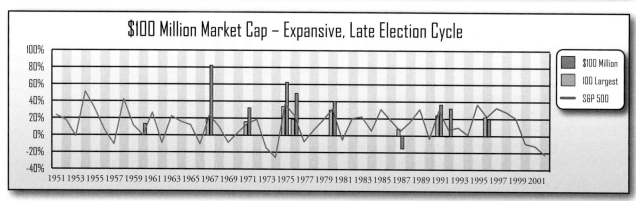

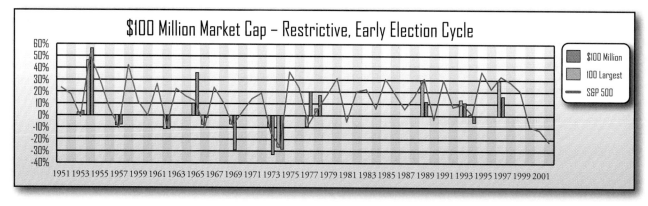

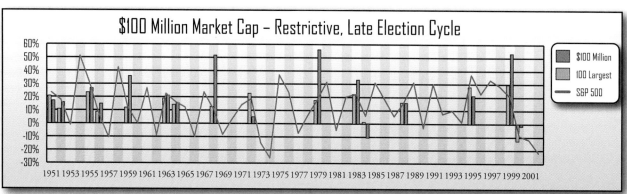

Exhibit 34C: Returns by Market Cap by Fed-Election Cycle – Prior Years' Rates
100 Smallest Market Caps Over $100 Million vs. 100 Largest

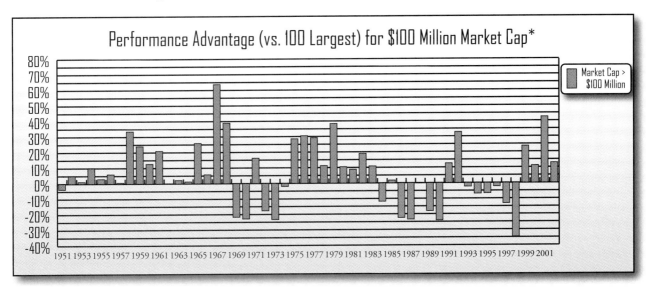

	Expansive	Aggressively Expansive	Restrictive	Aggressively Restrictive	All Years
$100 Million Market Cap*					
Early Election Cycle	12.3%	11.6%	5.5%	-26.9%	7.9%
Late Election Cycle	30.0%	31.0%	26.3%	39.2%	27.8%
All Years	22.0%	26.2%	15.2%	6.2%	17.9%
100 Largest Companies					
Early Election Cycle	6.4%	-4.3%	6.8%	-11.4%	6.6%
Late Election Cycle	16.5%	11.1%	15.7%	25.2%	16.1%
All Years	12.0%	7.3%	11.0%	6.9%	11.3%
Difference in Returns (Small Cap Minus Large Cap)					
Early Election Cycle	5.9%	15.9%	-1.2%	-15.5%	1.2%
Late Election Cycle	13.5%	19.8%	10.5%	14.1%	11.8%
All Years	10.1%	18.9%	4.3%	-0.7%	6.5%

100 smallest companies with inflation-adjusted market cap > $100 Million

Exhibit 34D: Returns by Market Cap by Fed-Election Cycle– Prior Years' Rates
100 Smallest Market Caps Over $100 Million vs. 100 Largest vs. S&P 500

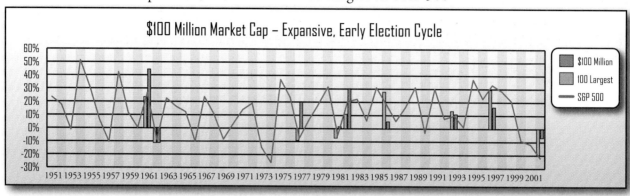

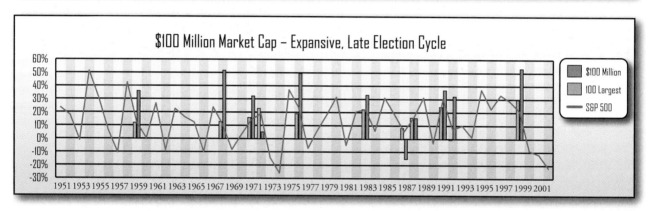

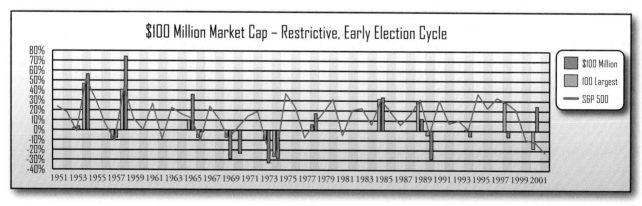

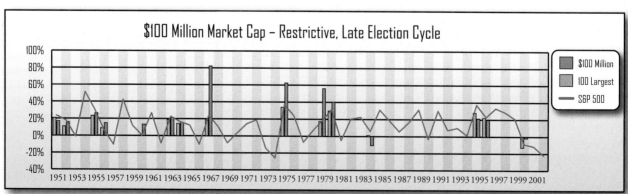

Exhibit 34E: Small Cap vs. Large Cap and the Fed-Election Cycle
100 Smallest Market Caps Over $100 Million– Best & Worst Years vs. 100 Largest

Fed Policy Analysis

	Current Year	Prior Year			Election Cycle	
		Expansive	Restrictive		Early	Late
The Best 15 Years for Small Cap:						
Expansive	9	5	4		4	5
Restrictive	6	4	2		2	4
Totals:					6	9
The Best 15 Years for Large Cap:						
Expansive	6	2	4		4	2
Restrictive	9	3	6		6	3
Totals:					10	5
Small Cap Minus Large Cap						
Expansive	3	3	0		0	3
Restrictive	-3	1	-4		-4	1
Totals:					-4	4

The Best 15 Years for Large Cap vs. Small Cap

The Best 15 Years for Large Cap Stocks:

Year	S&P 500 Returns	100 Largest Companies	Market Cap > $100 Million	Small Cap - Large Cap
1996	22.68%	22.07%	19.73%	-2.34%
1993	9.94%	13.39%	10.99%	-2.40%
1995	37.11%	27.97%	21.29%	-6.68%
1994	1.28%	1.49%	-5.44%	-6.93%
1984	5.97%	1.28%	-10.54%	-11.82%
1997	33.10%	29.44%	16.31%	-13.13%
1972	18.88%	22.78%	5.11%	-17.67%
1989	31.23%	29.96%	11.88%	-18.07%
1969	-8.32%	-7.28%	-28.96%	-21.68%
1986	18.54%	27.77%	5.37%	-22.40%
1970	3.33%	-0.53%	-23.36%	-22.83%
1973	-14.50%	-9.58%	-32.92%	-23.34%
1987	5.67%	8.20%	-15.28%	-23.48%
1990	-3.14%	-4.64%	-28.74%	-24.10%
1998	28.34%	28.67%	-6.03%	-34.70%
Average Returns	12.67%	12.73%	-4.04%	-16.77%

The Best 15 Years for Small Cap Stocks:

Year	S&P 500 Returns	100 Largest Companies	Market Cap > $100 Million	Small Cap - Large Cap
1967	23.73%	18.53%	82.23%	63.71%
2001	-11.85%	-17.83%	24.68%	42.51%
1968	10.84%	12.69%	51.64%	38.95%
1979	18.19%	17.67%	56.04%	38.38%
1958	42.44%	40.66%	74.19%	33.53%
1992	7.43%	-0.69%	32.14%	32.83%
1976	23.64%	18.91%	49.40%	30.50%
1977	-7.16%	-9.25%	19.96%	29.21%
1975	36.92%	33.98%	62.51%	28.53%
1965	12.27%	10.00%	35.90%	25.90%
1959	11.79%	11.89%	35.90%	24.01%
1999	20.88%	29.67%	53.30%	23.64%
1961	26.60%	23.50%	44.45%	20.95%
1982	20.37%	11.03%	30.03%	19.00%
1971	14.15%	15.87%	32.14%	16.27%
Average Returns	16.68%	14.44%	45.64%	31.19%

Exhibit 35A: Returns by Market Cap by Fed-Election Cycle– Current Years' Rates
100 Smallest Market Caps Over $250 Million vs. 100 Largest

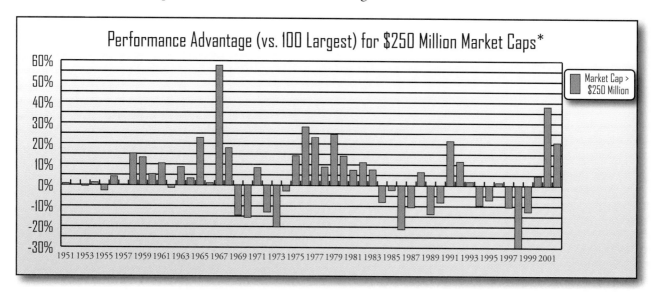

	Expansive	Aggressively Expansive	Restrictive	Aggressively Restrictive	All Years
$250 Million Market Caps*					
Early Election Cycle	12.7%	13.4%	3.0%	-11.2%	7.1%
Late Election Cycle	32.4%	56.7%	18.4%	36.5%	23.8%
All Years	22.1%	29.6%	11.0%	4.7%	15.4%
100 Largest Companies					
Early Election Cycle	10.3%	8.6%	3.9%	-2.4%	6.6%
Late Election Cycle	17.1%	25.6%	15.4%	15.2%	16.1%
All Years	13.6%	14.9%	9.8%	3.5%	11.3%
Difference in Returns (Small Cap Minus Large Cap)					
Early Election Cycle	2.4%	4.8%	-0.9%	-8.8%	0.5%
Late Election Cycle	15.2%	31.2%	3.0%	21.3%	7.7%
All Years	8.5%	14.7%	1.1%	1.2%	4.1%

100 smallest companies with inflation-adjusted market cap > $250 Million

Exhibit 35B: Returns by Market Cap by Fed-Election Cycle– Current Years' Rates
100 Smallest Market Caps Over $250 Million vs. 100 Largest vs. S&P 500

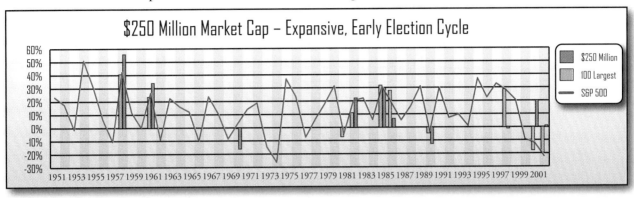

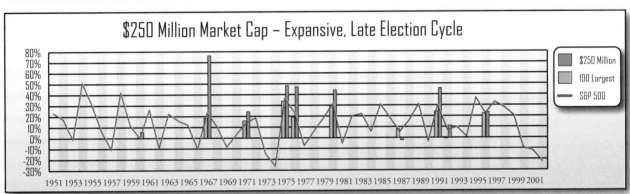

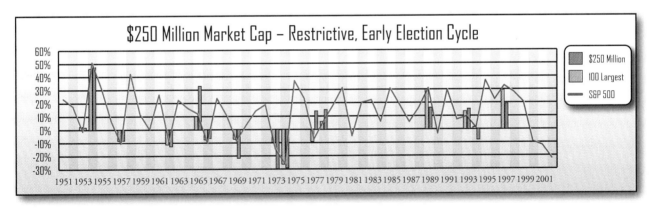

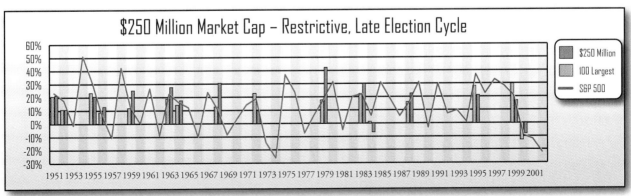

Exhibit 35C: Returns by Market Cap by Fed-Election Cycle– Prior Years' Rates
100 Smallest Market Caps Over $250 Million vs. 100 Largest

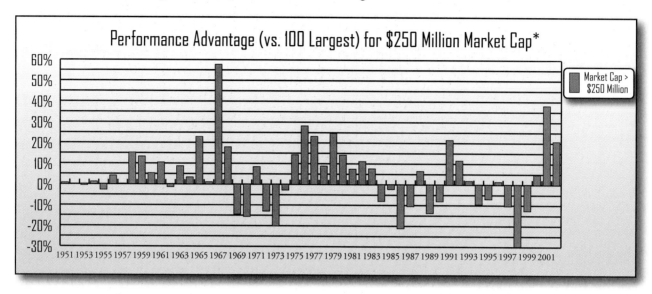

	Expansive	Aggressively Expansive	Restrictive	Aggressively Restrictive	All Years
$250 Million Market Cap*					
Early Election Cycle	11.1%	11.6%	5.0%	-22.4%	7.1%
Late Election Cycle	23.7%	22.6%	23.8%	35.8%	23.8%
All Years	18.0%	19.9%	13.8%	6.7%	15.4%
100 Largest Companies					
Early Election Cycle	6.4%	-4.3%	6.8%	-11.4%	6.6%
Late Election Cycle	16.5%	11.1%	15.7%	25.2%	16.1%
All Years	12.0%	7.3%	11.0%	6.9%	11.3%
Difference in Returns (Small Cap Minus Large Cap)					
Early Election Cycle	4.7%	15.9%	-1.7%	-11.0%	0.5%
Late Election Cycle	7.2%	11.5%	8.1%	10.6%	7.7%
All Years	6.0%	12.6%	2.9%	-0.2%	4.1%

* 100 smallest companies with inflation-adjusted market cap > $250 Million

Exhibit 35D: Returns by Market Cap by Fed-Election Cycle– Prior Years' Rates
100 Smallest Market Caps Over $250 Million vs. 100 Largest vs. S&P 500

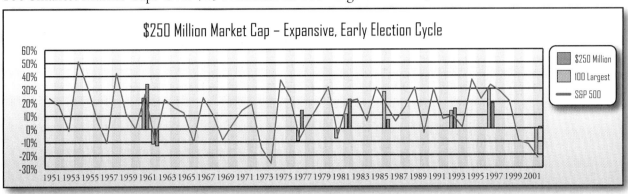

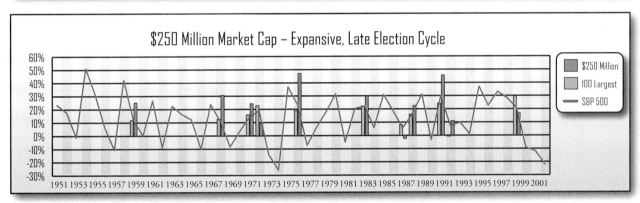

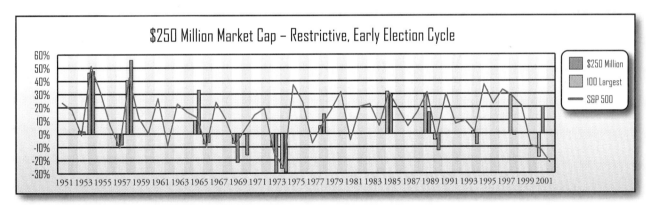

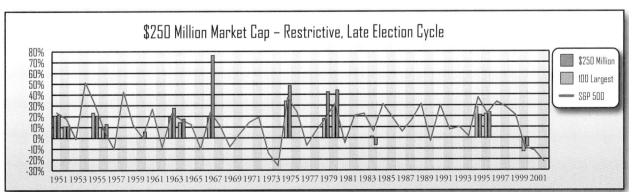

Exhibit 35E: Small Cap vs. Large Cap and the Fed-Election Cycle
100 Smallest Market Caps Over $250 Million– Best & Worst Years vs. 100 Largest

| | Fed Policy Analysis | | | Election Cycle | |
| | Current Year | Prior Year | | | |
		Expansive	Restrictive	Early	Late
The Best 15 Years for Small Cap:					
Expansive	10	5	5	4	6
Restrictive	5	3	2	2	3
Totals				6	9
The Best 15 Years for Large Cap:					
Expansive	5	2	3	4	1
Restrictive	10	3	7	6	4
Totals:				10	5
Small Cap Minus Large Cap					
Expansive	5	3	2	0	5
Restrictive	-5	0	-5	-4	-1
Totals				-4	4

The Best 15 Years for Large Cap vs. Small Cap

The Best 15 Years for Large Cap Stocks:

Year	S&P 500 Returns	100 Largest Companies	Market Cap > $250 Million	Small Cap - Large Cap
1974	-26.03%	-26.39%	-29.15%	-2.76%
1995	37.11%	27.97%	21.06%	-6.90%
1984	5.97%	1.28%	-6.70%	-7.97%
1990	-3.14%	-4.64%	-12.71%	-8.07%
1994	1.28%	1.49%	-8.10%	-9.59%
1997	33.10%	29.44%	19.10%	-10.35%
1987	5.67%	8.20%	-2.29%	-10.49%
1999	20.88%	29.67%	17.07%	-12.60%
1972	18.88%	22.78%	9.76%	-13.02%
1989	31.23%	29.96%	16.16%	-13.80%
1969	-8.32%	-7.28%	-21.77%	-14.48%
1970	3.33%	-0.53%	-16.15%	-15.61%
1973	-14.50%	-9.58%	-29.69%	-20.11%
1986	18.54%	27.77%	6.62%	-21.15%
1998	28.34%	28.67%	-1.16%	-29.83%
Average Returns	10.16%	10.59%	-2.53%	-13.12%

The Best 15 Years for Small Cap Stocks:

Year	S&P 500 Returns	100 Largest Companies	Market Cap > $250 Million	Small Cap - Large Cap
1967	23.73%	18.53%	76.28%	57.75%
2001	-11.85%	-17.83%	20.28%	38.10%
1976	23.64%	18.91%	47.12%	28.22%
1979	18.19%	17.67%	42.35%	24.68%
1977	-7.16%	-9.25%	13.87%	23.12%
1965	12.27%	10.00%	32.89%	22.89%
1991	30.00%	24.21%	45.69%	21.48%
2002	-21.97%	-19.65%	1.11%	20.77%
1968	10.84%	12.69%	30.59%	17.90%
1958	42.44%	40.66%	55.85%	15.19%
1975	36.92%	33.98%	48.21%	14.23%
1980	31.52%	29.86%	44.01%	14.15%
1959	11.79%	11.89%	25.19%	13.30%
1992	7.43%	-0.69%	10.90%	11.59%
1982	20.37%	11.03%	22.15%	11.13%
Average Returns	15.21%	12.13%	34.43%	22.30%

Exhibit 36A: Returns by Market Cap by Fed-Election Cycle– Current Years' Rates
100 Smallest Market Caps Over $500 Million vs. 100 Largest

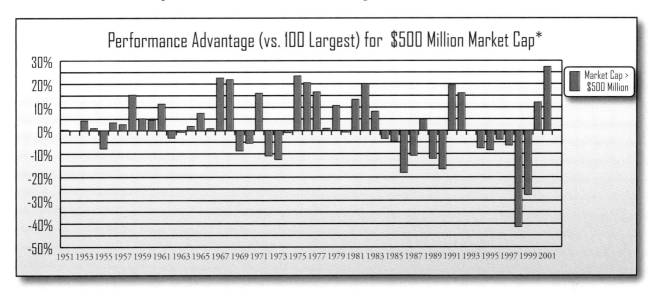

	Expansive	Aggressively Expansive	Restrictive	Aggressively Restrictive	All Years
$500 Million Market Cap*					
Early Election Cycle	10.4%	15.1%	2.7%	-9.4%	6.0%
Late Election Cycle	27.9%	47.4%	16.0%	31.5%	20.6%
All Years	18.7%	27.2%	9.6%	4.3%	13.3%
100 Largest Companies					
Early Election Cycle	10.3%	8.6%	3.9%	-2.4%	6.6%
Late Election Cycle	17.1%	25.6%	15.4%	15.2%	16.1%
All Years	13.6%	14.9%	9.8%	3.5%	11.3%
Difference in Returns (Small Cap Minus Large Cap)					
Early Election Cycle	0.1%	6.5%	-1.2%	-7.0%	-0.6%
Late Election Cycle	10.7%	21.8%	0.6%	16.3%	4.5%
All Years	5.2%	12.3%	-0.3%	0.8%	1.9%

* 100 smallest companies with inflation-adjusted market cap > $500 Million

Exhibit 36B: Returns by Market Cap by Fed-Election Cycle– Current Years' Rates
100 Smallest Market Caps Over $500 Million vs. 100 Largest vs. S&P 500

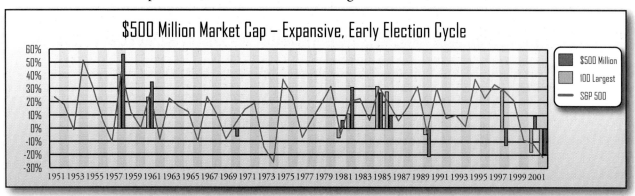

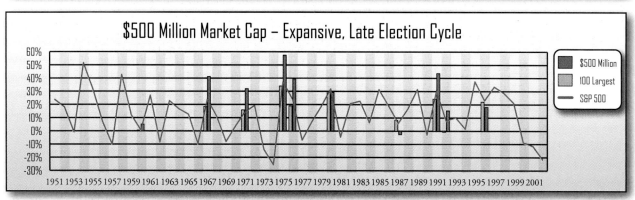

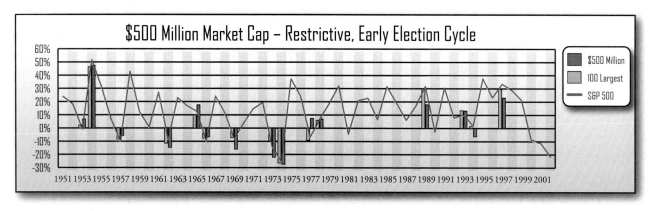

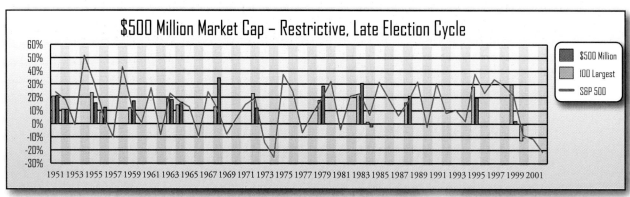

Exhibit 36C: Returns by Market Cap by Fed-Election Cycle – Prior Years' Rates
100 Smallest Market Caps Over $500 Million vs. 100 Largest

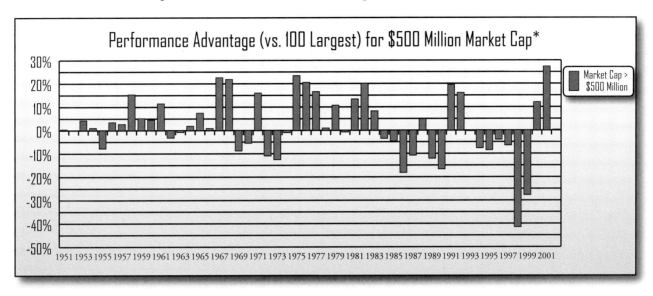

	Expansive	Aggressively Expansive	Restrictive	Aggressively Restrictive	All Years
$500 Million Market Cap*					
Early Election Cycle	10.1%	5.9%	3.8%	-16.5%	6.0%
Late Election Cycle	22.3%	22.6%	19.3%	25.7%	20.6%
All Years	16.8%	18.4%	11.1%	4.6%	13.3%
100 Largest Companies					
Early Election Cycle	6.4%	-4.3%	6.8%	-11.4%	6.6%
Late Election Cycle	16.5%	11.1%	15.7%	25.2%	16.1%
All Years	12.0%	7.3%	11.0%	6.9%	11.3%
Difference in Returns (Small Cap Minus Large Cap)					
Early Election Cycle	3.7%	10.2%	-2.9%	-5.1%	-0.6%
Late Election Cycle	5.7%	11.5%	3.6%	0.5%	4.5%
All Years	4.8%	11.2%	0.1%	-2.3%	1.9%

100 smallest companies with inflation-adjusted market cap > $500 Million

Exhibit 36D: Returns by Market Cap by Fed-Election Cycle– Prior Years' Rates
100 Smallest Market Caps Over $500 Million vs. 100 Largest vs. S&P 500

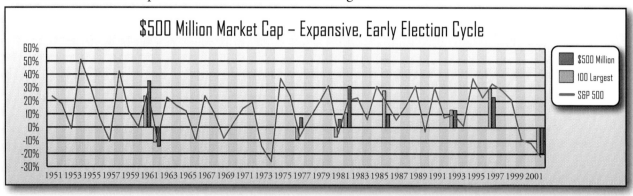

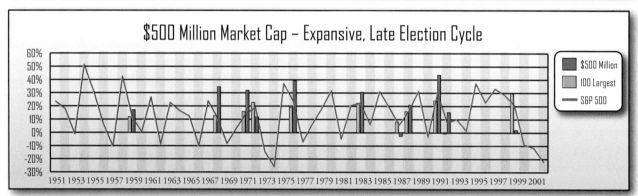

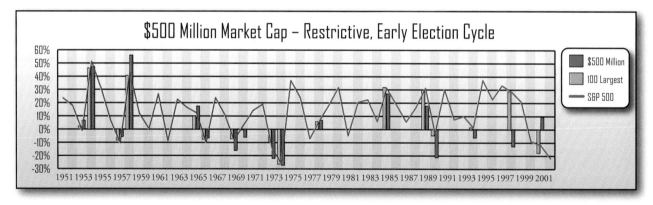

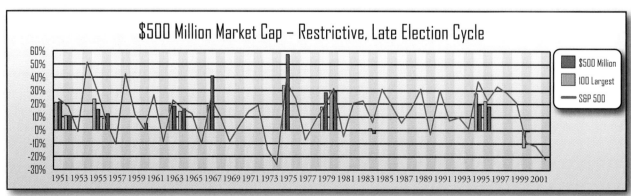

Exhibit 36E: Small Cap vs. Large Cap and the Fed-Election Cycle
100 Smallest Market Caps Over $500 Million– Best & Worst Years vs. 100 Largest

	Fed Policy Analysis			Election Cycle	
	Current Year	Prior Year		Early	Late
		Expansive	Restrictive		
The Best 15 Years for Small Cap:					
Expansive	11	7	4	5	6
Restrictive	4	2	2	1	3
Totals				6	9
The Best 15 Years for Large Cap:					
Expansive	6	2	4	5	1
Restrictive	9	3	6	5	4
Totals:				10	5
Small Cap Minus Large Cap					
Expansive	5	5	0	0	5
Restrictive	-5	-1	-4	-4	-1
Totals				-4	4

The Best 15 Years for Large Cap vs. Small Cap

The Best 15 Years for Large Cap Stocks:

Year	S&P 500 Returns	100 Largest Companies	Market Cap > $500 Million	Small Cap - Large Cap
1985	31.06%	31.75%	26.98%	-4.76%
1970	3.33%	-0.53%	-6.02%	-5.49%
1997	33.10%	29.44%	22.98%	-6.47%
1994	1.28%	1.49%	-6.15%	-7.64%
1955	30.96%	23.37%	15.58%	-7.79%
1995	37.11%	27.97%	19.48%	-8.48%
1969	-8.32%	-7.28%	-16.05%	-8.77%
1987	5.67%	8.20%	-2.58%	-10.78%
1972	18.88%	22.78%	11.83%	-10.94%
1989	31.23%	29.96%	17.85%	-12.10%
1973	-14.50%	-9.58%	-22.11%	-12.53%
1990	-3.14%	-4.64%	-21.28%	-16.63%
1986	18.54%	27.77%	9.61%	-18.15%
1999	20.88%	29.67%	2.00%	-27.67%
1998	28.34%	28.67%	-12.80%	-41.47%
Average Returns	15.63%	15.93%	2.62%	-13.31%

The Best 15 Years for Small Cap Stocks:

Year	S&P 500 Returns	100 Largest Companies	Market Cap > $500 Million	Small Cap - Large Cap
2001	-11.85%	-17.83%	9.55%	27.37%
1975	36.92%	33.98%	57.41%	23.43%
1967	23.73%	18.53%	41.13%	22.60%
1968	10.84%	12.69%	34.54%	21.85%
1976	23.64%	18.91%	39.43%	20.52%
1982	20.37%	11.03%	31.06%	20.04%
1991	30.00%	24.21%	43.69%	19.49%
1977	-7.16%	-9.25%	7.33%	16.58%
1992	7.43%	-0.69%	15.41%	16.09%
1971	14.15%	15.87%	31.91%	16.04%
1958	42.44%	40.66%	56.02%	15.36%
1981	-4.85%	-7.26%	6.13%	13.39%
2000	-9.03%	-12.75%	-0.64%	12.11%
1961	26.60%	23.50%	34.98%	11.49%
1979	18.19%	17.67%	28.41%	10.74%
Average Returns	14.76%	11.28%	29.09%	17.81%

Exhibit 37A: Returns by Market Cap by Fed-Election Cycle – Current Years' Rates
100 Smallest Market Caps Over $1 Billion vs. 100 Largest

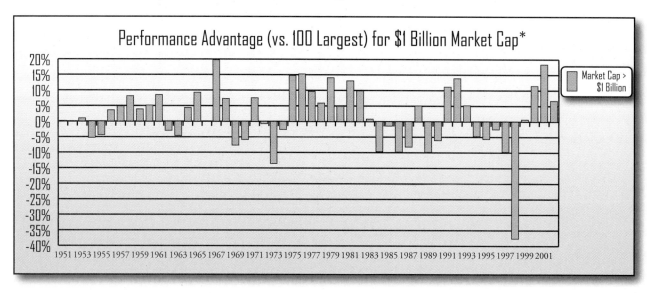

	Expansive	Aggressively Expansive	Restrictive	Aggressively Restrictive	All Years
$1 Billion Market Cap*					
Early Election Cycle	10.7%	13.3%	2.6%	-7.4%	6.0%
Late Election Cycle	25.3%	40.8%	17.0%	25.9%	20.2%
All Years	17.6%	23.6%	10.0%	3.7%	13.1%
100 Largest Companies					
Early Election Cycle	10.3%	8.6%	3.9%	-2.4%	6.6%
Late Election Cycle	17.1%	25.6%	15.4%	15.2%	16.1%
All Years	13.6%	14.9%	9.8%	3.5%	11.3%
Difference in Returns (Small Cap Minus Large Cap)					
Early Election Cycle	0.4%	4.8%	-1.4%	-5.0%	-0.6%
Late Election Cycle	8.2%	15.2%	1.6%	10.7%	4.2%
All Years	4.1%	8.7%	0.2%	0.2%	1.8%

100 smallest companies with inflation-adjusted market cap > $1 Billion

Exhibit 37B: Returns by Market Cap by Fed-Election Cycle– Current Years' Rates
100 Smallest Market Caps Over $1 Billion vs. 100 Largest vs. S&P 500

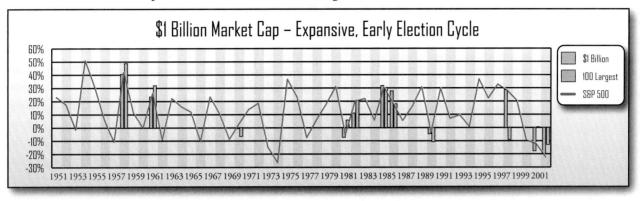

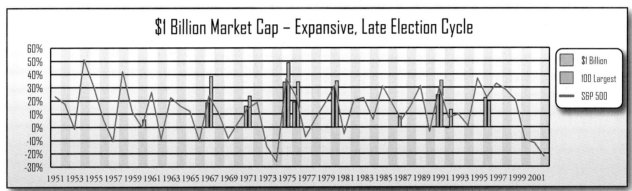

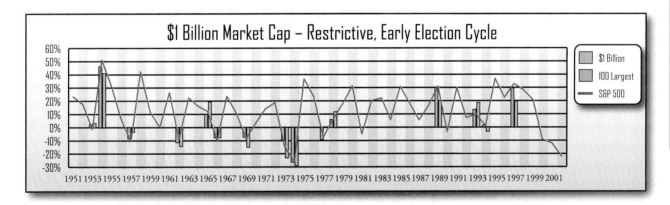

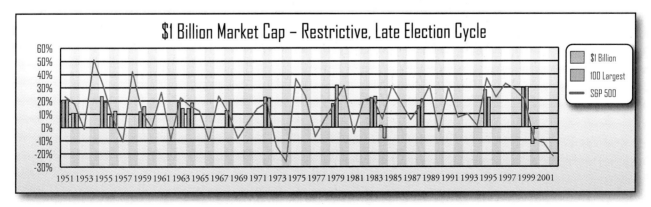

Exhibit 37C: Returns by Market Cap by Fed-Election Cycle – Prior Years' Rates
100 Smallest Market Caps Over $1 Billion vs. 100 Largest

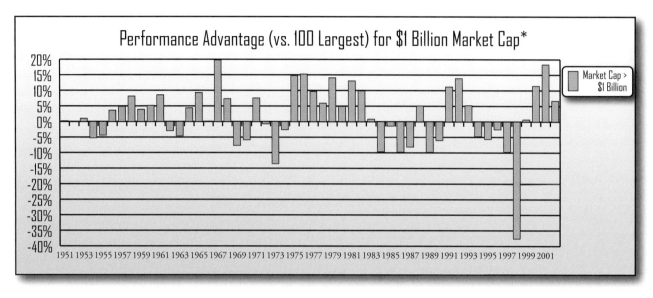

	Expansive	Aggressively Expansive	Restrictive	Aggressively Restrictive	All Years
$1 Billion Market Cap*					
Early Election Cycle	9.8%	4.0%	4.0%	-16.8%	6.0%
Late Election Cycle	21.7%	17.8%	19.1%	29.6%	20.2%
All Years	16.3%	14.3%	11.1%	6.4%	13.1%
100 Largest Companies					
Early Election Cycle	6.4%	-4.3%	6.8%	-11.4%	6.6%
Late Election Cycle	16.5%	11.1%	15.7%	25.2%	16.1%
All Years	12.0%	7.3%	11.0%	6.9%	11.3%
Difference in Returns (Small Cap Minus Large Cap)					
Early Election Cycle	3.4%	8.3%	-2.8%	-5.4%	-0.6%
Late Election Cycle	5.2%	6.6%	3.4%	4.4%	4.2%
All Years	4.4%	7.0%	0.1%	-0.5%	1.8%

* 100 smallest companies with inflation-adjusted market cap > $1 Billion

Exhibit 37D: Returns by Market Cap by Fed-Election Cycle– Prior Years' Rates
100 Smallest Market Caps Over $1 Billion vs. 100 Largest vs. S&P 500

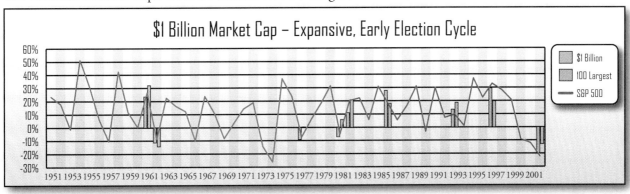

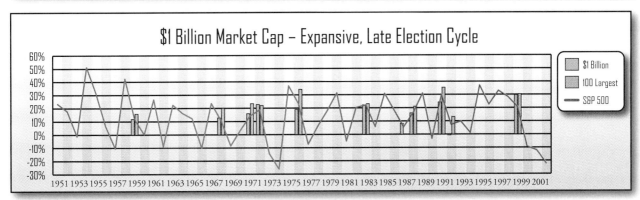

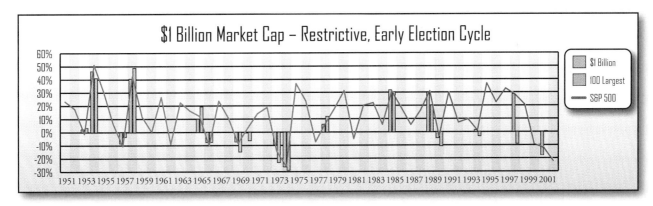

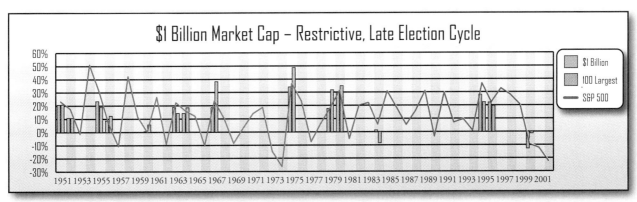

Exhibit 37E: Small Cap vs. Large Cap and the Fed-Election Cycle
100 Smallest Market Caps Over $1 Billion– Best & Worst Years vs. 100 Largest

	Fed Policy Analysis			Election Cycle	
	Current Year	Prior Year			
		Expansive	Restrictive	Early	Late
The Best 15 Years for Small Cap:					
Expansive	11	7	4	5	6
Restrictive	4	1	3	2	2
Totals				7	8
The Best 15 Years for Large Cap:					
Expansive	5	2	3	4	1
Restrictive	10	1	9	6	4
Totals:				10	5
Small Cap Minus Large Cap					
Expansive	6	5	1	1	5
Restrictive	-6	0	-6	-4	-2
Totals				-3	3

The Best 15 Years for Large Cap vs. Small Cap

The Best 15 Years for Large Cap Stocks:

Year	S&P 500 Returns	100 Largest Companies	Market Cap > $1 Billion	Small Cap - Large Cap
1955	30.96%	23.37%	18.98%	-4.39%
1963	22.50%	18.86%	14.25%	-4.61%
1994	1.28%	1.49%	-3.27%	-4.77%
1954	51.23%	46.32%	41.07%	-5.24%
1995	37.11%	27.97%	22.33%	-5.64%
1970	3.33%	-0.53%	-6.42%	-5.89%
1990	-3.14%	-4.64%	-10.71%	-6.07%
1969	-8.32%	-7.28%	-15.00%	-7.72%
1987	5.67%	8.20%	0.04%	-8.16%
1984	5.97%	1.28%	-8.40%	-9.68%
1997	33.10%	29.44%	19.66%	-9.78%
1986	18.54%	27.77%	17.98%	-9.79%
1989	31.23%	29.96%	20.12%	-9.83%
1973	-14.50%	-9.58%	-23.14%	-13.56%
1998	28.34%	28.67%	-8.96%	-37.63%
Average Returns	16.22%	14.75%	5.23%	-9.52%

The Best 15 Years for Small Cap Stocks:

Year	S&P 500 Returns	100 Largest Companies	Market Cap > $1 Billion	Small Cap - Large Cap
1967	23.73%	18.53%	38.29%	19.76%
2001	-11.85%	-17.83%	0.54%	18.36%
1976	23.64%	18.91%	34.14%	15.23%
1975	36.92%	33.98%	48.74%	14.76%
1979	18.19%	17.67%	31.71%	14.05%
1992	7.43%	-0.69%	13.17%	13.86%
1981	-4.85%	-7.26%	5.80%	13.06%
2000	-9.03%	-12.75%	-1.30%	11.45%
1991	30.00%	24.21%	35.36%	11.16%
1982	20.37%	11.03%	20.89%	9.86%
1977	-7.16%	-9.25%	0.40%	9.65%
1965	12.27%	10.00%	19.28%	9.27%
1961	26.60%	23.50%	32.03%	8.53%
1958	42.44%	40.66%	48.79%	8.13%
1971	14.15%	15.87%	23.42%	7.55%
Average Returns	14.86%	11.11%	23.42%	12.31%

Exhibit 38A: Returns by Market Cap by Fed-Election Cycle– Current Years' Rates
S&P 500 vs. 100 Largest– Graph & Table

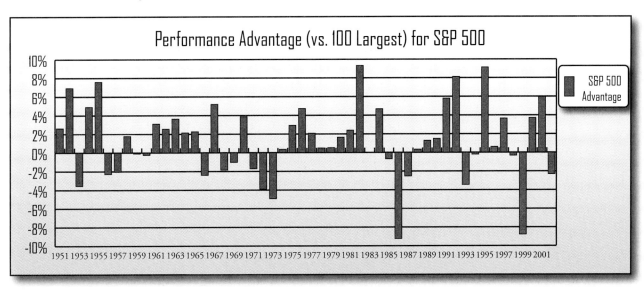

	Expansive	Aggressively Expansive	Restrictive	Aggressively Restrictive	All Years
S&P 500					
Early Election Cycle	11.7%	9.5%	3.9%	-3.8%	7.2%
Late Election Cycle	19.6%	30.2%	16.9%	14.5%	17.9%
All Years	15.5%	17.3%	10.6%	2.3%	12.6%
100 Largest Companies					
Early Election Cycle	10.3%	8.6%	3.9%	-2.4%	6.6%
Late Election Cycle	17.1%	25.6%	15.4%	15.2%	16.1%
All Years	13.6%	14.9%	9.8%	3.5%	11.3%
Difference in Returns (S&P 500 Minus Large Cap)					
Early Election Cycle	1.4%	1.0%	0.0%	-1.4%	0.6%
Late Election Cycle	2.5%	4.6%	1.5%	-0.7%	1.9%
All Years	1.9%	2.3%	0.8%	-1.2%	1.2%

Exhibit 38B: The Fed-Election Cycle and Market Cap– Current Years' Rates
S&P 500 vs. 100 Largest– Graphs

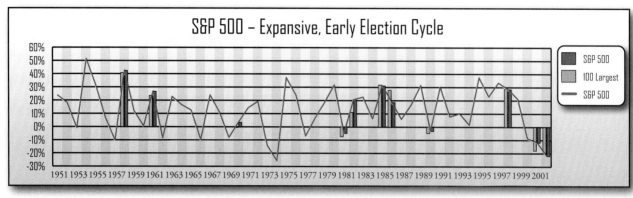

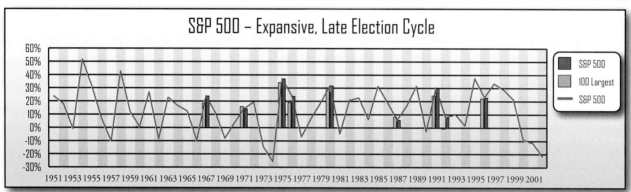

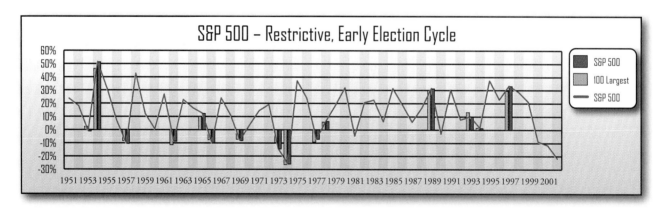

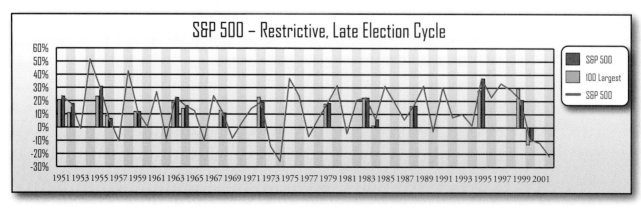

Exhibit 38C: Returns by Market Cap by Fed-Election Cycle– Prior Years' Rates
S&P 500 vs. 100 Largest– Graph & Table

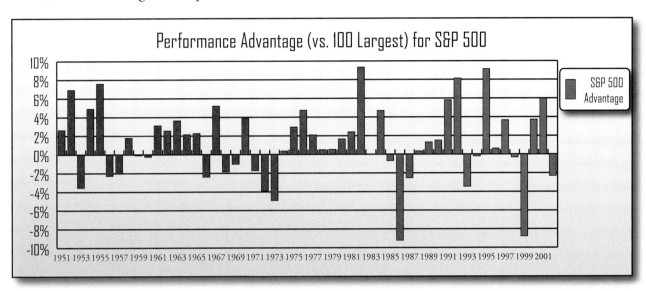

	Expansive	Aggressively Expansive	Restrictive	Aggressively Restrictive	All Years
S&P 500					
Early Election Cycle	7.3%	-0.8%	7.2%	-10.3%	7.2%
Late Election Cycle	16.5%	12.3%	19.0%	28.9%	17.9%
All Years	12.4%	9.0%	12.7%	9.3%	12.6%
100 Largest Companies					
Early Election Cycle	6.4%	-4.3%	6.8%	-11.4%	6.6%
Late Election Cycle	16.5%	11.1%	15.7%	25.2%	16.1%
All Years	12.0%	7.3%	11.0%	6.9%	11.3%
Difference in Returns (S&P 500 Minus Large Cap)					
Early Election Cycle	0.9%	3.5%	0.4%	1.1%	0.6%
Late Election Cycle	0.0%	1.1%	3.3%	3.8%	1.9%
All Years	0.4%	1.7%	1.8%	2.4%	1.2%

Exhibit 38D: Returns by Market Cap by Fed-Election Cycle– Prior Years' Rates
S&P 500 vs. 100 Largest– Graphs

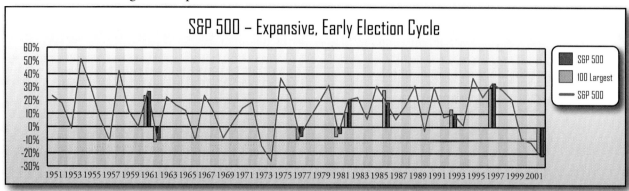

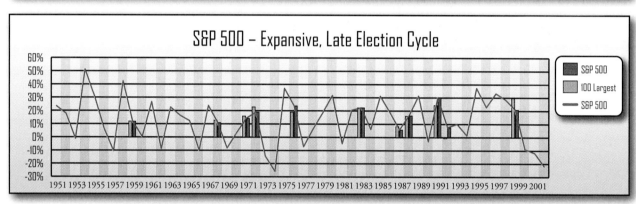

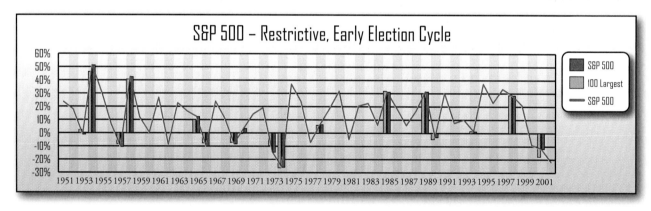

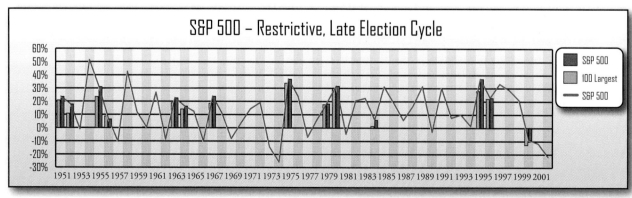

Exhibit 38E: Small Cap vs. Large Cap and the Fed-Election Cycle
S&P 500– Best & Worst Years vs. 100 Largest

	Fed Policy Analysis			Election Cycle	
	Current Year	Prior Year			
		Expansive	Restrictive	Early	Late
The Best 15 Years for Small Cap:					
Expansive	7	4	3	3	4
Restrictive	8	1	7	2	6
Totals:				5	10
The Best 15 Years for Large Cap:					
Expansive	5	4	1	3	2
Restrictive	10	4	6	6	4
Totals				9	6
Small Cap Minus Large Cap					
Expansive	2	0	2	0	2
Restrictive	-2	-3	1	-4	2
Totals				-4	4

The Best 15 Years for Large Cap vs. Small Cap

The Best 15 Years for Large Cap Stocks:

Year	100 Largest Companies	S&P 500 Returns	Small Cap - Large Cap
1985	31.75%	31.06%	-0.69%
1969	-7.28%	-8.32%	-1.03%
1971	15.87%	14.15%	-1.72%
1968	12.69%	10.84%	-1.85%
1957	-8.43%	-10.48%	-2.04%
1956	8.72%	6.44%	-2.28%
2002	-19.65%	-21.97%	-2.31%
1966	-7.59%	-9.99%	-2.40%
1987	8.20%	5.67%	-2.53%
1993	13.39%	9.94%	-3.45%
1953	2.38%	-1.17%	-3.55%
1972	22.78%	18.88%	-3.90%
1973	-9.58%	-14.50%	-4.92%
1999	29.67%	20.88%	-8.78%
1986	27.77%	18.54%	-9.23%
Average Returns	8.04%	4.67%	-3.38%

The Best 15 Years for Small Cap Stocks:

Year	100 Largest Companies	S&P 500 Returns	Small Cap - Large Cap
1982	11.03%	20.37%	9.34%
1995	27.97%	37.11%	9.14%
1992	-0.69%	7.43%	8.12%
1955	23.37%	30.96%	7.59%
1952	10.78%	17.71%	6.93%
2001	-17.83%	-11.85%	5.97%
1991	24.21%	30.00%	5.80%
1967	18.53%	23.73%	5.20%
1954	46.32%	51.23%	4.91%
1976	18.91%	23.64%	4.73%
1984	1.28%	5.97%	4.69%
1970	-0.53%	3.33%	3.87%
2000	-12.75%	-9.03%	3.72%
1997	29.44%	33.10%	3.66%
1963	18.86%	22.50%	3.64%
Average Returns	13.26%	19.08%	5.82%

The Fed-Election Cycle and Price/Earnings

Exhibit 39A compares the performance of low P/E stocks to that of high P/E stocks in each phase of the Fed-Election Cycle.

The bar chart at the top of the exhibit illustrates the performance advantage of low P/E stocks over high P/E stocks. Bars above the zero line indicate years in which low P/E stocks outperformed high P/E stocks.

During the 52 years from 1951 to 2002, low P/E stocks outperformed high P/E stocks 47 times (90.4% of the time), by an average of 26.0% per year in those 47 years. High P/E outperformed low P/E a total of five times (9.6% of the time), by an average of 9.8% per year.

Low P/E stocks averaged annual returns of 41.3% late in the Election Cycle, versus an average of 26.4% during the early years of the cycle. Low P/E stocks responded to an expansive Fed policy with average annual returns of 40.6%, versus the 29.2% they returned when Fed policy was restrictive.

The low P/E strategy made money, on average, in every phase of the Fed-Election Cycle.

High P/E stocks averaged annual returns of 23.3% in late Election Cycle years, versus a loss of 0.8% during the early years of the cycle. They responded to an expansive Fed policy with average annual returns of 14.1%, versus the 9.4% they returned when Fed policy was restrictive.

The high P/E strategy lost money, on average, early in the Election Cycle when Fed policy was expansive and eked out a tiny gain when Fed policy was restrictive (although it lost big during Extreme Panic Years). High P/E made money, however, late in the Election Cycle, whether Fed policy was expansive or restrictive.

Low P/E outperformed high P/E in all four primary phases of the Fed-Election Cycle. The superior performance of low P/E is most evident early in the Election Cycle and during periods of expansive Fed policy.

Low P/E stocks' best performance vis-à-vis high P/E occurred early in the Election Cycle when Fed policy was expansive. Low P/E's performance advantage during this phase was 36.1%. During the early Election Cycle years when Fed policy was aggressively expansive, low P/E stocks outperformed high P/E by 42.7%.

Low P/E stocks were far more likely to outperform high P/E stocks early in the Election Cycle. As we saw in **Exhibits 39A** and **39C**, average returns for high P/E stocks were dismally low early in the Election Cycle.

High P/E rarely outperformed low P/E, but when it did, this generally occurred late in the Election Cycle.

Exhibit 39B compares the performance of low P/E stocks to that of high P/E stocks (and compares them both to returns for the S&P 500) for each phase of the Fed-Election Cycle.

Exhibits 39C–39D are similar to **Exhibits 39A–39B,** except that the years are categorized according to Fed policy in the prior year.

The results presented in **Exhibits 39C–39D** are nearly identical to those we saw when we used the current years' rates to characterize Fed policy, with one exception. High P/E stocks actually outperformed low P/E stocks in late Election Cycle years which followed an aggressively restrictive year. This is significant, because high P/E stocks so rarely outperformed low P/E stocks.

Exhibit 39E compares the 15 best years for low P/E stocks to the 15 best years for high P/E stocks, ranking the years according to the differences between the annual returns for low P/E and high P/E stocks.

The 15 Best Years for High P/E Stocks

In their best 15 years, high P/E stocks returned an average of 23.5%, while the average annual return for the S&P 500 was 12.4%. Low P/E stocks actually outperformed high P/E stocks during these years, posting an average annual gain of 26.2%.

The S&P 500 had above-average returns in nine of the 15 best years for high P/E stocks. All but one of the nine years occurred late in the Election Cycle. Four of the six years in which the S&P 500 had below-average returns were restrictive years preceded by restrictive years.

Nine of the 15 best years for high P/E stocks occurred late in the Election Cycle. In eight of these nine years, the S&P 500 had above-average returns. In five of the six years occurring early in the Election Cycle, Fed policy was restrictive, and four of these five years were preceded by another restrictive year.

Fed policy was restrictive in 10 of the 15 best years for high P/E stocks, and seven of these 10 years were preceded by another restrictive year. Of the five remaining (expansive) years, all were preceded by a restrictive year, and four were years in which the S&P 500 had above average returns. Twelve of the 15 best years for high P/E stocks were preceded by a restrictive year.

In 15 of the 15 best years for high P/E stocks, Fed policy was restrictive in the current year, the prior year, or both (eight years being the corresponding figure for expansive policy).

Thus, high P/E stocks were most likely to outperform low P/E stocks when late Election Cycle bull markets occurred in strong—or at least inflated—economies (as evidenced by the tendency for high P/E stocks' best years to occur during, or immediately following, periods of restrictive Fed policy).

The 15 Best Years for Low P/E Stocks

During the 15 years in which low P/E stocks' performance advantage over high P/E stocks was greatest, low P/E stocks averaged returns of 43.0%, versus a loss of 2.1% for high P/E stocks. The S&P 500 annual average return during these years was 6.9%, well below its average of 12.6%.

The S&P 500 had below-average returns in 10 of the 15 best years for low P/E stocks. Four of the five years in which the S&P 500 had above-average returns occurred early in the Election Cycle, and four of the five were expansive years preceded by expansive years.

Eleven of the 15 best years for low P/E stocks occurred early in the Election Cycle. In seven of the 11 early Election Cycle years, the S&P 500 had below-average returns. Seven of the 11 early cycle years were expansive.

In nine of the 15 best years for low P/E stocks, Fed policy was expansive. Seven of these nine years were preceded by another expansive year. In fact, 11 of the 15 best years for low P/E stocks were preceded by an expansive year.

In 13 of the 15 best years for low P/E stocks, Fed policy was expansive in the current year, the prior year, or both (eight years being the corresponding figure for restrictive policy).

Low P/E stocks tend to outperform high P/E stocks in almost all circumstances, except in late Election Cycle years preceded by a year in which Fed policy was aggressively restrictive. The performance advantage of the low P/E strategy is likely to be greatest in early Election Cycle bear markets during periods of expansive monetary policy.

The Fed-Election Cycle and Price/Sales

Exhibit 40A compares the performance of low P/S stocks to that of high P/S stocks in each phase of the Fed-Election Cycle.

The bar chart at the top of the exhibit illustrates the performance advantage of low P/S stocks over high P/S stocks. Bars above the zero line indicate years in which low P/S stocks outperformed high P/E stocks.

During the 52 years from 1951 to 2002, low P/S stocks outperformed high P/S stocks 38 times (73.1% of the time), by an average of 31.3% per year. High P/S outperformed low P/S 14 times (26.9% of the time), by an average of 17.9% per year.

When **Exhibit 40A** is compared to the graph of low P/E versus high P/E shown in **Exhibit 39A,** two differences are apparent.

For one thing, low P/S did not outperform high P/S nearly as often as low P/E outperformed high P/E.

Also, it's clear from the graph in **Exhibit 40A** that something changed in the relationship between low P/S versus high P/S. Prior to 1980, high P/S was more likely to outperform low P/S. After 1980, low P/S was dominant.

As we will explain later in this chapter, there are good reasons to suspect that the relationship between high P/S and low P/S may revert back to what it was prior to 1980, i.e., that high P/S may begin to outperform low P/S more frequently than it has in the years since 1980. The explanation will have to wait, however, until we address the post-1980 decline in inflation and its effects on Wall Street.

Low P/S stocks averaged annual returns of 30.7% late in the Election Cycle, versus an average of 18.4% early in the cycle. Low P/S stocks responded to an expansive Fed policy with average annual returns of 33.6%, versus the 18.5% they returned when Fed policy was restrictive.

The low P/S strategy made money, on average, in every phase of the Fed-Election Cycle, except for years in which Fed policy was aggressively restrictive early in the Election Cycle.

High P/S stocks averaged annual returns of 21.1% in late Election Cycle years, versus a loss of 8.1% in the early years of the cycle. They responded to an expansive Fed policy with average annual returns of 5.6%, but they actually did better when Fed policy was restrictive (7.1%).

Regardless of whether Fed policy was expansive or restrictive, the high P/S strategy lost money, on average, early in the Election Cycle and made money late in the Election Cycle.

Low P/S stocks outperformed high P/S stocks in all four primary Fed-Election Cycle phases. As we saw with low P/E versus high P/E, the superior performance of low P/S stocks was most evident early in the Election Cycle and during periods of expansive Fed policy. During early Election Cycle years when Fed policy was expansive, low P/S outperformed high P/S by 40.1%.

However, when Fed policy was aggressively restrictive late in the Election Cycle, high P/S outperformed low P/S by 3.1%.

Exhibit 40B compares the performance of low P/S stocks to that of high P/S stocks (and compares them both to returns for the S&P 500) for each phase of the Fed-Election Cycle.

Exhibits 40C–40D are similar to **Exhibits 40A–40B,** except that the years are categorized according to Fed policy in the prior year.

The results presented in **Exhibits 40C–40D** display patterns similar to those we observed when using current years' rates to characterize Fed policy. High P/S outperformed low P/S by 32.8% in late Election Cycle years that followed aggressively restrictive years—the only circumstance in which high P/S prevailed.

Exhibit 40E compares the 15 best years for low P/S stocks to the 15 best years for high P/S stocks, ranking the years according to the differences between annual returns for low P/S and high P/S stocks.

The 15 Best Years for High P/S Stocks

In their best 15 years, high P/S stocks returned an average of 37.4%, while the average annual return for the S&P 500 was 13.5%. Low P/S stocks gained an average of 21.1% during those years.

The S&P 500 had above-average returns in 10 of the 15 best years for high P/S stocks. All 10 of these years occurred late in the Election Cycle. Fed policy was restrictive in four of the five years for which the S&P 500 had below-average returns.

Eleven of the 15 best years for high P/S occurred late in the Election Cycle. The S&P 500 had above-average returns in 10 of these years. Fed policy was restrictive in all four of the years which occurred early in the Election Cycle, and three of these four years were preceded by restrictive years.

Fed policy was restrictive in 10 of the 15 best years for high P/S stocks, and seven of these 10 years were preceded by another restrictive year. Of the five remaining (expansive) years, three were preceded by a restrictive year, and all were years in which the S&P 500 had above-average returns. Ten of the 15 best years for high P/S stocks were preceded by a restrictive year.

In 13 of the 15 best years for high P/S stocks, Fed policy was restrictive in the current year, the prior year, or both (eight years being the corresponding figure for expansive policy).

As was the case with high P/E versus low P/E stocks, high P/S stocks were most likely to outperform low P/S stocks when late Election Cycle bull markets occurred in strong—or at least inflated—economies (as evidenced by the tendency for high P/S stocks' best years to occur during, or immediately following, periods of restrictive Fed policy).

The 15 Best Years for Low P/S Stocks

During the 15 years in which low P/S stocks' performance advantage over high P/S stocks was greatest, low P/S averaged returns of 40.4%, versus a loss of 16.4% for high P/S stocks. The S&P 500 annual average return during these years was 10.6%, somewhat below its 52-year average of 12.6%.

The S&P 500 had below-average returns in nine of the 15 best years for low P/S stocks.

The 15 best years for low P/S stocks were about evenly divided between the early and late Election Cycle phases.

Fed policy was restrictive in eight of the 15 best years for low P/S and expansive in seven. The prior year's Fed policy was expansive in nine of the 15 best years.

In 12 of the 15 best years for low P/S stocks, Fed policy was expansive in the current year, the prior year, or both (11 years being the corresponding figure for restrictive policy).

The performance advantage of low P/S stocks tends to be greatest in early Election Cycle bear markets during periods of expansive monetary policy.

The Fed-Election Cycle and Price/Book Value

Exhibit 41A compares the performance of low P/BV stocks to that of high P/BV stocks in each phase of the Fed-Election Cycle.

The bar chart at the top of the exhibit illustrates the performance advantage of low P/BV over high P/BV. Bars above the zero line indicate years in which low P/BV stocks outperformed high P/BV stocks.

During the years from 1951 to 2002, low P/BV stocks outperformed high P/BV stocks 34 times (65.4% of the time), by an average of 36.4% during those 34 years. High P/BV outperformed low P/BV 18 times (34.6% of the time), by an average of 15.8% per year. Thus, high P/BV was the growth strategy with the most consistently strong record vis-à-vis its value-oriented antithesis.

Low P/BV stocks averaged annual returns of 31.6% late in the Election Cycle, versus an average of 21.2% during the early years of the cycle. Low P/BV stocks responded to an expansive Fed policy with average annual returns of 33.5%, versus the 21.6% they returned when Fed policy was restrictive.

The low P/BV strategy made money, on average, in every phase of the Fed-Election Cycle.

High P/BV stocks averaged annual returns of 19.7% in late Election Cycle years, versus a loss of 3.5% during the early years of the cycle. They responded to an expansive Fed policy with average annual returns of 10.3%, versus the 6.6% they returned when Fed policy was restrictive.

Regardless of whether Fed policy was expansive or restrictive, the high P/BV strategy lost money, on average, early in the Election Cycle and made money late in the Election Cycle.

Over the entire 52-year period included in our study, low P/BV stocks out-performed high P/BV stocks in all four primary phases of the Fed-Election

Cycle. Their superior performance was most evident early in the Election Cycle.

Exhibit 41B compares low P/BV performance to that of high P/BV stocks (and compares them both to returns for the S&P 500) for each phase of the Fed-Election Cycle.

Exhibits 41C–41D are similar to **Exhibits 41A–41B,** except that the years are categorized according to Fed policy in the prior year.

The results presented in **Exhibits 41C–41D** are similar to what we saw when using the current years' rates to characterize Fed policy, with one exception. High P/BV stocks outperformed low P/BV stocks in late Election Cycle years which followed an aggressively restrictive year.

Exhibit 41E compares the 15 best years for low P/BV stocks to the 15 best years for high P/BV stocks, ranking the years according to the differences between the annual returns for low P/BV and high P/BV stocks.

The 15 Best Years for High P/BV Stocks

In their 15 best years, high P/BV stocks returned an average of 33.9%, while the average annual return for the S&P 500 was 14.3%. Low P/BV stocks returned an average of 15.2% during these years.

The S&P 500 had above-average returns in 10 of the 15 best years for high P/BV stocks. All but one of the 10 years occurred late in the Election Cycle. Four of the six years in which the S&P 500 had below-average returns were restrictive years preceded by restrictive years.

Ten of the 15 best years for high P/BV stocks occurred late in the Election Cycle. In nine of these 10 years, the S&P 500 had above-average returns. Four of the five years occurring early in the Election Cycle were restrictive years preceded by restrictive years.

Fed policy was restrictive in nine of the 15 best years for high P/BV stocks, and eight of these nine years were preceded by another restrictive year. Of the six remaining (expansive) years, four were preceded by a restrictive year, and five were years in which the S&P 500 had above-average returns. Twelve of the 15 best years for high P/BV stocks were preceded by a restrictive year.

In 13 of the 15 best years for high P/BV stocks, Fed policy was restrictive in the current year, the prior year, or both (seven years being the corresponding figure for expansive policy).

High P/BV stocks were far more likely to outperform low P/BV stocks late in the Election Cycle. As we saw with the other growth strategies, high P/BV performed poorly early in the Election Cycle.

As was the case with high P/E and high P/S stocks, high P/BV stocks were most likely to outperform their value-oriented opposites (i.e., low P/BV stocks) when late Election Cycle bull markets occurred in strong—or at least inflated—economies (as evidenced by the strong tendency for high P/BV stocks' best years to occur during, or immediately following, periods of restrictive Fed policy).

The 15 Best Years for Low P/BV Stocks

During the 15 years in which low P/BV stocks' performance advantage over high P/BV stocks was greatest, low P/BV stocks averaged returns of 45.0%, versus a loss of 12.8% for high P/BV. The S&P 500 annual average return during these years was 8.0%, well below its average of 12.6%.

The S&P 500 had below-average returns in nine of the 15 best years for low P/BV stocks. Four of the six years in which the S&P 500 had above-average returns occurred early in the Election Cycle, and four were expansive years.

The 15 best years for low P/BV stocks were about evenly divided between the early and late Election Cycle phases.

In nine of the 15 best years for low P/BV stocks, Fed policy was expansive. Six of those nine years were preceded by expansive years. Ten of the 15 best years for low P/BV stocks were preceded by an expansive year.

In 13 of the 15 best years for low P/BV stocks, Fed policy was expansive in the current year, the prior year, or both (nine years being the corresponding figure for restrictive policy).

The performance advantage of the low P/BV strategy is likely to be greatest in bear markets during periods of expansive monetary policy.

The Fed-Election Cycle and Price/Cash Flow

Exhibit 42A compares the performance of low P/CF stocks to that of high P/CF stocks in each phase of the Fed-Election Cycle.

The bar chart at the top of the exhibit illustrates the performance advantage of low P/CF stocks over high P/CF stocks. Bars above the zero line indicate years in which low P/CF stocks outperformed high P/CF stocks.

During the 52 years from 1951 to 2002, low P/CF stocks outperformed high P/CF 43 times (82.7% of the time), by an average of 34.3% in those 43 years. High P/CF outperformed low P/CF nine times (17.3% of the time), by an average of 16.1%.

Low P/CF stocks averaged annual returns of 40.4% late in the Election Cycle, versus an average of 26.1% during the early years of the cycle. Low P/CF stocks responded to an expansive Fed policy with average annual returns of 40.2%, versus 28.6% when Fed policy was restrictive.

The low P/CF strategy made money, on average, in every phase of the Fed-Election Cycle, except for years in which Fed policy was aggressively restrictive early in the Election Cycle (i.e., Extreme Panic Years).

High P/CF stocks averaged annual returns of 20.7% in late Election Cycle years, versus a loss of 5.3% during the cycle's early years. High P/CF stocks responded to an expansive Fed policy with average annual returns of 7.8%, versus 7.6% when Fed policy was restrictive.

Regardless of whether Fed policy was expansive or restrictive, the high P/CF strategy lost money, on average, early in the Election Cycle and made money late in the Election Cycle.

Low P/CF stocks outperformed high P/CF stocks in every primary phase of the Fed-Election Cycle. As with the other low price ratios, the superior performance of low P/CF was most evident early in the Election Cycle. When Fed policy was expansive early in the Election Cycle, low P/CF outperformed high P/CF by 45.9%. When Fed policy was aggressively expansive early in the Election Cycle, low P/CF outperformed high P/CF by 56.8%.

Exhibit 42B compares the performance of low P/CF stocks to that of high P/CF (and compares them both to returns for the S&P 500) for each phase of the Fed-Election Cycle.

Exhibits 42C–42D are similar to **Exhibits 42A–42B** except that the years are categorized according to Fed policy in the prior year.

The results presented in **Exhibits 42C–42D** are similar to those we saw when we used the current years' rates to characterize Fed policy—with the same exception noted with the other price ratios. High P/CF stocks outperformed low P/CF stocks in late Election Cycle years which followed aggressively restrictive years.

Exhibit 42E compares the 15 best years for low P/CF stocks to the 15 best years for high P/CF stocks, ranking the years according to the differences between the annual returns for low P/CF and high P/CF stocks.

The 15 Best Years for High P/CF Stocks

In their best 15 years, high P/CF stocks returned an average of 26.4%, while the average annual return for the S&P 500 was 14.2%. Low P/CF stocks returned an average of 19.5% during these years.

The S&P 500 had above-average returns in 10 of the 15 best years for high P/CF stocks. All but one of the 10 years occurred late in the Election Cycle. Four of the five years in which the S&P 500 had below-average returns occurred early in the Election Cycle when Fed policy was restrictive.

Ten of the 15 best years for high P/CF stocks occurred late in the Election Cycle. In nine of these 10 years, the S&P 500 had above average returns. Of the five years occurring early in the Election Cycle, four were restrictive; all five were preceded by restrictive years.

Fed policy was restrictive in 10 out of the 15 best years for high P/CF stocks, and eight of these 10 years were preceded by restrictive years. Of the five remaining (expansive) years, four were preceded by a restrictive year and four were years in which the S&P 500 had above-average returns. Twelve of the 15 best years for high P/CF stocks were preceded by a restrictive year.

In 14 of the 15 best years for high P/CF stocks, Fed policy was restrictive in the current year, the prior year, or both (seven years being the corresponding figure for expansive policy).

As was the case with high P/E, high P/S, and high P/BV stocks, high P/CF stocks were mostly likely to outperform their value-oriented opposites (i.e., low P/CF stocks) when late Election Cycle bull markets combined with strong—or at least inflated—economies (as evidenced by the tendency for high P/CF stocks' best years to occur during, or immediately following, periods of restrictive Fed policy).

The 15 Best Years for Low P/CF Stocks

During the 15 years in which low P/CF stocks' performance advantage over high P/CF stocks was greatest, low P/CF stocks averaged returns of 52.5%, versus a loss of 7.1% for high P/CF stocks. The S&P 500 annual average return during these years was 8.0%, well below its 52-year average of 12.6%.

The S&P 500 had below-average returns in eight of the 15 best years for low P/CF stocks. Five of the seven years in which the S&P 500 had above-average returns occurred late in the Election Cycle, and five were years in which Fed policy was expansive.

The 15 best years for low P/CF stocks were about evenly divided between the early and late halves of the Election Cycle.

In 10 of the best 15 years for low P/CF stocks, Fed policy was expansive. In seven of those 10 years, Fed policy had been expansive during the previous year as well. Ten of the 15 best years for low P/CF stocks were preceded by an expansive year.

In 13 of the 15 best years for low P/CF stocks, Fed policy was expansive in the current year, the prior year, or both (eight years being the corresponding figure for restrictive policy).

Thus, the performance advantage of low P/CF stocks tends to be greatest in bear markets during periods of expansive monetary policy.

The Fed-Election Cycle and Value Versus Growth

Exhibit 43A compares the performance of the Value Index to that of the Growth Index in each phase of the Fed-Election Cycle.

The bar chart at the top of the exhibit illustrates the performance advantage of value stocks over growth stocks. Bars above the zero line indicate years in which value stocks outperformed growth stocks.

During the 52 years from 1951 to 2002, the Value Index outperformed the Growth Index 42 times (80.8% of the time), by an average of 29.4% in those 42 years. Growth outperformed value a total of 10 times (19.2% of the time), by an average of 13.8%.

The Value Index averaged annual returns of 36% late in the Election Cycle, versus an average of 23.0% during the early years of the cycle. Value stocks responded to an expansive Fed policy with average annual returns of 37%, versus the 24.5% they returned when Fed policy was restrictive.

The Value Index made money, on average, in every phase of the Fed-Election Cycle, except when the Fed was aggressively restrictive early in the Election Cycle (Extreme Panic Years).

The Growth Index averaged annual returns of 21.2% late in the Election Cycle, versus a loss of 4.4% during the early years of the cycle. Growth stocks responded to an expansive Fed policy with average annual returns of 9.5%, versus the 7.7% they returned when Fed policy was restrictive.

Whether Fed policy was expansive or restrictive, the Growth Index lost money, on average, early in the Election Cycle and made money, on average, late in the Election Cycle.

The Value Index outperformed the Growth Index in every phase of the Fed-Election Cycle. The superior performance of value stocks was most evident early in the Election Cycle and during periods of expansive Fed policy. Value outperformed growth by an average of 38.5% in early Election Cycle years when Fed policy was expansive. During early Election Cycle years when Fed policy was aggressively expansive, value's performance advantage was 48.5%.

The Growth Index's best performance relative to the Value Index occurred late in the Election Cycle when Fed policy was restrictive (Euphoric Years).

Exhibit 43B compares the performance of the Value Index to that of the Growth Index (and compares them both to returns for the S&P 500) for each phase of the Fed-Election Cycle.

Exhibits 43C–43D are similar to **Exhibits 43A–43B,** except that the years are categorized according to Fed policy in the prior year.

The figures presented in **Exhibits 43C–43D** follow the patterns we have seen with the various price ratios, as well as with those we saw when using the current years' rates to characterize Fed policy.

Growth stocks had their best years vis-à-vis value stocks late in the Election Cycle when the previous years' Fed policy was restrictive. On average, value outperformed growth by 9.9% during Prior Year Restrictive/Late Election Cycle years. However, if we only consider the late Election Cycle years when the prior year's Fed policy was aggressively restrictive, growth outperformed value by 18.2%.

Exhibit 43E compares the 15 best years for the Value Index to the 15 best years for the Growth Index, ranking the years according to the differences between the annual returns for the Value Index and those of the Growth Index.

The 15 Best Years for Growth

During the 15 best years for growth, the Growth Index gained 28.3% versus the Value Index's 20.3%, while the S&P 500 gained an average of 14.2%.

The S&P 500 had above-average returns in 10 of the 15 best years for growth stocks. Four of the five years in which the S&P 500 had below-average returns were restrictive years preceded by restrictive years.

Ten of the 15 best years for growth stocks occurred late in the Election Cycle. In nine of the 10 years occurring late in the Election Cycle, the S&P 500 had above-average returns. Four of the five years that occurred early in the Election Cycle were restrictive years preceded by restrictive years.

Fed policy was restrictive in 10 of the 15 best years for growth stocks, and, in eight of the 10 years, it had been restrictive during the previous year as well. Of the five remaining (expansive) years, four were preceded by a restrictive year, and three exhibited returns for the S&P 500 that were well above-average.

In 14 of the 15 best years for growth stocks, Fed policy was restrictive in the current year, the prior year, or both (seven years being the corresponding figure for expansive policy).

Thus, growth is most likely to outperform value in late Election Cycle bull markets that occur in strong—or at least inflated—economies (as evidenced by the tendency for growth stocks' best years to occur during, or immediately following, periods of restrictive Fed policy).

The 15 Best Years for Value

During the 15 years in which value's performance advantage over growth was greatest, the Value Index returned an average of 42.9%, versus a loss of 8.4% for the Growth Index. During these years, the S&P 500 returned an average of 7.9%, well below its 52-year average of 12.6%.

The S&P 500 had below-average returns in 10 of the 15 best years for value stocks. Three of the five years in which the S&P 500 had above-average returns were expansive years.

Exhibit 39A: Returns by Value & Growth by Fed-Election Cycle– Current Years' Rates
Price to Earnings

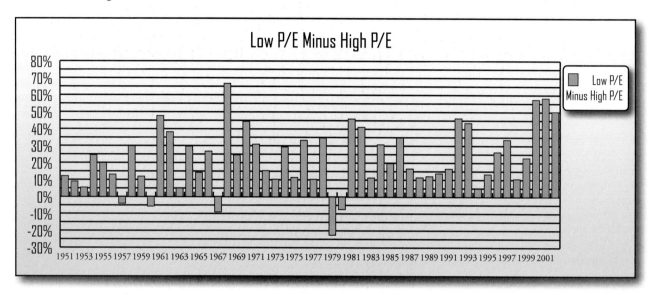

	Expansive	Aggressively Expansive	Restrictive	Aggressively Restrictive	All Years
Bottom 100 (Lowest Price to Earnings)					
Early Election Cycle	33.6%	40.0%	21.1%	2.6%	26.4%
Late Election Cycle	48.2%	81.1%	36.9%	68.1%	41.3%
All Years	40.6%	55.4%	29.2%	24.4%	33.8%
Top 100 (Highest Price to Earnings)					
Early Election Cycle	-2.5%	-2.7%	0.5%	-16.0%	-0.8%
Late Election Cycle	32.3%	74.8%	17.7%	46.1%	23.3%
All Years	14.1%	26.4%	9.4%	4.7%	11.3%
Lowest P/E Minus Highest P/E					
Early Election Cycle	36.1%	42.7%	20.6%	18.6%	27.1%
Late Election Cycle	15.9%	6.3%	19.2%	22.0%	17.9%
All Years	26.5%	29.0%	19.9%	19.8%	22.5%

Exhibit 39B: Returns by Value & Growth by Fed-Election Cycle– Current Years' Rates
Price to Earnings vs. S&P 500

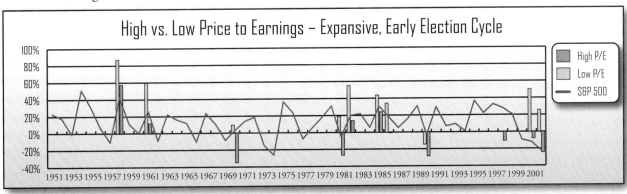

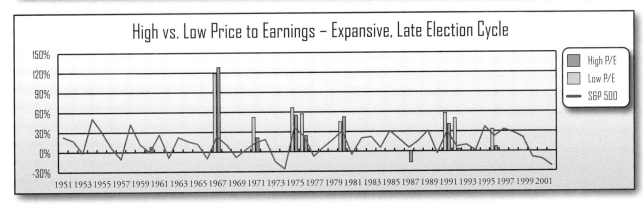

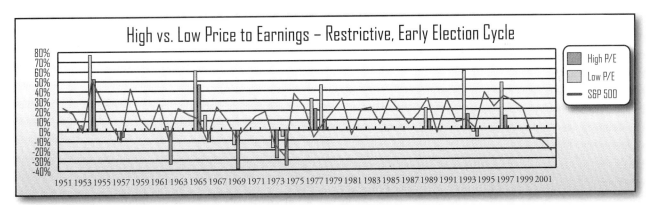

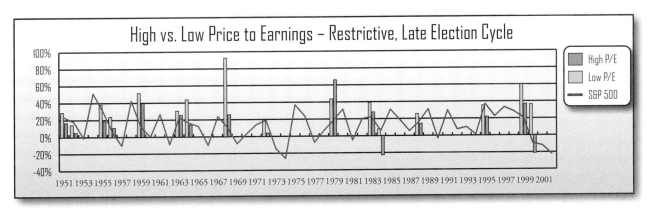

Exhibit 39C: Returns by Value & Growth by Fed-Election Cycle– Prior Years' Rates
Price to Earnings

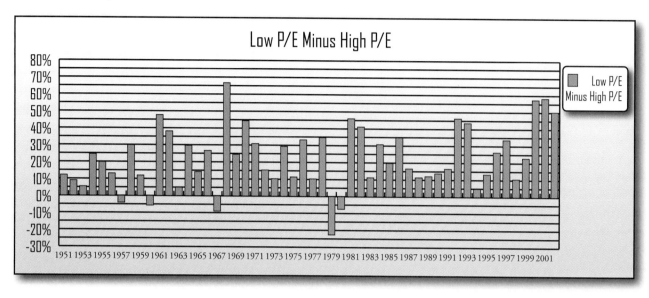

	Expansive	Aggressively Expansive	Restrictive	Aggressively Restrictive	All Years
Bottom 100 (Lowest Price to Earnings)					
Early Election Cycle	37.3%	40.4%	20.6%	-3.7%	26.4%
Late Election Cycle	45.9%	50.5%	37.9%	41.2%	41.3%
All Years	42.0%	48.0%	28.7%	18.8%	33.8%
Top 100 (Highest Price to Earnings)					
Early Election Cycle	-1.1%	-5.3%	-0.6%	-36.5%	-0.8%
Late Election Cycle	20.1%	16.3%	25.7%	46.8%	23.3%
All Years	10.6%	10.9%	11.8%	5.2%	11.3%
Lowest P/E Minus Highest P/E					
Early Election Cycle	38.4%	45.7%	21.1%	32.8%	27.1%
Late Election Cycle	25.7%	34.3%	12.2%	-5.6%	17.9%
All Years	31.4%	37.1%	16.9%	13.6%	22.5%

Exhibit 39D: Returns by Value & Growth by Fed-Election Cycle– Prior Years' Rates
Price to Earnings vs. S&P 500

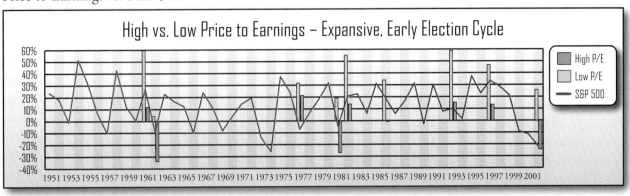

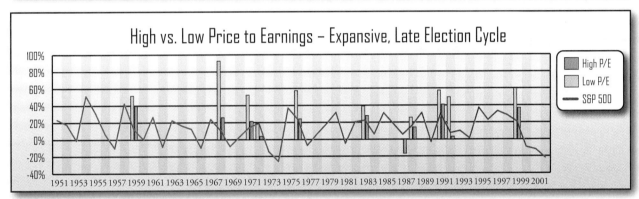

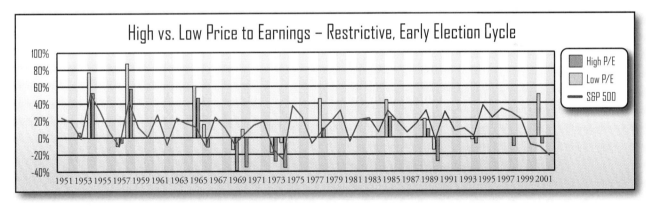

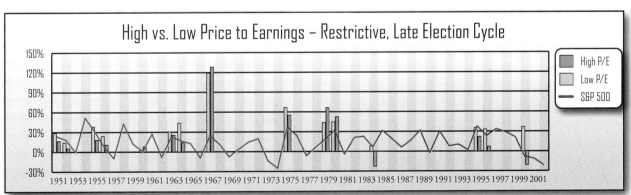

Exhibit 39E: Value vs. Growth and the Fed-Election Cycle
Price to Earnings– Best & Worst Years

| | Fed Policy Analysis | | | Election Cycle | |
| | Current Year | Prior Year | | | |
		Expansive	Restrictive	Early	Late
Best 15 Years for Value:					
Expansive	9	7	2	7	2
Restrictive	6	4	2	4	2
Totals:				11	4
Best 15 Years for Growth:					
Expansive	5	0	5	1	4
Restrictive	10	3	7	5	5
Totals				6	9
Value Minus Growth:					
Expansive	4	7	-3	6	-2
Restrictive	-4	1	-5	-1	-3
Totals				5	-5

The Best 15 Years for Growth vs. Value

The Best 15 Years for Growth Stocks:

Year	S&P 500 Returns	High P/E Strategy	Low P/E Strategy	High P/E - Low P/E
1979	18.19%	66.21%	43.61%	22.60%
1967	23.73%	128.33%	119.22%	9.10%
1980	31.52%	52.32%	44.81%	7.50%
1960	0.28%	7.99%	2.26%	5.73%
1957	-10.48%	-6.15%	-10.20%	4.05%
1994	1.28%	-7.66%	-2.75%	-4.91%
1963	22.50%	25.51%	30.51%	-5.00%
1953	-1.17%	0.41%	5.86%	-5.44%
1952	17.71%	5.31%	14.29%	-8.98%
1973	-14.50%	-28.17%	-17.86%	-10.32%
1977	-7.16%	21.39%	31.73%	-10.34%
1998	28.34%	-10.77%	-0.19%	-10.58%
1983	22.31%	27.84%	39.11%	-11.27%
1975	36.92%	55.21%	66.58%	-11.38%
1988	16.35%	14.23%	25.67%	-11.44%
Average Returns	12.39%	23.47%	26.18%	-2.71%

The Best 15 Years for Value Stocks:

Year	S&P 500 Returns	High P/E Strategy	Low P/E Strategy	High P E - Low P/E
1976	23.64%	24.18%	57.42%	-33.24%
1997	33.10%	13.30%	46.91%	-33.61%
1978	6.39%	10.67%	45.34%	-34.66%
1986	18.54%	-0.79%	34.05%	-34.85%
1962	-8.83%	-33.80%	4.37%	-38.17%
1982	20.37%	14.00%	55.15%	-41.15%
1993	9.94%	15.20%	58.80%	-43.60%
1970	3.33%	-34.86%	9.57%	-44.43%
1981	-4.85%	-26.95%	19.03%	-45.98%
1992	7.43%	3.20%	49.49%	-46.28%
1961	26.60%	11.92%	59.62%	-47.70%
2002	-21.97%	-24.51%	25.74%	-50.25%
2000	-9.03%	-21.04%	36.35%	-57.39%
2001	-11.85%	-8.04%	50.19%	-58.23%
1968	10.84%	25.93%	92.62%	-66.69%
Average Returns	6.91%	-2.11%	42.98%	-45.08%

Exhibit 40A: Returns by Value & Growth by Fed-Election Cycle– Current Years' Rates
Price to Sales

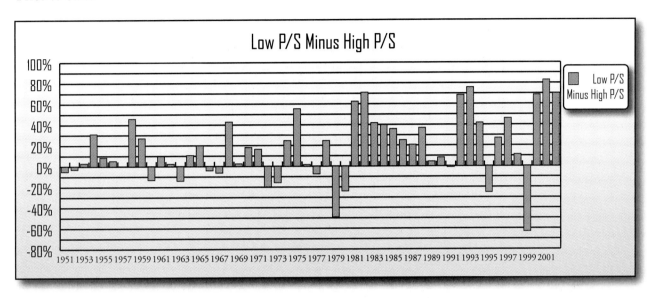

	Expansive	Aggressively Expansive	Restrictive	Aggressively Restrictive	All Years
Bottom 100 (Lowest Price to Sales)					
Early Election Cycle	27.6%	35.6%	11.8%	-5.7%	18.4%
Late Election Cycle	40.1%	78.7%	24.8%	61.6%	30.7%
All Years	33.6%	51.8%	18.5%	16.7%	24.6%
Top 100 (Highest Price to Sales)					
Early Election Cycle	-12.5%	-11.3%	-4.9%	-19.0%	-8.1%
Late Election Cycle	25.6%	62.7%	18.4%	64.7%	21.1%
All Years	5.6%	16.5%	7.1%	8.9%	6.5%
Lowest P/S Minus Highest P/S					
Early Election Cycle	40.1%	46.9%	16.7%	13.3%	26.6%
Late Election Cycle	14.5%	16.0%	6.4%	-3.1%	9.5%
All Years	27.9%	35.3%	11.4%	7.8%	18.1%

Exhibit 40B: Returns by Value & Growth by Fed Election Cycle– Current Years' Rates
Price to Sales vs. S&P 500

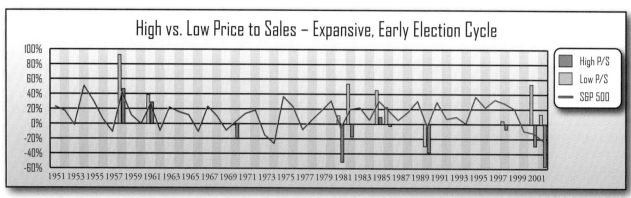

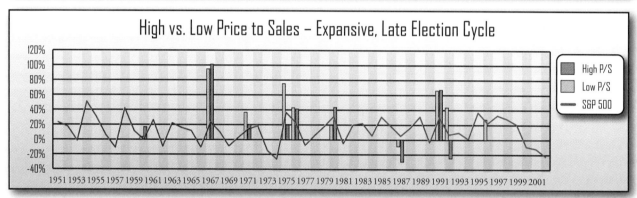

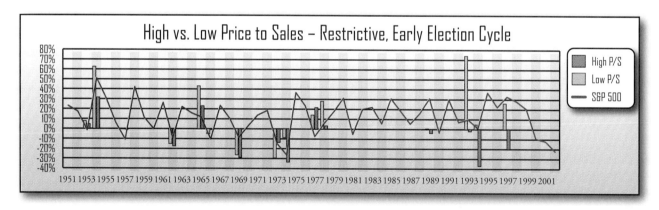

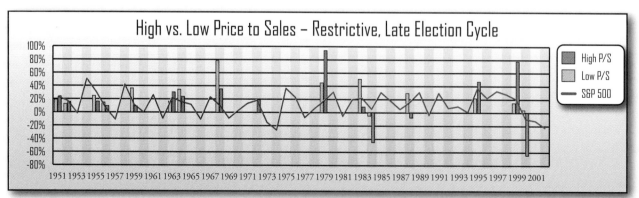

Exhibit 40C: Returns by Value & Growth by Fed-Election Cycle– Prior Years' Rates
Price to Sales

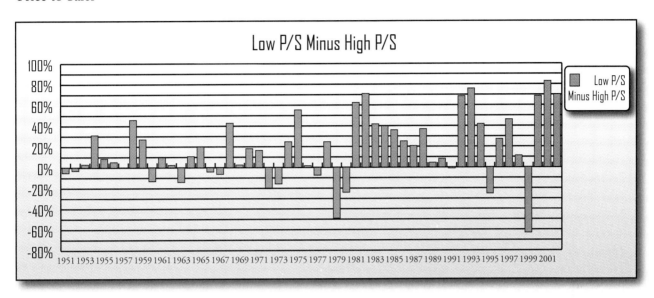

	Expansive	Aggressively Expansive	Restrictive	Aggressively Restrictive	All Years
Bottom 100 (Lowest Price to Earnings)					
Early Election Cycle	26.5%	33.5%	14.2%	-12.3%	18.4%
Late Election Cycle	35.3%	38.1%	27.2%	28.8%	30.7%
All Years	31.4%	36.9%	20.3%	8.3%	24.6%
Top 100 (Highest Price to Earnings)					
Early Election Cycle	-13.0%	-37.1%	-5.5%	-27.4%	-8.1%
Late Election Cycle	19.7%	8.5%	22.2%	61.5%	21.1%
All Years	5.0%	-2.9%	7.5%	17.1%	6.5%
Lowest P/S Minus Highest P/S					
Early Election Cycle	39.5%	70.6%	19.7%	15.1%	26.6%
Late Election Cycle	15.6%	29.5%	5.1%	-32.8%	9.5%
All Years	26.4%	39.8%	12.9%	-8.8%	18.1%

Exhibit 40D: Returns by Value & Growth by Fed-Election Cycle– Prior Years' Rates
Price to Sales vs. S&P 500

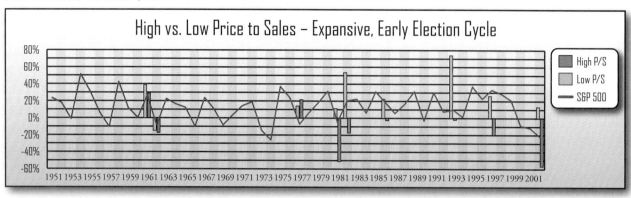

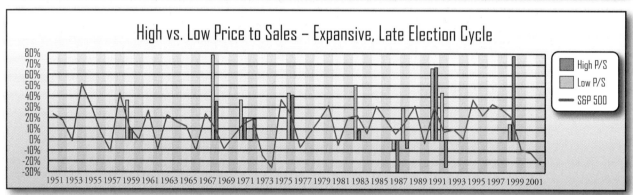

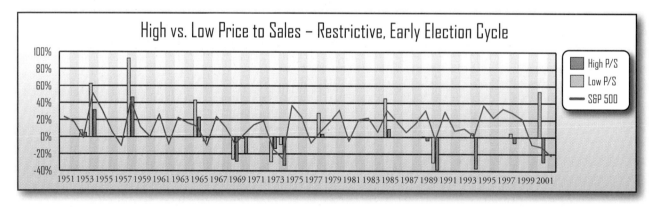

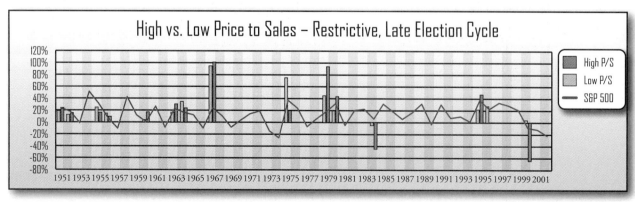

Exhibit 40E: Value vs. Growth and the Fed-Election Cycle
Price to Sales– Best & Worst Years

Fed Policy Analysis

Best 15 Years for Value:	Current Year	Prior Year Expansive	Restrictive
Expansive	7	4	3
Restrictive	8	5	3
Totals			
Best 15 Years for Growth:			
Expansive	5	2	3
Restrictive	10	3	7
Totals:			
Value Minus Growth:			
Expansive	2	2	0
Restrictive	-2	2	-4
Totals			

Election Cycle

	Early	Late
Expansive	5	2
Restrictive	3	5
Totals	8	7
Expansive	0	5
Restrictive	4	6
Totals:	4	11
Expansive	5	-3
Restrictive	-1	-1
Totals	4	-4

The Best 15 Years for Growth vs. Value

The Best 15 Years for Growth Stocks:

Year	S&P 500 Returns	High P/S Strategy	Low P/S Strategy	High P/S - Low P/S
1999	20.88%	77.85%	14.79%	63.06%
1979	18.19%	93.99%	44.92%	49.07%
1995	37.11%	47.10%	21.89%	25.21%
1980	31.52%	43.53%	19.54%	23.99%
1972	18.88%	19.05%	-0.68%	19.73%
1973	-14.50%	-13.60%	-29.33%	15.73%
1963	22.50%	30.46%	16.51%	13.95%
1960	0.28%	16.95%	3.85%	13.10%
1977	-7.16%	21.66%	14.17%	7.49%
1967	23.73%	101.16%	94.84%	6.32%
1966	-9.99%	-1.01%	-5.07%	4.07%
1952	17.71%	15.40%	12.38%	3.02%
1991	30.00%	67.22%	66.19%	1.03%
1957	-10.48%	-0.82%	-0.50%	-0.32%
1976	23.64%	41.24%	42.91%	-1.67%
Average Returns	13.49%	37.35%	21.09%	16.25%

The Best 15 Years for Value Stocks:

Year	S&P 500 Returns	High P/S Strategy	Low P/S Strategy	High P/S - Low P/S
1988	16.35%	-7.51%	29.48%	-36.99%
1984	5.97%	-44.74%	-4.91%	-39.83%
1983	22.31%	8.80%	50.57%	-41.78%
1994	1.28%	-36.99%	4.85%	-41.84%
1968	10.84%	35.33%	78.23%	-42.90%
1958	42.44%	46.51%	92.43%	-45.92%
1997	33.10%	-20.05%	26.13%	-46.18%
1975	36.92%	19.67%	75.14%	-55.46%
1981	-4.85%	-51.23%	11.22%	-62.45%
1992	7.43%	-24.98%	43.54%	-68.52%
2000	-9.03%	-64.49%	4.18%	-68.66%
2002	-21.97%	-56.73%	13.33%	-70.07%
1982	20.37%	-17.43%	53.64%	-71.06%
1993	9.94%	-1.92%	74.00%	-75.92%
2001	-11.85%	-29.44%	53.50%	-82.94%
Average Returns	10.62%	-16.35%	40.35%	-56.70%

Exhibit 41A: Returns by Value & Growth by Fed-Election Cycle – Current Years' Rates
Price to Book Value

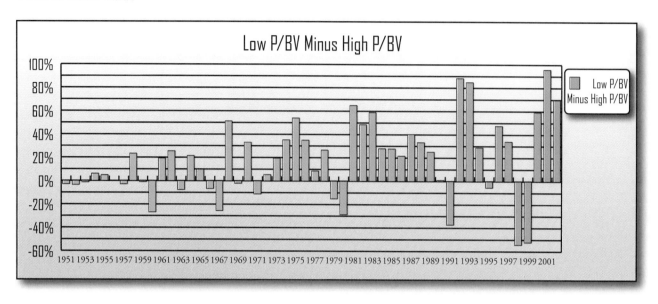

	Expansive	Aggressively Expansive	Restrictive	Aggressively Restrictive	All Years
Bottom 100 (Lowest Price to Book Value)					
Early Election Cycle	28.4%	37.9%	15.9%	0.4%	21.2%
Late Election Cycle	39.1%	58.7%	26.9%	63.0%	31.6%
All Years	33.5%	45.7%	21.6%	21.2%	26.4%
Top 100 (Highest Price to Book Value)					
Early Election Cycle	-3.5%	-9.8%	-3.5%	-17.8%	-3.5%
Late Election Cycle	25.6%	61.6%	16.0%	44.9%	19.7%
All Years	10.3%	17.0%	6.6%	3.1%	8.1%
Lowest P/BV Minus Highest P/BV					
Early Election Cycle	31.9%	47.7%	19.4%	18.2%	24.7%
Late Election Cycle	13.6%	-2.9%	10.9%	18.1%	11.9%
All Years	23.1%	28.7%	15.0%	18.2%	18.3%

Exhibit 41B: Returns by Value & Growth by Fed-Election Cycle– Current Years' Rates
Price to Book Value vs. S&P 500

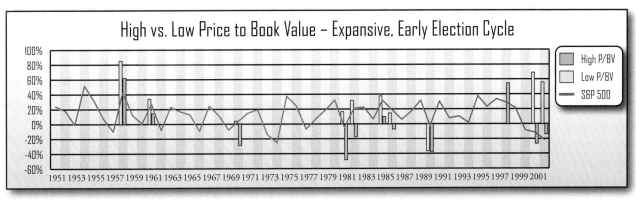

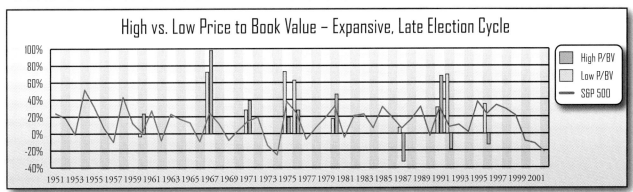

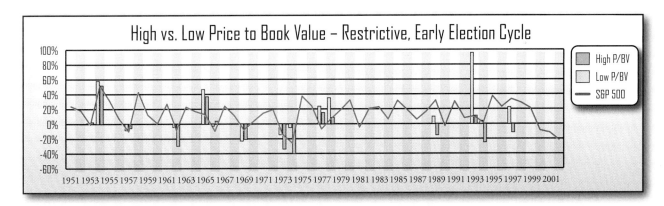

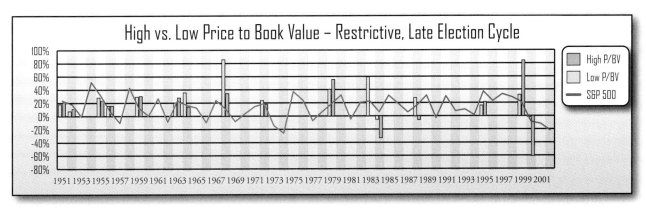

Exhibit 41C: Returns by Value & Growth by Fed-Election Cycle– Prior Years' Rates
Price to Book Value

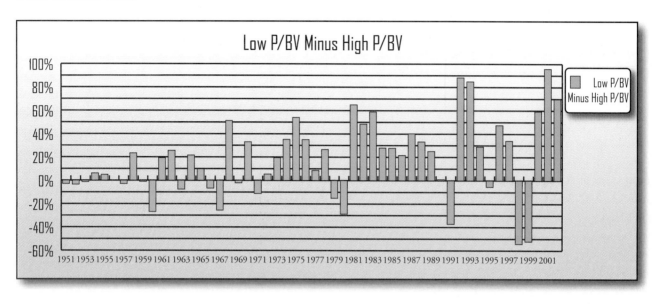

	Expansive	Aggressively Expansive	Restrictive	Aggressively Restrictive	All Years
Bottom 100 (Lowest Price to Book Value)					
Early Election Cycle	32.2%	43.7%	15.3%	-7.9%	21.2%
Late Election Cycle	41.3%	47.0%	24.5%	24.5%	31.6%
All Years	37.2%	46.1%	19.6%	8.3%	26.4%
Top 100 (Highest Price to Book Value)					
Early Election Cycle	-9.7%	-15.5%	-0.3%	-30.0%	-3.5%
Late Election Cycle	22.2%	13.2%	17.9%	40.9%	19.7%
All Years	7.8%	6.0%	8.3%	5.5%	8.1%
Lowest P/BV Minus Highest P/BV					
Early Election Cycle	41.9%	59.2%	15.6%	22.1%	24.7%
Late Election Cycle	19.2%	33.8%	6.6%	-16.4%	11.9%
All Years	29.4%	40.1%	11.4%	2.8%	18.3%

Exhibit 41D: Returns by Value & Growth by Fed-Election Cycle– Prior Years' Rates
Price to Book Value vs. S&P 500

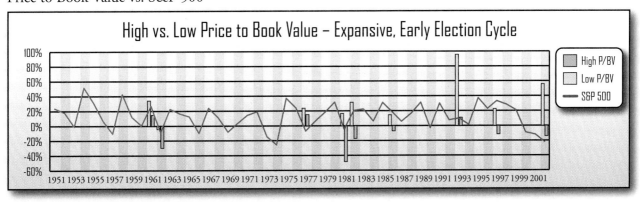

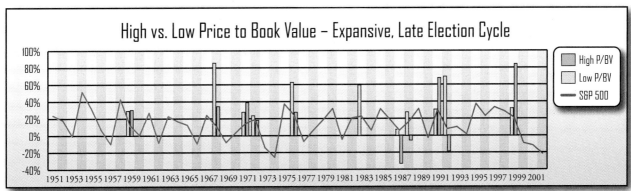

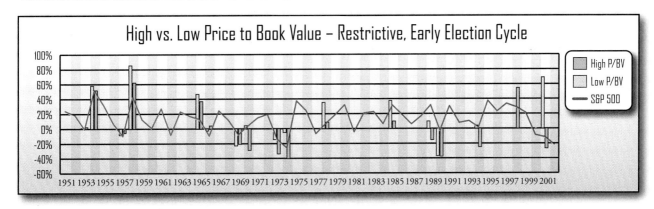

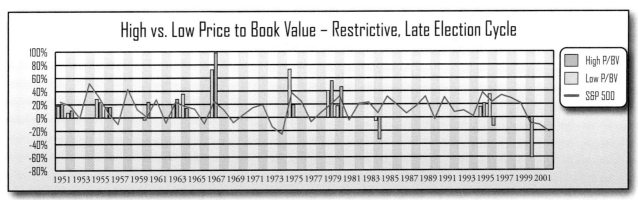

Exhibit 41E: Value vs. Growth and the Fed-Election Cycle
Price to Book Value– Best & Worst Years

Fed Policy Analysis / Election Cycle

	Current Year	Prior Year Expansive	Prior Year Restrictive	Early	Late
Best 15 Years for Value:					
Expansive	9	6	3	4	5
Restrictive	6	4	2	3	3
Totals				7	8
Best 15 Years for Growth:					
Expansive	6	2	4	1	5
Restrictive	9	1	8	4	5
Totals				5	10
Value Minus Growth:					
Expansive	3	4	-1	3	0
Restrictive	-3	3	-6	-1	-2
Totals				2	-2

The Best 15 Years for Growth vs. Value

The Best 15 Years for Growth Stocks:

Year	S&P 500 Returns	High P/BV Strategy	Low P/BV Strategy	High P/BV - Low P/BV
1998	28.34%	54.70%	0.40%	54.30%
1999	20.88%	84.20%	32.00%	52.20%
1991	30.00%	67.90%	30.60%	37.30%
1980	31.52%	46.10%	17.30%	28.80%
1960	0.28%	23.40%	-3.40%	26.80%
1967	23.73%	98.00%	72.50%	25.50%
1979	18.19%	55.40%	40.30%	15.10%
1971	14.15%	38.90%	27.70%	11.20%
1963	22.50%	27.80%	20.20%	7.60%
1966	-9.99%	4.00%	-2.70%	6.70%
1995	37.11%	21.20%	15.80%	5.40%
1952	17.71%	10.90%	7.40%	3.50%
1957	-10.48%	-5.60%	-8.50%	2.90%
1969	-8.32%	-20.80%	-22.90%	2.10%
1953	-1.17%	2.30%	1.00%	1.30%
Average Returns	14.30%	33.89%	15.18%	18.71%

The Best 15 Years for Value Stocks:

Year	S&P 500 Returns	High P/BV Strategy	Low P/BV Strategy	High P/BV - Low P/BV
1997	33.10%	-11.50%	22.50%	-34.00%
1976	23.64%	27.50%	62.60%	-35.10%
1974	-26.03%	-40.30%	-5.00%	-35.30%
1987	5.67%	-33.20%	7.10%	-40.30%
1996	22.68%	-13.10%	34.40%	-47.50%
1982	20.37%	-17.00%	31.50%	-48.50%
1968	10.84%	34.30%	85.60%	-51.30%
1975	36.92%	19.00%	73.00%	-54.00%
1983	22.31%	0.30%	59.20%	-58.90%
2000	-9.03%	-61.10%	-1.80%	-59.30%
1981	-4.85%	-48.40%	16.50%	-64.90%
2002	-21.97%	-14.00%	55.80%	-69.80%
1993	9.94%	10.90%	95.70%	-84.80%
1992	7.43%	-18.70%	69.50%	-88.20%
2001	-11.85%	-26.80%	68.90%	-95.70%
Average Returns	7.95%	-12.81%	45.03%	-57.84%

Exhibit 42A: Returns by Value & Growth by Fed-Election Cycle– Current Years' Rates
Price to Cash Flow

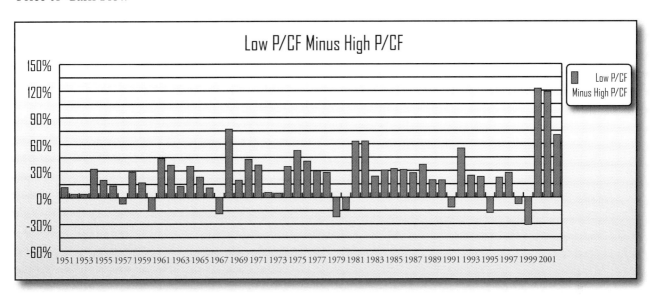

	Expansive	Aggressively Expansive	Restrictive	Aggressively Restrictive	All Years
Bottom 100 (Lowest Price to Cash Flow)					
Early Election Cycle	36.7%	46.4%	18.4%	-1.5%	26.1%
Late Election Cycle	44.1%	67.8%	38.1%	67.8%	40.4%
All Years	40.2%	54.4%	28.6%	21.6%	33.3%
Top 100 (Highest Price to Cash Flow)					
Early Election Cycle	-9.2%	-10.5%	-2.3%	-20.3%	-5.3%
Late Election Cycle	26.6%	60.2%	17.0%	40.4%	20.7%
All Years	7.8%	16.0%	7.6%	-0.1%	7.7%
Lowest P/CF Minus Highest P/CF					
Early Election Cycle	45.9%	56.8%	20.7%	18.8%	31.4%
Late Election Cycle	17.5%	7.6%	21.1%	27.4%	19.8%
All Years	32.4%	38.4%	20.9%	21.7%	25.6%

Exhibit 42B: Returns by Value & Growth by Fed-Election Cycle– Current Years' Rates
Price to Cash Flow vs. S&P 500

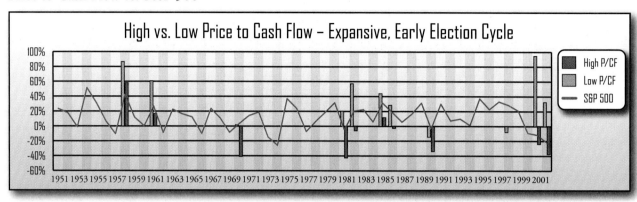

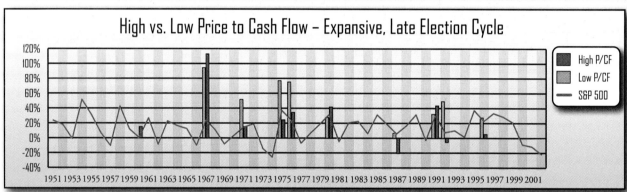

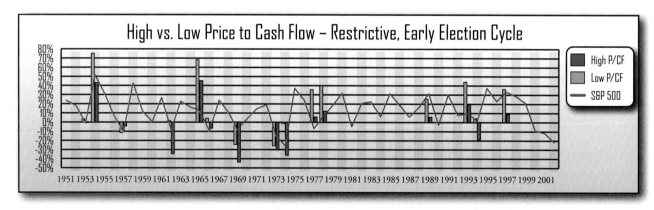

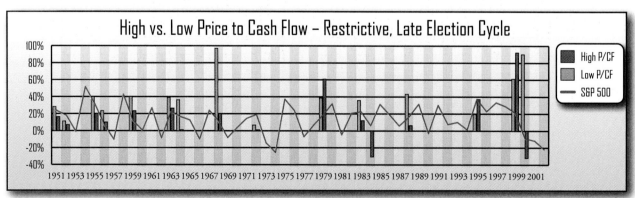

Exhibit 42C: Returns by Value & Growth by Fed-Election Cycle– Prior Years' Rates
Price to Cash Flow

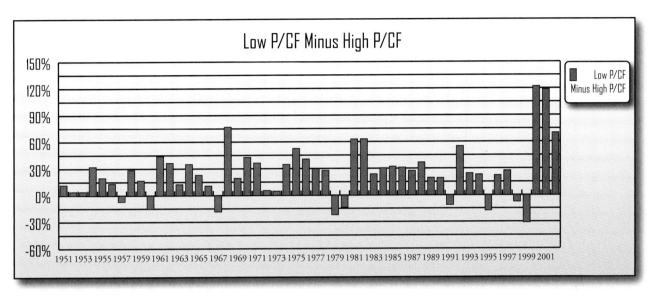

	Expansive	Aggressively Expansive	Restrictive	Aggressively Restrictive	All Years
Bottom 100 (Lowest Price to Cash Flow)					
Early Election Cycle	35.2%	44.8%	21.3%	-8.0%	26.1%
Late Election Cycle	45.3%	53.3%	36.8%	28.7%	40.4%
All Years	40.8%	51.1%	28.6%	10.3%	33.3%
Top 100 (Highest Price to Cash Flow)					
Early Election Cycle	-8.1%	-21.9%	-3.8%	-40.3%	-5.3%
Late Election Cycle	20.1%	11.1%	21.0%	46.6%	20.7%
All Years	7.4%	2.8%	7.9%	3.1%	7.7%
Lowest P/CF Minus Highest P/CF					
Early Election Cycle	43.3%	66.6%	25.1%	32.3%	31.4%
Late Election Cycle	25.2%	42.2%	15.8%	-17.9%	19.8%
All Years	33.3%	48.3%	20.7%	7.2%	25.6%

Exhibit 42D: Returns by Value & Growth by Fed-Election Cycle– Prior Years' Rates
Price to Cash Flow vs. S&P 500

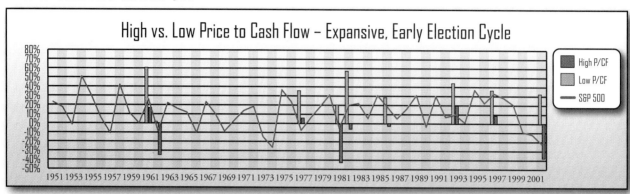

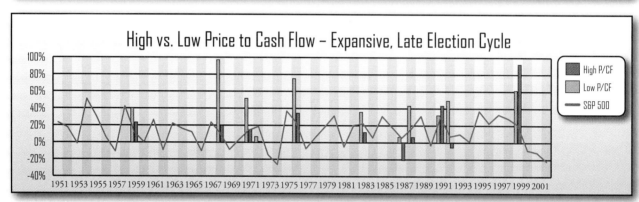

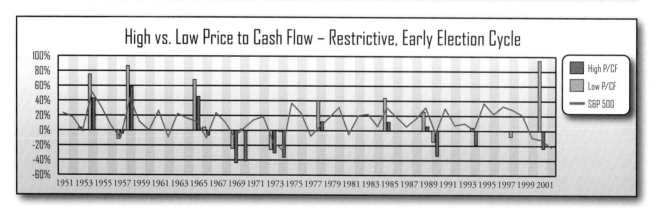

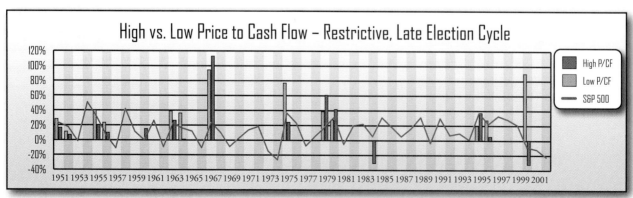

Exhibit 42E: Value vs. Growth and the Fed-Election Cycle
Price to Cash Flow– Best & Worst Years

Fed Policy Analysis

Best 15 Years for Value:	Current Year	Prior Year Expansive	Prior Year Restrictive
Expansive	10	7	3
Restrictive	5	3	2
Totals			

Best 15 Years for Growth:	Current Year	Prior Year Expansive	Prior Year Restrictive
Expansive	5	1	4
Restrictive	10	2	8
Totals			

Value Minus Growth:	Current Year	Prior Year Expansive	Prior Year Restrictive
Expansive	5	6	-1
Restrictive	-5	1	-6
Totals			

Election Cycle

Best 15 Years for Value:	Early	Late
Expansive	6	4
Restrictive	1	4
Totals	7	8

Best 15 Years for Growth:	Early	Late
Expansive	1	4
Restrictive	4	6
Totals	5	10

Value Minus Growth:	Early	Late
Expansive	5	0
Restrictive	-3	-2
Totals	2	-2

The Best 15 Years for Growth vs. Value

The Best 15 Years for Growth Stocks:

Year	S&P 500 Returns	High P/CF Strategy	Low P/CF Strategy	High P/CF - Low P/CF
1999	20.88%	92.20%	61.10%	31.10%
1979	18.19%	60.80%	38.60%	22.20%
1967	23.73%	112.90%	94.40%	18.50%
1995	37.11%	37.20%	19.60%	17.60%
1960	0.28%	15.10%	-0.20%	15.30%
1980	31.52%	41.70%	27.80%	13.90%
1991	30.00%	43.40%	32.10%	11.30%
1998	28.34%	-0.20%	-7.80%	7.60%
1957	-10.48%	-4.40%	-11.50%	7.10%
1952	17.71%	7.00%	11.20%	-4.20%
1953	-1.17%	-0.60%	3.60%	-4.20%
1973	-14.50%	-30.50%	-25.70%	-4.80%
1972	18.88%	1.10%	6.70%	-5.60%
1966	-9.99%	-6.70%	4.20%	-10.90%
1963	22.50%	26.40%	39.00%	-12.60%
Average Returns	14.20%	26.36%	19.54%	6.82%

The Best 15 Years for Value Stocks:

Year	S&P 500 Returns	High P/CF Strategy	Low P/CF Strategy	High P/CF - Low P/CF
1964	16.30%	1.10%	36.20%	-35.10%
1971	14.15%	15.20%	51.60%	-36.40%
1962	-8.83%	-34.80%	1.70%	-36.50%
1988	16.35%	6.40%	43.20%	-36.80%
1976	23.64%	34.40%	75.10%	-40.70%
1970	3.33%	-41.00%	1.80%	-42.80%
1961	26.60%	16.70%	60.70%	-44.00%
1975	36.92%	24.30%	76.90%	-52.60%
1992	7.43%	-5.80%	49.20%	-55.00%
1981	-4.85%	-42.70%	20.20%	-62.90%
1982	20.37%	-6.00%	57.10%	-63.10%
2002	-21.97%	-37.70%	32.40%	-70.10%
1968	10.84%	19.90%	96.90%	-77.00%
2001	-11.85%	-24.00%	94.70%	-118.70%
2000	-9.03%	-32.10%	90.10%	-122.20%
Average Returns	7.96%	-7.07%	52.52%	-59.59%

Exhibit 43A: Returns by Value & Growth by Fed-Election Cycle– Current Years' Rates
Value Index Minus Growth Index

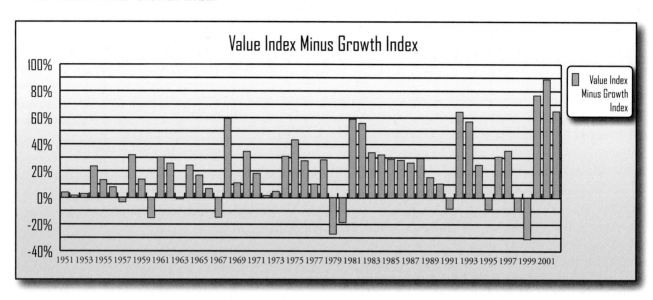

	Expansive	Aggressively Expansive	Restrictive	Aggressively Restrictive	All Years
Value					
Early Election Cycle	31.6%	40.0%	16.8%	-1.1%	23.0%
Late Election Cycle	42.9%	71.6%	31.7%	65.1%	36.0%
All Years	37.0%	51.8%	24.5%	21.0%	29.5%
Growth					
Early Election Cycle	-6.9%	-8.6%	-2.6%	-18.3%	-4.4%
Late Election Cycle	27.5%	64.8%	17.3%	49.0%	21.2%
All Years	9.5%	19.0%	7.7%	4.1%	8.4%
Value Minus Growth					
Early Election Cycle	38.5%	48.5%	19.3%	17.2%	27.4%
Late Election Cycle	15.4%	6.7%	14.4%	16.1%	14.8%
All Years	27.5%	32.9%	16.8%	16.9%	21.1%

Exhibit 43B: Returns by Value & Growth by Fed-Election Cycle– Current Years' Rates
Value Index vs. Growth Index vs. S&P 500

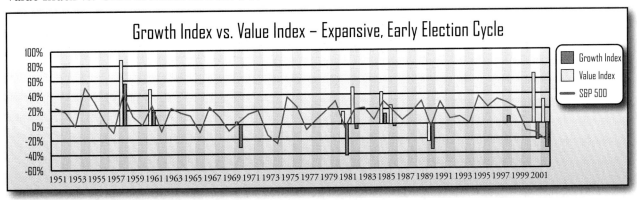

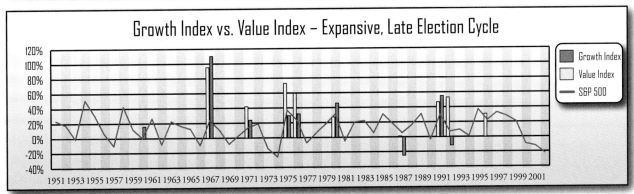

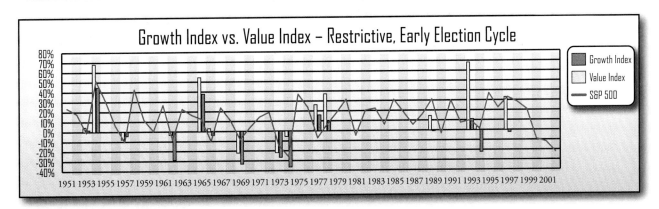

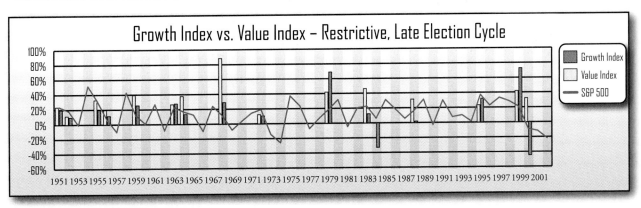

Exhibit 43C: Returns by Value & Growth by Fed-Election Cycle– Prior Years' Rates
Value Index Minus Growth Index

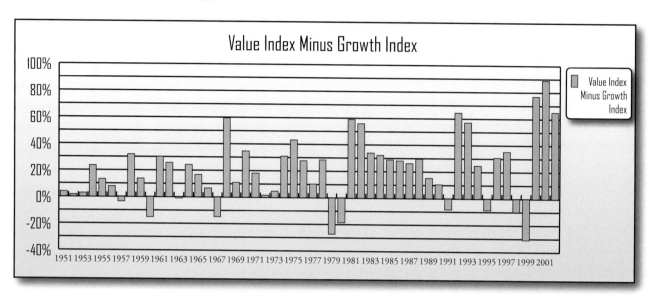

	Expansive	Aggressively Expansive	Restrictive	Aggressively Restrictive	All Years
Value					
Early Election Cycle	32.8%	40.6%	17.9%	-8.0%	23.0%
Late Election Cycle	42.0%	47.2%	31.6%	30.8%	36.0%
All Years	37.8%	45.6%	24.3%	11.4%	29.5%
Growth					
Early Election Cycle	-8.0%	-19.9%	-2.5%	-33.5%	-4.4%
Late Election Cycle	20.5%	12.3%	21.7%	49.0%	21.2%
All Years	7.7%	4.2%	8.8%	7.7%	8.4%
Value Minus Growth					
Early Election Cycle	40.8%	60.5%	20.4%	25.6%	27.4%
Late Election Cycle	21.4%	34.9%	9.9%	-18.2%	14.8%
All Years	30.1%	41.3%	15.5%	3.7%	21.1%

Exhibit 43D: Returns by Value & Growth by Fed-Election Cycle– Prior Years' Rates
Value Index vs. Growth Index vs. S&P 500

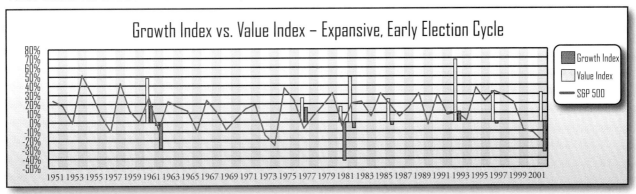

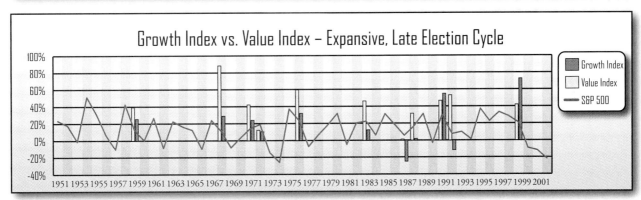

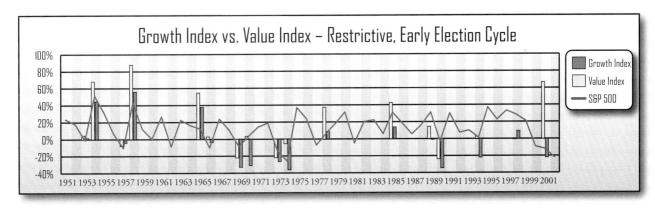

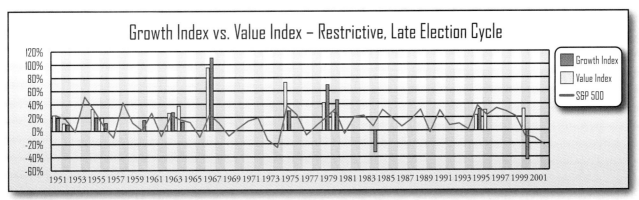

Exhibit 43E: Value vs. Growth and the Fed-Election Cycle
Value Index vs. Growth Index– Best & Worst Years

Fed Policy Analysis / Election Cycle

Best 15 Years for Value:	Current Year	Prior Year Expansive	Prior Year Restrictive	Early	Late
Expansive	8	4	4	6	2
Restrictive	7	4	3	3	4
Totals				9	6
Best 15 Years for Growth:					
Expansive	5	1	4	1	4
Restrictive	10	2	8	4	6
Totals				5	10
Value Minus Growth:					
Expansive	3	3	0	5	-2
Restrictive	-3	2	-5	-1	-2
Totals				4	-4

The Best 15 Years for Growth vs. Value

The Best 15 Years for Growth Stocks:

Year	S&P 500 Returns	Value Index	Growth Index	Value Index - Growth Index
1999	20.88%	41.91%	72.77%	-30.86%
1979	18.19%	41.86%	69.10%	-27.24%
1980	31.52%	27.36%	45.91%	-18.55%
1960	0.28%	0.63%	15.86%	-15.23%
1967	23.73%	95.24%	110.10%	-14.86%
1998	28.34%	-0.77%	9.24%	-10.02%
1995	37.11%	23.13%	31.85%	-8.72%
1991	30.00%	46.58%	54.85%	-8.27%
1957	-10.48%	-7.68%	-4.24%	-3.43%
1963	22.50%	26.55%	27.54%	-0.99%
1952	17.71%	11.32%	9.65%	1.66%
1972	18.88%	12.22%	10.55%	1.66%
1953	-1.17%	4.57%	1.73%	2.83%
1973	-14.50%	-21.87%	-26.59%	4.72%
1966	-9.99%	2.97%	-3.74%	6.71%
Average Returns	14.20%	20.27%	28.31%	-8.04%

The Best 15 Years for Value Stocks:

Year	S&P 500 Returns	Value Index	Growth Index	Value Index - Growth Index
1974	-26.03%	-5.40%	-36.40%	31.00%
1958	42.44%	87.92%	56.01%	31.91%
1984	5.97%	-0.62%	-32.87%	32.25%
1983	22.31%	46.17%	12.26%	33.91%
1970	3.33%	3.51%	-31.12%	34.62%
1997	33.10%	32.96%	-2.36%	35.32%
1975	36.92%	72.91%	29.54%	43.36%
1982	20.37%	49.35%	-6.61%	55.95%
1993	9.94%	68.15%	10.95%	57.20%
1981	-4.85%	16.74%	-42.32%	59.06%
1968	10.84%	88.34%	28.87%	59.47%
1992	7.43%	52.93%	-11.57%	64.50%
2002	-21.97%	31.82%	-33.24%	65.05%
2000	-9.03%	32.21%	-44.68%	76.89%
2001	-11.85%	66.82%	-22.07%	88.89%
Average Returns	7.93%	42.92%	-8.37%	51.29%

Nine of the 15 best years for value stocks occurred early in the Election Cycle. In six of the nine years occurring early in the Election Cycle, the S&P 500 had below-average returns.

Fed policy was expansive in eight of the 15 best years for value stocks, and, in four of the eight years, Fed policy had been expansive during the previous year as well.

In 12 of the 15 best years for value stocks, Fed policy was expansive in the current year, the prior year, or both (11 being the corresponding figure for restrictive policy).

The performance advantage of value over growth tends to be greatest in early Election Cycle bear markets when the Fed is expansive. Three of the four Expansive/Early Election Cycle years in which S&P returns were negative made value's Top 15 list. In those three years, value beat growth by an average of 70.7%. (In 1990, the only Expansive/Early Election Cycle/Negative S&P 500 year not on the list, value beat growth by 10.6%.)

The Fed-Election Cycle and Relative Strength

Exhibit 44A compares the performance of high relative strength to that of low relative strength in each phase of the Fed-Election Cycle.

The bar chart at the top of the exhibit illustrates the advantage of high relative strength over low relative strength. Bars above the zero line indicate years in which high relative strength outperformed low relative strength.

During the 51 years from 1952 to 2002, high relative strength outperformed low relative strength 38 times (74.5% of the time), by an average of 22.1% during those 38 years. Low relative strength outperformed high relative strength 13 times (25.5% of the time), by an average of 18.7% per year.

High relative strength averaged annual returns of 32.7% late in the Election Cycle, versus an average of 7.8% during the early years of the cycle. High relative strength responded to an expansive Fed policy with average annual returns of 23.7%, versus 17.4% when Fed policy was restrictive.

The high relative strength strategy made money, on average, in every phase of the Fed-Election Cycle, except when the Fed was aggressively restrictive early in the Election Cycle (i.e., in Extreme Panic Years).

Low relative strength averaged annual returns of 20.9% late in the Election Cycle, versus an average loss of 3.8% during the cycle's early years. Low relative strength responded to an expansive Fed policy with average annual returns of 11.9%, versus 5.8% when Fed policy was restrictive.

The low relative strength strategy lost money, on average, in the early half of the Election Cycle, and made money, on average, in the second half.

High relative strength outperformed low relative strength in every phase of the Fed-Election Cycle, except when the Fed was aggressively restrictive late in the Election Cycle (i.e., Extreme Euphoric Years).

Exhibit 44B compares the performance of high relative strength to that of low relative strength (and compares them both to returns for the S&P 500) for each phase of the Fed-Election Cycle.

Exhibits 44C–44D are similar to **Exhibits 44A–44B,** except that the years are categorized according to Fed policy in the prior year.

The results presented in **Exhibits 44C–44D** are similar to those we saw when we used the current years' rates to characterize Fed policy. Using current years' rates, low relative strength outperformed high relative strength only when Fed policy was aggressively restrictive. Using the prior years' rates, there were no phases of the Fed-Election Cycle in which low relative strength outperformed high relative strength. However, the gap between the two strategies narrowed considerably late in the Election Cycle when the prior year's Fed policy had been restrictive.

Exhibit 44E compares the 15 best years for high relative strength to the 15 best years for low relative strength, ranking the years according to the differences between the annual returns for high and low relative strength.

The 15 Best Years for Low Relative Strength

During its 15 best years, the low relative strength strategy returned an average of 29.2%, while the average annual return for the S&P 500 was 11.8%. High relative strength stocks returned an average of 13.3% during these years.

The S&P 500 had below-average returns in nine of the 15 best years for low relative strength stocks. Six of the nine years occurred early in the Election Cycle, and six were years in which Fed policy was restrictive. Four of the six years in which the S&P 500 had above-average returns occurred late in the Election Cycle.

The 15 Best Years for High Relative Strength

During its 15 best years, the high relative strength strategy returned an average of 37.7%, while the average annual return for the S&P 500 was 16.4%. Low relative strength stocks returned an average of 1.2% during these years.

The S&P 500 had above-average returns in 10 of the 15 best years for high relative strength stocks. Seven of the 10 years occurred late in the Election Cycle. In four of the five years in which the S&P 500 had below-average returns, Fed policy was restrictive.

Nine of the 15 best years for high relative strength stocks occurred late in the Election Cycle. Of these nine years, the S&P 500 had above-average returns in seven, and Fed policy was restrictive in six.

Fed policy was restrictive in 10 of the 15 best years for the high relative strength strategy. However, Fed policy was restrictive in only seven of the years preceding the 15 best years. This suggests that high relative strength tends to outperform low relative strength by a wider than usual margin in the first year of a restrictive policy.

Indeed, in the 10 years marking the onset of rate increases, high relative strength returned an average of 33.6% per year, versus the 11.7% average return for low relative strength. High relative strength outperformed low relative strength in seven of these 10 years.

The performance advantage of high relative strength over low relative strength tends to be greatest when the Fed initiates a restrictive policy during a late Election Cycle bull market. There were four Restrictive Policy Initiation/Late Election Cycle years with above-average S&P 500 returns. On average, high relative strength beat low relative strength by 33.4% during these years.

High relative strength also does particularly well vis-à-vis low relative strength when the Fed is neither aggressively expansive nor aggressively restrictive. This makes perfect sense because we should expect the future to replicate the past when important variables are held constant. If certain companies are prospering in today's monetary environment, we should expect that a continuation of this environment would contribute to their continued prosperity. If other companies are floundering in today's environment, why should we expect that more of the same will improve their performance?

Stocks tend to keep moving in whatever direction they are going, until something bumps them off course. Often, that something is a change in Fed policy.

Exhibit 44A: Returns by Relative Strength by Fed-Election Cycle– Current Years' Rates

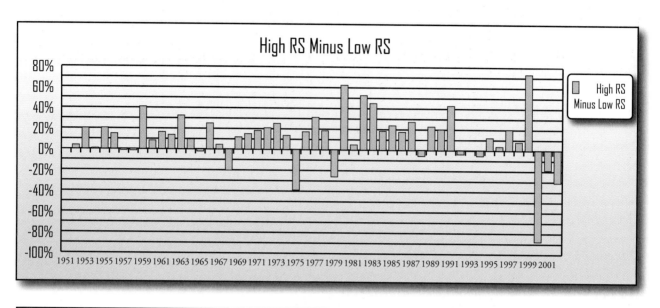

	Expansive	Aggressively Expansive	Restrictive	Aggressively Restrictive	All Years
Top 100 (Highest Relative Strength)					
Early Election Cycle	6.8%	2.9%	8.5%	-14.9%	7.8%
Late Election Cycle	42.4%	87.1%	26.2%	33.6%	32.7%
All Years	23.7%	34.5%	17.4%	1.2%	20.0%
Bottom 100 (Lowest Relative Strength)					
Early Election Cycle	-3.0%	-0.5%	-4.4%	-27.5%	-3.8%
Late Election Cycle	28.2%	84.3%	16.0%	56.7%	20.9%
All Years	11.9%	31.3%	5.8%	0.6%	8.3%
Highest RS Minus Lowest RS					
Early Election Cycle	9.8%	3.5%	13.0%	12.6%	11.6%
Late Election Cycle	14.2%	2.8%	10.2%	-23.2%	11.8%
All Years	11.9%	3.2%	11.6%	0.6%	11.7%

Exhibit 44B: Returns by Relative Strength by Fed-Election Cycle vs. S&P 500– Current Years' Rates

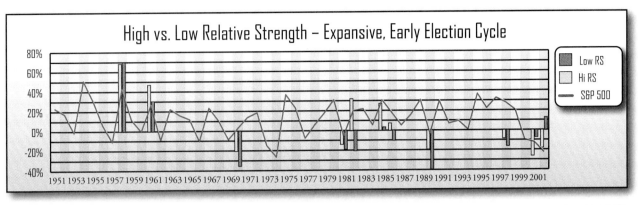

High vs. Low Relative Strength – Expansive, Early Election Cycle

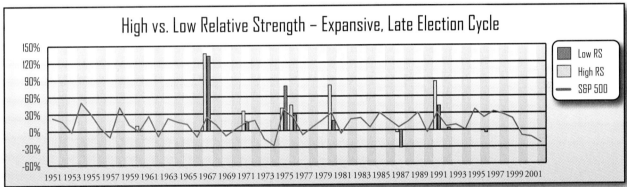

High vs. Low Relative Strength – Expansive, Late Election Cycle

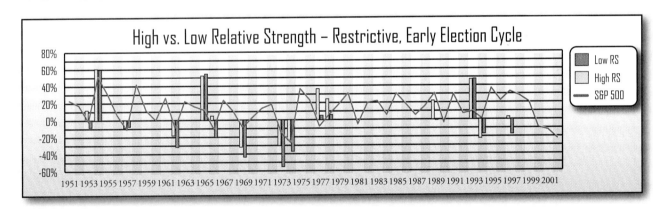

High vs. Low Relative Strength – Restrictive, Early Election Cycle

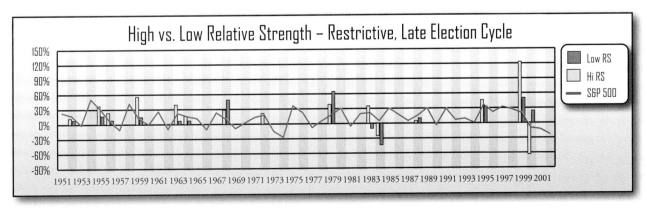

High vs. Low Relative Strength – Restrictive, Late Election Cycle

Exhibit 44C: Returns by Relative Strength by Fed-Election Cycle– Prior Years' Rates

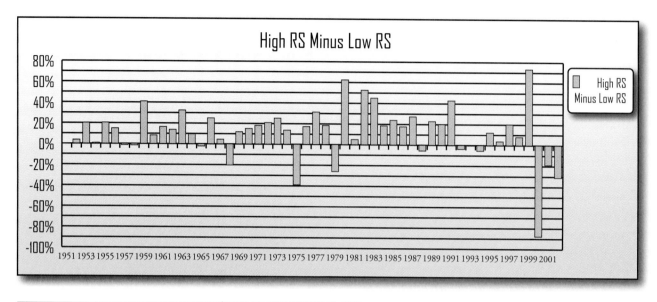

	Expansive	Aggressively Expansive	Restrictive	Aggressively Restrictive	All Years
Top 100 (Highest Relative Strength)					
Early Election Cycle	13.6%	6.8%	4.7%	-25.2%	7.8%
Late Election Cycle	39.0%	26.5%	27.7%	54.8%	32.7%
All Years	27.5%	21.6%	15.1%	14.8%	20.0%
Bottom 100 (Lowest Relative Strength)					
Early Election Cycle	-0.4%	-4.0%	-5.6%	-38.8%	-3.8%
Late Election Cycle	15.7%	13.2%	25.0%	38.5%	20.9%
All Years	8.4%	8.9%	8.2%	-0.1%	8.3%
Highest RS Minus Lowest RS					
Early Election Cycle	14.0%	10.8%	10.4%	13.6%	11.6%
Late Election Cycle	23.3%	13.3%	2.7%	16.2%	11.8%
All Years	19.1%	12.7%	6.9%	14.9%	11.7%

Exhibit 44D: Returns by Relative Strength by Fed-Election Cycle vs. S&P 500– Prior Years' Rates

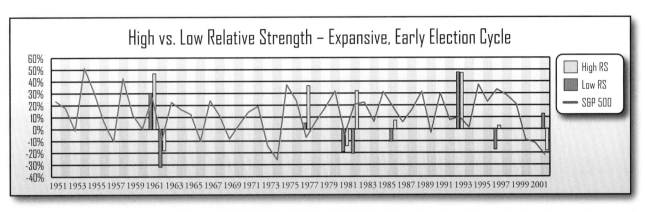

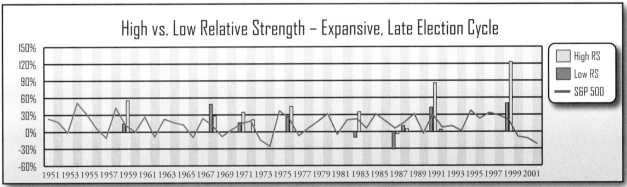

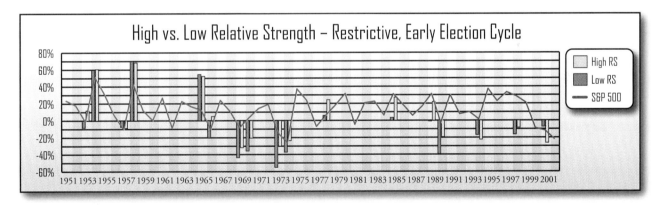

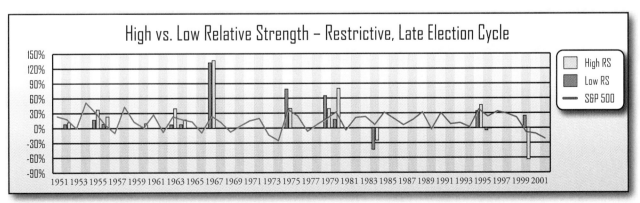

Exhibit 44E: High Relative Strength vs. Low Relative Strength and the Fed-Election Cycle
Best & Worst Years

	Fed Policy Analysis			**Election Cycle**	
	Current Year	Prior Year			
Years for High Relative Strength:		Expansive	Restrictive	Early	Late
Expansive	5	3	2	2	3
Restrictive	10	5	5	4	6
Totals				6	9
Years for Low Relative Strength:					
Expansive	6	2	4	3	3
Restrictive	9	3	6	5	4
Totals:				8	7
Low RS Minus High RS:					
Expansive	-1	1	-2	-1	0
Restrictive	1	2	-1	-1	2
Totals				-2	2

The Best 15 Years for High Relative Strength vs. Low Relative Strength

The Best 15 Years for High RS Stocks:

Year	S&P 500 Returns	High RS	Low RS	High RS - Low RS
1999	20.88%	123.22%	50.00%	73.22%
1980	31.52%	79.45%	17.03%	62.42%
1982	20.37%	31.98%	-20.65%	52.63%
1983	22.31%	34.96%	-10.12%	45.08%
1991	30.00%	85.61%	42.69%	42.93%
1959	11.79%	55.53%	14.56%	40.97%
1963	22.50%	39.43%	6.98%	32.45%
1977	-7.16%	36.34%	5.01%	31.33%
1987	5.67%	-3.86%	-31.18%	27.33%
1973	-14.50%	-29.95%	-55.13%	25.18%
1966	-9.99%	4.94%	-20.10%	25.05%
1985	31.06%	27.17%	3.29%	23.88%
1989	31.23%	21.95%	-1.00%	22.95%
1972	18.88%	21.34%	0.44%	20.90%
1955	30.96%	37.28%	16.82%	20.46%
Average Returns	16.37%	37.69%	1.24%	36.45%

The Best 15 Years for Low RS Stocks:

Year	S&P 500 Returns	High RS	Low RS	High RS - Low RS
1996	22.68%	-1.14%	-4.89%	3.75%
1954	51.23%	60.62%	59.74%	0.88%
1993	9.94%	47.27%	47.70%	-0.43%
1957	-10.48%	-8.71%	-7.44%	-1.28%
1958	42.44%	68.36%	69.91%	-1.55%
1965	12.27%	52.32%	54.51%	-2.19%
1992	7.43%	-0.21%	3.54%	-3.75%
1994	1.28%	-22.36%	-17.00%	-5.36%
1988	16.35%	4.57%	10.15%	-5.58%
2001	-11.85%	-26.31%	-7.44%	-18.87%
1968	10.84%	28.40%	48.74%	-20.34%
1979	18.19%	38.75%	64.73%	-25.98%
2002	-21.97%	-18.30%	12.67%	-30.98%
1975	36.92%	39.33%	78.29%	-38.96%
2000	-9.03%	-63.58%	24.13%	-87.71%
Average Returns	11.75%	13.27%	29.16%	-15.89%

The Fed-Election Cycle and Stock Selection Strategy

If we've learned anything from our review of historical performance data, it's that value usually outperforms growth, small companies usually outperform large companies, and high relative strength usually outperforms low relative strength.

These relationships held true throughout the Fed-Election Cycle's four primary phases, whether Fed policy was restrictive or expansive, and irrespective of the particular selection criteria used for market cap and value/growth styles.

Our analysis also revealed that the best times to switch into growth, large cap, and low relative strength styles corresponded to specific phases of the Fed-Election Cycle.

We saw that growth stocks were most likely to outperform value stocks in Euphoric Years (Restrictive/Late Election Cycle), times when the market was advancing despite the Fed's sustained and aggressive attempts to rein in an overheated economy. Growth was especially likely to outperform value late in the Election Cycle after an extended series of rate increases.

Large caps tended to outperform small companies in Panic Years (Restrictive/ Early Election Cycle), when the market was suffering from the combined impact of unaccommodating government policies and restrictive monetary policy.

Low relative strength was most likely to outperform high relative strength in Extreme Euphoric Years, the oddball sub-phase that so frequently renews investors' hopes in bad long-term strategies.

The Best Performing Styles for Each Phase of the Fed-Election Cycle

Exhibit 45 summarizes the key performance comparisons on which we have based our strategy for shifting styles according to the Fed-Election Cycle.

Two points should be kept in mind as we review this exhibit.

The first is that Fed policy and the economic conditions that drive it usually have opposite effects on the stock market. An expansive Fed policy may be bullish for stocks, but the economic weakness that prompted the Fed to lower rates will mitigate the impact of the rate cuts. Similarly, when the Fed adopts a restrictive policy to rein in an overheated economy, the bearish effects of monetary policy are often temporarily overwhelmed by euphoria over rising earnings expectations.

The second point is that market performance has little or no predictive value. Although we describe the conditions that favor each style in terms of Fed policy, the Election Cycle, and the overall strength of the market (i.e., the S&P 500) in order to explain why different conditions favor different styles, knowing that growth stocks tend to do well in bull markets does not, in itself, tell us when to shift to a growth style. (We might not know for sure whether we were in a bull market until it was too late to profit from that knowledge.) In practice, Fed policy and the Election Cycle signal when a change of styles is likely to be profitable.

As we review **Exhibit 45,** we'll describe the market environment in each phase of the Fed-Election Cycle, analyze the market's usual response, and then indicate the styles that have historically provided the best returns.

Early Election Cycle, Expansive Fed Policy

Scenario:

When Fed policy was expansive early in the Election Cycle, the market's performance reflected economic weakness, uncertainty over government economic policies, and a reduced level of fiscal stimulus. Returns for the S&P 500 were below-average (11.7%). This was the index's second worst performance of the four Fed-Election Cycle phases.

The Market's Reaction:

In this environment, investors tended to be somewhat defensive, preferring stocks that they perceived as safer and cheaper. Small companies outperformed large caps, but by very small margins, while value outperformed growth by a wide margin.

Nanocaps' performance advantage (3%) over large caps was the smallest of the four Fed-Election Cycle phases, while small caps ($100 million companies) had their second smallest performance advantage (3.2%).

Value stocks had their greatest performance advantage (38.5%) over growth in this phase.

High relative strength had its smallest performance advantage (9.8%) over low relative strength (consistent with a preference for bargain-priced stocks and a substantial shift into value).

Exhibit 45: The Fed-Election Cycle and Stock Selection Strategy

The Fed-Election Cycle and Stock Selection Strategy

Election Cycle

Fed Policy	Early	Late
Expansive (falling rates reflect economic weakness)	**3rd Best Returns for S&P 500 (11.7%)** Nanocaps' Smallest Performance Advantage (3.0%) Over Large Caps Small Caps' 2nd Smallest Performance Advantage (3.2%) Over Large Caps Value Index's Greatest Performance Advantage (38.5%) Over Growth Index High Relative Strength's Smallest Performance Advantage (9.8%) Over Low Relative Strength *Buy Nanocap Value. If insufficient Nanocap opportunities available, buy Small Cap Value. High Relative Strength less important than usual.*	**Best Returns for S&P 500 (19.6%)** Nanocaps' Greatest Performance Advantage (29.0%) Over Large Caps Small Caps' Greatest Performance Advantage (18.2%) Over Large Caps Value Index Beats Growth Index (by 15.4%) High Relative Strength's Greatest Performance Advantage (14.2%) Over Low Relative Strength *Buy Nanocap Value. If insufficient Nanocap opportunities available, buy Small Cap Value. High Relative Strength important.*
Restrictive (rising rates reflect economic strength)	**Panic Years. Worst Returns for S&P 500 (3.9%)** Nanocaps Beat Large Caps (by 6.6%) Small Caps Underperform Large Caps (by 0.2%) Value Index's 2nd Greatest Performance Advantage (19.3%) Over Growth Index High Relative Strength's 2nd Greatest Performance Advantage (13.0%) Over Low Relative Strength *Buy Nanocap Value. If insufficient Nanocap opportunities available, or if Fed is Aggressively Restrictive, buy Large Cap Value. High Relative Strength important.*	**Euphoric Years. 2nd Best Returns for S&P 500 (16.9%)** Nanocaps' 2nd Greatest Performance Advantage (10.4%) Over Large Caps Small Caps' 2nd Greatest Performance Advantage (7.8%) Over Large Caps Value Index's Smallest Performance Advantage (14.4%) Over Growth Index High Relative Strength's 2nd Smallest Performance Advantage (10.2%) Over Low Relative Strength *Buy Nanocap Value. If insufficient Nanocap opportunities available, buy Small Cap Value. Exception: shift to Growth when Fed policy was Agressively Restrictive in the prior year, otherwise buy Value. High Relative Strength less important than usual.*

Stock Selection Strategy:

In the Expansive/Early Election Cycle phase, nanocap value stocks would have provided the best returns of the styles we have considered. Whenever uninvested assets exceeded the availability of good nanocap opportunities, small company value stocks would have been the next best alternative. Large cap value stocks would have been safe bets (considering that the performance advantage of nanocaps and small caps over large caps was so small in this phase). High relative strength outperformed low relative strength by a smaller-than-usual margin.

Late Election Cycle, Expansive Fed Policy

Scenario:

When Fed policy was expansive late in the Election Cycle, the combination of accommodating government policies and monetary easing boded well for future growth in earnings. The performance figures reflected this surge in earnings expectations (if not actual earnings). The S&P 500 had its best performance of any Fed-Election Cycle phase.

The Market's Reaction:

In this environment, investors tended to buy stocks more for their future growth potential than for their relative cheapness.

Nanocaps had their greatest performance advantage (29%) over large caps of any phase, as did small caps (18.2%). Meanwhile, the performance advantage of value over growth narrowed, to 15.4%.

High relative strength had its greatest performance advantage (14.2%) over low relative strength, indicating that buyers focused on proven winners.

Stock Selection Strategy:

In the Expansive/Late Election Cycle phase, the odds favored nanocap value stocks with high relative strength. Whenever uninvested assets exceeded the availability of good nanocap opportunities, the next best alternative would have been to purchase small cap value stocks with high relative strength.

Early Election Cycle, Restrictive Fed Policy

Scenario:

When Fed policy was restrictive early in the Election Cycle, the performance figures reflected weak economic confidence. The Fed's anti-inflationary bias held earnings expectations in check, and little help was provided by fiscal stimulus. The S&P 500 had its worst returns of any phase of the Fed-Election Cycle, earning a scant 3.9% on average.

The Market's Reaction:

Investors reacted defensively to these Panic Years. In a stereotypical "flight to quality," they bid up the prices of large cap stocks with good value characteristics.

Nanocaps still managed to outperform large caps (by an average of 6.6%) during Panic Years. However, when the Fed was aggressively restrictive early in the Election Cycle (i.e., in Extreme Panic Years), the 100 largest companies outperformed nanocaps (by an average of 8.5%).

Large caps outperformed small caps by a slight margin in Panic Years (on average), but in Extreme Panic Years, when the Fed was aggressively restrictive, they outperformed small caps by an average of 10.2%.

The Value Index had its second greatest performance advantage (19.3%) over the Growth Index in Panic Years.

Also, high relative strength had its second greatest performance advantage (13%) over low relative strength, once again indicating investors' preference for proven winners, as they "flew" to quality.

Stock Selection Strategy:

Unless Fed policy was aggressively restrictive, the odds in Panic Years favored nanocap value stocks with high relative strength. However, whenever uninvested assets exceeded the availability of good nanocap opportunities, or if the Fed was aggressively restrictive, the best alternative would have been to buy large cap value stocks with high relative strength.

Late Election Cycle, Restrictive Fed Policy

Scenario:

When Fed policy was restrictive late in the Election Cycle, the performance figures reflected an economy that was growing fast enough to create inflationary pressures. Politically motivated fiscal stimulus added fuel to the fire. The S&P 500 achieved its second best performance, returning an average of 16.9% despite the Fed's restrictive policy. Even when the Fed was aggressively restrictive late in the Election Cycle, the S&P 500 still had above-average returns (14.5%).

The Market's Reaction:

When politically motivated economic policies overstimulate the economy, causing inflationary pressures to mount despite sustained and aggressive interest rate increases, the bull market that typically results often takes on a character we describe as "euphoric."

Euphoria—an exaggerated sense of well being—pervades the market when investors fail to acknowledge the unsustainability of accelerated earnings growth. Earnings growth accelerates when the economy expands quickly (despite the Fed's efforts to keep it from overheating). When an economic expansion is in full swing, the market tends to shrug off rate increases as earnings growth drives stock prices higher. In a euphoric market, investors project accelerating earnings growth too far into the future. They become willing to buy stocks at prices that reflect unrealistic growth rates, often failing to question whether the earnings expectations implied by high P/E ratios will ever be achieved.

During such times, buying interest has tended to focus on stocks that offered the most growth potential (and inflation hedge). These have included nanocaps, small caps, and growth stocks. Investors take on more risk in Euphoric Years, (in stark contrast to the extremely risk-averse behavior exhibited in Panic Years), but in a euphoric market, risk tends to be rewarded.

Nanocaps and small caps both had their second best performance advantage over large caps (10.4% and 7.8%, respectively) in Euphoric Years, while value had its smallest performance advantage (14.4%) over growth.

When Fed policy was aggressively restrictive, nanocaps outperformed large caps by a wide margin (55.9%), as did small caps (38.7%). And, the longer this scenario (booming economy, bull market, restrictive Fed policy) played out, the more likely it became that growth would outperform value.

High relative strength had its second smallest performance advantage (10.2%) over low relative strength, consistent with the market's appetite for risk and low quality in this phase.

When to Buy Low Relative Strength

Low relative strength is a particularly good bet in Extreme Euphoric Years that follow years in which returns for high relative strength were unusually high. Such circumstances may well be indicative of a bubble that the Fed is attempting to deflate. (If you should hear the Fed Chairman use the phrase "irrational exuberance" in reference to stock prices, that's another good clue.)

Stock Selection Strategy:

With regard to market cap, the best returns in this phase would have been provided by nanocaps (as usual) followed closely by small caps.

Generally speaking, value tended to outperform growth in Restrictive/Late Election Cycle years.

However, whenever the Fed maintained a sustained, aggressively restrictive policy and, despite this, the economy continued to grow and the market continued to rise, growth tended to outperform value. This was especially true as periods of economic expansion entered their later stages.

Under these circumstances—i.e., in Extreme Euphoric Years, low relative strength outperformed high relative strength by a wide margin (23.2%!).

Strategy for Shifting Styles According to the Fed-Election Cycle

We can summarize our strategy for shifting styles according to the Fed-Election Cycle as follows:

- When Fed policy is expansive early in the Election Cycle, buy nanocap value or small cap value stocks. Don't rule a stock out solely because it has low relative strength.

- In Panic Years (when Fed policy is restrictive early in the Election Cycle), buy nanocap or large cap value stocks with high relative strength.

- When Fed policy is expansive late in the Election Cycle, buy nanocap or small cap value stocks with high relative strength.

- In Euphoric Years (when Fed policy is restrictive late in the Election Cycle), buy nanocaps or small caps. Buy value unless Fed policy has been aggressively restrictive for more than a year; in that case, buy growth stocks. Buy high relative strength unless the Fed is aggressively restrictive. In Extreme Euphoric Years, buy low relative strength.

Predicting Style Shifts

A weatherman who knows only that the average rainfall in the month of April is 8.77 inches wouldn't be well prepared to predict the weather for this April. But if he knew that a large low-pressure trough had broken off from the jet stream and was slowly drifting his way, he could predict April showers with a high level of confidence.

Likewise, a simple comparison of the average annual performance of different styles in different phases of the Fed-Election Cycle doesn't tell us all we need to know to accurately predict when large caps would be likely to outperform small caps, or when growth would be likely to outperform value. For that, we need a better understanding of what causes these performance shifts.

Circumstantial evidence is provided by our association of the best and worst years for different selection strategies with specific market environments defined by Fed Policy, the Election Cycle, and the overall strength of the market (i.e., the S&P 500).

For example, our association of the best years for growth stocks with a late Election Cycle bull market, a strong economy, and rising short-term interest rates suggests that earnings expectations and interest rates were factors in the performance of the growth style. Digging a little deeper, it also suggests that the yield curve of interest rates and inflation were factors, as was investor psychology.

Let's look at these factors one by one.

Earnings Expectations

Stock prices rise and fall for many reasons, but—apart from the effects of broader market forces—sizable short-term price movements of individual stocks are generally driven by investors' expectations regarding earnings.

There is a direct relationship between the price ratios (i.e., price to earnings, price to sales, etc.) ascribed to a stock and investors' expectations of future changes in the growth rate of the company's earnings, sales, etc. Much of the spectacular performance of really big winners is attributable to increases in their price ratios arising from investors' belief that their earnings, sales, etc. will grow at an accelerating pace in the future.

At any point in time, the growth rate of a company's earnings, sales, book value, and cash flow will normally be reflected in its stock price. A company's past three years' results have far less effect on its stock's price than do expectations for the coming three years. Generally speaking, a company that is expected to grow quickly will command higher price ratios than one that is expected to grow more slowly.

Growth stocks sit at one end of the earnings expectations spectrum, while value stocks sit at the other. Growth stocks have higher price ratios because investors have high expectations for future operating performance. Comparatively speaking, not much is expected of value stocks.

When expectations for the future growth rate of a company change, its stock price—as well as its P/E, P/S, P/BV, and P/CF ratios—will change accordingly. The stock price of a company expected to grow its earnings at the rate of 5% per year will rocket higher if the expected growth rate rises to 10%. Meanwhile, the stock price of a company expected to grow its earnings at the rate of 20% per year will plummet if its expected growth rate falls to 15%.

Other things being equal, growth stocks outperform value stocks when the expectations for growth stocks' future operating performance are rising faster than the expectations for value stocks. It is quite difficult for a growth stock to foster rising expectations for extended periods of time because, by definition, a growth stock has already been blessed with above-average expectations. On the other hand, it is nearly as hard for a value stock to consistently generate lower expectations because, with the exception of companies heading for bankruptcy, an occasional positive surprise is almost inevitable.

One of the distinguishing characteristics of growth stocks is that a good deal of their ultimate promise– in the form of earnings growth strong enough to support their stock prices– resides in the distant future.

Recall that a company is ultimately worth the present value of its future cash flows. Positive cash flow comes from earnings, which either get paid out currently as dividends or are retained in the business and invested so as to produce growth in future earnings and dividends.

Growth companies retain most or all of their earnings and reinvest them in their businesses, thereby pushing the ultimate return to shareholders further and further into the future. This means that growth companies and their shareholders are placing relatively large bets on how the future will play out.

Thus, the prices of growth stocks, to a large extent, are based on expectations of earnings growth in the dim, distant future. By comparison, the prices of value stocks are often based on expectations that earnings will not grow at all (and may well decline) as time goes by.

Consequently, lower long-term interest rates will have more of a positive effect on growth stocks than on value stocks. On the other hand, a decline in short-term interest rates will normally have more of a positive effect on value stocks than it will on growth stocks.

The Yield Curve of Interest Rates

The yield curve is a graph of the interest rates charged on different maturities of debt. It normally depicts a positively-sloped line which rises from the rates for short-term debt to the rates for long-term debt.

Here is the yield curve for U.S. Treasury securities as of April 1, 2004.

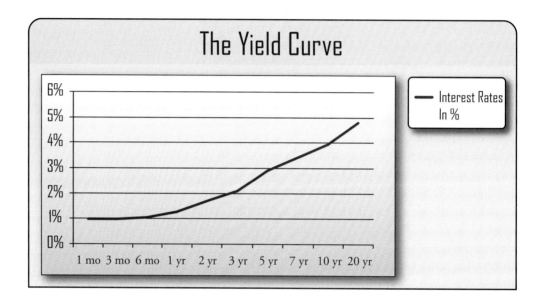

Long-term rates are normally higher than short-term rates because long-term money demands a higher return in exchange for the sacrifice of liquidity and– in the case of debt instruments not guaranteed by the U.S. government– a greater risk of default.

The Fed's control of interest rates, as we noted in Chapter 10, extends only to short-term rates. Long-term rates are determined by the buyers and sellers of debt instruments in the credit markets.

The Fed raises short-term interest rates when it determines that an overheated economy is leading to an unacceptable level of inflation. The bond market reacts quickly to any sign that the Fed is not raising rates fast enough to prevent an increase in inflation. When that happens, bond traders bid up long-term rates and the Fed often responds by raising short-term rates. Normally, when the Fed initiates a restrictive phase, short-term rates rise faster than long-term rates, causing the yield curve to flatten.

At some point, when bond traders become convinced that the Fed is bringing inflation under control, long-term rates begin to decline. Short-term rates, however, remain high for a time, as the Fed maintains an anti-inflationary bias. This causes the yield curve to become even flatter. In extreme cases, when long-term rates fall below short-term rates, the yield curve becomes inverted.

A normal, positively sloped yield curve places a higher relative value on near-term earnings and cash flow than a flat or inverted yield curve. (When short-term rates are lower than long-term rates, near-term cash flows are discounted at a lower rate than long-term cash flows.) Therefore, a positively sloped yield curve favors value over growth, because a value stock's price is based more on its near term earnings prospects than its long-term earnings prospects.

A flat or inverted yield curve, on the other hand, places a higher relative value on long-term earnings and cash flow than a normal yield curve. (When long-term interest rates are the same or lower than short-term rates, long-term cash flows are discounted at a relatively low rate compared to short-term cash flows.) Since a growth company's stock price is based more on its long-term earnings prospects than its near-term earnings prospects, a flattening yield curve favors growth over value.

A flattening or inverted yield curve is generally taken as a sign that interest rates and economic growth are about to decline.

The prospect that economic growth is about to decline probably favors growth over value as well, for reasons rooted in investor psychology. In fact, as we will explain more fully in Chapter 16, investors' tendency to overestimate the magnitude and persistence of rapid earnings growth is the principal reason why growth stocks tend to become overvalued. Although there is often a flight to quality when the reality of a recession hits home, the prospect of an economic slowdown leads some investors to buy stocks that they think can keep growing right through a recession. Naturally, these investors look for companies that have a history of superior earnings growth – i.e., growth stocks.

The yield curve is most likely to become flattened or inverted late in a restrictive phase, when the bond market decides that inflation is under control. As we have seen, this is precisely when growth performs best vis-à-vis value.

Inflation

Growth stocks suffer far more from inflation than do value stocks, but you would never know it from the way investors bid up the prices of growth stocks in inflationary periods.

Inflation is ultimately bad for growth stocks because a rising inflation rate erodes the value of cash flows in the distant future more than it does that of near-term cash flows.

Many investors make the mistake of believing that growth stocks provide a better hedge against inflation than value stocks. After all, growth stocks' earnings grow faster than value stocks' earnings, don't they? Shouldn't they be more likely to grow fast enough to beat inflation?

Actually, the above-average earnings growth that investors seem to take for granted in a growth stock rarely persists for as long as they assume it will when they pay the high prices these stocks command. Studies have shown that the half-life of above-average earnings growth is less than two years, and the growth rate of a growth company's earnings will decline to that of a typical value company's in about six years.

Nevertheless, investors continue to bid up growth stocks to astronomically high levels. Few ever take the time to calculate the growth rate implied by a P/E ratio of 100 to 1. In reality, an investor who pays $100 for a share of stock earning $1 is assuming that the company's earnings will grow 15-fold by 2030: that is, that they will grow at 11.5% year in and year out for the next 25[1] years (or significantly faster if the period of above-average growth is assumed to be less than 25 years).

Most of the time, growth stocks fail to live up to investors' overly optimistic expectations, and when this happens, their prices fall hard and fast.

Growth stocks are not a good hedge against inflation. During the 52-year period from 1951 to 2002, the compound annual rate of return for our Growth Index was 3.8%. During the same period, the annual rate of inflation was 4%.

Back in the days before the Fed tamed inflation "once and for all" in the early 1980's, growth stocks outperformed value stocks more often than they have during the most recent two decades. When an over-stimulated economy drove stock prices higher despite rising interest rates, investors responded to rising inflation by buying the stocks they perceived as having the fastest earnings growth: i.e., growth stocks.

[1]Assuming that all earnings will be paid out as dividends, that the company's stock will trade at a P/E of 20 at the end of the 25-year period, and that both long and short term interest rates are 7%.

Heteroskedasticity

In Chapter 5, as we reviewed the historical performance of growth strategies shown in **Exhibit 11-Exhibit 18**, it became apparent that a change occurred in the data sometime in the early 1980's. From 1951 to 1980, growth outperformed value fairly often, but in the years since 1980, this became a rare occurrence.

Statisticians have a term for this phenomenon: "heteroskedasticity." When heteroskedasticity is observed within a data series, it means, technically speaking, that the variance of the measure under study is not constant across observations.

Heteroskedasticity may indicate that one or more important explanatory variables have changed in fundamental ways, thereby undermining the validity of analyses that combine pre-change and post-change data.

In the case of our own analysis, heteroskedasticity was present in the comparison of growth and value. We believe its causes to have been the post-1980 decline in inflation rates and the growing market shares of mutual funds and brokerages.

In the years since 1980, declining inflation rates led to corresponding decreases in interest rates. During this period, as the yields on fixed income investments of all maturities fell, stocks were posting returns well above their historical norms. The stock market became increasingly attractive relative to bank deposits, insurance policies, and bonds.

The rise in equity prices which occurred in the 1980's and 1990's might have uniformly affected returns across all equity styles had it not been for the growing influence of mutual funds and retail brokerages. Large institutional investors and brokerage analysts focus their attention on a relatively small universe of stocks. The stocks they favor at any given time tend to rise sharply, but when they shift their attention to other stocks, their former favorites tend to fall.

Growth stocks are more affected by this phenomenon than value stocks. Were we to divide the market into a value half and a growth half using any of our price ratios (P/E, P/S, P/BV, P/CF), we would see that the growth stocks have been more widely held by mutual funds and more frequently recommended by brokerage analysts.

Why? Because growth stocks tend to be exciting, and value stocks tend to be boring. Excitement sells, boredom doesn't. Above all else, mutual funds and brokerages are sales organizations. Their profitability is determined by how much they can sell to their customers, not by how much money their customers make.

As massive amounts of capital flowed from banks and insurance companies into mutual funds and brokerage accounts, the fund companies and retail brokerage giants grew larger and more powerful. As they grew, their ability to cause booms and busts in individual stocks – most notably growth stocks – increased.

But then, in 2000, the bubble burst. Brokerage analysts and mutual funds lost much of their credibility with the investing pubic.

And what happened next?

2001-2002 were decent years for nanocaps (+29% and 12.5%, respectively) and value stocks (+66.8% and 31.8%), the very stocks that institutions had been most likely to snub.

The stocks favored by institutions, however, suffered losses of historic proportions. The S&P 500 lost 11.9% and 22% in 2001-2002, and our Growth Index lost 22.1% and 33.2%.

Exhibit 46 shows how often growth outperformed value during the "inflationary" years (1951 – 1980) compared to the "post-inflationary" years. It also shows separately the "post-inflationary" years that occurred during the dot.com frenzy of 1995 – 1999.

Leaving aside that five-year period of insanity, when investors' appetite for "new paradigms" seemed insatiable, growth outperformed value in just one year out of 17 post-inflationary years.

By comparison, growth was much more likely to outperform value during the pre-1980 period. And when it did, investors were far more likely to bid-up high P/S and high P/BV stocks than they were to chase high P/E or high P/CF stocks, proving once again that it's hardly ever a wise idea to pay too much for earnings or cash flow.

So what now?

Value Screening of High Relative Strength Stocks

Many institutional favorites temporarily develop high relative strength.

In *What Works on Wall Street*, Jim O'Shaugnessy found that subjecting high RS stocks to a value screen (low P/S) would have been effective in enhancing returns. This screen would, of course, weed out many companies whose high RS had resulted from fleeting institutional interest.

Exhibit 46: Growth *vs.* Value and Inflation

Growth vs. Value and Inflation

	1951 - 1980: Inflation Years 30 Years			1981 - 2002: Post-Inflation Years 22 Years			1995 - 1999: Dot.com Years
	# of Years Growth Beats Value	% of Years Growth Beats Value	Average Performance Advantage When Growth Beats Value	# of Years Growth Beats Value	% of Years Growth Beats Value	Average Performance Advantage When Growth Beats Value	Dot.com Years (1995 - 1999) When Growth Beats Value
Price to Earnings	5	16.7%	9.8%	0	0.0%	N/A	0
Price to Sales	11	36.7%	14.7%	3	13.6%	29.8%	2
Price to Book Value	14	46.7%	9.7%	4	18.2%	37.3%	3
Price to Cash Flow	5	16.7%	15.4%	4	18.2%	16.9%	3
Growth vs. Value Indices	6	20.0%	13.5%	4	18.2%	14.5%	3

Inflation may very well reverse its declines of the past two decades. Indeed, there are plenty of reasons to suspect that inflation will return, and that the Fed will be powerless to stop it.

The huge federal debt owed by America to foreigners is one factor beyond the Fed's direct control that might lead to inflation. The temptation to pay off that debt by devaluing the currency may become irresistible at some point, even at the cost of rising interest rates.

Energy shortages and the resulting price increases will likely be another source of inflation in the future. Population growth and the unsustainability of modern farming practices will almost certainly drive food prices higher. And the rapid modernization of economies in emerging nations such as China and India will increase worldwide demand for all kinds of commodities and manufactured products.

Faced with such enormous inflationary pressures, will the Fed be able to keep interest rates high enough to prevent inflation? And if it did, would the effect on economic growth be politically acceptable?

An increase in inflation would certainly be bad for stocks in general. And to the extent that rising inflation causes the yield curve to steepen, it would favor value over growth.

Does this mean that growth will rarely outperform value in the future?

Perhaps.

We suspect, however, that rising inflation will not dampen the enthusiasm many investors feel for fast-growing companies. In all likelihood, the widespread tendency to overestimate future earnings for these companies will delude many into thinking of growth stocks as inflation hedges.

From time to time, the market will become "irrationally exuberant," and euphoria will prompt otherwise sane people to buy into the excitement. Whenever this happens, growth will probably outperform value.

Large Caps Versus Small Company Stocks

We've considered some of the factors that underlie shifts in the performance of growth versus value. What about shifts between large caps and small company stocks? What causes them?

Two variables underlie these shifts: investors' tolerance for risk and the economic impact of politically motivated fiscal stimulus.

Large caps' best performance vis-à-vis smaller companies occurs early in the Election Cycle. This is also the phase in which value performs best versus growth.

The combination of "large cap" plus "value" implies "safety" to many investors, and, therefore, we see the early Election Cycle swing toward large cap value stocks as primarily a flight to quality, particularly when Fed policy turns restrictive early in the Election Cycle.

When the market is receiving little help from governmental stimulus or interest rate cuts, and, as a result, is moving sideways or down, investors become cautious. They become more concerned with avoiding losses than with missing out on opportunities.

There is nothing wrong with this line of reasoning, except insofar as it leads to the purchase of large caps "for safety."

Small company stocks, as a group, are not significantly more risky than large caps, just more volatile. That is, their returns fluctuate to a greater extent, but they do so around higher mean returns.

The 100 largest companies strategy lost money in 14 of 52 years between 1951 and 2002. The small cap ($100 million companies) strategy also lost money in 14 of 52 years. Nanocaps lost money in just 12 of 52 years. Moreover, as we saw in **Exhibit 25,** the risk of total failure—bankruptcy—by a nanocap company is surprisingly small.

Nevertheless, when the Fed was restrictive or aggressively restrictive early in the Election Cycle, large caps tended to outperform small companies. Whether this is a rational response to such a situation or not, there is little point in fighting the tape. While a small cap or nanocap strategy would outperform a large cap strategy over time, returns could be boosted somewhat by switching into large caps during Panic Years.

Exhibit 23's second graph illustrates the performance of large caps and small companies versus the S&P 500.

When small companies beat the market, they usually beat it by a lot. When they lose to the market, the margin tends to be relatively small.

Low-Risk Nanocap Investing

An asset allocation strategy involving 40% in money market securities and 60% in a highly diversified selection of nanocaps would be quite likely to outperform the S&P 500 on a consistent basis – with far less risk.

Of course, risk could be further reduced through appropriate management of the portfolio's value/growth and high/low relative strength characteristics, and by switching into large caps during Panic Years. The use of index puts to hedge against major market downturns would also reduce risk.

For most investors who want to maximize their risk-adjusted returns, large caps only make sense as a defensive move during Panic Years.

Small companies outperformed large caps by a wide margin late in the Election Cycle. A flight from quality often occurs when accommodating government policies boost economic confidence (and corporate earnings). In the bull markets that typically result, investors are emboldened to buy small company stocks they might otherwise consider too risky.

As we noted in Chapter 9, the "wind" of late Election Cycle governmental stimulus affects the performance of small company stocks more than it affects large cap returns.

Heteroskedasticity was also observed in the relative returns of nanocaps. These stocks' worst years (relative to large caps) were between 1980 and 2000.

Nanocaps' performance suffered during this period as mutual funds and brokerages funneled investment dollars into large, well-known companies.

Most mutual funds were (and are) simply too large to buy nanocaps. Brokerage analysts didn't recommended them, so brokers rarely sold them to their clients. In fact, clients who held nanocaps were often encouraged to sell.

Since 2000, as we have observed, nanocap stocks have outperformed large caps by a significant margin.

And the future looks even brighter for nanocaps. As growing numbers of investors utilize Information Age technologies to bypass mutual funds and full-service brokerages, improving access to information and the ability to execute online trades for less than $10 will increase the flow of money into these stocks.

Small companies and technological innovation have always been our country's engine of economic growth. As more and more investors learn to appreciate the superior investment opportunity they represent, and as technology improves their ability to keep investors informed, nanocaps' performance advantage over large caps will likely continue.

Greater investor awareness of and comfort with small companies would, of course, enhance their access to capital markets and thereby accelerate the pace of innovation. All in all, that will be a good thing for America.

Implementing the Fed-Election Cycle Strategy: Practical Considerations

Although a strategy of buying only small cap value stocks with high relative strength would have achieved superior performance compared to the other strategies we backtested, few investors approach the market with a 52-year planning horizon. As we have seen, even our best performing strategy would have underperformed alternative strategies from time to time. Thus we began our search for a strategy that would coordinate stock selection criteria with the two cycles that most powerfully influence performance.

But any attempt to implement such a strategy would raise a number of practical considerations.

Were we to consider wholesale realignment of our portfolio every time the Fed-Election Cycle entered a new phase, for example, trading costs might wipe out whatever gains we could hope to achieve by switching strategies. Consequently, any strategy for shifting stock selection criteria only applies to new purchases. Positions carried over from one phase to the next would get unwound according the trading tactics we spell out in Part Three.

More critical to the success of our strategy for shifting styles according to the Fed-Election Cycle is the risk of not accurately predicting the market's reaction to a phase shift.

We know that small company value stocks with high relative strength have outperformed the other strategies over time, but shifts between value and growth or between large caps and small caps are probabilistic. That is, the data only permit us to say that a shift is likely. In any given situation, a predicted shift in performance may fail to materialize, and we could wind up lowering our returns if we bet on such a prediction. We always have to weigh the prospect of improved returns if our prediction is accurate against the possibility of our returns suffering if we turn out to have been wrong.

In this regard, a performance shift in favor of large caps (from small companies) during Panic Years is somewhat more probable than a shift from value to growth during Euphoric Years. Growth is unlikely to outperform value very often. Still, it's worth knowing when a shift in favor of growth stocks is likely to occur: that is, in a late Election Cycle bear market on the cusp of a shift from a restrictive phase to an expansive one.

And should an opportunity arise to confidently predict a shift from value to growth, it's important to avoid making one of the biggest mistakes investors can make when buying growth stocks: paying too much.

Investing in growth stocks demands substantial due diligence before buying and active monitoring afterwards. Investors should always take care to verify that the market's enthusiasm is warranted before buying any stock with high price ratios.

Once a growth stock has been added to the portfolio, it is important to stay as informed as possible by monitoring news sources. And it's very important to sell at the first hint of disappointment.

It's also a good idea to remember that growth stocks can become too richly valued after they are bought (a nice problem to have). One should always be ready to sell when the expectations incorporated into the price ratios cross the line between optimism and fantasy.

Another potential pitfall with a growth stock is the possibility that the company will outrun its financial resources. Rapid growth tends to use cash, often leading to the need for additional financing. With good operating performance, new financing is usually available, but – depending on the condition of the financial markets, interest rates, and many other factors –it might not be available under ideal terms. It's easy to become so focused on the wonderful news about sales and earnings growth that the potential for significant dilution resulting from an offering of additional stock gets overlooked. Wise investors read balance sheets and keep an eye on cash flow.

The trick in buying growth stocks, then, is to buy after the market has recognized them but before they become overpriced, paying close attention to the companies' financial position and capital structure.

• Chapter 12 •

SELL-SIDE ANALYSTS' RESEARCH

In general, companies that receive little or no coverage by brokerage analysts present better opportunities, because analyst coverage tends to drive stock prices higher than they would otherwise be. Wall Street coverage reduces the potential for profiting from market inefficiencies and increases the likelihood of trading losses. (The absence of analyst coverage contributes to the superior performance of nanocaps. Few stocks with market caps under $100 million are well covered by analysts.) However, we nearly always avoid very large companies with minimal analyst coverage. Brokerage analysts tend to avoid covering large cap companies with problems, rather than issue neutral or negative reports on them.

When we began work several years ago on a precursor to this book, the stock market analysts' role was not as widely understood as it is now. Individual investors routinely bought shares on the basis of analysts' recommendations, little realizing that they were basing their decisions on the output of a badly flawed process that was never intended to help them make good choices.

But then, in the search for the culprits behind the dot.com collapse, the role analysts play in their firms' pursuit of brokerage commissions and investment banking fees suddenly became front page news. We saw analysts from the biggest Wall Street firms paraded before congressional investigating committees, listened to stories of internal brokerage house communications trashing the very stocks that were being touted to clients, and heard the hue and cry from all quarters to pass laws requiring firewalls between investment bankers and the analysts.

But despite this increase in public awareness of the problem, little substantive progress has been achieved in preventing flagrant abuses of investors' trust. Highly compensated brokerage analysts continue to collect information, issue recommendations, and forecast earnings in ways that serve the interests of almost everyone involved – except their firms' retail customers.

And it's clear that analysts' research reports continue to exert tremendous influence over the price movements of individual stocks. Investors who have become accustomed to basing their buying decisions on forecasts of future earnings continue to depend on this advice, perhaps because they have yet to discover any better alternatives.

In the face of massive evidence to the contrary, too many people continue to pretend that analysts' reports are what they purport to be, i.e., honest, expert opinions based on detailed fundamental analysis.

There are many reasons why analysts' opinions and forecasts are a poor basis for selecting stocks. In this chapter, we will briefly review some of the reasons we ignore analysts' recommendations when we select stocks to purchase, and why we think the best investment opportunities are usually companies that analysts ignore.

The Role of the Analyst in a Large Brokerage Firm

Supporting Brokerage Operations

Analysts are key contributors to the profitability of large, full-service brokerage firms.

The advertising campaigns of big full-service firms tout their superior ability to advise customers in selecting the best investments. The ads emphasize their analysts' deep understanding of financial markets and portray their brokers as capable, knowledgeable financial advisors.

In reality, no special financial expertise is required to become a broker in a large firm. Almost anyone willing and able to make 100 phone calls per day can become a securities salesperson (aka stockbroker or, in some firms, "financial consultant").

No doubt, some brokers are competent and honest financial advisors, but most are little more than telemarketers. Few sophisticated investors would respond to their sales pitches were it not for the façade of expertise provided by the firms' research departments.

Much of the time, when a broker calls to sell a client on the merits of a particular stock, he or she is merely reading the analysts' opinions from a computer screen. Analysts provide the credibility that brokers lack, thereby allowing the firm to economically leverage a few well-paid "experts" with large numbers of commission-driven salespeople.

Thus, one of the key functions of the analyst is to support brokerage operations with a steady flow of "new insights" that provide brokers with the material they need to pitch clients. (The analysts' insights also provide content for the firms' marketing and public relations efforts.)

The reality is, therefore, quite different from the conventional notion that the analyst's role is to provide expert, unbiased advice to individual investors. Rather than being independent judges of investment merit, analysts are more like advertising copywriters. It doesn't matter whether what they say is true; what matters is that it sells product (in this case, brokerage services).

Seen in this light, it's not surprising that analysts' support of brokerage operations creates an almost universal bias toward favorable recommendations. "Buy" recommendations generate more commission dollars than "sell" recommendations, because all investors are potentially in a position to buy. "Sell" recommendations can only be acted upon by clients who already own the stock in question or are part of the minority of investors willing to short sell.

Supporting Investment Banking Operations

Support of brokerage operations is the most visible of the analysts' functions, but it is not the only way they contribute to their firms' profitability. A major portion of the profits earned by large, full-service brokerage firms is derived from fees for investment banking services, and, as is now well-known, analysts have worked closely with investment bankers to promote this business.

Analysts' association with investment banking has done more to destroy the integrity of their work than any other factor. Huge banking fees create tremendous incentives to please corporate customers, and, despite protestations to the contrary, analysts do not operate independently of such pressures.

In some firms, the association has been blatant. Analysts have been required to seek formal approval from senior investment banking executives before changing their opinions. Organization charts have shown the head of the research department reporting to an executive in the investment banking organization.

In other cases, the association of analysts with investment banking is more subtle, but no less harmful.

Suppose, for example, that an analyst wanted to issue an unfavorable report on a particular biotech stock. His firm's management and investment bankers may well prevail upon him to keep a lid on that opinion, since a negative recommendation could undermine the firm's efforts to get underwriting business in the next wave of IPO's.

Analysts tend to be very well-compensated for the contributions they make to their firms' bottom lines, so they have a lot to lose from bucking the system. Brokerage analysts who fail to generate sufficient revenue from commissions and investment banking fees lose their jobs, no matter how insightful their research might be. In fact, highly original, insightful research is rarely rewarded and has no place in this scheme of things.

External Influences on Analysts' Opinions

Up to this point, we have been discussing how the analysts' role in a large brokerage firm determines the purposes to which their work will be put – purposes that have very little to do with providing unbiased advice to investors.

The independence and quality of analysts' work is further degraded by their dependence on corporate executives for "research material" and by the pressures placed upon them to remain in sync with their peers from competing firms.

Investors like to suppose that analysts have an inside track on information regarding the companies they follow. Presumably, this would give them special insight that they would pass along to their firms' clients.

Investors would be less sanguine about acting on this information if they knew the extent to which analysts merely repeat what industry executives tell them, without any effort to filter out spin, misinformation, and an obvious bias toward telling only the good news.

Analysts go to great lengths to cultivate the industry sources who provide the bulk of the information that goes into their research opinions, and they are loath to risk offending the corporate executives who spoon-feed them. As a practical matter, analysts who can't get information from industry sources have very little to say.

Occasionally, an analyst will do some actual independent research – perhaps talking with a company's customers and suppliers – but this is more for the sake of appearances than anything else. If it leads to conclusions that differ radically from the views expressed by the company's Chief Financial Officer, we are not likely to hear about them - especially if the company is also seen as a potential investment banking client.

An analyst's recommendations and earnings forecasts are strongly influenced by those of his peers. Whatever strong opinions an analyst might privately harbor about a stock often get watered down through a process known as groupthink.

The peer pressure generated by groups can often lead intelligent, moral individuals to do stupid, if not downright immoral things. Classic examples of groupthink include the Bay of Pigs debacle (which resulted from groupthink in JFK's cabinet), NASA's decision to go ahead with the ill-fated Challenger launch, and most riots.

Analysts avoid getting too far out of step with their peers from competing firms. Doing so risks a loss of credibility with their firms' investors, brokers, and investment banking clients. For analysts, the rewards associated with being the first to publicize sensational and correct findings regarding a stock are small compared to the penalties for being wrong.

Suppose one of the analysts following a stock puts out a favorable opinion with an earnings forecast well above the consensus. If the forecast is not met, his firm will have a lot of unhappy clients blaming the salespeople for their losses. If the analyst is foolish enough to repeat this mistake too often, the firm's salespeople will become gun-shy about passing his recommendations along to their clients. This will reduce the volume of "buy" orders generated from the analyst's recommendations.

Suppose, alternatively, an analyst wants to put out an unfavorable opinion with an earnings forecast well below the consensus. The firm's brokers might recommend that clients sell the stock. If the analyst turns out to be wrong, the clients will be unhappy about their lost opportunity, for which they'll blame the brokers. The brokers, of course, will think twice before calling their clients the next time the analyst issues a recommendation.

But that won't be the end of the trouble caused by the analyst's "Chicken Little" recommendation. Management at the company in question, whose compensation was probably affected by the fall in their stock's price, will be angry at the analyst, which will color their view of the entire firm. Even if the firm's investment bankers are able to smooth the executives' ruffled feathers, they will still have to deal with the consequences of the drop in the affected company's stock price, which might very well include a diminished capacity

> ## Analysts' Groupthink
>
> For more information on how analysts' opinions are influenced by their peers, see "Implications of Herding Behavior for Earnings Estimates, Risk Assessment, and Stock Returns," by Robert Olsen, *Financial Analysts Journal*, July/August 1996.

for making acquisitions and a reduced willingness to execute future stock offerings.

Whatever affects the stock price of one company usually affects the stocks of the other companies that operate in its industry. If an analyst issues an unfavorable report on Burger King, the stock price of Burger King will probably fall, but so will the prices of McDonald's and Wendy's. Thus, the difficulties that an analyst's downgrade might cause between his firm and the affected company could easily spread to the entire industry.

Many analysts specialize in just one industry. For them, the consequences of a single ill-considered downgrade could entail a career-ending disaster.

Analysts get paid to generate buying interest for the stocks they follow. By creating buying interest, they help produce commission revenue and support the stock prices of their firms' investment banking clients. Analysts who cannot generate buying interest lose their jobs.

On the other hand, the analyst who keeps his opinions and forecasts in line with those of his peers has a ready-made defense against any fallout from overly optimistic recommendations. He won't be singled out for blame if all his peers are just as wrong.

Analysts' Bias Toward Optimism

We have touched on some of the factors that cause a strong bias toward favorable analyst recommendations. Needless to say, this creates dangers for individual investors, who are advised to buy stocks on the basis of unrealistic expectations, but are rarely told when to sell.

The bias toward optimism that permeates the industry is a little like the problem of grade inflation at certain Ivy League colleges, where nobody fails and the worst students in the class graduate cum laude.

Investors are learning to discount analysts' recommendations, so that "strong buy" means "possibly interesting" and "hold" means "run for the exits." Instead of translating analysts' opinions in this way, it would be better for investors to see analysts' unfounded optimism as another indication of their recommendations' essential uselessness.

The analysts who earn seven-figure salaries for issuing such recommendations have strong incentives to filter out any negative comments that might offend either their firms' investment banking clients or the industry executives who

Churn, Churn, Churn

Clients are rarely told to sell on any objective basis related to the investment merits of their holdings.

But if a broker senses an opportunity to generate commission dollars by "repositioning" a client's portfolio, that client will be advised to sell, and buy, and sell, and buy...

are their sources of information. They realize that issuing negative opinions – however well-founded – can never make any of their key constituents happy, but can entail career-threatening consequences.

So they continue to feed favorable recommendations to their firms' brokerage operations, injecting only enough caution into their reports to maintain a modicum of credibility.

Analysts report what they are expected to say, not what they actually think.

Analysts' Slow Reaction to New Information

By now it should be clear that a wide gap exists between the reality of analysts' work and the public image they strive to maintain.

The reality is that most sell-side analysts will say and write whatever their corporate constituents want them to write, as long as it generates revenues for their brokerage firms.

By contrast, analysts portray themselves as well-informed sleuths with superior financial insights who perform acutely precise analyses in a sincere effort to help the firms' brokerage clients achieve superior investment returns. Striving to give the appearance of possessing Delphi-like omniscience, they have strong incentives to protect their opinions from whatever facts come along to contradict them.

An analyst's credibility with investors and brokers is his stock in trade. Therefore, even as circumstances change, analysts have a tendency to stick with opinions that get less and less valid, rather than admit their errors, because to do so might be interpreted as a sign of instability or unreliability.

When changing fundamentals ultimately compel a major change in an analyst's opinion or forecast, rarely will the change be given effect all at once. Instead, it will be announced over time in small increments.

For example, if a stock that an analyst has rated a "Strong Buy" runs into major problems, the analyst will typically lower the opinion in stages. Rather than going from "Strong Buy" to "Sell," the recommendation will go from "Strong Buy" to "Buy." Then, a few months later, the opinion will get lowered again from "Buy" to "Hold." A few months after that, instead of going from "Hold" to "Sell," the analyst might simply drop coverage on the stock, rather than admit his mistake.

Incremental changes, especially in the case of downward revisions, protect an analyst's credibility in two ways: they require less explanation than big changes, and they tend to keep an analyst's pronouncements more in line with those of his peers.

Decision Rules for Analyst Recommendations

Analysts' recommendations are influenced by many factors that have nothing whatever to do with providing good advice to investors, and, therefore, they should rarely, if ever, be accepted at face value or acted upon.

On the contrary, analyst coverage tends to reduce opportunities for profiting from market inefficiencies, due to the publicity and buying pressure it causes.

Large cap stocks covered by multiple analysts are not likely to be undiscovered bargains. Analysts prefer to cover companies with relatively large market values, because larger companies have greater potential to generate investment banking fees and brokerage commissions. As a result, normally, the larger a company is, the more analyst coverage it will receive. Analysts' recommendations, biased towards optimism, stimulate widespread buying interest in these stocks, causing them to be at least fairly priced, if not overvalued.

Investors seeking superior returns can find better opportunities among the small companies that analysts mostly ignore. The relative information vacuum surrounding such companies makes it possible for small investors to get a jump on the big institutional fund managers.

We can summarize our decision rules for dealing with analysts' recommendations as follows:

Rule #1: Never buy a stock simply because an analyst recommends it—the analyst is probably less interested in your profits than in his own bonus.

Rule #2: Search for undiscovered values in stocks that are not followed by analysts.

It is not difficult to construct a portfolio of companies with excellent earnings growth, strong balance sheets, and good management that are too small to attract much interest from analysts or that, for one reason or another, are considered "out of favor" by analysts and institutional investors.

But large companies with little or no analyst coverage should usually be avoided. It's usually safe to assume that any large company not followed by analysts has major flaws and is headed for trouble. Otherwise, analysts seeking banking fees and brokerage commissions would be all over it.

Earnings Forecasts

As we noted earlier, despite all that has come to light regarding analysts' multiple conflicts of interest, investors continue to buy and sell stocks on the basis of analysts' earnings forecasts. We believe that relying on analysts' earnings forecasts to inform trading decisions makes no more sense than selecting stocks according to their recommendations.

We don't think anyone can forecast a company's earnings with the precision implicitly claimed by most analysts. No amount of inside information or special insight could create the ability to see into the future that clearly. Even a company's own financial people can't do it consistently, despite having access to all of the company's financial records.

Analysts, however, can generate buying interest in a stock by raising their earnings estimates for a company from, say, $4.12 to $4.20 per share, even though their forecasts might have a $1.00 margin of error (or more).

Our own attempts to peer into the future are limited to evaluating whether news of some unexpected event will cause a company's earnings, sales, book value, or cash flow to go up or go down – or whether it will cause a company's growth rate to rise or decline. We might even go so far as to estimate the order of magnitude of a change, but we don't try to forecast specific amounts.

In other words, we sometimes try to project trends, but we are mindful that most earnings forecasts are not nearly as precise as analysts would have us believe, and we ignore any small changes that fall within a forecast's margin of error.

We listen carefully when the management of a company whose stock we own provides earnings guidance, but the screens we use to select the stocks for potential purchase are based solely upon actual published financial results, not on anyone's forecasts. We never base trading decisions solely on analysts' earnings forecasts.

Analyst Errors
Support for this assertion can be found in a 1995 *Financial Analysts Journal* article, "Analyst Forecasting Errors and Their Implications for Security Analysis" by David Dreman and Michael Berry. Dreman and Berry observed that 50% of all industries studied had median errors (i.e., differences between consensus forecasts and actual earnings) of more than 32%.

"Legal" Insider Trading

Though we acknowledge the influence corporate executives have on analysts' estimates, we are nevertheless loathe to rely on the analysts to be effective conduits of the information management reveals.

Whatever analysts say is likely to be old news by the time it reaches us.

Although analysts aren't allowed to explicitly tell their firms' best brokerage clients about impending recommendations and forecast changes, they still are able to tip off favored clients with their "body language." Were there no such advantage to be derived from speaking directly with analysts, professional money managers wouldn't waste their time doing it.

These ex parte conversations inure to the detriment of individual investors and flagrantly violate the spirit, if not the letter, of our securities laws. Someday, we hope, they will be banned.

Of course, banning them would have the effect of significantly reducing the ability of analysts to assist in the generation of brokerage commissions.

In fact, any changes in securities laws or industry practice that would be truly effective in improving the integrity of research would, in all likelihood, significantly reduce the role analysts' play in selling stocks and investment banking services.

Brokerage research might ultimately gain in integrity, as appropriate regulations are implemented, but its most competent practitioners will undoubtedly be leaving for greener pastures as time passes.

Earnings Surprises and the "Sergei Bubka Gambit"

Earnings surprises occur when a company's reported earnings differ from the analysts' consensus estimate. This often leads to predictable stock price movements.

There is an important distinction between basing investment choices on analysts' recommendations or forecasts - which we never do - and reacting when a company's actual performance diverges from analysts' predictions. In the first case all we have to go on are the predictions themselves, corrupted, as we have seen, by multiple unacknowledged influences. In the second case, we have real data to guide our decisions.

It is important to remember that analysts do not develop their earnings forecasts in a vacuum. We have noted how heavily analysts depend on corporate executives for information. Working together to create earnings estimates, the analysts and executives share a common interest in managing expectations so as to maintain a positive spin on the company's prospects, while taking care not to set the bar too high. The analysts maintain a pretense of independence when they announce the new forecast, but, in fact, they rarely challenge the estimates given by management.

Hence, a positive earnings surprise means that, in effect, the company outperformed its own expectations. A negative surprise means something went wrong that management was unable (or unwilling) to predict. In either event, the market response will be fairly predictable.

Positive Earnings Surprises

We know from extensive research and our own experience that positive earnings surprises often cause stock prices to rise over extended periods because, when results are better than predicted, more positive surprises generally follow as the story unfolds.

Corporate executives who beat their earnings forecast win accolades (and bonuses) for their demonstrated ability to manage their business. If nothing else, they have shown an ability to manage investors' expectations. Absent any major change in circumstances, they have compelling motivation for encouraging analysts to continue setting artificially low expectations that the company can easily surpass.

The analysts are only too happy to cooperate, because positive earnings surprises serve their interests as well. Instead of increasing their earnings estimate for a growing company in one large step, they announce a series of small increases over a period of time, hoping to keep their forecasts below the actual rate of earnings growth. Each announcement fosters goodwill with the company's executives, who are pleased with the positive press and happy that the Street's expectations remain eminently achievable.

At the same time, conveniently, analysts' predilection for incrementalism contributes to their support of brokerage operations. When an analyst raises his earnings estimate for a stock, the fact of the increase is more important than the amount. Even a small increase gives the firms' brokers an opportunity to call their clients and persuade them to buy more stock. A series of incremental increases multiplies the opportunities for generating brokerage commissions, and it increases buying interest by reinforcing clients' positive perception of the company.

Thus, by adjusting their earnings forecast to set up a string of positive earnings surprises, analysts are able to please all of their key constituencies: the corporate executives who supply essential information and may also be investment banking prospects, the brokers who generate commission revenue, and the brokerage clients who, along with everyone else, are delighted with the inevitable rise in the stock's price.

We call this approach the "Sergei Bubka Gambit" in honor of the Ukrainian pole-vaulter who set 35 world records in his event. Bubka had no real competition, and his sponsors paid him a bonus every time he set a new record. Consequently, with no incentive whatsoever to give his best effort, he opted to improve his record one centimeter at a time.

Analysts, emulating Sergei Bubka, in effect, earn bonuses for themselves every time they announce tiny, incremental increases in their forecasts. At the same time, they avoid the risk of going out on a limb with a large upward revision.

Analysts who employ the "Sergei Bubka Gambit" compound the market impact of corporate executives who sandbag their forecasts. When they understate earnings forecasts, they cause the market's reaction to actual earnings growth to be delayed. A positive earnings surprise may lead many investors to buy the stock, but few realize the full extent of the opportunity. They don't buy as aggressively as they might have, or more likely, they sell before the company's earning power is fully reflected in its stock price.

It Pays to Act Quickly

A better-than-expected earnings announcement often leads one or more analysts to issue a "buy" recommendation. And when one analyst issues a buy recommendation, it often leads to additional buy recommendations, as the other analysts who follow the stock fall in line.

As a result, it usually pays to react to a positive earnings surprise by immediately and aggressively buying the stock.

The wisdom of this approach is supported by an article entitled, "The Anatomy of the Performance of Buy and Sell Recommendations," by Scott Stickel, *Financial Analysts Journal,* September/October 1995.

In it, Mr. Stickel noted that analysts' buy and sell recommendations dated within five days of an earnings report tended to outperform recommendations dated at month-end by a wide margin.

Eventually, the company's operating performance will drive the stock price to a more appropriate level, as public perception catches up with reality. This scenario often creates prime opportunities for superior gains.

Therefore, if a stock meeting our initial screening criteria reports a positive earnings surprise, unless a review of the earnings announcement reveals that the better-than-expected performance is just a one-time event, we immediately and aggressively buy it.

This illustrates our tactic of buying stocks in response to good news stories. The utility of this approach derives from delay in investors' reactions to favorable developments. Delay may result when, as in the case of positive earnings surprises, the reality of the story is better than its telling. Delay might also result from a host of psychological factors, which we will explore in detail in Chapter 16.

Negative Earnings Surprises

Delay in releasing and reacting to new information can be even more pronounced in the case of a deteriorating situation. Very often, a negative earnings surprise is our first indication that things are going wrong with a company.

When a company's plans go awry, managers at all levels tend to put an overly optimistic spin on developments. Few divisional or regional sales managers are willing to risk their jobs by painting a bleak picture of their own unit's prospects. Prophets of doom are rarely rewarded, even if they do manage to keep their jobs, so unrealistically optimistic forecasts tend to get passed up the organization to the senior executives.

The senior executives, for their part, may be inclined to accept and repeat a rosy scenario, rather than face the consequences of going public with the truth. They would rather persuade analysts to defer cutting earnings estimates than go public with information that might well batter their stock and jeopardize their bonuses.

Analysts, as we have noted, react slowly to new information, and very few analysts are quick to blow the whistle on a deteriorating situation. This is especially true when the firm or its institutional clients hold significant positions in the stock, or when the firm's investment banking division is pursuing a deal with the company.

And, besides their need to protect themselves and their key constituents, analysts have a typical human aversion to admitting their mistakes. They will often delay downgrading a stock they have heavily touted until it has become obvious that something is amiss.

Thus, both the executives and the analysts have substantial incentives to keep the company's problems under wraps, buying time in the hope that things will get better.

A negative earnings surprise often represents the unmasking of long-standing problems that, in all probability, will continue to cause operating performance to deteriorate. Meanwhile, the executives and analysts will be motivated to continue whitewashing the earnings estimates, leading to more negative surprises in the future.

This creates an opportunity to profit from put options purchased upon the announcement of a negative earnings surprise. After the fall in price resulting from the negative surprise has run its initial course, the stock might recover temporarily as a result of the overly optimistic earnings forecasts, wishful thinking by investors who have lost money, and a reduction in margin call-related selling pressure, but then the stock will in all likelihood continue to drift lower as the full scope of the company's problems is gradually revealed.

The Brokerage Analyst's Future: Reform or Extinction?

We began this chapter by commenting on the recent controversy that has surrounded brokerage analyst research. During the writing of this book, stories have come to light of widespread, blatant trading of favorable research opinions for everything from investment banking deals to admission into exclusive nursery schools!

What we find especially striking about many of these stories is that no attempt was made by the participants to exercise even a minimum of discretion. Electronic correspondence explicitly spelling out quid pro quos or directing analysts to bring in more business in return for their favorable opinions reveals a world in which such practices have long been the established way of doing business– so long that most of those involved seem to have lost touch with ethical and legal concerns.

The sanctions imposed in the wake of the "analyst-gate" scandal were insignificant compared to the profits that firms derive from these corrupt practices. The guilty firms settled for what amounted to slaps on the wrist and then went on doing business just as they always have, albeit with perhaps a bit more discretion.

The glare of publicity led to many proposals for reforming the brokerage research function, but the major flaws that exist in the way analysts' jobs are structured and their work compensated go beyond anything that can be solved by new legislation or regulation. Without entering into a long discussion of each proposal's pros and cons, we'll simply state our opinion that it may not be possible to reform the present system in a way that reconciles all conflicts of interest.

Under the existing system, analysts' research provides the justification for the exorbitant commissions that full service brokerage firms charge. In other words, research is what retail investors get in return for paying several hundred dollars for a trade that they could have executed through a discount broker for as little as $7. But all too often, the "research" consists of little more than information obtained from public companies that is repackaged with minimal added value before being passed through the firms' brokers to their retail clients.

As brokerage clients become increasingly aware of how little value is added by the firms' research departments, more will begin to wonder why their broker's recommendations cost so much.

In the pre-Internet days, large brokerage firms could argue that they provided the most convenient, efficient way for information on public companies to get distributed to investors – even if the firms' analysts didn't add much value to the information, and even though it often got distorted by multiple conflicts of interest. As a practical matter, most investors had nowhere else to go.

Now, of course, the Internet has made the distribution of information much more efficient than ever before. Investors can get information on public companies for a tiny fraction of what it costs to obtain it through a full service brokerage firm.

A client of a full service brokerage firm might easily pay a commission of $300 to buy 100 shares of a stock that he could have purchased through a discount broker for $10. He would pay another $300 when those shares are sold. The difference between what it costs to establish and unwind such a position through a full service firm, versus what it would cost through a discount broker, is thus $580.

Thus, the client in our example would be paying $20 for brokerage services and $580 for research.

If he had been able to obtain that research through the Internet, rather than through a broker, would it cost $580?

Probably not.

So why do investors continue to get their research information through full service brokers?

The answer to this question probably lies in the brokerage firm's ability to organize and filter the information. Most of the information that is available through a broker is also available through the Internet, but in a form that is less organized and harder to access.

If, however, a small portion of the billions of dollars spent each year on full service brokerage commissions were to be diverted into the development of web-based systems that could provide individual investors with the information they need in an easily accessible format, there would rarely be any justification for $300 commissions. They would go the way of the $120 calculator and the $40 long-distance telephone call.

Besides being cheaper, web-based investment research could provide a number of other potential advantages over traditional methods.

It could offer public companies a range of presentation options (e.g., multi-media, interactive) to use in making their pitch to investors. It could provide investors with the ability to tailor the flow of information to their individual needs. And, it could facilitate collaboration between public companies' investor relations departments and independent, third-party analysts in the preparation of research materials.

But most of all, it could facilitate a total restructuring of the current perfidious system.

Analysts who sold their research reports directly to investors for a fee would be beholden to those investors, not to big institutions or corporate insiders. Their work would no longer be supported by transaction fees, so they wouldn't have any incentive to issue recommendations for the sole purpose of churning client accounts. The integrity of their work wouldn't be subordinated to the pursuit of huge investment banking fees, so they would no longer have any reason to avoid issuing sell recommendations when circumstances warranted. And, rather than being pressured to stay in line with their peers, analysts would compete with each other to provide the best, most insightful, most useful research to their customers.

If investors are to ever receive truly honest and insightful investment research, it would have to be provided by professionals with impeccable qualifications and ethics whose independence was secure from any undisclosed potential conflicts of interest.

The increasing numbers of CFA charterholders who are becoming independent investment advisors would meet these criteria.

Well-qualified professionals such as these, working under a strict code of ethics, could provide high quality independent research using Internet technologies to facilitate the development and distribution of their reports. Such a group could become the core of a new system for disseminating investment research.

To do this, they would need access to information beyond what is currently provided in annual reports and SEC filings, but, as we have said, most of this information is already available on the Internet.

Most public companies already post information on their products, markets, suppliers, and production facilities on their web pages. Ultimately, it could become the norm for them to add additional information, such as interactive video presentations of product demonstrations, plant tours, and management interviews.

It's not hard to imagine public companies competing with each other to provide the best package of information to support their stock prices. Partnering with independent, objective professionals in the production of investor research reports would legitimize the information, similar to the way a company's financial statements acquire legitimacy through being audited by CPA's.

The present unsatisfactory system, rather than being reformed by new laws and more rigorous enforcement, could be replaced by something entirely new that takes full advantage of Information Age technologies.

And, as more and more investors became aware of the advantages of web-based research, demand for the traditional forms of research hitherto provided by brokerage analysts would diminish.

In that case, brokerage analysts might very well fade into extinction.

Exhibit 47 shows how sell-side analysts interact with mutual funds and brokers to keep the market anything *but* efficient.

Exhibit 47

How Mutual Funds and Brokerages Keep the Market "Efficient"

Investment Bankers

Work for brokerages, generate huge fees from corporate securities issuers, expert salespeople

Corporate Issuers

Give investment banking business to firms whose analysts will best support their stock prices

Brokerage Executives

Focused on maximizing revenues, typically earn far more from investment banking fees than brokerage commissions

Pressure to make recommendations which please corporate issuers

May deny access to information if analyst does not support their stock prices

Pressure to support banking efforts

Conversations with institutional brokers and their clients in which "body language" indicating possible future recommendations is communicated (if not actual recommendations)

Brokerage Analysts

Expert salespeople with significant investment knowledge, ethics in doubt if not CFA charterholders or AIMR members

Institutional Stockbrokers

Expert salespeople with significant investment knowledge

Written Recommendations

Recommendations to buy and sell, retail brokers (and their clients) often get this information after the institutional brokers

Sell investments to mutual funds based upon recommendations of brokerage analysts

Mutual Fund Portfolio Managers

Expert investors with more assets than they can efficiently handle, resulting market impact outweighs benefits of preferred treatment from brokers

Retail Stockbrokers

Expert salespeople with superficial investment knowledge, typically have little or no fiduciary duty to clients (though clients *think* they do)

Recommend securities whose prices have already been driven up by institutions

Recommend mutual funds that already have excessive assets

Promote funds to stockbrokers and provide selling incentives

$

Cost controls and need to keep reportable expenses low (for marketing reasons) forces managers to rely upon brokerage research, whose costs are hidden from investors

Retail Clients of Full Service Broker

If they stop paying big fees for bad advice, the system breaks down

Mutual Fund Executives
(Sales, Marketing and Administrative)

Focus on gathering more assets and cutting costs

Chapter 13

PROFITING FROM DEFICIENCIES IN GAAP

We take advantage of differences between a company's true economic condition and performance, and its condition and performance as reported according to GAAP accounting principles.

Financial reporting scandals have filled the business sections and network news programs throughout the course of this book's development. As the parade of fraudulent accounting cases has made its way through the courts and across the front pages, thoughtful observers have expressed their concern that corporate executives who intentionally misreported their companies' performance - and the accountants who let them get away with it - may have undermined the integrity of our financial system.

And then, in the face of all of these reporting scandals, the market shot up– by 28% (during 2003) in the case of the S&P 500.

The stock market recovered, as it always has, because it provides a combination of liquidity, capital appreciation, and hedge against inflation that is hard to match.

The accounting scandals have had an effect on investors' behavior, though. At the merest whiff of smoke from cooked books, investors flee as if from a burning building. The penalty for being among the last out can be severe.

It remains to be seen whether recently enacted reforms will effectively protect investors from financial reporting chicanery, but we doubt that legislation will ever completely eliminate this problem. In the meantime, for investors who wish to avoid getting trampled in the exit from one of these disasters, the challenge is to become better equipped to spot weaknesses in the numbers before the rush for the door begins.

The ability to spot fraudulent reporting is just one of the useful benefits to be gained from learning to analyze financial statements, however. Learning to spot differences between a company's true economic condition and performance, on the one hand, and its condition and performance as reported according to GAAP accounting principles, on the other, can lead to the discovery of many wonderful investment opportunities.

The Information "GAAP"

GAAP: Generally Accepted Accounting Principles.

With all of today's technological wizardry, it is sometimes easy to forget that much of the instantly accessible financial information flowing through electronic media these days continues to be derived from financial statements produced by accountants in very traditional ways.

One of the most important things to know about the GAAP accounting rules that govern how financial statements are prepared is that they are definitely *not* designed to measure the economic or financial value of a company in any kind of scientifically rigorous way.

Having witnessed the destruction of a major public accounting firm (Arthur Andersen), we have been reminded that if a misleading financial statement causes someone to overvalue a company, the accountant who certified the statement can get sued for any losses that might result.

This is important to an understanding of GAAP. It is the reason GAAP accounting rules were designed to allow accountants to *lean in the direction of undervaluing companies,* to "play it safe."

CPA's claim that they do this to protect investors, but this bias primarily serves to protect auditors.

Of course, the recent scandals came about when auditors allowed companies such as Enron to be overvalued by falsely overstating earnings and understating liabilities, but this had little to do with the GAAP rules and everything to do with large fees earned by the consulting divisions of the accounting firms.

Fraudulent reporting aside, if the accountants truly desired to serve the interests of investors, they would create GAAP rules designed to accurately measure the true economic value of their clients' net worth and earnings.

Instead, the accounting profession developed what is known as the *conservatism principle*, which requires that CPA's certifying financial statements never overstate assets or earnings, or understate liabilities. (The profession failed, however, to develop a corresponding GAAP principle that would prevent assets and earnings from being *understated* with respect to their true economic values.)

In practice, this led to what is called *historical cost basis accounting*, which has the added benefit (for accountants) of making the measurement of values easier—but which unfortunately makes the financial information provided to investors significantly less meaningful.

Historical Cost Basis Accounting

To illustrate how historical cost basis accounting degrades the quality of financial reporting, let's take as an example two companies making identical products that, for the sake of our example, sell for identical prices.

Company A produces its product in a factory that it built 20 years ago, on land it owns, at a cost of $1 million. Its accountants decided to write off the cost of the plant over 25 years, so the depreciation amount included in cost of sales each year is $40,000. The plant would be reported on Company A's balance sheet at its historical cost of $1 million, minus 20 years' accumulated depreciation of $800,000, for a net value of $200,000. In addition to the plant, Company A's fixed assets would include the land, carried at its 1984 cost of $50,000.

Company B produces its product in a factory it paid $5 million to build just last year on land it recently purchased for a cost of $1 million. Its accountants plan to write the new plant off over 25 years as well, so Company B's annual depreciation cost is $200,000. Company B's factory would be carried on its balance sheet at a net value of $4.8 million.

Suppose, just to keep this exercise simple, that each company has $1 million in sales, and that direct manufacturing costs (material and labor) total $700K in both cases. In addition, let's assume that neither company carries any inventory on their books, and that both companies have zero selling, general, and administrative expenses—and no debt.

The following table summarizes some key financial figures:

	Company A	Company B
Net Fixed Assets	$250,000	$5,800,000
Sales	$1,000,000	$1,000,000
Direct Costs	$(700,000)	$(700,000)
Depreciation	$(40,000)	$(200,000)
Total Cost of Sales	$(740,000)	$(900,000)
Profit	$260,000	$100,000
Return on Assets	104%	2%

Now, suppose A and B have the same market cap, and you were asked to pick one of these two companies' stocks to purchase. Which one would you buy?

Based on these numbers, the obvious choice would be company A; it's far more profitable, with a much higher return on invested assets.

But would that be the right choice?

Actually, there is not enough information given to answer this question.

If these two companies happened to be semiconductor manufacturers, whose plants last only a few years before becoming obsolete, you would probably be better off with Company B because its plant is newer. On the other hand, they might be paper producers, in which case you could be just as well off with Company A, because paper mills last for decades.

The accountants chose to write both plants off over 25 years, but that doesn't necessarily tell us the actual useful life of the facilities. The choice of 25 years might simply be an artifact of the IRS code, or some similarly arcane financial accounting standard that may be misleading when applied to this particular industry or technology.

Both factories are carried on the companies' balance sheets at historical cost, less the accumulated depreciation, but their actual value today might be much greater, and they might have many more years of productive life.

Furthermore, Company A's factory was built on land it has owned for at least 20 years, but which is carried on the balance sheet at its original cost of $50,000. The land is most likely worth far more then $50,000. Nevertheless,

GAAP accounting rules do not allow long-lived assets to be "written up" to their current actual market value, so it's impossible to fairly compare Company A's balance sheet to Company B's balance sheet.

Oddly enough, the same GAAP conservatism rules that prevent Company A's land and factory from being carried at its full current value also cause the company's reported earnings to be higher than Company B's. Of course, in a real world case, much of this difference might be offset by the higher maintenance costs associated with operating an older plant and the savings produced by Company B's more efficient new plant.

Historical cost basis accounting produces significant distortions in financial reporting. The value of any assets acquired more than a few years ago are likely to be materially understated on the balance sheet, and the earnings produced by such assets are likely to be correspondingly overstated.

Real estate, in particular, tends to be grossly understated on the balance sheets of established businesses.

Other Distortions Caused by GAAP

GAAP rules distort financial reporting and make comparisons difficult in many other ways.

Consider the way certain expenditures are "conservatively" treated as expenses of the period in which they are made, instead of being applied to all of the periods over which benefit is derived. Examples of this include research, product development, marketing, and advertising to build brand awareness and loyalty.

It would be beyond the scope of this book to fully describe all of the ways in which GAAP can distort such key metrics as book value and earnings. Instead, we'll illustrate some of the more important facets of financial statement analysis by comparing two mythical companies, Hi-Q and Lo-Q.

Remarkably few investors go to the trouble of scrutinizing financial reports for disparities between GAAP presentation and economic reality, but those willing to expend the effort can gain significant advantages. Often, they can uncover hidden values, steer clear of weak companies, and avoid becoming the victims of fraudulent reporting.

Shrewd investors do not accept financial statements as presented. Instead, they adjust the figures as necessary to better reflect the economic realities of the companies under consideration.

Hi-Q Versus Lo-Q

To illustrate some of the distortions found in financial statements, we'll compare two fictitious firms, Hi-Q (i.e., High Quality) and Lo-Q (i.e., Low Quality).

The point of this illustration is to depict two firms of vastly divergent economic value whose financial statements, on the surface, appear substantially identical. This will provide examples of the distortions that careful financial analysis can reveal.

We'll begin by comparing the two companies' balance sheets, line by line.

Cash: Both Hi-Q and Lo-Q operate internationally and maintain large cash balances in banks throughout the world. However, Hi-Q's cash is held in banks in developed nations that allow unrestricted repatriation of cash, while Lo-Q's cash is mostly held in developing countries that restrict its repatriation.

Marketable Securities: Both Hi-Q and Lo-Q have large bond portfolios that their accountants treat as "Held to Maturity," which requires that they be carried on the balance sheet at their purchase cost (which happens to be the same for each firm). But Hi-Q's bonds are long-term U.S. Treasury securities purchased when interest rates were higher (so their current market value is much higher than what they cost), whereas Lo-Q's mix of Treasury and corporate issues were bought when rates were at their (relatively low) current level.

Inventory: Both companies are in the forest products business. Most of Hi-Q's timber inventory is carried at prices prevailing in 1900, when it acquired the bulk of its forests, while most of Lo-Q's inventory of timber is carried at the prices it paid when the property was acquired five years ago. For tax reasons, however, Hi-Q mostly cuts its more recently acquired, higher cost forests, so its reported profits from forest products are exactly the same as Lo-Q's.

In addition to the forest products businesses, both firms own commodity chemicals subsidiaries. Hi-Q's chemical subsidiary values its inventory on a LIFO (last-in, first-out) basis. Its inventory has slowly but constantly expanded, and so most of it is priced at historical costs from 30 years ago (a small fraction of its current market value). Lo-Q's chemical subsidiary, on the other hand, which also values its inventory on a LIFO basis, recently sold off all of its hydrochloric acid, which had been carried at 1973 prices, and began building a sulfuric acid inventory. (Coincidentally, the large profit Lo-Q earned from the sale of its hydrochloric acid inventory was exactly equal to the difference between its bond interest income and that of Hi-Q.)

Prepaid Expenses: Hi-Q prepaid for a variety of goods and services whose prices have risen significantly. Lo-Q paid a similar amount for goods and services whose prices have stayed the same.

Other Investments: Both firms have recently established venture capital subsidiaries that invariably hold 40% stakes in their portfolio companies, which they account for according to the Equity Method (which means that the investments are carried on the firms' balance sheets at cost plus or minus 40% of the portfolio companies' retained earnings). Although the earnings of the portfolio companies owned by each firm have been exactly equal to date, several of Hi-Q's holdings are likely to go public within the next year or two, while the investments owned by Lo-Q will not be ready to go public for at least another five years.

Fixed Assets: The value of fixed assets on each company's balance sheet is identical, but all of Lo-Q's fixed assets were acquired within the past five years, and their reported values closely approximate current market values. Hi-Q's fixed assets, on the other hand, include several hundred acres of prime urban real estate that it acquired as undeveloped woodlands at the end of the nineteenth century, which it is still carrying on its balance sheet at historical cost according to the GAAP rules. Hi-Q's new CEO is presently entertaining offers from several real estate developers who have expressed an interest in acquiring the vacant portions of this land, offering to pay hundreds of times the property's original cost.

Notes Payable and Long-Term Debt: Hi-Q and Lo-Q have the same amount of debt on their balance sheets, and they have been paying identical rates of interest on their debt. However, this will soon change, for two reasons.

Several years ago, in order to finance its major purchases of timberlands from competitors, Lo-Q agreed to some onerous bank loan covenants. Recently, its financial ratios have slipped to levels that breach those covenants, and, as a result, it will be forced to pay significantly higher interest rates until the company's financial ratios improve.

In addition, while both companies had issued publicly traded long-term bonds when market interest rates were higher, Hi-Q's bonds included a call provision but Lo-Q's did not. Consequently, Hi-Q will soon be able to re-finance its debt at lower current rates, while Lo-Q will go on paying higher rates on its bonds for years to come.

Shareholders' Equity: While both firms currently have an identical amount of equity and the same number of common shares issued and outstanding, Lo-

Q is about to experience substantial dilution due to the vesting of large numbers of incentive stock options held by its executives. Moreover, the "lockup" period for a substantial block of stock sold by Lo-Q in a private placement will soon expire, and it is expected that a large percentage of this stock will be sold on the open market shortly. Hi-Q, on the other hand, has just announced a major common stock repurchase program.

Next, let's look at some obligations that GAAP financial statements are particularly likely to present in misleading or uninformative ways: pensions and contingent liabilities.

Pension Plans: Pension benefit obligations are defined as the amount of money that must be invested today at an assumed rate of investment return in order to pay for future benefit payments as they come due—in other words, the present value of whatever future benefit payments have been earned to date by employees. (Future benefit payments calculations are based upon assumptions regarding the employees' future compensation growth, and the related expense and liability is accrued over time as employee length of service accumulates.)

Hi-Q and Lo-Q happen to do business in the same industries, in the same geographical regions, and offer identical pension benefits to their workers, who have substantially similar skill sets, compensation, turnover rates, and demographic profiles. Therefore, there is every reason to conclude that the cash outlays associated with pension benefits will be about the same for each firm. Furthermore, the firms' pension assets are currently identical.

Hi-Q, though, has elected to incorporate assumptions of much higher growth in its employees' future compensation and lower investment returns in recording and funding its pension obligations, compared to Lo-Q. As a result, its reported pension expense and liability will be higher than Lo-Q's, and its earnings lower.

However, Hi-Q's conservative pension fund assumptions give it superior earnings quality vis-à-vis Lo-Q, since Hi-Q is recognizing higher expenses currently to fund a liability that should ultimately be roughly equal for both companies. Hi-Q also has a higher book value quality than Lo-Q (with respect to its pension plan), for the same reason.

If Hi-Q's conservative assumptions prove to be accurate in the future, Lo-Q will be forced to increase its pension expense to make up for the shortfall. If Hi-Q's assumptions prove to be too conservative, its future pension costs will be lower than expected. Either way, Hi-Q will be better off than Lo-Q with respect to the future earnings impact of its pension plan.

Contingent Liabilities: Lo-Q is the defendant in a number of recently filed lawsuits concerning health problems allegedly caused by Lo-Q's improper disposal of carcinogenic waste products from its chemical plants. Due to the uncertainty surrounding the ultimate cost of these claims, the company did not feel it necessary to reflect them in its financial results, disclosing the information in a footnote instead.

The next task will be to compare the two companies' income statements, focusing on the two companies' "earnings quality."

Income Statement Items: In the comparison of Hi-Q's and Lo-Q's balance sheets, we have already alluded to several ways in which Lo-Q's earnings quality is lower than Hi-Q's:

- Some of the cash generated by Lo-Q's earnings is locked up in countries with restrictions on the repatriation of cash. Since that cash is therefore less available to its U.S. shareholders for dividend payments, stock repurchase, or reinvestment in productive assets, Lo-Q's earnings are worth less than earnings that are fully accessible.

- Lo-Q's earnings were temporarily inflated by the liquidation of an old LIFO layer of inventory with a cost far below current prevailing values.

- Hi-Q has been purposely lowering its reported earnings (to save taxes) by cutting timber from its more recently acquired properties, thereby recognizing a higher cost of sales. At some future date, it will resume cutting from the forests it acquired a century ago at low historical costs, which will drive up its GAAP earnings.

- Because Hi-Q prepaid for goods and services whose prices have risen, while Lo-Q prepaid for goods and services whose prices have remained constant, this will boost Hi-Q's future earnings relative to Lo-Q.

- Although the impact of the two firms' venture capital operations on their respective earnings has been identical thus far, it is apparent that the real economic impact on the value of each firm is substantially different. Eventually the reported financial results will show the difference, as Hi-Q's investments are sold at dazzling profits while Lo-Q's continue to muddle along.

Stock Repurchase Programs

Stock repurchase programs reduce the total number of shares outstanding, which shrinks the pool of shares over which earnings, dividends, etc., get divided.

If a company's stock truly is undervalued, repurchases are likely to benefit shareholders.

- For over a century, Hi-Q's worth has risen invisibly as the value of its land holdings increased, unreported in its financial statements.

- As noted, Hi-Q will realize an opportunity to reduce its borrowing costs by refinancing its debt, an opportunity that is unavailable to Lo-Q.

- Lo-Q's earnings per share will be subject to substantial dilution, from the employee stock options that are about to vest. Hi-Q's earnings per share may well be enhanced as it buys shares under its recently announced repurchase program.

- Lo-Q will inevitably face higher future pension expenses than Hi-Q.

- Lo-Q's contingent liabilities pose a number of problems from the standpoint of earnings quality. In addition to the possibility that the company will have to pay substantial claims for damages at some point in the future, it is almost certain to run up significant legal expenses defending itself over the next few years. It may also need to adopt costly remedial measures, and the price it pays for insurance will certainly rise. All of this may lead to additional borrowing, which it will be forced to finance at the higher rates previously noted.

We'll conclude our comparison of Hi-Q and Lo-Q with a look at their auditors' opinions.

Auditors Opinion: Hi-Q had a "clean" opinion from a major CPA firm which stated, without qualification, that the company's financial statements were fairly presented on a basis consistent with that of previous years.

Lo-Q's CPA firm, on the other hand, resigned from the audit and was replaced by a small regional firm. That firm issued a qualified opinion, which indicated a number of internal control weaknesses and exceptions.

As we said at the beginning of this illustration, the financial statements of these two companies would appear, at first glance, to be almost identical. Certainly, anyone who looked only at the reported earnings per share and balance sheet ratios would conclude that these two firms were equally desirable investments. Such an investor might look at Hi-Q and Lo-Q and decide to buy both stocks, "for diversification."

A more circumspect investor would avoid Lo-Q like the plague.

The Information GAAP – Conclusions:

Although some people continue to think of accounting rules as cut and dried, as unwavering as the rules of arithmetic, there is a growing public awareness of the tremendous amount of estimation and judgment involved in financial reporting. Without any intentional malfeasance, and strictly following Generally Accepted Accounting Principles, the reported book values and earnings of public companies can exhibit huge variations from their true economic values.

Such variations can be caused by, among other things:

- GAAP's requirement that assets and liabilities be presented at their historical costs (or principal amounts) rather than at their true economic values;

- Differences in the assumptions allowed by GAAP in calculating the present value of outcomes that are subject to significant degrees of uncertainty;

- GAAP's failure to require that any numbers at all be pinned on events whose outcomes are subject to extreme degrees of uncertainty;

- Differences in the credibility of accounting firms issuing audit opinions, as well as differences in the opinions themselves.

In order to overcome these difficulties and arrive at the best information attainable for making investment selections, investors need to adjust the published financial results in many cases.

With regard to book value, investors should focus on developing figures that represent:

- The current fair market value of the company's assets; less,

- The current fair market value of the company's liabilities; less,

- The current fair market value of any equity holdings in the company other than those associated with the company's outstanding common stock; plus (or minus),

- The present value of the expected proceeds (or payment obligations) associated with any contingent assets (or liabilities).

With regard to earnings, investors should focus on developing figures that represent the company's:

- After-tax earnings from normal, ongoing, day-to-day operations that are likely to continue recurring in the future; plus (or minus),

- Understatements (or overstatements) of after-tax earnings caused by overly conservative (or aggressive) assumptions regarding future events or events that are difficult to measure accurately; plus (or minus),

- The projected recurring after-tax earnings effect, including any related financing costs, associated with contingent assets or liabilities; plus,

- The additional after-tax income that could be realized by investing the after-tax proceeds from the sale of unused (or underutilized) assets.

If the company has recently changed auditors, if its auditor is not a major firm, and, most importantly, if the opinion is qualified in any way, the reported financial results should be interpreted with a great deal of skepticism.

This brings us to the darker topic of earnings manipulation: how to spot it and how to avoid being hurt by it.

Earnings Manipulation and Financial Reporting Fraud

It's important to recognize a distinction between earnings manipulation, on the one hand, and financial reporting fraud on the other.

Most companies "manage" their reported earnings to some extent. To most corporate managers, and even to many investors, this is an accepted business practice, a normal response to the overwhelming pressure on public companies to make their quarterly numbers.

Financial reporting fraud is an entirely different matter.

No one in their right mind would knowingly choose a liar or thief for a business partner, and no business owner would knowingly hire such a person to run their affairs, so why would an investor ever buy stock in a company run by dishonest managers?

Unfortunately, no clear boundary exists between the accepted form of "earnings management" and outright fraud. A good deal of this activity falls into a large gray area.

It would be unrealistic to condemn all forms of earnings manipulation, because, in practice, there is simply too much judgment involved in accounting and financial reporting for this to be practical.

For example, if a company sets up an inventory reserve for obsolescence, thereby reducing the current period's earnings, the existence and the amount of the reserve requires the exercise of professional judgment. If, in a future period, the company reduces the reserve, thereby increasing earnings, that is also a matter of professional judgment. Reasonable, honest professionals could easily disagree about the appropriate level at which to maintain the reserve.

Public companies make adjustments like this in almost every reporting period, partly to account for the cost of things like inventory obsolescence, and partly to smooth reported earnings from period to period.

As investors, we simply have to accept this situation and do our best to understand what management is up to, through careful analysis of the financial statements.

In some cases, no amount of analysis will reveal intentional misreporting. The executives of big companies like Enron or WorldCom who create byzantine webs of "special purpose" entities to hide fraudulent transactions, move losses, and erase debt off their books can fool even the most sophisticated analysts. Perhaps this is just one more reason for investors to avoid large cap stocks. The financial statements of small companies tend to be somewhat easier to interpret than those of large companies.

In many cases, however, the red flags that indicate accounting fraud can be spotted by a careful investor before the story hits the news media. You just have to know where to look for them.

How to Identify Questionable Financial Reports

We have compiled the following, by no means exhaustive, summary of "red flags" we have found to be reliable indicators of potential problems with reported numbers.

The number one red flag is a large, unexplained disparity between reported earnings and cash flow.

For example, if a company reports positive earnings and negative cash flow, and there are no large capital acquisitions or development projects that would explain where the cash went, the earnings are suspect. There should always be correspondence over time between earnings and cash flow unless the company is making significant investments in long-lived assets or is growing rapidly.

Large, unexplained changes in a company's gross margin percentage could also indicate earnings manipulation. Often, such changes are the result of undisclosed valuation adjustments to inventory. In order to spot these adjustments, inventory balances should be compared to sales figures to verify that there is

> ### Gross Margin
>
> Gross margin is equal to sales minus cost of goods sold, and the percentage margin is gross margin divided by sales.

a constant relationship between the two. If, over time, inventory is growing significantly faster than sales, it may be an indication of reporting fraud.

It is often useful to track percentage gross margin and the relationship between inventory and sales over time.

A company's gross margin percentage is usually a reliable indicator of its competitive position within its industry. A high gross margin percentage– compared to its competitors– indicates pricing power, which arises from competitive advantages (see Chapter 14). If a reduction in the gross margin percentage is observed over time, it could indicate declining competitiveness, or it could merely reflect general weakness in the industry, or in the broader economy.

However, any significant variations in the ratio of gross margin to sales or the ratio of inventory to sales which is not adequately explained by management could also indicate potential reporting fraud.

A sudden, dramatic change in a company's net earnings which is not adequately explained by management is another red flag.

Suppose, for example, that a company which has earned profits every quarter for three consecutive fiscal years suddenly reports a loss in the first quarter. Suppose that just about the time this loss was being reported, the general manager of a major division was replaced by a newcomer.

In a situation like this, it is quite possible that the deterioration in earnings actually started in the prior year. The former general manager might have delayed disclosure of his problem by recording questionable shipments at year-end. The first quarter's operating results might then have suffered from the impact of customer returns (of shipments they hadn't ordered, or of products they had received in an unfinished or defective condition). In addition, the first quarter's sales might have been reduced by the amount of production required to make good on sales that were recorded in the prior year, but which had never left the company's dock.

When earnings are manipulated at year-end through the recording of revenue which has not been earned (or the deferral of expenses that have already been incurred), investors who continue to hold the stock until the next reporting cycle suffer the consequences. In many cases, however, they could have found clues buried in the year-end financial statements.

In our example, the clue would have been an unusually low year-end inventory. In the case of inappropriately deferred expenses, reporting fraud might be indicated by unexplained changes in the ratios of expenses to sales.

Any significant change in reported earnings, especially a reduction, which is not accompanied by a credible explanation should raise concerns about possible reporting fraud.

Accounts Receivable balances that, over several periods, have grown out of proportion to the growth in cash receipts could indicate the recording of phony sales. Similarly, large year over year increases in the ratio of Accounts Receivable to Sales could also indicate overstated revenues.

Investors should pay particular attention to any accounts labeled "Unbilled Revenue" or the like. The existence of such an account indicates that sales which have not been billed to customers are being recorded. The recording of revenue on a schedule which is different from that used to bill costumers might be a perfectly legitimate accounting practice for a company engaged in long-term contracts whose progress billings are based on specific project milestones, but investors should be wary of large, unexplained changes in this account.

Rapidly growing companies should be subjected to special scrutiny by investors seeking to protect themselves from reporting irregularities, because the intense pressure placed on these companies to maintain their growth rates can create the temptation to record fraudulent sales. As we observed in earlier chapters, growth companies that falter are severely punished by the market. Exacerbating this pressure is the likelihood that these companies' internal control systems will not have kept pace with their rapid growth.

Balance sheets should be scrutinized for the appearance of growth of any assets other than the usual Current Assets (i.e., Cash, Accounts Receivable, Inventory, and Prepaid Expenses) and Fixed Assets (i.e., Property, Plant, and Equipment). The existence of unusual asset accounts may be a sign that operating costs are being improperly capitalized.

The use of reserve accounts to shift earnings from one reporting period to another is a widespread practice. Investors should always be wary of large year over year changes in accounts such as the Allowance for Doubtful Accounts Receivable or the Reserve for Inventory Obsolescence. Reserves should be held at a more or less constant percentage of the asset accounts with which they are associated, and should remain in proportion to the size of the business (as measured by Sales and Total Assets). Any significant shift in these proportions may indicate earnings manipulation.

The Allowance for Depreciation merits special attention. Companies frequently change either their depreciation methods or their assumptions concerning assets' useful lives in order to manipulate earnings. If Depreciation Expense doesn't maintain a reasonably constant ratio to the value of Fixed Assets, it's probably worthwhile to investigate further.

It is often useful to review a company's debt structure and loan covenants to evaluate the potential for loan covenant violations. Companies facing covenant violations have tremendous motivation to consider fraudulent reporting, because the alternative may well entail onerous penalties. Desperate people often do desperate things.

Investors should always suspect the possibility of reporting fraud in the case of companies that make abrupt or frequent changes in auditing firms, especially if the new firm is smaller and less well-known than its predecessor. Often, this is a sign that the auditors and management don't see eye-to-eye on how things should be accounted for.

Most disputes between auditors and management involve managements' desire to present numbers that are rosier than justified. Astute investors prefer to bet on teams that do their scoring on the playing field, rather than by rewiring the scoreboard.

Finally, any significant lapses in SEC-required reporting should be treated as a possible indication of reporting fraud. The annual and quarterly SEC reports are intended to include, among other things, managements' explanations for just the kinds of reporting anomalies and discrepancies we have been discussing in this chapter. Any failure to provide those explanations in a timely manner should raise suspicion.

Smart investors concerned about financial reporting fraud rely on a combination of two essential protections:

a) certification– and a clean opinion– by a large, well-known CPA firm; and
b) their own analysis.

• Chapter 14 •

FUNDAMENTAL ANALYSIS

We employ fundamental analysis to evaluate news stories within the context of the subject firms' industry attractiveness, competitive position, financial resources, and management quality. This helps us assess the impact of new developments on critical earnings and cash flow trends.

In this chapter, we will explain how we analyze a company's "fundamentals."

By "fundamentals," we mean all of the factors that create the ability to grow profits and survive financially. This would include the company's competitive position within its industry, the attractiveness of the industry, the company's financial strength, and the quality of its management team.

Some authors lump fundamental analysis and financial statement analysis together, but we treat them as two distinct research methods with different, but related, purposes.

As we explained in Chapter 13, financial statement analysis can yield insights into a company's financial strengths and weaknesses, provide context for evaluating its current market valuation, and, in some cases, reveal malfeasance, ranging from reporting abuses to outright fraud.

Financial reports can tell us a lot about how a company has performed in the recent past, but not much about how the business will be doing a few years down the road. Furthermore, financial statement analysis is, by its nature, limited to internal issues that are specific to the company.

Quantitative vs. Qualitative Analysis

In practice, we typically buy and sell stocks on the basis of a "quick and dirty" financial statement analysis coupled with a rapid appraisal of breaking news.

Recognizing this reality, we have created a sharper distinction than most authors between the quantitative and qualitative aspects of fundamental analysis.

The implications of breaking news for a company's industry and competitive position constitute our most common brush with the issues raised in this chapter. Rather than attempting a complete review of a company's fundamentals, we are typically looking for just one important change in its industry or competitive position. Perhaps some of its largest suppliers or customers are merging (bad) or a competitor is raising prices (good). (cont'd.)

Or Wal-Mart is about to become a competitor (very bad).

The rapid pace of day-to-day trading precludes a comprehensive fundamental analysis in most cases.

Nevertheless, for the sake of convenience in presentation, we have spelled out the principal tasks involved in a comprehensive analysis so that readers can become more familiar with the individual lines of inquiry.

More importantly, a company's annual and quarterly reports do not supply all the information needed to assess how its products and strategies stack up against those of its competitors, or how the industry in which it operates fits into broader economic and technological trends.

Fundamental analysis incorporates and builds upon financial statement analysis. It is used to assess a company's future within the context of its industry and the wider economy. Properly done, it will lead to a better understanding of the broader forces affecting the company's prospects, thereby establishing either a firmer basis for projecting existing trends into the future, or an indication that things are likely to change.

The Role of Fundamental Analysis in Our Stock Selection Strategy

It would not be possible—nor would it be desirable—to undertake a comprehensive fundamental analysis of every stock we might consider for purchase. Fundamental analysis is time-consuming, and, as we will emphasize in Part Three, most trading situations call for quick reaction. In most cases, by the time we would have completed a rigorous fundamental analysis, the opportunity would have passed us by.

However, from time to time, we come across opportunities to invest in stocks with tantalizing prospects of substantial gains, but whose futures are clouded by ambiguous circumstances. A stock that satisfies our initial screening criteria and appears to be an excellent value might be the subject of a series of news stories that raise questions regarding its future performance or viability—questions such as whether an established earnings trend will persist (or improve), or whether the company's financial resources are adequate to meet its future needs. Fundamental analysis can help to resolve the ambiguity, giving us a clearer picture of the company's future.

We use fundamental analysis to project a company's trajectory—i.e., whether earnings or cash flow will grow or shrink—but, unlike many other investors and analysts, we make no attempt to forecast the actual numbers.

As we have previously emphasized, we are highly skeptical of any attempt to predict precise earnings figures. Any investor who would buy a stock simply because a brokerage analyst has forecast earnings of $4.10—but who would not have bought it if the analyst's forecast was $3.90—places far too much faith in the analyst's ability to foresee the future. Even the company's managers, who presumably have the ability to influence their numbers (either legitimately, or through accounting manipulations), cannot predict next year's earnings with such precision in most cases. Too much uncertainty surrounds the multiplicity of factors that go into the calculation of earnings per share.

While we recognize that expectations for a company's future financial performance drive its stock price, we also acknowledge our inability to estimate future earnings with certitude. Consequently, for the most part, we select stocks on the basis of measurable characteristics– calculated using actual, reported financial results– that have been reliable predictors of superior performance for long periods in the past. We prefer to base our investment decisions on hard data, rather than on dubious attempts to predict earnings numbers.

We employ fundamental analysis to determine whether circumstances generally favor or generally impede future growth in earnings and cash flow, and to clear up questions concerning the prospects of companies that otherwise meet our criteria.

The Importance of a Systematic Approach

Our objective in this chapter will be to present a systematic approach for evaluating the fundamental factors that determine a company's likely earnings and cash flow trajectory.

We cannot overstate the importance of approaching fundamental analysis systematically and methodically. Fundamental analysis can absorb a lot of time—and generate more confusion than illumination in complex situations—if the analysis is not undertaken with a clear understanding of the questions that need to be answered.

The complexity and sheer volume of information available on the typical public company can be overwhelming. It's very easy to get distracted by the "trees"—details like FDA approvals, product announcements, new store openings, etc.—and lose sight of whether the "forest" is growing or dying.

Accordingly, we usually begin with an assessment of the industry in which the company in question operates. The profit potential of an industry determines the aggregate profit potential of the individual firms that operate in that industry, but industries come and go as technology and society change over time. In order to get necessary perspective on a *company's* potential, we need to know whether its *industry* is young and growing, mature and stable, or on the decline.

Once we have evaluated the industry's potential, our next task will be to assess the company's competitive position within its industry. What is the company's strategy? How does it stack up against the other firms in its industry? Is it gaining or losing market share? Our objective is to get a general idea of how this company's strategy compares to its competitors, and whether the market is responding favorably or not.

Finally, we need to determine whether the company has the financial and management resources to execute its strategy. We assess the trajectory of the company's cash flow relative to its current resources to identify potential requirements for additional capitalization (bearing in mind that rapid growth can eat up financial resources even faster than losses). Management quality is usually harder to measure, except in extreme cases, but no fundamental factor has greater potential importance. Good managers can overcome unforeseen setbacks by adapting strategies to fit changed circumstances. Bad managers can screw up the best of companies.

In the rest of this chapter, we will explain in detail how we assess these four key factors: industry attractiveness, competitive position, financial resources, and management quality. Then, we will close with a few thoughts on how to obtain the information required to objectively analyze a company's "fundamentals."

Industry Attractiveness

According to traditional microeconomic analysis, a company's earnings growth will ultimately be determined by the profitability of its industry and by the firm's ability to compete for a share of the industry's profits.

Harvard Business School professor Michael Porter created a process for evaluating an industry's attractiveness (i.e., its profit potential) based on an analysis of competitive factors. These included:

- The likelihood of entry by new competitors

- The competitive threat posed by substitute products

- Customers' and suppliers' power to bargain for price adjustments, and

- The degree of rivalry existing among current competitors

An industry has *unattractive* prospects for future earnings growth to the extent that it is likely to attract new competitors, is vulnerable to substitute products, has customers or suppliers in strong bargaining positions, or is characterized by strong rivalry among the firms in the industry. Competitive pressures, whether caused by new entrants, rivalry among existing firms, or substitute products, will tend to drive down the prices (and therefore profits) that the industry's firms can realize for their products. Customers with strong bargaining power can likewise drive down prices, while suppliers with strong bargaining power can lower profits by raising costs.

New firms will be less likely to enter an industry that has high barriers to entry, such as high start-up costs or government-imposed barriers. Existing firms' economies of scale or strong brand loyalty will also discourage new competitors, as will obstacles that block the newcomers' access to distribution channels.

The existence of substitute products threatens an industry's profit potential to the extent that customers might perceive advantages in switching to the substitutes. Customers will be less willing to switch if the substitute products are less effective or efficient, or if switching involves high costs.

Customers have strong bargaining power when sales are concentrated among a relatively small number of buyers, i.e., when the ratio of suppliers to customers is high. Customers' bargaining power is also enhanced when their cost of switching suppliers is low, when substitute products are available at a competitive cost, and when product differentiation is low. Customers who can vertically integrate—i.e., who have the technical capability and financial resources to bring production in-house—are often in a particularly strong position relative to their suppliers. On the other hand, customers with low income, or whose purchases constitute a high percentage of their total costs, can derive bargaining power from their lack of flexibility, because supplier price increases would threaten their viability. Finally, customers who know a lot about their suppliers' technology, production methods, and costs will be in a stronger bargaining position than the customers of suppliers who cannot obtain access to this information.

Suppliers have strong bargaining power when the ratio of suppliers to customers is low (the extreme case being a monopoly). They also can derive bargaining power from posing a credible threat to enter their customers' industry as a competitor. Suppliers' bargaining power is stronger when their customers' cost of switching suppliers is high, or when substitute products are not available at a competitive cost. The bargaining power of a supplier who sells to high-income customers is enhanced by the customers' ability to pay higher prices, and a supplier who sells a highly differentiated, highly necessary product is in a very strong position indeed. As noted above, suppliers who are able to keep proprietary information secret maintain a stronger bargaining position than those whose products and processes are widely understood.

Rivalry among competing firms is greater when, on an industry-wide basis, fixed costs are high. In such a situation, each firm has a strong incentive to increase sales by cutting its prices, because, on a marginal basis, each dollar of additional revenue would result in a relatively larger contribution to gross profit. This is especially true where industry-wide sales growth is slow, because buying market share with lowered prices may be the firms' only option for growing earnings. Rivalry would also be higher in an industry where brand identity is weak, product differentiation is minimal, and the products are easily understood and copied. As might be expected, industries with large numbers of competitors tend to have high levels of rivalry. Rivalry will also be higher where the cost of exiting the business is high, because competitors will be more willing to live with lower profits.

Definition of an Industry

In evaluating an industry's attractiveness from an investment standpoint, much depends on how we define an industry.

We wince whenever we hear someone speak about the "high tech industry," as though companies making genetically engineered pharmaceuticals had anything to do with contract electronics manufacturers. Even a more narrowly defined "industry," for example, "the software industry," includes too wide a range of products and services to be meaningful for the purpose of fundamental analysis. Firms selling enterprise resource planning systems cannot be considered competitors of firms writing data communications algorithms.

We define an industry as a group of companies that compete for the same market, by offering products or services with similar functions to essentially the same pool of customers.

In most cases, an attractive industry has, at most, two or three strong competitors. Industries with more than three major competitors tend to have profits driven down to the point where the industry is no longer attractive to investors.

However, there are exceptions to this rule. Industries that are by their nature geographically dispersed, have government-imposed barriers to entry, or are little threatened by substitute products or services can often include relatively large numbers of profitable companies. Examples can be found in broadcasting, utilities, and many service businesses. Industries that sell to customers with limited bargaining power (e.g., life insurance) may also support numerous competitors.

Nevertheless, it is unusual for an industry to offer attractive investment opportunities *and* be accommodating to more than two or three competitors.

Division of Profits Across Industries

In the preceding discussion, we presented a framework for assessing an industry's attractiveness through an analysis of the competitive environment within the industry. What about competition between industries?

Many complex products undergo a long process of intermediate steps between the gathering of raw materials and their purchase by consumers. At each step along the way, value is added to the original raw materials by a different industry. The production of an automobile starts with the mining of iron ore. It requires the efforts of the steel, glass, rubber, battery, automotive electronics, and a great many other industries before the "auto industry" assembles the final product and ships it off to the auto dealership. A similar situation exists with regard to the production of airplanes, computers, houses, and other big ticket items.

Industries that produce different sub-components of the same complex product compete with each other for a share of the profit from the final sale. Thus, all of the industries involved in the production and sale of automobiles compete for a share of the price ultimately paid by a car buyer. The tire industry is competing with the automotive electronics industry and the auto body industry for a finite pool of profits from auto sales.

Ultimately, profits from sales of complex products are divided among the related industries according to the competitiveness of the industries' structures.

Competitiveness between related industries is measured according to the same criteria we used earlier. In other words, the industries that will capture the biggest share of the total profit for a complex product will be the ones that have:

- The lowest likelihood of entry by new competitors,

- The least rivalry among current competitors,

- The least competitive threat by substitute products, and

- The least bargaining power among customers and suppliers.

Consider as an example the industries involved in the production of desktop computer systems. Which of these industries make the most money when a typical PC is sold?

The industries that best fit our criteria for success are those that produce the microprocessor and the operating system software – the industries dominated by Intel and Microsoft, respectively.

It is unlikely that significant new competitors will enter either of these industries any time soon, and, since Intel and Microsoft have no strong competitors, they face relatively little rivalry. The two firms' products are not seriously threatened by potential substitutes (AMD and Linux notwithstanding). Therefore, the customers and suppliers that deal with Intel and Microsoft have very little bargaining power, because they have few realistic alternatives.

It should come as no surprise, then, that these two industries, the microprocessor industry and the operating system software industry, retain the largest share of the purchase price every time a personal computer is sold.

Thus, the attractiveness of an industry is significantly enhanced if it is in a strong competitive position vis-à-vis related industries.

The Company's Competitive Position

Strategy and Execution

Merely being *involved* in an attractive industry, however, is no guarantee of profitability—or survival, for that matter. A lot of companies that have been involved in the highly attractive microprocessor industry have either failed, withdrawn from the industry, or continued as marginal players.

A company will only be attractive to an investor to the extent that it can successfully *compete*. Its *competitive position* depends on its choice of strategy and its ability to execute that strategy—relative to the strategies and execution of its competitors.

Apart from financially driven strategies (for example, acquiring competitors), a company can adopt one of two fundamental strategies for competing. It can compete by offering a "better" (i.e., differentiated) product, or can compete on the basis of price.

A successful product differentiation strategy typically requires a certain amount of ingenuity in addition to investments in product development, specialized production facilities, marketing campaigns, etc.

Competing on price requires the ability to become a low cost producer.

Generally speaking, an industry can have only one successful industry-wide, low-price competitor. If more than one firm adopts the low-price strategy, the resulting price competition will usually depress profitability and earnings growth for the entire industry.

On the other hand, a number of firms can compete successfully on the basis of product differentiation. Product differentiation can arise from actual differences in product features, services, or method of delivery, or from perceived product differences created by differentiated marketing methods.

Even the marketers of highly standardized goods and services can create perceived differences in their products. For example, casinos in Las Vegas differentiate their product by offering a variety of 25-cent slot machines through which highly similar bets can be placed. In addition, the casinos create perceived differences through differentiated marketing, styling their facilities as Egyptian, Arabian, circus, etc.

Along with the fundamental choice of whether to compete primarily on the basis of product differentiation or primarily on the basis of price, the company must decide whether it will pursue the entire market that its industry serves or just a segment (niche) of that market.

The niche strategy, if widely adopted, can increase profitability for all of an industry's participants. In the case of the Las Vegas casinos, their attempts to differentiate stylistically would not prevent a certain amount of price competition if they all pursued the same group of gamblers. They avoid price competition by dividing their market into niches. Caesar's Palace and Luxor offer relatively high stakes games and luxury accommodations to attract high rollers. Circus Circus, on the other hand, offers lower stakes games and inexpensive accommodations that attract a more budget-conscious clientele. Since they are pursuing different groups of customers, Caesar's Palace and Circus Circus have little incentive to poach each other's market share through aggressive price-cutting.

If a company adopts a niche strategy, the desirability of the niche it chooses is a critical determinant of its potential profitability and earnings growth. All market niches are not created equal.

Some niches may be small and shrinking, while others might be large and growing. Some niches may offer higher margins, especially those that place a premium on product differentiation.

Oddly enough, companies competing in the least attractive (in terms of profitability) niches often provide the best investment opportunities. Such companies tend to have below-average P/E ratios, and since the least attractive niches are the easiest to defend from competitors, they often exhibit above-average earnings growth as competition dwindles over time.

Highly attractive niches, on the other hand, tend to attract the most competition. The companies that compete in highly attractive niches often carry the highest P/E multiples, even as the entry of new competitors threatens earnings growth. Furthermore, attractive niches spur the development of substitute products and competing technologies, and thus are particularly vulnerable to changes in customer preferences.

As we noted earlier, a company's competitive position is determined partly by its choice of strategy, but, perhaps even more importantly, by how well it executes that strategy.

Companies that successfully execute their chosen strategies generally have strong corporate cultures, policies, resources, and core competencies that are compatible with those strategies. Companies that successfully execute a low-price strategy, for example, tend to be finance- and manufacturing-driven, while companies that successfully execute product differentiation strategies tend to be engineering- and marketing-driven.

Firms that adopt strategies inconsistent with their core capabilities are not likely to execute them successfully. For example, a technology company that has embarked on a strategy of product differentiation will probably not succeed if it is located in an area with few qualified engineers. A company whose manufacturing costs include a significant labor component will probably not succeed in becoming a low-cost producer if it has a history of unresolved disputes with a heavily unionized workforce.

How can we tell if a company is successfully executing its strategy?

Following our usual practice, we look for objective evidence that the company is winning against its competitors. We look for gross and net margins that are improving faster than industry averages, and for gains in market share. We take particular note of competitors' withdrawals from the industry, especially from an industry with apparently bright prospects. This is often a sign that one firm is gaining a dominant competitive position. (Think of the way Intel's success drove its competitors out of the microprocessor industry.)

On the other hand, we generally discount management's (or brokerage analysts') version of events, in which strategies are often "retroactively redefined" to fit the circumstances.

Companies that achieve dominant positions in their industries can produce superior investment results over many years. Some well-known "buy and hold" investors have achieved success by limiting their stock selections to industry leaders—either the top firm in the industry, or a strong number two. As the saying goes, "If you're not one of the lead dogs, the view never changes."

The Company's Competitors

Our understanding of a company's competitive position within its industry would not be complete without comparing the firm's plans, products, and pricing to those of its competitors.

The more we can learn about a firm's competitors, the better we will understand its prospects. In particular, we want to identify and assess threats to the firm's major sources of profit.

We begin by comparing - niche by niche - each competitor's core strategy (i.e., whether it competes primarily on the basis of product differentiation or primarily on the basis of price) to that of the firm we are analyzing.

If the subject firm competes primarily on the basis of price, we examine trends in competitors' prices and costs, and we assess their potential for adopting production and delivery innovations that would lower their costs. We generally avoid industries in which multiple firms are pursuing a low price strategy, because profits in such industries tend to spiral downward.

If the subject firm competes primarily on the basis of product differentiation, we attempt to learn as much as we can about potential buyers' perceptions of its products' features, benefits, and delivery methods. Our goal is to compare customers' perceptions of the firm's products to those of its competitors, and to assess whether perceived differences are consistent with price differences.

We also evaluate the firm's product development plans and capabilities relative to those of its competitors. We try to evaluate how easy it would be for a competitor to copy the firm's products, or create attractive substitutes, by comparing expenditures on research and development, track records of product development, product development pipelines, and the status of each firm's intellectual property. We pay particular attention to the potential effects of patent or copyright expirations.

Finally, our evaluation of the firm's competitors includes an assessment of the potential impact of impending mergers, spinoffs or other ownership changes. Such transactions can affect an individual firm's competitive position in ways that are not always easy to predict. Consolidation can lead to improved profitability industry-wide by reducing competition. On the other hand, it can also weaken the firm's position if competitors are able to broaden their product lines, improve their distribution channels, or create economies of scale in production and marketing.

The Company's Competitive Position—Additional Considerations

Beyond a company's choice of strategy and our general sense of whether its management is successfully executing that strategy, there are a number of specific factors affecting the firm's competitive position that are important to evaluate. These include the company's:

- Customers
- Products (or services)
- Distribution channels
- Tangible assets
- Intangible assets
- Suppliers and sub-contractors
- Labor
- Legal and regulatory issues

Customers

We want to know as much about the firm's customers as we can discover, (though, admittedly, this information can be difficult to obtain).

We want to know who they are, where they are, and why they buy the company's products. We want to know how they perceive the company and its products. For example, do they see the company's products as mundane, essential items, purchased with little thought, or are they drawn in by advertising and led to think of the company's brand as something special? If the firm's customers are industrial producers, are their purchase decisions driven more by price, quality, or on-time delivery?

We want to assess customer loyalty. Does the firm primarily sell to customers who have bought its products many times over a number of years, or does it rely on a steady stream of new customers? What creates customer loyalty? Do customers really love the products, or do they buy because of personal loyalty to the firm's owners or employees?

We want to know if the firm's customer base is concentrated or diversified, wholesale or retail. If the customer base is concentrated, how are those customers doing? Are they financially healthy and growing stronger, or are their incomes shrinking?

Products (or Services)

In addition to developing a good understanding of who buys the company's products and why they buy them, it's important to learn more about the products themselves.

Perhaps the most relevant piece of information concerning a firm's products is where they stand in their product life cycles. Every product has a life cycle that starts when it is invented and ends when it is no longer needed by anybody. Portable computing devices are young, refrigerators are mature, and typewriter ribbons are in rigor mortis. Knowing a product's life cycle stage helps us to evaluate whether demand for the product will grow, hold steady, or shrink in the next five to 10 years.

Since fundamental analysis is intended to provide a window into the future, we also want to know about any new products in the pipeline. This leads us to inquire into the company's product development capabilities. How much is the firm investing in new product development? How much of the total budget is absorbed by maintenance on existing products?

Distribution Channels

By studying a company's distribution channels, we can learn a lot about the firm's ability to grow in the future. In addition to determining whether existing distribution channels are adequate for current needs, we want to assess whether they are adequate to support future growth, especially with regard to new products. Furthermore, we want to assess the complexity, and hence the vulnerability, of the distribution channels. How close are customers to production facilities, and how hard is it to get products into their hands? How sensitive is the firm's profitability to its distribution costs? Would a modest increase in distribution costs cause a big drop in earnings?

Tangible Assets

Most firms that produce products, as well as many that provide services, require a significant investment in tangible assets.

The availability of adequate production facilities can be the single most critical constraint on growth for a manufacturing company. The firm's ability to finance expansion of its production facilities is just one factor to consider. If expansion is required, the availability of land at an acceptable price, the availability of skilled construction workers, and the lead times associated with environmental and other regulatory processes must also be considered. Once the building has been constructed, the lead times and costs involved with acquiring and developing specialized production equipment and processes can create significant additional bottlenecks.

Companies that require significant investments in tangible assets are always facing the question of whether to invest in maintenance and repairs or acquire new facilities. Our fundamental analysis of such a company must include an evaluation of its maintenance and repair programs, including their cost.

Companies trying to boost short-term earnings (or that are squeezed for cash) often cut back on maintenance and repairs, which creates future problems that are not always obvious to investors. Normally, maintenance and repairs expense will grow as a percentage of fixed assets as the assets age. At some point, it becomes more economical to replace the assets.

Furthermore, in many industries, investment in new assets is required to stay current with technology. We typically avoid companies that report significant reductions in repairs and maintenance which are unaccompanied by announced intentions to replace aging assets. Any tangible asset-dependent company that is not continuously investing in new assets is not investing in its future.

Intangible Assets

While the profitability of many companies is highly dependent on maintaining efficient, up-to date tangible assets, other companies' profits arise primarily from intangible assets: intellectual property such as patents, copyrights, trademarks, and licensing agreements. For many firms, intellectual property includes brand identity. And, just as tangible asset-dependent companies must continuously invest in maintenance and modernization of their assets' bases, so too must intellectual property-dependent companies continuously invest in the maintenance of their intangible assets.

Maintenance of intellectual property requires regular expenditures on legal and regulatory processes. In addition to fighting off challenges from those who would encroach on its intellectual property, the firm must face the certainty that intellectual property "wears out," in the sense that patents and copyrights expire. The company needs to maintain a pipeline of new intellectual property, or else expect a drop-off in profitability when its patents and copyrights expire.

Evidence that a firm is maintaining its portfolio of patents and copyrights can be found in the number of lawsuits it successfully pursues to defend its rights and in the sustaining of its research and development expenditures. For companies whose profits are heavily dependent on "brand awareness," significant expenditures on advertising and other marketing expenses to maintain those brands is evidence of a commitment to future profitability.

Suppliers and Sub-Contractors

Few companies are so self-sufficient that they can function without assistance from suppliers and sub-contractors. Most depend to some degree on outside suppliers of raw materials, sub-components, or services.

The nature of a company's relationships with its suppliers and sub-contractors is certainly one of the fundamental factors that can generally favor or generally impede future growth in earnings and cash flow. Indeed, a firm's relationships with its suppliers and subcontractors can be a major competitive strength or a strategic weakness.

Many firms have adopted the "just in time" management technique to minimize their investments in inventory and to reduce working capital requirements. A modern manufacturing plant can be shut down within hours of a disruption in raw materials deliveries. Even if the availability of raw materials is reasonably assured, price fluctuations can wreak havoc on earnings and competitive position. In a highly competitive industry, firms may be unable to pass along raw materials price increases to their customers. (Consider, for example, the impact of fuel price increases on airline profits.) On the other hand, when raw materials prices are volatile, firms with solid, long-term supply contracts can obtain significant competitive advantages over competitors who purchase their materials on the spot market.

Therefore, assessing the quality of a firm's relationships with its suppliers and sub-contractors is a key part of our fundamental analysis. We assess the availability of raw materials supplies both in terms of reliability and price stability. We look for the existence of potential alternative materials, and we try to assess what technological developments and capital investments might be required to make switching to alternatives practical.

We are particularly interested in the firm's bargaining power relative to its suppliers. A firm that is one of many small competitors buying from a few big suppliers has very little bargaining power. A firm that dominates its market but is supplied by many small vendors has tremendous bargaining power. (We are aided in our assessment of relative bargaining power by the required footnote disclosure of supplier relationships.)

The greater a firm's dependence on it suppliers (i.e., the less bargaining power it has), the more information we will want to gather on the suppliers. This would include examining the financial statements of key suppliers and sub-contractors, where available, to evaluate their financial health and long-term viability. We want to know how long they have been supplying the subject firm and whether they operate under any long-term agreements.

It's also a good idea to examine recent and impending ownership transactions, to determine if there are any trends favoring consolidation or fragmentation in the suppliers' industries, or whether events indicate a trend toward vertical integration.

Labor

A firm's attitude toward, and relationships with, its labor force can say a lot about management's opinion of the company's future.

In companies where management seems to be perpetually at war with its workers, there tends to be a focus on squeezing out short-term profits at the expense of the future. A bad relationship between management and labor leads to high employee turnover, pressures for unionization where workers are not organized, and strikes where workers are unionized. The inevitable result will ultimately be higher labor costs, lower productivity, lower product quality, and, over time, a worsening of the firm's competitive position.

Contrast this view of labor with that expressed a few years ago by a software industry executive, who described his business as one where "the assets walk out the door every night at five o'clock." Companies that foster good relations with their workers seem to be saying they are in business for the long haul. They strive to build their future on the most talented, best motivated workers they can find. They invest in worker training and employee retention because they believe these investments lead to higher productivity, higher product quality, lower *unit* labor costs, and, ultimately, a strengthening of their competitive positions.

Other things being equal, we would rather invest in a firm that strives for good relations with its workers, because we believe such a company will be better equipped to compete in the future.

On the other hand, we are wary of firms that must go to unusual lengths to attract and retain workers. In some cases, this can indicate a problem with labor supply. Perhaps the firm is located in a sparsely populated area, or perhaps it faces too much competition from other employers for a limited pool of workers. The unavailability of qualified workers can severely limit a company's ability to grow profitably.

Furthermore, no matter how skilled and motivated a firm's work force might be, the workers' capabilities must be in line with the company's strategy. If the firm's strategy relies on low costs, it better have good manufacturing people. If the strategy is based on product differentiation, the firm must have good engineering people to be successful. If the strategy is based on building brands through clever marketing, the firm should have bright, creative marketing and advertising people. And, in almost every case, companies that achieve profitable growth have a sales force that is talented, motivated, and properly supported.

Legal and Regulatory Issues

Despite the best efforts of well-meaning politicians to periodically prune government regulation of business, public companies continue to be burdened by an ever-growing accumulation of laws, regulations, reporting requirements, inspections, and audits. Since the accounting scandals that began with the Enron debacle, this trend has accelerated.

No doubt, most of the laws and regulations are initiated with the best of intentions, to protect workers, investors, and the public. Nevertheless, it is becoming increasingly difficult for corporate leaders who want to do the right thing to keep up with governmental requirements, and a growing portion of potential earnings is absorbed by the inefficiency and overhead attributable to regulation.

Consequently, it would be unrealistic for us to make any blanket statements about avoiding the stocks of companies that fail to live up to *all* regulatory requirements. Some corporate transgressions are more deserving of investors' attention than, for example, violations of Department of Labor statistical reporting requirements, or minor OSHA infractions.

On the other hand, any failure to adhere to SEC regulations and file the required reports accurately, completely, and on time may be an indication that management has something to hide. Therefore, we would usually avoid the stock of a company that is not up to date on its 10-K's, 10-Q's, etc. The new requirement for public companies to document their internal control procedures will be another area deserving of attention by fundamental analysts.

Trouble with the IRS can also be a sign that management may not be playing by the rules. IRS penalties can have a significant impact on a company's current earnings, and an IRS order to change tax accounting methods could reduce its future earnings as well. Consequently, major trouble with the IRS would be another reason to avoid a stock.

Environmental regulation is another area of concern. Like contaminated soil and water underneath a factory, violations of environmental regulations can remain hidden until it is too late to avoid the consequences. A thorough fundamental analysis would typically include an evaluation of the company's potential exposure to environmental liabilities.

If the company operates in an environmentally sensitive industry, we would normally expect it to publicize the efforts it makes to protect the environment from harm. For example, a process manufacturing operation might be expected to tout its investments in waste water treatment facilities. Silence might be interpreted as a sign that the company is not doing all that it should to follow the regulations.

Certain industries are subject to special regulatory attention from such agencies as the Food and Drug Administration, the Federal Communications Commission, the Department of Transportation, etc. A fundamental analysis of any firm operating in one of these highly regulated industries should also include a review of foreseeable changes in the regulations that might have an impact on the firm's profits. Trade publications and the agencies' web sites are good sources of information on any new rules under consideration.

Almost every company becomes involved in legal disputes from time to time, and a pending lawsuit is not in itself a reason to avoid investing in a company's stock. However, any lawsuit that carries the potential for very large financial impact is certainly worthy of further research, and an excessive involvement in legal disputes would be good reason to avoid the stock altogether.

A lot of investors focus on earnings when they evaluate stocks as investments. Others base their trades on charts of daily stock price movements. We rarely encounter an investor who focuses primarily on cash flow.

While it's true that earnings expectations drive a company's stock price, few events can drive its price down faster than a liquidity crisis. We tend to associate cash flow problems with money-losing firms, but, in fact, it's not uncommon even for a rapidly growing, profitable company to run short of cash.

The information necessary to estimate the likelihood of a cash crunch - and to gauge a company's ability to survive such a crisis - is usually available from the financial statements.

An analysis of a company's cash flow would normally include a review of recent cash flow trends, an evaluation of the firm's actual and potential financial resources, and an assessment of the adequacy of cash flows into the foreseeable future.

Recent Cash Flow Trends

We start with an analysis of cash flow over the recent past, usually at least two years. Our primary concern is to confirm that net cash flow from operations has been positive, that growth in positive cash flow has been proportionate with growth in sales and earnings, and that operating cash flow has been adequate to meet debt service obligations.

If the company has not been producing positive operating cash flow, it could be due to investments in expansion (such as the opening of additional field sales offices, growth in customer service operations, expenditures for advertising and promotion, etc.) - or it may be an indication that something is seriously amiss (e.g., declining margins).

Regardless of how good management's reasons for incurring negative cash flow might be, however, a situation such as this always entails significant risk. The managers of rapidly growing companies have been known to overspend on expansion, and it is very difficult to rein in spending fast enough when revenue growth falters. Similar concerns apply when operating cash flow has been positive, but trending down.

Evaluation of Financial Resources

Once a good picture of the firm's cash flow situation has been developed, the next step is to evaluate its financial resources, to see whether they are adequate to meet existing financial commitments and operating needs. An assessment of the firm's ability to tap additional financial resources (should they be needed) is another important factor to consider.

An evaluation of a firm's financial resources (and its creditors' claims on them) should take into account off-balance sheet financing activities and commitments as well as reported assets and liabilities. It should also include a check of the firm's compliance with its bank loan covenants and an assessment of its obligations to preferred shareholders and holders of options, warrants, and rights.

The evaluation begins with a comparison of the firm's current assets to its short-term liabilities. This comparison provides a good indication of the firm's ability to remain current with its short-term obligations. The ratio of current assets to short-term liabilities should normally be in the range of at least 1.5 to 2.0 for a healthy company. Less than 1.0 is often an indication of a liquidity crisis in the making; it is certainly cause for further investigation.

After satisfying ourselves that the firm is able to meet its current operational needs, the next step would be a review of the company's long-term investment needs and capital structure.

Most businesses require a regular stream of new investments in long-term assets. Firms make investments in long-term assets - which include everything from plant and equipment to whole companies - in order to support their growth, maintain and enhance their competitive position, and improve their profitability. A company's ability to sustain a commitment to capital investment is a critical determinant of its long-term prospects.

Normally, we would question a sharp decline in new investment as much as we would a sudden increase. When managers get nervous about their company's near-term future, investment in long-term assets is one of the first places they cut. This can provide investors an early warning of future difficulties. Conversely, a large increase in expenditures for long-term assets means that management is taking on major new commitments that will have to be supported by future growth. This adds additional risk.

A firm can sustain a commitment to long-term capital investment only to the extent that it can finance the program. Few companies are profitable enough to finance all of their capital investment requirements without resort to long-term financing (whether through borrowing or the sale of additional stock).

A company's ability to obtain additional long-term financing at reasonable terms depends, to a large extent, on its capital structure. One method for evaluating a firm's capital structure is the debt to equity ratio. This ratio (of long-term debt to owners' equity) is widely used by lenders to assess a firm's ability to support additional long-term debt. The debt to equity ratio can easily be calculated by dividing long-term liabilities by stockholders' equity (using the figures reported on the balance sheet).

In most industries, a debt to equity ratio significantly above 3.0 is a sign that the firm has become overextended, meaning that few lenders would loan additional funds at acceptable terms. A firm that has reached its borrowing limit is dangerously close to a major liquidity crisis. One or two quarterly losses might be all that is necessary to push it over the edge. A debt to equity of between 1.0 and 3.0 indicates that the firm is leveraged, but not overly so. Debt to equity below 1.0 is usually considered rock-solid, unless the company is losing money. Most lenders are unwilling to advance credit to unprofitable companies.

Using reported balance sheet figures to calculate the debt to equity ratio may not yield the most accurate result in all cases. As we pointed out in Chapter 13, historical cost accounting often leads to significant differences between the values of assets and liabilities reported on the balance sheet and their actual, fair market values. Adjustments are often required to correct for these differences between market values and reported values. Additional adjustment may be necessary to reflect items that GAAP accounting rules leave off the balance sheet entirely.

Examples of items requiring adjustment include real estate carried on the books at old historical costs and special purpose equipment that has lost value faster than it has been depreciated on the books.

Additional adjustments may be required to correct the values of financial assets, such as pension plan investments, whose values are sensitive to external forces (e.g., stock market movements, interest rate changes, and foreign exchange risks). Hedging strategies and exposure to derivatives can also affect a company's financial strength in ways that aren't reflected on its balance sheet. And if the company leases its products to customers, the value of its receivables will require adjustment to reflect any unrecorded vulnerability to early lease terminations.

Certain liabilities, such as contingent liabilities (e.g., loan guarantees provided to other entities, potential losses arising from legal disputes, etc.) and operating lease obligations are generally not reported on the balance sheet under GAAP accounting rules. The valuation of other liabilities, such as warranty and pension obligations, is based on estimates. In order to accurately gauge the company's ability to borrow funds, it may be necessary to adjust for discrepancies in these liability values. Obligations to preferred shareholders may necessitate additional adjustments.

Adjusting for unrecorded or misreported assets and liabilities sometimes reveals opportunities or risks that are not immediately apparent from a quick review of the financial statements. This can create trading opportunities for astute investors.

A firm's capacity for assuming additional debt depends on factors beyond the value of its assets, liabilities, and its financial leverage. Its ability to borrow additional funds is also constrained by market forces. A company with a lot of debt and lease obligations (relative to its assets) may be able to raise additional cash at acceptable terms when credit markets are relaxed, but might be unable to obtain the cash it needs when credit markets are tight. Bank loan covenants can become so tight that they constrain management's ability to operate the business at peak efficiency, which, together with higher interest rates, can further degrade its financial strength.

Once a firm has reached its practical borrowing limit, any additional financial requirements must be met through the sale of equity. The firm's ability to attract equity funding through an additional offering of stock is much harder to measure than its capability to borrow money. It depends on market conditions as much as it depends on the firm's attractiveness as an investment.

In any case, the dilutive effects of a new stock offering must be carefully weighed, along with any dilution caused by commitments to the holders of convertible securities, stock options, and warrants. Too many investors in rapidly growing companies overlook the dilution that will be caused when those companies make their predictable return to the equity market for additional funding. The companies' growth in sales and earnings might meet their most optimistic projections but still produce only mediocre investment returns due to the issuance of additional shares.

Adequacy of Future Cash Flows

After we have reviewed a company's recent cash flow trends and evaluated its financial resources, we will have reached a fairly good assessment of its current financial strength. If our assessment shows the company to be in poor or marginal condition, we probably won't give it any further consideration.

Consequently, when we reach the point where we are assessing a company's future cash flows, we are invariably looking at a financially strong company. Our assessment of its cash flow trajectory would therefore be limited, in most cases, to a review of factors that have the potential to affect the availability of financial resources in a major way.

A significant reduction in projected revenues would certainly have a major effect on a company's future cash flows.

Thus, we might begin by reviewing macroeconomic factors such as demographics, emerging technologies, economic trends, international trade relations, government spending policies, and environmental regulations that could affect the company's markets.

Pricing developments within the company's industry could also affect its revenues and cash flow. Suppose, for example, that a competitor cut its prices by 20%. Would the company be able to match the price reduction and still generate enough cash to remain afloat?

It is almost always helpful to compare the financial strengths and weaknesses of competitors and potential competitors. A financially strong company may run into trouble if it faces even stronger competitors that choose to invest heavily in product development, distribution channels, or marketing efforts. On the other hand, it would be useful to know that a competitor's financial weakness is likely to prevent it from cutting prices.

In other words, a company's relative financial strength (compared to its competitors) may be the most important factor to consider in assessing the adequacy of its future cash flows.

A potential need for significant investments in expansion or modernization would be another important factor to consider. When companies grow rapidly, they tend to develop needs for additional financing. Rapid growth isn't the only reason a company might need to plan for a major capital expenditure, though. An old, slow-growing company operating out of a run-down, old facility might have capital needs just as great as its faster growing neighbor, due to its need to modernize.

Major capital investment requirements demand special efforts to estimate the amounts in question and to determine the source of funding, because a failure by the company to meet these needs could very well destroy its investment value. If the source of adequate financing at reasonable terms is not readily identifiable, the stock may carry an unacceptable level of risk.

Maintaining a competitive level of customer service can also place significant demands on a company's future resources. Rapid sales growth can cause costs for order fulfillment, returns, and warranty obligations to skyrocket. Failure to provide adequate financial resources for customer service could limit a promising company's ability to achieve its potential.

In most cases, the factors having the greatest impact on a company's future cash flows will be its revenues and capital investments. For many companies, semi-variable costs related to growth—such as the expansion of distribution channels and the ramp-up of customer service—would also merit scrutiny.

Of course, there are many other factors that could significantly affect the adequacy of a company's future cash flows. A review of all major contracts with the company's suppliers, workers, landlords, and customers, with special attention paid to future cost increases and balloon payments, would reveal additional demands on a company's resources. Any restrictions on cash balances or transfers that are demanded by banks, foreign governments, or contractual obligations should also be considered in assessing future cash flows.

The Quality of the Management Team

Most private equity investors (venture capitalists, for example) will tell you that the first and most important factor they consider when deciding whether to invest in a company is the quality of the management team.

Technological windows of opportunity can open and close, development projects can fail to realize their promise, and unforeseen difficulties and opportunities regularly occur in the life of any business venture. Business plans make perfect sense—until the day after they are written, then everything changes.

Capable managers can adapt, solving new problems and seizing new opportunities as they arise.

Ineffective managers cannot.

Of course, it's much easier to acknowledge than to assess the critical importance of "management quality." As investors in public companies, we rarely get to know the executives who run "our" businesses. We must do the best we can with publicly available information to learn more about a company's executives.

Generally, except for some highly visible "superstar" CEO's, we rely on the background information provided in SEC reports as our starting point. The SEC reports tell us where each senior executive worked in the past and a little bit about what they accomplished in their prior jobs.

Further digging is often useful in evaluating the experience claimed in the 10-K. For example, if an executive is reported as having been Senior Vice President of Sales at XYZ Corp. for five years in the 1990's, it might be a good idea to look up XYZ Corp.'s history of sales growth during the years of his tenure. It's always a good idea to find out as much as practically possible about the companies in which the managers previously worked. The corporate culture and relative success of the executives' previous employers can tell us a lot about how the executives will perform in their current jobs.

Once we have assembled information on each senior executive, we rate the company's management on three key questions:

- Is each key functional role filled by an executive with a strong track record of success in his or her area?

- Is the team effectively led by an experienced CEO with a strong record of successful leadership?

- Does the group function effectively as a team?

Each key role should be filled by a manager with a job history of progressively responsible positions and a verifiable track record of accomplishments in successful organizations with corporate cultures that are compatible with the current employer. It's usually better if the experience was gained in the same industry as the current employer, because the executive will have formed industry contacts with prospective customers, suppliers, and employees. None of the executives should have any record of legal problems, bankruptcies, or other skeletons in their closets.

The CEO should have a strong record of developing leaders and a record of creating shareholder value through growth of sales and profits. Because the CEO's personality has a lot to do with the corporate culture that will develop, we prefer a CEO who radiates a passion for the firm's mission and whose personal style is both energetic and ethical.

The executive group must be able to function well as a team. A well-integrated group of B-level executives that has worked together for ten years would be preferable to a recently assembled bunch of A-level prima donnas. The team should collectively possess all the skills necessary to grow the business. There should be no gaps in expertise or unfilled positions on the management team.

It is desirable for the team to have at least one member who would be capable of stepping up to the CEO position should anything happen to the incumbent. A company with a designated successor will generally have stronger leadership than a company with a large capability gap between the CEO and the executive team. Having a designated successor is a sign that the CEO can develop leaders. When the time comes for the inevitable change in leadership, the company and its shareholders will enjoy a smoother transition.

The company's board of directors, advisory committees, and major shareholders should be actively involved in the firm's management. A strong, active board is generally indicative of a well-managed company. Board members who bring in relationships with customers, suppliers, joint venture partners, and others can significantly enhance a company's value.

Finally, a company whose executives and board members have significant ownership stakes in the company will have greater congruity between the interests of management and shareholders. It is preferable for management's ownership to be in the form of restricted stock rather than options structured for a "quick hit." The closer management's compensation is tied to long-term appreciation of the share price, the better.

• Chapter 15 •

FINAL THOUGHTS ON STOCK SELECTION STRATEGIES

We'll conclude Part Two, "Our Data Driven Stock Selection Strategy," by briefly summarizing what we've learned from our research about picking stocks and clarifying the role stock selection plays in our approach to investing.

Our "data driven" philosophy leads us to adopt stock selection strategies that have consistently produced market-beating returns in the past, because these are the very strategies that offer the best odds of beating the market in the future.

Most of the time, this means selecting small company value stocks with high relative strength.

Over time, as we have seen, small company stocks have outperformed large caps by a wide margin. Occasionally, large caps outperform small companies, most typically in Panic Years, (i.e., when the Fed raises interest rates early in the Election Cycle). Our strategy of switching to large caps in Panic Years is designed to avoid the losses that nanocap strategies often experience during such risk-averse times.

The long-term superiority of value over growth is even more pronounced than that of small company stocks over large caps. The high P/E strategy outperformed the low P/E strategy in just five out of 52 years, the last time being in 1980! Growth strategies are most likely to outperform value strategies in Euphoric markets, i.e., Late Election Cycle bull markets occurring toward the end of a period of aggressively restrictive policy. High P/S and high P/BV strategies have a much better track record vis-à-vis their value counterparts than do either high P/E or high P/CF.

Buying high relative strength is normally a market-beating strategy, except during "Extreme Euphoric" years (or in the year-end "tax selling season").

Looking back, a strategy of shifting stock selection criteria according to phase changes in the Fed-Election Cycle would have outperformed a small company, high relative strength value strategy.

However, in practice it rarely makes sense to re-construct the entire portfolio when the cycle shifts into a new phase. The performance advantage gained by shifting into large caps or growth stocks during the periods when they outperform small cap value stocks must be weighed against the trading costs associated with shifting assets. In most cases, it's advisable to make appropriate adjustments in the selection criteria for *new purchases* when the Fed-Election Cycle enters a new phase, rather than re-casting the entire portfolio to fit a different style.

Quantitative stock selection criteria are just the starting point in our methodology for identifying stocks to be purchased. Using criteria based on P/E, market cap, etc. to develop our preliminary "watch list" of stocks, we winnow the group of stocks eligible for consideration down from the thousands of public companies in existence to the one or two thousand companies that have winning characteristics.

And, frankly, this is the easy part. Almost anyone can pick good stocks to buy simply by running a screen for low price ratios and small market cap.

But picking good stocks does not guarantee that we will beat the market. We might pick excellent stocks, but if we buy or sell them at the wrong time or for the wrong price, we can still perform poorly.

Remember, successful investing goes well beyond stockpicking. How we trade them is just as important as picking potential winners.

And that's why we wrote Part Three of *Data Driven Investing— Professional Edition*.

In Part Three, *Trading Tactics,* we'll study the psychology of decision-making as it applies to investing, because human nature is at the heart of most, if not all, of the stock market inefficiencies we've studied. We'll emphasize the competitive nature of stock trading as we draw links between specific market inefficiencies and the innate flaws in human thought processes that lead us to make irrational choices.

News and Fundamentals

Although, in organizing this book, we grouped financial statement and fundamental analysis with stock selection strategies, in practice we create our watch lists using only quantitative selection criteria. We rarely analyze financial statements or fundamentals until after a news story breaks.

At that point, however, a quick review of the company's financial statements and fundamentals is often critical to our assessment of the market's reaction to the story.

Our trading tactics emphasize a *swift and sure response* to breaking news stories. We need to evaluate a story's market impact before we commit to a trade, but we must act quickly to seize the opportunity before it fades. Consequently, our time for analyzing financial statements and fundamentals is quite limited.

In the absence of breaking news, financial statement and fundamental analysis might be good ways to select stocks—for someone who has unlimited time or a large research staff.

However, any investor would benefit from acquiring a familiarity with these important disciplines, especially those who intend to trade on news stories. In most cases, our ability to decipher a breaking story depends on a modest amount of research guided by the principles laid out in Chapters 13 and 14.

Irrational behavior can be observed in the market every day. An understanding of investor psychology enables us to out-trade our fellow investors, and in Chapter 16, "Understanding the Psychology of Investing," we'll identify numerous ways to apply this knowledge in different trading situations.

Then, in Chapter 17, we'll get into the nuts and bolts of our trading tactics. We'll start by defining, in detail, the critical role breaking news plays in our **Data Driven Investing**™ approach to investing. We'll describe how we use a combination of psychological, financial statement, and fundamental analysis to evaluate news stories and predict the market's reaction, emphasizing the vital importance of reacting swiftly and surely to breaking news stories and significant price movements.

Next, we'll explain the ins and outs of placing buy and sell orders, show how we price our bids and asks, and list seven simple rules for reacting to news and significant price movements.

Once we've covered all the basic mechanics of our trading tactics, we'll pay a visit to our trading room.

Successful trading is as much an art as it is a science, and, as such, it's impossible to reduce to a simple set of decision rules. We'll illustrate the art in our trading tactics by taking our readers through a "typical" trading day, using specific (hypothetical) examples of different trading situations to give readers a "feel for the game."

Next, we'll review several well-established trading patterns that continue to provide good opportunities for investors, including calendar-based patterns and patterns associated with corporate spin-offs.

Finally, we'll close Chapter 17 by discussing some of the "big picture" issues involved with trading stocks. These include the management of buying power, the minimization and deferral of taxes, and the management of risk.

Part Three

OUR DATA DRIVEN
TRADING TACTICS

In Part Three, we describe our day-to-day trading tactics. We outline the psychological factors that influence investors' behavior and explain how to profit by anticipating the reactions of fellow traders. We emphasize the competitive nature of trading stocks and the critical importance of reacting swiftly and confidently to news stories. We also show when and how to profit from the impatience of others by providing liquidity in thinly-traded issues, and we review well-established trading patterns that continue to provide good opportunities for informed investors. We provide tips and techniques for managing buying power, minimizing investment-related taxes, and managing risk.

• Chapter 16 •

UNDERSTANDING THE PSYCHOLOGY OF INVESTING

In this chapter, we will explain how we apply psychological principles to improve our investment returns.

We developed this approach to trading through a review of academic research concerning the ways people make choices under conditions of uncertainty. The principles derived from this research explain many of the patterns of behavior we regularly observe in our day-to-day trading, and, more significantly, they enable us to profit by anticipating the likely reactions of our fellow traders in various situations.

Most finance professors would have us believe that psychology has no place in a serious discussion of investing. Academic finance has long been dominated by adherents to the Efficient Market Hypothesis, who maintain (among other assertions) that analyzing and trading upon the emotions and cognitive quirks of fellow investors is not a course that can lead to market-beating performance.

However, evidence against the preposterous notion of an efficient market has been mounting, and links between behavioral patterns and market inefficiencies have been established. In one recent experiment, the psychophysiological responses of traders were monitored as they made trading decisions involving large sums of real money. Fluctuations in the traders' heart rate, blood pressure, respiration, etc. were correlated with market events (e.g., price volatility), suggesting that the traders' decisions were affected by their emotional responses.[1]

Trading stocks is an intensely competitive activity.

---

[1] "The Psychophysiology of Real-Time Financial Risk Processing," by Andrew Lo and Dmitri Repin. *Journal of Cognitive Neuroscience*, April 2002, pgs. 323-339.

Yet, when we enter an order to buy or sell a stock, it's often easy to think we are casting our trade into a nameless, faceless, disembodied market that operates more like a machine than a person.

On the contrary, even when we are trading the largest of the widely held companies, we are interacting with real people who are motivated by the same psychological factors that drive us all. Even a rudimentary understanding of investor behavior can help us to identify decision-making patterns of fellow market participants that we can exploit to our advantage.

This opportunity continues to exist because even investors who are aware of psychological biases do not generally exploit them. We all find it difficult to overcome the psychological underpinnings - prejudice, preference, fear, and illusion - that impair our ability to make rational decisions, especially decisions affecting our financial well-being. And even those who should know better frequently allow their investment decisions to be driven by irrational impulses.

Nevertheless, investors can learn to recognize and avoid unprofitable tendencies in their own decision-making patterns by studying the psychological factors that influence investor behavior and applying the lessons appropriately. In most trading situations, investors will make better decisions if they pause to consider the impact of psychological factors prior to choosing a course of action (or inaction). Biases can be overcome if they can be identified. Half-blind reactions to incomplete or misinterpreted information can give way to purposeful action guided by rigorous analysis of historical data.

Most of the strategies and tactics we write about and use are rooted in investor psychology. Psychological factors help explain the persistence of exploitable market inefficiencies related to the Fed Effect, the Election Cycle, and calendar-related trading patterns. They have a big impact on the performance of strategies based on value, growth, and relative strength, and they are largely responsible for the outstanding performance of nanocaps.

In addition, investor psychology underlies one of our most useful trading tactics, reacting quickly to news stories. Many of the psychological factors we will discuss cause error and delay in reacting to new information. In Chapter 17, we will explain how to profit by reacting swiftly and confidently to new information with appropriately priced orders, but first we need to establish an understanding of the psychological factors that cause this tactic to work as well as it does.

Four Major Psychological Biases

Four major categories of bias drive investor behavior:

- Trend biases

- Loss aversion biases

- Conservatism biases

- Cognitive biases

Trend Biases

Trend biases lead people to believe that established trends will continue to prevail. These biases cause investors to overreact in the short-term—by motivating them to buy what has risen and to sell what has fallen. In Chapter 7, we discussed one well-known manifestation of trend bias, momentum investing.

Most people feel some degree of pressure to adopt the beliefs of those around them. In some cases, that pressure is real—that is, there are explicit negative consequences associated with not fitting in or following the herd. In most cases, probably, this pressure is self-inflicted, caused by our instinctive desire to remain part of the group.

Over the course of human development, this bias probably contributed to a survival advantage and may still serve us well in some respects. When we see a crowd of people running away from something, it generally behooves us not to run toward that something. On Wall Street, though, the reverse often holds true, i.e., it usually pays to gravitate toward the places that most investors flee.

Trend bias can make overvalued assets become more overvalued and undervalued assets more undervalued. Sometimes trend bias can cause valuations to reach truly absurd levels. Consider the tulip bulb mania in 17th century Holland (when a single bulb could trade for 12 acres of fertile farmland), the Tokyo real estate bubble of the 1980's (when the value of downtown Tokyo was theoretically worth more than the entire state of California), and, of course, the recent dot.com bubble.

In all of these examples, prices went up mainly because they had gone up yesterday, and the day before, etc.—and because everyone wanted to be in on the easy money.

Trend biases lead investors to discount or ignore information that might indicate the trend will come to an end. Trend biases are therefore a significant contributor to the tendencies of growth stocks to rise outrageously high and value stocks to fall unreasonably low.

Loss Aversion Biases

Loss aversion biases cause investors to become irrationally protective of their gains, or obsessed with breaking even when their positions are down.

These biases often cause investors to sell their winners for lower prices than they should, creating opportunities for others to buy stocks whose prices have been depressed by profit taking. And these same biases cause investors with paper losses to hold on to their losers, hoping to recover their investments, even when this hope has no basis in fact.

Loss aversion biases cause rising stocks to rise more slowly, and falling stocks to fall more slowly, than they otherwise would. Thus, loss aversion biases tend to counteract the effect of trend biases.

Conservatism Biases

Conservatism biases arise from investors' comfort with the status quo, as well as from their tendency to require unnecessarily large amounts of data when making decisions.

Conservatism biases cause delays in the market's reaction to new information. They also contribute to the overvaluation of growth stocks and the undervaluation of value stocks.

Cognitive Biases

Cognitive biases are caused by innate flaws in the processes through which we perceive and interpret information.

Some cognitive biases cause investors to overemphasize information that supports their biases and de-emphasize information that doesn't. Others cause investors to ignore important data altogether. And some create mental processing errors, leading investors who may have properly perceived and rationally weighed data to draw incorrect conclusions.

All cognitive biases have the potential to cause delays and mistakes in the market's reaction to new information.

Each of the psychological factors we will discuss in this chapter can be associated with at least one of these four categories. Human psychology being as complex as it is, most of the factors are interrelated and tend to enhance or weaken the effects of the others. While the market impact of each one may be quite predictable when taken in isolation, it's rarely possible to observe a single psychological factor operating in isolation. Nevertheless, it is possible, with experience, to get a fairly good sense of the factors that are likely to be in play in any given situation, in a way that allows us to make sufficiently reliable predictions.

Generally speaking, trend biases tend to cause overreaction to new information, while loss aversion, conservatism, and cognitive biases tend to cause underreaction. All psychological biases tend to create error and confusion, but also opportunity. Since, over time, all of these psychological biases are likely to affect the market for any given stock in response to the ebb and flow of events, opportunities abound for those who understand how the market thinks.

Five Classes of Psychological Factors

For convenience in study, we will re-shuffle the psychological factors associated with these biases and classify them into the following five groups:

- Narrow-minded stubbornness

- Devotion to status quo

- Loss aversion

- Inattentiveness

- Unsupported optimism

Narrow-Minded Stubbornness

Selective Perception (a Cognitive/Conservatism Bias)

Selective perception, along with selective exposure, selective attention, selective interpretation, and selective retention, causes us to see the world in ways that conform to our pre-existing beliefs.

We selectively expose ourselves to sources of information that reinforce what we already believe to be true. Catholics don't spend much time in mosques. And relatively few liberals listen to Rush Limbaugh on a regular basis.

The new information that attracts our attention tends to be consistent with what we already know (or believe). When we encounter ambiguities, we tend

Selective Perception & Sales

We see things the way we expect to see them, rather than as they actually exist. Politicians, magicians, and salespeople have relied on this for millennia, telling us what we expect to hear and showing us what we expect to see.

Large financial services firms profit from selective perception when they run ads extolling their client-centered competence and rectitude. The vast majority of individual investors who own mutual funds and full-service brokerage accounts believe what they see in the ads, because that's the image they want to have of the firms that hold their nest eggs. They overlook the high commissions and fees, lackluster performance, and general mismanagement they often endure as clients of these firms.

Wall Street has been telling the same half-truths for so long that they have become conventional wisdom. The Efficient Market Theory, for example, dictates maximum diversification.

But leaving aside the question of whether any market as decentralized and complex as the U.S. stock market could ever be deemed efficient, the truth is that when brokers and mutual fund salespeople urge their clients to diversify, in most cases they're really just interested in selling whatever is trendy and pays a hefty commission. The net effect on the client's well-being is, more often than not, negative - what some wags have called "deworsification."

Much of what we write about in this book strikes at the core of Wall Street's belief system, and we expect a significant number of securities industry veterans to ignore or downplay the significance of our ideas.

That is how selective perception works.

to interpret them in ways that minimize any need for adjusting our views of the world. And we recall best that information with which we are most comfortable; that is, information that doesn't force us to question, adjust, or reform our views and opinions. Consequently, when we encounter new information that is inconsistent with our preconceived notions, we tend to ignore it or downplay its significance.

Selective perception has been demonstrated in a variety of academic research studies. In one, a group of students were shown news clips of the 1982 killings of Palestinians in Lebanon's refugee camps and then asked to count the number of favorable and unfavorable references to Israel. The pro-Arab students counted 1.6 favorable references for every unfavorable reference, while the pro-Israeli students counted 3.5 unfavorable references for every favorable reference.

People generally interpret news in ways that fit their preconceptions. They tend to discount stories that contradict what they believe. Sometimes they blame the news source for a lack of objectivity, as they did in the study of reactions to the attack on Palestinians. (Academics refer to this form of selective perception as the "hostile media effect."[2])

Selective perception creates opportunities to buy small company stocks (especially nanocaps) cheaply. The widespread misconception that only large company stocks are suitable investments leads "serious" investors to ignore favorable developments at small companies. (Large brokerage firms, which rarely follow any company that isn't a potential investment banking client, perpetuate this misconception by dismissing small caps as "speculative." And imagine the chaos that would quickly ensue were a 10,000 salesperson firm to start pounding the table about a stock that normally trades 1,000 shares a day.)

A lag always exists between the release of news and market reaction. It takes at least a few seconds to analyze a press release and punch in an order. But the lag can be much longer when the true nature or significance of the news is not readily perceived. Thus, selective perception causes delay in the market's reaction to surprising news, creating opportunities for investors to profit by reacting quickly to news stories.

The Halo Effect (a Cognitive Bias)

We have a tendency to let our overall opinion of a person—or of one of his outstanding traits—color our impression of every feature of that person. This tendency is known as the "halo effect." If we have an especially strong like or

2 "The Hostile Media Phenomenon: Biased Perception and Perceptions of Media Bias in Coverage of the Beirut Massacre," *Journal of Personality and Social Psychology*, 49, pgs. 577-585, by Vallone, Ross, and Lepper, 1985.

dislike of the person or trait, the halo effect will be even more likely to over-shadow our opinion of other features.

Halo effect can be positive or negative, and it can apply to organizations or things as well as people.

Polls conducted after the 1960 Kennedy-Nixon presidential debate showed that most people who heard the debate on the radio thought Nixon had won, while a majority of the television watchers thought Kennedy had prevailed. The television watchers were charmed by Kennedy's telegenic good looks and put off by Nixon's haggard appearance. Their opinions of the candidates' substance were colored by assessments of physical attributes.

Because of the halo effect, we instinctively ascribe all sorts of positive attributes to physically attractive people, and all sorts of negative attributes to the less attractive. Tall people tend to get promoted faster and make more money than short people, but are there any studies proving that tall people are smarter or work harder?

The halo effect is so compelling that even when we have a special duty to make objective evaluations of another person's capabilities, traits, etc., we regularly fail to distinguish and rate them separately. A study of the evaluations given to Army officers by their superiors showed strong correlation between such unrelated traits as intelligence and character, intelligence and leadership ability, and even intelligence and physique.[3]

Just as we evaluate politicians more on their style than their substance, and people more on their appearance than their character and ability, we investors often evaluate stocks on the basis of considerations that, by any objective standard, would be considered irrelevant. It's easy for us to fall into the trap of thinking good companies make good investments, or that bad companies make bad investments.

There are many examples of companies whose reputations—based on their management, their products, or their advertising—grow out of proportion to the growth of their earnings or cash flow. Under the influence of the halo effect, investors buy these companies for their reputations rather than their financial performance, causing them to become overvalued.

In a similar way, negative halo effect (which we like to call "horns effect") causes other companies to be undervalued. Peter Lynch made a lot of money for Magellan investors by applying this principle. As he pointed out in *One Up on Wall Street*, companies that have unfavorable reputations or produce

[3] "A Constant Error in Psychological Ratings," *Journal of Applied Psychology*, 4, pgs. 25-29, by E. Thorndike, 1920.

products with unpleasant connotations often make excellent investments. He cited as examples Philip Morris (tobacco) and Service Corp. of America (caskets).

Once we make up our minds that something is good (or bad), we tend to hold on to that point of view, jealously guarding and defending our opinions even as evidence mounts that we are wrong. But a company can lose its halo and grow horns, or vice versa. This creates opportunities for investors who recognize the change early in the process.

The stock price of a company with overall positive halo effects tends to react quickly to good news, but slowly to bad news. Conversely, the stock price of a company with negative halo effects will tend to react quickly to bad news, but slowly to good news.

Furthermore, stocks with positive halo effects are likely to have less perceived risk than they deserve. From time to time, we hear about companies being "too big to fail"—Enron and WorldCom come to mind.

On the other hand, stocks with negative halo effects are likely to suffer from high levels of perceived risk – even in the absence of real risk associated with such fundamental factors as financial leverage, etc.

Some of the factors leading to halo effects include:

- **Size**– Large companies are often thought to be better investments than small companies (although, as we have seen, the opposite is usually true).

- **Price Momentum**– A company whose stock price is rising is generally thought to be a good investment.

- **Growth**– Companies whose sales are growing rapidly are usually thought to be better investments than their slower growing peers.

- **Publicity**– Positive media coverage is a prime contributor to halo effect.

- **Industry**– Companies in glamorous, fast-growing industries are thought by many to be better investments than companies in stodgy industries.

- **Market**– When the market is going up, investors tend to be more optimistic and forgiving. When it's going down, they are quicker to sell and slower to buy.

A large, rapidly growing company which operates in a glamorous industry and whose stock price is rising sounds like the perfect investment to many investors. In fact, this is a typical profile for an overvalued growth company.

A small, slowly growing company which operates in a boring or unsavory industry and whose stock price doesn't move very far or very fast will be overlooked by most investors, although this is a fairly typical profile of an attractively priced value company.

Confirmation Bias (a Cognitive/Conservatism Bias)

As we noted with regard to selective perception, our attitude toward new information is strongly influenced by what we already believe to be true. Confirmation bias leads us to actively look for facts that support our beliefs.

Confirmation bias has been demonstrated in a number of research studies. In one[4], subjects were given identical information about a woman who alternated between extroversion and introversion. Later, the subjects were asked whether the woman would be better suited for selling real estate or for library research. Some of the subjects were told that the woman had applied for a real estate sales job, while others were told she had applied for a library job.

Most of the subjects who were told she had applied for the sales job thought she would be good at it because of her extroverted personality. Most of the subjects who were told she had applied for the library job cited evidence of her introverted nature as being more significant. In other words, both groups gave the most weight to confirming data rather than to disconfirming data.

In a related experiment, subjects were asked to list the questions they would ask to judge a person's suitability for these jobs. For prospective real estate sales people, "How outgoing is the candidate?" was asked with much greater frequency than "How shy is the candidate?" Actually, both questions get at the same personality issue, but from two different angles. The preference for the first question showed the bias toward the collection of confirming data, rather than disconfirming data.

As a result of confirmation bias, an "out of favor," value stock (i.e., one with low ratios of price to earnings, sales, etc.) will tend to react slowly to a positive news story, while an "in favor," growth stock (one with high price ratios) will tend to react slowly to a negative news story. In both cases, most investors discount or ignore the validity of the news because it does not confirm their preexisting beliefs, which causes delay in the market's response.

---

[4] "Testing Hypotheses About Other People: The Use Of Historical Knowledge," *Journal of Experimental Social Psychology*, 15, pgs.330-342, by M. Snyder and N. Cantor, 1979.

Devotion to Status Quo

Cognitive Dissonance (a Cognitive Bias)

According to cognitive dissonance theory, we all struggle to maintain consistency between our beliefs and actions. Any inconsistency between what we think and what we do creates distress, which drives us to find some way of reconciling the inconsistency.

There are two forms of cognitive dissonance: "pre-decisional dissonance" and "post-decisional dissonance." Pre-decisional dissonance can oblige us to choose the course of action which is most consistent with our prior actions and beliefs. Post-decisional dissonance leads us to adjust our beliefs in order to rationalize our prior actions. We strive for consistency of thought, word, and deed, not so much to disguise behavior that might appear foolish to others, but in order to appear reasonable to ourselves.

Consider the post-decisional dissonance of the fox in Aesop's "Fox and the Grapes" fable. He tries and tries, but he can't reach the grapes. Then, he gives up, concluding that he didn't want them anyway because they were too sour. In this way, the fox rationalizes his decision to quit trying.

When investors get burned on a stock, they are less likely to rush back into it later when good news breaks, due to their need to avoid cognitive dissonance. They often have made up their minds that the stock is irredeemably bad, and they are invested in defending their evaluation.

Post-decisional dissonance frequently arises after we have made a commitment, when we experience "morning after" doubts or "buyer's remorse." Our attempts to reconcile dissonance between the choice we have made and all of the potential reasons why it might not have been the best course of action lead us to attitudinal changes, much like Aesop's fox.

In a study involving horse track bettors, those who had actually placed their bets had a much higher level of confidence that their horse would win than those who were in line to bet but had not actually done so.[5]   Similarly, Canadian voters had higher opinions of the candidates they favored, in terms of both suitability for the job and chances of winning, after casting their votes than before.[6]

These studies show that post-decisional attitude adjustments can lead us to become irrationally confident in the correctness of our decisions. We tend to develop overly favorable impressions of the alternatives we select, and overly negative impressions of the alternative we reject, especially if the decision was

[5] "Postdecision Dissonance At Post Time," *Journal of Personality and Social Psychology,* 8, pgs. 319-323, by Robert Knox and James Inkster, 1968.

[6] "Post-Decision Dissonance At the Polling Booth," *Canadian Journal of Behavioural Science,* 8, pgs. 347-350, by O.J. Frenkel and A.N. Doob, 1976.

a close call. Our overconfidence can cause us to react slowly to developments that contradict the convictions upon which our earlier decisions were based.

Cognitive dissonance theory suggests that our assessment of an item's value will be consistent with the price paid or effort expended to acquire it. Even in the face of contradictory evidence, we minimize dissonance by striving to maintain our original appraisal.

In an experiment investigating this principle, 24 discount stores were divided into twelve pairs. In each pair, one store introduced mouthwash at 39 cents a bottle, while the other store priced it at 25 cents. Nine days later, the stores with the 25 cent mouthwash conformed with the other stores by raising the price to 39 cents. In 10 of the 12 pairs, the store that initially charged 39 cents sold more mouthwash than the one with the 25 cent introductory price. Similar experiments were conducted with other products, and, in each case, the products with high introductory prices outsold those with lower introductory prices that were subsequently raised.

We often think that if something costs more, it must be worth more. Consumers who bought the mouthwash at the introductory price of 39 cents continued to buy it at that price; their actions were consistent with their prior decisions and, presumably, with their view of the product's value. Consumers who had been offered the 25 cent introductory price apparently saw the mouthwash as worth 25 cents but overpriced at 39 cents. This created pre-decisional dissonance, which caused many of them to stop buying the product.[7]

In the stock market, the need to avoid cognitive dissonance causes investors who have bought a stock at $30 to be slower to sell if it goes down to $25. These investors would tend to believe the stock's fair value to be at least whatever they paid for it, just like the consumers who bought the 39 cent mouthwash. If the price drops below their purchase price, they might buy more shares. They will discount any suggestion that the stock is worth less than what they paid, because that would create dissonance with their earlier decision. On the other hand, investors who considered buying the stock at $30 - but decided to hold off - will tend to be even less likely to buy if the price goes up to $35, because this would create dissonance with their earlier opinion that the stock was worth less than $30.

Thus, investor psychology will tend to keep that stock trading fairly close to $30 until some other factor causes it to break out of its narrow trading range. Of course, none of this has anything to do with the "intrinsic" value of the stock. For stocks with relatively stable prices, the influence of cognitive dis-

---

[7] "Effect Of Initial Selling Price On Subsequent Sales," *Journal of Personality and Social Psychology*, 11, pgs. 345-350, by Doob, Carlsmith, Freedman, Landauer, and Tom, 1969.

sonance on investors' behavior tends to slow the fall of stock prices that are unjustifiably high and slow the rise of prices that are unjustifiably low.

We call this effect "value-oriented dissonance" to distinguish it from "momentum-oriented dissonance."

Momentum-oriented dissonance can have the opposite effect on unjustifiably high prices, i.e., it can cause them to keep rising. Momentum investors are strongly influenced by recent trends in stock prices, rather than absolute price levels. They buy a stock whose price went from $100 to $120 last week because they see it as one that can go to $140 this week (i.e., a "$20 a week price appreciator"). Any objective measure of value that might lead to the thought that it could stop rising - or even fall - would be dissonant with their reason for buying it.

Ultimately, though, the price stops going up and momentum investors begin to head for the exits. The crash of a momentum-driven stock is more akin to the derailment of a very long train than to an egg hitting a brick wall. Momentum investors want to believe, even when the momentum underlying their original purchase decisions has turned against them. They often buy on dips, temporarily buoying the price of a falling stock, and creating opportunity for put buyers.

To summarize, avoidance of cognitive dissonance causes investors to underestimate the long-term effects of unexpected events and to delay their reaction to news that is inconsistent with their preconceived notions.

Conservatism (a Conservatism Bias)

People tend to be slow to revise their opinions when additional information becomes available to them. This impediment to good decision-making is known as "conservatism."

In 1968, Ward Edwards conducted an experiment that illustrates this bias toward delayed reaction to new information.

He asked subjects to envision two very large containers filled with many tons of poker chips. In one of the containers, red chips outnumber blue chips 7:3. In the other, blue chips outnumber red 7:3. He asked the subjects to imagine one of these containers being picked at random and 12 chips being randomly pulled from it.

Subjects were then asked to estimate the chances (in percentage terms) that the container with 70% red chips had been selected, assuming that 8 of the chips drawn were red and 4 were blue.

When asked this question, most people incorrectly guess the answer to be somewhere in the area of 75%. In fact, through application of Bayes' theorem, it can be proven that the probability of the chips having come from the container with mostly red chips is about 97%.

Imagine yourself choosing a container and drawing chips from it. Suppose the first chip you draw is red. You would begin to think that the container chosen was the one holding mostly red chips. As you drew additional chips, the majority of them red, you would upwardly revise your estimate that the chips came from this container. However, your subjective estimate of this probability would probably not increase as rapidly as the carefully calculated probability.

Just as our minds' processing of the probabilities associated with complex events is inherently flawed, our ability to revise our estimates of probabilities in light of new information is flawed.

Edwards noted this delayed response, estimating that his subjects were requiring 100% to 400% more data to revise their opinions than was actually necessary.[8]

When an "in favor" stock is the subject of unfavorable news, conservatism often delays a fall in the stock's price while investors wait for additional confirmation. Similarly, when an "out of favor" stock is the subject of favorable news, there is typically a lag between the timing of the announcement and full incorporation of the news into the stock's price.

> ### Conservatism
>
> Conservatism also affects analysts and corporate managements, leading them to underestimate the impact of new developments. This is yet another good reason to buy quickly on good news and sell quickly on bad news.

Anchoring (a Conservatism/Cognitive Bias)

Whenever a value for anything has been established or proposed, however outrageous the amount might be, anchoring causes our perception to be influenced by that value, and it will continue to influence us even if we later obtain contradictory information. We have all encountered anchoring in such commonplace experiences as buying a car, real estate, or anything else whose price is open to negotiation. The price set by the seller at the beginning strongly influences what we are willing to pay.

This has been demonstrated in numerous research studies. In one study, several dozen real estate agents were asked to estimate the value of a home with

---

[8] "Conservatism In Human Information Processing," by W. Edwards, *Formal Representation Of Human Judgment* ed. B. Kleinmuntz, John Wiley and Sons 1968.

an appraised value of $135,000. They each got 20 minutes to inspect the home and its surroundings, along with all of the information that would normally go into conducting an actual appraisal. The agents were not told the appraised value, but instead were told the home's listing price. However, the agents were given different amounts for the listing price.

The listing prices given to each group of agents and their estimates of the value are given in the following table:

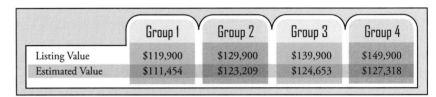

	Group 1	Group 2	Group 3	Group 4
Listing Value	$119,900	$129,900	$139,900	$149,900
Estimated Value	$111,454	$123,209	$124,653	$127,318

Clearly, the agents' estimates of the home's value were influenced by the listing prices they were given.[9]

The applicability of the anchoring phenomenon to stock market investing should be obvious. If a stock has been trading in a narrow range for several months, most investors will be convinced that it is fairly priced no matter what evidence exists to the contrary.

The effect of this behavior on stock prices will be to delay reaction to new information, creating opportunities for investors who react quickly to breaking news.

Loss Aversion

Psychological Accounting (a Loss Aversion/Cognitive Bias)

The term "psychological accounting" refers to our method of mentally projecting and tracking the outcomes of our decisions. The way we evaluate outcomes can dramatically affect the choices we make, making it probable that some methods of psychological accounting would lead to stock market inefficiencies.

Our psychological accounting "frames" our evaluation of decision outcomes, similar to the way in which we might frame a photograph. We expand the scope of our evaluation in the same way we reveal more of a picture, by widening the frame.

According to theorists, there are three basic ways to keep our psychological accounts.

---

[9] "Experts, Amateurs, and Real Estate: An Anchoring-and-Adjustment Perspective On Property Pricing Decisions," *Organizational Behavior and Human Decision Processes,* 39, pgs. 84-97, by Norcraft and Neale, 1987.

One approach is to separately track outcomes from every decision. For example, we could consider selling a particular stock without regard to the sale's impact on the portfolio as a whole. This is referred to as the "minimal" account method of psychological accounting.

Alternatively, we might evaluate the outcomes of a decision in relation to its context. For example, we could consider selling a stock in light of its performance versus a benchmark (such as the S&P 500) or of its role in the diversification of our portfolio. This is the "topical account" method.

The third method is to evaluate the outcomes of each decision in light of all relevant factors. In this case, we might consider selling the stock with regard given to our personal financial goals, requirements, and tax situation, our overall portfolio performance and strategy, investment alternatives, market conditions, and so on. This is the "comprehensive account" method.[10]

In a well-known study, participants were asked whether they would drive to a store 20 minutes away to save $5 on an item costing $15. 68% of the respondents said yes, they would make the drive. A similar group was asked whether they would be willing to make the same drive to save $5 on an item costing $125, but, in this case, only 29% responded affirmatively.

Obviously, if 20 minutes of a person's time is worth a $5 savings, the price of the item shouldn't matter, but framing the question in reference to a $15 item versus a $125 item (i.e., in a topical account) made a big difference to the study participants.

Researchers have theorized that a "ratio-difference principle" could explain such illogical behavior. In effect, saving $5 on a $15 item is somehow more "meaningful" to people than saving $5 on a $125 item, because the first case represented a savings of 33%, whereas the second example involved a savings of only 4%.[11]

If psychological accounting leads an investor to keep separate psychological "accounts" for each stock in his portfolio, the ratio-difference principle magnifies the level of anxiety associated with each holding. Tracking gains and losses on individual stocks in percentage terms can cause investors to become distraught over losses that may be small both in absolute terms and as a percentage of total portfolio value. As a result, an investor may be far more worried about the prospect of losing 100% on a $1,000 investment than losing 5% on a $100,000 holding (a loss of $5,000).

---

[10] "The Framing of Decisions and the Psychology of Choice," *Science*, 211, pgs. 453-458, by Tversky and Kahnemann, 1981.

[11] "Contrasting Rational and Psychological Analyses of Political Choice," *American Political Science Review*, 82, pgs. 719-736, by Quattrone and Tversky, 1988.

A large body of evidence suggests that this is exactly how most investors view their portfolios, i.e., as a collection of individual investments, rather than a single, inclusive account. Indeed, this psychological bias is reflected in the Prudent Man Rule, which once legally mandated the prudence of each individual investment made by a fiduciary. It was only recently that regulators changed their view of prudence to encompass entire portfolios rather than focusing upon individual holdings.

Psychological accounting causes otherwise sensible people to shy away from nanocap stocks, despite the marked superiority of nanocap performance over other market cap categories. Many investors simply cannot deal with the possibility of taking a 100% loss on any one of their investments, no matter how well their portfolio as a whole might perform. If one of their stocks goes down, psychological accounting leads them to think of it in isolation, as an uncompensated loss, rather than as an inevitable cost of achieving better overall performance. As a consequence, the market consistently undervalues nanocaps, which are seen as being more likely to go bust than large caps.

Our accounting for decision outcomes may vary according to time frame, as well as to context. The period over which we measure results is subjectively determined, as is the contextual data we incorporate in the measurement process.

A bettor at a racetrack can either "close his account" after each race, or he can close it at the end of the day. If, after losing $140 on earlier races, he is considering whether to bet $10 on a 15:1 long shot in the last race, he can evaluate his alternatives as either:

a. A chance to break even for the day versus losing $150, or

b. A chance to gain $140 versus losing $10.

According to theory, the first option will induce more risk taking, which is borne out by surveys showing that long shot gambles are more popular on the last race of the day.

This helps to explain why so many investors hang on to losing investments even as they sell their winners. As Peter Lynch once said, they "pull their flowers and water their weeds," because closing out a psychological (or real) account at a loss is decidedly unpleasant. As long as the account can be left open, the loss does not have to be fully and finally faced.

Psychology at the Track

If you're going to bet on long-shot horses, do it at the beginning of the day, when the odds are better. And bet on favorites toward the end of the day. In racetrack betting, as on Wall Street, it generally pays to be a contrarian.

In our decision-making processes, any significant amount of potential loss outweighs an equivalent amount of potential gain. This is the essence of prospect theory.

Let's consider an extreme example. Suppose you are a person of relatively modest means who has managed to save, over 20 years of patient frugality, $100,000. You have the opportunity to make an investment that has two equally likely outcomes:

a. You can get back $600,000, making a $500,000 profit; or

b. You can lose the entire $100,000.

Would you do it? Probably not. Most people would pass on such an opportunity because the prospect of losing one's entire life savings far outweighs the benefits of possibly making a 500% profit.

Nevertheless, if you were to make this investment 100 times you would probably come out ahead by $20 million (50 winners of $500,000 minus 50 losers of $100,000). The average of these 100 outcomes would equal the expected value, a gain of $200,000.

Perhaps it would be unreasonable to expect people to gamble their entire life savings on such a chancy proposition. Suppose, instead, that the offer involved risking $5,000 for a 50% chance of receiving $30,000? A lot of people with $100,000 in savings would still decline.

The psychological bias that underlies prospect theory causes many investors to shy away from risks that ought to be acceptable to them. They abandon rational thinking, ignore their ability to cheaply hedge most investment risks (through diversification, put options, etc.), and succumb to irrational fears of loss. Prospect theory provides yet another explanation for why most investors avoid nanocaps in favor of underperforming, allegedly safer investments. This sets the stage for huge gains on nanocaps as they grow, get acquired, etc.

The Endowment Effect (a Loss Aversion/Cognitive Bias)

The endowment effect causes us to place a higher value on the things we own than on the things we do not own. We tend to think, perhaps subconsciously, that our ownership of a thing endows it with additional value.

This principle applies to the stocks in our portfolio. It causes us to be biased in favor of hanging on to the stocks we own, even when an objective appraisal of their prospects would induce us to sell. Generally speaking, we hold our stocks too long because, due to the endowment effect, we think they are worth more than the market is willing to pay.

The endowment effect causes delay in the market's reaction to bad news. We are especially unwilling to sell our stocks when they go down. As the owners of a falling stock, we delude ourselves into seeing value in it that the market does not, and we may even buy even more of it. Selling would involve both recognizing the diminution of value and admitting that we were wrong. When unfavorable events occur, such irrational behavior can cause a stock's price to fall more slowly than it otherwise would.

On the other hand, the endowment effect can cause investors to become risk-averse with respect to their paper gains. We may overvalue the gain itself simply because we own it, which can lead us to sell sooner than we should. Thus, the endowment effect can cause a stock's price to rise more slowly than it should when favorable events occur, due to premature profit taking.

Inattentiveness

Failure to Recognize Regression Phenomena (a Trend/Cognitive Bias)

In Chapter 11, we pointed out that a stock's price ratios are directly related to investors' expectations regarding the company's future earnings growth rates. Investors' expectations for earnings growth, however, are subject to problems we all have in recognizing and applying regression phenomena in our everyday experience.

In particular, we fail to apply the lesson that virtually any statistic has a tendency, over time, to revert to its mean. Instead, we project the most extreme circumstances indefinitely into the future. Then, when extreme conditions inevitably give way to average conditions, we struggle to find the cause for the "sudden" change.

Economists teach that a firm can earn "abnormal" profits only for a limited period of time. Eventually, competitive pressures force earnings to revert to "normal" levels (consistent with the firm's capital investment, prevailing interest rates, industry-specific risk, and so on).

Abnormal profits can be abnormally high or abnormally low. If a firm is earning abnormally high profits - because it has invented or discovered new products, methods of providing services, markets, etc. - eventually other firms will offer competing products or services, thereby taking away market share, and driving down prices and operating margins. If a firm is earning abnormally low profits, perhaps because it is involved in an unprofitable market niche, eventually competitors will abandon that niche, allowing prices and margins to rise.

The period over which a firm can earn abnormal profits is often surprisingly short. Nevertheless, investors routinely buy stocks with P/E ratios so high that decades of rapid earnings growth would be required to repay their investments.

To illustrate this point, it is necessary to understand the financial life cycle of a firm. At the firm's inception, it might sell stock to raise money to invest in the assets, technologies, etc., that it needs to bring its products to market. Product sales generate earnings which, in the early years, tend to get re-invested in additional assets required by the business's growth. Eventually, growth slows as the firm and its market matures. When this happens, there is no more gain to be had by re-investing profits back into the business, so profits are instead paid out to shareholders in the form of dividends. Of course, real firms tend to find new markets to enter, repeating the cycle, but, in theory at least, eventually the original market dies, the firm is liquidated (i.e., its assets are converted to cash), and the cash is paid out to shareholders.

Thus, ownership of a share of stock ultimately represents a claim on future cash dividend payments, and the fair value of a share would be equal to the discounted present value of those payments.

Suppose you are evaluating for possible purchase two different stocks, each with trailing 12-month earnings of $1. Let's assume that both short-term and long-term interest rates are 7%, that all earnings will be paid out as dividends for the next 25 years, and that both companies will trade at 20 times trailing earnings 25 years from now, when you plan to sell. Company A's shares are trading for a price to earnings ratio (P/E) of 20 (i.e., its current market price is $20 a share). Company B is a "hot" biotech company whose shares trade at a P/E of 100 (i.e., $100 a share).

If you buy a share of Company A for $20 and Company A's earnings grow at an average annual rate of 2% (all of which gets paid out as dividends), your investment will earn the 7% long-term bond yield. Too stodgy, you say, you want something with more upside. But before you buy Company B's stock for a price of $100, consider that Company B's earnings would have to grow by 11.5% per year for decades to come in order to achieve the same result.

Present Values of Projected Cash Flows for Company A and Company B

Company A

Dividends $14.23
Stock Sale.............................. 6.05
Total.................................. $20.28

Company B

Dividends $44.62
Stock Sale............................ 56.02
Total.............................. $100.63

If Company B grows its earnings at a compounded rate of 5% rather than 11.5%, the present value of its cash flows falls to $32.22 (i.e., by more than 2/3).

If, on the other hand, Company A grows its earnings at a compounded rate of 5% rather than 2%, the present value of its cash flows rises to $32.22 (almost a 60% gain).

In other words, the P/E of 20 on Company A's stock implies expectations of a compounded annual earnings growth rate of 2%. By choosing Company B over Company A, you would be betting that B will grow its earnings at a compounded rate of more than 11.5% year in and year out for the next 25 years. It takes a lot of confidence in company B's management team (and its successors), markets, products, etc., to justify paying $100 for a share of its stock.

Investors do not seem to recognize the implications of very high P/E ratios. They often fail to realize just how fast earnings will have to grow to justify such prices, and they do not consider how soon today's high growth can deteriorate into tomorrow's average growth. When the company eventually fails to hit its lofty growth target, both the P/E and the stock's price drop precipitously.

On the other hand, investors who buy stocks with P/E's substantially below the market average P/E can make handsome profits as these companies' earnings growth rates rise to the market average.

Investors' failure to understand regression phenomena, particularly their tendency to ignore the likelihood that performance will regress to the mean, contributes to the tendency of growth stocks to become overvalued, and to the long-term superiority of value stocks over growth stocks.

Availability and Vividness (Cognitive/Trend Biases)

The easier it is to imagine a thing happening – that is, the greater its availability - the higher the probability of its occurring is perceived to be, quite apart from any objective assessment of probability.

"Vividness" magnifies the effect of availability in cases where the circumstances involved in the event in question are viewed as concrete, exciting, interesting, and/or emotionally involving.

For example, prior to September 11, 2001, most Americans would have assessed the probability of planes being intentionally crashed into the World Trade Center as close to zero. Having experienced this tragedy, some of us have come to think of it as having a relatively high probability of happening to other tall buildings. It has become easier to imagine, i.e., more available. And, having seen it on television over and over again, in excruciating slow motion detail, the vividness of the event made some people consider a repeat occurrence so likely that they are not even willing to visit a city with tall buildings.

Without question, publicity increases availability. Deaths caused by anthrax poisoning are still extremely rare, but massive amounts of resources have been committed to prevent them, because the media's coverage made them seem more likely. In more mundane times, headlines focused on murders and traffic fatalities. Most of us would be surprised to learn that diabetes and stomach cancers (rarely reported in the media) cause twice as many deaths as homicide and car accidents. We overestimate the probability of being killed by a murderer or in a horrible traffic accident, not just because murder and fatal accidents get more media coverage, but also because violent death is more vivid.

Vividness often contributes to halo effects. For investors, there are few events that rival the vividness of making a big score or taking a big loss on a stock. In particular, losing money on a stock is likely to give rise to a negative halo effect that persists for a very long time. No matter how good an investment that stock might become, someone who took a big loss on it in the past will be very unlikely to buy it again.

Moreover, although the investor with a big loss might be slow to close out that position (due to other psychological biases, such as post-decisional dissonance), when he finally does sell he is likely to compound his loss by engaging in panic selling. Rather than trading patiently and holding out for a fair price, he may dump his stock at whatever price the market will give him. This is yet another good reason for selling out as quickly as possible whenever a stock is the subject of a negative news story.

The availability of past earnings growth rates leads some investors to give them disproportionate weight when projecting future growth. If a company has grown its earnings 15% annually over the past five years, it's easier to imagine 15% growth for the next five years. The projection of past trends (whether favorable or unfavorable) too far into the future leads investors to pay too much for fast-growing companies and too little for slow growers.

An especially vivid positive or negative corporate development will have a disproportionate influence on an investor's assessment of a stock. News stories that the investor finds especially interesting or exciting, or personal experiences or connections with the company, will also have big impacts on trading decisions.

Inaccurate Evaluation of Disjunctive Versus Conjunctive Events (a Cognitive Bias)

When we are faced with a complex situation involving a series of events, our ability to accurately assess the probability of a particular outcome depends on how well we understand the relationship among the events.

If an outcome depends on occurrence of any one of several mutually exclusive events, the events are said to be disjunctive. For example, a bet on a horse to "show" in a race wins if the horse finishes first, second, or third.

Alternatively, if the outcome requires the occurrence of all of the events, the events are said to be conjunctive. Here's an example of an outcome based on conjunctive events. Suppose you were to make a pre-season bet on your favorite college basketball team to win the NCAA Championship in the annual 64-team tournament. Seven separate events must all occur to make this a winning bet:

1. Your team must do well enough in the regular season to be invited to the tournament in the first place,

2. Your team must be one of the 32 teams that win in the first round of the tournament,

3. Your team must be one of the 16 teams that win in the second round of the tournament,

4. Your team must be one of the eight teams that win in the third round of the tournament,

5. Your team must be one of the teams that makes it to the "Final Four",

6. Your team must be one of the two teams that makes it to the finals, and

7. Your team must win the championship game.

Research shows that people consistently underestimate the probability of outcomes based on disjunctive events and consistently overestimate the probability of outcomes based on conjunctive events. We simply cannot accurately estimate these probabilities unless we perform the necessary calculations.[12]

Mathematically, the correct way to analyze the probability of an outcome based on disjunctive events is to add the probabilities of each event. In the horse race example, suppose you knew that the horse had a one in 10 chance of winning the race, a one in four chance of placing second, and a one in two

[12] "On the Subjective Probability of Compound Events," *Organizational Behavior and Human Performance*, 9, pgs. 396-406, by Bar-Hillel, 1973.

chance of coming in third. The horse's probability of "showing" could then be calculated as:

> 10% (odds of winning) plus 25% (odds of placing second) plus 50% (odds of running third)

Given these probabilities (but without actually performing the calculation), would you have guessed that the horse has an 85% chance of showing? Most of us would have guessed a lower probability.

The correct procedure for calculating the probability of an outcome based on conjunctive events is to multiply the probabilities associated with each event. For your college basketball team, if the probability of success at any one of our seven levels is 50%, the probability of winning the championship would be slightly less than 0.8%.

Yet, without doing the calculation, if you thought your team had a 50-50 chance of making the tournament and an even chance of beating each team it faced throughout the tournament, you would have probably guessed that the odds of your team going all the way would be much better than just 1 in 128.

Many investment decisions depend on estimates of probabilities in complex situations, but few of us spend the time necessary to actually perform the calculations. As a consequence, we often base our decisions on predictably bad estimates.

Suppose, for example, we are considering buying a stock because a respected hedge fund manager said in a television interview that he expected the company's earnings to triple over the next five years. After analyzing all of the publicly available information, we conclude that, in order to triple its earnings, the company would have to:

- Reduce cost of sales as a percentage of revenue by 10%,

- Reduce selling and administrative expenses by 10%,

- Double unit sales in North America,

- Triple unit sales in Asia, and

- Achieve these sales increases without lowering prices.

The company has an experienced management team that seems capable of achieving these targets, so suppose we assign a probability of 75% to each objective. Without going any further, we might easily conclude that the company is likely to triple its earnings, as predicted. We would probably buy the stock, even though its price has risen considerably since the fund manager's interview was broadcast.

But, in fact, the probability that all of these objectives would be achieved is only 24% (i.e., 0.75 x 0.75 x 0.75 x 0.75 x 0.75). If we did the calculation, we would see that a tripling of earnings was not likely enough to justify a rapid price advance.

Optimistic earnings projections are usually based on conjunctive events, which can cause them to seem more achievable than a careful calculation of their probabilities would indicate. Investors should be suspicious of rosy scenarios that are based on more than one or two critical factors. The probability of success of any plan is inversely proportionate to its complexity, and our tendency to overestimate probabilities associated with conjunctive events can easily lead us to buy into overpriced growth or turnaround stories.

Illusory and Invisible Correlations (Trend/Conservatism/Cognitive Biases)

Correlation involves expressing a dependent variable as a function of an independent variable, so that the value of the dependent variable can be predicted when the value of the independent variable is known.

For example, if we can express a stock's historical one-year return (the dependent variable) as a function of its P/E ratio at the beginning of each year (the independent variable), we can then make a very rough, but nevertheless useful, prediction of the stock's performance over the coming year, based on its current P/E ratio.

Our data driven approach to investing involves backtesting investment strategies with historical market data to search for correlations that help us predict which strategies are most likely to succeed. Many of the strategies described in this book are based on correlations that we have discovered (or at least confirmed) by this method (the correlations between Federal Reserve policy and the performance of different investment styles, for example).

As humans, our innate ability to discern correlation is profoundly flawed. We consistently overlook the existence of very highly correlated variables (i.e., invisible correlations), yet time and again we perceive illusory correlations where, in reality, none exist.

In one research study, subjects were asked to estimate the correlation of different groups of data pairs that exhibited actual correlation ranging from 0.00 (i.e., no correlation) to 1.00 (i.e., perfect correlation). The participants were unable to regularly perceive correlation at levels below 0.60 (which is a very significant degree of correlation). Actual levels of correlation ranging from 0.20 to 0.40 were estimated to be between 0.04 and 0.08, and even very high levels of correlation were consistently underestimated. For example, samples with correlation greater than 0.80 elicited a mean estimate of just 0.50, and the correlation of data pairs that were in fact perfectly correlated was estimated to be less than 0.85.[13]

This and other studies have demonstrated that, unless we perform the calculations, we tend to underestimate correlation, and, furthermore, that even highly significant levels of correlation can remain practically invisible to us. The success of data driven investment strategies based on invisible correlations is likely to continue until either a) these correlations are discovered by investors, or b) the underlying factors responsible for the success of these strategies go away.

Quantitative research has long been used by big institutional investors and hedge fund managers because it provides insight into hidden relationships – invisible correlations – among the factors that drive stock prices. The results of this research tend to remain secret, although we suspect that very little of it has been focused on nanocap stocks.

But now, access to quantitative methodology is no longer limited to big investors with large research budgets. The revolution in information technology has put sophisticated analytical tools and nearly instantaneous access to vast amounts of financial data into the hands of ordinary investors. Those who make use of these tools can develop new strategies that are likely to remain profitable because most investors will continue to overlook these hidden relationships.

Another way to make money in the stock market is to take advantage of other investors' illusory correlations.

Illusory correlations appear to have their psychological roots in the availability effect. The easier it is for a person to imagine a thing happening, the higher the perceived probability of occurrence is likely to be, separate and apart from any objective assessment of probability. Thus, if something in our experience makes it easy to imagine that two things might be related, we will overestimate the degree of correlation between them.

An experiment was conducted in which participants were shown 12 word pairs, one pair at a time. The first word in the pair was always either "bacon," "blossoms," "boat," or lion." The second word was always either "eggs," notebook,"

13   "Informal Covariation Assessment: Data-Based versus Theory-Based," *Judgments, Judgment Under Uncertainty: Heuristics and Biases*, eds. by Kahnemann, Slovic, and Tversky, by Jennings, Amabile, and Ross 1982.

or "tiger." Each of the possible 12 word pairs was shown the same number of times. However, the subjects believed that "bacon" was paired with "eggs" almost half (47%) of the time, when, in fact, this occurred exactly one third of the time. They also overestimated the correlation between "lion-tiger."[14]

Other studies involved the stereotypes shared by clinical psychologists. For example, 91% of the clinicians surveyed thought that the eyes drawn by suspicious people taking the Draw-A-Person psychological test would be unusual, while 82% felt that people who worry about their own intellectual ability would emphasize the head in their drawings. In neither case were the beliefs supported by the evidence – instead, the clinicians' beliefs caused them to perceive illusory correlations.[15]

Investors take this kind of intellectual shortcut all too often. Illusory correlations cause companies and industries to become "in favor" and "out of favor." In the late 1990's, for instance, illusory correlation led many to associate "technology stocks" with "guaranteed profits." Many investors continue to perceive illusory correlations between "small company stock portfolio" and "extremely risky" or between "value stock" and "low return." These "correlations" are taken for granted by much of Wall Street, and the constant retelling of these falsehoods makes them more "available" in a psychological sense. Though they sometimes hold true, over long periods of time, they don't; thus, they are illusory.

Learn to separate the true correlations from the illusory. Then, when a stock market pundit makes a pronouncement based on an illusory correlation, you can watch for the flurry of trading and sudden, dramatic price movement, and take a contrarian position when the trend loses momentum.

We recommend that investors either learn to apply quantitative research methodology themselves, or consider working with an investment advisor who understands and uses these techniques. The best way to uncover invisible correlations that can lead to profitable investment strategies is to examine actual data. The data driven strategies we have presented in this book provide some examples of how this can be done.

The best way to avoid over- or underestimating the degree of correlation is to examine actual data and run the numbers. Mental shortcuts or over-reliance on subjective estimates of correlation will usually lead to faulty assessments of the relationships between stock prices and the factors that drive them.

---

[14] "Illusory Correlation in Observational Report," *Journal of Verbal Learning and Behavior*, 6, pgs. 151-155, by Chapman 1967.

[15] "Genesis of Popular but Erroneous Psychodiagnostic Observations," *Journal of Abnormal Psychology*, 72, pgs. 193-204 by Chapman and Chapman.

Overconfidence and Calibration (Cognitive Biases)

Most of us overestimate the accuracy of our judgments. If we are 98% certain of being right, we probably have only a 67% chance of actually being correct, according to researchers who have measured our tendency to be overconfident.[16]

In one experiment, participants were given information on a dozen stocks and then asked which ones would go up and which would go down within a specified period. The subjects were, on average, 65% sure of their responses, but correctly predicted the outcome just 47% of the time.[17]

Paradoxically, the more we know about a subject, the more likely we are to be overconfident in our judgment.

In a study of this phenomenon, psychologists and psychology students were asked to read a four-part biographical case study, and then, after reading each part, to answer a set of multiple choice questions. The same set of questions was asked each time, and, after answering the questions, the participants were instructed to estimate the probability that they had answered each question correctly.

The questions related to the facts of the case and required the study participants to develop professional judgments regarding the subject's psychological history. As the participants read each part of the case, they gained more information, and, presumably, more insight into the subject's psychological history.

Not surprisingly, their confidence in the accuracy of their answers increased steadily with each section read. However, their answers were not significantly more accurate after reading all four sections than they had been after reading just one. Thus, the difference between their confidence and their accuracy (i.e., their overconfidence) steadily increased as more information became available. After reading all four parts of the case, participants were, on average, more than 50% certain of their answers but less than 30% accurate. More than 90% of them were overconfident in estimating their accuracy.[18]

Investing requires the exercise of judgment in virtually every decision we make. Perhaps it is a little discouraging to note that learning more about a stock (or an investment strategy) does not necessarily improve our chances of making an accurate appraisal of its prospects as much as it increases overconfidence in our own judgment. That should not keep us from gathering all the

16 "Calibration of Probabilities: The State of the Art to 1980," *Judgment Under Uncertainty: Heuristics and Biases*, eds Kahnemann, Slovic, and Tversky, by Lichtenstein, Fischoff, and Phillips, 1982.

17 "Do Those Who Know More Also Know More About How Much They Know?" *Organizational Behavior and Human Performance*, 20, pgs. 159-183, Lichtenstein and Fischoff, 1977.

18 "Overconfidence in Case Study Judgments," *Journal of Consulting Psychology*, 29, pgs. 261-265, Oskamp, 1965.

information we reasonably can, of course, but it ought to warn us that our increasing confidence should not be mistaken for improved judgment.

There are several things we can do to avoid the obvious dangers of overconfidence.

First, we can base our decisions on hard data as much as possible, instead of relying on our intuition. For example, instead of selecting stocks on the basis of how brilliantly CEO's handle TV interviews, we can base our selection on the historical performance of stocks with certain measurable characteristics in similar market conditions (i.e., the Fed Cycle, Election Cycle, etc.).

Secondly, to the extent we do rely on subjective judgment, we should factor in the tendency to be overconfident by discounting our optimism. For example, suppose we are 70% sure that a company will get FDA approval for its new drug. Before we buy the stock, we ought to consider whether it would still be a good deal if we had only a 50% chance of being right.

Finally, we can monitor the results of our decisions and revise our decision methodology as new data becomes available. This is "calibration," the process of continuously adjusting and improving our decision model based on feedback. In order to do this, we need a good system for capturing feedback.

People who regularly estimate the odds of their predictions being right - for example, meteorologists and Las Vegas oddsmakers – are much less prone to overconfidence than the general population. This is because they have means for regularly comparing their predictions with the actual results, and because they use this information to make better predictions the next time.

The essential elements of a feedback loop for investors would include documentation of the assumptions on which decisions are made. The assumptions would be compared to what actually occurred, and, for each decision, the system would record what worked, what didn't work, and why. Finally, there would be some means of summarizing the conclusions that could be drawn from experience.

Admittedly, most investors will not find the time or motivation to implement a formal feedback system such as the one just described. Nevertheless, it might be a helpful exercise for those who find themselves repeating mistakes arising from overconfidence.

Overconfidence is one of the driving forces that cause growth stocks to become overvalued. It also afflicts many who are attracted to turnaround situations, often causing troubled companies to be valued on the basis of optimistic scenarios that seem more likely than they actually are.

Calibration

This is a skill shared by experienced stock traders. No matter how good you are, the market will teach you humility. But, if you pay attention, it will also teach you to recognize when the odds are in your favor.

Unsupported Optimism

Valence Effect (a Cognitive Bias)

A group of college students were asked to compare their chances of enjoying one or more of 18 positive life experiences, or suffering any of 24 negative life experiences, against the odds that their classmates would have these experiences.

On average, the students figured their chances of enjoying the successes, rewards, and pleasures of life were 15% better than their peers. On the other hand, they estimated their chances of suffering from the failures, penalties, and afflictions – the slings and arrows of outrageous fortune – to be 20% lower than their unfortunate associates.[19]

Other things being equal, we tend to judge favorable outcomes as more likely than negative outcomes. This psychological phenomenon is called the "Valence Effect."

Valence affects investors in predictable ways. It can lead to overoptimism in the estimation of any company's future earnings, particularly the earnings of fast-growing companies, which contributes to their potential for becoming overpriced. When negative news affects growth companies, investors' reaction is often delayed because their tendency is to interpret all news that affects their future prospects as being better than it is. Merely "good news" is often interpreted as "extremely good news," leading to buyer overreaction (i.e., overpricing).

The valence effect enhances the profits of investors who react quickly to breaking news stories. The market's delay (often brief) in reacting to bad news can give nimble investors a chance to sell a stock before the price drops significantly. And the market's overreaction to good news regularly provides an opportunity to make substantial profits for those who buy in quickly and sell when the momentum fades.

Investment Trap (a Loss Aversion/Cognitive Bias)

The investment trap is also referred to as the sunk cost effect.

Every student of introductory microeconomics is taught that "sunk costs" are irrelevant for decision-making purposes. And yet, many senior leaders of large organizations—bright, successful executives who rarely make a wrong move otherwise—regularly violate this basic principle year after year. Investors do it all the time, at great cost.

---

[19] "Unrealistic Optimism About Future Life Events," *Journal of Personality and Social Psychology*, 39, pgs. 806-820, Weinstein, 1980.

The principle is simply this: tax consequences aside, it does not matter what you have already spent - or made - on an investment, it only matters what you will spend - or make - in the future. Whatever costs you incurred in the past are completely irrelevant and should be ignored.

Like the endowment effect and post-decisional dissonance, the investment trap can cause investors to ascribe inflated values to what they own. Even when we find ourselves owning an investment that is essentially worthless, we are likely to overvalue it if it is associated with a significant prior investment of our time, effort, or cash.

The investment trap causes delay in reaction to negative events. Our prejudice is always toward hanging on to the stocks we already own, especially if they go down in value. Owners of the stock who are affected by the investment trap are likely to delay selling, thus providing an opportunity for savvy investors to get out at a better price.

Don't fall into the investment trap! Sell the affected stock *immediately* when a negative news story breaks!

Exhibit 48 shows how psychological factors cause overreaction, underreaction, and delayed reaction to news.

Exhibit 48

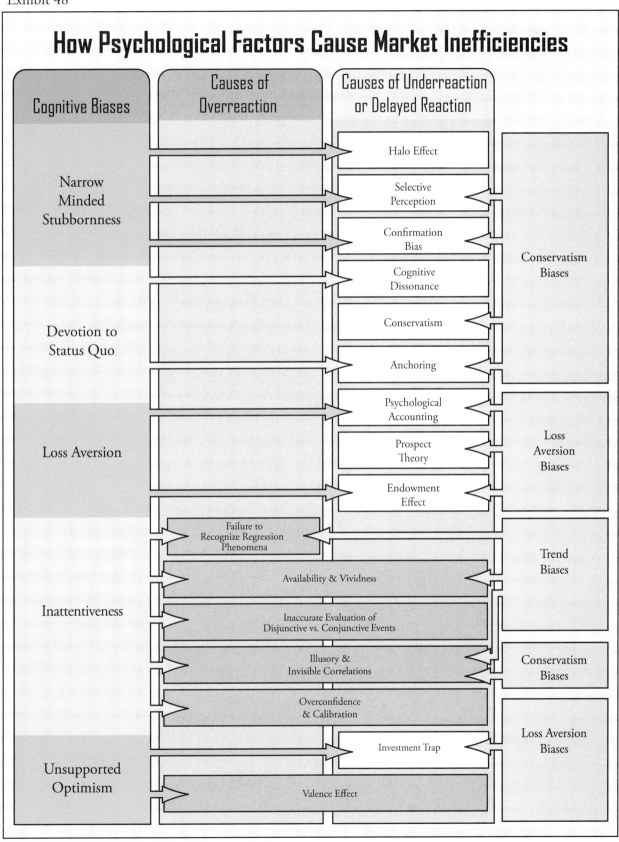

How Psychological Factors Cause Market Inefficiencies

Chapter 17

TRADING TO WIN

We react swiftly and surely to news stories that affect the companies on our watch list. We monitor the actions of other traders, noting the direction and volume associated with price movements, and we profit from their impatience by making shopkeeper trades.

Reacting to News Stories

General Patton once said that a good plan immediately and violently executed always beats a perfect plan executed next week. The same goes for analyzing and acting upon news stories.

Stock traders need to view information much the same as a reporter racing to meet a deadline or a general fighting a battle. The key to using information effectively is to determine in advance what your reaction will be to certain kinds of information, and then, when information becomes available, to react faster than the competition. For active traders, success requires timely, accurate information and swift, sure reactions to news.

We live in the Information Age, and news is more available than it ever has been. Information timely enough to justify active trading was once only available to investment professionals, but now individual investors have up-to-the-minute access through the Internet and numerous financial programs on television.

However, the huge volume of news stories, routine corporate announcements, and PR puff pieces has the potential to overwhelm our ability to identify and interpret important news. With so much information being delivered electronically every day, we need to find ways to separate the important from the useless.

For our purposes as traders, a news story is only important if it causes a stock's price to move.

It is often difficult to tell whether a particular news story will cause a stock to rise or fall. A lot depends on context. For example, an announcement stating that a company's earnings were 20% higher than last year could be bad news if the market was expecting a 25% increase.

The market's reaction to a news story is the ultimate judge of whether the news is good, bad, or neutral. If a story causes a stock's price to go up, by definition it is good news. If the stock price goes down in reaction to a story, it is bad news.

Simply knowing whether news is good or bad– and picking stocks appropriately– does not create trading profits, however. What really matters is how quickly we react to the news. Our goal is to react before other investors do, which means we generally cannot afford to wait and see how the market interprets the story.

In Chapter 16, we reviewed a number of psychological factors that could slow an investor's reaction to news: selective perception, halo affect, cognitive dissonance, conservatism, anchoring, endowment effect, etc. These psychological factors help to explain why so many investors wait to act until their judgments are confirmed (or disproved) by the actions of other traders. Traders who react decisively to news stories can earn profits (and avoid losses) at the expense of these unsure, slow-to-react investors.

This opportunity is nowhere so evident as in the trading of nanocaps. Few investors – and very few analysts – follow the stocks of the smallest companies. Information sufficient to make informed investment decisions may be available, but, relatively speaking, nobody is paying any attention. Moreover, these stocks are often so thinly-traded that the actions of individual investors can influence prices. With a thinly-traded stock, we can often discern the moves of individual traders, decipher their likely intentions, and then beat them to the punch.

Reacting to news stories is a key element of our trading tactics, especially in the trading of nanocaps.

Front-Running Short Sellers

With a thinly-traded stock, we can generally assume there is at least one short seller betting against the stock whenever the asked price is only a penny higher than the bid and the last trade was executed at the current bid. Why? Because a short sale can only occur on an uptick.

When we identify a large short seller of a stock we own, we typically start selling small amounts of that stock. If the short seller's asking price continues to drop with the stock's price, we'll continue to sell until the price falls to a level we consider unjustifiably low. At that point, we begin replacing the stock we've sold by buying what the short seller is offering.

Perhaps the short seller is acting upon an impending news story and the stock will continue to fall. Or maybe the stock's price will bounce back to where it was prior to the short sales. In either case, we will be better off for having sold our shares at higher prices than we paid to buy them back.

In essence, we are front-running the short sellers (legally) in this sequence of trades. The uptick rule allows us to learn of the short sellers' intention to sell, enabling us to step in front of them with our own sell orders.

Monitoring News and Price Movements

In Part Two, we explained how we select stocks according to investment strategies that have, historically, produced superior returns during different phases of the Federal Reserve monetary and Presidential Election Cycles.

Using strategies appropriate to the current phase of the Fed-Election Cycle, we typically calibrate our selection criteria to produce a list of between 1,000 and 2,000 stocks that, generally speaking, we would be willing to own. These stocks, together with the stocks we have already purchased, comprise our watch list, which is updated frequently.

Focusing on our watch list companies, we monitor information sources for news stories and significant price movements more or less continuously. Every morning before the market opens, and throughout the trading day, we search the Internet (using proprietary software) for news stories involving these companies. We also monitor televised business news programs and keep tabs on significant price changes. We watch prices closely because significant price changes often presage an impending story. All too often, the pattern of trading in these cases seems to indicate that some investors are getting wind of the story before its release.

In monitoring news and price movements, our goal is always to be among the first to discover, interpret, and act upon the information, before the opportunity fades away.

Decision Points

A breaking news story or significant price movement can represent one of five situations that might require action:

- An unambiguously good or unambiguously bad news story on a stock we own.

- An ambiguous news story on a stock we own.

- A significant price change on a stock we own.

- An unambiguously good or unambiguously bad news story on a stock we do not own (but which is on our watch list and thus meets our selection criteria).

- A significant price change on a stock we do not own (but which is on our watch list and thus meets our selection criteria).

A story that is "unambiguously good" is news that will likely cause the stock's price to rise. An "unambiguously bad" story is news that will likely cause the stock's price to fall.

When we discover a news story that is unambiguously good or bad for a stock we own, we are faced with a decision of whether to buy more, sell, or hold. With an ambiguous story, we must usually wait to see the market's reaction, armed with a clear understanding of the circumstances under which we would buy, sell, or hold – and be prepared to act very quickly.

When a stock we own records a significant price increase, we need to decide whether it heralds a soon-to-be-released good news story that will result in further gains (in which case we might want to buy more) or just a nice improvement in our position, but not the beginning of a sustained advance (in which case we would probably hold). If a stock we own records a significant price decrease, we need to decide whether a bad news story is coming soon (which would lead us to sell immediately), or whether the decline is merely a random event (which would lead us to hold our position or perhaps buy more).

For the stocks on our watch list that we do not already own, the decisions are simpler. An unambiguously good news story will usually lead us to buy a stock on our watch list, but if the news is ambiguous or unambiguously bad, we simply do not buy the stock. In some circumstances, we will sell short or buy put options in response to an unambiguously bad news story.

Occasionally, large price changes in watch list stocks occur in the absence of news. In these circumstances, we look to trading volume for guidance, on the theory that volume legitimizes direction. A large price increase on a watch list stock that we do not own might lead us to buy the stock if its trading volume is heavy, even if there is no news. A large price decrease on light volume and no news may also constitute a buying opportunity.

The decisions to be made in each of these five situations depend on multiple factors, which we will survey later in this chapter. We will also explain how and why each factor weighs on the decisions to be made. But first, we need to discuss what constitutes good and bad news, and explain the fundamentals of how orders get placed and priced.

Evaluating News

The first decision we have to make upon discovering a breaking news story affecting one of our watch list stocks is to determine whether it is good news, bad news, or ambiguous.

Since trading profits arise from acting swiftly, decisively, and without regard for the opinions of others, we must rely on judgment – based on experience – to determine whether news is likely to be favorable or unfavorable for a stock's price. We do not have the luxury of waiting for more information or for the market's confirmation of our judgment. If we wait for more certainty, we will miss the opportunity.

Over the course of many trading decisions, we have learned that it is usually better to trust our instincts – abetted by some "back of the envelope" analysis of the company's financial statements and fundamentals – and act quickly.

After placing our orders, we closely monitor the market's reaction to both the news and to our orders. We watch to see whether our orders get filled (and at what price), and to see whether the stock price moves in the expected direction (and with what volume).

We always consider volume in our evaluation of the market's reaction. Market reactions confirmed by high volume are more credible and likely to be sustained than reactions accompanied by low volume. Low volume generally amounts to a non-reaction.

If we buy or sell a stock in reaction to a news story and the price does not move as expected, we do not hesitate to admit our error and close out the position. If the stock moves counter to our expectation with significant volume, inevitably other traders will have made the same mistake we did. This often provides an opportunity for us to cut our losses by being quicker than they are to sell, usually allowing us to avoid losing more than 10% on any one position. Closing our losing positions also tends to increase the overall relative strength of our portfolio, and it generates short-term capital losses in the current tax year to offset our heavily-taxed short-term capital gains.

Over years of trading, we have observed that certain kinds of news stories occur with regularity and have predictable effects on stock prices.

Good News Stories

Some examples of commonly occurring news stories that are reliable indicators of an impending stock price increase include:

- A positive earnings surprise, or anything that is likely to give rise to an unexpected earnings increase.

- A positive sales surprise, or anything that is likely to give rise to an unexpected sales increase. (Note that for some companies, the important sales number is shipments or billings. For other companies with longer order fulfillment cycles, the important number to watch might be new bookings. For typical retailers, the most important sales numbers are same store sales and period-to-period comparisons of same store sales.)

- An unexpected announcement of a major new contract or of a promising new product or technology.

- Insider buying, particularly of a sizable amount, is always good news.

- Stock repurchase plans for deep value stocks (especially very low P/BV stocks) are very good news, except when the company is buying stock from an insider, especially the CEO.

- A positive earnings or sales surprise announced by a competitor or customer.

Examples of Bad News

Some examples of commonly occurring news stories that tend to reliably predict a stock price fall include:

- A negative earnings surprise, or anything that is likely to cause earnings to fall or to not grow as fast as expected.

- A negative sales surprise, or anything that is likely to cause sales to fall or to not grow as fast as expected.

- An unexpected cancellation of a major contract.

- Newly discovered financial reporting irregularities.

- Problems involving legal or regulatory issues.

- Insider selling among high-level executives and directors who own relatively small stakes in their companies.

- Unexpected announcements of plans to issue additional shares or convertible debt.

- Credit concerns, such as downward changes in debt rating or failure to meet bank covenants.

How to Place Orders

Successful trading on news stories involves more than staying informed, evaluating news stories, anticipating the market's reaction, and then acting quickly and decisively. It is also important to place the correct type of order and price it properly.

Professional stock traders know that controlling the price of a trade—and setting the right price—is usually just as important as knowing whether, and when, to buy or sell a particular stock. They also know when to sacrifice their control of pricing for the sake of speed in execution.

A basic familiarity with the mechanics of trading is required to fully understand how we place trades in response to news stories and significant price changes. Accordingly, we will briefly review the mechanics of placing orders before proceeding with our discussion.

Mechanics of Placing Orders

The typical full service stockbroker encourages the widely held misperception that stocks have but one price—the "market price"—at any given point in time. When a broker tells his client that XYZ Corporation is trading "at 12½," it does not necessarily mean that the client can buy or sell XYZ Corporation for that price. All it means is that the last transaction was executed for a price of $12.50.

In fact, every stock has a "bid" price and an "offering" price. (The offering price is often referred to as the "asked" price.) The bid price is the highest amount a buyer of the stock is willing to pay for one share, and the offering price is the lowest price a seller is willing to accept for one share.

The difference between the bid and offering price is called the "spread," or the "dealer's spread." The dealer's spread is the profit a dealer (or "market maker") earns by buying shares at a lower (i.e., bid) price and selling them at a higher (offering) price, much the same way that a shopkeeper buys merchandise at wholesale and sells it at retail.

An investor who wishes to buy or sell stock has the option of specifying the price that he or she is willing to pay or accept, or, alternatively, of entering the trade "at the market." If a price is specified, the trade gets executed when the buyer's bid price matches a seller's offering price. Shares are bought and sold only to the extent that the number of shares offered for sale matches the number of shares that buyers are willing to purchase. Thus, a trade may or may not get executed, or it may only get partially executed.

A simplified example will illustrate how this works. Note that, for the purpose of this example, we will ignore the effects that this series of trades would have on other traders' willingness to enter additional orders. In an actual trading scenario, the downward movement of the stock's price would usually induce traders to enter additional orders to buy or sell.

The table below summarizes a typical book of outstanding orders for a thinly-traded stock.

Bids		Offers	
Shares	Price	Shares	Price
200	$7.50	100	$8.05
300	$7.45	400	$8.10
200	$7.35	900	$8.25
700	$7.00	200	$8.30
100	$6.95	500	$9.00

At this point, no trades will be executed, because none of the bids equal or exceed the lowest offering price.

Now, suppose a trader enters an order to buy 200 shares, specifying a price not to exceed $8.05. Only 100 shares are currently being offered at this price, so a trade for 100 shares will be executed at a price of $8.05. After the execution, the order book would look like this:

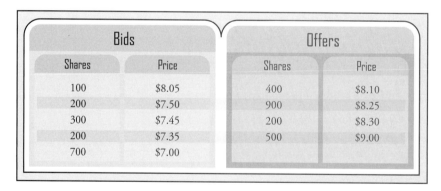

Bids		Offers	
Shares	Price	Shares	Price
100	$8.05	400	$8.10
200	$7.50	900	$8.25
300	$7.45	200	$8.30
200	$7.35	500	$9.00
700	$7.00		

Next, suppose another trader enters an order to sell 700 shares for a price of not less than $7.40. Only 600 shares are currently being bid at a price of $7.40 (or better). This seller will receive $8.05 per share for 100 shares, plus $7.50 per share for 200 shares, plus $7.45 per share for 300 shares. After the executions, the order book would look like this:

Bids		Offers	
Shares	Price	Shares	Price
200	$7.35	100	$7.40
700	$7.00	400	$8.10
		900	$8.25
		200	$8.30
		500	$9.00

Now, suppose the next trader wants to sell 500 shares "at the market." Market orders to sell (almost) always get executed to the extent to which there are buyers available. The seller is willing to accept whatever price the available bidders are bidding, so this seller will receive $7.35 per share for 200 shares plus $7.00 per share for another 300 shares.

In the preceding example, one buyer specified $8.05 as the highest price he was willing to pay for shares in the company. Another order had the seller specifying $7.40 as the lowest price he was willing to accept. When a buyer or seller specifies the best price he is willing to pay or accept, the order is referred to as a "limit order." The price specified is referred to as the "limit price." Note that it is not necessary to use the term "limit" when placing the order. The fact that a price was specified makes it a limit order.

If no price is specified when an order is placed, it is considered a market order. A market order is an instruction to execute the trade as quickly as possible at the best available price.

Most stockbrokers would prefer that every trade get entered as a market order, because, in that case, they know the trade will almost certainly get executed, earning them their commission or dealer profit. Limit orders only get executed when another investor agrees to the price on the other side of the transaction. Large numbers of market orders get placed and filled every day, so, apparently, many investors think this is the best – or only – way to enter a trade.

In fact, however, market orders are appropriate only in certain situations. Most of the time, limit orders are better.

How many things would you be willing to buy or sell without knowing beforehand – prior to agreeing to the deal – the price you would pay or receive? Would you agree to sell your car, or buy a house, without knowing the price in advance? Even when we make minor purchases, most of us insist on knowing the price we are being asked to pay, yet stock market investors routinely engage in transactions worth many thousands of dollars without knowing the price beforehand.

We enter most of our trades as limit orders, because controlling the price we are willing to pay or receive is key to our trading success. This is especially true when we buy or sell thinly-traded nanocap stocks. When we trade large cap stocks with narrow spreads and greater volume, it is less important.

In most cases, we want to make sure that the price we specify in our limit order is the best available at that time, so we will be first in line to get our trades executed. Suppose, for example, that the highest bid for a stock is currently $7.50 and the lowest offering is $8.00. If we want to buy the stock, we might place a limit order for, say, $7.60. If we want to sell, we might place a limit order for $7.90. Then, if another investor were to enter a market order to buy, our order would be the first to be filled.

Any time another investor enters a market order for a stock on which we have placed a limit order, he concedes to us the ability to control the price of the transaction. The ability to control pricing provides us many opportunities to earn profits or limit losses.

One way we benefit from our fellow traders' willingness to enter market orders is a tactic we call "shopkeeper trading." Similar to the way an operator of a corner store provides a quick, convenient way to purchase a quart of milk, we earn profits on stocks with wide spreads between bid and ask prices by supplying convenience – i.e., liquidity – in the form of standing orders to buy or sell shares. We will explain this tactic more fully later in this chapter.

For the most part, we enter market orders only when we want to sell out of a liquid stock very quickly in reaction to a bad news story. In such a situation, getting out of the position quickly – and with the certainty that our order will be filled – outweighs the opportunity to dicker over price. We rarely enter buy orders at the market, doing so only when we have compelling reasons for owning a liquid stock that is moving up rapidly.

There are other types of orders besides limit orders and market orders that bear mentioning, while we are on the topic.

A "stop order" is an order to buy or sell if, and only if, a trade gets executed at or through the price specified (the "trigger price") in the stop order. For example, if a stop order is entered to buy at $20, the order will become executable if any other trade occurs at or above $20. If a stop order is entered to sell at $15, the order will become executable if a trade occurs at or below $15.

A stop order cannot trigger its own execution. It will not be executed until a different order is transacted at or through the trigger price. Note that a stop order is not necessarily executed at the price specified. When the stop order is "triggered," it becomes a market order to buy or sell as soon as possible at the best available price.

A couple of simple examples will illustrate how a stop order works.

Suppose that XYZ Corp. stock is trading at $5.50 bid, $5.75 offered. Joe Jones enters a stop order to buy 100 shares of XYZ Corp. at $6.25. In other words, Joe wants to buy 100 shares if XYZ Corp. trades at or above $6.25. Now, suppose the following six trades are executed at the prices indicated:

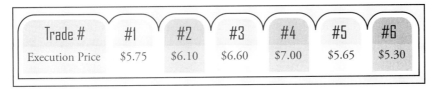

Trade #	#1	#2	#3	#4	#5	#6
Execution Price	$5.75	$6.10	$6.60	$7.00	$5.65	$5.30

As this series of executions shows, the price of XYZ Corp. climbed smartly until, after trade #4, a severe downdraft occurred. It could have been the result of a news story or rumor affecting XYZ Corp., or it could have been a sudden turn in the overall market. Joe's stop order became executable when a trade occurred at or above the stop price, i.e., when trade #3 was executed. At that point, Joe's order to buy 100 shares became a market order, which was executed (trade #4) at $7.00. As it turned out, that happened to have been the peak price for the day. Afterwards, XYZ Corp. drifted down, closing at $4.90.

Stop orders are sometimes used to limit losses or protect profits. For example, an investor may enter a stop order to sell if the stock drops below a certain price. This is sometimes referred to as a "stop loss" order. Buying stop orders can be used to establish a long position when a stock rises through a specified level, or to limit a loss or protect a profit on a short position.

Stealth Sales

The sale that doesn't sound like a sale and the sales commission that doesn't sound like a sales commission are the basis for some of Wall Street's most successful mutual fund products.

How about the "no load" funds with the "contingent deferred sales charges?" There is, of course, nothing contingent about the inescapability of these charges. The broker gets paid right away, and the commission of 4%, 5%, or more is taken out of your account over time, unless you sell out of the fund. When you sell, you pay the "contingent" sales charge immediately. ("Contingent deferred sales charges" are, in fact, "contingent accelerated sales charges.")

Or how about closed-end bond funds? The broker will tell you that these funds are better than bonds, because they are professionally managed, diversified, and have the liquidity of stocks. And if you buy them on their initial offerings, you don't even have to pay a sales commission!

What isn't often mentioned is that a large percentage (often 6%) of the initial offering price is, in effect, the sales commission, which comes directly out of the funds' net asset value. It's also rarely mentioned that hefty fees will be taken out of the fund on a regular basis.

The market price of these funds consistently falls a month or so after their initial offering. During the funds' first month, brokerage firms support their prices through open market purchases. And they take back the brokers' commissions if their clients sell within that month. Brokers don't generally mention this fact either.

Stop orders can be dangerous. If a stock price temporarily falls due to a misreported news story or unfounded rumor, a stop order to sell can result in an execution at the bottom of the dip. Likewise, a buy stop order can result in a purchase getting executed at a temporary peak. We do not enter stop orders for the same reasons we avoid market orders. As we have said, a stop order becomes a market order when it is triggered, and we prefer to maintain control over the pricing of our trades in most cases.

It is possible to place a stop order and to specify a price for the trade. A "stop limit" order combines the features of stop orders and limit orders. Like a stop order, a stop limit order is triggered if, and only if, a trade gets executed at or through the trigger price. However, when a stop limit order gets triggered, it becomes a limit order rather than a market order.

Stop limit orders are used for much the same purposes as stop orders. They allow an investor to instruct the broker to act in a predetermined way if the market for a stock rises or falls to specified levels. The investor can initiate long and short positions based on price movements, limit losses, and protect profits without having to constantly monitor the stock's price.

The primary advantage of a stop limit order over a stop order is the ability to maintain control over pricing. This eliminates much of the danger that a purchase will be executed at a temporary peak or that a sale will be executed at a temporary trough. The primary disadvantage of a stop limit order (vis-à-vis a stop order) is that the trade may never get executed, depending on how the stop and limit prices are specified, and on how fast the price rises or falls.

Stop orders and stop limit orders have a way of being executed at the worst possible time. They are the best way we know to increase your odds of selling when the market is at its most panicky and buying when it's at its most euphoric. These order types are, in fact, the antithesis of our shopkeeper trades. A significant portion of the profits we earn from shopkeeper trades are derived from the mindless buying and selling dictated by stop orders and stop limit orders.

Brokers, of course, absolutely love stop orders, because they plant the seeds of future commissions that will be earned automatically through transactions that can be effected without the inconvenience of obtaining additional approval from the client. The broker is, in effect, making a sale that doesn't sound like a sale.

We have never placed any type of stop order in trading the test portfolio, and we do not recommend them. Stop orders are primarily used to limit risk, but we consider them the single worst risk-reducing idea imaginable. Investors who wish to reduce the risk in their portfolios should focus on buying a diversified portfolio of value stocks, avoiding companies with operating losses, hedging through the use of put options, and reducing the size of their margin debt.

Pricing Orders Appropriately

Pricing orders is an art. There is no such thing as a "correct" price to bid or ask. Pricing trades is akin to betting in a poker game; the actions and intentions of the other players must always be considered.

Nevertheless, we have developed some broad guidelines derived from our experience pricing tens of thousands of trades.

When buying on good news, we often bid at or above the asking price. This enables us to step in front of other buyers who hesitate to pay significantly more than the price of the previous trade, even when breaking news justifies doing so.

When selling on bad news, we often ask the bid price or less. Again, we do this to step in front of other traders who tend to hesitate before selling for less than the previous trade.

Generally speaking, the price we bid in reaction to a good news story is limited by the magnitude of the new development's effect on earnings. For example, if a company's earnings were expected to be $1.00 per share but it reports earnings of $1.10 per share, we wouldn't bid more than 10% above yesterday's closing price (i.e., the pre-news price) to buy the stock. In fact, to be conservative, we would rarely bid more than 5% above yesterday's closing price in such a situation.

In the case of a negative surprise, aggressive action is usually required. It's not uncommon for a 5% shortfall in expected earnings to trigger a 20% one day drop in a company's stock price, with further declines to follow. It rarely makes sense to second-guess the market's judgment of a bad news story, and in the event of catastrophically bad news, we do our best to be among the first out the door. We sell as aggressively as we can, entering offers at or even below the highest bid price in order to scoop up more buyers. In rare instances, we'll even enter market orders to get out of a particularly odious situation.

However, false alarms are not uncommon, and bad news stories often contain kernels of good news that get overlooked in the headlines. When a company we own announces a negative surprise, we're usually willing to sell as much of our position as we can at or above 15% less than the pre-news price. In some cases we sell down to that level and then wait and see whether the market will stabilize before selling more. Nevertheless, unless some new information surfaces to change our assessment of the negative surprise, our objective is to close out the position by the end of the trading day.

The decision to unload a position in response to a bad news story quickly, taking whatever we can get, or to sell in a more orderly fashion requires judgment. More often than not, we opt for the quick exit, occasionally to our regret. Nevertheless, the tally of bullets we dodge far outnumbers our occasions for nostalgia over missed opportunities.

We always have to take into account a stock's price movements in the days leading up to an earnings surprise or other unexpected news. In many cases, the stock has already traded up or down in anticipation of the news. When this occurs, our reaction to the news story is tempered accordingly: we bid less aggressively.

We also consider long-term historical price trends and ratios for the stock, its industry, and for the market as a whole. Other things being equal, if a non-seasonal company traded at a price of 100 a year ago after reporting quarterly earnings of $2, its industry P/E and the overall market P/E are both up 10%, and the company has just reported earnings of $2.50, we would feel comfortable bidding 125. To our way of thinking, a fair value for the stock would be in the neighborhood of 137.50 (25% growth in earnings times a 10% increase in the market P/E, times the prior year price of 100). By paying anything less than 137.50, we'd be acquiring a stock with significant short-term appreciation potential.

In general, we are more aggressive when bidding on or selling highly liquid stocks than we are when dealing with thinly-traded issues. If we overbid on a liquid stock, the negative consequences are limited, unless there are lots of other buyers who are also overbidding. If we overbid on an illiquid stock, however, we are far more likely to single-handedly (and temporarily) drive the price to an inappropriately high level.

If we already own a significant position in a stock, we won't bid as aggressively as we might to acquire a new position. As a rule, the bigger a position becomes, the smaller the percentage return on it will ultimately be. The more we buy, the more we pay per share, because as we buy more shares, we are dealing with sellers who are progressively less motivated. The more we sell, the less we receive, especially if we have to sell quickly. Unloading a large nanocap position quickly and at a reasonable price can be challenging, to say the least. Therefore, before adding to any long position in a thinly-traded stock, we carefully consider the market's capacity for reabsorbing the shares.

We bid less aggressively in response to a good news story which occurs shortly after another recent positive surprise. Whenever this happens, it always seems that some investors knew in advance that two positive developments were in the offing and priced that information into the stock upon release of the first announcement. In any event, although multiple good news stories spaced several months apart can sustain a rising price, good news stories bunched closely together have less cumulative impact.

Most of our trading decisions are influenced by tax considerations.

Unless bad news breaks, we hold our winners until they qualify for long-term capital gains treatment. We do this even at the expense of deteriorating prices in most cases, betting that any price declines will not exceed the 20% tax difference between short-term and long-term capital gains treatment.

When we have large year-to-date short-term capital gains, especially as year-end approaches, we are a more aggressive bidder and a more aggressive seller. We bid aggressively because 35% of our short-term losses will be subsidized by the IRS, in return for which they'll only require 15% of our long-term capital gains (in a future year). We sell losing positions aggressively to capture short-term losses in the current year; any reduction in the price we receive is more than offset by the 35% tax benefit of the entire loss. We aren't concerned about selling stocks in December whose prices have already been driven down by other tax-motivated sellers, even if we expect those prices to rebound in January. We're better off taking the tax loss and putting the proceeds into other low relative strength stocks that are likely to rebound.

Tax-motivated trading patterns affect the pricing of our orders around year-end.

We bid less and ask less for high relative strength stocks in late December, since these stocks tend to be driven down in January by tax-deferred selling. We bid more aggressively for low relative strength stocks in late December because these stocks are likely to rebound in the new year from their temporarily depressed (by tax selling) year-end lows.

When we find ourselves owning a low relative strength stock in early December that has bad news, we are particularly aggressive in selling it, since the combination of bad news and year-end tax selling is likely to hammer its price in the coming weeks.

Starting in mid-January, we bid more and ask more for high relative strength stocks, and we bid less and ask less for low relative strength stocks – the opposite of what we do in December.

From time to time, we bid on non-watch list stocks. For example, we might buy a large cap or mid cap stock announcing a very large positive earnings surprise, and then sell it a day or two later. This maneuver succeeds because it often takes brokerage analysts a while to upwardly revise their earnings estimates after an unusually large earnings surprise. The embarrassment of being wrong by so great an amount causes them to rethink their opinions of the company. Institutional buyers tend to be slow to respond, too; many of them need to hold committee meetings before entering their orders.

After 9:30am, we bid less aggressively and sell more aggressively whenever we trade large or mid cap stocks. The effects of positive news stories are reflected more rapidly in the stock prices of large companies than in those of smaller companies. We sell more aggressively because we generally are not interested in holding these stocks for very long.

The first step in properly pricing an order in response to breaking news is gauging the magnitude of surprise that the news will create. In theory, stocks are worth the present value of their future cash flows to shareholders. A tradable surprise is any piece of news that causes investors, explicitly or implicitly, to significantly change their assumptions regarding the timing or amounts of these cash flows.

An announcement of earnings from continuing operations equal to 45 cents (per share) may represent an upside surprise of 12.5% if the consensus estimate was 40 cents. On the other hand, the market may have perceived the 40 cent estimate to be downwardly biased or based on stale information. Perhaps the unpublished consensus (the "whisper number") is 50 cents.

In that case, the stock price would probably plummet when the company announced 45 cents. Investors would (theoretically, at least) plug that lower than expected earnings figure into their valuation spreadsheets, and the consequences of that 5 cent shortfall would ripple through their cash flow projections for decades to come. Some investors might assume that the 10% earnings shortfall would lower all future cash flows by 10%. Others might reduce their assumptions of future earnings growth rates in addition to reducing their models' starting points by 10%, deflating their calculations of the stock's "true" value by more than 10% (possibly much more).

Suppose the whisper number in this example was 30 cents. In that case, the market might collectively raise its cash flow projections by at least 50%. The 50% positive surprise might lead some to adjust their growth assumptions to the point where they're willing to pay double (or more) the pre-news price.

An earnings number, of course, results from the adding and subtraction of many component numbers. The figures that should most profoundly affect cash flow models are those which arise from activities that are integral, recurring features of a company's day-to-day operations.

However, earnings are also affected by events that are unlikely to recur with regularity, or ever again. A five cent per share loss arising from a one-time accounting adjustment or a 100-year flood should rarely cause a stock's price to fall much more than five cents.

It is often impossible to immediately sort out all the components of an earnings figure and discern which met, exceeded, or failed to meet expectations. Quite often, market participants disagree on what is recurring and what isn't.

Consequently, earnings releases often result in chaotic market conditions. Sometimes the most optimistic interpreters of these releases bid stocks prices up to excessive levels. Sometimes the pessimists are in control. And sometimes everyone is so confused that nobody wants to make the first move.

We never want to pay or receive "true" value when we trade. Our intent is to pay less than the figure implied by the cash flow assumptions ultimately reached by the market. And we want to sell for more than the price that these assumptions imply.

We have found it profitable to "split the surprise" with our initial responses to news. In the case of a buy order, this means setting a bid price in the neighborhood of 5% higher than the last trade pre-news if we estimate a 10% positive surprise. If all goes according to plan, the stock will rise by 10% plus another increment attributable to an increasing growth assumption.

Of course, bidding 105 for a stock that closed at 100 yesterday will probably not result in acquiring stock for precisely 105. The stock might open at 110 and never fall to the bid price. On the other hand, we may get our shares for substantially less than 105.

Sometimes investors can't figure out whether to bid 108 or 110, so they wait to see what everyone else is doing. When other buyers delay their decisions, this creates wonderful opportunities for low-ball bidders like us to bid 105 and buy the stock for 102 or less.

There's no such thing as a "called strike" in trading. If we bid 105 on a stock that opens at 107 and goes straight to 125, we haven't lost anything. It's far preferable to occasionally miss a winner than to routinely overpay. Excessive zeal when buying generally leads to costly mistakes.

Thus, we rarely submit a bid that exceeds the previous day's closing price by more than 15% -- even in the event of upside surprises exceeding 30%. The possible cost of being wrong is just too great.

A little bit of zeal when selling on bad news, though, is often beneficial. Unless we own so much of a stock that we risk single-handedly driving it down to unwarranted depths, we generally try to "give the entire surprise" (and often more) to the market. We're usually willing to surrender the greater of 15% of the pre-news price or the percentage by which the bad news affects earnings.

For example, if the pre-news price was 10 and the earnings miss was 30%, our initial reaction would be to sell as low as 7. If the market lowers its consensus estimate of future growth rates in addition to reducing base period cash flow by 30%, even a 30% haircut will leave us better off than we would have been otherwise.

Placing a limit sell order at 7 will allow us to pick off buyers until either the stock price goes below our limit or, preferably, until our order is completely filled. If we can't sell everything we have at this limit price, it often makes sense to wait a few hours and start selling small amounts of stock into the market for whatever is being bid.

The rationale for waiting is that panic and margin calls often result in falling stocks hitting extraordinarily low lows within the first hour of post-news trading. Rather than adding to this panic through overanxious selling, it often makes sense to step away from the situation for a while and give the stock's equilibrium a chance to return.

It is, however, imperative that all of a "bad news stock" be sold during the first day of post-news trading. Research by others, as well as our own observations, suggest that the prices of these stocks continue to deteriorate in the following days.

Seven Simple Rules

The seven rules that guide our responses to news and significant price changes are:

1. Buy aggressively on good news.

2. Sell aggressively on bad news.

3. Expect large price moves on light volume to reverse themselves (especially if there is no news to account for the price change).

4. Expect large price moves on heavy volume to be sustained (especially if the price change occurred in reaction to a news story).

5. Be a less aggressive buyer of a stock in which a substantial position has been established.

6. Be a less aggressive seller when realizing short-term capital gains.

7. When in doubt, do nothing.

The market typically overreacts slowly. Most of the psychological biases affecting the behavior of investors tend to dampen the effect of news on stock prices. Moreover, most investors do not efficiently receive relevant breaking news, analyze it properly, and respond with appropriate orders.

In the absence of a news story, large price moves on light volume are likely to be caused by factors other than changes in a company's prospects, but large price moves on heavy volume are likely to be caused by impending news. Price moves accompanied by news stories are likely to be sustained.

Always remember that anything bought must eventually be sold. Limiting each position to a manageable size allows us to hasten our exit and reduces market impact costs (i.e., the amount by which our own selling reduces the proceeds from our subsequent sales).

The high tax rates on short-term gains advise patience when closing out a position with a large unrealized short-term gain. By shorting against the box rather than selling outright, it is possible to lock in gains while deferring them long enough to receive long-term capital gain tax treatment. The major downside to doing this is that short sales can only be executed on upticks. When bad news hits, stock prices often dive precipitously with no upticks. In these cases, it is usually preferable to sell rather than short sell because the prices during free fall will inevitably be higher than the price of the first upticks.

Be Careful When Shorting Against the Box

The Taxpayer Relief Act of 1997 placed a number of restrictions on the practice of shorting against the box to defer taxes and/or transform short-term gains into long-term gains. Please check with your tax advisor before attempting this maneuver.

If you can't make an airtight case to yourself for buying a stock, don't do it. The trade may or may not wind up being successful, but whether it is successful or not, you'll still have to pay commissions. As we've said, there's no such thing as a "called strike" in this business. When you have doubts, your best bet is to rest your bat on your shoulder until more compelling opportunities arise. They always do.

The rules for selling are different. When bad news breaks, don't procrastinate. Bad news is like a 92 mile an hour fastball aimed at your head. If you don't get out of its way, it's going to hurt you. It could even put you out of the game.

Shopkeeper Trades

Consider the mechanics of the marketplace. Sellers have asking prices. Buyers make bids. When they reach agreement, items of value change hands. Both parties are better off at that point. At least they perceive themselves to be better off; otherwise, they presumably wouldn't have entered into their deal in the first place.

Other things being equal, when sellers ask less or buyers bid more, more transactions occur. More people walk away happy.

With thinly-traded stocks, a wider gap typically exists between bid and asked prices than exists with larger, more actively traded issues. Anything that narrows that gap will bring more buyers and sellers together, and more transactions will occur. And whoever facilitates that increase in transactions is in a position to profit.

In its simplest form, this is how securities dealers make their money. They buy shares from those who wish to sell at a relatively low price and sell to those interested in buying for a relatively high price, pocketing the difference.

But it isn't necessary to become a broker/dealer to play this game. Now that online discount brokerage firms and easy access to information are available via the Internet, any investor can "make a market" in a thinly-traded stock and pick up the difference between bid and ask prices whenever impatience or ignorance leads a fellow trader to enter a market order.

Our term for the tactic of patiently trading on the spread between bid and ask prices is "shopkeeping." We maintain standing orders to buy and sell at the best bid and ask prices available. In doing so, we narrow the spread, enhance liquidity, and provide a convenience for other traders.

The economics of shopkeeping involve a comparison of the probability distribution of future price movements with the premium that other parties might be willing to pay for the luxury of entering into transactions at their convenience. Other things being equal, the smaller the risk of holding an item in inventory relative to the premiums for transaction convenience, the more profit a shopkeeper is likely to make from that item.

Investors may have any number of motivations for wanting to buy or sell a stock immediately. They may be in a rush to buy because they fear missing an impending rally. They may have to sell quickly because of an emergency need for cash. Whoever stands ready with the lowest asking price for the stock they want to buy – or the highest bid for the stock they need to sell – is providing them a valuable service.

An investor who is unable or unwilling to engage in patient, hands-on trading might very well prefer to pay a significant premium to own a stock right away. An investor with an urgent need for cash has no alternative but to accept whatever price the market offers.

Consider the market for automobiles. Few people are willing to spend days on end dickering for the best price when they buy and sell cars. They're generally willing to leave a few bucks on the table for the convenience of dealing with someone who will close the deal ASAP.

A lot of investors approach buying and selling stocks in the same way. As a result, hands-on traders are in a position to buy at wholesale and sell at retail – to make money by virtue of their willingness to provide convenience for impatient investors. Rather than simply betting on the direction of future price movements, a hands-on investor can set up the Wall Street equivalent of a used car dealership.

This tactic is most profitable for stocks with large spreads, a common characteristic of thinly-traded nanocap stocks.

One of our current shopkeeping trades involves a stock with a bid price of 6.70 and an asked price of 7.40 – and yes, that is us on both sides of the market. If this stock's price goes absolutely nowhere, we are in a position to make $.70 for every share we are able to buy at the bid and sell at the asked.

We generally limit shopkeeper trades to value stocks (i.e., those with low multiples of earnings, sales, book value, and cash flow) so that any shares we buy will be unlikely to crash overnight.

However, when a significant news story hits, we generally close down our shop immediately. If it's bad news, we don't want anyone accepting our bid for the stock – and if it's good news, we may want to pay someone else's asking price to own more of it.

A Visit to the Trading Room

Trading involves at least as much art as science, and like any art, it simply isn't possible to learn all there is to know about the subject by reading a book. Becoming proficient requires personal experience.

We have created what we hope will be the next best thing to personal experience: a "visit" to our trading room. We'll illustrate our approach to trading with a virtual walk-through of a typical trading day.

In some ways, learning to trade stocks successfully can be likened to learning to play chess. While there is no substitute for the experience of playing, a great deal of insight can be gained by observing the pros and studying their best moves.

However, trading stocks is different from playing chess in that, with stock trading, the rules are constantly evolving, whereas in chess the rules have been static for centuries. When one of our tactics loses its effectiveness, we analyze what went wrong and then modify or discontinue the practice.

In this sense, successful traders are like third base coaches who are good at stealing the other team's signals. The utility of any information gained may not extend beyond today's game (indeed, the opposing team might change signals in the middle of the game).

Similarly, many of our trading tactics are based on patterns that involve a specific stock or industry. Many of these patterns fade, disappear, or reverse themselves as other traders become aware of them. Successful traders are students of the market, always on the lookout for events that have predictable effects on stock prices, and perceptive enough to realize when the predictive power of these events is no longer strong enough to be useful.

Virtually anything that happens anywhere in the world has the potential to affect stock prices. Consequently, the more knowledge you effectively work into your decision-making process, the more profitable your trading will be.

On the other hand, successful trading can also be defined simply as the exploitation of other investors' fear, greed, impatience, and ignorance - without being done in by one's own tendencies to let emotions override rational thought. Or, even more simply, to do immediately what the market is going to do later.

Making educated guesses about what other investors feel and know – and having the inner strength to take risks that flout convention – puts us in a good position to make the trades that others will want to make later.

The stock market is an inherently chaotic place. But the very chaos that brings some investors to ruin can be the key to great wealth for those who have the knowledge, empathy, and emotional stability to exploit it systematically.

Welcome to our trading room!

7:00 AM Turn on CNBC

Televised business news offers many advantages to traders, not the least of which is the media's capacity for providing up to the minute coverage. CNBC is one of the best televised news sources currently available.

Although we get our corporate earnings news from many different sources, CNBC's coverage of earnings announcements is particularly valuable to us because it provides context along with the numbers. CNBC's reporters separate operating earnings from non-recurring items before comparing the adjusted numbers with analyst estimates. They also ferret out patterns we might otherwise miss.

CNBC often reports on industry-specific patterns of earnings surprises, information that can help traders dodge some very expensive bullets. It's important to know, for example, that the last five homebuilders to report have beaten analyst estimates, and that, therefore, it won't really be a positive earnings surprise when the next homebuilder reports above-consensus earnings. In this case, knowing the context behind the story prevents us from bidding aggressively for a company that beat the consensus forecast by 10% while its competitors were beating the estimates by 20%.

This kind of information is especially useful when trading nanocaps, whose names are rarely mentioned on the air. Upon learning that several large homebuilders have reported blowout positive earnings surprises, we can start looking for nanocap homebuilders that haven't reported their earnings yet – especially if their stock prices have not been moving up in sympathy with their large cap peers. Chances are excellent that these companies will not only report solid earnings, but also that the market will treat their earnings announcements as significant positive surprises.

Many of the news items CNBC covers in depth have huge impact on the stock market but are little noticed by the average investment professional. Their coverage of the University of Michigan Consumer Confidence Survey, the Fed's Beige Book, and Department of Labor reports includes interviews with experts who can tell us what the reports mean. It would not be efficient for us to develop expertise in divining the meaning of these reports, so we rely on CNBC to provide access to smart people with the specific expertise we need to make sense of recent developments in the economy, labor markets, etc.

It's useful to know, for instance, if most of this month's CPI increase is attributable to higher oil prices rather than to overall strengthening of the economy. The CPI report's meaning to the Fed (and, thus, its likely impact upon interest rates and stock prices) is often hidden in the details.

Trading opportunities lay hidden in correlations between the content of these reports and the subsequent price movements of specific industries and individual stocks. A $10 million market cap company might, for instance, have a history of big gains on days when unexpectedly high consumer confidence figures are announced. This sort of information is usually priced into large cap stocks before we can take advantage, but small cap stock prices often take hours (or even days) to adjust.

When CNBC airs a breaking news story affecting a multi-billion dollar company, dozens of institutional investors are ready to buy or sell within seconds. But the effects of a news story on the thousands of stocks that are too small for most institutions to hold get ignored by research analysts. And since the individual investors who mostly own these smaller companies tend to have other things occupying their time, nobody is standing by to promptly bid them up on good macroeconomic news (or sell them on bad news).

CNBC often interviews the CEO's of publicly traded companies during market hours. Sometimes these people slip up and reveal more than they intend. In one recent case, a CEO appeared to inadvertently give an earnings estimate that was significantly above the analysts' consensus. We were able to get our buy order filled a short time later, before the market had a chance to adjust.

In December 2000, pundit after pundit appeared on CNBC and predicted that the market would emerge from its funk when the Fed got around to cutting rates. On January 3, 2001, the Fed announced a surprise inter-meeting rate cut, which was immediately covered by CNBC. As the story was being

---

Test Your Broker

If you don't believe us, give your brokers a call during market hours soon after an important (i.e., something that moves the S&P or S&P futures by ½% or more) bit of economic news is announced and dissected on CNBC.

See if they can explain:

a. what the news was, and
b. why it is affecting (or not affecting) the specific stocks in your portfolio.

broadcast, we entered a large market order to buy GE stock in the test portfolio, an order that was filled seconds before the stock's price spiked upward. Few other news sources could have created that opportunity for us.

Although plenty of people are watching CNBC during market hours, relatively few of them are prepared to immediately assess and act upon news as it breaks. A serious data driven investor, though, knows in advance what constitutes a trading opportunity and is ready to act right away when one presents itself.

In trading stocks, the more data you efficiently process and effectively act upon, the more successful you will be. There is no substitute for the immediacy and quality of a televised news source such as CNBC.

7:05 AM Fire up Computer and Log on to TheFlyOnTheWall.com

The Fly is an equity research site run by some very smart people in New Jersey. It contains a news feed, updates on analyst reports at major firms, actual versus consensus comparisons for companies that have already reported earnings, consensus earnings estimates for companies due to report shortly, a syndicate calendar (i.e., a listing of upcoming equity offerings), and many, many other useful features.

There is no fluff in The Fly's news feed – there's nothing about this or that company's latest public service award or how the company's product was voted best in its class by someone or other. It's all news that is relevant to our data driven style of investing. We scan it regularly, just to see if any patterns are emerging, and it regularly leads us to tradable ideas.

The best indication that a company (or industry) is about to announce a positive earnings surprise is an upward earnings estimate revision by one or more analysts. The Fly reports what the analysts are saying, enabling us to buy into companies and sectors whose prospects are improving and sell out of those that are deteriorating.

As we noted in Chapter 12, we pay no heed to analysts' buy, sell, and hold recommendations, but we studiously attend changes in earnings estimates. A stock's price will generally rise immediately after an analyst upwardly revises an earnings estimate. Nevertheless, we are often willing to pay that higher price, especially when a large revision is involved, because a large revision by one analyst often emboldens others to follow suit. And their revisions typically result in further stock price increases.

Finding Value in Analysts' Estimates

We never rely on an analyst's estimate figure, in and of itself, to trigger a trade. Revisions however, while not ideal indicators, have value in that they are allow us to exploit the "Sergei Bubka" phenomenon. Revisions also provide raw material for analysis of industry-wide trends.

The information provided by The Fly frequently reveals industry-wide patterns of estimate revisions, which not only affords us the opportunity to buy into companies whose earnings are likely to be upwardly revised in the near future, but also leads us to buy small cap stocks in industries that are gaining in favor with analysts. Though it may be years before any analyst even looks at these small caps, improving analyst sentiment with respect to their industries often portend favorable near term earnings announcements that drive up their stock prices.

On any given day, CNBC compares actual earnings to consensus estimates for just a tiny fraction of the companies that are reporting. The Fly provides these comparisons for many more companies. (For stocks that aren't covered by either CNBC or The Fly, we have found the First Call information in AOL's Personal Finance area to be useful.)

The Fly's syndicate calendar is of tremendous use in assessing the likely direction and potential size of short-term market moves. Although the theoretical value of a stock is equal to the present value of its future cash flows, in the very short-term, stock prices are set by supply and demand. If everything else is held constant while supply is increased, prices are virtually guaranteed to fall.

Whenever large amounts of money are being raised through stock offerings, the overall market weakens. In essence, selling stock to the public (whether through IPO's or seasoned offerings) alters the balance of supply and demand. Other things being equal, we tend to place larger bets on the market rising when the syndicate calendar is light and become more bearish when especially large amounts of supply are scheduled to hit the market.

7:10 AM Begin Running our News Searches

The groundwork for running our news searches is laid on weekends when we download data from the various financial databases to which we subscribe and run the stock screens used to create our watch list.

Our next step is to load the watch list into our proprietary news search software, which is configured to search the Internet for news stories on these stocks throughout the trading day.

7:15 AM Scan the Wall Street Journal

We also scan the *Wall Street Journal* for stories we can trade on.

Generally speaking, it is next to impossible to make money on the companies written about in the *Journal*, because anything published in a newspaper

Neglected Companies

Many companies are, of course, not followed by analysts and don't have consensus estimates.

tends to be old news by the time we receive it and because too many other traders are trying to place the same orders we would want to enter.

Nevertheless, articles in the *Wall Street Journal* provide good background information on emerging trends, industry-specific developments, and the like. Whether or not any of this amounts to a tradable opportunity, it's often information that becomes useful later on, when we are evaluating breaking news according to the principles of fundamental analysis outlined in Chapter 14. Occasionally, when a company-specific story appears in the *Journal*, it can lead us to opportunities with the company's less well-known competitors, suppliers, or customers.

7:30 AM – 9:30 AM Develop and Place Orders

By 7:30 AM, we are working with information from CNBC, The Fly, our news searches, and the *Wall Street Journal*. Our **Data Driven Investing**™ process generates most of its value added between now and 9:30, when the major U.S. markets open.

The bulk of the actionable news we analyze involves corporate earnings. Most companies report earnings outside of market hours (i.e., after 4 PM or before 9:30 AM). Our goal is to analyze every available earnings report issued by the companies on our watch lists before 9:30 AM. This allows us to be "standing in line" with our orders when the market opens.

As we pointed out in Chapter 16, most of us have biases that prevent us from bidding $10 for a stock worth $20 if it closed yesterday at $5. These biases prevent most investors from aggressively bidding on stocks that look to open significantly above yesterday's closing price. As a result, we are often able to secure tremendous bargains by bidding aggressively on "good news" stocks when the market opens. In our view, this is the best time to buy the incremental value of the good news for a fraction of its true worth.

A company that reports quarterly operating earnings of $.50 when Wall Street was expecting $.40, raises guidance from $2 to $2.50 for next year, and goes on to say that the causes for this improved profitability will persist for the foreseeable future will usually lead analysts to conclude that its stock is now worth at least 25% more than whatever it was worth when expectations were lower. Accelerating earnings growth might even cause the P/E to rise, which would lead to a stock price increase of more than 25%.

If the stock's price chart for the past month shows that it has tracked its industry (or the overall market), we can be confident that no significant trading was done on leaks of the new earnings and guidance figures. Therefore, if the stock closed at $40 yesterday, it is likely to hit $50 in the near future.

We generally perform two more bits of due diligence before entering our order, though.

First, we consider the tendency of other companies in the industry to beat expectations. If the company's industry peers have been reporting earnings that are in line with or below expectations, that's a plus. It means that, in all likelihood, the market will have been pleasantly surprised by the company's announcement. If, on the other hand, the company's competitors have also been beating expectations by 25%, we would be forced to conclude that the element of surprise has been lost. In that case, we would probably back off.

In most cases, we subtract the average positive surprise of the industry from our preliminary target price for the stock. Thus, if the company's competitors have recently announced earnings surprises averaging 10%, we would adjust our company's 25% surprise downward to 15%, giving us a target price of $46 instead of $50.

Then, in order to set a benchmark for reasonableness, we would look at the year-ago ratios of price to quarterly operating earnings and price to projected annual operating earnings. Let's say that the company reported earnings of $.30 for the same quarter last year and gave guidance of $1.50 for this year – and that its stock traded around 30 after the announcement. This gives us the following ratios:

Price to quarterly operating earnings: $30/$.30 = 100x

Price to projected annual operating earnings: $30/$1.50 = 20x

Some adjustment is called for, though, because the average price/earnings ratio for the industry may have changed. If it has increased from 20 to 25, we need to multiply last year's ratios by 25/20 to create useful benchmarks:

Price to quarterly operating earnings: 100x times (25/20) = 125x

Price to projected annual operating earnings: 20x times (25/20) = 25x

Were the stock to reach our target price of $46 in the near future, these ratios would become:

Price to quarterly operating earnings: $46/$.50 = 92x

Price to projected annual operating earnings: $46/$2.50 = 18.4x

Since the ratios associated with a $46 price are well below last year's adjusted ratios, it appears that this is, if anything, a very conservative target price.

Accounting for Profits

We think of our gains in terms of "profit on the buy" (which arises from buying at a favorable price– either on news or, in the case of shopkeeper trades, at a price below the midpoint of the bid and asked prices), "profit on the sell" (which arises from selling at a favorable price), and "profit on the hold."

If $46 is the "fair value" of this stock, we obviously want to bid something less. After all, if we always bought and sold our stocks for what they were worth, we'd never beat the market. And if all we wanted to do was match the market, we'd buy an index fund and be done with it.

The amount we are willing to bid also depends upon how much buying power we have in our account. If we only have enough buying power for one or two trades, we will bid less than we would had we enough for 50 trades. The rationale for this is that, in order to put large amounts of money to work, we can't be as fussy as is appropriate when we can focus our buying power on a small number of situations.

Since we happen to have plenty of buying power, we'll bid $44 (assuming that no market-moving events occur before the open). The $4 premium over yesterday's closing price represents 2/3 of the value inherent in the company's earnings report. If we get our stock, the predicted value of our profit "on the buy" will be at least $2 per share ($46 "fair value" minus $44 bid).

However, if CNBC reports that the S&P 500 futures are up 1% at 9:25, indicating a strong opening for the market, we would adjust our bid up to $44.44 (101% of $44). On the other hand, if S&P 500 futures were down 1%, we would bid only $43.56 (99% of $44).

We also consider the stock's recent trading volume before entering our order. If the stock trades 1000 shares a day, we might only bid for 200 shares. We might also lower our bid somewhat. If it turns out that the stock is worth only $42, we can't rely on the rest of the market to save us from our ignorance if our order constitutes a large percentage of the stock's activity.

Sometimes a highly liquid, deep value stock reports surprisingly good news. If we have sufficient buying power, we may decide to "bet the limit" on it. Our limit is 5% of account equity in any one stock, in order to keep company-specific risk at a reasonable level.

Responding to bad earnings news on stocks we own is, by far, the most complex part of our investment process – especially when we are making money on them.

The first question we need to answer is whether we should sell short against the box (i.e., maintaining our existing long position while creating an offsetting short position) or sell the position outright. In theory, shorting against the box allows us to protect short-term gains until they are long-term gains, which saves on taxes. Things can go wrong with this strategy, though.

Avoiding Overconcentration

We regularly monitor the values of our individual positions and are quick to sell off portions of any that grow to more than 5% of account equity.

We Reiterate Our Previous Warning

Please check with your tax advisor before attempting to short against the box.

The biggest problem with shorting against the box is that short sales can only occur on an uptick. If a stock's price is plummeting, no short sales can occur until there is a pause in its descent. Whereas an outright sale might yield $10 a share, a simultaneously placed short sale order on a deteriorating stock might yield $9.50 or less.

Another problem is that short sellers are occasionally forced to involuntarily cover their shorts. The mechanics of short selling involve borrowing stock from someone else. If someone whose stock you borrowed needs to get it back – perhaps because they want to sell it – your broker's operations people will try to maintain your short position, trying to replace the original lender's stock by borrowing stock from someone else. Sometimes, though, there isn't any additional stock available for borrowing. Your only alternatives are to either cover the short with the stock you own (realizing the taxable gain at that point) or to cover it with stock purchased in the open market (which exposes you to future declines in the price of your stock).

When deciding whether to sell short against the box or sell outright, the following considerations guide our thinking:

- The size of our unrealized gain in the position. The larger the unrealized gain, the more likely we are to sell short.

- The size of our total year-to-date realized short-term gain. If we have accumulated short-term losses or only small short-term gains, selling short would probably be a mistake.

- Proximity to year-end. Shorting against the box late in the year is more likely to achieve income deferral than doing so earlier in the year. There's less chance of our having to involuntarily cover the short prior to the achievement of our income deferral objective.

- Liquidity of the stock. When bad news is announced, liquid stocks are more likely than illiquid stocks to experience upticks shortly after they open – largely because they tend to open at prices more reflective of the news. Illiquid stocks often fall to this level gradually, but without pause. Other things being equal, we are more likely to short liquid stocks against the box. Shorts involving illiquid stocks are far more likely to be involuntarily covered.

- How bad is the news? If the news is really bad, we may stand to lose more while waiting for an uptick than we are likely to save in taxes. Thus, the worse the news, the more inclined we are to sell outright rather than against the box.

Once we've decided whether to short sell or sell outright, we still have to figure out how to time, size, and price our order.

The basic rules we use for pricing, sizing, and timing bids also apply to sales, except that we turn up the aggressiveness a few notches. Whereas no money is lost when a good buying opportunity is missed, the cost of failing to promptly sell a stock on bad news can be enormous.

Timing and sizing a sale in response to bad news is relatively straightforward. Before the market opens, we place orders to sell the entire position, regardless of how illiquid the stock might be.

We generally break up our orders into smaller lots: 2500 shares or less. Smaller orders seem to get filled more quickly than very large orders. And if we are trying to unload a plummeting stock, even a split-second of delay can cost us thousands of dollars.

The target price set by the formula we use when buying stocks on good earnings news is likely to overstate the near-term value of a "bad news" stock. In other words, the target price is likely to be significantly higher than the price at which the stock will close on the day of the announcement. Since bad news stocks are likely to fall even further in the days and months ahead, we resign ourselves to the necessity of asking the target price – or even 5-10% less.

By selling aggressively at the opening bell, we are exploiting a variety of psychological phenomena, as well as an asymmetrical distribution of information.

Many of the investors who know about the bad earnings news are in denial. Before the market opens, they can not fathom the extent to which the news will pummel their stock, nor can they readily accept their error in holding on as long as they did. Other investors, some of whom have open buy orders, don't even know that there was an earnings report. Still others read the press release and saw "record earnings" but failed to realize that these earnings were below consensus. They put in buy orders before they left for work.

After we have assessed and reacted to all of the earnings-related news stories affecting watch list stocks, our last bit of pre-9:30 business is to deal with the non-earnings news. In evaluating these stories, we are primarily looking for events that have significant potential to enhance or detract from the future earnings per share of the companies on our watch lists. We are also interested in items indicative of management and shareholder confidence (or its lack).

The most commonly reported items with meaningful implications for future earnings per share include sales reports, new contract announcements, and acquisitions.

Don't Trade in the Pre-Market

When we suggest that orders be placed before the market opens, we are most emphatically not encouraging you to transact business in the pre-market.

The liquidity in the pre-market is unacceptably light for most stocks. Moreover, the participants in this market tend to be much shrewder than the average investor who trades during normal market hours.

If you enter a large, aggressive sell order in the pre-market, you may well create panic among other sellers and discourage potential bidders– which will cost you money when 9:30 comes.

Retailers regularly report "same store sales," a comparison of this year's sales to last year's sales for stores that were in operation during both periods. In addition, First Call publishes consensus estimates of changes in same store sales.

If a company beats expectations by 10%, this often (though not always) implies that its earnings are likely to exceed the consensus estimate by at least 10%. With respect to entering buy and sell orders, we act on this information in the same way we would were we acting upon an earnings report or a management update to earnings guidance.

In the case of other developments affecting earnings per share, we are similarly interested in calculating an updated earnings estimate. A company with $10 million in annual sales which lands a new customer worth $1 million per year would expect to grow earnings by at least 10% (possibly much more). Furthermore, the market may reward this boost to its growth with a higher P/E multiple.

In such a case, we would generally feel comfortable bidding 5% more than the price of its last pre-announcement trade. But if the stock has already been running up in anticipation of the new contract, or if the S&P 500 futures are down in the pre-market, we might bid somewhat less (or not at all).

Acquisitions that are accretive to earnings are good news, and those which are dilutive to earnings are bad news. In either case, we calculate our target price as:

Most Recent Stock Price × (Previous Earnings Guidance For Next Year + Next Year's Projected Earnings Impact of Acquisition) ÷ Previous Earnings Guidance For Next Year

In responding to news of acquisitions, we employ the same procedures for order timing, pricing, and sizing that apply in our responses to earnings announcements.

Events that are indicative of management and shareholder confidence (or its lack) include:

- Insider stock sales and purchases;
- Announcement of convertible debt or secondary stock offerings;
- Announcement of repurchase plans; and
- Self-tender offer results.

Insider selling is frequently – but not always - a sign of impending trouble. Executives who have the vast majority of their net worth invested in their companies' stocks have legitimate reasons to diversify. Moreover, they risk running afoul of insider trading laws if they sell too aggressively prior to the release of bad news. Consequently, insider selling does not automatically trigger selling on our part.

However, when we observe selling by high-level executives who own relatively small amounts of their company's stock, we get nervous. In such circumstances, we sell our holdings patiently but purposefully. If we have large short-term capital gains, we short against the box. We try to sell at the high end of the bid/asked spread, but when the spread narrows we are willing to sell at the bid price.

Insider buying is always good news. Here again, we trade patiently but purposefully when we buy these stocks. We try to buy at the low end of the bid/asked spread, but when the spread narrows we are willing to pay the asked price.

When a company announces a decision to issue additional shares or convertible debt, we generally take it as a sign that management thinks the stock is fairly valued (if not overvalued). In any event it is almost invariably dilutive to earnings per share. Consequently, we usually sell aggressively when a stock offering or the issuance of convertible debt is announced. With large caps, we usually price our sell orders 1-2% below the most recent closing price; with small companies, we are even more aggressive in selling.

Repurchase Announcements
In an October 1993 working paper, David Ikenberry, Josef Lakonishok, and Theo Vermaelen concluded that high BV/P stocks significantly outperformed their peers following repurchase announcements, while low BV/P stocks slightly underperformed.

Stock repurchase plans may or may not be good news. Their announcement tends to portend above-market returns for value stocks, but below-market returns for growth stocks. Since value stocks tend to outperform growth stocks, one might reasonably conclude that value companies with repurchase programs are smarter investors than growth companies who buy back shares– and that this would be reflected in returns to their investors.

One might also argue that returning cash to shareholders – either through dividends or stock repurchases – is more in keeping with the mission of value companies. Growth companies, presumably, can better use their cash by investing in their businesses, which have to grow quickly to justify high stock valuations.

When a value company announces a share repurchase program, we usually take it as an indication of management's confidence in the continuing viability of the company. (If they anticipated hard times ahead, we would expect them to keep their cash in the business.)

However, when a growth company announces a repurchase program, it's more likely to be a temporary measure designed to buoy a sinking stock price. Even worse, it could indicate management's inability to identify future growth opportunities – a catastrophe for believers in the company's ability to grow earnings quickly enough to justify the high valuation typically ascribed to a growth stock.

As is the case with our responses to insider buying and selling, we react to stock repurchases with patient purposefulness. We buy value companies and sell (or buy puts on) growth companies who repurchase stock.

Occasionally, companies buy back stock through self-tender offers, rather than on the open market. The terms of a typical self-tender might indicate a company's willingness to repurchase up to 1,000,000 shares for $5 each.

Under-subscribed self-tenders represent wonderful opportunities if the company's stock is selling near or below the price offered.

If only 900,000 shares are tendered for the $5 offered, this indicates that the reservoir of potential sellers at $5 has been largely drained. Any large shareholders who were aware of imminent problems likely to send the stock tumbling below $5 would presumably have taken this opportunity to bail out (rather than face the difficulties associated with getting a good price for their stock in the open market).

If we can buy a stock like this for $5.25 or less, we are very likely to do it. In most such cases, we can safely presume that management believes its stock is worth considerably more than the price being offered.

Over-subscribed self-tenders can be good short selling opportunities if the company's stock is selling at or above the price offered – and we would normally sell immediately if we happened to own the stock.

If 5,000,000 shares are tendered at the $5 offering price, this means that there is a 4,000,000 share reservoir of stock remaining to be sold at $5. Large shareholders who responded to the self-tender offer may be aware of imminent problems likely to send the stock tumbling below $5. They may prefer to bail out through the tender, rather than face the difficulties associated with getting a good price for their stock in the open market.

If we can short the stock for $4.85 or more, we are likely to do it. The price is unlikely to rise far above $5 anytime soon, due to the supply available at that price. And the stock's price is likely to fall as either the company reports the bad news feared by the major shareholders or these shareholders decide to sell their stock on the open market.

9:30AM – 4:00PM Market Hours

Having entered our orders, it's time for us to wait and watch as our trades either get executed or not. Nevertheless, we remain vigilant for news stories throughout the trading day.

A few companies like to report earnings shortly before or after 9:30. On one hand, this creates a lot of stress as we feverishly attempt to analyze the news and act upon it before the rest of the market. But, on the other hand, news arriving in the midst of the market's opening is likely to be ignored, misinterpreted, or analyzed only later by many investors. Unlike these investors, we are prepared to analyze this news and respond quickly.

We often bid successfully on a stock, only to see its price fall below the previous day's closing price. This is what we call a "mistake." When we make a mistake, we don't wait and see what will happen next. If the mistake is a buy, we sell immediately; if the mistake is a short sale, we cover immediately.

Chances are that we're not the only people who made this same mistake. If we can undo our mistake faster than the others who fell into the same trap, we view that as something of a victory – even if, overall, we net less from the sale than we paid for the buy.

When we successfully bid on a stock and its price rises above what we paid for it, we resist the temptation to take profits. Very often, we add to our position.

When a stock falls below what we paid but remains above the previous day's closing price, we closely watch its trading activity. Until we can identify the cause of this price decline (or until the price falls below that of the previous day's close, which would generally trigger a sell), no action is taken.

However, when a stock price falls sharply during a company's investor conference call, we assume that management said something to cause the decline. We are quick to sell, on the assumption that others will be selling as whatever was said is analyzed and passed on.

After the chaos of the open has subsided, we start running our TradeStation® programs. We developed these programs to search for trading opportunities using a system available through TradeStation Securities. One such program searches for wide bid/asked spreads on value stocks (for shopkeeping). Another one seeks out stocks with big price moves on light volume.

If our "shop" is going to be holding stocks in "inventory" that were not bought on good news, we need to take reasonable precautions to minimize risk. We believe that value stocks are less likely to fall precipitously than growth stocks, so we focus our shopkeeping efforts on value stocks. In addition, we limit our exposure to no more than $5000 worth of any one stock unearthed by our TradeStation shopkeeping program.

Shopkeeping, as we explained earlier, involves nothing more than placing Good 'Til Cancel orders to buy stocks for a few cents more than the current bid – and, once we own them, to sell for a few cents less than the current asked price. Frequently, we have open orders to buy and sell the same stock. Frequently, too, both our buy and sell orders are filled within a matter of minutes.

Consequently, we regularly check our account for newly executed shopkeeper trades. We like to make sure that our shelves are well-stocked at all times!

We typically own put options to hedge us against major market downturns, and during periods we expect to be bullish, we also own call options. The worst possible scenario for our option holdings would be for the market to be range-bound between now and their expiration.

Our shopkeeping strategy, on the other hand, is most profitable in the conditions least favorable for our options. The best scenario for shopkeeper trades is a directionless market that bounces back and forth rapidly and violently. As such, it affords a novel means of risk reduction.

As noted above, our TradeStation program informs us when stocks make big price moves on light volume and no news. We often profit from betting that these moves will reverse themselves.

Oftentimes, we suspect, these moves result from individual traders who are impatient to buy or sell illiquid stocks. If the spread is sufficiently narrow – and we own such a stock that has risen sharply– we typically place an order to sell at– or even a bit below– the bid price.

When stocks make big price moves on heavy volume and no news, we don't bet on a reversal of these moves. In fact, our tendency is to trade in anticipation of the move continuing.

Because we focus so much on companies with breaking news, we are in an especially good position to see how often their stock prices move sharply up or down immediately before the news is released – and how rarely such moves are to the upside prior to the release of bad news (or down prior to the release of good news).

Often, we'll notice that one of our holdings is up or down sharply on heavy volume. We can't find any news stories to account for this, prices are stable for other stocks in the company's industry, and no analysts are changing their earnings estimates or recommendations on the company. But then we notice that the company is scheduled to report earnings the following day. Aha!

Our educated guess is that someone is already trading on the as yet unreleased earnings figure, so our response is to sell if the stock is down and buy more if the stock is up. This strategy isn't 100% foolproof, but so far it's been right often enough to warrant continued use.

Until 4:00 PM, we'll continue to monitor CNBC, The Fly, and our news searches, looking for more trading opportunities along the lines we have described. Things really slow down after 11:00 AM, though, giving us time to think about "big picture issues."

Big Picture Issues

Big picture issues do not require our immediate attention, as breaking news does. Nevertheless, handling them properly can significantly boost our after-tax returns, as well as afford us protection in adverse market conditions.

Big picture issues include:

- Devising and acting upon strategies that exploit calendar-related trading patterns;

- Risk management;

- Buying power management; and

- Tax minimization.

Exploiting Calendar-Related Trading Patterns

Over the years, a variety of pronounced stock price patterns have emerged. They range from such phenomena as the strong January performance of stocks hitting 52-week lows in December to the Super Bowl Effect, which holds that the stock market will be strongest in years when NFC teams win the Super Bowl.

Some of these patterns, like the strong January performance of downtrodden stocks, seem to exist for good reason. Many investors sell their losers in December in order to take tax losses. This selling drives the prices of beaten-down stocks to unreasonably low levels, thus enabling them to bounce back strongly in January when tax-motivated selling subsides.

The Super Bowl Effect, though, is a product of data mining. If you attempt to correlate stock prices with a large enough number of data sets, you are bound to find patterns that would have made you money had you acted on them in the past – even if the data sets have no discernible connection to anything that might conceivably move markets.

There is no telling, of course, when any stock price pattern will stop recurring. What is certain, though, is that if enough investors suddenly attempt to exploit one pattern in particular, that course of action will immediately cease to be profitable.

Significant price patterns resulting from understandable cause and effect relationships have the best odds of recurring reliably enough to make us money. If a pattern meets these criteria and strategies based upon it have a lengthy track record of profitability, so much the better.

Our favorite pattern-based strategies include:

- Buying losers in late December,

- Aggressively buying small companies in December,

- Being more bearish between June and September,

- Selling Friday afternoon and buying Monday morning, and

- Buying spinoffs about one month after they begin trading.

Buy Losers in Late December

As we noted, many investors sell their losers before year-end in order to take

tax losses, thus driving down the prices of these stocks to unrealistically low levels. When this selling pressure subsides after year-end, the prices of these stocks tend to bounce back. Indeed, they are often repurchased by the very same investors who sold them in December, after the expiration of an IRS-mandated 30-day period between the sale and repurchase (i.e., the "wash sale" rule).

Tax-motivated selling in December is a big part of the explanation for the well-known, widely researched January Effect. As numerous studies have confirmed, a significant portion of the stock market's annual gains occur in the month of January. And, the stocks which perform best in January are often the very same ones that investors dumped in December.

For readers who are not familiar with the January Effect, here's some background.

The January Effect has been known to academics since at least April 1942, when it was identified in a study published in *The Journal of Business* entitled "Certain Observations on Seasonal Movements in Stocks Prices." Despite its having been well-known for over 60 years, the January Effect continues to exert a strong influence on investment returns.

The University of Iowa's Michael Rozeff and William Kinney revisited the January Effect in an October 1976 *Journal of Financial Economics* article "Capital Market Seasonality: The Case of Stock Returns." Their study analyzed the 1904-1975 performance of all NYSE stocks and determined that January's average return (excluding dividends) was 3.48%, more than five times the period's overall average monthly return of .68%.

Several academic studies have confirmed that losers bought in late December are often big winners in January. A 1983 *Journal of Finance* article by Tel Aviv University's Dan Givoly and Arie Ovadia entitled "Year-End Tax-Induced Sales and Stock Market Seasonality" addressed this subject. It indicated that, between 1945 and 1979, stocks reaching two-year lows in December provided average excess returns of 4.94% in January.

And more recently, a similar study published in the 1999 *Stock Trader's Almanac* looked at the December 1974 to February 1998 period, analyzing the mid-December to mid-February performance of NYSE stocks hitting new lows "around December 15." These stocks' prices increased, on average, 12.2% during the 2-month holding period, while the NYSE averaged gains of only 5.2%. Significantly, the "December low" stocks outperformed the NYSE Composite in 20 years out of 24.

Our approach to profiting from the January Effect is to buy low relative strength stocks in December, preferably those trading at or near their 52-week low. In doing so, we emphasize the acquisition of small company stocks.

Aggressively Buying Small Companies in December

We almost always have a bias toward buying small companies, but in December we buy them with a single-minded focus.

This is a logical thing to do because many portfolio managers sell off small caps in December for reasons that have nothing to do with these stocks' inherent value.

Professional money managers typically receive year-end bonuses based on performance. Many of them attempt to lock in their bonuses prior to year-end by shifting assets to lower-risk securities. But when January rolls around, these managers buy back into higher-risk assets, driving up the prices of all equities, particularly the prices of small cap stocks.

Stocks, in general, tend to do well in January, but small companies tend to do especially well.

A study published in the January/February 1996 *Financial Analysts Journal* by University of California professors Robert Haugen and Phillippe Jorion showed that small caps tend to benefit more from the January Effect than large caps. Their article, "The January Effect: Still There After All These Years," observed that the smallest market cap decile of NYSE stocks averaged January returns of 13.58%(!) between 1926 and 1993. The largest market cap decile, in contrast, averaged returns of just 1.35%. Thus, the smallest NYSE decile outperformed the largest by a margin of more than 10:1!

Without exception, average returns for the 68 years decreased as market cap increased. Bearing in mind that these results were based on many thousands of January return observations, their consistency is quite remarkable.

Following this strategy has also served our test portfolio well. Its January 2001, 2002, 2003, and 2004 returns (assuming a .2% hypothetical fee) were, respectively, 18.3%, 10.2%., 0%, and 8.5%. These returns beat the S&P 500's total returns by, respectively, 14.7%, 11.7%, 2.6%, and 6.7%.

Being More Bearish Between June and September

The summer months are the worst time of the year to invest in stocks, especially small cap stocks.

Many of us become less focused on building our stock portfolios when the weather warms up and vacation time is upon us. During these months, many individual investors prefer to put their money into boats, summer homes, and expensive trips, rather than into mutual funds and individual stocks.

Many of us aren't at home to answer the phone when securities salespeople call with their buy recommendations. And, realizing this, they don't make nearly as many calls.

Consequently, the public has more reasons to sell (to finance summer spending) and fewer reasons to buy (because fewer investment pitches are being made).

As **Exhibit 4** indicates, the S&P 500 returns for June through September averaged just .4% per month during expansive periods, compared to 1.9% per month for October through May. During restrictive periods, the S&P 500 returned .4% for June through September versus .8% per month for the October – May period.

Institutional investors, of course, are more consistent in their investment activities than retail investors. As a result, we would expect the large cap stocks they typically buy to outperform small caps, which are, to a much greater extent, the domain of the small investor.

The *Stock Trader's Almanac 2001* graphs the relative returns of the Russell 2000 (small caps) and Russell 1000 (large caps) throughout an average year, based upon 1979-1999 daily data. On average, the Russell 2000 underperformed the Russell 1000 by about 3% between June and September.

Selling Friday Afternoon and Buying Monday Morning

When investors have a weekend at home to focus upon their portfolios (or upon spouses' opinions of their investing prowess), they often become terrified by their losing positions - or obsessed with a desire to protect the profits on their winning positions. This frequently leads them to sell first thing Monday morning, often at the lowest prices of the week.

This behavior is consistent with data presented in the *Stock Trader's Almanac 2001*. Between 1987 and 1999, the Dow opened down most of the time on Mondays, while opening up most of the time on every other day of the week. Despite its slow starts, Monday still managed to have higher average Dow returns than every other day of the week during this period.

Our experience indicates that this phenomenon is, if anything, exaggerated for small caps. One panicky small investor unloading $5,000 worth of a thinly-traded stock can create a huge price decline.

Therefore, other things being equal, we try to sell on Friday afternoon – front-running the investors who will be selling on Monday. And we try to buy on Monday morning, especially if we sense that unwarranted panic selling is depressing prices.

Buying Spinoffs About One Month After They Begin Trading

Sometimes publicly traded companies find it beneficial to "spin off" portions of their businesses, creating new subsidiaries whose stocks also trade publicly. The spinoff process typically makes shareholders owners of both the post-spinoff parent entity and the subsidiary that the parent has spun off (i.e., the spinoff).

The investment characteristics of spinoffs are likely to be quite different from those of their parents. Among other differences, spinoffs tend to be much smaller than their parents and pay far smaller dividends than their parents.

Consequently, a significant number of the parent company shareholders receiving spinoff shares may find these shares to be unsuitable for their needs. They sell those shares, leading to downward pressure on the prices of spinoff shares immediately after they start to trade publicly. Subsequently, though, spinoff shares whose prices fall lower than their fundamentals should merit can produce exceptional returns as their prices rebound to more appropriate levels.

The tendency of spinoff stocks to perform well after an initial period of decline was confirmed by the findings of Keith Brown and Bryce Brooke in their September/October 1993 *Financial Analysts Journal* article "Institutional Demand and Security Price Pressure: The Case of Corporate Spinoffs."

Brown and Brooke found 74 cases of spinoffs that occurred between January 1980 and April 1990 in which both the parent and the spinoff were publicly traded and for which complete data on investment characteristics such as institutional ownership, dividend yields, and S&P stock ratings were available.

The 74 spinoffs studied by Brown and Brooke:

- Had, on average, market caps roughly 82% lower than those of the parent companies ($387.6 million versus $2106.2 million), with median market caps that were about 84% lower ($154.2 million versus $965.2 million)

How Brokers Handle Spinoffs

Bill Matson observed, while working as a retail broker, that his colleagues often cited the small market caps and low dividend payouts of spinoff securities as evidence of unacceptable risk and "lack of fit" with retail client portfolios. These salespeople, of course, were able to generate commission dollars from both the sales of the spinoff shares and their clients' purchases of "more suitable" investments.

- Were not in the S&P 500 (i.e., they were 0 for 74 in this respect), while 31 of the 74 parent companies were included in the S&P 500

- Had average dividend yields of .81% (versus 2.65% for the parent companies), and;

- Were not rated by S&P, whereas the parent companies had an average S&P stock rating of A-.

Would these differences in investment characteristics be likely to render spinoff securities unsuitable for institutional investors?

Brown and Brooke cited research indicating that professional investors have tended to require investments to be restricted to dividend-paying stocks in order to satisfy criteria for prudence.[1] They also noted that investment professionals attempt to reduce their exposure to liability arising from their fiduciary duties by self-imposing restrictions on the investments they select. They seek to prove their prudence by investing only in companies that meet such criteria as minimum market capitalization and dividend yield.[2]

The researchers went on to find evidence that these differences in investment characteristics actually were causing significant institutional selling of spinoff shares. Median institutional ownership of spinoff shares was 42.5% when public trading commenced (i.e., equal to median institutional ownership of the parent companies). Within about three months, this figure declined to 19.0% (a decrease of more than 55%).

Moreover, the median number of institutions owning spinoff shares was 123.5 when public trading commenced. But within roughly three months, this figure declined to 28.5 – indicating a median exodus exceeding 75% of all institutional owners.

Finally, Brown and Brooke confirmed that this selling was, indeed, creating profitable investment opportunities. During Days 31 through 60 of public trading, the 31 spinoffs with S&P 500-member parents averaged excess returns of 2.68%. Interestingly, this 2.68% represents a rebound almost exactly equal to 1/3 of the –8.04% negative excess returns that these stocks experienced, on average, during their first 30 days of trading.

Though the Brown and Brooke study did not analyze returns after 60 days of trading, our belief is that spinoffs of S&P 500 parents are likely to continue providing significant excess returns thereafter. We say this because the excess returns for Days 31 through 60 were only 1/3 of the negative excess returns experienced by these stocks, on average, during their first 30 days of trading.

[1] "The Dividend Puzzle" by Fischer Black, *Journal of Portfolio Management*, 1976.

[2] "Patterns of Institutional Investment, Prudence, and the Managerial 'Safety-Net' Hypothesis" by S. Badrinath, G. Gay, and J. Kale, *Journal of Risk and Insurance*, 1989.

Also, as a 1993 *Journal of Financial Economics* article by Patrick Cusatis, James Miles, and J. Randall Woolridge, "Restructuring Through Spinoffs," indicated, returns from spinoff stocks exceeded those of both their industries and the S&P 500 by roughly 10% annually during their first 36 months of trading. These findings were based on a Penn State study that analyzed 25 years of data between 1963 and 1988.

And, as Joel Greenblatt notes in *You Can Be A Stock Market Genius*, "In the Penn State study, the largest stock gains for spinoff companies took place not in the first year after the spinoff but in the second."

Buying Power Management

This is a simple, but nevertheless vitally important task.

In order to place buy orders before 9:30 AM, we need to have buying power (i.e., additional margin we can borrow to fund stock purchases). Typically, 10% of account equity is sufficient to take advantage of the day's opportunities, this amount being enough to fund one typical purchase of a highly liquid stock and two or three purchases of moderately liquid stocks. But when unusually large numbers of earnings reports are expected, it's generally advisable to have even more buying power available.

In order to free up sufficient buying power, we regularly sell our losing positions (patiently trading our way out of illiquid stocks). We take this approach primarily to keep the portfolio concentrated in high relative strength stocks, but it also makes a lot of sense from a tax perspective.

If we still need more buying power after selling our losing positions (i.e., whatever losers we are able to sell at reasonable prices), we sell stocks with long-term gains (taking the smallest gains first). The last stocks we sell are those with large, unrealized short-term capital gains.

Tax Minimization

Our aim is always to minimize taxes at the short-term capital gain rate.

More often than not, we're better off holding a position in which we have an unrealized short-term gain until it qualifies as a long-term gain (i.e. for more than one year). By holding, we run the risk that the stock's price may decline, erasing some or all of the gain. On the other hand, the difference between the tax rate on short-term gains versus that charged on long-term gains is (currently) equal to 20% of the gain, and that 20% tax difference is a sure thing. Thus, we're betting the possibility of the value of our position falling more than 20% of the gain against the certainty of the tax.

In the absence of bad news, this is normally a good bet to make. Of course, there is always the possibility that a major market decline will affect the outcome of our bet, but, generally speaking, unless bad news breaks, we're comfortable holding a large, unrealized gain until it qualifies for long-term treatment (especially in the case of a value stock that we bought on a good news story).

Our strategy for creating buying power – i.e., selling losers first, selling positions in which we have large short-term gains last – tends to accelerate the realization of short-term losses. This helps us to minimize and defer our tax liability by offsetting the current year's short-term gains.

In addition, we continuously review our holdings for positions with gains that have recently achieved long-term status. Then, unless we have a compelling reason to hang on to the stock (something that would have induced us to buy the stock if we didn't already own it), we sell.

Our trading decisions are guided by our objective of maximizing after-tax returns, and we employ a variety of methods to minimize our tax liability. Nevertheless, it is difficult to recommend specific tax avoidance measures. Individual situations vary, and, moreover, our tax laws are complex and subject to constant change. We recommend that investors check with their tax advisors before implementing any tax-advantaged strategy.

Risk Management

Used judiciously, margin borrowing can provide a huge boost to returns. It can also wipe out a portfolio with breathtaking speed.

In the long run, a prudently leveraged and diversified portfolio managed according to our decision rules is likely to outperform an unleveraged portfolio run in an otherwise similar fashion. Over the course of many years, even small amounts of leverage can result in enormous enhancements of one's end result.

Raising our compounded annual return from 9% to 12% doesn't sound like a huge difference. But, in fact, this allows an investment to double in value every six years rather than every eight. In one case, $10,000 grows to $80,000 in 24 years; in the other, it grows to $160,000.

Given that the average stock market returns are much more than the rates typically charged for margin loans, it would appear that borrowing as much as possible on margin and keeping it all invested in stocks would be a sensible strategy.

However, the problem with this strategy is that the average return on a portfolio will always be greater than its geometric return, and the greater the volatility of the portfolio, the greater this difference will be.

Here's what we mean. Let's say that you have average returns of 100% for three years. This sounds great, but it may not be nearly as good as it sounds. What if I told you that the returns in those three years were +200%, +200%, and –100%? It's quite possible, you see, to go broke on average returns of 100% a year.

The key to building long-term wealth is to maximize potential appreciation, while reducing risk wherever possible and all but eliminating the potential of catastrophic loss.

In our test portfolio, we maximized appreciation potential by staying fully invested. That is, we were fully margined most of the time, except for the liquidity needed to invest in new opportunities.

We reduced risk by:

- Diversifying– Only rarely has any one stock accounted for more than 5% of the account's equity.

- Buying value stocks– Companies with low P/S and low P/BV tend to decline less in weak markets.

- Buying into good news– Companies reporting good news today are more likely than the average company to have additional good news to report in the future.

- Selling quickly on bad news– Much of the price declines resulting from bad news can be avoided if affected stocks are sold promptly.

- Selling losers quickly– When a trade doesn't work out, it usually makes sense to sell quickly. Often, a stock's price will drift lower because someone is trading on bad news that has yet to be announced. Selling losers quickly also allows us to concentrate our portfolio in high relative strength stocks, which, as a group, tend to lose money less often than low relative strength stocks.

- Adopting a more conservative stance in bearish phases of the Fed-Election Cycle, as well as in historically bearish months (i.e., June through September).

- Becoming more conservative when unusually large amounts of new stock (i.e., IPO's and seasoned offerings) are being brought to market.

We have also bought puts on growth indices and growth stocks with bad news, thereby reducing our exposure to market risk.

If the market goes down 30% and leverage causes our portfolio to decline 50%, we need to make back 100% just to break even. By buying puts, we can dramatically reduce the probability of this scenario ever happening.

As this is being written, the test portfolio has roughly $2.4 million in equity invested as follows:

- Long stock positions: $4.7 million;

- Short stock positions: $1 million;

- Call option positions: $50,000 ($200,000 notional value); and

- Put option positions: $80,000 ($1,900,000 notional value).

If the market were to go up 20% and our stock positions (and the stocks underlying our options) were to match the market, the gain on the stocks would be ($4.7 million - $1 million) × 20% = $740,000. The call position is deep in the money, so the gain on it would be about $40,000, and the puts would expire worthless. All told, the portfolio would be up $700,000, a return of about 29% on today's equity (before deducting margin interest).

Consider, though, what would happen if the market declined 20%. If the market were to drop 20% and our stock positions (and the stocks underlying our options) were to match the market, the loss on the stocks would be ($4.7 million - $1 million) × 20% = $740,000. The call position is deep in the money, so the loss on it would be about $40,000.

Half the puts are at the money and the other half are 5% out of the money. So, in essence, we've got $1.9 million in insurance (the notional value of the options, equal to the number of puts × 100 shares per put × the average strike price) with a 2.5% deductible (2.5% being the average amount by which the puts are out of the money).

A 20% decline in their underlying stocks would cause the puts to be worth $332,500.[3] Since the puts are currently worth $80,000, the gain on them would be $252,500.

---

[3] $1.9 million × (20%-2.5%) = $332,500

Thus, in the event of a 20% market free fall, the overall portfolio's loss (before margin interest) would be $527,500, the net effect of:

- A $740,000 loss on the stock positions, plus

- A $40,000 loss on the call options, minus

- A $252,500 gain on the put options.

This would work out to a return on today's equity of -22% before margin interest.

To the extent that the stocks we are long outperform the stocks on which we own puts, the ultimate payoffs will be skewed in our favor. On the other hand, there is always the possibility that we will get things backwards and lose a lot more than we project.

Perhaps the best way to assess risk is to go through the kind of analysis we just performed, and then ask yourself if you can live with a loss that's 50% greater than what your analysis tells you. When markets go into panic mode, very few things work out as planned. Panicky brokers may suddenly tighten up their margin policies and sell your securities without warning at fire sale prices. And who knows what the bid/asked spread is likely to be if you need to sell those puts in the midst of market turmoil.

Ultimately, the role of your portfolio is to help you and your family to achieve whatever goals you have set for yourselves. If you already have all the wealth you'll ever need to be happy, you should set a relatively conservative course for yourself. If, on the other hand, you have a high tolerance for risk and a compelling need to accumulate wealth quickly, a much more aggressive approach is probably in order.

• Afterword •

VIDEOFINANCIALS & THE FUTURE OF WALL STREET

Our VideoFinancials product (available in 2005) will be an online successor to Bill Matson's Virtual Company Visits venture which, in 1993, was putting information about publicly traded companies on CD-ROM discs in a video format (facilities tours, product demos, management interviews, and interactive spreadsheet analyses).

In 1993, investors scratched their heads and wondered why anyone would ever need this sort of presentation when it was so much more convenient to rely upon the reports of brokerage analysts. Ten years later, the answer to this question has become painfully obvious.

The VideoFinancials vision is to ultimately build a critical mass of multilingual, video/audio/transcribed audio presentations for thousands of publicly traded companies. Each presentation would consist of a standardized software template, into which several dozen video clips would be placed, along with interactive spreadsheets designed to facilitate "what if" analyses.

VideoFinancials would provide visual information, as well as management comments on major balance sheet and income statement items - through facilities tours, product demos, and management interviews. In addition, these presentations would contain management explanations of contingencies that might have material impact upon their businesses (including natural disasters, extreme weather, currency and commodity price fluctuations, legal/regulatory/political developments, competitors' actions, etc.). Users would then be able to continuously search the "Risks, Opportunities & Contingencies" sections of all corporate presentations in the database, seeking out whatever keywords apply to breaking news.

For instance, if there's a major earthquake whose epicenter is in Pusan, South Korea, it is worth a lot of money to know *immediately*:

1. That there was a significant earthquake in Pusan; and

2. Which companies are vulnerable to disruptions caused by their Pusan-area plants going down (as well as which competitors stand to benefit).

It took the market several days to appropriately price the stock of McGrath RentCorp after the Northridge quake on 1/17/94 (4:30 AM PST). If a VideoFinancials capability existed back then, a user could have known immediately that a California earthquake would provide a major boost to McGrath (which rents modular buildings), bought the stock, and made a big profit. (McGrath stock closed at $7.25 on 1/17 (volume: 18,400), up only $.13 from its previous close on 1/14 (volume: 3000). It was unchanged on 1/18 (volume: 18,200) and went up only to $7.50 by the 1/19 close (1/19 volume: 11,800). On 1/20, though, McGrath closed at $8.12 on volume of 301,200 shares, rising to $8.25 and $8.37, respectively, at the closes of 1/21 (volume: 47,800) and 1/24 (volume: 28,800).)

The number of good opportunities that thousands of news sources (versus the five news sources we currently use) could generate in conjunction with a large VideoFinancials database is mind-boggling -- especially for investors in small companies. When such a system becomes available, it will dramatically increase the asset management capacity of individual portfolio managers; that is, a small cap manager might be able manage $1 billion as effectively as he can now manage $100 million.

Independent investment advisors could link their online analyses to the corporate VideoFinancials presentations. Not only would these analyses generate revenue on a pay-per-view basis, but they would also be effective in building investor awareness of the advisors (which would help them in securing new money management clients).

Though some nimble mutual fund organizations might be able to adjust their business models to profitably employ this new paradigm, it's hard to envision a place for traditional full-service brokerage firms. There would be little room for any organization not focused on creating insightful analyses.

Even the investment banking function would be rendered largely irrelevant. Through use of VideoFinancials (coupled with an online auction capability), securities issuers would be able to:

1. Avoid the enormous fees exacted by investment bankers;

2. Provide investors with more useful information than would be possible through road shows and prospectuses;

3. Expose more potential investors to this information than would be possible through syndicate members' sales forces;

4. Conduct online auctions that fairly price their securities from the moment they go public, bypassing the immense corruption that has pervaded the IPO process; and

5. Ignore brokerage analysts' phone calls, focusing on running their businesses without fear of what disgruntled analysts might do to their stocks' prices AND reducing their exposure to inadvertent violations of Reg FD.

Obviously it will take years for VideoFinancials (or something like it) to change the way Wall Street does business. But it *will* happen.

Exhibit 49 shows this new paradigm, in which unbiased research will be efficiently distributed to investors, enabling them to capitalize on opportunities hitherto available only to insiders.

Exhibit 49

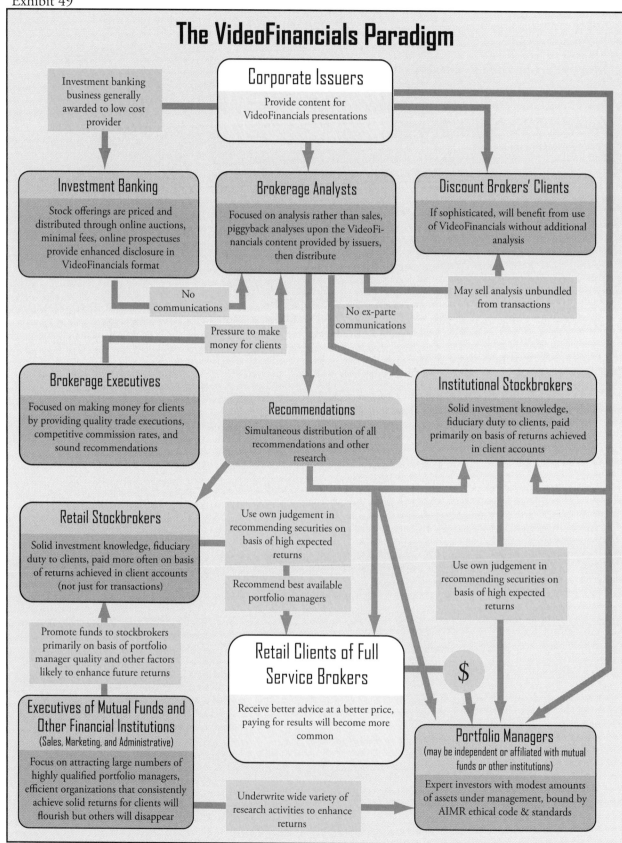

The VideoFinancials Paradigm

Corporate Issuers
Provide content for VideoFinancials presentations

Investment banking business generally awarded to low cost provider

Investment Banking
Stock offerings are priced and distributed through online auctions, minimal fees, online prospectuses provide enhanced disclosure in VideoFinancials format

Brokerage Analysts
Focused on analysis rather than sales, piggyback analyses upon the VideoFinancials content provided by issuers, then distribute

Discount Brokers' Clients
If sophisticated, will benefit from use of VideoFinancials without additional analysis

No communications

May sell analysis unbundled from transactions

No ex-parte communications

Pressure to make money for clients

Brokerage Executives
Focused on making money for clients by providing quality trade executions, competitive commission rates, and sound recommendations

Recommendations
Simultaneous distribution of all recommendations and other research

Institutional Stockbrokers
Solid investment knowledge, fiduciary duty to clients, paid primarily on basis of returns achieved in client accounts

Use own judgement in recommending securities on basis of high expected returns

Retail Stockbrokers
Solid investment knowledge, fiduciary duty to clients, paid more often on basis of returns achieved in client accounts (not just for transactions)

Recommend best available portfolio managers

Use own judgement in recommending securities on basis of high expected returns

Promote funds to stockbrokers primarily on basis of portfolio manager quality and other factors likely to enhance future returns

Retail Clients of Full Service Brokers
Receive better advice at a better price, paying for results will become more common

$

Executives of Mutual Funds and Other Financial Institutions
(Sales, Marketing, and Administrative)
Focus on attracting large numbers of highly qualified portfolio managers, efficient organizations that consistently achieve solid returns for clients will flourish but others will disappear

Underwrite wide variety of research activities to enhance returns

Portfolio Managers
(may be independent or affiliated with mutual funds or other institutions)
Expert investors with modest amounts of assets under management, bound by AIMR ethical code & standards

• Appendix A

WHAT DO PERFORMANCE FIGURES REALLY MEAN?

Performance figures have meaning, but, in the absence of context, they are more likely to mislead than inform.

Consider the 788% returns achieved in our test portfolio over the 45 months ended March 31, 2004, a period during which the S&P 500 fell by about 18%.

Does this represent skill on a par with Warren Buffett or Peter Lynch?

More to the point: could we be counted on to consistently do this well in the future?

Many observers of the stock market have noted the tendency of investment strategies and styles to lose effectiveness after a run of good performance. Superior returns result from the taking of positions before the majority of investors react, so, naturally, the performance of any strategy will decline as more and more investors adopt it.

Data Driven Investing™ is our way of staying ahead of the curve by continuously updating and refining our investment style as new data become available.

We believe this is the best way to develop stock selection strategies and trading techniques that are likely to perform better than major market indices (over the long term).

Nevertheless, a number of factors would work against our ability to sustain the test portfolio's level of performance in the future, especially if we were managing significantly greater assets.

We will review a few of these factors in this appendix, in order to give our readers a better understanding of how investment advantages that lead to superior returns are gained and lost.

Our Performance Calculation Method

In calculating out test portfolio's monthly returns, we assumed that all deposits were made at the beginning of the month and that all withdrawals were made at month-end. This assumption tends to overstate returns in down months and understate them in up months. It does, however, allow us to present conservative and readily confirmable performance figures.

The Advantages of a Small Fund

When we started our test portfolio in 2000, it was funded with well under a million dollars. Being small is the single most important advantage any money manager can have.

The manager of a small fund can be more selective than the manager of a large fund in choosing investments. No matter how extensive (or expensive) a fund's research effort might be, only a limited number of first-rate opportunities will be discovered on any given day. After positions have been taken in all of the best opportunities, any uninvested funds that remain will have to be placed in less promising alternatives. Thus, as assets under management increase, more of the money gets placed in progressively less desirable investments.

A small fund also has the advantage of being able to invest a greater proportion of its assets in nanocaps, the market cap grouping with by far the best historical returns. At some point, a fund becomes too large to invest in nanocaps at all.

Consider the manager of a multi-billion dollar fund, who has responsibility for investing tens of millions of dollars per week. It would be impossible to invest that kind of money in a series of $20,000 trades. Even if it took only 10 minutes to assess each stock and place an order to buy, it would take over 400 man-hours (or about 17 man-days) to invest $50 million.

The manager of a big fund does not have the option of simply buying a bigger position in each small company either. There are at least three reasons why this cannot be done.

For one thing, a very large order would disrupt trading in the stock, and the price would fluctuate wildly. An order to buy $50,000 worth of a nanocap stock that averaged only a few thousand dollars per day of trading volume would cause its price to temporarily skyrocket, due to the gross imbalance between supply and demand. An order to sell off a large position in a nanocap stock would similarly cause its price to crash temporarily.

For another thing, there might not be enough sellers to get a large buy order executed, even with the additional sellers that a skyrocketing price would attract.

A third reason that big funds cannot easily move in and out of large positions in nanocap stocks is the additional regulatory scrutiny given to major ownership changes in public companies. Rules requiring the acquisition or sale of a significant interest to be promptly reported impede trading in very small companies by large investment funds, which are typically not in the business of exercising control over the companies whose stock they purchase.

Since a multi-billion dollar fund can't efficiently buy nanocaps in either large amounts or small amounts, it can't buy them at all.

Even a small fund is limited in how much of a nanocap stock it can profitably acquire in a short time. When we enter a buy order with a limit price above the current asked price, we get the first few hundred shares for the asked price, but then, the next few hundred shares costs a penny or two more per share. The cost per share continues to rise until either the order is filled or there is no longer stock available at the price we're willing to pay. We might be unable to acquire more than $2000 or $3000 worth of the stock at or below our limit price.

We could raise our limit price to buy more shares, but, of course, that would ultimately lower our returns. Furthermore, we might someday need to quickly sell out of the position in response to breaking news. The more shares we needed to sell, the lower our average selling price would be.

It is feasible for the manager of a fund many times larger than our test portfolio to successfully trade nanocaps, as long as assets under management do not exceed a few hundred million dollars (and trading is supported with appropriate automation). The returns would tend to be lower than what we achieved because the threshold of what is considered an attractive, investable idea would have to be lowered to include more stocks. With a fund the size of our test portfolio (under $2.5 million), all of the assets can be invested in opportunities we consider A+'s. A larger fund might have to be allocated, to some extent, into A- or B+ situations.

Every investment advisor faces this problem. The more money he is asked to manage, the harder it is for him to find really good places to invest all of the funds. In this respect, investment advisors are like jockeys: the bigger they get, the less competitive they become.

The Effect of Leverage

Our use of leverage (i.e., buying on margin) significantly affected the performance of our test portfolio.

The impact of leverage on performance is difficult to measure precisely, because it would require distinguishing between those gains and losses on individual transactions that were attributable to margin debt and those that were not.

Calculating the Benefits of Margin

Distinguishing between gains and losses that are attributable to margin debt versus those that aren't would require more than just careful record keeping – it would also involve knowing the investor's motivation for incurring the margin debt, as well as some fairly arbitrary choices.

Suppose, for example, that you were holding 100 shares of Company S that you purchased with cash, and then saw a good opportunity to buy Company T, which would require a margin loan. Furthermore, suppose you liked Company T so much better than Company S that you would be willing to sell S to buy T if no margin loan were available. However, since you do have the ability to buy on margin, you go ahead and buy T and continue to hold S. Did you incur the margin debt to buy T, or did you incur it so that you could hold S? If T turns out to be a big winner, how much of your performance is attributable to leverage?

Or, what if, upon starting a day with no margin debt and no cash, you entered orders to buy Company X and sell Company Y. If your buy order got executed in the morning, would you consider any gains or losses ultimately realized from your position in X to be attributable to the use of margin, even though your order to sell Y got executed later that afternoon, and you ended the day with zero margin?

It is difficult to predict the effect leveraging might have on any portfolio, because the amount of additional assets that can be purchased on margin depends on multiple factors.

In general, a fully margined portfolio consisting of stocks that are gaining in value will perform better than an unleveraged portfolio holding proportionately reduced positions in the same stocks.

A fully margined portfolio of stocks that are falling in value will perform worse than an unleveraged portfolio holding proportionately reduced positions in the same stocks. Indeed, it could perform much worse - buying on margin entails the possibility that falling prices will trigger margin calls that force stocks to be sold at inopportune times, further degrading performance.

The additional risk associated with margin debt can be hedged by purchasing put options on market indices or individual stocks. That way, losses caused by a sudden downdraft will be offset by gains in the options. Of course, the cost of this portfolio insurance often reduces performance to some degree.

In our test portfolio, we used leverage aggressively, staying fully margined most of the time, but we also hedged against major market declines.

Some investors may be uncomfortable with the additional risk associated with buying on margin or may not wish to utilize margin debt as aggressively as we did in the test portfolio. In other cases, statutory or contractual limitations may preclude their use of margin. For example, retirement accounts (IRA's, 401k's, etc.) are not permitted to buy stocks on margin.

Investors who do not or cannot authorize trading on margin should realize that, to the extent that our test portfolio performance was attributable to leverage, it would not be representative of the performance one might expect to achieve in an unleveraged account.

Difficulty of Aligning Investment Style with Market Environment

Our stock selection strategies are based on our understanding of certain key factors (such as the Fed-Election Cycle) that drive stock prices, which was derived from extensive analysis of long-term market data.

While we are always seeking to improve our performance through a continuous effort to analyze historical data, we are also very disciplined in following the strategies we have adopted. We change our stock selection criteria when the Fed-Election Cycle enters a new phase, not when surges of emotion push the market temporarily in one direction or another.

Data Driven Investing™ allows us to avoid mistakes arising from emotion, but it can also leave us vulnerable to first-time phenomena with no history to analyze (such as the unpredictable flows of investor cash precipitated by, in rapid succession, the burst of a financial bubble, an unprecedented terrorist attack on U.S. soil, accounting scandals, war in Iraq, a West Coast dockworkers' strike, and North Korean nuclear mischief).

No amount of data or analysis will ever make it possible to create an investment strategy that is perfectly aligned with the market at all times. History never goes down precisely the same path more than once. Yet, we are convinced that human beings and their institutions can be relied upon to react more or less predictably most of the time. People and organizations, it seems, have an inexhaustible capacity for finding new ways of doing what they have always done.

As we strive to align our investment strategies with the market environment of the future, the past is the only objective guide we have, statistical analysis the only tool for discovering hidden patterns of behavior.

Data Driven Investing™ provides a factual basis for predicting the market's reaction to changes in key factors (like interest rates) and quantitative criteria for selecting stocks that are likely to achieve superior performance in a particular market environment, but it may be more effective in certain market environments—or with certain types of stocks—than others.

For example, during the period in which we ran the test portfolio, the market environment strongly favored value investing in very small cap companies. As it happened, two of these years also coincided with a meltdown of large cap companies, especially large cap growth companies (particularly in the technology sector).

We suspect that a lot of the money fleeing from large cap growth stocks may have found its way into small cap value stocks, buoying the test portfolio's holdings. Therefore, it is entirely possible that small cap value stocks will underperform market averages when investors get comfortable with large cap growth again.

Furthermore, our quantitative approach to stock selection might be more suitable to value stocks than growth stocks. With value stocks, it is all about the numbers. With growth stocks, fantasy, spin, and emotion enter the picture.

In a market environment that favored value stocks, **Data Driven Investing**™ achieved very good performance. In a market environment that favors growth stocks, **Data Driven Investing**™ may be less effective.

Our analysis of historical data indicates that some phases of the cycle are better for stocks than others. The key factors that drive stock prices sometimes drive them down. And, while we strive to identify and employ the best performing strategies for whatever phase we happen to be in at the time, there may be other key factors or cycles that we failed to identify, that confound our expectations.

Window Dressing, and the Valuation of Thinly-Traded Issues

Window dressing is the practice of adjusting the composition of a portfolio near the end of a reporting period in order to make it appear to have been managed better than was actually the case. The portfolio manager who engages in window dressing buys stocks that have done well during the period and sells those that have done poorly, to make it seem like he was making smart decisions all along.

With thinly-traded issues, it is relatively easy for an unscrupulous portfolio manager to temporarily drive up the price of a stock in which he has a large position, in order to boost performance figures (and earn a big performance bonus).

It is often difficult to determine a realistic value for a thinly-traded stock whose price is apt to fluctuate widely in response to relatively small orders. The monthly returns of any thinly-traded stock in our test portfolio could be significantly affected by just one end-of-month order.

We did not engage in any window dressing or intentional manipulation of stock prices in our test portfolio. Our performance figures are based on Fidelity Discount Brokerage's valuation of the stocks we held at the close of each month. Nevertheless, it is still possible that any particular stock could be significantly overvalued or undervalued, depending on whether the last order of the month was a buy or sell. Of course, over time, and over a large number of positions, significant overvaluations and undervaluations would tend to cancel each other out.

Investors who suspect their investment advisor of manipulating the performance numbers should review their account statements regularly and ask lots of questions if they ever find that the advisor has bought several percent of any thinly-traded company.

Taking a large position in a thinly-traded stock is not in itself a bad thing, if the company is sound and the stock was either bought in response to positive news or purchased near the bottom of the bid-asked range. We would get very suspicious, though, if we saw this kind of stock being bought at the top of the bid-asked range in the absence of a compelling news story—particularly if it were bought on the last trading day of the month.

Investment Management Fees

Our test portfolio's performance figures have been adjusted by the amount of fees (roughly 1.5% annually) that might have been charged if the portfolio had been an individually managed account under the direction of an investment advisor.

It should be noted that 1.5% - 2% is a fairly typical fee arrangement for an actively managed equity portfolio, and also that the typical actively managed equity portfolio is not as heavily invested in nanocaps as was our test portfolio. Hypothetically, a portfolio manager might need to charge a larger fee to compensate for the additional effort and time required to invest heavily in nanocaps.

It is much more time-consuming to invest in nanocaps than in large caps. A million dollars worth of GE can be bought in seconds, but efficiently buying a million dollars worth of nanocap stocks can take days, if not weeks. Consequently, if $15,000 is considered a fair amount to charge annually for managing a $1 million portfolio of large cap equities, then the same $1 million invested in nanocaps should theoretically cost substantially more.

A 1.5% fee may be unrealistically low for the management of a portfolio which is as heavily weighted toward nanocaps as was our test portfolio. If so, our test portfolio's performance would not be representative of the results an investor might achieve in such an account, by the amount that the management fees assumed to have been charged are understated.

Taxes

The performance figures we quote for our test portfolio do not reflect any Federal or state income taxes.

The gains we report were real, so Federal income tax was certainly paid, but every individual investor's tax situation is different. The test portfolio, for example, has been located in New Hampshire, which does not have a state income tax, since 2002. Had it remained across the border in Massachusetts

Taxable Gain Reporting

In some cases, the statements in Appendix C may understate short-term gains and/or overstate long-term gains. Fidelity's reporting system does not typically discern short sales against the box that give rise to constructive sales.

(where it was in 2000-2001), its short-term gains would have continued being taxed at 12%!

Because of the differences in individual tax situations, adjusting the test portfolio's performance for taxes paid would not be representative of the after-tax performance that another taxpayer might achieve by following the same strategy.

It should also be noted that our trading tactics involve a high level of activity, which generates large amounts of short-term capital gains. This is one of the biggest drawbacks to active trading, compared to a buy and hold strategy.

Commissions

The commission rates that were paid by the test portfolio might not be representative of the rates that might be paid by an investor in an individually managed account under the direction of an investment advisor. The online broker we used, Fidelity, currently charges different rates for individual accounts and advisory accounts.

The minimum charge per trade in Fidelity advisory accounts has, at times, been higher than the minimum charges applicable to the test portfolio account. This advantage of non-advisory accounts may be partially offset in some cases by a percentage of principal ceiling that would make it more economical to buy very low priced stocks in advisory accounts.

The S&P 500 is Not an Ideal Benchmark

Performance should be compared to a benchmark that accurately reflects the strategy employed. That having been said, there is no perfect benchmark against which we could compare our test portfolio.

We chose to compare our performance to the S&P 500 index because it is well-known and includes a large cross-section of American industry.

The Russell 2000 Value Index might be more reflective of the test portfolio's holdings, but it would no longer be appropriate when a tightening Fed leads us to shift our style from value to growth, or when circumstances dictate that we invest heavily in large caps, puts, and commodities.

Idiot's Luck?

How much of a role did luck play in the performance of our test portfolio?

Suppose that in July 2000 you had thrown a dart at the Wall Street Journal and bought whatever you hit. There would have been a small chance that the stock you bought would have outperformed our portfolio.

If you had thrown the dart twice and split your money between the two stocks you hit, you would have had a significantly smaller chance of outperforming us.

If you were throwing "buy darts" and "sell darts" dozens of times every week— and had to pay $8 (or more) every time you threw one—we suspect that the odds against outperforming our test portfolio would be quite steep.

Of course, your odds of achieving superior performance would be significantly improved if you were standing close to the target and had a very good idea of what you needed to hit.

That, as we see it, is the nature of our advantage. Based on historical data, we identify areas of the market we believe are likely to pay the best returns. These are the areas we aim for. We fire off a lot of trades in the direction of these areas, and we have many more misses than hits.

Up to now anyway, the hits have been profitable enough to support the idea that we are on the right track with **Data Driven Investing™**. That said, there is always the slight possibility that we are not as good as our numbers say we are, just lucky.

Appendix B

OUR BACKTESTING METHODOLOGY

Our study period ran from 1950 to 2002. We backtested strategies on an annual basis from 1951 to 2002.

We used the Standard & Poor's Compustat database, including the Compustat Basic North America, Research Quarterly & PDE, and Backdata Annual & Quarterly data files. This gave us access to data on over 20,000 companies.

We defined *market cap* as: Common Shares Outstanding times Price Per Common Share. Companies with market caps falling below $10,000,000 in December 2002 dollars at the time of portfolio construction (deflated using the CPI) were ineligible for inclusion in the portfolios backtested.

Our other formulas were defined as follows:

Price/Book Value: Closing Price Per Share divided by Common Equity

Price/Cash Flow: Closing Price Per Share divided by (Income Before Extraordinary Items & Discontinued Operations plus Depreciation & Amortization)

Price/Earnings: Closing Price Per Share divided by Basic Earnings per Share excluding Extraordinary Items

Price/Sales: Closing Price Per Share divided by Sales

Relative Strength: Based on Total Return (see Total Return calculation below)

Total Return: Calculated by adding (End of Period Stock Price divided by Beginning of Period Stock Price) to (Dividends divided by Beginning of Period Stock Price) and subtracting 1

The effects of transaction costs (i.e., fees, commissions, and market impact costs) and taxes were ignored.

By including actual brokerage statements in the Appendices, we hoped to show the real-life costs entailed by the trading strategies we advocate. Note that these statements present information on taxable gains, as well as on commissions and fees.

Though market impact costs are essentially unknowable, researchers may arrange access to much of the trade-by-trade detail behind these statements by contacting us (and paying us a nominal fee to cover copying, postage, etc.). This data shows, among other things, how execution prices worsen as incremental shares are bought or sold, as well as the profitability of shopkeeping.

Bias and Error

Though Compustat data is the gold standard of stock market data, it isn't 100% perfect for backtesting purposes. Rather than being paralyzed into inaction by these imperfections or expending inordinate amounts of time and resources trying to correct them, we have opted to disclose them and base our conclusions upon some simplifying assumptions that we consider reasonable. Compared to the leaps of faith taken by respected academics who routinely assume an efficient market, our assumptions are but mincing shuffles.

In many cases, several periods of data were backfilled when companies were added to the Compustat database. This introduces a survivorship bias, since companies that failed or muddled along are, in effect, being systematically excluded.

This bias is particularly strong in the 1950's and 1960's, since the database originally contained historical data only on active companies. Survivorship bias was mitigated as some of these companies began to fail. However, additional bias was introduced in subsequent years, when data was backfilled for newly included companies.

I'm sure that the great majority of users appreciate having access to backfilled data; otherwise, Compustat wouldn't expend the considerable effort entailed in providing it. This data does create difficulties for backtesters, though.

The best way to address this issue, we believe, is to understand that small, money-losing, or otherwise risky companies are the biggest beneficiaries of survivorship bias (appearing, as a group, to have better returns than they actually do), while large, stable ventures gain the least.

For much of our 52-year sample period, only annual data was available to us. This forced us to choose between, for example, 1951 or 1952 data in predicting 1953 returns. Using the 1951 data increases survivorship bias and entails the disadvantages of stale data. On the other hand, using 1952 data introduces look-ahead bias, since final year-end data is not available until financial statements have been prepared, audited, and released.

We opted to risk look-ahead bias, using data for the preceding year (rather than lagging it by a year) to predict returns. Two or three quarters of actual data plus one or two quarters of estimated data would normally be available at year-end. In most cases, we believe, this blend of actual and estimated data would have given a highly reliable indication of the final year-end figures; moreover, this approach minimizes survivorship bias and avoids stale data issues.

When a company, in the absence of a merger, acquisition, LBO, or going private transaction, stops trading and filing with the SEC, its stock may still have value. Unfortunately, Compustat generally can not say what that value is. (Nor does Compustat provide comprehensive data on stock values subsequent to merger, acquisition, LBO, and going private transactions.)

To the extent that other flaws exist in our analyses, we suspect they are primarily caused by random error, rather than by any systematic bias. Considering how many millions of pieces of information we are dealing with it would, indeed, be quite surprising if either we or Compustat had zero errors. If our computers were to hiccup for a nanosecond or two in the midst of their heroic number-crunching labors, this might very well go unnoticed.

In order to minimize random error and its consequences, we selected Compustat as our data provider and checked our work through extensive sampling. We will promptly post errata notices to our website when errors are brought to our attention.

• Appendix C

BROKERAGE STATEMENTS

Test Portfolio Performance

Exhibit 50A summarizes the performance of the test portfolio from July 2000 to March 2004. The detailed monthly performance calculation is presented in Exhibit 50B. The figures presented in Exhibits 50A and 50B are corroborated by the brokerage statements reproduced on the pages which follow.

The test portfolio earned a compound annual return of 79.0% during the 45 months from July 2000 to March 2004, a period in which the S&P 500 lost 5.1% compounded. The year-end account summaries reproduced in this appendix provide evidence of the kinds of investments and level of diversification maintained in the portfolio.

The authors of *Data Driven Investing – Professional Edition* wish to emphasize that the test portfolio's performance was achieved with real money. Therefore, all of the trading costs associated with our active style of investing are reflected in these figures. In addition, the performance calculations reflect a hypothetical 1.5% annual management fee in order to make them more comparable to what might be achieved in an individually managed account under the direction of an independent investment advisor.

This management fee is the only thing "hypothetical" about the test portfolio's performance. Without adjusting for it, the test portfolio would have earned a compound annual return of 81.4%.

Through publication of the brokerage statements reproduced in this appendix, the returns we cite for our test portfolio are among the most comprehensively documented investment performance claims ever made in any book about investing. The authors wish to acknowledge Fidelity Investments for permitting their reproduction and publication.

Source: Fidelity Investments. Fidelity is not responsible for the subject matter of this publication and has not reviewed its content for accuracy. Fidelity has not examined, nor does it endorse, any trading strategy discussed in this publication. The Fidelity Investments and Pyramid Logo is a registered trademark of FMR Corp.

Exhibit 50A: Test Portfolio Performance Summary

Test Portfolio Performance (Less Hypothetical Management Fee)* vs. S&P 500

Period	Test Portfolio		S&P 500		Performance Advantage	
	Percentage Returns	Growth of $1	Percentage Returns	Growth of $1	Percentage Returns	Growth of $1
July - December 2000	13.4%	$1.13	-8.7%	$0.91	22.1%	$0.22
2001	104.1%	$2.31	-11.9%	$0.80	116.0%	$1.51
2002	24.9%	$2.89	-22.1%	$0.63	47.0%	$2.26
2003	153.9%	$7.34	28.7%	$0.81	125.3%	$6.53
January - March 2004	21.0%	$8.885	1.7%	$0.820	19.3%	$8.06
Compound Annual Returns	79.0%		-5.1%		84.2%	

Adjusted for hypothetical management fee of approximately 0.375% per quarter.

Test Portfolio Performance (Without Management Fee) vs. S&P 500

Period	Test Portfolio		S&P 500		Performance Advantage	
	Percentage Returns	Growth of $1	Percentage Returns	Growth of $1	Percentage Returns	Growth of $1
July - December 2000	14.2%	$1.14	-8.7%	$0.91	22.9%	$0.23
2001	106.7%	$2.36	-11.9%	$0.80	118.6%	$1.56
2002	26.7%	$2.99	-22.1%	$0.63	48.8%	$2.36
2003	157.0%	$7.69	28.7%	$0.81	128.3%	$6.88
January - March 2004	21.4%	$9.33	1.7%	$0.820	19.7%	$8.51
Compound Annual Returns	81.4%		-5.1%		86.6%	

Exhibit 50B: Test Portfolio Monthly Returns vs. S&P 500

Month	Beginning Market Value of Investments	Additions	Withdrawals	Fees & Comms	Interest Paid	Investment Value Change	Debit/Short Change	Adj's	Ending Market Value of Investments	Debit Balance	Ending Net Account Balance	Monthly Returns Test Portfolio[1]	Monthly Returns S&P 500	Test Portfolio Performance Advantage[2]	Hypothetical Quarterly Management Fees[3]	Monthly Returns Adjusted for Management Fees[4]	Test Portfolio Performance Advantage After Adj. for Fees[5]
Jul-00	$273,954	$341,588	$8,000	$2,076	$6	$11,138	$19,625		$636,222	$19,625	$616,598	1.5%	-1.6%	3.0%		1.5%	3.0%
Aug-00	$636,222	$10,000	$10,007	$2,431	$20	$51,577	$(19,625)	$(314)	$665,402	$(314)	$665,716	7.8%	6.2%	1.6%	$2,308	7.8%	1.6%
Sep-00	$665,402			$3,712	$60	$12,455		$314	$674,382	$(17)	$674,399	1.4%	-5.3%	6.6%		1.0%	6.3%
Oct-00	$674,382		$5,000	$1,485		$(4,388)		$(17)	$663,509	$(17)	$663,526	-0.9%	-0.4%	-0.4%		-0.9%	-0.4%
Nov-00	$663,509		$10,000	$2,103		$(14,603)			$636,803		$636,803	-2.5%	-7.9%	5.4%		-2.5%	5.4%
Dec-00	$636,803			$3,040	$285	$45,451	$240,179	$3	$919,112	$240,179	$678,933	6.6%	0.5%	6.1%	$2,520	6.2%	5.7%
Jan-01	$919,112		$19,000	$2,518	$1,812	$129,715	$63,425		$1,088,924	$303,604	$785,319	18.5%	3.5%	14.9%		18.5%	14.9%
Feb-01	$1,088,924		$20,000	$4,855	$2,207	$(33,581)	$(12,892)		$1,015,387	$290,712	$724,675	-5.2%	-9.1%	3.9%	$2,528	-5.2%	3.9%
Mar-01	$1,015,387			$3,207	$1,511	$41,393	$(17,060)		$1,035,003	$273,652	$761,351	5.1%	-6.3%	11.4%		4.7%	11.1%
Apr-01	$1,035,003		$10,000	$3,328	$1,597	$94,686	$(117,598)		$997,165	$156,054	$841,111	11.8%	7.8%	4.0%		11.8%	4.0%
May-01	$997,182		$10,000	$3,418	$1,018	$113,034	$62,486		$1,158,265	$218,539	$939,726	12.9%	0.7%	12.2%	$2,824	12.9%	12.2%
Jun-01	$1,158,265		$53,693	$3,559	$657	$18,516	$(23,241)		$1,095,631	$195,298	$900,333	1.5%	-2.4%	4.0%		1.2%	3.7%
Jul-01	$1,095,631	$30	$10,100	$2,177	$975	$40,431	$18,765		$1,141,605	$214,064	$927,542	4.1%	-1.0%	5.1%		4.1%	5.1%
Aug-01	$1,141,605	$3,000	$3,000	$968	$878	$(9,053)	$(16,600)		$1,111,107	$197,464	$913,643	-1.2%	-6.3%	5.1%	$3,326	-1.2%	5.1%
Sep-01	$1,111,107		$11,000	$3,740	$810	$(38,300)	$(62,092)		$998,165	$135,372	$862,794	-4.7%	-8.1%	3.4%		-5.0%	3.0%
Oct-01	$998,165		$8,000	$5,664	$748	$138,172	$47,176		$1,169,101	$182,547	$986,553	15.3%	1.9%	13.4%		15.3%	13.4%
Nov-01	$1,169,101		$10,000	$6,103	$830	$125,319	$102,649		$1,380,137	$285,197	$1,094,940	12.0%	7.7%	4.3%	$3,173	12.0%	4.3%
Dec-01	$1,380,137		$10,000	$4,278	$1,267	$92,101	$149,228		$1,605,919	$434,424	$1,171,495	7.9%	0.9%	7.0%		7.6%	6.7%
Jan-02	$1,605,919		$20,000	$6,319	$1,047	$129,354	$(93,311)		$1,614,596	$341,113	$1,273,483	10.4%	-1.5%	11.9%		10.4%	11.9%
Feb-02	$1,614,596		$13,000	$6,003	$1,228	$13,594	$289,845		$1,897,805	$630,958	$1,266,847	0.5%	-1.9%	2.4%	$4,295	0.5%	2.4%
Mar-02	$1,897,805		$16,000	$4,667	$2,171	$182,136	$226,724	$(16)	$2,283,827	$857,682	$1,426,146	13.8%	3.8%	10.1%		13.5%	9.7%
Apr-02	$2,283,827		$40,000	$6,438	$2,714	$215,274	$47,521		$2,497,477	$905,203	$1,592,274	14.5%	-6.1%	20.5%		14.5%	20.5%
May-02	$2,497,477		$21,574	$9,987	$2,633	$89,553	$58,421		$2,611,257	$963,624	$1,647,633	4.8%	-0.7%	5.6%	$5,208	4.8%	5.6%
Jun-02	$2,611,257		$27,000	$7,540	$3,091	$115,013	$(17,763)	$14	$2,670,889	$945,860	$1,725,029	6.3%	-7.1%	13.5%		6.0%	13.1%
Jul-02	$2,670,889		$28,000	$11,178	$3,346	$(169,436)	$(123,966)		$2,334,963	$821,894	$1,513,068	-10.7%	-7.8%	-2.9%		-10.7%	-2.9%
Aug-02	$2,334,963		$144,000	$9,226	$2,843	$16,599	$102,631		$2,298,124	$924,525	$1,373,600	0.3%	0.7%	-0.4%	$6,270	0.3%	-0.4%
Sep-02	$2,298,124		$22,000	$5,541	$2,987	$(114,366)	$(369,739)		$1,783,491	$554,786	$1,228,706	-8.9%	-10.9%	1.9%		-9.4%	1.5%
Oct-02	$1,783,491		$20,000	$7,741	$1,918	$7,749	$40,105		$1,801,686	$594,890	$1,206,796	-0.2%	8.8%	-9.0%		-0.2%	-9.0%
Nov-02	$1,801,686			$4,668	$2,154	$54	$93,670		$1,888,588	$688,560	$1,200,028	-0.6%	5.9%	-6.4%	$4,422	-0.6%	-6.4%
Dec-02	$1,888,588			$3,365	$3,036	$(29,119)	$37,210		$1,890,278	$725,770	$1,164,508	-3.0%	-5.9%	2.9%		-3.3%	2.5%
Jan-03	$1,890,278			$4,273	$1,355	$8,232	$(212,590)		$1,680,292	$513,180	$1,167,112	0.2%	-2.6%	2.8%		0.2%	2.8%
Feb-03	$1,680,292		$27,500	$7,622	$1,779	$(3,666)	$62,908	$60	$1,702,633	$576,089	$1,126,544	-1.1%	-1.5%	0.4%	$4,172	-1.1%	0.4%
Mar-03	$1,702,633		$55,000	$5,057	$1,433	$(11,533)	$(206,200)		$1,423,410	$369,889	$1,053,521	-1.6%	1.0%	-2.6%		-2.0%	-2.9%
Apr-03	$1,423,410	$11,154	$10,000	$7,393	$1,209	$115,619	$(154,725)	$(81,314)	$1,528,557	$376,864	$1,151,693	10.1%	8.2%	1.9%		10.1%	1.9%
May-03	$1,528,557	$15	$25,000	$8,649	$1,210	$136,521	$(48,538)		$1,581,756	$328,327	$1,253,430	11.0%	5.3%	5.7%	$3,749	11.0%	5.7%
Jun-03	$1,581,756		$40,100	$8,373	$1,272	$99,077	$(54,475)		$1,606,714	$273,852	$1,332,862	7.1%	1.3%	5.8%		6.8%	5.5%
Jul-03	$1,606,714		$50,000	$8,676	$979	$303,183	$274,454		$2,053,283	$548,306	$1,504,977	15.9%	1.8%	14.2%		15.9%	14.2%
Aug-03	$2,053,283		$46,400	$10,649	$1,417	$206,871	$(154,725)		$2,043,363	$393,581	$1,649,782	12.9%	2.0%	11.0%	$4,714	12.9%	11.0%
Sep-03	$2,043,363		$80,000	$6,719	$1,367	$23,240	$267,855	$88,867	$2,368,839	$661,436	$1,707,403	6.3%	-1.1%	7.4%		6.0%	7.1%
Oct-03	$2,368,839		$73,000	$3,923	$2,146	$330,166	$140,442	$404	$2,753,782	$801,878	$1,951,903	19.0%	5.7%	13.4%		19.0%	13.4%
Nov-03	$2,753,782		$92,000	$6,253	$3,183	$245,958	$(57,247)	$(18)	$2,860,038	$744,631	$2,115,407	12.1%	0.9%	11.2%	$5,990	12.1%	11.2%
Dec-03	$2,860,038		$30,000	$5,740	$6,685	$194,358	$233,242	$(4,681)	$3,178,533	$977,874	$2,200,659	8.4%	5.2%	3.1%		8.1%	2.9%
Jan-04	$3,178,533		$35,000	$6,361	$4,135	$196,751	$136,971	$4,960	$3,471,719	$1,114,845	$2,356,873	8.7%	1.8%	6.9%		8.7%	6.9%
Feb-04	$3,471,719		$105,000	$5,310	$6,907	$205,954	$31,168		$3,666,623	$1,146,013	$2,520,610	8.2%	1.4%	6.8%	$7,633	8.2%	6.8%
Mar-04	$3,666,623			$8,131	$5,858	$95,436	$91,669		$3,734,738	$1,237,682	$2,497,056	3.2%	-1.5%	4.7%		2.9%	4.4%

1 Monthly Return = (Investment Value Change − Fees − Interest + Adjustments) ÷ (Beginning Net Account Balance + Additions).

2 Performance Advantage = Amount by which Test Portfolio Monthly Returns exceed Monthly Returns for the S&P 500.

3 Hypothetical Management Fees = 0.375% per quarter applied to Beginning Net Account Balance and first month's Additions. Including foregone investment returns, the cumulative cost of these fees would have been $208,212.

4 For a detailed explanation of the calculation of Monthly Returns Adjusted for Management Fees, please visit our website, www.DataDrivenPublishing.com.

5 Performance Advantage = Amount by which Test Portfolio Monthly Returns (after adjustment for Hypothetical Management Fees) exceed Monthly Returns for the S&P 500.

Investment Report

July 1, 2000 - July 31, 2000

Online www.fidelity.com
FAST(sm)-Automated Telephone 800-544-5555
Customer Service 800-544-6666

Messages:

Find out about 10 Uncommon Values(R) 2000 Portfolio, a Unit Investment Trust comprised of 10 stocks that Lehman Brothers believes will outperform the S&P 500(R). Visit Fidelity.com or call 800-544-6666 for a prospectus.

WILLIAM NICHOLAS MATSON

Ultra Service Account

WILLIAM N MATSON - INDIVIDUAL

Congratulations. You've earned lower commissions based on your rolling 12-month trading activity. Your account pricing has been upgraded and you will receive deeper discounts on your stock and option trades. The enclosed commission schedule details your new pricing. Thank you for your continued business.

Income Summary

	This Period	Year to Date
Taxable		
Dividends	$1,497.34	$1,497.34
Interest	109.53	173.66
Total	**$1,606.87**	**$1,671.00**

Account Summary

Beginning market value as of Jul 1	$273,953.63
Additions	100,866.62
Withdrawals	-8,000.00
Transaction costs, loads and fees	-2,075.99
Net adjustments	-83,092.22
Margin interest paid	-5.60
Transfers between Fidelity accounts	323,813.18
Change in investment value	11,138.28
Change in debit balance	19,624.56
Ending market value as of Jul 31	636,222.46
Debit balance	-19,624.56
Ending Net Value	**$616,597.90**

Your commission schedule

	Active Trader
Minimal annual trade requirement	36
Eligible trades from Aug 1999 - Jul 2000	62
Current rate on debit balance	10.55%
Additional amount you can borrow	$200,151.41

August 2000

WILLIAM NICHOLAS MATSON

Investment Report

August 1, 2000 - August 31, 2000

Online
FAST(sm)-Automated Telephone
Customer Service

www.fidelity.com
800-544-5555
800-544-6666

Ultra Service Account

WILLIAM N MATSON - INDIVIDUAL

Congratulations. You've earned lower commissions based on your rolling 12-month trading activity. Your account pricing has been upgraded and you will receive deeper discounts on your stock and option trades. The enclosed commission schedule details your new pricing. Thank you for your continued business.

Income Summary

	This Period	Year to Date
Taxable		
Dividends	$367.69	$1,865.03
Interest	100.25	273.91
Total	**$467.94**	**$2,138.94**

Account Summary

Beginning market value as of Aug 1	$636,222.46
Additions	10,000.00
Withdrawals	-10,007.28
Transaction costs, loads and fees	-2,431.45
Margin interest paid	-20.13
Change in investment value	51,576.75
Change in credit balance	-313.53
Change in debit balance	-19,624.56
Ending market value as of Aug 31	665,402.26
Credit balance	313.53
Ending Net Value	**$665,715.79**

Your commission schedule	**Gold Circle**
Minimal annual trade requirement	72
Eligible trades from Sep 1999 - Aug 2000	133
Current rate on debit balance	10.05%
Additional amount you can borrow	$198,509.36

Investment Report

September 1, 2000 - September 30, 2000

Online	www.fidelity.com
FAST(sm)-Automated Telephone	800-544-5555
Customer Service	800-544-6666

Messages:

Phase II of decimalization began on September 25, 2000. For detailed information about the securities participating in each phase, please refer to the insert in this statement or www.fidelity.com.

WILLIAM NICHOLAS MATSON

WILLIAM N MATSON - INDIVIDUAL

Ultra Service Account

Account Summary

Beginning market value as of Sep 1	$665,402.26
Transaction costs, loads and fees	-3,712.35
Margin interest paid	-59.70
Change in investment value	12,454.97
Change in credit balance	296.62
Ending market value as of Sep 30	674,381.80
Credit balance	16.91
Ending Net Value	**$674,398.71**

Your commission schedule	Gold Circle
Minimal annual trade requirement	72
Eligible trades from Oct 1999 - Sep 2000	232
Current rate on debit balance	10.55%
Additional amount you can borrow	$80,282.84

Income Summary

	This Period	Year to Date
Taxable		
Dividends	$721.91	$2,586.94
Interest	532.87	806.78
Total	$1,254.78	$3,393.72

Realized Gain/Loss from Sales

	This Period	Year to Date
Short-term gain	$51,055.01	$97,131.08
Short-term loss	-23,024.86	-51,506.70
St disallowed loss	698.19	1,598.54
Net short	$28,728.34	$47,222.92

This may not reflect all of your gains/losses because of incomplete cost basis.

October 2000

WILLIAM NICHOLAS MATSON

Investment Report

October 1, 2000 - October 31, 2000

Online	www.fidelity.com
FAST(sm)-Automated Telephone	800-544-5555
Customer Service	800-544-6666

Ultra Service Account

WILLIAM N MATSON - INDIVIDUAL

Fidelity BillPay(SM) - one of many features you can get with your Fidelity Brokerage(R) account. Send bill payments electronically to virtually any business, merchant, or individual. Even schedule recurring fixed-amount payments, like mortgages, all through Fidelity.com. And best of all, BillPay can be FREE. Visit Fidelity.com/goto/billpay for details and to enroll now.

Account Summary

Beginning value as of Oct 1	$674,381.80
Withdrawals	-5,000.00
Transaction costs, loads and fees	-1,484.66
Change in investment value	-4,388.17
Change in credit balance	16.91
Ending value as of Oct 31	$663,525.88

Your commission schedule

Gold Circle	
Minimal annual trade requirement	240
Eligible trades from Nov 1999 - Oct 2000	292

Amount you can borrow	$189,555.20
Maximum rate that could currently apply	10.55%

Income Summary

	This Period	Year to Date
Taxable		
Dividends	$965.64	$3,552.58
Interest	1,427.60	2,234.38
Return of capital	450.00	450.00
Total	**$2,843.24**	**$6,236.96**

Realized Gain/Loss from Sales

	This Period	Year to Date
Short-term gain	$11,392.44	$108,523.52
Short-term loss	-17,525.74	-69,032.44
St disallowed loss	621.47	2,220.01
Net short	**-$5,511.83**	**$41,711.09**

This may not reflect all of your gains/losses because of incomplete cost basis.

WILLIAM NICHOLAS MATSON

Investment Report

November 1, 2000 - November 30, 2000

Online   www.fidelity.com
FAST(sm)-Automated Telephone   800-544-5555
Customer Service   800-544-6666

WILLIAM N MATSON - INDIVIDUAL

Ultra Service Account

Congratulations. You've earned lower commissions based on your rolling 12-month trading activity. Your account pricing has been upgraded and you will receive deeper discounts on your stock and option trades. The enclosed commission schedule details your new pricing. Thank you for your continued business.

Account Summary

Beginning value as of Nov 1	$663,525.88
Withdrawals	-10,000.00
Transaction costs, loads and fees	-2,102.66
Change in investment value	-14,602.99
Ending value as of Nov 30	$636,820.23

Your commission schedule	Gold Circle
Minimal annual trade requirement	240
Eligible trades from Dec 1999 - Nov 2000	423

Amount you can borrow	$307,775.98
Maximum rate that could currently apply	10.55%

Income Summary

	This Period	Year to Date
Taxable		
Dividends	$180.00	$3,732.58
Interest	857.00	3,091.38
Return of capital	0.00	450.00
Total	$1,037.00	$7,273.96

Realized Gain/Loss from Sales

	This Period	Year to Date
Short-term gain	$19,661.87	$128,185.39
Short-term loss	-35,880.85	-104,913.29
St disallowed loss	1,496.18	3,716.19
Net short	-$14,722.80	$26,988.29

This may not reflect all of your gains/losses because of incomplete cost basis.

WILLIAM NICHOLAS MATSON

Investment Report

December 1, 2000 - December 31, 2000

Online	Fidelity.com
FAST(sm)-Automated Telephone	800-544-5555
Customer Service	800-544-6666

Messages:

To help you manage your taxes, Fidelity now offers online year-to-date tax information on your brokerage account. Log in to Fidelity.com, click on the account you want to review, and choose "Tax Information".

Ultra Service Account

WILLIAM N MATSON - INDIVIDUAL

Congratulations. You've earned lower commissions based on your rolling 12-month trading activity. Your account pricing has been upgraded and you will receive deeper discounts on your stock and option trades. The enclosed commission schedule details your new pricing. Thank you for your continued business.

Account Summary

Beginning market value as of Dec 1	$636,820.23
Transaction costs, loads and fees	-3,039.58
Net adjustments	3.00
Margin interest paid	-284.85
Change in investment value	45,451.43
Change in debit balance	240,179.07
Ending market value as of Dec 31	919,129.30
Debit balance	-240,179.07
Ending Net Value	**$678,950.23**

Your commission schedule	**Gold Circle**
Minimal annual trade requirement	240
Eligible trades from Jan 2000 - Dec 2000	589
Current rate on debit balance	8.80%
Additional amount you can borrow	$11,582.80

Income Summary

	This Period	Year to Date
Taxable		
Dividends	$847.50	$4,580.08
Interest	173.79	3,265.17
Return of capital	0.00	450.00
Total	**$1,021.29**	**$8,295.25**

Realized Gain/Loss from Sales

	This Period	Year to Date
Short-term gain	$23,165.36	$151,350.75
Short-term loss	-21,574.46	-126,487.75
St disallowed loss	7,219.11	11,715.56
Net short	**$8,810.01**	**$36,578.56**

This may not reflect all of your gains/losses because of incomplete cost basis.

2000 Investment Report

January 1, 2000 - December 31, 2000

Realized Gain/Loss from Sales

Short-term gain	$151,350.75
Short-term loss	-126,487.75
St disallowed loss	15,986.59
Net short	**$40,849.59**

This may not reflect all of your gains losses because of incomplete cost basis

Ultra Service Account

WILLIAM N MATSON - INDIVIDUAL

Income Summary

Taxable		
Ordinary Dividends		$4,414.89
Dividends	3,265.17	
Interest	62.80	
Lt cap gain	102.39	
Return of capital		
Total		**$7,845.25**

Foreign taxes paid on funds you owned are included in Ordinary Dividends. Detailed reporting and instructions to help you file your federal tax return are found on your Form 1099-DIV.

2000 Account Summary

Beginning market value as of Jan 1	$0.00
Additions	396,376.62
Withdrawals	-56,779.28
Transaction costs, loads and fees	-14,946.69
Net adjustments	-83,089.22
Margin interest paid	-370.29
Transfers between Fidelity accounts	323,213.18
Change in investment value	113,845.90
Change in debit balance	240,179.07
Ending market value as of Dec 31	919,129.30
Debit balance	-240,179.07
Ending Net Value	**$678,950.23**

Your commission schedule

	Gold Circle
Minimal annual trade requirement	240
Eligible trades from Jan 2000 - Dec 2000	589

2000 Annual Summary

2000 Investment Report

January 1, 2000 - December 31, 2000

WILLIAM N MATSON - INDIVIDUAL

Ultra Service Account

Holdings (Symbol as of 12/31)	% of Holdings	Income Earned	Quantity	Price per Unit	Total Cost Basis	Total Value
M AMERICA FIRST APT INV L P BEN UNIT CTF (APRCZ)	2%	0.00	2,000.00000	9.5000	19,294.85	19,000.00
M AMERICAN VANGUARD CP (AVD)	1%	0.00	500.00000	12.5630	4,232.75	6,281.50
M AMTECH SYSTEMS INC (ASYS)	2%	0.00	2,000.00000	8.0000	17,207.50	16,000.00
M APPLE COMPUTER INC NFS LLC IS A MARKET MAKER IN THIS SECURITY (AAPL)	2%	0.00	1,000.00000	14.8750	14,451.50	14,875.00
M APPLIED INDUSTRIAL TECH (AIT)	2%	120.00	1,000.00000	20.5630	16,576.50	20,563.00
M ASTRONICS CORP (ATRO)	3%	0.00	2,000.00000	12.0000	19,352.45	24,000.00
M ASTRONICS CORP CL B (NON TRANSFERABLE) (ATROB)	0%	0.00	200.00000	10.0000		2,000.00
M AVERT INC (AVRT)	2%	0.00	1,500.00000	13.2500	17,260.75	19,875.00
M BARNWELL INDUSTRIES INC (BRN)	0%	20.00	200.00000	20.7500	3,564.00	4,150.00
M BEAZER HOMES USA INC (BZH)	2%	0.00	500.00000	40.0000	15,076.50	20,000.00
M BOB EVANS FARMS INC (BOBE)	1%	45.00	500.00000	21.3130	9,319.69	10,656.50
M CIRCUIT CITY STORES INC CARMAX GROUP (KMX)	3%	0.00	6,000.00000	3.9380	24,001.50	23,629.00
M COHESANT TECHNOLOGIES INC (COHT)	1%	0.00	4,100.00000	2.3750	10,317.45	9,737.50
M COMTECH TELECOMMUNICATIONS CORP COM NEW (CMTL)	1%	0.00	500.00000	15.5630	6,014.00	7,781.50
M CROWN GROUP INC (CNGR)	1%	0.00	2,000.00000	4.4380	9,020.00	8,976.00
M ECOLOGY & ENVIRONMENT INC CL A (EEI)	1%	0.00	1,000.00000	5.7500	5,951.50	5,750.00
M ESTERLINE TECH CORP (ESL)	1%	0.00	500.00000	26.2500	10,899.00	13,125.00
M EVERLAST WORLDWIDE INC COM (EVST)	1%	0.00	7,000.00000	1.9060	14,703.02	13,342.00
M FFP MARKETING CO INC (FMM)	0%	0.00	1,000.00000	3.3750	3,514.00	3,375.00
M FRISCHS RESTAURANTS (FRS)	3%	0.00	1,900.00000	15.0000	20,597.70	28,500.00
M GENERAL BEARING CORP (GNRL)	1%	0.00	1,000.00000	5.1250	5,514.00	5,125.00
M GREATER COMMUNITY BANCORP (GFLS)	2%	236.26	1,575.00000	9.0000		14,175.00
M HARVEY ELECTRONICS INC (HRVE)	1%	0.00	7,000.00000	0.9380	6,333.00	6,566.00
M HIGH PLAINS CORP (HIPC)	2%	0.00	6,000.00000	3.1250	14,305.75	19,750.00

2000 Annual Summary

2000 Investment Report

January 1, 2000 - December 31, 2000

Ultra Service Account

WILLIAM N MATSON - INDIVIDUAL

Holdings (Symbol) as of 12/31	% of Holdings	Income Earned	Quantity	Price per Unit	Total Cost Basis	Total Value
M HOVNANIAN ENTERPRISE INC CL A (HOV)	1%	0.00	1,000.00000	9.3750	9,389.00	9,375.00
M INTERPOOL INC (IPX)	2%	37.50	1,000.00000	17.0630	11,707.45	17,063.00
M LIFSCHULTZ INDS INC (LIFF)	2%	0.00	1,100.00000	14.7500		16,225.00
M MAGELLAN PETE CORP (MPET)	0%	0.00	3,000.00000	0.9690	2,467.50	2,907.00
M MARINEMAX INC (HZO)	3%	0.00	4,000.00000	5.8750	22,610.50	23,500.00
M MAX & ERMAS RESTRNTS (MAXE)	1%	0.00	1,300.00000	8.7500	11,391.45	11,375.00
M MEDIA ARTS GROUP INC (MDA)	2%	0.00	5,000.00000	4.3130	22,062.00	21,565.00
M MET PRO CORP (MPR)	2%	0.00	2,000.00000	10.3000	20,938.00	20,600.00
M NATIONAL HOME HEALTH CARE CORP (NHHC)	2%	0.00	4,000.00000	5.2190	22,213.64	20,876.00
M NEOGEN CORP (NEOG)	3%	0.00	3,000.00000	9.1250	22,385.75	24,375.00
M NITCHES INC (NICH)	1%	0.00	1,000.00000	5.6880	5,576.50	5,688.00
M OHIO CASUALTY CORP (OCAS)	1%	120.00	1,000.00000	10.0000	8,514.00	10,000.00
M OUTLOOK GRAPHICS CRP (OUTL)	3%	0.00	4,000.00000	5.8750	23,790.00	23,500.00
M RESEARCH INC NEW (RESR)	1%	0.00	1,700.00000	3.5000	6,840.50	5,950.00
M REX STORES CORP (RSC)	2%	0.00	1,000.00000	16.6250	16,371.75	16,625.00
M RICKS CABARET INTL INC (RICK)	0%	0.00	3,000.00000	1.1250	4,905.00	3,375.00
M RIVIANA FOODS INC (RVFD)	1%	0.00	300.00000	19.6250	5,095.25	5,887.50
M ROCKY MTN CHOCOLATE FACTORY INC NEW COM PAR $0.03 (RMCF)	0%	0.00	1,100.00000	3.4390	4,414.00	3,781.80
M ROTTLUND CO (RH)	2%	0.00	3,000.00000	5.5000	17,280.00	16,500.00
M STV GROUP INC FRMLY STV ENGINEERS INC (STV)	1%	0.00	2,000.00000	6.6250	15,908.95	13,250.00
M SAPPI LTD SA REPSRTG 10 ORD (SPP)	2%	0.00	2,000.00000	7.1250	12,770.00	14,250.00
M SINGING MACHINE CO INC (SING)	2%	0.00	4,000.00000	3.7500	13,489.20	15,000.00
M SMITHFIELD FOODS INC (SFD)	3%	0.00	1,000.00000	30.4000	27,014.00	30,400.00
M SPORT CHALET INC (SPCH)	1%	0.00	2,100.00000	5.2500	13,548.25	11,025.00
M STANDARD COMMERCIAL CORPORATION (STW)	1%	25.00	2,000.00000	6.8130	10,706.51	13,626.00
M STRATUS SVCS GROUP INC (SERV)	1%	0.00	1,000.00000	4.7500	4,014.00	4,750.00

2000 Annual Summary

Ultra Service Account

2000 Investment Report

January 1, 2000 - December 31, 2000

WILLIAM N MATSON - INDIVIDUAL

Holdings (Symbol) as of 12/31	% of Holdings	Income Earned	Quantity	Price per Unit	Total Cost Basis	Total Value
M TEKTRONIX INC (TEK)	2%	0.00	500.00000	33.6890	14,045.25	16,844.00
M TRIO TECHNOLOGY INTERNATIONAL (TRT)	1%	0.00	2,000.00000	3.1250	6,403.00	6,250.00
M VICCORP RESTAURANTS INC (VRES)	2%	0.00	1,000.00000	17.7500	17,514.00	17,750.00
M WILLIAMS INDS INC (WMSI)	2%	0.00	7,300.00000	2.7500	19,699.75	20,075.00
Other						
M CHELSEA GCA RLTY INC (CCG)	2%	375.00	500.00000	36.8750		18,437.50
M IRT PPTY CO (IRT)	3%	0.00	3,000.00000	8.1250	24,284.00	24,375.00
M MID-ATLANTIC RLTY TR SH BEN INT (MRR)	2%	222.50	1,500.00000	12.1880	17,653.00	18,282.00
M ROBERTS REALTY INVESTORS INC (RPI)	1%	110.00	1,000.00000	7.8750	7,639.95	7,875.00

Total Market Value as of December 31, 2000 $919,129.30

Total income earned on positions no longer held   5,933.99

2000 Income Earned   **$7,845.25**

Debit balance   -240,179.07

Total Net Value   **$678,950.23**

M - Position held in margin account

Investment Report

January 1, 2001 - January 31, 2001

Online		Fidelity.com
FAST(sm)-Automated Telephone		800-544-5555
Customer Service		800-544-6666

WILLIAM NICHOLAS MATSON

WILLIAM N MATSON - INDIVIDUAL

Ultra Service Account

Account Summary

Beginning market value as of Jan 1	$919,129.30
Withdrawals	-19,000.00
Transaction costs, loads and fees	-2,517.57
Margin interest paid	-1,811.77
Change in investment value	129,715.33
Change in debit balance	63,425.31
Ending market value as of Jan 31	1,088,940.60
Debit balance	-303,604.38
Ending Net Value	**$785,336.22**

Your commission schedule

	Gold Circle
Minimal annual trade requirement	240
Eligible trades from Feb 2000 - Jan 2001	729
Current rate on debit balance	8.30%
Additional amount you can borrow	$16,060.63

Income Summary

	This Period	Year to Date
Taxable		
Dividends	$602.50	$602.50
Return of capital	450.00	450.00
Total	**$1,052.50**	**$1,052.50**

Realized Gain/Loss from Sales

	This Period	Year to Date
Short-term gain	$54,693.37	$54,693.37
Short-term loss	-20,472.95	-20,472.95
St disallowed loss	12,845.40	12,845.40
Net short	**$47,065.82**	**$47,065.82**

This may not reflect all of your gains/losses because of incomplete cost basis.

February 2001

Investment Report

February 1, 2001 - February 28, 2001

Online	Fidelity.com
FAST(sm)-Automated Telephone	800-544-5555
Customer Service	800-544-6666

WILLIAM NICHOLAS MATSON

WILLIAM N MATSON - INDIVIDUAL

Ultra Service Account

Account Summary

Beginning market value as of Feb 1	$1,088,940.60
Withdrawals	-20,000.00
Transaction costs, loads and fees	-4,855.48
Margin interest paid	-2,207.43
Change in investment value	-33,581.10
Change in debit balance	-12,892.29
Ending market value as of Feb 28	1,015,404.30
Debit balance	-290,712.09
Ending Net Value	**$724,692.21**

Your commission schedule	Gold Circle
Minimal annual trade requirement	240
Eligible trades from Mar 2000 - Feb 2001	1,019
Current rate on debit balance	7.80%
Additional amount you can borrow	$3,589.04

Income Summary

	This Period	Year to Date
Taxable		
Dividends	$2,010.00	$2,612.50
Return of capital	0.00	450.00
Total	$2,010.00	$3,062.50

Realized Gain/Loss from Sales

	This Period	Year to Date
Short-term gain	$117,008.29	$171,701.66
Short-term loss	-83,521.26	-103,994.21
St disallowed loss	47,949.70	61,113.44
Net short	$81,436.73	$128,820.89

This may not reflect all of your gains/losses because of incomplete cost basis.

Investment Report

March 1, 2001 - March 31, 2001

Online — Fidelity.com
FAST(sm)-Automated Telephone — 800-544-5555
Customer Service — 800-544-6666

WILLIAM NICHOLAS MATSON

WILLIAM N MATSON - INDIVIDUAL

Ultra Service Account

Account Summary

Beginning market value as of Mar 1	$1,015,404.30
Transaction costs, loads and fees	-3,206.67
Margin interest paid	-1,510.77
Change in investment value	41,393.30
Change in debit balance	-17,060.46
Ending market value as of Mar 31	1,035,019.70
Debit balance	-273,651.63
Ending Net Value	$761,368.07

Your commission schedule

	Gold Circle
Minimal annual trade requirement	240
Eligible trades from Apr 2000 - Mar 2001	1,202
Current rate on debit balance	7.30%
Additional amount you can borrow	$54,473.04

Income Summary

	This Period	Year to Date
Taxable		
Dividends	$0.00	$2,612.50
Return of capital	0.00	450.00
Total	$0.00	$3,062.50

Realized Gain/Loss from Sales

	This Period	Year to Date
Short-term gain	$42,671.33	$214,372.99
Short-term loss	-79,084.05	-183,078.26
St disallowed loss	77,908.63	145,160.69
Net short	$41,495.91	$176,455.42

This may not reflect all of your gains/losses because of incomplete cost basis.

Investment Report

April 1, 2001 - April 30, 2001

Online
FAST(sm)-Automated Telephone
Premium Services Team 76
8am - 8pm ET, Mon - Fri

Fidelity.com
800-544-5555
800-544-4442

WILLIAM NICHOLAS MATSON

WILLIAM N MATSON - INDIVIDUAL

Ultra Service Account

Account Summary

Beginning market value as of Apr 1	$1,035,019.70
Withdrawals	-10,000.00
Transaction costs, loads and fees	-3,328.17
Margin interest paid	-1,597.33
Change in investment value	94,685.57
Change in debit balance	-117,597.72
Ending market value as of Apr 30	997,182.05
Debit balance	-156,053.91
Ending Net Value	**$841,128.14**

Your commission schedule   Gold Circle

Minimal annual trade requirement	240
Eligible trades from May 2000 - Apr 2001	1,415
Current rate on debit balance	6.80%
Additional amount you can borrow	$34,534.36

Income Summary

	This Period	Year to Date
Taxable		
Dividends	$111.00	$2,723.50
Return of capital	0.00	450.00
Total	$111.00	$3,173.50

Realized Gain/Loss from Sales

	This Period	Year to Date
Short-term gain	$57,995.67	$272,368.66
Short-term loss	-99,202.84	-282,281.10
St disallowed loss	78,726.46	224,087.84
Net short	$37,519.29	$214,175.40

This may not reflect all of your gains/losses because of incomplete cost basis.

WILLIAM NICHOLAS MATSON

Investment Report

May 1, 2001 - May 31, 2001

Online
FAST(sm)-Automated Telephone
Premium Services Team 76
8am - 8pm ET, Mon - Fri

Fidelity.com
800-544-5555
800-544-4442

WILLIAM N MATSON - INDIVIDUAL

Ultra Service Account

Account Summary

Beginning market value as of May 1	$997,192.05
Withdrawals	-10,000.00
Transaction costs, loads and fees	-3,417.78
Margin interest paid	-1,018.27
Change in investment value	115,033.76
Change in debit balance	62,485.54
Ending market value as of May 31	1,158,255.30
Debit balance	-218,539.45
Ending Net Value	**$939,725.85**

Your commission schedule	Gold Circle
Minimal annual trade requirement	240
Eligible trades from Jun 2000 - May 2001	1,605
Current rate on debit balance	6.30%
Additional amount you can borrow	$36,302.30

Income Summary

	This Period	Year to Date
Taxable		
Dividends	$1,652.00	$4,375.50
Return of capital	0.00	450.00
Total	**$1,652.00**	**$4,825.50**

Realized Gain/Loss from Sales

	This Period	Year to Date
Short-term gain	$49,718.83	$322,087.49
Short-term loss	-81,543.17	-363,824.27
St disallowed loss	36,911.73	269,297.46
Net short	**$5,087.39**	**$227,560.68**

This may not reflect all of your gains/losses because of incomplete cost basis

Your Portfolio Details

Ultra Service Account

WILLIAM N MATSON - INDIVIDUAL

Account Summary

Beginning market value as of Jun 1	$1,158,265.30
Withdrawals	-53,693.00
Transaction costs, loads and fees	-3,559.05
Margin interest paid	-656.61
Change in investment value	18,515.93
Change in debit balance	-23,241.12
Ending market value as of Jun 30	1,095,631.45
Debit balance	-195,298.33
Ending Net Value	**$900,333.12**

Your commission schedule

	Gold Circle
Minimal annual trade requirement	240
Eligible trades from Jul 2000 - Jun 2001	1,793
Current rate on debit balance	5.00%
Additional amount you can borrow	$38,400.96

Income Summary

	This Period	Year to Date
Taxable		
Dividends	$665.00	$5,040.50
Return of capital	0.00	450.00
Total	**$665.00**	**$5,490.50**

Investment Report

June 1, 2001 - June 30, 2001

Realized Gain/Loss from Sales

	This Period	Year to Date
Short-term gain	$30,806.02	$352,893.51
Short-term loss	-32,417.84	-396,242.11
St disallowed loss	13,878.54	292,134.73
Net short	**$12,266.72**	**$248,786.13**

This may not reflect all of your gains losses because of incomplete cost basis

WILLIAM NICHOLAS MATSON

Investment Report

July 1, 2001 - July 31, 2001

Online
FAST(sm)-Automated Telephone
Premium Services Team 76
8am - 8pm ET, Mon - Fri

Fidelity.com
800-544-5555
800-544-4442

Messages:

Enter for a chance to Win a 2001 Saab and play Chart ClimberSM (a Fidelity Investments game that tests your investment knowledge). Register by August 17, 2001 at Fidelity.com.goto.chartclimber. No purchase necessary.

Ultra Service Account   WILLIAM N MATSON - INDIVIDUAL

Due to an erroneous calculation last month, Fidelity customers were not charged for Margin interest on June 9th or June 10th. The calculation has been corrected and is reflected in your debit balance and on this month's statement.

Account Summary

Beginning market value as of Jul 1	$1,095,631.45
Additions	29.90
Withdrawals	-10,100.00
Transaction costs, loads and fees	-2,177.21
Margin interest paid	-975.20
Change in investment value	40,431.02
Change in debit balance	18,765.34
Ending market value as of Jul 31	1,141,605.30
Debit balance	-214,063.67
Ending Net Value	**$927,541.63**

Your commission schedule

	Gold Circle
Minimal annual trade requirement	240
Eligible trades from Aug 2000 - Jul 2001	1,870
Current rate on debit balance	5.00%
Additional amount you can borrow	$11,206.84

Income Summary

	This Period	Year to Date
Taxable		
Dividends	$851.50	$5,892.00
Return of capital	475.00	925.00
Total	**$1,326.50**	**$6,817.00**

Realized Gain/Loss from Sales

	This Period	Year to Date
Short-term gain	$23,749.39	$376,684.15
Short-term loss	-29,498.55	-425,740.66
St disallowed loss	10,627.97	303,247.50
Net short	**$4,878.81**	**$254,190.99**

This may not reflect all of your gains losses because of incomplete cost basis

August 2001

Investment Report

August 1, 2001 - August 31, 2001

Online   Fidelity.com
FAST(sm)-Automated Telephone   800-544-5555
Premium Services Team 76   800-544-4442
8am - 8pm ET, Mon - Fri

WILLIAM NICHOLAS MATSON

Messages:

ACT NOW TO AVOID THE FIDELITY FUNDS ANNUAL MAINTENANCE FEE FOR SMALL BALANCES. SEE LAST PAGE OF STATEMENT FOR DETAILS.

Ultra Service Account

WILLIAM N MATSON - INDIVIDUAL

Account Summary

Beginning market value as of Aug 1	$1,141,605.30
Withdrawals	-3,000.00
Transaction costs, loads and fees	-967.50
Margin interest paid	-878.16
Change in investment value	-9,052.52
Change in debit balance	-16,600.37
Ending market value as of Aug 31	1,111,106.75
Debit balance	-197,463.30
Ending Net Value	**$913,643.45**

Your commission schedule

	Gold Circle
Minimal annual trade requirement	240
Eligible trades from Sep 2000 - Aug 2001	1,841
Current rate on debit balance	5.00%
Additional amount you can borrow	$3,231.07

Income Summary

	This Period	Year to Date
Taxable		
Dividends	$454.33	$6,346.33
Return of capital	0.00	925.00
Total	**$454.33**	**$7,271.33**

Realized Gain/Loss from Sales

	This Period	Year to Date
Short-term gain	$5,295.83	$391,979.98
Short-term loss	-1,998.06	-427,638.72
St disallowed loss	1,233.69	304,635.88
Net short	**$4,631.46**	**$258,977.14**

This may not reflect all of your gains/losses because of incomplete cost basis.

WILLIAM NICHOLAS MATSON

Investment Report

September 1, 2001 - September 30, 2001

Online
FAST(sm)-Automated Telephone
Premium Services Team 76
8am - 8pm ET, Mon - Fri

Fidelity.com
800-544-5555
800-544-4442

Ultra Service Account

WILLIAM N MATSON - INDIVIDUAL

Account Summary

Beginning market value as of Sep 1	$1,111,106.75
Additions	3,000.00
Withdrawals	-11,000.00
Transaction costs, loads and fees	-3,739.73
Margin interest paid	-810.04
Change in investment value	-38,299.95
Change in debit balance	-62,091.68
Ending market value as of Sep 30	998,165.45
Debit balance	-135,371.62
Ending Net Value	**$862,793.83**
Your commission schedule	Gold
Account eligible trades from Oct 2000 - Sep 2001	1,982
Current rate on debit balance	4.75%
Additional amount you can borrow	$66,477.59

Income Summary

	This Period	Year to Date
Taxable		
Dividends	$735.00	$7,081.33
Return of capital	0.00	925.00
Total	**$735.00**	**$8,006.33**

Realized Gain/Loss from Sales

	This Period	Year to Date
Short-term gain	$14,106.41	$396,036.39
Short-term loss	-99,301.70	-516,940.42
St disallowed loss	18,741.93	323,377.81
Net short	**-$56,453.36**	**$202,523.78**

This may not reflect all of your gains losses because of incomplete cost basis

Investment Report

October 1, 2001 - October 31, 2001

Online — Fidelity.com
FAST(sm)-Automated Telephone — 800-544-5555
Premium Services Team 76 — 800-544-4442
  8am - 8pm ET, Mon - Fri
Participant Stock Services — 800-544-9534
  9:00 am - 12:00 am EST, Mon - Fri.

WILLIAM NICHOLAS MATSON

WILLIAM N MATSON - INDIVIDUAL

Ultra Service Account

Account Summary

Beginning market value as of Oct 1	$998,165.45
Withdrawals	-8,000.00
Transaction costs, loads and fees	-5,664.45
Margin interest paid	-749.46
Change in investment value	138,172.37
Change in debit balance	47,175.87
Ending market value as of Oct 31	1,169,100.78
Debit balance	-182,547.49
Ending Net Value	**$986,553.29**
Your commission schedule	Gold
Account eligible trades from Nov 2000 - Oct 2001	2,207

Income Summary

	This Period	Year to Date
Taxable		
Dividends	$1,016.35	$8,097.68
Return of capital	0.00	925.00
Total	**$1,016.35**	**$9,022.68**

Realized Gain/Loss from Sales

	This Period	Year to Date
Short-term gain	$40,889.62	$436,976.01
Short-term loss	-42,308.99	-559,249.41
St disallowed loss	15,112.97	342,143.16
Net short	**$13,693.60**	**$219,869.76**

This may not reflect all of your gains/losses because of incomplete cost basis

Investment Report

November 1, 2001 - November 30, 2001

Online   Fidelity.com
FAST(sm)-Automated Telephone   800-544-5555
Premium Services Team 76   800-544-4442
8am - 9pm ET, Mon - Fri

WILLIAM NICHOLAS MATSON

WILLIAM N MATSON - INDIVIDUAL

Ultra Service Account

Account Summary

Beginning market value as of Nov 1	$1,169,100.78
Withdrawals	-10,000.00
Transaction costs, loads and fees	-6,102.98
Margin interest paid	-829.53
Change in investment value	125,318.95
Change in debit balance	102,649.32
Ending market value as of No. 30	1,380,136.54
Debit balance	-285,196.81
Ending Net Value	**$1,094,939.73**
Your commission schedule	Gold
Account eligible trades from Dec 2000 - Nov 2001	2,415
Current rate on debit balance	3.87%
Additional amount you can borrow	$29,419.97

Income Summary

	This Period	Year to Date
Taxable		
Dividends	$759.00	$8,856.68
Return of capital	0.00	925.00
Total	**$759.00**	**$9,781.68**

Realized Gain/Loss from Sales

	This Period	Year to Date
Short-term gain	$92,862.01	$529,838.02
Short-term loss	-63,766.46	-623,015.87
St disallowed loss	35,974.83	385,551.88
Net short	**$65,070.38**	**$292,374.03**

This may not reflect all of your gains/losses because of incomplete cost basis.

December 2001

Investment Report

December 1, 2001 - December 31, 2001

Online
FAST(sm)-Automated Telephone
Premium Services Team 76
8am - 8pm ET, Mon - Fri

Fidelity.com
900-544-5555
800-544-4442

WILLIAM NICHOLAS MATSON

WILLIAM N MATSON - INDIVIDUAL

Ultra Service Account

Account Summary

Beginning market value as of Dec 1	$1,380,136.54
Withdrawals	-10,000.00
Transaction costs, loads and fees	-4,277.76
Margin interest paid	-1,267.38
Change in investment value	92,100.55
Change in debit balance	149,227.50
Ending market value as of Dec 31	1,605,919.45
Debit balance	-434,424.31
Ending Net Value	**$1,171,495.14**
Your commission schedule	Gold
Account eligible trades from Jan 2001 - Dec 2001	2,512
Current rate on debit balance	3.87%
Additional amount you can borrow	$12,990.64

Income Summary

	This Period	Year to Date
Taxable		
Dividends	$543.00	$9,399.68
Return of capital	0.00	925.00
Total	**$543.00**	**$10,324.68**

Realized Gain/Loss from Sales

	This Period	Year to Date
Short-term gain	$20,975.89	$550,813.91
Short-term loss	-84,432.74	-707,448.61
St disallowed loss	52,978.27	439,972.42
Net short	**-$10,478.58**	**$283,337.72**
Long-term gain	$1,743.31	$1,743.31

This may not reflect all of your gains/losses because of incomplete cost basis.

WILLIAM NICHOLAS MATSON

2001 Investment Report

January 1, 2001 - December 31, 2001

Online — Fidelity.com
FAST(sm)-Automated Telephone — 800-544-5555
Premium Services Team 76 — 800-544-4442
8am - 8pm ET, Mon - Fri

Your 2001 Investment Report summarizes activity in your Fidelity account for the past year. To assist you in tax preparation. **COST BASIS** information is located in the section entitled *Realized Gain-Loss and Cost Basis Information from Sales*. You will receive your **Forms 1099** under separate cover.

WILLIAM N MATSON - INDIVIDUAL

Ultra Service Account

2001 Account Summary

Beginning market value as of Jan 1	$919,129.30
Additions	3,029.90
Withdrawals	-164,793.00
Transaction costs, loads and fees	-43,814.35
Margin interest paid	-14,310.95
Change in investment value	712,433.31
Change in debit balance	194,245.24
Ending market value as of Dec 31	1,605,919.45
Debit balance	434,424.31
Ending Net Value	**$1,171,495.14**

Your commission schedule — Gold
Account eligible trades from Jan 2001 - Dec 2001 — 2,512

Income Summary

Taxable		
Ordinary Dividends		
Dividends		$9,399.68

Realized Gain/Loss from Sales

Short-term gain	$550,813.91
Short-term loss	-707,448.61
St disallowed loss	440,276.06
Net short	**$283,641.36**
Long-term gain	$1,743.31

This may not reflect all of your gains/losses because of incomplete cost basis.

Ultra Service Account

2001 Investment Report

January 1, 2001 — December 31, 2001

WILLIAM N MATSON - INDIVIDUAL

Stocks

Holdings (Symbol as of 12/31)	% of Holdings	Income Earned	Quantity	Price per Unit	Total Cost Basis	Total Value
M NOVEL DENIM HLDG LTD ISIN #USG6674P1098 (NVLD)	3%	$0.00	4,600.00000	$11.7000	$43,060.49	$53,820.00
M CARLISLE HOLDINGS LIMITED NEW ISIN #BZP212771018 (CLHL)	0%	0.00	3,000.00000	2.2000	5,978.00	6,600.00
M AOL TIME WARNER INC (AOL)	1%	0.00	500.00000	32.1000	16,139.00	16,050.00
M ACTION PRODS INTL INC (APII)	0%	0.00	1,500.00000	0.8900	1,099.00	1,335.00
M ADAMS RES & ENERGY INC COM NEW (AE)	0%	0.00	500.00000	7.8000	3,264.00	3,900.00
M ALMOST FAMILY INC (AFAM)	2%	0.00	2,000.00000	15.1300	24,424.00	30,260.00
M AMAZON.COM INC (AMZN)	1%	0.00	1,500.00000	10.8200	16,522.00	16,230.00
M AMCAST INDL CORP (AIZ)	0%	0.00	1,000.00000	5.3800	5,064.00	5,380.00
M AMERICAN MED TECHNOLOGIES INC (ADLI)	0%	0.00	2,500.00000	1.3300	1,398.00	3,325.00
M AMTECH SYSTEMS INC (ASYS)	3%	0.00	6,000.00000	7.1600	36,738.46	42,960.00
M APPLIANCE RECYCLING CTRS AMER INC (ARCI)	2%	0.00	6,400.00000	3.8500	22,119.20	24,640.00
M ASTRONICS CORP CL B (NON TRANSFERABLE) (ATROB)	1%	0.00	750.00000	11.1000		8,325.00
M AVALON CORRECTIONAL SVCS INC COM (CITY)	0%	0.00	300.00000	1.9900	606.67	597.00
M BACK YD BURGERS INC (BYB!)	8%	0.00	32,273.00000	3.9800	66,522.56	128,446.54
M CIRCUIT CITY STORES INC CARMAX GROUP (KMX)	2%	0.00	1,500.00000	22.7400	22,205.33	34,110.00
M COHESANT TECHNOLOGIES INC (COHT)	7%	0.00	27,353.00000	.4300	68,933.32	119,767.90
M COMMUNITY FINL GRP INC (CFGI)	4%	2,108.00	3,700.00000	15.2500	48,468.70	56,425.00
M CONOLOG CORP COM PAR $.01 (CNLG)	0%	0.00	1,500.00000	0.5900	934.00	885.00
M DEWEY ELECTRS CORP (DEWY)	3%	0.00	12,231.00000	4.0500	47,583.96	49,535.55
M DIXON TICONDEROGA CO (DXT)	0%	0.00	2,500.00000	1.5000	3,813.00	3,750.00
M DOCUCORP INTL INC (DOCC)	4%	0.00	10,500.00000	6.2000	55,813.44	65,100.00
M DYNEGY INC HLDG CO (DYN)	1%	0.00	500.00000	25.5000	11,624.00	12,750.00

2001 Investment Report

January 1, 2001 - December 31, 2001

Ultra Service Account

WILLIAM N MATSON - INDIVIDUAL

Holdings (Symbol) as of 12-31	% of Holdings	Income Earned	Quantity	Price per Unit	Total Cost Basis	Total Value
M ELXSI CORP COM NEW (ELXS)	0%	0.00	236.00000	7.6200	1,477.20	1,798.32
M E M C CORP MASS (EMC)	1%	0.00	1,500.00000	13.4400	20,299.00	20,160.00
M EBAY INC (EBAY)	1%	0.00	300.00000	66.9000	19,769.00	20,070.00
M EDISON CTL CORP (EDCO)	2%	0.00	4,600.00000	7.0000	19,458.00	32,200.00
M EQUITY OIL CO (EQTY)	0%	0.00	1,500.00000	1.8000	2,844.00	2,700.00
M EVERLAST WORLDWIDE INC COM (EVST)	0%	0.00	1,000.00000	2.3500	2,284.00	2,350.00
M FIBERMARK INC (FMK)	1%	0.00	2,000.00000	5.7200	9,253.00	11,440.00
M FIRETECTOR INC NEW (FTEC)	1%	0.00	12,066.00000	1.5200	18,602.04	18,340.32
M FOODARAMA SUPERMARKETS (FSM)	3%	0.00	1,200.00000	40.5000	31,795.00	48,600.00
M GP STRATEGIES CORP (GPX)	0%	0.00	1,000.00000	3.8000	3,364.00	3,800.00
M GREATER COMMUNITY BANCORP (GFLS)	1%	885.66	1,300.00000	11.7500	15,335.40	15,275.00
M HIRSCH INTERNATIONAL CORP CL A (HRSH)	0%	0.00	3,000.00000	0.4600	1,343.00	1,330.00
M HURCO CO FRMLY HURCO MFG INC 3-14-1985 (HURC)	0%	0.00	2,500.00000	2.2000	5,307.70	5,500.00
M IFR SYS INC (IFRS)	0%	0.00	1,500.00000	1.2500	859.00	1,875.00
M INTEGRATED ELECTRICAL S VCS INC (IEE)	0%	0.00	1,500.00000	5.1200	6,224.00	7,680.00
M INTEGRITY INC CL A N C FROM 45813H104 (ITGR)	2%	0.00	5,600.00000	6.3000	23,545.13	35,280.00
M JLM COUTURE INC (JLMC)	1%	0.00	5,900.00000	2.1700	11,236.23	12,803.00
M MPW INDUSTRIAL SERVICES GROUP INC (MPWG)	2%	0.00	10,500.00000	2.3000	12,007.60	24,150.00
M MARINE PRODUCTS CORP (MPX)	6%	1,200.00	20,000.00000	4.4500	59,172.00	89,000.00
M MINUTEMAN INTL INC (MMAN)	1%	0.00	1,000.00000	8.4600	8,578.00	8,460.00
M NATIONAL HOME HEALTH CARE CORP (NHHC)	4%	0.00	5,700.00000	12.4500	33,616.66	70,965.00
M OPTA FOODS INGREDIENTS INC (OPTS)	0%	0.00	1,000.00000	1.0200	1,034.00	1,020.00
M POLYMER SOLUTIONS INC (PYSU)	0%	0.00	13,833.00000	0.2570	4,387.22	3,555.08
M R & B INC (RBIN)	4%	0.00	8,700.00000	6.9500	40,454.06	60,465.00
M RAVEN INDS INC (RAVN)	5%	868.00	3,200.00000	23.1500	47,424.08	74,080.00

2001 Investment Report

January 1, 2001 - December 31, 2001

Ultra Service Account

WILLIAM N MATSON - INDIVIDUAL

Holdings (Symbol) as of 12/31	% of Holdings	Income Earned	Quantity	Price per Unit	Total Cost Basis	Total Value
M REX STORES CORP (RSC)	4%	0.00	2,500.00000	28.0200	51,000.00	70,050.00
M RICKS CABARET INTL INC (RICK)	3%	0.00	13,604.00000	3.0600	37,146.49	41,628.24
M ROCKY MTN CHOCOLATE FACTORY INC NEW COM PAR $0.03 (RMCF)	1%	0.00	1,450.00000	14.2500	12,677.00	20,662.50
M SHILOH INDS INC (SHLO)	0%	0.00	1,500.00000	1.9000	2,567.75	2,850.00
M STEARNS & LEHMAN INC (SLHN)	1%	0.00	1,500.00000	6.0100	5,414.80	9,015.00
M SUN MICROSYSTEMS INC (SUNW)	1%	0.00	900.00000	12.3000	10,930.10	11,070.00
M SUPREME INDS INC CL A (STS)	1%	0.00	3,000.00000	4.2000	12,368.00	12,600.00
M TRANS-LUX CORP (TLX)	2%	35.00	4,500.00000	5.7500	26,768.76	25,875.00
M VILLAGE SUPERMKT INC CL A NEW (VLGEA)	2%	0.00	1,000.00000	24.7400	24,226.00	24,740.00
M WESTERBEKE CORP (WTBK)	0%	0.00	1,000.00000	1.5500	1,474.00	1,550.00
M WILLIAMS INDS INC (WMSI)	5%	0.00	15,500.00000	4.8000	63,273.50	74,400.00
M WORLD FUEL SERVICES CORP (INT)	2%	0.00	2,000.00000	18.3000	30,937.00	36,600.00
M YAHOO INC (YHOO)	1%	0.00	1,000.00000	17.7400	18,038.75	17,740.00

Total Market Value as of December 31, 2001 $1,605,919.45

Total income earned on positions no longer held   4,303.02

2001 Income Earned $ 9,399.68

Debit balance   -434,424.31

Total Net Value $1,171,495.14

M - Position held in margin account.

WILLIAM NICHOLAS MATSON

Investment Report

January 1, 2002 - January 31, 2002

Online — Fidelity.com
FAST(sm)-Automated Telephone — 800-544-5555
Premium Services Team 76 — 800-544-4442
9am - 8pm ET, Mon - Fri

WILLIAM N MATSON - INDIVIDUAL

Ultra Service Account

Account Summary

Beginning market value as of Jan 1	$1,605,919.45
Withdrawals	-20,000.00
Transaction costs loads and fees	-6,318.53
Margin interest paid	-1,047.05
Change in investment value	129,353.70
Change in debit balance	-93,311.20
Ending market value as of Jan 31	1,614,596.37
Debit balance	-341,113.11
Ending Net Value	**$1,273,483.26**
Your commission schedule	Gold
Account eligible trades from Feb 2001 - Jan 2002	2,778
Current rate on debit balance	3.87%
Additional amount you can borrow	$160,482.99

Income Summary

	This Period	Year to Date
Taxable		
Dividends	$1,068.50	$1,068.50

Realized Gain/Loss from Sales

	This Period	Year to Date
Short-term gain	$222,437.07	$222,437.07
Short-term loss	-66,255.94	-66,255.94
St disallowed loss	25,446.44	25,446.44
Net short	**$181,627.57**	**$181,627.57**
Long-term gain	$28,642.82	$28,642.82

This may not reflect all of your gains losses because of incomplete cost basis.

Investment Report

February 1, 2002 - February 28, 2002

Online
FAST(sm)-Automated Telephone
Premium Services Team 76
9am - 8pm ET, Mon - Fri

Fidelity.com
800-544-5555
800-544-4442

WILLIAM NICHOLAS MATSON

WILLIAM N MATSON - INDIVIDUAL

Ultra Service Account

Account Summary

Beginning market value as of Feb 1	$1,614,596.37
Withdrawals	-13,000.00
Transaction costs, loads and fees	-2,002.61
Margin interest paid	-1,227.59
Change in investment value	13,594.03
Change in debit balance	285,844.82
Ending market value as of Feb 28	1,897,805.02
Debit balance	-630,957.93
Ending Net Value	**$1,266,847.09**
Your commission schedule	Gold
Account eligible trades from Mar 2001 - Feb 2002	2,809
Current rate on debit balance	3.87%
Additional amount you can borrow	$46,154.06

Income Summary

	This Period	Year to Date
Taxable		
Dividends	$434.00	$1,502.50
Return of capital	312.50	312.50
Total	$746.50	$1,815.00

Realized Gain/Loss from Sales

	This Period	Year to Date
Short-term gain	$27,965.68	$250,402.75
Short-term loss	-50,061.53	-116,311.27
St disallowed loss	19,600.71	46,013.16
Net short	-$2,494.94	$180,098.64
Long-term gain	$2,350.77	$31,493.59

This may not reflect all of your gains/losses because of incomplete cost basis

Investment Report

March 1, 2002 - March 31, 2002

Online   Fidelity.com
FAST(sm) Automated Telephone   800-544-5555
Premium Services Team 76   800-544-4442
9am - 3pm ET, Mon - Fri

WILLIAM NICHOLAS MATSON

WILLIAM N MATSON - INDIVIDUAL

Ultra Service Account

Account Summary

Beginning market value as of Mar 1	$1,897,805.02
Withdrawals	-16,000.00
Transaction costs, loads and fees	-4,667.24
Margin interest paid	-2,170.55
Change in investment value	192,136.26
Change in debit balance	226,723.69
Ending market value as of Mar 31	2,293,827.19
Debit balance	-857,681.61
Ending Net Value	**$1,436,145.58**
Your commission schedule	Gold
Account eligible trades from Apr 2001 - Mar 2002	2,921
Current rate on debit balance	3.87%
Additional amount you can borrow	$124,462.63

Income Summary

	This Period	Year to Date
Taxable		
Dividends	$1,527.00	$3,029.50
Return of capital	0.00	312.50
Total	**$1,527.00**	**$3,342.00**

Realized Gain/Loss from Sales

	This Period	Year to Date
Short-term gain	$39,676.18	$290,078.93
Short-term loss	-48,397.86	-164,715.13
St disallowed loss	28,698.40	75,506.39
Net short	**$19,976.72**	**$200,870.19**
Long-term gain	$11,728.12	$43,221.71

This may not reflect all of your gains/losses because of incomplete cost basis

April 2002

WILLIAM NICHOLAS MATSON

Investment Report

April 1, 2002 - April 30, 2002

Online
FAST(sm) - Automated Telephone
Premium Services Team 76
8am - 8pm ET, Mon - Fri

Fidelity.com
800-544-5555
800-544-4442

WILLIAM N MATSON - INDIVIDUAL

Ultra Service Account

Account Summary

Beginning market value as of Apr 1	$2,283,827.19
Withdrawals	-40,000.00
Other Tax Withheld	-16.43
Transaction costs, loads and fees	-6,437.53
Margin interest paid	-2,714.48
Change in investment value	215,296.73
Change in debit balance	47,521.36
Ending market value as of Apr 30	2,497,476.84
Debit balance	-905,202.97
Ending Net Value	**$1,592,273.87**
Your commission schedule	Gold
Account eligible trades from May 2001 - Apr 2002	3,038
Current rate on debit balance	3.87%
Additional amount you can borrow	$153,669.79

Income Summary

	This Period	Year to Date
Taxable		
Dividends	$1,415.19	$4,444.69
Return of capital	0.00	312.50
Total	**$1,415.19**	**$4,757.19**

Realized Gain/Loss from Sales

	This Period	Year to Da
Short-term gain	$58,469.40	$348,551.27
Short-term loss	-46,250.95	-208,416.57
St disallowed loss	16,323.45	89,983.69
Net short	**$28,541.90**	**$230,118.39**
Long-term gain	$142,465.53	$185,687.24
Long-term loss	-38.17	-38.17
Net long	**$142,427.36**	**$185,649.07**

This may not reflect all of your gains/losses because of incomplete cost basis.

May 2002

WILLIAM NICHOLAS MATSON

Investment Report

May 1, 2002 - May 31, 2002

Online   Fidelity.com
FAST(sm) - Automated Telephone   800-544-5555
Premium Services Team 76   800-544-4442
8am - 8pm ET, Mon - Fri

WILLIAM N MATSON - INDIVIDUAL

Ultra Service Account

Account Summary

Beginning market value as of May 1	$2,497,476.84
Withdrawals	-21,574.00
Transaction costs, loads and fees	-9,986.53
Margin interest paid	-2,632.50
Change in investment value	89,552.50
Change in debit balance	58,420.75
Ending market value as of May 31	2,611,257.06
Debit balance	-963,623.72
Ending Net Value	**$1,647,633.34**
Your commission schedule	Gold
Account eligible trades from Jun 2001 - May 2002	3,253
Current rate on debit balance	3.87%
Additional amount you can borrow	$166,552.54

Income Summary

	This Period	Year to Date
Taxable		
Dividends	$605.00	$5,049.69
Return of capital	0.00	312.50
Total	**$605.00**	**$5,362.19**

Realized Gain/Loss from Sales

	This Period	Year to Date
Short-term gain	$68,249.74	$416,801.01
Short-term loss	-87,714.47	-296,131.04
St disallowed loss	38,834.36	130,524.96
Net short	**$19,369.63**	**$251,194.93**
Long-term gain	$52,819.62	$238,506.86
Long-term loss	0.00	-38.17
Net long	**$52,819.62**	**$238,468.69**

This may not reflect all of your gains/losses because of incomplete cost basis.

June 2002

Investment Report

June 1, 2002 - June 30, 2002

Online
FAST(sm) - Automated Telephone
Premium Services Team 76
8am - 8pm ET, Mon - Fri

Fidelity.com
800-544-5555
800-544-4442

WILLIAM NICHOLAS MATSON

WILLIAM N MATSON - INDIVIDUAL

Ultra Service Account

Account Summary		
Beginning market value as of Jun 1	$2,611,257.06	
Withdrawals	-27,000.00	
Transaction costs, loads and fees	-7,540.37	
Net adjustments	14.00	
Margin interest paid	-3,090.88	
Change in investment value	115,012.61	
Change in debit balance	-17,763.30	
Ending market value as of Jun 30	2,670,889.12	
Debit balance	-945,860.42	
Ending Net Value	**$1,725,028.70**	
Your commission schedule	Gold	
Account eligible trades from Jul 2001 - Jun 2002	3,272	
Current rate on debit balance	3.87%	
Additional amount you can borrow	$63,973.61	

Income Summary	This Period	Year to Date
Taxable		
Dividends	$2,618.23	$7,667.92
Return of capital	**0.00**	**312.50**
Total	**$2,618.23**	**$7,980.42**

Realized Gain/Loss from Sales	This Period	Year to Date
Short-term gain	$99,575.71	$516,376.72
Short-term loss	-48,483.29	-343,069.45
St disallowed loss	34,490.36	165,293.70
Net short	**$85,582.78**	**$338,600.97**
Long-term gain	$21,171.39	$259,678.25
Long-term loss	0.00	-38.17
Net long	**$21,171.39**	**$259,640.08**

This may not reflect all of your gains/losses because of incomplete cost basis.

WILLIAM NICHOLAS MATSON

Investment Report

July 1, 2002 - July 31, 2002

Online
FAST(sm) - Automated Telephone
Premium Services Team 76
8am - 8pm ET, Mon - Fri

Fidelity.com
800-544-5555
800-544-4442

WILLIAM N MATSON - INDIVIDUAL

Fidelity Account

Account Summary	
Beginning market value as of Jul 1	$2,670,889.12
Withdrawals	-28,000.00
Transaction costs, loads and fees	-11,178.41
Margin interest paid	-3,346.20
Change in investment value	-169,435.70
Change in debit balance	-123,966.04
Ending market value as of Jul 31	2,334,962.77
Debit balance	-821,894.38
Ending Net Value	**$1,513,068.39**

Your commission schedule	Gold
Account eligible trades from Aug 2001 - Jul 2002	3,507
Current rate on debit balance	3.87%
Additional amount you can borrow	$59,138.06

Income Summary

	This Period	Year to Date
Taxable		
Dividends	$2,472.84	$10,140.76
Return of capital	0.00	312.50
Total	**$2,472.84**	**$10,453.26**

Realized Gain/Loss from Sales

	This Period	Year to Date
Short-term gain	$67,683.54	$584,060.26
Short-term loss	-196,809.88	-539,879.33
St disallowed loss	64,827.05	230,120.75
Net short	**-$64,299.29**	**$274,301.68**
Long-term gain	$8,262.04	$267,940.29
Long-term loss	0.00	-38.17
Net long	**$8,262.04**	**$267,902.12**

This may not reflect all of your gains/losses because of incomplete cost basis.

August 2002

Investment Report

August 1, 2002 - August 31, 2002

Online
FAST(sm)-Automated Telephone
Premium Services Team 76
8am - 8pm ET, Mon - Fri

Fidelity.com
800-544-5555
800-544-4442

WILLIAM NICHOLAS MATSON

WILLIAM N MATSON - INDIVIDUAL

Fidelity Account

Account Summary	
Beginning market value as of Aug 1	$2,334,962.77
Withdrawals	-144,000.00
Transaction costs, loads and fees	-9,225.75
Margin interest paid	-2,842.57
Change in investment value	16,599.48
Change in debit balance	102,630.56
Ending market value as of Aug 31	2,298,124.49
Debit balance	-924,524.94
Ending Net Value	**$1,373,599.55**
Your commission schedule	Gold
Account eligible trades from Sep 2001 - Aug 2002	3.895
Current rate on debit balance	3.87%
Additional amount you can borrow	$54,519.41

Income Summary	This Period	Year to Date
Taxable		
Dividends	$242.85	$10,383.61
Return of capital	**0.00**	**312.50**
Total	**$242.85**	**$10,696.11**

Realized Gain/Loss from Sales	This Period	Year to Date
Short-term gain	$27,104.69	$611,164.95
Short-term loss	-126,107.93	-665,987.26
St disallowed loss	31,835.40	264,691.35
Net short	**-$67,167.84**	**$209,869.04**
Long-term gain	$8,181.12	$276,121.41
Long-term loss	0.00	-38.17
Net long	**$8,181.12**	**$276,083.24**

This may not reflect all of your gains/losses because of incomplete cost basis.

Investment Report

September 1, 2002 - September 30, 2002

Online
FAST(sm) - Automated Telephone
Premium Services Team 76
8am - 8pm ET, Mon - Fri

Fidelity.com
800-544-5555
800-544-4442

Messages:

Fidelity has expanded its mutual fund product line to give you more choices for your investment needs.

WILLIAM NICHOLAS MATSON

Fidelity Account

WILLIAM N MATSON - INDIVIDUAL

Account Summary

Beginning market value as of Sep 1	$2,298,124.49
Withdrawals	-22,000.00
Transaction costs, loads and fees	-5,540.68
Margin interest paid	-2,986.64
Change in investment value	-114,366.49
Change in debit balance	-369,739.43
Ending market value as of Sep 30	1,783,491.25
Debit balance	-554,785.51
Ending Net Value	**$1,228,705.74**

Your commission schedule
Account eligible trades from Oct 2001 - Sep 2002

Gold
3,966

Income Summary

	This Period	Year to Date
Taxable		
Dividends	$1,209.50	$11,593.11
Return of capital	0.00	312.50
Total	**$1,209.50**	**$11,905.61**

Realized Gain/Loss from Sales

	This Period	Year to Date
Short-term gain	$16,168.26	$627,333.21
Short-term loss	-88,007.57	-753,994.83
St disallowed loss	21,512.03	287,313.07
Net short	**-$50,327.28**	**$160,651.45**
Long-term gain	$10,084.02	$286,205.43
Long-term loss	0.00	-38.17
Net long	**$10,084.02**	**$286,167.26**

This may not reflect all of your gains/losses because of incomplete cost basis.

October 2002

WILLIAM NICHOLAS MATSON

Investment Report

October 1, 2002 - October 31, 2002

Online
FAST(sm) - Automated Telephone
Premium Services Team 10
8am - 8pm ET, Mon - Fri

Fidelity.com
800-544-5555
800-544-4442

Fidelity Account

WILLIAM N MATSON - INDIVIDUAL

Account Summary

Beginning market value as of Oct 1	$1,783,491.25
Withdrawals	-20,000.00
Transaction costs, loads and fees	-7,740.99
Margin interest paid	-1,917.63
Change in investment value	7,748.77
Change in debit balance	40,104.66
Ending market value as of Oct 31	1,801,686.06
Debit balance	-594,890.17
Ending Net Value	**$1,206,795.89**
Your commission schedule	Gold
Account eligible trades from Nov 2001 - Oct 2002	4,035
Current rate on debit balance	3.87%
Additional amount you can borrow	$8,015.61

Income Summary

	This Period	Year to Date
Taxable		
Dividends	$1,989.30	$13,582.41
Return of capital	0.00	312.50
Total	**$1,989.30**	**$13,894.91**

Realized Gain/Loss from Sales

	This Period	Year to Date
Short-term gain	$24,565.26	$651,898.47
Short-term loss	-77,736.60	-831,731.43
St disallowed loss	20,512.81	311,244.96
Net short	**-$32,658.53**	**$131,412.00**
Long-term gain	$4,219.57	$290,425.00
Long-term loss		-119.22
Lt disallowed loss	81.05	81.05
Net long	**$4,219.57**	**$290,386.83**

This may not reflect all of your gains/losses because of incomplete cost basis.

WILLIAM NICHOLAS MATSON

Investment Report

November 1, 2002 - November 30, 2002

Online
FAST(sm) - Automated Telephone
Premium Services Team 10
8am - 8pm ET, Mon - Fri

Fidelity.com
800-544-5555
800-544-4442

Fidelity Account

WILLIAM N MATSON - INDIVIDUAL

Account Summary

Beginning market value as of Nov 1	$1,801,686.06
Transaction costs, loads and fees	-4,667.52
Margin interest paid	-2,154.03
Change in investment value	53.99
Change in debit balance	93,669.70
Ending market value as of Nov 30	1,888,588.20
Debit balance	-688,559.87
Ending Net Value	**$1,200,028.33**
Your commission schedule	Gold
Account eligible trades from Dec 2001 - Nov 2002	3,977
Current rate on debit balance	3.77%
Additional amount you can borrow	$52,277.14

Income Summary

	This Period	Year to Date
Taxable		
Dividends	$184.33	$13,766.74
Return of capital	0.00	312.50
Total	**$184.33**	**$14,079.24**

Realized Gain/Loss from Sales

	This Period	Year to Date
Short-term gain	$24,104.01	$676,002.48
Short-term loss	-96,337.89	-928,069.32
St disallowed loss	40,838.27	355,973.00
Net short	**-$31,395.61**	**$103,906.16**
Long-term gain	$12,881.92	$303,306.92
Long-term loss	0.00	-119.22
Lt disallowed loss	0.00	81.05
Net long	**$12,881.92**	**$303,268.75**

This may not reflect all of your gains/losses because of incomplete cost basis.

December 2002

WILLIAM NICHOLAS MATSON

Investment Report

December 1, 2002 - December 31, 2002

Online — Fidelity.com
FAST(sm)-Automated Telephone — 800-544-5555
Premium Services Team 10 — 800-544-4442
8am - 8pm ET, Mon - Fri

Fidelity Account — WILLIAM N MATSON - INDIVIDUAL

Account Summary

Beginning market value as of Dec 1	$1,888,588.20
Transaction costs, loads and fees	-3,365.42
Margin interest paid	-3,036.06
Change in investment value	-29,119.12
Change in debit balance	37,210.13
Ending market value as of Dec 31	1,890,277.73
Debit balance	-725,770.00
Ending Net Value	**$1,164,507.73**
Your commission schedule	Gold
Account eligible trades from Jan 2002 - Dec 2002	3,920

Income Summary

	This Period	Year to Date
Taxable		
Dividends	$2,667.50	$16,434.24
Return of capital	0.00	312.50
Total	**$2,667.50**	**$16,746.74**

Realized Gain/Loss from Sales

	This Period	Year to Date
Short-term gain	$13,014.59	$689,017.07
Short-term loss	-41,511.92	-969,581.24
St disallowed loss	15,262.70	373,735.45
Net short	**-$13,234.63**	**$93,171.28**
Long-term gain	$27,972.23	$331,279.15
Long-term loss	0.00	-119.22
Lt disallowed loss	0.00	81.05
Net long	**$27,972.23**	**$331,240.98**

This may not reflect all of your gains/losses because of incomplete cost basis.

Fidelity Account

WILLIAM N MATSON - INDIVIDUAL

2002 Annual Report

January 1, 2002 - December 31, 2002

2002 Account Summary

Beginning market value as of Jan 1	$1,605,919.45
Withdrawals	-351,574.00
Other Tax Withheld	-16.43
Transaction costs, loads and fees	-82,671.58
Net adjustments	14.00
Margin interest paid	-29,166.18
Change in investment value	456,426.78
Change in debit balance	291,345.69
Ending market value as of Dec 31	1,890,277.73
Debit balance	-725,770.00
Ending Net Value	**$1,164,507.73**
Your commission schedule	Gold
Account eligible trades from Jan 2002 - Dec 2002	3,920

Income Summary

Taxable		
Ordinary Dividends		
Dividends		$16,434.24

Foreign taxes paid on securities you owned are included in Ordinary Dividends. Detailed reporting and instructions to help you file your federal tax return are found on your Form 1099-DIV.

2002 Investment Report

Realized Gain/Loss from Sales

Short-term gain	$536,150.97
Short-term loss	-965,622.69
St disallowed loss	370,960.14
Net short	**-$58,511.58**
Long-term gain	$331,279.15
Long-term loss	-119.22
Lt disallowed loss	81.05
Net long	**$331,240.98**

This may not reflect all of your gains/losses because of incomplete cost basis.

2002 Annual Report

2002 Investment Report

January 1, 2002 - December 31, 2002

Fidelity Account

WILLIAM N MATSON - INDIVIDUAL

2002 Account Summary

Beginning market value as of Jan 1	$1,605,919.45
Withdrawals	-351,574.00
Other Tax Withheld	-16.43
Transaction costs, loads and fees	-82,671.58
Net adjustments	14.00
Margin interest paid	-29,166.18
Change in investment value	456,426.78
Change in debit balance	291,345.69
Ending market value as of Dec 31	1,890,277.73
Debit balance	-725,770.00
Ending Net Value	**$1,164,507.73**
Your commission schedule	Gold
Account eligible trades from Jan 2002 - Dec 2002	3,920

Income Summary

Taxable		
Ordinary Dividends		
Dividends		$16,434.24

Foreign taxes paid on securities you owned are included in Ordinary Dividends. Detailed reporting and instructions to help you file your federal tax return are found on your Form 1099-DIV.

Realized Gain/Loss from Sales

Short-term gain	$536,150.97
Short-term loss	-965,622.69
St disallowed loss	370,960.14
Net short	**-$58,511.58**
Long-term gain	$331,279.15
Long-term loss	-119.22
Lt disallowed loss	81.05
Net long	**$331,240.98**

This may not reflect all of your gains/losses because of incomplete cost basis.

Holdings (Symbol) as of 12/31	% of Holdings	Income Earned	Quantity	Price per Unit	Total Cost Basis	Total Value
Stocks						
M LJ INTERNATIONAL INC (JADE)	0%	$0.00	4,000.000	$1.250	$5,032.00	$5,000.00
M ATP OIL & GAS CORP (ATPG)	0%	0.00	100.000	4.070	320.00	407.00
M ABLEST INC (AIH)	1%	0.00	3,000.000	5.450	12,706.00	16,350.00
M AMTECH SYSTEMS INC (ASYS)	0%	0.00	100.000	3.170	349.00	317.00
M ANGELICA CORP (AGL)	4%	400.00	3,500.000	20.650	61,492.00	72,275.00
M ASTRONICS CORP CL B (NON TRANSFERABLE) (ATROB)	0%	0.00	450.000	6.250		2,812.50
M BIG DOG HOLDINGS INC (BDOG)	1%	0.00	5,680.000	2.462	16,317.50	13,984.16
M BLAIR CORP (BL)	2%	1,500.00	1,500.000	23.320	26,103.00	34,980.00
M BLUEGREEN CORP (BXG)	1%	0.00	8,000.000	3.510	26,113.93	28,080.00
M CTI INDS CORP NEW (CTIB)	2%	0.00	6,000.000	6.260	13,264.84	37,560.00
M CALLOWAYS NURSERY INC (CLWY)	0%	0.00	2,000.000	0.880	1,688.00	1,760.00
M CANNONDALE CORP (BIKE)	0%	0.00	2,300.000	1.070	2,094.00	2,461.00
M CASTLE A M & CO MARYLAND(CAS)	0%	0.00	1,000.000	4.550	4,514.00	4,550.00

2002 Investment Report

January 1, 2002 - December 31, 2002

Fidelity Account

WILLIAM N MATSON - INDIVIDUAL

Holdings (Symbol) as of 12/31	% of Holdings	Income Earned	Quantity	Price per Unit	Total Cost Basis	Total Value
M CD&L INC (CDV)	0%	0.00	3,000.000	0.600	1,797.03	1,800.00
M COHESANT TECHNOLOGIES INC (COHT)	0%	0.00	1,689.000	3.900	5,943.10	6,587.10
M COMARCO INC (CMRO)	2%	0.00	4,500.000	8.650	37,709.63	38,925.00
M CONCEPTS DIRECT INC (CDIR)	0%	0.00	3,000.000	0.580		1,740.00
M CONTROL CHIEF HLDGS INC COM NEW (DIGM)	0%	0.00	40.000	110.000	12,101.60	4,400.00
M DECKERS OUTDOOR (DECK)	1%	0.00	5,800.000	3.340	19,198.00	19,372.00
M DREW INDS INC COM NEW (DW)	3%	0.00	3,000.000	16.050	39,877.61	48,150.00
M EDISON CTL CORP (EDCO)	1%	0.00	3,700.000	5.000	22,137.76	18,500.00
M FEDERAL SCREW WKS (FSCR)	4%	1,200.00	1,600.000	42.000	59,690.74	67,200.00
M FIRST ALBANY COS INC (FACT)	1%	287.50	2,231.000	6.980	unknown	15,572.38
M FIRSTWAVVE TECHNOLOGIES INC NEW (FSTW)	1%	0.00	1,700.000	15.920	4,374.40	27,064.00
M GSE SYSTEMS INC (GVP)	0%	0.00	1,500.000	1.050	1,534.00	1,575.00
M GREATER COMMUNITY BANCORP (GFLS)	2%	522.32	2,363.000	16.000	31,557.47	37,808.00
M GREEN MOUNTAIN PWR CORP (GMP)	2%	380.00	1,800.000	20.970	34,603.00	37,746.00
M GUNDLE SLT ENVIRONMENTAL INC (GSE)	3%	0.00	6,000.000	8.840	36,585.00	53,040.00
M HARTMARX CORP (HMX)	3%	0.00	21,000.000	2.440	43,174.00	51,240.00
M IOMED INC (IOX)	0%	0.00	6,500.000	1.340	5,705.00	8,710.00
M ISHARES TR RUSSELL 2000 VALUE INDEX FD (IWN)	4%	0.00	600.000	111.500	67,730.01	66,900.00
M JLM COUTURE INC (JLMC)	3%	0.00	16,800.000	3.500	44,472.00	58,800.00
M JO ANN STORES INC CL A (JASA)	4%	0.00	3,000.000	22.970	51,938.00	68,910.00
M K2 INC (KTO)	1%	0.00	2,000.000	9.400	15,328.00	18,800.00
M KINARK CORP (KIN)	1%	0.00	10,300.000	1.470	13,445.51	15,141.00
M MPW INDUSTRIAL SERVICES GROUP INC (MPWG)	1%	0.00	10,500.000	1.800	12,007.60	18,900.00
M MARGO CARIBE INC (MRGO)	0%	0.00	1,800.000	3.770	5,602.22	6,786.00
M MATRIX SVC CO (MTRX)	2%	0.00	4,000.000	9.420	33,385.00	37,680.00
M MOORE MED CORP (MMD)	1%	0.00	2,500.000	7.150	18,247.85	17,875.00
M MOVIE STAR INC (MSI)	0%	0.00	1,500.000	0.520	739.00	780.00

2002 Annual Report

2002 Investment Report

January 1, 2002 - December 31, 2002

Fidelity Account

WILLIAM N MATSON - INDIVIDUAL

Holdings (Symbol) as of 12/31	% of Holdings	Income Earned	Quantity	Price per Unit	Total Cost Basis	Total Value
M NAPCO SECURITY SYS INC (NSSC)	3%	0.00	6,500.000	9.250	55,305.22	60,125.00
M NATIONAL HOME HEALTH CARE CORP (NHHC)	1%	0.00	1,500.000	9.999	13,243.00	14,998.50
M NOLAND COMPANY (NOLD)	1%	0.00	500.000	30.280	13,664.00	15,140.00
M OMEGA PROTEIN CORP (OME)	3%	0.00	12,300.000	3.950	47,126.88	48,585.00
M OUTLOOK GRAPHICS CRP (OUTL)	2%	235.00	5,400.000	5.970	27,108.50	32,238.00
M PC CONNECTION INC (PCCC)	4%	0.00	13,800.000	5.070	74,094.46	69,966.00
M PC MALL INC (MALL)	1%	0.00	7,600.000	3.450	21,888.05	26,220.00
M PIONEER STD ELECTRS INC (PIOS)	1%	0.00	2,500.000	9.180	19,494.15	22,950.00
M POLYMER SOLUTIONS INC (PYSU)	0%	0.00	1,433.000	0.266	427.27	381.17
M R & B INC (RBIN)	5%	0.00	9,400.000	10.110	54,136.40	95,034.00
M RF INDUSTRIES INC (RFIL)	0%	0.00	4,000.000	2.100	8,246.00	8,400.00
M RAINBOW TECHNOLOGIES INC (RNBO)	0%	0.00	1,000.000	7.170	4,955.00	7,170.00
M RAVEN INDS INC (RAVN)	4%	1,998.00	2,300.000	34.448	58,379.18	79,230.40
M RAWLINGS SPORTING GOODS INC (RAWL)	4%	0.00	8,300.000	8.810	43,484.30	73,123.00
M REXHALL INDS INC (REXL)	0%	0.00	2,000.000	3.501	7,002.00	7,002.00
M SANDS REGENT (SNDS)	1%	0.00	7,200.000	3.340	22,807.20	24,048.00
M STEEL TECHNOLOGIES INC (STTX)	8%	1,400.00	9,000.000	16.960	90,777.80	152,640.00
M STEIN MART INC (SMRT)	1%	0.00	2,000.000	6.100	12,084.00	12,200.00
M SUPER VISION INTL IN CL A (SUPVA)	0%	0.00	1,000.000	1.990	2,014.00	1,990.00
M SYMS CORP (SYM)	3%	0.00	8,000.000	7.090	51,567.00	56,720.00
M TECHE HOLDING CO (TSH)	4%	1,062.50	2,500.000	27.370	53,401.00	68,425.00

2002 Investment Report

January 1, 2002 - December 31, 2002

Fidelity Account

WILLIAM N MATSON - INDIVIDUAL

Holdings (Symbol) as of 12/31	% of Holdings	Income Earned	Quantity	Price per Unit	Total Cost Basis	Total Value
M TUMBLEWEED INC (TWED)	0%	0.00	1,000.000	0.630	598.00	630.00
M V S E CORP (VSEC)	2%	78.08	3,952.000	10.760	35,144.13	42,523.52

Total Market Value as of December 31, 2002			**$1,890,277.73**
Total income earned on positions no longer held	7,370.84		
2002 Income Earned	**$ 16,434.24**		
Debit balance			-725,770.00
Total Net Value			**$1,164,507.73**

M - Position held in margin account.

January 2003

WILLIAM NICHOLAS MATSON

Investment Report

January 1, 2003 - January 31, 2003

Online Fidelity.com
FAST(sm)-Automated Telephone 800-544-5555
Premium Services 800-544-4442
 8am - 8pm ET, Mon - Fri

Fidelity Account

WILLIAM N MATSON - INDIVIDUAL

Account Summary			
Beginning market value as of Jan 1	$1,890,277.73		
Transaction costs, loads and fees	-4,273.48		
Margin interest paid	-1,354.61		
Change in investment value	8,232.42		
Change in debit balance	-212,589.65		
Ending market value as of Jan 31	1,680,292.41		
Debit balance	-513,180.35		
Ending Net Value	**$1,167,112.06**		
Your commission schedule	Gold		
Account eligible trades from Feb 2002 - Jan 2003	3,787		

Income Summary		This Period	Year to Date
Taxable			
Dividends		$1,328.30	$1,328.30

Realized Gain/Loss from Sales	This Period	Year to Date
Short-term gain	$34,300.57	$34,300.57
Short-term loss	-42,612.49	-42,612.49
St disallowed loss	15,337.97	15,337.97
Net short	**$7,026.05**	**$7,026.05**
Long-term gain	$5,770.91	$5,770.91

This may not reflect all of your gains/losses because of incomplete cost basis.

WILLIAM NICHOLAS MATSON

Investment Report

February 1, 2003 - February 28, 2003

Online
FAST(sm)-Automated Telephone
Premium Services
8am - 8pm ET, Mon - Fri

Fidelity.com
800-544-5555
800-544-4442

Fidelity Account

WILLIAM N MATSON - INDIVIDUAL

Account Summary		This Period	Year to Date
Beginning market value as of Feb 1	$1,680,292.41		
Withdrawals	-27,500.00		
Transaction costs, loads and fees	-7,621.77		
Margin interest paid	-1,779.48		
Change in investment value	-3,666.44		
Change in debit balance	62,908.37		
Ending market value as of Feb 28	1,702,633.09		
Debit balance	-576,088.72		
Ending Net Value	**$1,126,544.37**		

Your commission schedule Gold
Account eligible trades from Mar 2002 - 3,798
Feb 2003

Income Summary

	This Period	Year to Date
Taxable		
Dividends	$269.63	$1,597.93

Realized Gain/Loss from Sales

	This Period	Year to Date
Short-term gain	$61,080.22	$95,380.79
Short-term loss	-44,098.43	-86,710.92
St disallowed loss	22,683.08	38,022.47
Net short	**$39,664.87**	**$46,692.34**
Long-term gain	$0.00	$5,770.91
Long-term loss	-1.16	-1.16
Lt disallowed loss	1.16	1.16
Net long	**$0.00**	**$5,770.91**

This may not reflect all of your gains/losses because of incomplete cost basis.

March 2003

Investment Report

March 1, 2003 - March 31, 2003

Online   Fidelity.com
FAST(sm) - Automated Telephone   800-544-5555
Premium Services   800-544-4442
8am - 8pm ET, Mon - Fri

WILLIAM NICHOLAS MATSON

Fidelity Account   WILLIAM N MATSON - INDIVIDUAL

Account Summary

Beginning market value as of Mar 1	$1,702,633.09
Withdrawals	-55,000.00
Transaction costs, loads and fees	-5,057.13
Margin interest paid	-1,433.05
Change in investment value	-11,532.94
Change in debit balance	-206,199.71
Ending market value as of Mar 31	1,423,410.26
Debit balance	-369,889.01
Ending Net Value	**$1,053,521.25**
Your commission schedule	Gold
Account eligible trades from Apr 2002 - Mar 2003	3,793
Current rate on debit balance	3.77%
Additional amount you can borrow	$22,002.24

Income Summary

	This Period	Year to Date
Taxable		
Dividends	$1,190.27	$2,788.20

Realized Gain/Loss from Sales

	This Period	Year to Date
Short-term gain	$18,876.37	$114,257.16
Short-term loss	-67,014.03	-153,724.95
St disallowed loss	49,570.21	89,157.95
Net short	**$1,432.55**	**$49,690.16**
Long-term gain	$14,578.61	$20,349.52
Long-term loss	0.00	-1.16
Lt disallowed loss	0.00	1.16
Net long	**$14,578.61**	**$20,349.52**

This may not reflect all of your gains/losses because of incomplete cost basis.

WILLIAM NICHOLAS MATSON

Investment Report

April 1, 2003 - April 30, 2003

Online
FAST(sm) - Automated Telephone
Premium Services
  8am - 8pm ET, Mon - Fri

Fidelity.com
800-544-5555
800-544-4442

Messages:

President Bush's proposal to end the double tax on dividends is good for individual investors. We encourage you to learn more, support it, and voice your support with Congress at: fidelity.com/dividendtaxrelief.

WILLIAM N MATSON - INDIVIDUAL

Fidelity Account

Congratulations. You've earned lower commissions based on your assets and trading with Fidelity. Your pricing has been upgraded and you will receive deeper discounts on your stock and option trades. The enclosed commission schedule details your new pricing. Thank you for your continued business.

Account Summary

Beginning market value as of Apr 1	$1,423,410.26
Additions	1,154.25
Withdrawals	-10,000.00
Transaction costs, loads and fees	-7,393.43
Margin interest paid	-1,208.90
Change in investment value	115,619.33
Change in debit balance	6,975.36
Ending market value as of Apr 30	1,528,556.87
Debit balance	-376,864.37
Ending Net Value	**$1,151,692.50**
Your commission schedule	Gold
Account eligible trades from May 2002 - Apr 2003	3,894

Income Summary

	This Period	Year to Date
Taxable		
Dividends	$811.30	$3,599.50

Realized Gain/Loss from Sales

	This Period	Year to Date
Short-term gain	$36,443.50	$150,700.66
Short-term loss	-53,158.85	-206,883.80
St disallowed loss	25,573.39	116,307.06
Net short	**$8,858.04**	**$60,123.92**
Long-term gain	$35,462.56	$55,812.08
Long-term loss	0.00	-1.16
Lt disallowed loss	0.00	1.16
Net long	**$35,462.56**	**$55,812.08**

This may not reflect all of your gains/losses because of incomplete cost basis.

Investment Report

May 1, 2003 - May 31, 2003

Online	Fidelity.com
FAST(sm) -Automated Telephone	800-544-5555
Premium Services	800-544-4442
8am - 8pm ET, Mon - Fri	

WILLIAM NICHOLAS MATSON

Fidelity Account   WILLIAM N MATSON - INDIVIDUAL

Account Summary

Beginning market value as of May 1	$1,528,556.87	
Additions	14.95	
Withdrawals	-25,000.00	
Transaction costs, loads and fees	-8,649.44	
Net adjustments	60.00	
Margin interest paid	-1,209.52	
Change in investment value	136,521.13	
Change in debit balance	-48,537.53	
Ending market value as of May 31	1,581,756.46	
Debit balance	-328,326.84	
Ending Net Value	**$1,253,429.62**	
Your commission schedule	Gold	
Account eligible trades from Jun 2002 - May 2003	3,895	

Income Summary

	This Period	Year to Date
Taxable		
Dividends	$305.25	$3,904.75

Realized Gain/Loss from Sales

	This Period	Year to Date
Short-term gain	$44,099.14	$194,799.80
Short-term loss	-42,697.90	-249,581.70
St disallowed loss	18,066.19	135,917.24
Net short	**$19,467.43**	**$81,135.34**
Long-term gain	$12,901.99	$68,714.07
Long-term loss	-352.34	-353.50
Lt disallowed loss	227.95	229.11
Net long	**$12,777.60**	**$68,589.68**

This may not reflect all of your gains/losses because of incomplete cost basis.

Investment Report

June 1, 2003 - June 30, 2003

Online
FAST(sm)-Automated Telephone
Premium Services
8am - 8pm ET, Mon - Fri

Fidelity.com
800-544-5555
800-544-4442

WILLIAM NICHOLAS MATSON

WILLIAM N MATSON - INDIVIDUAL

Fidelity Account

Account Summary		This Period	Year to Date
Beginning market value as of Jun 1	$1,581,756.46		
Withdrawals	-10,000.00		
Transaction costs, loads and fees	-8,372.84		
Margin interest paid	-1,272.08		
Change in investment value	99,077.44		
Change in debit balance	-54,475.17		
Ending market value as of Jun 30	1,606,713.81		
Debit balance	-273,851.67		
Ending Net Value	**$1,332,862.14**		

Income Summary		This Period	Year to Date
Taxable			
Dividends		$0.00	$3,904.75

Realized Gain/Loss from Sales	This Period	Year to Date
Short-term gain	$94,259.28	$289,059.08
Short-term loss	-65,556.58	-315,138.28
St disallowed loss	27,172.23	164,258.63
Net short	**$55,874.93**	**$138,179.43**
Long-term gain	$41,902.07	$80,616.14
Long-term loss	0.00	-353.50
Lt disallowed loss	0.00	229.11
Net long	**$11,902.07**	**$80,491.75**

Your commission schedule — Gold
Account eligible trades from Jul 2002 - Jun 2003 — 4,115

Current rate on debit balance — 3.77%
Additional amount you can borrow — $34,716.04

This may not reflect all of your gains/losses because of incomplete cost basis.

July 2003

WILLIAM NICHOLAS MATSON

Investment Report

July 1, 2003 - July 31, 2003

Online — Fidelity.com
FAST(sm)-Automated Telephone — 800-544-5555
Premium Services — 800-544-4442
8am - 8pm ET, Mon - Fri

Messages:

FUND UPDATE: Looking for a way to tap into the value of America's top companies? Ask about our new Fidelity Blue Chip Value Fund.

Fidelity Account — WILLIAM N MATSON - INDIVIDUAL

Account Summary

Beginning market value as of Jul 1	$1,606,713.81
Additions	4,273.48
Withdrawals	-40,100.00
Transaction costs, loads and fees	-8,675.84
Net adjustments	-85,587.25
Margin interest paid	-979.34
Change in investment value	303,183.42
Change in debit balance	274,454.40
Ending market value as of Jul 31	2,053,282.68
Debit balance	-548,306.07
Ending Net Value	**$1,504,976.61**

Your commission schedule	Gold
Account eligible trades from Aug 2002 - Jul 2003	4,164
Current rate on debit balance	3.77%
Additional amount you can borrow	$33,206.70

Income Summary

	This Period	Year to Date
Taxable		
Dividends	$496.00	$4,400.75

Realized Gain/Loss from Sales

	This Period	Year to Date
Short-term gain	$97,249.39	$386,308.47
Short-term loss	-61,795.66	-376,933.94
St disallowed loss	20,035.05	184,643.60
Net short	**$55,488.78**	**$194,018.13**
Long-term gain	$82,644.54	$163,260.68
Long-term loss	0.00	-353.50
Lt disallowed loss	0.00	229.11
Net long	**$82,644.54**	**$163,136.29**

This may not reflect all of your gains/losses because of incomplete cost basis.

WILLIAM NICHOLAS MATSON

Investment Report

August 1, 2003 - August 31, 2003

Online
FAST(sm) - Automated Telephone
Premium Services
   8am - 8pm ET, Mon - Fri

Fidelity.com
800-544-5555
800-544-4442

Messages:

Beginning in September, all trades in your brokerage account executed on the same business day will be aggregated onto one confirmation statement.

Fidelity Account — WILLIAM N MATSON - INDIVIDUAL

Account Summary

Beginning market value as of Aug 1	$2,053,282.68
Withdrawals	-50,000.00
Transaction costs, loads and fees	-10,648.97
Margin interest paid	-1,416.65
Change in investment value	206,871.01
Change in debit balance	-145,481.35
Change in short balance	-9,243.31
Ending market value as of Aug 31	2,043,363.41
Debit balance	-402,824.72
Short balance	9,243.31
Ending Net Value	**$1,649,782.00**

Your commission schedule	Gold
Account eligible trades from Sep 2002 - Aug 2003	4.126
Current rate on debit balance	3.77%
Additional amount you can borrow	$40,790.89

Income Summary

	This Period	Year to Date
Taxable		
Dividends	$557.00	$4,957.75

Realized Gain/Loss from Sales

	This Period	Year to Date
Short-term gain	$63,995.52	$450,303.99
Short-term loss	-90,874.51	-467,808.45
St disallowed loss	41,523.90	226,851.47
Net short	**$14,644.91**	**$209,347.01**
Long-term gain	$14,108.10	$177,368.78
Long-term loss	0.00	-353.50
Lt disallowed loss	0.00	229.11
Net long	**$14,108.10**	**$177,244.39**

This may not reflect all of your gains/losses because of incomplete cost basis.

September 2003

WILLIAM NICHOLAS MATSON

Investment Report

September 1, 2003 - September 30, 2003

Online   Fidelity.com
FAST(sm)-Automated Telephone   800-544-5555
Premium Services   800-544-4442
8am - 8pm ET, Mon - Fri

Messages:

Fidelity has created more descriptive names and updated the definitions for the Investment Objectives of customer accounts. Please see the last page for the updated names and definitions. No action is required.

WILLIAM N MATSON - INDIVIDUAL

Fidelity Account

Account Summary

Beginning market value as of Sep 1	$2,043,363.41
Withdrawals	-46,400.00
Transaction costs, loads and fees	-6,719.07
Net adjustments	88,866.80
Margin interest paid	-1,366.59
Change in investment value	23,239.54
Change in debit balance	329,799.15
Change in short balance	-61,944.29
Ending market value as of Sep 30	2,368,838.95
Debit balance	-732,623.87
Short balance	71,187.60
Ending Net Value	**$1,707,402.68**
Your commission schedule	Gold
Account eligible trades from Oct 2002 - Sep 2003	4,184
Current rate on debit balance	3.77%
Additional amount you can borrow	$64,955.89

Income Summary

	This Period	Year to Date
Taxable		
Dividends	$2,105.68	$7,063.43

Realized Gain/Loss from Sales

	This Period	Year to Date
Short-term gain	$53,147.73	$503,451.72
Short-term loss	-59,884.11	-527,692.56
St disallowed loss	12,504.32	239,640.28
Net short	**$5,767.94**	**$215,399.44**
Long-term gain	$5,919.74	$183,288.52
Long-term loss	0.00	-353.50
Lt disallowed loss	0.00	229.11
Net long	**$5,919.74**	**$183,164.13**

This may not reflect all of your gains/losses because of incomplete cost basis.

Investment Report

October 1, 2003 - October 31, 2003

Online	Fidelity.com
FAST(sm) - Automated Telephone	800-544-5555
Private Access Team 73	800-544-5704

WILLIAM NICHOLAS MATSON

WILLIAM N MATSON - INDIVIDUAL

Fidelity Account

Account Summary

Beginning market value as of Oct 1	$2,368,838.95	
Withdrawals	-80,000.00	
Transaction costs, loads and fees	-3,922.91	
Net adjustments	403.94	
Margin interest paid	2,146.24	
Change in investment value	330,165.66	
Change in debit balance	209,733.28	
Change in short balance	-69,291.15	
Ending market value as of Oct 31	2,753,781.53	
Debit balance	-942,357.15	
Short balance	140,478.75	
Ending Net Value	**$1,951,903.13**	
Your commission schedule	Gold	
Account eligible trades from Nov 2002 - Oct 2003	4,123	
Current rate on debit balance	3.77%	
Additional amount you can borrow	$85,191.56	

Income Summary

	This Period	Year to Date
Taxable		
Dividends	$871.52	$7,934.95

Realized Gain/Loss from Sales

	This Period	Year to Date
Short-term gain	$33,087.18	$536,538.90
Short-term loss	-42,688.46	-570,381.02
St disallowed loss	5,065.69	245,844.51
Net short	**-$4,535.59**	**$212,002.39**
Long-term gain	$4,366.77	$187,655.29
Long-term loss	0.00	-353.50
Lt disallowed loss	0.00	229.11
Net long	**$4,366.77**	**$187,530.90**

This may not reflect all of your gains/losses because of incomplete cost basis.

November 2003

WILLIAM NICHOLAS MATSON

Investment Report

November 1, 2003 - November 30, 2003

	Fidelity.com
Online	800-544-5555
FAST(sm) - Automated Telephone	800-544-5704
Private Access Team 73	

Fidelity Account

WILLIAM N MATSON - INDIVIDUAL

Account Summary

Beginning market value as of Nov 1	$2,753,781.53
Withdrawals	-73,000.00
Other Tax Withheld	-18.00
Transaction costs, loads and fees	-6,252.94
Margin interest paid	-3,183.48
Change in investment value	245,957.95
Change in debit balance	402,951.82
Change in short balance	-460,198.75
Ending market value as of Nov 30	2,860,038.13
Debit balance	-1,345,308.97
Short balance	600,677.50
Ending Net Value	**$2,115,406.66**
Your commission schedule	Gold
Account eligible trades from Dec 2002 - Nov 2003	4,222
Current rate on debit balance	3.77%
Additional amount you can borrow	$130,874.48

Income Summary

	This Period	Year to Date
Taxable		
Dividends	$855.00	$8,789.95
Liquidations	33,058.00	33,058.00
Total	**$33,913.00**	**$41,847.95**

Realized Gain/Loss from Sales

	This Period	Year to Date
Short-term gain	$65,129.87	$597,490.25
Short-term loss	-68,527.79	-628,220.79
St disallowed loss	22,983.68	263,017.87
Net short	**$19,585.76**	**$232,287.33**
Long-term gain	$1,916.90	$189,572.19
Long-term loss	0.00	-353.50
Lt disallowed loss	0.00	229.11
Net long	**$1,916.90**	**$189,447.80**

This may not reflect all of your gains/losses because of incomplete cost basis.

WILLIAM NICHOLAS MATSON

Investment Report

December 1, 2003 - December 31, 2003

Online
FAST(sm) - Automated Telephone
Private Access Team 73

Fidelity.com
800-544-5555
800-544-5704

Messages:

Visit Fidelity.com to read about various issues facing the mutual fund industry and Fidelity's position on them.

WILLIAM N MATSON - INDIVIDUAL

Fidelity Account

Account Summary

Beginning market value as of Dec 1	$2,860,038.13
Withdrawals	-92,000.00
Transaction costs, loads and fees	-5,739.54
Net adjustments	-4,681.00
Margin interest paid	-6,685.28
Change in investment value	194,357.84
Change in debit balance	575,775.68
Change in short balance	-342,533.21
Ending market value as of Dec 31	3,178,532.62
Debit balance	-1,921,084.65
Short balance	943,210.71
Ending Net Value	**$2,200,658.68**
Your commission schedule	Gold
Account eligible trades from Jan 2003 - Dec 2003	4,531
Current rate on debit balance	3.77%
Additional amount you can borrow	$37,660.86

Income Summary

	This Period	Year to Date
Taxable		
Dividends	$2,928.21	$11,718.16
Liquidations	0.00	33,058.00
Total	**$2,928.21**	**$44,776.16**

Realized Gain/Loss from Sales

	This Period	Year to Date
Short-term gain	$37,229.51	$634,719.76
Short-term loss	-177,995.09	-806,215.88
St disallowed loss	122,476.49	385,532.58
Net short	**-$18,289.09**	**$214,036.46**
Long-term gain	$141,559.22	$331,131.41
Long-term loss	0.00	-353.50
Lt disallowed loss	0.00	229.11
Net long	**$141,559.22**	**$331,007.02**

This may not reflect all of your gains/losses because of incomplete cost basis.

2003 Annual Report

2003 Investment Report

January 1, 2003 - December 31, 2003

Fidelity Account   WILLIAM N MATSON - INDIVIDUAL

2003 Account Summary

Beginning market value as of Jan 1	$1,890,277.73
Additions	5,442.68
Withdrawals	-509,000.00
Other Tax Withheld	-18.00
Transaction costs, loads and fees	-83,327.36
Net adjustments	-937.51
Margin interest paid	-24,035.22
Change in investment value	1,648,026.36
Change in debit balance	1,195,314.65
Change in short balance	-943,210.71
Ending market value as of Dec 31	3,178,532.62
Debit balance	-1,921,084.65
Short balance	943,210.71
Ending Net Value	**$2,200,658.68**
Your commission schedule	Gold
Account eligible trades from Jan 2003 - Dec 2003	4,531

Income Summary

Taxable		
Ordinary Dividends		
Dividends		$11,718.16
Liquidations		**33,058.00**
Total		**$44,776.16**

Foreign taxes paid on securities you owned are included in Ordinary Dividends. Detailed reporting and instructions to help you file your federal tax return are found on your Form 1099-DIV.

2003 Investment Report

January 1, 2003 - December 31, 2003

Fidelity Account

WILLIAM N MATSON - INDIVIDUAL

Holdings (Symbol) as of 12/31	% of Holdings	Income Earned	Quantity	Price per Unit	Total Cost Basis/Proceeds	Total Value
Stocks						
M INTERWAVE COMMUNICATIONS INTL LTD SHS ISIN #BMG4911N3000 SEDOL #2631624 (IWAV)	0%	$0.00	4,500.000	$4.411	$9,986.00	$19,849.50
M ECTEL LTD (ECTX)	0%	0.00	1,000.000	4.960	4,777.80	4,960.00
M ICTS INTL N V FRMLY ICTS HOLLAND PROD (ICTS)	0%	0.00	2,000.000	3.420	5,193.00	6,840.00
M ELAMEX S A DE C V ISIN #MXP36209I078 SEDOL #2304595 (ELAM)	0%	0.00	1,000.000	2.500	2,578.00	2,500.00
M A A R CORP (AIR)	2%	0.00	5,000.000	14.950	62,846.00	74,750.00
M ACR GROUP INC (ACRG)	0%	0.00	1,000.000	0.900	488.00	900.00
M AMX CORP NEW (AMXC)	0%	0.00	2,500.000	7.970	5,219.00	19,925.00
S AMX CORP NEW (AMXC)	0%	0.00	-2,500.000	7.970	-19,030.10	-19,925.00
M AMERICAN BUSINESS FINL SVCS INC SHS DTD PRIOR TO 5/3/93 ARE SUBJECT TO A 1 FOR 547.70 REVERSE SPLIT (ABFI)	0%	0.00	1,000.000	4.300	3,556.00	4,300.00
M AMISTAR CORP (AMTA)	0%	0.00	3,000.000	2.240	6,152.20	6,720.00
M ANGELO & MAXIES INC (AGMX)	0%	0.00	500.000	1.420	1,391.00	710.00
M ASTREX INC COM NEW (ASXI)	0%	0.00	1,000.000	0.280	284.00	280.00
M ASTRONICS CORP CL B (NON TRANSFERABLE) (ATROB)	0%	0.00	305.000	4.500	547.00	1,372.50
M AUGUST TECHNOLOGY CORP (AUGT)	1%	0.00	2,000.000	18.600	31,081.00	37,200.00
S AUGUST TECHNOLOGY CORP (AUGT)	0%	0.00	-2,000.000	18.600	-34,175.50	-37,200.00
M BIG DOG HOLDINGS INC (BDOG)	0%	0.00	3,000.000	3.730	9,287.00	11,190.00
M BIOLOK INTL INC (BLLI)	0%	0.00	1,500.000	0.250	418.00	375.00
M BLUEGREEN CORP (BXG)	0%	0.00	3,000.000	6.240	9,034.00	18,720.00
M BOGEN COMM INTL INC (BOGN)	2%	0.00	15,100.000	5.000	76,406.90	75,500.00
M BOYDS COLLECTION LTD (FOB)	0%	0.00	1,500.000	4.250	6,583.00	6,375.00
M BRIDGFORD FOODS CORP (BRID)	0%	0.00	1,000.000	7.850	7,044.00	7,850.00
M CARMEL CONTAINER SYS LTD (KML)	0%	0.00	1,500.000	3.500	4,513.00	5,250.00
M CIRCOR INTL INC (CIR)	1%	112.50	1,000.000	24.100	14,418.89	24,100.00

2003 Investment Report

January 1, 2003 - December 31, 2003

Fidelity Account

WILLIAM N MATSON - INDIVIDUAL

Holdings (Symbol) as of 12/31	% of Holdings	Income Earned	Quantity	Price per Unit	Total Cost Basis/Proceeds	Total Value
M COACHMEN INDS INC (COA)	2%	180.00	5,000.000	18.110	75,381.36	90,550.00
S COACHMEN INDS INC (COA)	0%	0.00	-2,000.000	18.110	-34,808.32	-36,220.00
M COAST DISTRIBUTION SYSTEM DEL (CRV)	0%	0.00	3,500.000	5.510	8,406.00	19,285.00
S COAST DISTRIBUTION SYSTEM DEL (CRV)	0%	0.00	-3,500.000	5.510	-20,417.02	-19,285.00
M COHESANT TECHNOLOGIES INC (COHT)	1%	2,197.25	9,289.000	6.500	35,894.57	60,378.50
M COLGATE-PALMOLIVE CO (CL)	0%	0.00	300.000	50.050	14,945.00	15,015.00
M COMMERCIAL METALS CO (CMC)	2%	0.00	3,000.000	30.400	85,524.00	91,200.00
M CORE MOLDING TECH INC (CMT)	0%	0.00	1,500.000	2.920	3,139.00	4,380.00
M CRYPTOLOGIC INC (CRYP)	1%	120.00	2,000.000	11.910	16,548.00	23,820.00
M CUTTER & BUCK INC (CBUK)	2%	0.00	9,500.000	9.430	65,865.00	89,585.00
M DXP ENTERPRISES INC NEW (DXPE)	1%	0.00	5,400.000	4.092	10,805.33	22,096.80
M DATATEC SYSTEMS INC (DATCE)	0%	0.00	10,000.000	0.700	5,296.00	7,000.00
M DECKERS OUTDOOR (DECK)	1%	0.00	2,700.000	20.500	13,139.40	55,350.00
M DOCUCORP INTL INC (DOCC)	1%	0.00	5,000.000	10.160	48,384.20	50,800.00
M DYNATRONICS CORP (DYNT)	0%	0.00	1,600.000	1.800	1,854.60	2,880.00
M ELECSYS CORP COM (ASY)	0%	0.00	3,000.000	1.070	3,336.00	3,210.00
M ELECTRONIC TELE COMMUNICATIONS INC CL A (ETCIA)	0%	0.00	3,588.000	0.460	1,646.96	1,650.48
M EMTEC INC (ETEC)	0%	0.00	10,500.000	0.780	7,362.00	8,190.00
M EYE DYNAMICS INC (EYDY)	1%	0.00	44,101.000	0.500	8,874.71	22,050.50
M FACTORY 2 U STORES INC (FTUS)	0%	0.00	5,000.000	1.371	5,498.00	6,855.00
M FEDERAL SCREW WKS (FSCR)	1%	1,302.50	700.000	37.750	24,439.00	26,425.00
M FIBERMARK INC (FMK)	0%	0.00	2,500.000	1.750	3,148.00	4,375.00
M FIRST ALBANY COS INC (FACT)	1%	341.20	2,031.000	14.010	unknown	28,454.31
M FIRST INVESTORS FINANCIAL SERVICES GROUP INC (FIFS)	0%	0.00	1,300.000	4.530	5,569.38	5,889.00
M FIRSTWAVVE TECHNOLOGIES INC NEW (FSTW)	0%	0.00	1,500.000	5.340	6,086.00	8,010.00
M FIVE STAR PRODUCTS INC (FSPX)	0%	0.00	6,895.000	0.130	912.00	896.35

2003 Investment Report

January 1, 2003 - December 31, 2003

Fidelity Account

WILLIAM N MATSON - INDIVIDUAL

Holdings (Symbol) as of 12/31	% of Holdings	Income Earned	Quantity	Price per Unit	Total Cost Basis/Proceeds	Total Value
M FROZEN FOOD EXPRESS INDS INC (FFEX)	1%	0.00	4,000.000	6.640	22,641.00	26,560.00
M GSV INC (GSVI)	0%	0.00	1,500.000	0.080	212.00	120.00
M G-III APPAREL GROUP (GIII)	1%	0.00	4,000.000	9.200	36,697.07	36,800.00
S G-III APPAREL GROUP (GIII)	0%	0.00	-1,000.000	9.200	-9,399.54	-9,200.00
M GTSI CORP (GTSI)	1%	0.00	3,000.000	13.851	34,358.10	41,553.00
M GADZOOKS INC (GADZ)	0%	0.00	7,500.000	1.550	8,794.00	11,625.00
M GRAHAM CORP (GHM)	0%	0.00	1,000.000	10.200	8,906.00	10,200.00
M GREATER COMMUNITY BANCORP (GFLS)	0%	272.60	130.000	16.890	2,207.45	2,195.70
M HAROLDS STORES INC (HLD)	0%	0.00	1,000.000	3.350	3,197.00	3,350.00
M HARTMARX CORP (HMX)	2%	0.00	23,100.000	4.170	47,358.28	96,327.00
M HARVEY ELECTRONICS INC (HRVE)	0%	0.00	100.000	0.910	100.27	91.00
M HEALTHCARE SERVICES GROUP INC (HCSG)	1%	390.00	3,000.000	19.230	37,621.98	57,690.00
S HEALTHCARE SERVICES GROUP INC (HCSG)	0%	0.00	-1,000.000	19.230	-18,391.13	-19,230.00
M HOME PRODS INTL INC (HOMZ)	0%	0.00	2,500.000	1.300	2,718.50	3,250.00
M HOMETOWN AUTO RETAILERS CL A (HCAR)	0%	0.00	2,000.000	1.200	3,064.10	2,400.00
M HUMAN PHEROMONE SCIENCES INC (EROX)	0%	0.00	1,032.000	0.210	174.48	216.72
M ILX RESORTS INC (ILX)	0%	0.00	1,000.000	7.070	6,858.00	7,070.00
M IKONICS CORP (IKNX)	0%	0.00	600.000	6.300	3,975.77	3,780.00
M IMPERIAL INDS INC (IPII)	0%	0.00	30,000.000	0.260	9,316.60	7,800.00
M INDUSTRIAL SVCS OF AMERICA INC (IDSA)	0%	0.00	2,800.000	4.300	9,774.08	12,040.00
S INDUSTRIAL SVCS OF AMERICA INC (IDSA)	0%	0.00	-2,800.000	4.300	-12,083.38	-12,040.00
M INFORMATION RES INC LITIGATION CONTINGENT PMT RTS TR CONTINGENT VALUE RT (IRICR)	1%	0.00	20,197.000	1.750	unknown	35,344.75
M INTERLAND INC MINN (INLD)	0%	0.00	1,000.000	6.530	6,088.00	6,530.00

2003 Annual Report

2003 Investment Report

January 1, 2003 - December 31, 2003

Fidelity Account

WILLIAM N MATSON - INDIVIDUAL

Holdings (Symbol) as of 12/31	% of Holdings	Income Earned	Quantity	Price per Unit	Total Cost Basis/Proceeds	Total Value
M INTERNATIONAL ABSORBENTS INC COM NO PAR ISIN #CA45885E2033 SEDOL #2749118 (IAX)	0%	0.00	2,500.000	4.400	10,588.00	11,000.00
M JLM COUTURE INC (JLMC)	1%	0.00	4,832.000	5.100	15,993.43	24,643.20
M JPS INDUSTRIES INC FRMLY JPS TEXTILE GRP INC (JPST)	0%	0.00	70.000	2.530	154.00	177.10
M JEWETT-CAMERON TRADING CO LTD NEW ISIN #CA47733C2076 SEDOL #2471778 (JCTCF)	0%	0.00	300.000	5.100	1,520.00	1,530.00
M JOHNSON OUTDOORS INC CL A (JOUT)	1%	0.00	3,500.000	14.960	34,769.00	52,360.00
S JOHNSON OUTDOORS INC CL A (JOUT)	0%	0.00	-3,500.000	14.960	-51,586.83	-52,360.00
M JOULE INC TENDER OFFER FROM CUSIP 48110106	0%	0.00	3,100.000	1.510	4,203.00	4,681.00
M KSW INC (KSWW)	0%	0.00	1,000.000	0.620	828.00	620.00
M KIRLIN HLDG CORP NEW (KILN)	2%	0.00	7,386.000	10.800	34,210.12	79,768.80
M LA BARGE INC (LB)	1%	0.00	5,100.000	5.460	21,620.36	27,846.00
M LANCER ORTHODONTICS INC COM NEW (LANZ)	0%	0.00	2,000.000	0.580	1,252.00	1,160.00
M LAZARE KAPLAN INTL INC (LKI)	0%	0.00	1,000.000	6.950	6,798.00	6,950.00
M LESCO INC OHIO (LSCO)	1%	0.00	4,500.000	12.990	46,653.90	58,455.00
M LOTTERY & WAGERING SOLUTIONS INC (LWSL)	0%	0.00	1,100.000	1.300	1,185.00	1,430.00
M MGP INGREDIENTS INC (MGPI)	1%	0.00	2,500.000	15.750	25,863.00	39,375.00
M MANNING GREG AUCTION INC (GMAI)	0%	0.00	1,000.000	11.839	5,964.00	11,839.00
M MARKWEST HYDROCARBON INC (MWP)	1%	0.00	3,000.000	11.280	21,138.00	33,840.00
M MARSH SUPERMARKETS INC CL A (MARSA)	0%	0.00	1,000.000	10.850	10,808.00	10,850.00
M MASONITE INTL CORP (MHM)	2%	0.00	3,500.000	26.650	68,910.00	93,275.00
M MATRIX SVC CO (MTRX)	3%	0.00	7,000.000	18.110	48,087.00	126,770.00

2003 Investment Report

January 1, 2003 - December 31, 2003

Fidelity Account

WILLIAM N MATSON - INDIVIDUAL

Holdings (Symbol) as of 12/31	% of Holdings	Income Earned	Quantity	Price per Unit	Total Cost Basis/Proceeds	Total Value
S MATRIX SVC CO (MTRX)	0%	0.00	-6,000.000	18.110	-82,427.40	-108,660.00
M MAXCO INC (MAXC)	0%	0.00	700.000	2.800	2,044.00	1,960.00
M MEADOW VALLEY CORP (MVCO)	1%	0.00	13,400.000	1.710	19,737.91	22,914.00
M MERISEL INC (MSEL)	0%	0.00	110.000	5.910	542.00	650.10
M MICROS TO MAINFRAMES INC (MTMC)	0%	0.00	15,800.000	1.111	19,663.28	17,553.80
M MOD PAC CORP (MPAC)	1%	0.00	3,426.000	8.000	unknown	27,408.00
M MOVIE STAR INC (MSI)	0%	0.00	3,100.000	1.500	5,454.76	4,650.00
S MOVIE STAR INC (MSI)	0%	0.00	-3,000.000	1.500	-5,732.71	-4,500.00
M NAPCO SECURITY SYS INC (NSSCE)	0%	0.00	1,000.000	8.850	7,558.00	8,850.00
M NATIONAL R V HLDGS INC (NVH)	0%	0.00	1,900.000	9.950	16,806.00	18,905.00
M NEW FRONTIER MEDIA INC (NOOF)	3%	0.00	13,000.000	9.300	19,694.47	120,900.00
S NEW FRONTIER MEDIA INC (NOOF)	0%	0.00	-13,000.000	9.300	-104,477.55	-120,900.00
M NOLAND COMPANY (NOLD)	0%	95.52	1.000	41.500	35.24	41.50
M NORTHERN STATES FINL CORP (NSFC)	0%	0.00	500.000	28.640	14,644.00	14,320.00
M PC MALL INC (MALL)	3%	0.00	7,600.000	16.230	26,610.05	123,348.00
S PC MALL INC (MALL)	0%	0.00	-1,000.000	16.230	-13,141.38	-16,230.00
M PDS GAMING CORP FORMERLY PDS FINL CRP TO 05/11/01 (PDSG)	0%	0.00	7,500.000	1.919	14,872.00	14,392.50
M PRG SCHULTZ INTL INC (PRGX)	0%	0.00	2,000.000	4.900	9,358.00	9,800.00
M PAC-WEST TELECOM INC (PACW)	1%	0.00	11,000.000	1.920	16,437.38	21,120.00
S PAC-WEST TELECOM INC (PACW)	0%	0.00	-11,000.000	1.920	-24,118.86	-21,120.00
M PAR TECHNOLOGY CORP (PTC)	0%	0.00	1,000.000	7.990	6,364.00	7,990.00
S PAR TECHNOLOGY CORP (PTC)	0%	0.00	-700.000	7.990	-5,587.13	-5,593.00
M PARLUX FRAGRANCES INC (PARL)	0%	0.00	1,000.000	5.150	3,696.63	5,150.00
M PATRIOT TRANSN HLDG INC (PATR)	1%	0.00	806.000	33.000	25,266.02	26,598.00
M PHARMANETICS INC (PHAR)	0%	0.00	2,500.000	1.877	3,718.00	4,692.50
M PHARMCHEM INC (PCHM)	0%	0.00	200.000	0.140	64.53	28.00
M PLEXUS CORP (PLXS)	1%	0.00	2,000.000	17.170	28,574.06	34,340.00
S PLEXUS CORP (PLXS)	0%	0.00	-500.000	17.170	-9,071.57	-8,585.00
M PRICESMART INC (PSMT)	0%	0.00	2,000.000	6.260	10,918.00	12,520.00
M PURE WORLD INC (PURW)	0%	0.00	1,500.000	2.511	2,940.00	3,766.50
M QUANEX CORP (NX)	2%	255.00	1,500.000	46.100	57,376.00	69,150.00

2003 Investment Report

January 1, 2003 - December 31, 2003

Fidelity Account

WILLIAM N MATSON - INDIVIDUAL

Holdings (Symbol) as of 12/31	% of Holdings	Income Earned	Quantity	Price per Unit	Total Cost Basis/Proceeds	Total Value
M R & B INC (RBIN)	1%	0.00	3,700.000	15.500	38,071.29	57,350.00
S R & B INC (RBIN)	0%	0.00	-1,000.000	15.500	-14,077.33	-15,500.00
M ROCKY SHOES & BOOTS INC (RCKY)	4%	0.00	7,800.000	22.390	76,544.60	174,642.00
S ROCKY SHOES & BOOTS INC (RCKY)	0%	0.00	-3,500.000	22.390	-65,410.86	-78,365.00
M ROFIN SINAR TECH INC (RSTI)	1%	0.00	1,000.000	34.560	27,343.38	34,560.00
S ROFIN SINAR TECH INC (RSTI)	0%	0.00	-1,000.000	34.560	-29,130.62	-34,560.00
M RONSON CORP COM NEW (RONC)	1%	0.00	10,992.000	2.470	19,240.67	27,150.24
M RUSHMORE FINL GROUP INC (RFGI)	0%	0.00	1.000	0.370	unknown	0.37
M SBE INC COM NEW (SBEI)	2%	0.00	12,500.000	6.910	16,290.00	86,375.00
S SBE INC COM NEW (SBEI)	0%	0.00	-12,500.000	6.910	-88,900.69	-86,375.00
M SI INTL INC (SINT)	2%	0.00	3,500.000	19.570	60,620.00	68,495.00
M SCITEX LTD ORD (SCIX)	1%	0.00	9,000.000	5.060	42,053.00	45,540.00
M SERVOTRONICS INC (SVT)	0%	0.00	1,000.000	2.900	2,008.00	2,900.00
M SHILOH INDS INC (SHLO)	2%	0.00	10,000.000	6.300	26,783.00	63,000.00
M SIGMATRON INTL INC (SGMA)	3%	0.00	4,000.000	26.130	19,566.40	104,520.00
S SIGMATRON INTL INC (SGMA)	0%	0.00	-3,230.000	26.130	-71,933.08	-84,399.90
M SINGING MACHINE CO INC (SMD)	0%	0.00	2,500.000	2.390	4,890.00	5,975.00
M SMITH & WOLLENSKY RESTAURANT GROUP INC (SWRG)	0%	0.00	2,500.000	6.380	11,332.00	15,950.00
M SMITH-MIDLAND CORP (SMID)	0%	0.00	6,000.000	0.840	5,388.00	5,040.00
M SOUTHERN UNION CO NEW COM (SUG)	1%	0.00	2,000.000	18.400	34,618.00	36,800.00
M SPARTAN STORES INC (SPTN)	2%	0.00	12,500.000	5.000	48,369.00	62,500.00
M SPORT CHALET INC (SPCH)	0%	0.00	1,100.000	9.800	8,366.00	10,780.00
M STIFEL FINL CORP (SF)	3%	0.00	6,000.000	19.500	87,391.00	117,000.00
M STORAGE ENGINE INC (SENG)	0%	0.00	11.000	0.330	6.97	3.63
M STORAGENETWORKS INC NO STOCKHOLDER EQ 11/03/03	0%	33,058.00	20,000.000	------	unknown	unavailable
M TII NETWORK TECHNOLOGIES INC (TII)	1%	0.00	12,000.000	2.120	23,865.62	25,440.00
M T J T INC (AXLE)	1%	0.00	70,000.000	0.800	55,774.05	56,000.00
M TRM CORP (TRMM)	2%	0.00	9,000.000	8.530	23,540.50	76,770.00
M TARGET LOGISTICS INC (TARG)	0%	0.00	1,500.000	0.550	643.00	825.00

2003 Investment Report

January 1, 2003 - December 31, 2003

Fidelity Account

WILLIAM N MATSON - INDIVIDUAL

Holdings (Symbol) as of 12/31	% of Holdings	Income Earned	Quantity	Price per Unit	Total Cost Basis/Proceeds	Total Value
M TOUCHTUNES MUSIC CRP CL A (TTMC)	0%	0.00	3,500.000	0.210	930.00	735.00
M TRANS INDS INC (TRNI)	0%	0.00	1,500.000	2.750	3,423.00	4,125.00
M TRIMERIS INC (TRMS)	0%	0.00	500.000	20.940	9,998.00	10,470.00
M TROPICAL SPORTWEAR INTL (TSIC)	0%	0.00	2,500.000	2.180	6,109.00	5,450.00
M TUFCO TECHNOLOGIES INC (TFCO)	1%	0.00	6,500.000	7.050	40,813.45	45,825.00
M UFP TECH INC (UFPT)	0%	0.00	2,500.000	1.840	4,276.00	4,600.00
M US ONCOLOGY INC (USON)	1%	0.00	2,000.000	10.760	15,996.85	21,520.00
S US ONCOLOGY INC (USON)	0%	0.00	-2,000.000	10.760	-18,733.11	-21,520.00
M UBIQUITEL INC (UPCS)	1%	0.00	8,557.000	2.689	13,595.08	23,009.77
M ULTIMATE ELECTRS INC (ULTE)	0%	0.00	1,500.000	7.630	10,482.00	11,445.00
M UNI MARTS INC (UNI)	0%	0.00	3,000.000	1.560	5,072.00	4,680.00
M UNITED ST LIME & MINERALS INC (USLM)	1%	0.00	6,600.000	6.750	33,082.68	44,550.00
M VLPS LIGHTING SERVICES INTL INC (LITE)	1%	519.92	13,899.000	4.100	42,930.25	56,985.90
M V S E CORP (VSEC)	1%	600.68	3,555.000	13.250	31,681.92	47,103.75
M VODAVI TECHNOLOGY (VTEK)	2%	0.00	16,160.000	5.800	63,702.19	93,728.00
S VODAVI TECHNOLOGY (VTEK)	0%	0.00	-16,160.000	5.800	-129,110.18	-93,728.00
M WSI INDUSTRIES INC (WSCI)	0%	487.50	1,500.000	2.490	3,127.00	3,735.00
S WSI INDUSTRIES INC (WSCI)	0%	0.00	-1,500.000	2.490	-4,226.78	-3,735.00
M WASTE TECHNOLOGY CORP (WTEK)	0%	0.00	1,000.000	0.200	246.00	200.00
M WILSONS THE LEATHER EXPERTS (WLSN)	0%	0.00	1,500.000	3.460	4,978.00	5,190.00
M ZEVEX INTL INC DEL (ZVXI)	0%	0.00	3,000.000	3.980	11,030.60	11,940.00
S ZEVEX INTL INC DEL (ZVXI)	0%	0.00	-3,000.000	3.980	-11,581.43	-11,940.00
M ZUNICOM INC (ZNCM)	1%	0.00	20,445.000	1.350	10,552.88	27,600.75
Options						
M PUT SINA CORP REG SHS JAN 30 (NOQMF)	0%	0.00	50.000	0.450	2,333.00	2,250.00
M PUT AKAMAI TECH JAN 12 1/2 (UMUMV)	0%	0.00	15.000	1.750	2,505.50	2,625.00
M PUT AMERICA WEST HLDGS JAN 12 1/2 (AWAMV)	0%	0.00	25.000	0.750	2,295.50	1,875.00

2003 Investment Report

January 1, 2003 - December 31, 2003

Fidelity Account

WILLIAM N MATSON - INDIVIDUAL

Holdings (Symbol) as of 12/31	% of Holdings	Income Earned	Quantity	Price per Unit	Total Cost Basis/Proceeds	Total Value
M PUT ASK JEEVES INC JAN 20 (AUKMD)	0%	0.00	12.000	2.050	2,426.00	2,460.00
M PUT BRIGHTPOINT INC JAN 17 1/2 (ULNMW)	0%	0.00	20.000	1.050	2,146.00	2,100.00
M PUT CERADYNE INC JAN 35 (AUEMG)	0%	0.00	15.000	2.200	2,355.50	3,300.00
M CALL(LEAP 2005) (ZAV DIAMONDS TRUST SER I JAN 76 (100 SHS)(ZAV (ZAVAX)	1%	0.00	20.000	28.700	27,663.00	57,400.00
M PUT DOBSON JAN 7 1/2 (QDMMU)	0%	0.00	20.000	1.250	2,538.00	2,500.00
M PUT ECOLLEGE.COM JAN 17 1/2 (EGUMW)	0%	0.00	1.000	0.650	73.00	65.00
M PUT (DBO) ERESEARCH TECHNOLOGY JAN 25 (150 SHS) (DBOME)	0%	0.00	20.000	1.150	3,488.00	3,450.00
M PUT FARO TECHNOLOGIES JAN 25 (QEJME)	0%	0.00	20.000	1.450	2,638.00	2,900.00
M PUT (FLU) FLAMEL TECH SA ADR JAN 25 (100 SHS) (FLUME)	0%	0.00	27.000	0.750	1,938.50	2,025.00
M PUT (MUL) MOBILITY ELECTRONICS JAN 10 (100 SHS) (MULMB)	0%	0.00	20.000	1.250	2,338.00	2,500.00
M PUT OXIGENE INC JAN 10 (QYOMB)	0%	0.00	13.000	1.900	2,497.50	2,470.00
M PUT PRIMUS TELECOMMS GP JAN 10 (PWUMB)	0%	0.00	50.000	0.400	2,341.00	2,000.00
M PUT SONUS NETWORKS INC JAN 7 1/2 (UJSMU)	0%	0.00	50.000	0.300	1,312.50	1,500.00
M PUT TRADESTATION GROUP JAN 10 (ULRMB)	0%	0.00	20.000	1.200	2,338.00	2,400.00
M PUT (SHV) TRIDENT MICROSYSTEMS JAN 16 5/8 (150 SHS) (SHVMV)	0%	0.00	30.000	0.800	3,653.00	3,600.00

2003 Investment Report

January 1, 2003 - December 31, 2003

Fidelity Account

WILLIAM N MATSON - INDIVIDUAL

Holdings (Symbol) as of 12/31	% of Holdings	Income Earned	Quantity	Price per Unit	Total Cost Basis/Proceeds	Total Value
M PUT XM SATELLITE RADIO JAN 25 (QSYME)	0%	0.00	20.000	0.600	2,238.00	1,200.00
Total Market Value as of December 31, 2003						**$3,178,532.62**
Total income earned on positions no longer held		4,843.49				
2003 Income Earned		**$ 44,776.16**				
Debit balance						-1,921,084.65
Short balance						943,210.71
Total Net Value						**$2,200,658.68**

M - Position held in margin account. S - Position held in short account.

WILLIAM NICHOLAS MATSON

Investment Report

January 1, 2004 - January 31, 2004

Online	Fidelity.com
FAST(sm)-Automated Telephone	800-544-5555
Private Access Team 73	800-544-5704

Fidelity Account — WILLIAM N MATSON - INDIVIDUAL

Account Summary

Beginning market value as of Jan 1	$3,178,532.62
Withdrawals	-35,000.00
Transaction costs, loads and fees	-6,360.92
Net adjustments	-4,960.00
Margin interest paid	-4,135.41
Change in investment value	196,750.87
Change in debit balance	420,178.81
Change in short balance	-283,207.36
Ending market value as of Jan 31	3,471,718.61
Debit balance	-2,341,263.46
Short balance	1,226,418.07
Ending Net Value	**$2,356,873.22**
Your commission schedule	Gold
Account eligible trades from Feb 2003 - Jan 2004	4,614
Current rate on debit balance	3.42%
Additional amount you can borrow	$51,866.87

Income Summary

	This Period	Year to Date
Taxable		
Dividends	$434.38	$434.38

Realized Gain/Loss from Sales

	This Period	Year to Date
Short-term gain	$115,657.16	$115,657.16
Short-term loss	-193,834.77	-193,834.77
St disallowed loss	77,787.58	77,787.58
Net short	**-$390.03**	**-$390.03**
Long-term gain	$1,333.39	$1,333.39

This may not reflect all of your gains/losses because of incomplete cost basis.

WILLIAM NICHOLAS MATSON

Investment Report

February 1, 2004 - February 29, 2004

Online	Fidelity.com
FAST(sm) - Automated Telephone	800-544-5555
Private Access Team 73	800-544-5704

WILLIAM N MATSON - INDIVIDUAL

Fidelity Account

Account Summary

Beginning market value as of Feb 1	$3,471,718.61
Withdrawals	-30,000.00
Transaction costs, loads and fees	-5,309.92
Margin interest paid	-6,907.26
Change in investment value	205,954.22
Change in debit balance	-403,570.43
Change in short balance	434,737.97
Ending market value as of Feb 29	3,666,623.19
Debit balance	-1,937,693.03
Short balance	791,680.10
Ending Net Value	**$2,520,610.26**
Your commission schedule	Gold
Account eligible trades from Mar 2003 - Feb 2004	4,681
Current rate on debit balance	3.77%
Additional amount you can borrow	$72,285.01

Income Summary

	This Period	Year to Date
Taxable		
Dividends	$2,256.68	$2,691.06

Realized Gain/Loss from Sales

	This Period	Year to Date
Short-term gain	$292,768.33	$408,433.49
Short-term loss	-111,362.89	-305,095.66
St disallowed loss	63,094.27	154,993.23
Net short	**$244,499.71**	**$258,331.06**
Long-term gain	$4,695.21	$6,028.60

This may not reflect all of your gains/losses because of incomplete cost basis.

March 2004

Investment Report

March 1, 2004 - March 31, 2004

Online
FAST(sm) - Automated Telephone
Private Access Team 73

Fidelity.com
800-544-5555
800-544-5704

WILLIAM NICHOLAS MATSON

WILLIAM N MATSON - INDIVIDUAL

Fidelity Account

Account Summary

Beginning market value as of Mar 1	$3,666,623.19
Withdrawals	-105,000.00
Transaction costs, loads and fees	-8,131.30
Margin interest paid	-5,858.36
Change in investment value	95,435.52
Change in debit balance	291,638.12
Change in short balance	-199,969.17
Ending market value as of Mar 31	3,734,738.00
Debit balance	-2,229,331.15
Short balance	991,649.27
Ending Net Value	**$2,497,056.12**
Your commission schedule	Gold
Account eligible trades from Apr 2003 - Mar 2004	5,163
Current rate on debit balance	3.77%
Additional amount you can borrow	$273,364.90

Income Summary

	This Period	Year to Date
Taxable		
Dividends	$1,508.76	$4,199.82

Realized Gain/Loss from Sales

	This Period	Year to Date
Short-term gain	$355,816.60	$764,250.09
Short-term loss	-249,820.62	-554,916.28
St disallowed loss	142,231.97	305,577.66
Net short	**$248,227.95**	**$514,911.47**
Long-term gain	$133,717.29	$139,745.89

This may not reflect all of your gains/losses because of incomplete cost basis.

Appendix D

GLOSSARY

Abnormal Earnings Growth– Earnings growth which is either greater or less than the mean for companies with similar dividend payout ratios.

Accelerated Depreciation– Any depreciation method which causes depreciation expense to be highest during the initial years of an asset's assumed useful life.

Accruals– Accounting entries that are not associated with the receipt or disbursement of cash. Also, the income statement and balance sheet items generated by accrual entries. "Accrued Interest Revenue" and an "Accrued Interest Asset," for example, are often accounted for monthly in connection with bond investments that actually pay interest only twice per year.

Actively Managed Mutual Fund– A mutual fund whose intent is to outperform relevant market indices by buying low and selling high.

ADR– American Depository Receipts. A means through which U.S. investors may invest in non-U.S. companies.

Amortization– The accounting expense associated with the writing-off of intangible assets.

Anchoring– The inclination of decision makers to continue being influenced by "starting point" values for irrationally long periods of time, even when they are given additional data that render these values irrelevant (and even if the "starting point" values are clearly outrageous from the outset).

Anomaly– In a stock market context, any strategy that has consistently resulted in returns exceeding those attainable through investment in market indices possessing similar levels of risk

Asset– A thing of value

Asset Quality– A term used to describe the relationship between the economic value of an asset (or collection of assets) and its accounting valuation (i.e., balance sheet value). Low quality assets, for instance, are worth less than the accountants say they are.

Asymptotic– Referring to any relationship in which a dependent variable approaches but never actually reaches a maximum (or minimum) value as an independent variable is increased (or decreased). Example: 1/x approaches but never reaches 0 as x is increased.

Audit Opinion– The conclusion of a Certified Public Accountant (CPA) with respect to whether or not a company's financial statements are fairly presented in accordance with Generally Accepted Accounting Principles – accompanied by a statement describing the scope of the CPA's audit examination.

Availability– The easier it is for a person to imagine a thing happening, the higher its perceived probability of occurrence is likely to be. The Availability Effect predicts that this higher probability of occurrence will be assigned by decision makers separate and apart from any assignment of probability arising from objective analysis.

Average Cost– An inventory valuation method that values all identical items according to the average costs of all such items currently carried in inventory.

Backward Integration– A strategy through which a business assumes a function that, in the past, was performed by an outside supplier. When a newspaper buys a company that makes ink, it is engaging in backward integration.

Bayes Theorem– A statistical technique by which it is possible to assess the probability of an initial condition existing, given our knowledge of the outcome that arose from the condition. If we don't know how Barry Bonds did yesterday, but we see that the Giants scored only one run, application of Bayes Theorem would lead us to conclude that he probably did not hit a home run. Through application of Bayes Theorem, we might estimate this probability by dividing (Bonds's home run total for the year-to date) by (the total year-to date number of Giant at-bats which caused runs to be scored).

Behavioral Trap– A situation in which a person is biased toward continuing an irrational course of action because of his or her past investments (of time, money, or emotional commitment) in that course of action.

Beta– The change in a dependent variable per unit of change in an independent variable. An example: Assume that Total Expected Return on Stock A is our dependent variable and S&P 500 Return is the independent variable. We determine through regression analysis that:

Stock A's Total Expected Return =

5%

+ the S&P 500 Return times Stock A's Beta

The greater Stock A's Beta is, the more sensitive its Total Expected Return is to changes in the S&P 500 return.

Bid-Asked Bounce- Consider a stock that always trades at 9 bid, 10 asked. If it closes one month on a 100 share trade at the bid price, it will be either unchanged or up 1 as of the next month-end. Conversely, if it closes another month on a 100 share trade at the asked price, it will be either unchanged or down 1 at the end of the following month.

The fundamental concept to remember is that if a stock's period-end trade (this period) is at the asked price, this lowers the stock's expected return for the upcoming period – if we measure return as the difference between period-end closing prices. Similarly, if the last trade (this period) is at the bid price, this increases the expected return for the upcoming period.

Other things being equal, any study based on unadjusted closing prices will exaggerate the short-term reversal phenomenon (which indicates that price movements in the recent past are negatively correlated with near-term future price movements). Such a study would also tend to understate the positive correlation between intermediate term price changes and near-term future price movements.

Bid-Asked Spread– In any marketplace, there is a price that buyers are willing to pay (the bid price) and a price that sellers are willing to accept (the asked price). The difference between these two prices is the bid-asked spread. The greater the number of buyers and sellers, the smaller this spread tends to become.

Book Value– Book value is synonymous with the shareholders' equity value on the balance sheet. Book value is also equal to assets minus liabilities.

Book Value/Price– This ratio equals a company's book value divided by the market value of its outstanding common stock. It may also be calculated by developing a book value per share figure (book value divided by number of common shares outstanding) and dividing this figure by the stock's current market price.

Brokerage Analysts– These people work for brokerage firms. Their job descriptions typically include: estimating future earnings of the companies they cover, developing investment recommendations, helping their firms' salespeople generate brokerage commissions, and assisting in the development of investment banking business. Their pronouncements have enormous impact on stock prices, but it is important to note that their opinions often lack objectivity (due to the conflicting interests of those whom they serve).

BV/P– See Book Value/Price.

Calibration Bias– Most people are overconfident when assessing the accuracy of their judgments. Studies indicate that we are typically accurate half the time when we think we are being 67% accurate – and 75% accurate when we think we are being 99% accurate.

Call Option– The right (but not the obligation) to buy a specified number of shares at a specified price within a specified period of time.

Capital Asset Pricing Model– One widely held theory is that the stock market is perfectly efficient. Consequently, the returns an investor may expect are purely attributable to prevailing rates of risk-free return, in combination with overall market return expectations and the investor's willingness to assume risk. According to this theory:

> Total Expected Return =
>
> > Risk-Free Return
>
> + [Expected Market Return minus Risk-Free Return] times [Market Beta of Portfolio]

Capital Expenditure– An expenditure associated with the acquisition of fixed assets, such as property, plant, and equipment.

Capital-Intensive– Companies or industries characterized by large investments in fixed assets.

Capitalized Costs– Costs deemed by GAAP to have substantial benefits after the current period. These costs are treated as assets and either depreciated or amortized over time, rather than being fully expensed in the current period.

CAPM– See Capital Asset Pricing Model.

Cash Flow– Often, this term refers to Free Cash Flow, which can be calculated as:

> Net Income
>
> + Non-Cash Expenses
>
> - Additions To Working Capital
>
> - Capital Expenditures

For purposes of running the backtests in this book, we opted to define Cash Flow as: Income Before Extraordinary Items Available To Common Shareholders

> + Depreciation (a non-cash expense)
>
> + Amortization (another non-cash expense)

We wanted to capture Cash Flow figures that represented sustainable cash-generating power. In our view, Capital Expenditures and Working Capital Additions are items which not only may fluctuate wildly from quarter to quarter, but are also, in large measure, under the direct control of management. Depreciation and amortization charges, in contrast, tend to fluctuate very little. And income is subject to relatively little manipulation by management (in theory, anyway).

While it is true that Working Capital Additions are not optional for a fast-growing company, we believe that their inclusion in Cash Flow calculations: a) penalizes fast-growing companies excessively, because their growth rates (and resultant needs for Working Capital Additions) are typically not sustainable and b) rewards fast-shrinking companies excessively, because their ability to shrink (and, thus, their ability to reduce working capital) is also limited.

Clean Opinion– An audit opinion with no qualifications as to either scope of examination or fairness of the financial statements' presentation in accordance with GAAP.

Closed-End Fund– A mutual fund that trades like a stock. Unlike open-end funds, closed-end funds sell a fixed number of shares on a one-time only basis. Nor do closed-end funds redeem investors' shares. The price of closed-end fund shares is set in the marketplace by supply and demand.

Cognitive Bias– Any psychological phenomenon that interferes with a person's ability to accurately perceive and/or interpret available data.

Cognitive Dissonance– A psychological bias arising from need to minimize inconsistencies in one's perceptions of available data. Most of us, for example, tend to become more confident in our assessment of a stock's (or other thing's) value after we buy it. This would be consistent with the need many of us feel to believe that we are competent decision-makers.

Common Shares– Common shares allow their owners to participate more fully than other securities' owners in both the risks and the rewards of their companies. In general, common shareholders stand last in line for payment of dividends (after preferred shareholders are paid-in-full), as well as for any distributions in bankruptcy/liquidation situations. On the other hand, common shareholders have the most to gain when their companies are successful.

Company-Specific– Attributes that relate to one specific company, rather than to a group of companies.

Compromise Response– A manifestation of selective perception. Example: Some research subjects have looked at red sixes of spades (i.e., the wrong color) and reported seeing purple sixes of hearts or purple sixes of spades.

Confidence Level– The likelihood that, if tested an infinite number of times, the conclusion reached by the researcher would be correct. With respect to regression results, confidence level applies to the probability that an observed relationship between dependent and independent variables actually does exist (i.e., that the beta of the independent variable is not zero).

Confirmation Bias– This bias predisposes decision makers toward gathering and considering data which confirms (rather than disconfirms) the beliefs they currently hold.

Conjunctive Event– An event which is dependent upon two or more events taking place. The Patriots winning the Super Bowl, for example, would be viewed as a conjunctive event at the beginning of the football season. This event can not occur unless 1) the Patriots win enough regular season games to reach the playoffs, 2) win all of their pre-Super Bowl playoff games, and 3) win the Super Bowl itself. To calculate the probability of a conjunctive event, one must multiply the probabilities of all prerequisite events.

Consensus Earnings Estimate– The average of brokerage analysts' earnings estimates for a company. First Call is the most commonly used source of consensus earnings estimates.

Conservatism Bias– Refers to either a bias belonging to the conservatism family of biases or to the tendency of decision makers to alter their beliefs more slowly than new data would warrant.

Contingent Asset/Contingent Liability– An asset or liability whose value is subject to such significant uncertainties that it is only reflected in financial statement footnotes, rather than in the financial statement figures (e.g., the amount at stake in a pending lawsuit).

Covenant– A promise. Loan covenants typically require borrowers to maintain certain financial ratios (e.g., debt/equity) or refrain from undertaking certain activities (e.g., acquisitions) in order to lessen the likelihood of default.

Covered Call– A call option sold by the owner of an asset that, if necessary, can be used to satisfy an exercise of the call option. The owner of GE stock, for example, can earn additional income by selling calls on the stock – the downside being that this limits potential for gain if the stock rises sharply. If one sells a call without owning the underlying asset, the theoretical exposure to liability is unlimited.

Cowles Index– A predecessor of the Dow Jones Industrial Average.

Current Assets– Cash and assets likely to give rise to cash inflows (or to be consumed) during the current operating cycle of the business (typically within one year). Such non-cash current assets typically include accounts receivable, inventory, and prepaid expenses. Note that the current assets of a whiskey maker might well include inventory that must age for several years before being sold.

Current Liabilities– Liabilities likely to give rise to cash outflows during the current operating cycle of the business (typically within one year). Such non-cash current liabilities typically include accounts payable, accrued items (e.g., vacation pay), the current portion of long-term debt, unearned revenues (i.e., advances from customers), and taxes payable.

Data Mining– A process that involves testing the relationships between a dependent variable and a wide variety of independent variables. If one tests enough independent variables, pure coincidence alone will cause strong apparent correlations to emerge. These correlations, however, will have zero practical value in helping us to either predict or understand the dependent variable.

Day Trader– A very short-term investor. Day traders often turn over their portfolios several times during the course of a single day. They tend to buy on the basis of price momentum, rarely analyzing the financial ratios, earnings quality, and other fundamentals of the stocks they trade. They tend to lose money, even in bull markets.

Debt/Equity Ratio– A measure of financial risk. Typically the ratio of total company borrowings divided by shareholders' equity.

Decay Period Of Growth Differential– The period of time over which a company's abnormally high (or low) rate of EPS growth is expected to revert to the mean rate of EPS growth of companies with comparable dividend payout rates.

Decile– A subgroup constituting 10% of a population. Formed by the division of a population into 10 subgroups, sorted according to a specified characteristic.

Depreciation– An accounting expense which reflects the writing-off of an asset's value over the course of its assumed useful life. Note that some depreciable assets actually appreciate in value over time (e.g., some office buildings). When such assets are depreciated, this results in GAAP book values that grossly understate their economic values.

Discount Rate– The rate at which future cash flows are discounted when calculating the present value of these cash flows. For example, a cash flow of $110 that occurs in one year has a present value of $100 when a discount rate of 10% is used. $110 divided by (100% + the 10% discount rate) equals $100. We can check this by observing that the present value of $100 today will grow to the $110 future value when invested for one year at 10%.

Discounting– The process of calculating present value. See Discount Rate for a detailed description of this process.

Disjunctive Event– An event which can occur if one of two or more events take place. The Patriots not winning the Super Bowl, for example, would be viewed as a disjunctive event at the beginning of the football season. This event can occur if 1) the Patriots do not win enough regular season games to reach the playoffs, 2) lose a pre-Super Bowl playoff game, or 3) lose the Super Bowl itself. Generally, the easiest way to calculate the probability of a disjunctive event is to calculate the probability of the disjunctive event not occurring and subtract this probability from 1.

Diversified Investment Portfolio– A portfolio that is not concentrated in any one security, but spread among a variety of issues. Diversification generally reduces risk.

Diversifying Away Of Company-Specific Risk– Individual stocks are subject to the unique risk profiles associated with their issuers. The overall risk to one's portfolio that arises from the risk specific to any one company decreases as the portfolio becomes more diversified. In a highly diversified portfolio, such as the S&P 500, company-specific risk is minimized. The risk that remains in an S&P 500 portfolio is market risk, which can not be diversified away (except through investments other than long positions in American stocks, such as puts, bonds, commodities, real estate, foreign stocks, and foreign currencies).

Dividend Payout Ratio– The ratio of dividends paid to common shareholders divided by EPS.

Dividend Yield– The ratio of dividends paid to common shareholders divided by stock price.

Dividends As A % Of Earnings– See Dividend Payout Ratio.

Dow Jones Industrial Average– A widely followed index derived from price changes in a portfolio of 30 large U.S. industrial companies' stocks.

Dummy Variable– Some regression models involve independent variables that are not numbers. In some cases, the independent variable takes the form of a question that can be answered with a "Yes" or "No." In regression models that test the January Effect, for example, the dummy variable takes the value of 1 for January data points and 0 for data points drawn from other months. The same method is also employed in testing the implications of other non-numerical variables, such as the predictive value of buy recommendations issued with upward earnings estimate revisions versus those issued without revised earnings estimates.

Earnings Per Share– This figure equals:

> Net income plus/minus adjustments (for such items as preferred stock dividends)
>
> Divided by
>
> Common shares outstanding plus/minus adjustments (for such items as unexercised options, warrants, and rights)

Earnings Quality– The sustainability of the circumstances that generate a company's earnings. For example, earnings derived from the sale of a factory would typically be of lower quality than earnings arising from product sales.

Economies of Scale– Unit cost reductions that arise when activity levels and/ or the size of inputs to business processes are increased (i.e., increases in such factors as advertising expenditures, production volumes, average transaction amounts, and so on). Example: It costs much less to assemble Ford Explorers on a high volume assembly line than it would cost to have a small number of workers build them one at a time.

Efficient Market Theory– The widely held and thoroughly discredited notion that the stock market immediately and accurately factors all available information into stock prices. Proponents of Efficient Market Theory believe that any attempt to improve returns through active management will prove futile in the long run.

Endowment Effect– The bias that causes most people to ascribe irrationally high values to the things they currently own. The endowment effect tends to result in delayed investor reactions to adverse developments, causing stock prices to fall slower than they would in an efficient market.

EPS– See Earnings Per Share.

Equity– Assets minus liabilities. Also see Book value.

Equity Method– A method used by a parent company to account for subsidiaries in which it holds between 20% and 50% ownership. This method calls for the parent company to recognize a share of the subsidiary's income (or loss) in proportion to its ownership (e.g., $3,000,000 if the parent owns 30% of a subsidiary that earns $10,000,000). It also calls for the parent to show an "Investment in Subsidiary" asset on its balance sheet equaling its share of the subsidiary's shareholders' equity (e.g., $30,000,000 if the parent owns 30% of a subsidiary with shareholders' equity of $100,000,000).

Equivalent Shares– The denominator in the EPS equation, equaling common shares outstanding plus/minus adjustments for items such as unexercised options, warrants, and rights.

Excess Return– The difference between actual returns and the returns on an appropriate index portfolio used for purposes of comparison.

Exit Costs– The costs associated with withdrawing from an industry or discontinuing a line of business. High exit costs tend to intensify competition by forcing entities to participate in industries from which they would prefer to withdraw.

Expected Return– An amount calculated by 1) multiplying each possible outcome by its probability of occurrence and 2) adding these figures together. For example, a course of action might have a 20% chance of a $50,000 loss and an 80% chance of a $30,000 gain. Its expected return would be (.2 x -$50,000) + (.8 x $30,000), which equals (-$10,000 + $24,000) or $14,000.

Extrapolation– A means of estimating or projecting, based upon the extension of past trends.

Fair P/E– "Fair P/E" equals:

> A stock's estimated, discounted future cash flows to investors (over all future periods)

> Divided by

> EPS projected for the next profitable year

Any stock whose Fair P/E exceeds its actual P/E is, by definition, undervalued. Bear in mind, however, that Fair P/E is almost always a theoretical figure – since most of the variables in the Fair P/E equation are, under normal circumstances, impossible to know with certainty. Fair P/E analysis can be valuable in delineating the range of assumptions under which a stock may be fairly priced. To the extent that the assumptions implied by a stock's current price are not reasonable, the stock is likely to be mispriced (i.e., either undervalued or overvalued).

Fair Price/Earnings Multiple– See Fair P/E.

Fair Value– A company's Fair P/E multiplied by the EPS projected for its next profitable year.

FIFO– First-in, first-out. An inventory valuation method for handling identical units which assumes that the first units placed in inventory are the first units sold. During periods of inflation, FIFO valuation maximizes accounting income (by basing Cost of Goods Sold expense upon the least expensive units). It also maximizes assets and shareholders' equity by valuing unsold units at the costs associated with the most expensive units (i.e., those entering inventory most recently).

Fixed Costs– Costs that will not vary in the short-term with a company's sales volume. Examples include rent, depreciation, and employees' health insurance benefits.

Forward Integration– A strategy through which a business assumes a function that, in the past, was performed by a customer. When a company that makes ink buys a newspaper, it is engaging in forward integration.

Friendly Takeover– An acquisition made with the cooperation of the acquired company's management.

GAAP– See Generally Accepted Accounting Principles.

Generally Accepted Accounting Principles– The allowable methods for recording transactions and presenting audited financial information. Generally Accepted Accounting Principles may vary significantly from country to country.

Goodwill– Goodwill is treated as an intangible asset for accounting purposes in the U.S. It equals the difference between the purchase price paid for an acquired company and the acquired company's book value. In some countries, it is expensed immediately. Other things being equal, this causes the income of acquirers using these countries' GAAPs to be lower in the current year and higher in future years. Note that goodwill only arises when the "purchase" method is used to account for an acquisition (as opposed to the "pooling of interests" method). A complex set of rules dictate which accounting method is used.

Gross Margin– Typically the difference between an item's sales price and the cost at which it is carried in inventory.

Groupthink– A bias associated with the decision-making processes of groups which either overtly or tacitly enforce conformity among their members. Groupthink is inherent in the decision-making processes of many institutional investors, especially those which make decisions by committee. It may cause delayed market reaction to new information that conflicts with widely held beliefs, as well as overconfidence in courses of action consistent with these beliefs.

Growth Stock– A stock that provides or is expected to provide unusually high returns. Also, a stock with high price ratios.

Halo Effect– A bias that causes a favorable (or unfavorable) impression regarding one characteristic of a person or thing to influence opinion regarding another characteristic of that person or thing. For example, in the absence of other information, the halo effect predisposes many of us to believe that an attractive person is more intelligent than an unattractive person. Investors often tend to believe that well-managed companies are also likely to be good investments (which may or may not be the case). Consequently, the halo effect contributes to the overvaluation of "in favor" companies and the undervaluation of "out of favor" companies.

Hedge– To take actions designed to reduce one's losses in the event of adverse developments. For example, buying put options on a stock that one currently owns is a good way to hedge against the possibility of declines in the stock's price.

Held To Maturity Securities– Fixed income securities (e.g., government bonds) that are expected to be held until maturity. Even if rising interest rates or other circumstances diminish the market value of these securities (or falling interest rates increase their market value), they are carried on their owners' financial statements at historical cost. This GAAP-compliant accounting method can often cause large disparities between the accounting and economic values of these assets.

Herding– The tendency of analysts to be influenced by other analysts' earnings estimates.

Herding Index– A measure of the tendency to herd.

High Flyer– An "in favor" stock. Typically such a stock has a high P/E and is involved in a glamorous industry. On average, high flyers provide abnormally low returns while subjecting their owners to unusually high levels of risk.

High Relative Price Strength– Better-than-average recent price appreciation (usually measured over a period of months, if not years).

High Relative Value– Higher-than-average value ratios, such as earnings/price and book value/price.

Holding Period– The period that passes between the time a security is purchased and the time it is sold.

Hostile Media Effect– A bias that causes those who favor a given point of view to perceive the media (including brokerage analysts) as being prejudiced against that point of view. This bias may cause reluctance to believe reports of unexpected developments. Such reluctance may, in turn, lead to delayed market reaction—an inefficiency that fast-acting investors may profitably exploit.

Hypergrowth– Earnings growth which is greater than the mean for companies with similar characteristics.

Illusory Correlations– Correlations that are perceived where, in fact, none actually exist.

Implied Outcome– The outcome that must occur in order to justify a specified P/E. Also, the range of assumptions under which a stock may be fairly priced.

Inclusive Account– A mental account that includes more than one investment. That is, an inclusive account tracks investments in the context of a portfolio, rather than viewing each one in isolation.

Index Fund– A passively managed investment portfolio that seeks to mimic the returns of an index (such as the S&P 500, Dow Jones Industrial Average, or Russell 3000), rather than employing active management in an attempt to outperform.

Individually-Managed Accounts– Accounts that are actively managed in accordance with the needs of an individual client. Such an approach is especially useful in circumstances calling for sensitivity to the client's tax situation. In contrast, mutual funds handle all shareholders' accounts in exactly the same way and can not accommodate individual clients with special needs.

Inefficient Market- A market that does not immediately and accurately factor all available information into prices. Many investors believe that active management may improve returns through exploitation of market inefficiencies.

Insider– A corporate officer, board member, or other person whose association with a company entails restrictions and/or reporting requirements with respect to trading in the company's stock. Since insiders have special knowledge of their companies' prospects, it is generally wise to buy what insiders are buying and to sell what insiders are selling. Many studies have documented the effectiveness that such a strategy would have achieved in the past.

Institution/Institutional Investor– Any investor other than an individual. Major institutional investors include such entities as insurance companies, banks, endowments, and pension funds.

Institutional Investor All-America Team– Analysts who get more votes than their peers in a poll of institutional investors conducted by *Institutional Investor* magazine. As befits the conflicted nature of the analysts' job description, it is difficult to establish by any objective measure exactly how All-America Team members are superior to their peers (other than in their ability to collect votes in this poll).

Internally-Generated Funds– Cash flow generated by sources other than borrowing and the issuance of additional equity. Growth that can be financed with internally-generated funds typically results in faster EPS growth (and higher valuations) than growth that requires external financing.

Interpolation– A means of estimating the value of a data point, based upon one's knowledge of the data points surrounding the data point being estimated.

Investment Banks– Organizations that help businesses to raise money in the capital markets. They also act as advisors to businesses involved in mergers, acquisitions, and other complex financial transactions. Often, they are affiliated with brokerages, which play a key role in selling securities to the public. Companies typically seek to do business with the investment banks whose brokerage analysts can give their stocks the most attention and support (i.e., the analysts who can do the most to keep their stock prices high). Given the multi-million dollar fees that investment banking engagements often entail, huge potential for conflict exists between the interests of securities issuers and those of the investors who rely upon analysts' recommendations.

Investment Style– The type of stocks in one's portfolio. Style types include "value," "growth," "small cap," and "large cap." When evaluating portfolio performance, it is useful to identify the style being employed – since different styles may produce very different results in any given time period.

Investment Trap– See Behavioral Trap.

Invisible Correlations– Significant correlations that people fail to perceive. This phenomenon plays a key role in the persistence of stock market inefficiencies. That is, because most investors fail to see the correlations between certain factors and superior returns, these correlations do not influence their investment strategies. If the return advantages associated with these factors were widely exploited, they would disappear. Because they are not, inefficiencies continue to persist.

IPO– An initial public offering (i.e., the offering of a company's stock to the public for the first time).

January Barometer– The correlation between January stock market returns in the U.S. and returns during the following 11 months of odd-numbered years. This correlation is thought to result from the market's delayed response to major political events occurring during January in these years (such as the convening of a new Congress and the occasional inauguration of a new president).

January Effect– The tendency of January to produce a disproportionate share of total stock market returns. In general, January has been an especially good month for small cap stocks, as well as for stocks hitting 12-month or 24-month lows in December. Possible causes of this effect include year-end tax loss selling, which often occurs in November or December. Such selling is often followed by January buybacks of these issues, since buybacks within 30 days of sales would result in IRS disallowance of tax loss deductions (under "wash sale" rules).

Large Cap Stock– A stock with a large market capitalization (typically greater than $5 billion).

Last-In, First-Out (LIFO)– An inventory valuation method for handling identical units which assumes that the last units placed in inventory are the first units sold. During periods of inflation, LIFO valuation minimizes accounting income (by basing Cost of Goods Sold expense upon the most expensive units). It also minimizes assets and shareholders' equity by valuing unsold units at the costs associated with the least expensive units (i.e., those entering inventory first).

Liabilities– Items expected to generate future cash outflows. Examples include: bank borrowings, accounts payable, and accrued interest liabilities.

LIFO– See Last-In, First-Out.

Limit Order– An order that specifies a maximum price an investor is willing to pay for a stock or a minimum price at which an investor is willing to sell.

Liquidity– The ease with which an asset may be converted to cash. The liquidity of a stock is generally indicated by such factors as trading volume (high volumes indicating high liquidity) and bid-asked spread (small spreads indicating high liquidity). Long-term investors are likely to earn higher returns from illiquid stocks than from liquid issues, since a premium generally must be paid for liquidity (and liquidity is more valuable to investors who trade frequently than to investors with long holding periods).

Lockup Period– A period during which certain holders of a company's stock may be prohibited from selling their stock.

Long-Term Debt– Typically bond liabilities and other borrowings that will not come due during the coming year.

Look-Ahead Bias– A potential problem with models that use historical data to backtest the effectiveness of various investment strategies. This bias occurs when a study purports to predict stock price movements with data that would not have been available prior to the occurrence of the price movements being predicted (e.g., using year-end data that becomes available in February to predict January price movements).

Loss Aversion Bias– A family of biases that includes the Endowment Effect, as well as the effects of Prospect Theory, Psychological Accounting, and Investment Traps. They tend to delay the stock market's reaction to new developments. In general, loss aversion refers to an aversion to recognizing losses. It differs from risk aversion in that a loss averse investor experiencing losses on paper will actively seek risk in an effort to break even. The difference between losing $1,000 and breaking even may, in the loss averse investor's mind, exceed the difference between losing $1,000 and losing $2,000.

March Barometer– A predecessor of the January Barometer. Applies to 1909, 1913, 1921, 1929, and 1933, years when new presidents were inaugurated in March. The convening of new Congresses was also timed to coincide with these inaugurations, leading to a set of circumstances highly similar to that which has prevailed since 1935 in the January of odd-numbered years.

Market Capitalization– The market price of a stock multiplied by the total number of shares outstanding.

Market Impact– The effect of one's order on the market price of a stock. Buying causes the asked price to rise (bad if you can't fill your entire order at the current asked price), and selling causes the bid price to fall (bad if you can't fill your entire order at the current bid price). Market impact can cause significant adverse pricing effects even on relatively small orders involving illiquid stocks (e.g., orders to sell 200 shares when the highest bidder only wants 100 shares). It can also be a problem for large orders involving highly liquid stocks.

Market Inefficiency– A predictable circumstance in which the market does not immediately and accurately factor all available information into prices. Some investment strategies have been able to consistently outperform market averages by exploiting these inefficiencies.

Market Order– An order to buy a stock at the asked price (whatever that price may be) or to sell a stock at the bid price (whatever it may be). Though some brokerage firms offer discounted commissions for market orders, it makes more sense to enter limit orders in most situations. It is particularly dangerous to enter market orders involving thinly-traded stocks, since the bid and asked prices may fall or rise sharply if your order happens to hit the market at an illiquid moment (or if your order is relatively large).

Market Risk– There are a variety of factors that affect the great majority of U.S. stocks—such as interest rates, oil prices, and mutual fund cash flows. Consequently, most stocks tend to be up when the S&P 500 is up, and most stocks tend to go down when that index is down. The extent to which a stock or portfolio moves with the market determines its level of market risk (also known as its beta). By diversifying, it is possible to eliminate company-specific risk, but diversification within a universe of U.S. stocks can not eliminate market risk. Nor is it possible to fully eliminate market risk through international diversification - since foreign markets generally show strong correlation with the U.S. market. It is, however, possible to enhance expected return per unit of risk assumed through international diversification.

Material Non-Public Information– Information which 1) is not publicly available and 2) could reasonably be expected to affect an investor's evaluation of a stock. Unless you (or your advisor) develop it through the analysis of publicly available data, trading on the basis of material non-public information is generally illegal. (The SEC has rules about this sort of thing.) In view of the above-market returns that can be earned by mimicking corporate insiders, it appears that these people often make trades that are guided by their knowledge of material non-public information. Their trades may or may not be legal, but following their lead is legal – and likely to be profitable.

Mean– The average.

Median– The data point in the middle of a distribution. In a distribution with nine data points, the fifth-highest P/E ratio would be the median P/E ratio. That is, there would be four higher P/E ratios and four lower P/E ratios.

Minimal Account– A mental account that includes only one investment. That is, an investor using minimal accounts tracks each investment in isolation, rather than in the context of a portfolio.

Momentum– A pattern of recent performance. In a stock market context, momentum is generally defined as very recent stock price performance (i.e., over a period of days, hours, or even minutes).

Momentum Investor– An investor who invests in stocks exhibiting strong price performance in the very recent past.

Momentum-Oriented Dissonance– A bias which leads many momentum investors to project that past trends will persist in the future for unreasonably long periods of time. This bias leads them to pay too much for fast-growing companies and too little for slow-growers.

Multiple-Factor Regression– Regression that involves more than one independent variable.

Negative Surprise– A negative surprise occurs when a company reports a quarterly earnings figure that is less than the consensus earnings estimate. Most negative surprises are followed by significant decreases in stock price.

Neglected Stock Effect– The tendency of stocks with little or no analyst coverage to outperform stocks with heavier coverage. Recent research suggests that this effect fades as market cap increases. In general, analyst neglect of small cap stocks is associated with superior performance, while analyst neglect of large cap stocks is predictive of below-average returns.

New Economy– In general, the portion of the economy that is heavily engaged in Internet-related and other digitally-intensive activities (as opposed to "Old Economy" activities, such as traditional manufacturing). The line between New Economy and Old Economy has become quite blurred, as growing numbers of Old Economy businesses have become heavy users of New Economy technologies. It appears that these technologies have played an instrumental role in enhancing productivity and lowering unit labor costs in recent years, thus reducing inflationary pressures in the U.S.

Niche Market– A small market or a segment of a large market. Many highly successful companies owe their success to a focus upon a niche market that others have either overlooked or failed to properly serve. Niche markets often offer limited potential for growth, but they are also less likely than larger markets to generate intense competition.

Nonmarket Risk– Risk that is specific to individual companies. This risk can be largely eliminated through diversification.

Non-Recurring Items– Unsustainable circumstances that generate earnings or expense. For example, earnings derived from the sale of a factory would be a non-recurring item, as would be the expenses associated with repairing damage caused by a "100 year" flood.

Normal EPS Growth– EPS growth equal to the projected long-term mean for companies with similar dividend payout ratios.

November Barometer– A predecessor of the January Barometer. Applies to 1901, 1903, 1905, 1907, 1915, 1923, 1925, 1927, and 1931, years when new Congresses were convened in either November or December.

Options– The right (but not the obligation) to buy (in the case of a call option) or sell (in the case of a put option) an asset (such as a stock) at a specified price during a specified period of time.

Out-of-Favor Companies– Typically such stocks have low P/E multiples and are involved in unglamorous industries. On average, they provide abnormally high returns while subjecting their owners to unusually low levels of risk.

Overconfirmation Bias– The tendency of decision makers to alter their beliefs more slowly than new data would warrant.

Percentage-of-Completion Basis– An accounting method for recognizing project revenue on an ongoing basis (rather than waiting for the project to be completed). It might involve:

> Multiplying the total price to be billed for a project
>
> by
>
> The percentage of total project work performed during the accounting period

If a $2,000,000 project requires 20,000 hours of work, and 10,000 hours are performed during this accounting period, $1,000,000 in revenue would be recognized (10,000/20,000 x $2,000,000 = $1,000,000).

Positive Surprise– A positive surprise occurs when a company reports a quarterly earnings figure that is more than the consensus earnings estimate. Most positive surprises are followed by significant increases in stock price.

Postdecisional Dissonance– A bias that causes confidence in the correctness of a decision to increase after one becomes irrevocably committed to the course of action associated with the decision. In a stock market context, this bias may lead to delay in reacting to new information which contradicts the premises upon which an investment has already been made (or foregone).

Predecisional Dissonance– The inclination of decision makers to be influenced by historical data, even if this data is irrelevant. A stock that sells for $1 and quickly rises to $3 will still be remembered by some as a $1 stock. People who evaluate the stock in this manner will not be inclined to pay $3 for it, even if it is, by every measure other than its price history, worth at least $5.

Present Value– The discounted value of future cash flows.

Presidential Election Cycle Effect– The tendency of stock markets to show abnormally high returns during presidential election years and the year preceding presidential election years—as well as abnormally low returns in the two years following presidential elections. It is widely believed that this effect is caused by deliberate presidential effort to manipulate the stock market for political advantage.

Presidential Party Effect– The tendency of the stock market to provide higher returns during Democratic administrations than in Republican administrations. Also, the tendency of small cap stocks to outperform large cap stocks during Democratic presidencies, with the reverse being true during Republican presidencies.

Private Placement– An issuance of securities to a small number of qualified (i.e., wealthy) investors. Such securities are typically subject to restrictions regarding sale and transfer.

Product Differentiation– A strategy that allows a company or industry to compete on a basis other than price. Las Vegas casinos, which use a variety of motifs (Arabian, Egyptian, Roman, etc.) in targeting specific niches (Caesar's Palace targeting high-rollers, Circus Circus targeting the budget-conscious, and so on) offer a wonderful example of how an industry can differentiate a very basic set of products (i.e., slots, roulette, craps, table games, and sports betting). Products that can not be differentiated in meaningful ways (e.g., low cost air travel) often are associated with industries that experience intense price competition. Consequently, they tend to be only marginally profitable for even their most successful entrants.

Projected Benefit Obligation– The present value of future employee pension obligations. Though reflective of projected salaries (when companies' benefits are a function of average career salary or final year salary), this figure considers only benefits earned as of the balance sheet date.

Prospect Theory– Prospect theory holds that loss aversion differs from risk aversion—in that a loss averse investor experiencing losses on paper will actively seek risk in an effort to break even. The difference between losing $1000 and breaking even may, in the loss averse investor's mind, exceed the difference between losing $1000 and losing $2000.

Prudent Man Rule– An aspect of law regulating the investments made by those entrusted with fiduciary responsibility. According to the Prudent Man Rule, every investment made by a fiduciary on behalf of a client was expected to be prudent. For the most part, this rule has been supplanted by other regulations (such as ERISA and the Prudent Investor Rule) that can allow highly risky investments to be made within the context of a prudently managed portfolio.

Psychological Accounting– How we keep track of things. The Minimal Account method of accounting for investment results considers each investment in isolation. The Topical Account method, in contrast, focuses upon the results of the entire portfolio. The Minimal Account method can magnify the effects of loss aversion biases, since individual investments are likely to be much more volatile than portfolios are. Volatility, of course, inevitably raises anxiety levels and affords increased opportunity for loss aversion biases to come into play.

Psychological Biases – Widely held tendencies that affect decision-making in predictable ways. Investment strategies that involve buying the stocks that bias-afflicted investors are selling, while selling the stocks that they are buying, have tended to be profitable.

Publicly Traded Companies– Companies whose stocks trade on exchanges, NASDAQ, and/or other public markets.

Put Option– The right (but not the obligation) to sell a specified number of shares at a specified price within a specified period of time.

Qualified Opinion– An audit opinion that either 1) is based upon an examination of limited scope or 2) mentions one or more ways in which the financial statements fail to conform with GAAP.

Quartile– A subgroup constituting 25% of a population. Formed by the division of a population into four subgroups, sorted according to a specified characteristic.

Quintile– A subgroup constituting 20% of a population. Formed by the division of a population into five subgroups, sorted according to a specified characteristic.

Ratio-Difference Principle– A facet of psychological accounting which causes many investors to worry about large percentage losses, even when the amount of money involved is relatively inconsequential. Due to the ratio-difference principle, a 50% loss on a $1,000 investment in call options ($500) can create more anxiety and regret than a 2% loss on a $100,000 investment ($2,000).

Regression Analysis– A mathematical technique used to discern cause and effect relationships between independent and dependent variables. Regression analysis is particularly useful in identifying factors that have, historically, been predictive of superior investment returns.

Regression Toward The Mean– The tendency of both abnormally poor and abnormally rapid EPS growth to become average over time. Investors often underestimate this tendency when evaluating high P/E stocks that are experiencing rapid growth, causing them to overpay for these stocks. In addition, they often underestimate the tendency of slow-growers to improve when evaluating low P/E stocks, which causes these stocks to be undervalued.

REIT– Real Estate Investment Trust. A REIT is a managed portfolio of properties that trades like a stock.

Repatriation– The transfer of assets (such as cash) from a foreign country to one's home country. Some countries limit the ability of businesses to repatriate assets. Other things being equal, a company subject to repatriation restrictions will be worth less than a company unencumbered by such restrictions.

Reported Earnings– The net income and EPS figures reported in corporate financial statements. It often makes sense to adjust these figures in order to determine the portion of a company's earnings that is sustainable.

Required Return– The rate of return that investors expect to earn on an investment. This rate varies from investor to investor, and it also varies according to the risks inherent in the investment.

Restricted Stock– Stock sold through private placements that has restrictions associated with its sale or transfer. Restricted stock is typically sold at a significant discount to the issuer's publicly traded stock.

Retained Earnings– The portion of a company's earnings to date that have not been distributed in the form of dividends.

Revenue– Sales of goods and services.

Revenue Recognition– Revenue is generally recognized as soon as a company has completed all its obligations associated with the sale of its goods or services. In the case of companies with ongoing warranty and service responsibilities, it is typically acceptable to recognize revenue at the time of sale, while also recognizing a warranty or service liability (and related expense).

Under some circumstances involving lengthy projects, it is acceptable to use the "percentage of completion" revenue recognition method.

Rights– The right (but not the obligation) to buy a stock at a specified price during a specified period of time.

Risk Aversion– The tendency to avoid risk. Risk aversion differs from loss aversion—in that a loss averse investor experiencing losses on paper will actively seek risk in an effort to break even. The difference between losing $1000 and breaking even may, in the loss averse investor's mind, exceed the difference between losing $1000 and losing $2000. The investor who is truly risk averse (rather than loss averse) would care more about avoiding future risk than about breaking even.

Risk Premium– The difference between the required return on an investment and the risk-free rate. This premium is necessary in order to entice investors to accept risk.

Risk-Free Rate of Return– Typically the rate associated with short-term debt obligations of the U.S. Government.

Rivalry– A characteristic associated with highly competitive industries. Usually rivalry takes the form of price competition. Other things being equal, a company in a rivalry-intensive industry will experience slower EPS growth than a company in an industry with less rivalry. Rivalry is especially intense in industries having low levels of product differentiation, low variable costs, and high exit costs (such as the airline industry).

Robustness– If a regression model (or other predictive model): 1) may be applied to any time period and 2) works properly without requiring manipulation of one or more variables, it may be said to possess robustness. Results derived from models that are not robust should be viewed with suspicion.

Russell 3000– The Russell 3000 is an index based upon a portfolio of 3000 U.S. stocks. The average market cap of Russell 3000 companies is smaller than those of companies included in the Dow Jones Industrial Average and S&P 500.

Securities Analyst Societies– Organizations affiliated with the Association for Investment Management Research that provide investment professionals with information, networking, and professional development opportunities. Such organizations have been organized in financial centers throughout the world. They often afford publicly traded companies the opportunity to make presentations to their members.

Selective Perception– A bias that interferes with our ability to perceive information that conflicts with our expectations and beliefs. It can lead to delay in stock market reaction to unexpected developments.

Shareholders' Equity– Assets minus liabilities. Also see Book value.

Short-Term Reversal Phenomenon– The tendency of last month's biggest stock market winners to become this month's biggest stock market losers— and for last month's biggest stock market losers to become this month's biggest stock market winners. This phenomenon is largely attributable to momentum investors, who often cause prices to overreact to news. Reversals occur when the stock prices affected by such overreaction return to more appropriate levels.

Short Seller– An investor who borrows someone else's stock (usually through a broker) and sells it, then buying it back (and replacing it) at a later date. Such an investor makes money if the stock's price goes down. That is, if the stock can be bought back at a lower price than the price at which it was originally sold, the short sale will be profitable.

Skewness– A property possessed by a population having an unusually large number of its members that differ greatly from the mean (with respect to the characteristic being analyzed).

Small Cap Stock– A company with a small market capitalization (typically under $1 billion).

Spinoff– A portion of a parent company that is given autonomy and functions from then on as an independent company. Shares in spinoffs are typically distributed to the parent company's shareholders. Many shareholders tend to sell their spinoff shares soon after receiving them. This depresses their prices and often results in buying opportunities that can be profitably exploited. On average, spinoff shares have provided superior returns when purchased 30 days after they start to trade publicly.

Standard Deviation– A measure of dispersion. Stocks associated with large standard deviations in their returns are considered risky.

The mathematics of calculating standard deviation involve:

a. Calculating the mean of the population (i.e., the average of all data points);

b. Calculating the difference between each data point and the mean,

c. Squaring each of these differences;

d. Adding together each of the figures calculated in **c**;

e. Dividing [the figure calculated in **d**] by [the number of data points in the population – 1]; and

f. Calculating the square root of the figure calculated in **e**.

Statistical Significance– Possessing a high confidence level, typically 95% or more.

Stock Index Future– A security that allows investors to participate in the price movement of an entire index (such as the S&P 500).

Stock Option– The right (but not the obligation) to buy (in the case of a call option) or sell (in the case of a put option) a stock at a specified price during a specified period of time.

Stock Repurchase Program– A mechanism through which companies re-purchase their own stock.

Straight-Line Depreciation– A depreciation method which causes depreciation expense to be equal during each year of an asset's assumed useful life.

Structural Changes– Fundamental changes in the economic environment that can cause relationships between independent and dependent variables to change or disappear. Changes in the tax code, for instance, can alter the strength of the January Effect, since this phenomenon is caused, to some extent, by tax-motivated, year-end selling.

Style-Based Index– An index based on the price movements of a portfolio composed of stocks whose attributes are consistent with a specified investment style.

Substitute Products– To the extent that the products of a company or industry face competition from substitute products, this will have a negative impact upon future EPS growth prospects. Examples of products that can be substituted for each other to some degree include beer/wine, air travel/train travel, aluminum/steel, and paper/plastic.

Sunk Cost– An investment made in a course of action. Except for their ability to provide tax benefits, the amounts we have paid for investments in the past should have no relevance to the decisions we make in the future. A behavioral trap adversely affects decision-making when it causes someone to continue an inferior course of action in seeking to recoup sunk costs.

Super Bowl Indicator– An example of the hazards of data mining. According to this indicator, the market is likely to do well in years that the NFC team wins the Super Bowl.

Survivor Bias– A problem that arises when data associated with companies whose stocks stop trading during the study period is ignored or eliminated. This bias tends to make factors associated with risky businesses (such as negative earnings and high debt/equity ratios) appear to be more predictive of high returns than they deserve to be – since the risky companies that go out of business are ignored.

Sustainable Earnings– Earnings derived from transactions and circumstances that are likely to recur in the future.

Tax-Loss Selling– Selling of stocks that is motivated by a desire to realize losses during the current tax year.

Terminal Valuation– The cash that one expects to generate by selling an asset at a specified future date.

Thinly-Traded– A term used to describe a stock with low average daily trading volume.

Total Return– A performance figure that includes return from dividends, as well as return from price appreciation.

Transaction Costs– Commissions are a relatively small component of total transaction costs, which also include market impact costs and a portion of the bid-asked spread. Investors who seek to execute transactions immediately will maximize their exposure to costs associated with market impact and the bid-asked spread. More patient investors can reduce these costs significantly by placing limit orders, as well as by building and unwinding their positions over extended time periods. The downside to patient trading is that it tends to reduce the advantage to be gained by reacting quickly to new information. Limit orders, in fact, will never be executed if the stock does not reach the price limit specified.

Treasury Bill– A short-term debt security backed by the full faith and credit of the U.S. Government.

Trend Biases– A family of biases that cause investors to overreact in the short-term – buying what has risen and selling what has fallen.

T-Ratio/T-Statistic– If several regressions are run with different samples drawn from the same population, calculated betas will differ. The t-ratio is equal to:

Factor Beta minus Hypothesized Beta (usually 0)

Divided by

Standard Beta Error (the square of the standard deviations of the calculated betas)

Thus, the value of the t-ratio 1) increases as beta increases and 2) decreases as the variability of beta increases. Confidence levels are ascertained by comparing the t-ratio with the critical t-statistics found in the Student's t Distribution Table. A t-ratio of more than 1.96 indicates a 95%+ confidence level that the beta is greater than 0 (or some other hypothesized value), with t-ratios of more than 2.66 indicating confidence levels of 99% or more.

Uneven Intra-Month Cash Flow Effect– A predictable effect upon stock prices caused by employer-sponsored retirement plan investments at the beginning and middle of each month (when plan participants are normally paid).

Valence Effect– A bias that causes highly favorable events to seem more likely to occur in the future—and highly unfavorable events to seem less likely. Consequently, decision makers assign higher probabilities to highly favorable occurrences than objective analyses of the facts would warrant (and inappropriately low probabilities to highly unfavorable outcomes). The Valence Effect contributes to the overvaluation of stocks associated with the potential for spectacular success (and equally spectacular failure) and to the relative undervaluation of companies with expectations of modest, but predictable growth.

Valuation Model– A quantitative model that evaluates securities, based upon assumptions provided by the user.

Value Stock– A stock possessing strong value characteristics, such as low P/E ratio, high book value/price ratio, and/or high sales/price ratio.

Value-Oriented Dissonance– A bias causing a stock's price history to have a lingering effect upon its current price. If a company's stock has traded at 100 in the recent past, investors tend to feel there is legitimate reason to believe that it is worth 100—however much it may have risen or fallen from 100 and however much the company's prospects may have changed. This bias can cause delayed market reaction to new information.

Variable Costs– Costs that vary in direct proportion to sales (as opposed to fixed costs, which are the same regardless of what sales might be).

Vividness Effect– A bias that causes things, events, and ideas which are particularly memorable or emotionally involving to seem more likely to occur in the future. Consequently, decision makers assign higher probabilities to these occurrences than objective analyses of the facts would warrant. The vividness effect contributes to the overvaluation of stocks associated with exciting products and to the undervaluation of companies associated with highly memorable bad news.

Volatility– The propensity of a security or portfolio to exhibit large price swings. Often expressed in terms of standard deviation in returns.

Volume Effect– The tendency of stocks that have risen on heavy volume to, in the days ahead, outperform those that have risen on light volume. Also, the tendency of stocks that have fallen on heavy volume to underperform those that have fallen on light volume. It has been proposed that heavy volume serves to "legitimize" the initial price movement, indicating that the movement was caused by a significant change in business prospects rather than by a small amount of trading arising from investors' personal needs, hopes, and fears.

Warrant– The right (but not the obligation) to buy a specified number of shares at a specified price within a specified period of time.

Working Capital– Current assets minus current liabilities. Working capital components such as inventory and accounts receivable typically increase at roughly the same rate as a company's sales growth. Though these increases are generally offset to some extent by increases in current liabilities (such as accounts payable and accrued employee compensation items), working capital typically increases as sales grows.

Increases in working capital are a drain upon cash. If they can not be financed through internally-generated funds, such financing must come from outside sources (such as borrowing and the sale of stock).

Write-Down– An accounting entry that reduces the balance at which an asset is carried on a company's financial statements. Write-downs are often associated with bad debts, the obsolescence of inventory, or changes in business strategy which reduce the usefulness of plant and equipment.

Index

A

Accrual 466

Aggressively Expansive 125

Aggressively Restrictive 115, 121, 123, 125

Amortization 468

Analyst xxi, 4, 9, 10, 69, 70, 229, 231, 232 - 236, 239, 241, 264, 349, 351, 352, 481

Anchoring 307, 308, 328, 464

Anomaly 464

AOL 352

April xxviii, 19, 216, 218, 295, 365, 368, 409, 425, 442

Asset xxxiii, 121, 225, 261, 276, 277, 338, 376, 464, 469, 470, 471, 473, 474, 479, 482, 479, 490, 492

Audit 256, 257, 465, 468, 485

Availability vi, xii, 74, 95, 96, 212, 213, 276 - 278, 285, 314, 315, 319, 465

B

Bad News 10 - 12, 302, 307, 312, 323, 328 - 331, 336, 339 - 342, 344 - 346, 348, 350, 356 - 359, 361, 363, 372, 491

Bayes Theorem 465

Bearish xiii, 366

Best Years xi, 122, 123, 127, 128, 163, 164, 166, 167, 169, 170, 172, 173, 175, 202, 203

Beta 71, 465 - 467, 469, 480, 490

Bid-Asked 385, 466, 479, 490

Book Value (*see* BV)

Brokerage xix, xxii, xxiv, xxv - xxviii, xxxii - xxxvi, 4, 5, 9, 69, 70, 74, 75, 221, 222, 229 - 232, 235 - 239, 241 - 244, 264, 273, 300, 338, 342, 346, 375 - 377, 389, 393, 466, 469, 476, 477, 480

Bubka, Sergei xi, 238, 239, 351

Bullish 101, 131, 209, 362

Buying Power 11, 291, 293, 355, 370

BV (*see also* P/BV) ix, xi, xiv, 22, 23, 27, 29, 31, 36, 40, 43, 46, 54, 108, 117, 168, 169, 170, 172, 217, 221, 222, 289, 332, 359, 372, 389, 467

C

Calibration xiii, 321, 322, 469

Call xxvi, xxxiv, 7, 10, 11, 75, 110, 115, 239, 241, 243, 253, 264, 301, 305, 306, 336, 350, 352, 361, 362, 367, 373, 467, 469, 470, 482, 485, 489

Capitalize 377

Cash Flow (*see also* P/CF) 4, 10, 21, 22, 29, 36, 43, 58, 171, 216, 217, 219, 222, 228, 237, 259, 263 - 266, 277, 281, 282, 285, 301, 342 - 344, 347, 389, 467, 468, 471

CEO 253, 287, 288, 322, 332, 350

CFA v, xxvii, 244, 498

CFO 10

Closed-End 338, 468

CNBC 349

Cognitive Bias 300, 307, 308, 311, 312, 316, 323, 468

Cognitive Dissonance 304, 468

Company-Specific 468

Competition 70, 86, 239, 269, 271, 272, 274, 279, 327, 473, 482, 484, 487, 489

Compromise Response 469

Compustat vi, xxxiv, xxxv, 23, 66, 108, 117, 119, 389 - 391

Confidence Level 469

Confirmation 303, 307, 331

Confirmation Bias 303, 469

Conflict 478

Conjunctive Event 469

Consensus 469

Conservatism xii, xiii, 249, 251, 297 - 299, 303, 306, 307, 318, 328, 469

Contingent Liability 255, 469

Convertible Debt 358, 359

Cost of Goods Sold 259, 474, 479

Covenant 262, 469

CPA v, 244, 248, 249, 256, 262, 465, 498

Current Assets 282, 470

Current Liabilities 470, 492

D

Data Mining 364, 470, 489

Debt/Equity 469, 470, 489

December xiii, 9, 17, 19, 57, 61, 105, 341, 342, 350, 363, 364, 365, 366, 371, 389, 401, 417, 433, 450, 452, 454, 456, 458, 478, 482

Depreciation 249, 250, 262, 464, 471, 474, 489

Differentiation 267, 268, 270, 271, 272, 273, 279, 484, 487

Discount xxvi, 5, 15, 17, 74, 95, 96, 97, 98, 234, 242, 273, 298, 300, 303, 305, 346, 384, 471, 486

Disjunctive Event 471

Diversification xxxiv, 3, 35, 47, 66, 73, 90, 256, 300, 309, 311, 393, 471, 480, 482

Dividend 255, 313, 368, 369, 464, 470, 482

E

Early Election Cycle xi, 110, 111, 113, 115, 121 - 123, 127, 128, 201, 209, 210, 212, 213

Earnings ix, xi, xii, xiv, xvi, xxvi, 3, 4, 8, 10, 15, 21 - 24, 29, 35 - 37, 57, 58, 74, 88, 98, 101, 118, 125, 162, 210, 212 - 214, 216, 217, 219, 220, 222, 224, 226, 228, 230, 233, 236 - 241, 248, 249, 251, 253 - 266, 268, 271, 272, 276, 277, 279, 280, 281, 284, 301, 303, 312 - 315, 317, 318, 323, 328, 332, 339, 340, 342 - 344, 347, 349 - 355, 357, 358 - 361, 363, 370, 389, 464, 466, 469, 470, 472, 476, 481 - 483, 486, 489, 490

Economies of Scale xxvi, 267, 274, 472

Efficient Market Hypothesis 295

Efficient Market Theory xxii, 3, 4, 66, 300, 472

Endowment xii, 311, 312, 324, 328, 473, 479

EPS (*see also* Earnings) 470, 471, 473, 474, 477, 482, 485 - 487, 489

Equity vi, xxiv, xxv, xxvi, xxvii, xxxv, 4, 8, 15, 80, 93, 95, 108, 116 - 118, 131, 221, 253, 257, 283, 284, 286, 351, 355, 370, 372 - 374, 385, 466, 469, 470, 473, 474, 477, 479, 489, 498

Ethics xxvii, 244

Euphoric Years 115, 125, 130, 131, 174, 202, 209, 214, 215, 227; Extreme Euphoric Years 125, 130, 202, 209, 214, 215

Excess Return 473

Exit Costs 473, 487

Expansive xi, 100, 103, 111, 112, 115, 121, 125, 128, 201, 210, 212

Expectations xxi, xxii, 9, 57, 103, 118, 129, 210, 212 - 214, 216, 217, 220, 228, 234, 238, 239, 265, 281, 312, 314, 343, 353, 354, 358, 384, 467, 487, 491

Expected Return 473

Extrapolation 473

Extreme Euphoric Years 125, 130, 202, 209, 214, 215

Extreme Panic Years 123, 126, 130, 162, 171, 174, 201, 213

F

Federal Reserve Bank 9, 15, 17, 34, 46

Fees xxii, xxvii, xxxii, 75, 229, 231, 232, 236, 237, 243, 248, 300, 338, 377, 385, 389, 390, 478

FIFO 474

Fixed Costs 474

Friday xiii, 364, 367, 368

G

GAAP (*see* General Accepted Accounting Principles)

Generally Accepted Accounting Principles viii, xii, 10, 27, 247 - 249, 251, 253 - 255, 257, 283, 284, 465, 467, 468, 471, 474 - 485

Good News 10, 11, 12, 232, 240, 302, 304, 307, 323, 328, 330 - 332,

339, 341, 345, 348, 353, 355, 358, 359, 362, 363, 372

Gross Margin 259, 475

Groupthink 233, 475

Growth viii, ix, x, xi, xiv, xvi, xvii, xxix, xxxiv, 11, 13, 15, 20, 21, 23, 24, 27, 34 - 37, 43, 46 - 49, 54, 57 - 59, 62, 88, 93 - 101, 103, 107, 108, 110 - 113, 115 - 117, 119, 131, 162, 168, 170, 173 - 175, 201, 209, 210, 212 - 217, 219, 220 - 222, 224 - 228, 236, 237, 239, 254, 261, 265, 266, 268, 271, 272, 275 - 277, 279, 281, 282, 284 - 287, 289, 290, 296, 298, 301 - 303, 312 - 315, 318, 322, 323, 340, 342 - 344, 353, 358 - 360, 362, 371, 372, 383, 384, 386, 464, 468, 470, 475 - 478, 482, 485, 487, 489, 491, 492; Growth Index xvii, 46, 49, 111, 173, 174, 175, 213, 220, 222, 371; Growth Stock 35, 36, 46, 49, 217, 220, 228, 303, 360

Guidance 237, 330, 353, 354, 358

H

Halo Effect 300 - 302, 315, 475

Hedge 11, 12, 214, 220, 225, 247, 311, 317, 319, 362, 371, 475

Held To Maturity 475

Heteroskedasticity 221

Holding Period 365, 476

Horns Effect 301

Hostile Media Effect 300, 476

I

Illiquid 10, 340, 356, 357, 362, 370, 479, 480

Illusory Correlation 318, 319, 320, 476

Inclusive Account 310, 476

Index Fund 4, 37, 40, 355, 476

Industry vi, xix, xxii - xxv, xxviii, xxxii, xxxvi, 4, 10, 35, 40, 65, 66, 75, 232, 234, 238, 250, 260, 263 - 274, 277, 278, 280, 285, 287, 300, 302, 303, 312, 340, 348, 349, 351 - 354, 363, 386, 473, 476, 484, 487, 489, 498

Inefficient Market xxiv, 477

Inflation 23, 27, 66, 81, 82, 96, 99, 100, 108, 118, 120, 124, 165, 214, 216, 218 - 221, 224, 234, 247, 474, 478

Insider xxii - xxiv, 238, 332, 358 - 360, 477

Institution 477

Integration 278, 463, 474

Investment Banks 477

Investment Trap xiii, 323, 324, 478

Invisible Correlations xiii, 318 - 320, 478

IPO 232, 352, 372, 377, 478

J

January 11, 17, 19, 61, 77, 341, 342, 350, 363 - 366, 368, 371, 406, 422,
    438, 439, 460, 461, 472, 478 - 480, 482, 489; January Barometer 478,
    480, 482; January Effect 11, 365, 366, 472, 478, 489

K

L

Large Caps 62, 71 - 74, 76, 90, 93, 94, 108, 110, 111, 113, 116, 120
    - 129, 210, 212 - 214, 216, 224 - 227, 289, 290, 310, 359, 366, 367,
    385, 478
Late Election Cycle xi, 111 - 113, 115, 121, 125, 130, 131, 174, 203, 209,
    212, 213, 215, 289
Liabilities xxxiii, 27, 248, 249, 254 - 258, 280, 282 - 284, 466, 470, 473,
    479, 487, 492
LIFO 252, 255, 478, 479
Limit Order 335, 336, 338
Liquidity vi, 10, 80, 101, 102, 218, 247, 281 - 283, 293, 336, 338, 346,
    357, 372, 479
Lockup 254, 479
Long-Term Debt 218, 283, 470, 479
Look-ahead 23, 105, 119, 121, 391, 479
Loss Aversion 298, 299, 479, 484, 486

M

Manipulation 29, 34, 258, 259, 262, 384, 468, 487
Margin 11, 12, 46, 47, 97, 111, 113, 115, 122, 123, 125, 126, 203, 210,
    212 - 215, 225, 226, 237, 239, 241, 259, 260, 289, 339, 344, 366,
    370, 371, 373, 374, 381, 382
Market Cap (see also Market Capitalization) 10, 66, 69, 71, 89, 108, 111,
    117, 119, 123, 124, 126, 128, 129, 209, 215, 250, 290, 310, 350, 366,
    380, 389, 481, 487
Market Capitalization 9, 20, 54, 59, 65, 66, 69, 93, 110, 369, 478, 480,
    498
Market Impact 4, 239, 290, 299, 345, 389, 390, 480, 490
Market Order 11, 335 - 338, 346, 351, 480
May 367, 410, 426, 443
Minimal Account 481
Momentum 57, 58, 131, 297, 306, 320, 323, 470, 481, 487
Monday xiii, 11, 364, 367, 368
Mutual Fund vi, xxii, xxiii, xxvi, xxviii, xxxii, xxxiii, 35, 47, 66, 69, 70,
    300, 338, 376, 464, 468, 480

N

Nanocaps xxxiii, xxxvi, 9, 69, 70, 71, 73 - 76, 90, 93, 94, 108, 110, 111, 113, 116, 120 - 126, 128 - 131, 212 - 215, 222, 225, 226, 229, 296, 300, 310, 311, 328, 349, 380, 381, 385
Negative Surprise 238, 241, 339, 340, 481
Neglected Stock Effect 481
News Search 352
Niche 271, 273, 313, 482
Non-Recurring 349, 482
November 17, 19, 400, 416, 432, 449, 478, 482

O

October xxi, 10, 15, 17, 84, 97, 239, 359, 365 - 368, 399, 415, 431, 448
Open-End xxxiii, 468
Opinion xxxiv, 232, 233, 235, 242, 256, 258, 262, 278, 300, 301, 305, 468, 475, 485
Option 95, 268, 310, 333, 362, 373, 380, 469, 482, 489
Out-of-Favor 126, 236, 303, 307, 320, 475, 482
Overconfirmation Bias 482

P

P/BV (Price to Book Value) ix, xi, 22, 23, 27, 29, 31, 36, 40, 43, 46, 54, 108, 117, 168 - 170, 172, 217, 221, 222, 289, 332, 372
P/CF (Price to Cash Flow) ix, xi, 22, 23, 29, 31, 34, 36, 43, 46, 108, 117, 171 - 173, 217, 221, 222, 289
P/E (Price to Earnings) 22 - 24, 27, 29, 31, 34, 36, 37, 40, 43, 46, 47, 49, 54, 63, 108, 115, 117, 118, 162 - 167, 170, 172, 214, 217, 220 - 222, 272, 289, 290, 313, 314, 318, 340, 353, 358, 473, 474, 476, 481, 482, 485, 491
P/S (Price to Sales) ix, xi, 22 - 24, 27, 29, 31, 36, 40, 43, 46, 49, 108, 117, 165 - 168, 170, 172, 217, 221, 222, 289, 372
Panic Years 11, 110, 113, 115, 116, 123, 126 - 128, 130, 162, 171, 174, 201, 209, 213 - 215, 225, 226 - 289; Extreme Panic Years 123, 126, 130, 162, 171, 174, 201, 213
Pension Plans 254
Percentage-of-Completion Basis 483
Performance Advantage 17, 23, 24, 34, 36, 37, 48, 61, 65, 111, 112, 120, 121, 123 - 125, 128, 162, 164, 165, 167, 168, 170, 171, 173 - 175, 201, 203, 210, 212 - 214, 226, 290
Performance Figures vi, xxvii, xxix, 118, 129, 212, 213, 379, 384, 385
Positive Surprise 217, 341, 343, 354, 483
Postdecisional Dissonance 483
Pre-Market 357, 358

Predecisional Dissonance 483

Present Value 29, 98, 101, 217, 254, 257, 313, 314, 342, 352, 471, 483, 484

Presidential Election Cycle xxxiv, 4, 9, 13, 19, 20, 77, 79, 80, 94, 100, 483

Prospect Theory 311, 484

Prudent Man Rule 484

Psychological Accounting 484

Psychological Biases 297, 485

Put xxii, xxvii, xxxiv, xxxvi, 11, 12, 57, 232, 233, 240, 241, 301, 306, 311, 319, 330, 339, 346, 355, 357, 362, 367, 371, 373, 382, 475, 482, 489

Q

QQQ 11

Qualified Opinion 256, 485

Quality xxxvi, 10, 27, 75, 90, 111, 121, 126, 130, 213, 214, 219, 225, 226, 232, 244, 249, 254 - 256, 263, 266, 275, 278, 279, 286, 287, 351, 464, 470, 472

R

Regression 312, 314, 465, 469, 472, 487

Regulation xxiii, xxvi, xxxii, xxxiii, 81, 242, 279, 280

Reg FD xxvi, 377

Relative Strength 9, 13, 20, 54, 57 - 59, 61 - 63, 93, 94, 103, 108, 110, 112, 115 - 117, 119, 201 - 203, 209, 210, 212 - 215, 222, 225, 227, 289, 290, 296, 331, 341, 342, 365, 370, 372

Repatriation 252, 255, 486

Reported Earnings 486

Repurchase 254 - 256, 332, 358 - 360, 364, 489

Restricted Stock 486

Restrictive/Early 110, 111, 115, 121 - 123, 127, 209; Aggressively Restrictive/Early 115, 121, 123

Restrictive/Late 111 - 113, 115, 125, 130, 131, 174, 209, 215; Aggressively Restrictive/Late 115, 125

Retained Earnings 486

Revenue 4, 232, 234, 239, 260, 261, 268, 281, 317, 376, 464, 483, 486

Risk Aversion 479, 484, 486

Rivalry 487

Russell 3000 476, 487

S

S&P 500 vi, xxv, xxvi, xxix, 4, 15, 17, 19, 22 - 24, 27, 29, 31, 34, 36, 37, 40, 43, 46, 48, 49, 54, 59, 61, 66, 69, 71, 77, 79, 80, 83, 87, 100, 102, 103, 105, 107, 111, 117, 121 - 123, 127 - 131, 163, 164, 166, 167,

169 - 175, 201 - 203, 210, 212 - 214, 216, 222, 225, 247, 309, 355, 358, 366, 367, 369, 370, 379, 386, 465, 466, 471, 476, 480, 487, 488

Same Store Sales 332, 358

Screen 59, 61, 63, 222, 231, 290

Selective Perception 299, 300, 487

Self-Tender 360

Shopkeeper 10, 327, 333, 336, 338, 347, 354, 346, 362

Skewness 488

Small Cap vi, 11, 62, 63, 65, 66, 69, 89, 90, 94, 111, 112, 117, 123, 124, 212, 215, 225, 227, 290, 350, 352, 366, 376, 383, 478, 481, 483, 488

Spinoff 11, 368, 369, 370, 488

Stock Index Future 488

Stock Repurchase Program 489

Stock Selection xxxiv, xxxvi, 1, 5, 11, 20, 22, 27, 29, 31, 36, 40, 43, 46, 47, 54, 58, 62, 94, 95, 116 - 118, 119, 227, 289, 290, 379, 382, 383

Stop Order 337, 338

Structural Changes 489

Style xxxiv, 21, 35, 46, 119, 210, 216, 287, 290, 301, 351, 379, 386, 393, 478, 489

Substitute 266, 267, 268, 269, 272, 348, 351, 489

Sunk Cost 323, 489

Super Bowl Indicator 489

Survivor Bias 489

Sustainable 95, 468, 486, 490

Switching 11, 225, 227, 267, 278, 289

T

Tax xxvii, 9, 11, 19, 48, 57, 59, 61, 84, 252, 257, 258, 280, 290, 309, 324, 331, 341, 342, 345, 363, 364, 370, 371, 385, 386, 477, 478, 489, 490

Technical Analysis 8

Test Portfolio vi, xxviii, xxix, xxxiii, 19, 66, 73, 76, 338, 351, 366, 372, 373, 379, 380 - 387, 393, 498

TheFlyOnTheWall.com 351; The Fly 351 - 353, 363

Thinly-Traded vi, 3, 10, 11, 63, 74, 293, 328, 334, 336, 340, 341, 346, 347, 368, 384, 385, 480, 490

Total Return 15, 17, 23, 131, 490

Transaction Costs 490

Treasury Bill 490

Trend Biases 58, 297, 490

U

Unsupported Optimism 323
Uptick 328, 356

V

Valence Effect 323, 491
Valuation Model 491
Value-Oriented Dissonance 306, 491
Value Index 34, 46, 49, 111, 115, 173, 174, 175, 213, 386
Value Stock 21, 491
Variable Costs 491
VideoFinancials 375 - 377
Vividness xii, 314, 315, 491
Vividness Effect 491
Volatility 90, 484, 492
Volume Effect 492

W

Wall Street Journal xx, xxiv, 352, 353, 387
Warrant 492
Whisper Number 342
Window Dressing 384
Working Capital 492

X

Y

Y2K 79
Yield 118, 216, 218, 219, 224, 263, 283, 313, 356, 369; Yield Curve 218

Z

• About the Authors •

BILL MATSON & MITCHELL R. HARDY

Bill Matson, MBA, CPA, CFA, FLMI

Bill Matson is the Chief Executive Officer of **Data Driven Investment Management, LLC** and co-author of *Data Driven Investing– Professional Edition*. Mr. Matson is also the owner and manager of the test portfolio described in this book, which returned **788%** between July 2000 and March 2004.

Mr. Matson's career in finance spans over 30 years, including stints as an accountant, corporate loan officer, retail stockbroker, and executive for several start-up companies. Bill has worked at *General Electric, Arthur Andersen & Co., Chemical Bank, Dean Witter,* and *Merrill Lynch*.

In addition, he has founded or co-founded a variety of companies. One of these companies, *Virtual Company Visits*, pioneered (in 1993) the development of equity research CD-ROM's featuring video clips of management interviews, product demonstrations, and facilities tours.

Mr. Matson is a Certified Public Accountant and a Chartered Financial Analyst charterholder. He earned his MBA from Harvard Business School and his B.S. in Accounting from Babson College.

Mitchell R. Hardy

Mitch Hardy is the President and Chief Operating Officer of **Data Driven Investment Management, LLC** and co-author of *Data Driven Investing– Professional Edition*.

Over the past 30 years, Mr. Hardy has held senior executive-level financial positions with a number of high technology manufacturing firms, providing leadership in rapidly growing businesses, established firms, and turn-around situations. He has guided strategic planning and business development efforts for companies ranging in size from start-ups to NYSE-listed firms and is an expert in operational reporting for complex enterprises.

During the 1990's, Mr. Hardy owned and operated *Willowdale Specialty Products*, a specialty producer and marketer to the upscale hospitality industry.

Mr. Hardy is a graduate of Bentley College.